L-13 ,50

OREGON • WASHINGTON
BRITISH COLUMBIA

# GOING PLACES

## FAMILY GETAWAYS IN THE PACIFIC NORTHWEST

ANN BERGMAN
ROSE WILLIAMSON
NANCY THALIA REYNOLDS

## THE ULTIMATE GUIDE FOR TRAVELING IN THE PACIFIC NORTHWEST WITH KIDS

FOURTH EDITION

BOOKS FOR PARENTS
PUBLISHING

SEATTLE, WASHINGTON

**PARENT REVIEWERS:**
Conrad Alexandrovicz, Shelley Arenas, Ann Bergman, Amy Berman, Colleen Bollen, Cheryl Murfin Bond, Mari Brockhaus, Christine Chmielewski, Liz DeSimone, Stephanie Dunnewind, Jo Fjellman, Kathy Foster, Anne Doss Hardy, Jennifer Harry, High Heermans, Kathleen Koler, Shirley Kricheldorf, Alice Madsen, Shawn McDonald, Jill Orendorff, Carolyn Quigley, Nancy T. Reynolds, Lenore Sargent, Lori-Lynn Searle, Virginia Smyth, Scott Stolnack, Alayne Sulkin, Merrily Sutton, Shawn West, Rose Williamson, Pamela S. Wolter.

Printed in the United States of America.

Distributed by Sasquatch Books

Books for Parents Publishing
Seattle, Washington
www.booksforparents.com

ISBN: 0-9614626-8-X

Art Direction/Design: John Rusnak
Cover Illustration/Maps/Icons: Cary Pillo Lassen
Layout: John Rusnak
Indexing: Nancy D. Donnelly, IndexesForYou

# How to Use this Book

We all have a different idea of the perfect vacation spot. We wrote this book to give parents reliable information about the whole range of possibilities available to a parent planning a getaway with the kids in the Pacific Northwest.

## Places to Stay

We selected the places to stay featured in this edition by asking parents about their favorite family vacation spots and sending parent reviewers to check out the facilities. We kept in mind the diverse needs of parents traveling with babies, teens and everything in between.

Accommodation rates were classified as follows:

Inexpensive—Family of four under $85

Moderate—Family of four $85-$140

Expensive—Family of four over $140

Use our price range to get a rough idea of the cost, but if you are interested in a certain place, call and get an exact quote. Rates will vary dramatically depending on the time of the year, ages of your children and the type of accommodations you want. Unfortunately, school holidays are typically the busiest and most expensive periods. You can save substantially by going in an off-season.

Many of the places in this book have families that go back year after year. Be sure to make reservations as early as possible and pay close attention to cancellation policies.

## Places to Eat

When a grownup is brave or foolish enough to venture into a restaurant with a child, we believe they deserve all the good food and helpful service they can possibly get. To be recommended in this book a restaurant had to have good food, moderate to low prices, genuinely welcome kids and have fast service. Entertainment, such as a box of crayons or a balloon is an added bonus.

## Things to See and Do

Figuring out what to do once you arrive at your destination can be more work that any parent wants to do on a vacation. We checked out the popular tourist attractions as well as the lesser-known places of interest recommended by fellow parents. Of course we include cost, hours, addresses and phone numbers so you could spend less time doing the research and more time having fun.

**EVERYTHING CHANGES.**

Prices, owners, facilities—we expect them to change. Use us as a guide, but check out the details with a phone call or letter. Describe your family and what you are expecting to confirm that a place will meet your expectations.

**SHARE YOUR EXPERIENCES.**

If you know of other places that we should include in future editions of Going Places, or if you have comments about one of the places we included, please write us. We'd like to hear from you.

Books for Parents
Seattle, WA
www.booksforparents.com

# TABLE OF CONTENTS

## OREGON STATE

While Oregon shares many geographic, historic, and cultural characteristics with both Washington and British Columbia, it also differs in a number of ways, some of which will impact visitors to the state. In many ways, modern-day Oregon exhibits a pioneer spirit worthy of its history.

**HISTORY.** The territory now known as Oregon was "discovered" in 1579 (at the time, there were more than 100 Native American tribes living in the region) by the British admiral Frances Drake. The Lewis and Clark Expedition of 1805-06 furthered the knowledge of this frontier, and paved the way for an influx of trappers and fur trading companies. In 1811, John Jacob Astor established a trading post near modern-day Astoria, on Oregon's northern coast.

The single largest impact on the growth of the state was the influx of emigrants who came via the Oregon Trail during the mid-1800s (see sidebar). A territorial government was enacted in 1849, and Oregon became the 33rd state admitted to the Union in 1859. World War I encouraged further growth, reflecting the increased demand on the timber and shipbuilding industries. During this time, Portland became a major West Coast port. Again during World War II, newcomers flocked to Oregon to fill jobs in the shipyards.

### History at Your Feet:
### Following the Oregon Trail

**THE OREGON TRAIL THEN.** The first travelers on what was to become the Oregon Trail were missionaries seeking to establish Christianity among the native tribes. In 1836, Marcus and Narcissa Whitman settled near modern-day Walla Walla, Washington. Seven years later there began a tidal wave of emigration to the Oregon Territory, and during the next three decades, upwards of 200,000 pioneers made the arduous journey, driven by stories of rich agricultural land and, beginning about 1850, gold. The route was a difficult one, however, and an estimated one in 10 travelers perished along the way. Completion of the transcontinental railroad in 1869 stemmed the tide of wagons flowing along the Oregon Trail.

It would be difficult to underestimate the importance of the Oregon Trail in terms of the history of the United States. As the only practical route into the Oregon Territory, the trail served as gateway to the entire western region of the country. Without it, the area represented today by Oregon, Washington, Idaho, California, Utah, and Nevada might well have become a part of Canada or Mexico.

**A MODERN-DAY JOURNEY.** Retracing the steps of Oregon Trail pioneers is a moving experience. Several museums have been established to tell the Oregon Trail story, and there are many historical sites as well. Some of the sites are listed below, arranged from east to west (for obvious reasons). However, families can adjust the exploration to fit their own time-frame and interests.

- Begin in the small town of Vale, about 15 miles west of the Oregon-Idaho border on Highway 20. Tour the **RINEHART STONE HOUSE** and get directions to **KEENEY PASS** (10 miles away), an excellent place to view deep wagon ruts left by travelers on the Trail. For more information, see "Eastern Oregon: Ontario/Vale."

- Make your way back to I-84 and head northwest to **FAREWELL BEND STATE PARK** (off I-84 near the town of Huntington). At this point, the emigrants left the Snake River (which they had followed for 330 miles) and ascended the Burnt River Canyon. The park is nice, and there are kiosks and a recreated "prairie schooner."

- Continuing on I-84, plan to stop at the **NATIONAL HISTORIC OREGON TRAIL INTERPRETIVE CENTER,** on Flagstaff Hill east of Baker City. This is where Oregon Trail travelers first caught sight of the "Promised Land." Families can visit the museum, which recreates life along the Oregon Trail, and hike the interpretive path past scenic overlooks and historic sites, including ruts left by thousands of wagon wheels. See "Eastern Oregon: Baker City, Excursions" for more information.

- Near La Grande, take Exit 248 from I-84 and head west to the **OREGON TRAIL VISITOR PARK AT THE BLUE MOUNTAINS.** This interpretive site overlooks a portion of the Oregon Trail as it climbs through the forested slopes of the Blue Mountains, and includes one-half mile of paved paths with interpretive panels. On most weekends, visitors are greeted by living history characters.

- Traveling northwest on I-84 to Pendleton, you'll find the Oregon Trail story told from a different perspective-that of the Native American—at **TAMASTSLIKT CULTURAL INSTITUTE.** For details about this lovely museum, see "Eastern Oregon: Pendleton, Excursions."

- Cross the Deschutes River and continue on I-84 to The Dalles, where emigrants faced a difficult decision: to raft down the Columbia River, or to take the rugged Barlow Road around Mount Hood. Unless you're driving an amphibian vehicle, you'll choose to follow the Barlow Road route. Take Highway 197 south from The Dalles to Dufur. At **TYGH VALLEY** (where emigrants camped on the banks of Badger Creek and traded with the local Tygh Indians), head west through Wamic to Mount Hood.

- When you intersect Highway 35, travel south over **BARLOW PASS,** head west on Highway 26. In Rhododendron, you can stop to see a replica of the original tollgate that marked the final segment of the Trail. Stop at the **JONSRUD VIEWPOINT** in Sandy, for an overlook of the trail you've just traveled—all the way back to Mount Hood.

- To end your journey, stop into **THE END OF THE OREGON TRAIL CENTER** in Oregon City, an attractive museum which recaptures the flavor of historic Abernethy Green, the site of arrival and welcoming for emigrants for more than 150 years. A living history interpreter helps the journey come alive for visitors. The Center is described in detail under "Portland, Excursions."

**GEOGRAPHY.** Portland, the largest city in Oregon, is located in the northeastern part of the state, near the border with Washington. The Columbia River defines three-quarters of the state's northern boundary, carving a deep gorge and providing agricultural oases along the way. Passing through Portland, it ends its journey near Astoria on the Oregon Coast.

For the most part, Oregon's geographic and climatic regions are defined by its mountain ranges. The Cascades divide the state into two distinct climatic zones-the cool, wet western zone and the warm, dry eastside. The Coastal Range defines the Oregon Coastal region, which runs the full length of the state. In the northeast, the Blue, Wallowa, and Umatilla ranges run southwest to the state's central plateau.

Among these ranges are scattered a number of diverse regions. The central "high desert" is marked by volcanic geology, as is the semiarid plateau of the southeastern region. In the southwest, the wild and scenic Rogue River cuts through a drier region that more resembles California than the rest of western Oregon.

The six sections of this chapter relate to these geographic divisions, and are listed in this order: Portland, Oregon Coast, Willamette Valley, Southern Oregon, Mount Hood/Columbia Gorge, Central Oregon, Eastern Oregon.

**SPECIAL FEATURES.** Politically, Oregon is a progressive state. At the forefront in terms of land-use legislation and environmental causes, the state has enacted several laws that will impact tourists as well as residents:

- Legislation passed in 1967 set aside all beachfront property on the Oregon Coast for "free and uninterrupted use" by the public.
- The 1971 Bottle Bill (the first of its kind in the nation) encourages recycling by offering refunds for glass and aluminum products.
- Oregon has no sales tax, which makes a trip to the state more affordable. While the impact is small in terms of a single room or meal, visitors spending a week or more here will appreciate the savings.
- If you are traveling by car, note that Oregon State does not allow drivers to pump their own gas.

## STATEWIDE RESOURCES

### OREGON TOURISM COMMISSION
775 Summer St. NE
Salem, Oregon  97310
800/547-7842; www.traveloregon.com
This Website is excellent, with links to points of interest throughout the state.

### OREGON STATE PARKS AND RECREATION DEPARTMENT
1115 Commercial St. NE
Salem  97310
503/378-6305; 800/551-6949

# PORTLAND

Portland, the largest city in Oregon, is situated on the Willamette and Columbia rivers, at the state's northern border. It is a city that reflects exceptionally good urban planning—short city blocks, wide sidewalks, and lots of parks and open spaces. Somehow Portland's thriving commercial and cultural sectors don't detract from the relaxed, unpretentious atmosphere. In short, the Rose City is a wonderful place to visit with kids.

## GETTING THERE

**BY CAR.** From Seattle, drive south on I-5, 175 miles. Plan on a 3 1/2-hour drive, allowing time for a short stop.

**ROADSIDE ATTRACTIONS.** About halfway between Seattle and Portland, just when your backseat passengers can't bear another minute in the car, take advantage of the refueling wonderland of Centralia, Exit 82. Turn right and watch for **Country Cousin Family Restaurant,** two blocks ahead on the right. It serves family fare, well prepared, and serves it quickly (unless there's a line). Alternatively, turn right at Country Cousin and drive a block to **Andree's** (look for the Dutch windmill) for pastry, soup and sandwich, or a choice of salads (eat here or take out). Parents can get an espresso drink to pump them up, and kids will enjoy perusing the small gift shop, which features novelties from Holland.

If you have the time, cruise through the adjacent **Factory Outlet Center.** Several stores, such as the Carter's Outlet, sell deeply discounted children's clothing and shoes. Toy Liquidator offers discontinued brand-name items, including a good selection of car games and beach toys, at rock-bottom prices.

**BY TRAIN.** Amtrak (800/872-7245) operates six trains a day along the Seattle-Portland corridor. Trains depart Seattle in the morning, late morning, and evening, and return in the morning, afternoon, and evening. The trip takes about four hours. Round-trip adult fares vary considerably depending upon the time of year; it is often possible to find a special promotional rate. Generally, children ages two to 15 ride for half-price. Reservations are required.

## GETTING AROUND

The Columbia River separates Washington and Oregon. In the Portland area, you can cross the Columbia on one of two interstates: I-5 and, to the east, I-205. If you're going into Portland, stay on I-5.

It's particularly easy to get around in Portland, because the city is neatly subdivided into five sections: southwest, southeast, north, northwest, and northeast. These sections are delineated by the Willamette River, dividing east from west (11 bridges cross the river at various points), and by Burnside Street, separating north from south. The directional indicator in a street address correlates with the section of the city in which it is located. Major thoroughfares include Grand Avenue, Sandy Boulevard, SE 82nd Street, and Highway 26 (also known as the Sunset Highway).

The Tri-Met transit system, which serves a three-county area, includes buses, MAX (Metropolitan Area Express) light rail, and vintage trolleys. A 300-square-block section of downtown has been designated a fareless zone. Elsewhere, exact-change fares are payable upon boarding. For more information, call the Tri-Met hot-line, 238-RIDE, or visit Tri-Met's Web site at www.trimet.com.

### PLACES TO STAY

#### PORTLAND MARRIOTT
*1401 SW Naito Pkwy., 97201*
*503/226-7600, 800/228-9290*
*Rates: Moderate to expensive*
*FYI: Restaurant; refrigerators; indoor pool (open 24 hours); exercise facility; pets OK; baby-sitting*

This large, bustling hotel features conference facilities and a popular sports bar, but is nevertheless a good bet for families. With a prime location across the street from Waterfront Park and the Willamette River, it's within walking distance of downtown. For an added treat, request a room with a river view.

Champions Sports Bar is open to minors for lunch and dinner until 6 p.m. A better bet for families is the hotel's restaurant, Allie's, where the separate kids' menu comes with an activity booklet.

### 66 PARENT COMMENTS
*"Every time we go to Portland we stay here—they often have good weekend deals. We love the nice big pool, and the location is excellent."*

## RIVERSIDE INN

*50 SW Morrison, 97204*
*503/221-0711, 800/899-0247*
*Rates: Moderate*
*FYI: Restaurant; kitchen (suite); complimentary use of health club; small dogs OK (fee); complimentary off-street parking*

Like the Marriott to the south, this smaller (140-unit) hotel is well situated opposite Waterfront Park and the Willamette River, and within easy walking distance of most downtown activities. For families, there is one suite available. Formerly a one-bedroom residential apartment, it has a full kitchen. Larger families can also take advantage of the Riverside's many adjoining rooms. The restaurant has a lovely view of the river.

**❝ PARENT COMMENTS**
*"The suite is spacious and well-suited to a family."*

## RESIDENCE INN BY MARRIOTT

*1710 NE Multnomah St., 97232*
*503/288-1400, 800/331-3131*
*Rates: Moderate to expensive*
*FYI: Complimentary continental breakfast buffet; kitchens; fireplaces; outdoor pool (May-Sept.); sports court; laundry; pets OK (deposit and fee); free on-site parking and grocery shopping service*

This eastside hotel, designed primarily for longer stays, is also ideal for families who prefer to save money on meals. Rooms are spacious and comfortable, with full kitchens. Here you have several choices: a studio with a queen bed and hide-a-bed, a one-bedroom unit, or a two-bedroom/two-bath suite. Kids have several entertainment options: pool, sport court (for basketball, volleyball, and badminton), and a collection of games and books available at the desk.

A complimentary breakfast buffet is served daily in the lobby, and numerous family restaurants are in the area. Lloyd Center (see "Stroll & Browse, Downtown"), with its ice rink and cinemas, is within walking distance. The light-rail line that crosses the river to downtown is just two blocks away.

**❝ PARENT COMMENTS**
*"Very comfortable and friendly. The fabulous athletic facilities and breakfast buffet were a big treat for our two middle-schoolers."*

### RESIDENCE INN PORTLAND SOUTH
*15200 SW Bangy Road, Lake Oswego 97034*
*503/684-2603*
*Rates: Moderate to expensive*
*FYI: Complimentary continental breakfast; kitchens; fireplaces; outdoor pool (May-Sept.); sports court; laundry; pets OK (fee); free parking*

If you like the idea of a Residence Inn, but prefer to stay outside the city, this spot is for you. Located 8 miles southwest of downtown Portland, this Residence Inn offers the same choice of accommodations as its downtown counterpart. Lake Oswego is one of Portland's nicest suburban areas, with restaurants and activities nearby.

**66 PARENT COMMENTS**

*"One thing we really like about Residence Inns is the floor plan. The rooms are set up around a large, light lobby, where the breakfast buffet is served. This afforded our kids (aged six and eight) a good deal of independence. They could come and go from our room while we ate, and we could keep track of them."*

*"Residence Inn didn't just tolerate the family dog, they welcomed her. There was even a basket of dog treats at the desk!"*

### EMBASSY SUITES
*9000 SW Washington Square Road, Tigard 97223*
*503/644-4000, 800/362-2779*
*Rates: Expensive*
*FYI: Complimentary breakfast; refrigerators/microwaves; indoor pool; pets OK*

Located in a suburb 25 miles southwest of Portland, this attractive 10-story hotel works hard to make families feel welcome. The two-room suites are especially comfortable for families, and the complimentary "cook-to-order" breakfast buffet includes a number of kid favorites. Eat in your own room, in the large, central atrium, or poolside while the kids swim. Want to cook meals in your room? Utensils and dishes are available upon request.

**66 PARENT COMMENTS**

*"The hotel pool so thoroughly captivated our three children that it was hard to get them to leave. We could sit in the atrium having breakfast and watch our daughters go up in the glass elevator and walk to the door of our room! The atrium and the pool area are a very nice place to host visitors."*

*"The surrounding countryside abounds with biking and wine-tasting opportunities."*

## THE GREENWOOD INN

*10700 SW Allen Blvd., Beaverton 97005*
*503/643-7444, 800/289-1300; www.greenwood.inn*
*Rates: Moderate to expensive*
*FYI: Restaurant; two outdoor pools; weight room; pets OK (fee, first night only); complimentary parking and shuttle*

Located near Washington Square Mall and Cinemas in a western suburb, the Greenwood Inn is 10 to 15 minutes by car from downtown Portland. This independently managed 20-year-old hotel prides itself on its Northwest character, evident in original artwork, décor, and landscaping characteristic of the region. Families have several options here, including adjoining rooms, a one-room studio with kitchen, or a two-room apartment with kitchen.

The glass-enclosed atrium of The Pavilion Bar & Grill (open Sun.-Thurs., 6:30 a.m.-10 p.m.; Fri.-Sat., 7 a.m.-11 p.m.) is airy and inviting. The kids' menu features reasonably priced entrées; adults can order from a light bistro menu or an eclectic menu of entrées that showcase fresh Northwest ingredients.

**❝ PARENT COMMENTS**
*"We reserved an adjoining room for our teenagers, and everyone was happy with the arrangement. The kids had the privacy they wanted, and we were able to keep half an eye on them."*

## PLACES TO EAT

Portland has its share of chain restaurants that cater to families. Look for Fuddruckers, Tony Roma's, Cucina! Cucina!, Macheezmo Mouse, and Olive Garden, to name a few. But to get a truer taste of Portland, try one of the following:

### AZTEC WILLIE AND JOEY ROSE TAQUERIA

*1501 NE Broadway*
*503/280-8900*
*Hours: Lunch, dinner daily*

This spot is named after the owners' sons, who specified that "their" restaurant would have a playroom. Accordingly, a glassed-in area along the far wall features child-sized furniture, a wooden play kitchen, and a small, well-worn collection of toys. Almost as entertaining is the restaurant's cafeteria line.

Hoist your little ones up to see myriad culinary choices and to watch nimble-fingered chefs roll hearty burritos. There's something here for adventurous and picky eaters alike.

This is a popular neighborhood hangout and may be crowded, especially on Friday nights. If there's a wait, the playroom will provide welcome diversion. One hint about the décor: The small, round glass tables and tippy metal chairs are more aesthetic than practical. To avoid disaster, suggest your kids demonstrate their best restaurant manners while at the table.

### CHEVYS

*8400 SW Nimbus Ave., Beaverton*
*(and four other area locations)*
*503/626-7667*
*Hours: Lunch, dinner daily*

In terms of area restaurant chains that cater to families, Chevys is the "big enchilada." The Mexican fare is fresh and tasty, and the south-of-the-border ambiance suits parents and their unpredictable tablemates. While other restaurants may offer balloons and crayons, Chevys has the ultimate entertainment: a tortilla machine. Adults and little ones alike are fascinated watching it work. Kids can even request a wad of tortilla dough to shape and sculpt while awaiting their food. (Isn't edible Play-doh every parent's dream?)

There are five Chevys in the Portland area, but the Beaverton restaurant—with a capacity of 320—is arguably the best one for families. Service is consistently efficient, and reservations are accepted!

### CHEZ JOSE

*2200 NE Broadway*
*503/280-9888*
*8502 SW Terwilliger Blvd.*
*503/244-0007*
*Hours: Lunch, dinner daily*

Hip, healthful Mexican food is the specialty at the two Chez Jose cafés. They're out to please each member of the family. For the refined palate, there are specialty dishes such as chipotle-honey camarones (shrimp), lime chicken enchiladas and squash enchiladas with peanut sauce. Yet these trendy eateries make an effort to appeal to tot taste buds as well, with cheese quesadillas, bean burritos, and chimidogs. Best of all, children seven and under eat free, 5 to 7 p.m. daily.

You may find there's a wait at Chez Jose, particularly on weekends. But the staff is great about providing crayons and toys, and children will be entertained by the zany, colorful décor and noisy hustle-bustle.

### HARBORSIDE RESTAURANT & PILSNER ROOM
*0309 SW Montgomery*
*503/220-1865*
*Hours: Lunch, dinner daily*

Part of the McCormick & Schmick empire, this restaurant wins accolades for design. Huge plate-glass windows and tiered seating provide everyone with an excellent view of the Willamette River. It's quite chic, a good place to take kids old enough to appreciate a finer meal out. The separate children's menu includes a coloring page (crayons are provided) and such choices as cheeseburger and fries, mini-pizza, chicken quesadilla, and fish and chips (all include an ice cream sundae). The "grown-up" menu is á la carte and emphasizes fresh Northwest seafood.

### THE IVY HOUSE
*1605 SE Bybee Blvd.*
*503/231-9528*
*Hours: Lunch, dinner daily; brunch Sat.-Sun.*

The creative minds behind The Ivy House belong to Brian and Lisa Quinn, two chefs who are also the parents of young children. The Quinns have created what they longed for as diners: a charming restaurant that serves ambitious entrées to adults and conventional favorites to kids.

Housed in a quaint older home festooned with vines, this two-story restaurant reserves upstairs seating for families. Tables here are set with tablecloths and linen napkins, but there's also a tot-sized plastic table for the smallest members of the family. An adjacent alcove harbors a nice collection of toys and, if agreement is reached with other diners, a curtain can be pulled back to reveal a television/VCR. Have these amenable owners thought of everything? Yes! There's even a changing table with diapers and wipes, and a settee that provides a private spot for nursing!

### JAMIE'S GREAT HAMBURGERS
*838 NW 23rd Ave.*
*503/248-6784*
*1337 NE Broadway*
*503/335-0809*

*11900 SW Beaverton-Hillsdale Hwy., Beaverton*
*503/643-1771*

Drop a quarter in the jukebox, then slip into one of the red banquettes and order burgers all around. You'll feel like you're on the set of *Happy Days*. This '50s-style soda fountain is sure to delight youngsters. Kids' meals come in colorful cardboard cars with big fins, and imaginative diners will find numerous uses for them.

The only thing here that's not completely '50s is the menu. Oh sure, Jamie's serves a thick, juicy burger on a bed of fries, but you can also order a veggie burger or an entrée salad. The service may not have finesse, but the teen-age servers are personable and accommodating: Want a milkshake instead of a small sundae? Sure. More root beer in your float? No problem. Their friendly attitude suits the laid-back surroundings to a tee.

#### Newport Bay

*0425 SW Montgomery*
*503/227-3474*
*Hours: Lunch, dinner daily; Sun. brunch*

Although Newport Bay boasts seven branches in the area, this location is the jewel in the crown. Floating on the Willamette River, with views of the marina, this circular restaurant occupies a prime bit of real estate. Considering the location, the prices are very reasonable. The kids' menu features fish and chips, fried shrimp, burgers, and chicken tenderloins. Sunday brunch choices include Belgian waffles and scrambled eggs and bacon. Pasta, steak, seafood, and salad are among the entrées available for adults.

#### Old Wives' Tales

*1300 E. Burnside*
*503/238-0470*
*Hours: Breakfast, lunch, dinner daily*

The menu at Old Wives' Tales stresses healthful, multiethnic cuisine (the candy jar at the cash register holds sugar-free lollipops). The menu for each meal fills two pages, with options for children ranging from sandwiches and natural turkey franks to burritos and noodles in a Parmesan cream sauce. Adults have many choices, too, including Greek and Mexican specialties, seafood sandwiches, tofu Shepherd's pie and East Indian soup. The salad bar features daily ethnic specialties, plus fresh rolls and rice cakes.

While the food here is good, the playroom is great! Kids will find a colorful circus-train play structure with navigational controls, peekaboo windows, stairs, and a tunnel. The playroom is well-suited to preschoolers, but when the restaurant is busy, it can become a free-for-all; parents will want to supervise toddlers lest they end up at the bottom of the heap. (Families are seated near the playroom for easy access.)

### OLD SPAGHETTI FACTORY

*0715 SW Bancroft St.*
*503/222-5375*
*Hours: Lunch, dinner daily*

Even the parents of energetic little ones can relax at the Old Spaghetti Factory. The combination of a relaxed atmosphere; simple, good food; and friendly, efficient service makes it a hit with the whole family. This flagship of the 30-restaurant chain is spacious, seating 450 guests at capacity. Even so, guests regularly wait up to 45 minutes for seating. To avoid the crowds, families are encouraged to arrive before 6 p.m. or call ahead to inquire about waiting times. If you do get stuck with a long wait, the kids can go upstairs where, in view of the lobby, they can watch G-rated videos and play video games.

Served on plastic dinosaur plates, Kiddie Meals (for ages two to five) feature spaghetti with choice of sauce, applesauce, a drink, a cookie and ice cream or a Popsicle. Junior meals offer spaghetti, salad, a drink, and ice cream. Adults can choose from a variety of pasta and chicken dishes.

### THE ORIGINAL PANCAKE HOUSE

*SW 24th & SW Barbur Blvd.*
*503/246-9007*
*Hours: Breakfast, lunch Wed.-Sun.*

Not much has changed at this well-known spot in the 40 years it's been in business. The owners, not to mention the die-hard regulars, prefer it that way. The dining room is comfortable and homey, the food is good, and the servings are generous. Try a house specialty, a thick, fluffy apple pancake doused in cinnamon sauce, or a sweet, lemony German pancake (these may take an extra 20 minutes to prepare), or opt for one of the less exotic dishes.

If you suspect that little eyes are bigger than little stomachs, suggest that your children share a helping; the Original Pancake House encourages family-style dining. (Be aware there may be an extra charge when diners over age six choose to split an entrée.) Or consider the only menu item especially for children: three buttermilk pancakes with sausage or an egg.

Wondering if there's a downside to this spot? There is: It's so popular that there's almost always a wait. Parents are wise to come armed with books and lap games; but if you forget, don't despair. Ask the hostess to unearth the coloring book and crayons she keeps tucked away in her desk.

### THE ORIGINAL PORTLAND ICE CREAM PARLOUR & RESTAURANT

*1613 NE Weidler St.*
*503/281-1271*
*Hours: Lunch, dinner daily*

Patterned after the Farrell's restaurants baby boomers may remember from their childhood, this parlor offers a wide variety of ice cream confections served in a Gay '90s setting. Choose a light entrée and follow it with sweet treats, or come just for a soda or a sundae. Either way, kids will be entertained by the activity around them, especially the fanfare that accompanies birthday parties. (If you'd just as soon avoid the bells and whistles, your best bet is to come on a weekday afternoon or early evening, when the energy level is less frenetic.)

### RED ROBIN BURGERS AND SPIRITS

*1139 NE Grand Ave.*
*503/231-9223*
*20th Pl. & Burnside*
*503/ 222-4602*
*Hours: Lunch, dinner daily*

Although Red Robin has a chain of restaurants along the West Coast, there are only two in Portland and they deserve mention. This is "the home of the gourmet burger," but the great thing is that there are pages of other choices as well, and the food is universally good. The kids' menu, both extensive and inexpensive, includes meat, pasta, chicken, and fish entrées.

These joints are always jumping, which creates an entertaining atmosphere; even the coloring page sometimes goes untouched as the little ones are busy watching the people around them. Even if there is an upset or two, parents needn't worry that noise from their table will disturb others. One word of warning: These restaurants do their best to separate lounge from eating areas, but if your family is particularly sensitive to smoke, you may want to request a table well away from the lounge.

## WHAT TO SEE & DO

### STROLL & BROWSE

**DOWNTOWN PORTLAND.** The best way to experience downtown Portland is on foot. Two walking-tour maps are available. *Powell's Walking Map of Downtown Portland,* published by Portland's famous book emporium, is free. Pick it up at Powell's City of Books (1005 W. Burnside St.; 503/228-4651) or at Powell's Travel Store at Pioneer Courthouse Square (SW 6th Ave. & Yamhill; 503/228-1108). Or stop by the Regional Arts and Culture Council (620 Main St., Ste. 420; 503/823-5111) for a complimentary copy of its *Public Art Walking Tour.* The Portland/Oregon Visitors Association (26 SW Salmon St., at Front Ave.; 503/275-9750; www.pova.com) can also provide brochures and information.

A walking tour of downtown Portland offers many potential delights for children. Check out the magnificent statue *Portlandia,* which leans out over the street from its perch on the Art Deco-style **Portland Building** (1120 SW 5th Ave.). Stand beneath and look up at the giant lady, the nation's second-largest hammered copper sculpture. Or climb to the second floor of the Portland Building, where the Metropolitan Center for Public Art showcases a full-size plaster cast of the statue's head and photos of her arrival by barge.

The **Pioneer Courthouse Square** (SW Broadway & Yamhill), erected in 1984 on the former site of a parking lot, is a good example of forward-thinking civic planning. To fund its construction, more than 63,000 personalized bricks were sold; check them out as you walk through the square. Look for the *Weather Machine* in the northwest corner. Every day at noon a two-minute fanfare announces the forecast. Children also find the *Mile Post* amusing (SW 6th Ave.). It lists distances to Portland's nine sister cities and other whimsical destinations.

The Square serves as a town common, so you'll see everything from brown-bagging executives to teens playing hacky-sack and mothers watching their toddlers romp. **Pioneer Courthouse** (SW 6th Ave. & Yamhill), the oldest U.S. courthouse on the West Coast, is still in use today. From its glass-enclosed cupola you can catch a view of the city and mountains beyond. Flanking the old courthouse, directly opposite the square, are pools decorated with life-size birds and beasts cast in bronze; little ones love to climb on them. If weather permits, include several of the downtown fountains in your walk (see Sidebar).

The **South Park Blocks,** the area along South Park Street from Portland State University (Jackson St.) to the Performing Arts Center (Salmon St.), form downtown Portland's cultural core. They are punctuated by sculptures; look for statues of Abraham Lincoln and Teddy Roosevelt, and for *In the Shadow of the Elms*, a subtle granite inlay at Park Avenue and Clay Street.

If shopping is on your itinerary, downtown Portland has everything from large, national department stores to small, local boutiques. Ideally situated in central downtown, **Pioneer**

## *Water, Water Everywhere. . .*

In addition to the many natural waterways in the area, downtown Portland offers a number of fountains kids will find intriguing. Weather allowing, be sure to include one or two on your walking tour. (And pack an extra towel or two; the little ones aren't likely to stand by and admire the design.)

Children love to wade and play in the IRA KELLER FOUNTAIN (SW 3rd & Market, across from the Civic Auditorium). The naturalistic creeks and tumbling waterfalls are reminiscent of the Northwest landscape, and have the effect of bringing a little wilderness into the urban core. A few blocks south you'll find the LOVEJOY FOUNTAIN (SW 3rd & Hall), another cascade of fun.

At SALMON STREET SPRINGS (SW Front Ave. & Salmon St.), the kids will be bewitched and bewildered by the 185 water jets that are programmed by computer to keep youngsters on their toes. Just when they think they've got the rhythm down, they'll be surprised by a whole new set of jets erupting, perhaps right under their feet!

"ESSENTIAL FORCES," a fountain of legendary proportions, was a gift to the city from multibillionaire Paul Allen. Located at the main entrance to the Rose Garden (One Center Ct.), this huge computerized fountain features 500 water jets and two towers that emit geyser-force blasts of water. There are no trees or lawns in the immediate area, so bring a blanket to sit on and plenty of sunscreen!

**Place** (SW 5th Ave. & Taylor) is an upscale shopping center with a particularly nice mix of local family favorites, including Scooter & Beanbag children's clothing and Mimi Maternity. When you need a break, try the lovely food court with cascading water fountains. Finicky eaters will have lots of choices here, and parents can refuel with a coffee drink or snack. There is one drawback: On weekdays, crowds of businesspeople arrive at lunch hour, and it can get very noisy.

Then, before little legs wear out, walk the few blocks to **Finnegan's Toys and Gifts** (922 SW Yamhill; 503/221-0306). This is the toy store every kid dreams about, with toys and books stacked high on the shelves, toys out on display, and plenty of inexpensive knickknacks on which to blow two weeks' allowance.

At the northern edge of downtown, stop in at **Powell's City of Books** (1005 W. Burnside St.; 503/228-4651), the first destination of visiting book lovers. Occupying a full city block, Powell's displays new and used books side by side on its floor-to-ceiling shelves. The store has a lived-in feeling that's more alluring to bibliophiles than the antiseptic atmosphere of its competitors, and the children's literature section virtually overflows with classics and picture books. Tots are welcome to settle in and browse (and even try out the pop-up books). For a light pick-me-up, stop next door at the Annie Hughes Coffee Shop. Also in this neighborhood is **Hanna Andersson** (327 NW 10th Ave.; 503/242-0920), the popular all-cotton kids' clothing company. The Swedish-inspired fashions are colorful, comfortable and durable-if a bit pricey. And no one who sews for children will want to miss nearby **Daisy Kingdom** (207 NW Park; 503/222-4281), featuring row upon row of fun fabrics and the Daisy Kingdom line of patterns for clothes, dolls, and stuffed animals.

From downtown Portland, you can ride a vintage trolley across the river to **Lloyd Center** (NE Multnomah & 11th Ave. NE; 503/282-2511). Recently refurbished, this enclosed shopping mall is built around a large ice-skating rink. Board the trolley along Southwest Morrison, Yamhill, or 1st Avenue. The free rides are offered on the half hour (Mon.-Fri., 9:30 a.m.-3 p.m.; Sat.-Sun., 10 a.m.-6 p.m.).

**NORTHWEST 23RD AVENUE** is a chic neighborhood of boutiques, cafés, antique stores, and bakeries. There are several shops of special interest to kids, including **Child's Play** (907 NW 23rd Ave.; 503/224-5586) and **New Renaissance Book Shop** (1338 NW 23rd Ave.; 503/224-4929). If it's togs your little ones need, try **Mako** (732 NW 23rd Ave.; 503/274-9081). When hunger strikes, you can snack at a coffee shop or deli, or stop into **Jamie's Great Hamburgers** (838 NW 23rd Ave.; 503/248-6784) for a burger and a hit of '50s nostalgia (see "Places to Eat").

**SATURDAY MARKET.** One of the oldest open-air craft fairs in the country is still happening 10 months a year in Portland. Some 300 craft and food vendors cluster under the west end of the Burnside Bridge to sell handmade goods, and stage and street performers abound. Much of what's available is ethnic in flavor, from Peruvian wall hangings to Chinese lo-mein. Do keep close tabs on the kids, who will inevitably tend to scatter, attracted by the many sights and smells. It's easy to lose sight of them amid the crowds and warren of booths.

*Under the west end of the Burnside Bridge; 503/222-6072. Open March-Dec. Sat., 10 a.m.-5 p.m.; Sun., 11 a.m.-4:30 p.m. Free.*

**SOUTHEAST HAWTHORNE BOULEVARD** is funky and earthy, with dusty antique shops and tofu-and-sprouts eateries. Take the kids into **Pastaworks** (3731 SE Hawthorne Blvd.; 503/232-1010), where they can watch chefs preparing noodles and drool over the cheeses, savories, and desserts. Treat them to a toy stop, at **Kids at Heart** (3435 SE Hawthorne Blvd.; 503/231-2954) or a new book at **Powell's on Hawthorne** (3747 SE Hawthorne Blvd.; 503/238-1668). The **Bagdad Theatre & Pub** (3702 Hawthorne Blvd.; 503/230-0895) serves a full menu of multi-ethnic entrées inside a renovated theater. Call for film titles and times; minors are welcome at weekend family matinées only.

### PARKS

**CRYSTAL SPRINGS RHODODENDRON GARDEN.** Surrounded by a golf course and fed by 13 springs, these peaceful gardens are planted with hundreds of rhododendron and azaleas, which bloom in April and May. It's a bird paradise, where you're likely to spot all manner of waterfowl. Bring binoculars and cracked corn (no bread, please) and walk the winding, paved paths that loop around lakes, over bridges, past waterfalls and fountains, and along a lagoon. The boxes you see nailed to trees are either for wood ducks (with round door openings) or for bats. There are no tables or shelters here, but picnicking is allowed on the lawns.

*SE 28th Ave., one block north of Woodstock. 503/771-8386. Open daily, 10 a.m.-6 p.m. (March-early Sept.) Cost: $2/adult; free/Tues.-Wed.*

**FOREST PARK,** the largest natural area in any U.S. city, is a tangle of firs, alders, and maples, crisscrossed by some 50 miles of trails. It runs half the length of the city, on the west side of the Willamette River. Plan ahead, though, because few of the paths make loops; many will prove too long for little legs. While you're in the area, visit the Portland Audubon Wildlife Sanctuary (see "Animals, Animals").

*Travel west on NW Lovejoy St. until it becomes NW Cornell Road. Watch for signs.*

**GRANT PARK.** Portland's Grant Park is the site of the Beverly Cleary Sculpture Garden for Children, which immortalizes the award-winning author and her whimsical tales. A native of Portland, Cleary is the author of such childhood favorites as *Beezus and Ramona, Henry Huggins, and Otis Spofford.* Portland artist Lee Hunt sculpted clay statues of three of Cleary's most beloved characters-Ramona, Henry and Henry's mongrel, Ribsy—and then had them cast in bronze. There are fountains under Ramona's and Ribsy's feet; if the weather's nice, little ones can enjoy a splash.

Grant Park has a small, neighborhood feel and is located just four blocks from the Klickitat Street that Cleary made famous in her stories. Look for the sculpture garden just south of the playground.

*NE 33rd Ave., between Knott St. and Broadway, adjacent to Grant High School.*

**HOYT ARBORETUM.** Established in 1928, this 175-acre arboretum boasts the largest collection of conifers in the country. Many of its 10 miles of trails dip into neighboring Forest Park and Washington Park. The Vietnam Veterans Memorial Trail and Bristlecone Pine Trail are wheelchair accessible; most other trails are fairly rugged and may be steep in places.

To orient yourself to these large woods, stop first at the visitors' center (daily, 9 a.m.-3 p.m.). For a nominal fee, you can pick up self-guided tour booklets, maps for spring wildflowers and fall foliage, and trail maps of nearby Forest Park. Free, guided 90-minute tours are offered on weekends at 2 p.m., April through October.

*4000 SW Fairview Blvd. 503/228-8733.*

**TOM MCCALL WATERFRONT PARK,** named for the Oregon governor credited with a progressive vision for civic development, stretches for 22 blocks along the Willamette River and is popular with strollers, joggers, skaters, and picnickers. Don't miss Salmon Springs, a fountain where water play is encouraged (see sidebar). Continuing south to RiverPlace, you'll find a small marina, restaurants (see "Places to Eat"), and shops.

**TRYON CREEK STATE PARK.** Nestled in a shady canyon between Lewis and Clark College and Lake Oswego, this 645-acre forest has 14 miles of walking/running trails and a twisted maze of bike paths. It's heavily wooded, and home to a variety of fauna and flora, from woodpeckers to wildflowers. The paved half-mile *Trillium Trail* is perfect for the short-legged members of your family. Here you can visit the state park system's only Nature House, which features changing displays, nature programs, slide shows and a library.

*11321 SW Terwilliger (1 mile west of Hwy. 43). 503/636-4398.*

**WASHINGTON PARK** tops the itinerary of most families visiting Portland. Set in the hills to the west of downtown, it offers spectacular vistas of the city and, on a clear day, Mount Hood. In addition to its rolling lawns and miles of winding trail, Washington Park offers the following special attractions:

**INTERNATIONAL ROSE TEST GARDEN AND CHILDREN'S PARK.** Not only is the panoramic view breathtaking from here but, beginning in early summer, the air is heady with the fragrance of more than 400 varieties of roses. On weekends you're likely to see bridal parties posing for photographers against the stunning backdrop.

The innovative Children's Park, the first of its kind in the nation, was designed to serve the needs of physically challenged children and their families, as well as the community at large. Located next to the International Rose Test Garden, the 3.5-acre park features a clock tower, water play area, undulating bridges, fanciful ladders, and dozens of other colorful components, all wheelchair accessible. Paved trails link the park to the nearby Zoo Train, Children's Amphitheater, and the refurbished Elephant House, where you'll find picnic tables and restrooms.

*400 SW Kingston Ave. 503/223-1321. Open daily. Free.*

**JAPANESE GARDEN.** In 1990, the ambassador from Japan proclaimed this "the most beautiful and authentic Japanese garden in the world outside of Japan." It's the place to come for serenity, when the hurry and scurry of a modern city get you down. Kids love the hide-and-seek trails, fish ponds, and cascading streams. Leave the stroller in the car; backpacks will work better on the uneven, pebble-covered paths.

*611 SW Kingston Ave. 503/223-1321. Open daily, 10 a.m.- 6 p.m. (fall and spring); 9 a.m.-8 p.m. (summer); 10 a.m.-4 p.m. (winter). Cost: $6/adult, $4/senior 62 and over, $3.50/student, free/under 6.*

**OREGON ZOO.** See "Animals, Animals."

## MUSEUMS
### CHILDREN'S MUSEUM AND CHILDREN'S CULTURAL CENTER.

Housed in what was once a dormitory, this three-story museum has an intimate quality that's inviting to kids, teachers, and parents alike. Everything in this creative play center is tactile and "let's pretend"—from the basement-level Clayshop to the Kid City Thriftway (grocery store) and Bistro (eatery). Omokunle Village, a Nigerian town exhibit, is on permanent display in the annex. The environment within can get chaotic, so strollers will just be in the way. If the energy gets too high, change the venue: adjacent to the museum is a nice outdoor play area.

*3037 SW 2nd Ave. 503/823-2227. Open daily, 9 a.m.-5 p.m. Cost: $4/person, free/under 1.*

### END OF THE OREGON TRAIL INTERPRETIVE CENTER.

The second of four Oregon Trail history centers in the state, this Interpretive Center is visible from the freeway: Watch for the three Paul Bunyan-size covered wagons that mark the site. Inside the three main buildings are guides dressed in period clothing, a multimedia presentation dramatizing life on the trail, and the Provisioner's Depot, where kids learn what preparations were made by those who undertook the 2,000-mile trek. Complete your visit in the gallery, with its small collection of artifacts, including clothing, tools, and household items used by early settlers.

*1726 Washington St., Oregon City. 503/657-9336; www.teleport.com/~eotic. Open Mon.-Sat., 9 a.m.-5 p.m.; Sun., 10 a.m.-5 p.m. Cost: $5.50/adult, $4.50/senior 65 and over, $3/child 5-12, free/under 5.*

**OREGON HISTORY CENTER.** Located across Park Avenue from the Portland Art Museum and operated by the Oregon Historical Society, the Oregon History Center is the first place to come to learn about the state's rich heritage. The multisensory adventure, *Portland!*, provides an entertaining introduction to the Rose City's past. The museum presents permanent and changing exhibits that will bring Oregon history alive for little ones.

*1200 SW Park Ave. 503/222-1741; www.ohs.org. Open Mon.-Fri., 8:45 a.m.-5 p.m. (Thurs. until 8 p.m.); Sat., 10 a.m.-5 p.m.; Sun., noon-5 p.m. Cost: $6/adult, $1.50/student 6-12, free/under 6.*

**OREGON MUSEUM OF SCIENCE AND INDUSTRY.** This ambitious, state-of-the-art facility, housed in a gleaming steel-and-glass building, affords sweeping views of the Willamette River from its eastside location. Inside there's something for everyone: six exhibit halls with lots of hands-on activities, a five-story OMNIMAX theater, multimedia planetarium shows, laser light shows, and a rotating schedule of demonstrations. Discovery Space-an area for exploratory play-is reserved for children ages seven and under. Be sure to tour the *U.S.S. Blueback*, a 219-foot Navy submarine permanently docked here. With so much to see and do, you may want to plan a meal break at the attractive riverfront café.

*1945 SE Water Ave. 503/797-OMSI; www.omsi.edu. Open Tues.-Sun., 9:30 a.m.-5:30 p.m. (Thurs. until 8 p.m.). Cost: $6.50/adult, $4.50/senior and youth 3-17, free/under 3, two-for-one/Thurs., theater/planetarium tickets extra.*

**PORTLAND ART MUSEUM.** If you're not in the habit of sharing art with your children, this museum might be a good place to start. Founded in 1892, it is the oldest art museum in the Pacific Northwest. The collections are small but sterling: Northwest Coast Native American art, African art from the Cameroons, Asian art, and prints, drawings, and photographs by masters-old and modern.

Especially for families is the museum's series of Sunday open houses, where hands-on crafts, demonstrations, and performances introduce children to the art of other cultures. The open houses are held bimonthly, September through June.

*1219 SW Park Ave. 503/226-2811; www.pam.org. Open Tues.-Sun., 10 a.m.-5 p.m. (first Thursday of month until 9 p.m.) Cost: $7.50/adult, $6/senior & student 16 and over,*

*$2.50/student under 16, free/under 2, $10/family, free/first Thursday of month, 4-9 p.m.*

## ANIMALS, ANIMALS

**OREGON ZOO.** Like the nation's best "natural-style" parks, the zoo invites visitors to wander and discover. With a whole day—and lots of energy—you can tour the entire facility. But it may be more fun to pick several favorite habitats (African Rain Forest, Savanna, Antarctica, Alaska Tundra, Cascade Range) or animals. If possible, save time to let the kids clamber on the sculptures and somersault on the amphitheater lawn. For a meal break, visit the indoor cafeteria, which overlooks lush vegetation and colorful tropical birds in an enclosed aviary. Strollers and wagons are available for rent.

*4001 SW Canyon Road. 503/226-1561. Open daily, 9:30 a.m.-4 p.m. (winter); 9:30 a.m.-6 p.m. (summer). Cost: $5.50/adult, $4/senior 65 and over, $3.50/youth 3-11, free/under 3, free/second Tuesday of month, 3 p.m.-closing. Zoo Train Loop, $1.75/adult, $1.25/senior & youth 3-11, free/under 3.*

**PORTLAND AUDUBON WILDLIFE SANCTUARY.** Nestled against Forest Park's southwestern flank, the sanctuary is home to the Giant Pacific salamander (it barks like a dog and grows up to a foot long), bats (look for the wooden bat houses high up in the trees), and a variety of bird species. The 150 acres of dense forest encompass 4 miles of rugged trails that weave and loop over bridges and boardwalks along Balch Creek. Aspiring park rangers will want to visit the Wildlife Care Center, located at the trailhead, where volunteers tend injured birds and other forest creatures.

*5151 NW Cornell Road (West on NW Lovejoy St. until it becomes NW Cornell Road. Watch for signs.).*

*503/292-6855. Open Mon.-Sat., 10 a.m.-6 p.m.; Sun., 10 a.m.-5 p.m. Free.*

## KID CULTURE

**DANCE.** Young hoofers and aspiring ballet dancers will delight in seeing their wildest dancing dreams come true on stage. In Portland, the **Oregon Ballet Theatre** (503/2-BALLET) is the flagship dance company, offering an annual season of four productions at Civic Theater (SW 3rd Ave. & Clay) and Newmark Theater (1111 SW Broadway). But the "most inspirational dance" award must go to the **Jefferson Dancers** (503/916-5180), an ensemble composed of the most talented dance students in the Jefferson High School Performing and Visual Arts Magnet Program. This dance troupe, which maintains a repertoire of works in all dance styles, offers a series of performances in late spring at Newmark Theater (1111 SW Broadway).

**MUSIC.** If you have a budding young musician, or music critic, Portland is a great place to further his or her appreciation. The **Oregon Symphony** (503/228-1353) and **Portland Opera** (503/241-1802) both make a habit of reaching out to young audiences. The symphony offers its popular Kids Concerts series of one-hour performances at the Schnitzer Concert Hall (SW Broadway & Main). The Opera struts its "anything but stuffy" stuff at Civic Auditorium (SW 3rd Ave. & Clay). Its five-show season tends to blend traditional and innovative opera.

The nation's oldest youth orchestra, **Portland Youth Philharmonic** (503/223-5939) offers an ambitious repertoire mirroring those of major professional orchestras. It performs four concerts a year at Schnitzer Concert Hall (SW Broadway & Main). The **Metropolitan Youth Symphony** (503/228-9125) boasts student musicians from kindergarten to college age. The annual schedule features three major concerts at the Schnitzer Concert Hall (SW Broadway & Main) in December, March and June.

**THEATER.** Portland has several bright stars in children's theater. The **Northwest Children's Theater** (503/222-4480) is a nationally recognized company that has cornered the Portland youth theater market with alternatives for all interests, age levels, and budgets. With a reputation for showcasing classic plays and original adaptations of children's literature, NWCT now offers a four-production season that runs September through May at The Main Street Playhouse (904 SW Main St.).

Another big player is **Oregon Children's Theatre Company** (503/228-9571), a nonprofit professional theater company that presents two full-scale productions, November through May, in the Civic Auditorium (SW 3rd Ave. & Clay).

**Tears of Joy Theater** (530/248-0557 in Portland; 360/695-3050 in Vancouver, Washington), one of the nation's preeminent puppet troupes, develops inspirational programs that educate kids about faraway lands and peoples. The puppets themselves are custom-built for each show, and kids can visit with the puppeteers after the show to examine these creations and learn how they are manipulated. The company typically performs four shows a year, November through April, at the Vancouver Arts Center (400 W. Evergreen Blvd., Vancouver, Washington) and the Winningstad Theatre (1111 SW Broadway).

After 30 years in the children's theatre business, **Ladybug Theater** (503/232-2346) has become a Portland institution. Committed to offering preschoolers their first theater experiences, Ladybug's core of a half-dozen adult improvisation actors have adopted an informal style that invites audience participation. The troupe performs November through May at Oaks Amusement Park (SE Spokane St.). Wednesday matinées are a special bargain price.

**Tygres Heart Shakespearean Company** (503/222-9220) has developed a reputation for presenting fresh, bold theater. Though full-length performances may be overwhelming for many kids, the company's abridged Sunday Family Matinée series serves as a fine introduction to the works of the Bard. Productions are staged in the intimate, courtyard setting of the Winningstad Theatre (1111 SW Broadway).

Finally, if you're after something a little more avant-garde, check out **Imago Theatre** (503/231-9581). Recognized as one of the nations's most innovative mask ensembles, Imago established its reputation with the family favorite, Frogs, Lizards, Orbs, and Slinkys. The company performs August through May, at their own theater (17 SE 8th Ave.).

### SPECTATOR SPORTS

**THE PORTLAND TRAIL BLAZERS.** A National Basketball Association franchise, the Trail Blazers have recently settled into their new home in the Rose Garden. One of the league's glitziest venues, the Rose Garden is comfortable, roomy-and expensive. Most parents would agree that a ticket to a Blazers game is a special treat for a child. If you're going to go, though, think twice about buying the cheap seats, which may put you in the rafters. Instead, consult a ticket agent and ask about special discounts.

*Rose Garden, One Center Ct. 503/231-8000. Oct.-May. Cost: $15-80/seat.*

**THE PORTLAND ROCKIES.** This baseball team, a member of the northwest Single-A League, moved to Portland from Bend, Oregon, in 1995. Fans hope they never look back. Being new to the local sport scene, the Rockies offer very affordable entertainment for families. For bleacher seats, arrive just before the National Anthem, and settle in near the left-field line, just above the opposing team's bullpen. Bring your own treats or buy snacks or a kid's meal at the ballpark.

*Civic Stadium, 1844 SW Morrison. 503/223-2837. Mid-June-early Sept. Cost: $6.50/reserved, $4.50-5.50/general admission, $1-2.50/bleachers (day of game only).*

**THE PORTLAND WINTER HAWKS,** members of the Western Hockey League, play a fast-paced, rough game, peppered with the requisite brawls. On the West Coast, where kids are less likely to grow up on ice skates, hockey is an acquired taste. But the Winter Hawks, a Portland fixture for 22 years, enjoy a loyal following.

*Rose Garden, One Center Ct., or Memorial Coliseum, 1401 N. Wheeler Ave. 503/236-HAWK. Late Sept.-March. Cost: $9-14/seat.*

**LOCAL UNIVERSITIES** also offer a host of men's and women's competitions. Portland State University (724 SW Harrison; 503/725-5677) is best known for football and men's basketball. The University of Portland (5000 N. Willamette; 503/283-7525, Wed.-Fri., 1-5 p.m.) features soccer, basketball, volleyball, and baseball.

## EXCURSIONS

**COLUMBIA RIVER GORGE.** Although the Willamette River flows right through the middle of Portland, it's the Columbia that gets most of the attention. Just 40 miles east of town, along the Columbia River Gorge, is some of the state's finest scenery-fir-speckled cliffs and granite outcroppings, bubbling brooks and waterfalls. If time allows, drive up via the *Historic Columbia River Highway.* A masterpiece of engineering when it was built in 1915, this 22-mile road winds along a high bluff, past a dozen waterfalls and six state parks. A number of nice vistas and winding wooded trails are sprinkled along the way (see "Mount Hood/Columbia River Gorge").

*From Portland take I-84 east. If time allows, take Exit 17 from I-84 to Hwy. 30 and follow signs for the Columbia River Scenic Highway.*

**ENCHANTED FOREST.** Located on a wooded hillside near Salem (45 miles south), Enchanted Forest features a storybook land, built in a wooded setting, and a clever recreation of a mining town. School-aged children will enjoy the rides and haunted house. The whole family can enjoy Fantasy Fountains, a water-and-light show. (For more information, see "Willamette Valley: Salem.")

*8462 Enchanted Way SE, Turner (take I-5 south from Portland to Exit 248: Turner). 503/363-3060. Open daily, March 15-Sept., 9:30 a.m.-6 p.m. Cost: $6.50/adult, $4.95/senior, $5.75/child 3-12, free/under 3 (some rides are extra).*

**FORT VANCOUVER** was the northwest headquarters for the Hudson's Bay Company from 1818 to 1860. Its warehouses stocked supplies for the fur brigades and for Indian and settler trade. The stockade and five major outbuildings were reconstructed in 1966 after fires and decay destroyed the original fort. Visit the blacksmith shop, bakery, Indian trade shop, wash house, Chief Factor's residence, kitchen, and bastion. For special events, volunteers dressed in period costumes perform "living history" dramas. The Fort is located in Vancouver, Washington, a short trip north on I-5.

*612 E. Reserve St., Vancouver, Washington. 360/696-7655; 800/832-2599 (toll-free from Oregon only). Open daily, 9 a.m.-4 p.m. (winter); 9 a.m.-5 p.m. (summer). Cost: $4/family, $2/adult (summer), free (winter).*

**MOUNT HOOD.** At 11,247 feet, Mount Hood is the tallest peak in Oregon. Ski lifts here run year-round; even if you don't ski, the trip to the top is rewarding. At the end of the entrance road sits Timberline Lodge (Timberline; 503/231-5400, 800/547-1406). Built during the Depression as a showcase for the talents of local craftsmen, it is a masterpiece of hewn logs and great stone fireplaces. A slide show highlights the lodge's handiwork and architectural themes. Children with energy to burn can explore the three lobby areas, and there's a tabletop shuffleboard game. Perhaps the best meal option for families is at Government Camp. Owned and operated by Timberline, **The Brew Pub** (on Hwy. 26, Government Camp; 503/272-3724) serves pizza, hamburgers, salads, sandwiches, and chili in an informal chalet setting.

*From Portland take I-84 east to Hwy. 26, approx. 55 miles. At Government Camp, watch for signs to Timberline Lodge.*

**MOUNT ST. HELENS NATIONAL VOLCANIC MONUMENT.** The Monument's 110,000 acres include the volcano itself and the surrounding area devastated by the 1980 eruption. The Spirit Lake Memorial Highway stretches 45 miles east from I-5 at Castle Rock; traction devices may be required here during the winter months. Five miles east of Castle Rock is the

Monument Visitor Center, on the shore of Silver Lake. Here a walk-in model of a volcano, interpretive material, and films offer a fine introduction to the mountain. A short nature trail outside the center leads to a viewpoint where you can orient yourself to this amazing mountain.

There are two other visitor centers and miles of scenic road in the National Monument. If time allows an overnight excursion, see "Washington: Mount St. Helens. "

*From Portland, drive north on I-5 to the Castle Rock exit (approximately two hours), then 5 miles east.*

**SAUVIE ISLAND AND BYBEE HOUSE.** Sauvie Island, which sits in the Columbia River just north of the city, is a haven for bicyclists, bird-watchers, and sunbathers (there are four beaches along the northeastern shore). It's also the place to go in season to pick or buy fresh produce, especially berries, apples, pumpkins, and a variety of vegetables.

In summer you can tour the historic **Bybee House.** Built in 1858 by pioneers who arrived via the Oregon Trail, this nine-room Classic Revival dwelling was restored in 1966 by the Oregon Historical Society. Highlights include a series of living-history events titled *A Day in the Country*; and the Agricultural Museum, where children can explore horse-drawn farming equipment, and harness and woodworking shops. Even when the house is closed to the public, visitors are welcome to explore the grounds and neighboring wetlands.

*From Portland, drive northwest on Hwy. 30 to the Sauvie Island Bridge. Bybee House: Oregon History Center, Howell Park Road. 503/222-1741. Open Sat.-Sun., noon-5 p.m. Suggested donation: $3/adult, $2/child.*

**THE GREAT OUTDOORS**

**BOATING.** Although Portland's reliance on shipping for economic vitality is waning, the rivers continue to be focal points of local tourism (much to the delight of kids). **Cascade Sternwheelers** (503/223-3928) maintains an active schedule of narrated boat trips aboard authentic replicas of period sternwheelers, on the Willamette River (year-round) and the Columbia River (summer). Cruises leave from two downtown docks and one at Cascade Locks. Children have access to the pilot house and can stand aft to watch the paddlewheel up close.

**Great Rivers Cruises and Tours** (503/228-6228; 800/720-0012) maintains a 132-passenger catamaran that takes a seven-and-a-half-hour adventure to Bonneville Dam and back, May through late November. Another option is the three-hour lunch cruise on Saturdays. School-age children are entertained by the lively narration and open pilot house; younger ones tend to be put to sleep by the undulating currents. The **Sternwheeler Rose** (503/286-7673) is a jaunty little red-and-white paddle-wheeler that accommodates up to 130 passengers on its cruises south to Lake Oswego. Families might prefer the hour-long harbor tours. All cruises depart from the Oregon Museum of Science and Industry (1945 SE Water Ave.).

## *Design Your Own Boating Adventure*

If it's a more personal experience you're after, why not rent a craft and navigate the waters yourself? Rivers crisscross the region-you might sail the Columbia, canoe the Tualatin, or raft the Sandy. When you rent, ask for pointers from the staff (be sure to let them know the ages of family members), and request maps. And always, ALWAYS, wear personal flotation devices.

There are several choices for renting; phone ahead to make sure the craft you want will be available. **ALDER CREEK KAYAK & CANOE** (250 NE Tomahawk Island Dr.; 503/285-0464) rents only to paddlers with prior experience. Boaters put in on the Columbia River. If you need a brush-up on boating, ask about their classes and tours. At **EBB AND FLOW PADDLESPORTS** (0604 SW Nebraska; 503/245-1756), you can choose canoes or double kayaks. For convenience, you can cross the street and put in on the Willamette River, near Ross Island. **ISLAND SAILING CLUB** (503/285-7765) has a fleet of 28 sailboats; knowledge of sailing is required. **RIVER TRAILS** (336 Columbia River Hwy., Troutdale; 503/667-1964) offers both canoes and rafts.

Visiting in June or July? On weekends, **Oxbow Park** (503/797-1834) offers guided raft trips along the Sandy River. Ideally suited to beginners and families, these eight-hour trips cover 11 miles along a Class I (no white water) stretch of the river from Oxbow Park to Lewis and Clark State Park.

**BIKING.** Voted most bicycle-friendly city in the United States by *Bicycling Magazine*, Portland works hard to maintain its comprehensive network of bikeways. Bicycle trails wind through most city parks; particularly popular is the *Nature Trail* in Forest Park (see "Parks"). For maps and information, phone Portland Parks & Recreation (503/823-2223). To rent bikes for the whole family, try the **Bike Central Coop** (835 SW 2nd Ave.; 503/227-4439), **Bike Gallery** (821 SW 11th Ave.; 503/222-3821), or **Fat Tire Farm** (2714 NW Thurman; 503/222-3276).

**SNOW FUN.** You've heard a lot about Portland's wet weather; the good news is that, at a certain altitude, all that wetness guarantees SNOW. And Mount Hood, the state's highest peak, is within easy reach of the city. Always check weather conditions before heading up, and be prepared with traction devices and emergency supplies. For weather and road information, call the Oregon Department of Transportation (503/889-3999) or Slope Talk (800/593-2021).

## TIPS

It's convenient to rent equipment on the slopes, but remember that you may not find exactly what you need. If you have the means of transporting it, you may want to rent equipment in town. Several outdoor retail stores in Portland rent snow equipment; call ahead to make sure they have the children's equipment you need. Try **REI** (1798 Jantzen Beach Center; 503/283-1300), **BREEZE WINTER SPORTS RENTALS** (8100 SW Beaverton-Hillsdale Hwy.; 503/296-0504), or sports outlets on the way up the mountain—in Sandy, Welches, and Government Camp.

Mount Hood boasts some of the nation's most extensive ski resorts, and many sweeten the pot for parents by allowing kids under age seven to ski for free. **Cooper Spur Ski and Recreation Resort** (11000 Cloud Cap Road, Mount Hood; 541/352-7803), a smaller resort located on the eastern slope, is a popular family destination. Sole access to the 10 ski runs here is via T-bar, so this is a good spot for novice skiers. And the price is right; this is the least expensive resort around.

Another good spot for beginners is the **Summit Ski Area** (near Government Camp; 503/272-0256). Its chairlift and rope tow provide access to six runs of varying challenge. Lesson packages here are inexpensive and include rental of alpine ski or snowboard equipment.

By contrast, **Mount Hood Meadows Ski Resort** (Hwy. 35, Mount Hood; 503/337-2222), with 10 chair lifts, 82 runs, and 2,150 acres, is the largest day ski resort in the United States. **Mount Hood Ski Bowl** (near Government Camp; 503/272-3206; 503/222-BOWL) is the nation's largest night-ski area, with 34 lit runs.

Perhaps the best known ski resort in the area is **Timberline** (Hwy. 26, Timberline; 503/231-7979). Grand, historic Timberline Lodge sits near the summit of Mount Hood, over-looking activity on six chairlifts and 32 trails. Timberline hosts the nation's longest spring/summer ski season.

## CALENDAR

### FEBRUARY
International Film Festival, Portland Art Museum.

### MAY
Cinco de Mayo: Food and continuous entertainment with Mexican flair, Waterfront Park.

### JUNE
Portland Rose Festival: Twenty-four days of parades, concerts, air shows, and car races.

### JUNE-AUGUST
Outdoor Concerts, at Pioneer Courthouse Square, Washington Park Zoo and Oregon Square.

### JULY
Fort Vancouver July Fourth Celebration: Fireworks and fun at historic fort, Vancouver, Washington.

Riverfest: Waterfront Blues Festival.

Multnomah County Fair: Rides, crafts, animals, food, and fun.

### AUGUST
The Bite, A Taste of Portland: Northwest bands and selections from Portland restaurants, Waterfront Park.

### SEPTEMBER
Artquake: A celebration of visual arts, music, theatre, and dance; downtown.

Mount Hood Jazz Festival: Features big-name performers, Mount Hood Community College, Gresham.

Horst Mager Oktoberfest: Bavarian food and music and lots of activities for kids, Oaks Amusement Park.

Wintering-in Harvest Festival: Crafts, food, and tours, Bybee House on Sauvie Island.

**OCTOBER**

ZooBoo!: Two weeks of train rides, games, crafts, and food, Oregon Zoo.

**NOVEMBER**

Meier & Frank Holiday Parade, downtown.

Young People's Film and Video Festival, Portland Art Museum.

**DECEMBER**

Christmas at Fort Vancouver: Scottish and Irish music in historic setting, Vancouver, Washington.

Zoolights Festival: Outdoor holiday light display, Oregon Zoo.

"Nutcracker" Performances: Oregon Ballet Theatre performs 22 shows in three weeks.

Portland Parade of Ships: Festively decorated boats on the Columbia and Willamette rivers.

## RESOURCES

**PORTLAND/OREGON VISITORS ASSOCIATION**
26 SW Salmon St., Portland 97204
503/275-9750; 877/678-5263; www. pova.com

**ROAD CONDITIONS**
503/222-6721

**TRI-MET,** bus & light-rail transportation information
503/238-RIDE; Web site: www.trimet.org

**WEATHER INFORMATION**
503/275-9792

**BABY-SITTING SERVICES**
Auntie Fay Agency, 503/293-6252
Care Givers Placement Agency Inc., 503/244-6370
Northwest Nannies Inc., 503/245-5288

**BOOKS AND PUBLICATIONS**
*Portland Parent* (503/645-6508), a free monthly newsmagazine for parents, contains a complete calendar of local activities and outings for families. It is available at most children's shops and libraries in the greater Portland area.

*Out and About Portland with Kids,* by Elizabeth Hartzell DeSimone, is the definitive family guide to the Rose City, written by the former editor of Portland Parent.

## YAMHILL

Yamhill is 40 miles southwest of Portland-probably too far away, if seeing Portland is your focus. But from here you have the option of a day-long excursion into the city, if you choose; or drive west to the ocean and spend a day in the sands.

### FLYING M RANCH
*23029 NW Flying M Road, 97148*
*503-662-3222; www.Flying-M-Ranch.com*
*Rates: Inexpensive to moderate*
*FYI: Full kitchens (most cabins); trail rides; landing strip*

The Mitchell family has owned this land, 40 miles southwest of Portland, for more than a century. At one time, a hotel here served weary travelers on the Trask Mountain Stagecoach route. Since 1985, the ranch has offered families a choice of cabin or motel-style accommodations in a beautiful, serene setting, at the end of the road in the Coast Range. Go for a day trip or for a week's vacation, and take advantage of the ranch's trail rides (year-round) and ranch-style cuisine (open daily, April-Oct., breakfast, lunch, and dinner; open Nov.-March, Thurs., lunch and dinner; Fri.-Sun., breakfast, lunch, and dinner).

This is an old-fashioned, dude-ranch kind of experience. The seven cabins are rustic and neat, sleeping from two to 10 people each. Most have kitchens and woodstoves; a few have a TV; one ("Honeymoon") has a Jacuzzi. The 24 rooms in the bunkhouse all have two queen beds and a private bath, but lack the Western charm of the cabins. If you happen to own a small airplane, you might consider flying in; the ranch has its own private airstrip.

**66 PARENT COMMENTS**

*"The kids discovered good fishing holes and swimming holes, not far from the cabins."*

*"We had a ball on the trail rides, although we had sore bottoms for two days. Next time we hope to take the trail that goes all the way out to the coast!"*

*"This is a quick getaway, for a long weekend or for two weeks. There's a nice balance between quiet times and active times, and enough to do that the kids can stay active the whole time if they want."*

## OREGON COAST

The Oregon Coast is one of the Northwest's most scenic and entertaining places to go with children. The wind-battered shoreline is magnificent, with miles of sandy beach, rocky outcroppings, sand dunes, and sea stacks. There is something special to see around each bend—capes and observation points, lighthouses, little roadside museums, tide pools, wildlife, tiny beach towns, and quirky little shops. Vacation spots are as diverse as the 360-mile coastline—from grassy dunes to redwood groves, first-class resorts to funky cabins on the beach.

One word of warning: On weekends in the spring and all summer long, accommodations along the coast fill up fast. Make your reservations early.

### GETTING THERE

As you drive I-5, the major north-south corridor west of the Cascades, there are several highways that head west to the coast. An efficient route from up north is to leave I-5 at Longview-Kelso, take Highway 433 across the Columbia River bridge at Longview, and connect with Highway 30 to Astoria and Highway 101 (the coastal highway). Travel time from Seattle to Astoria is about 4 1/2 hours.

From Portland, a popular route is Highway 26 (also known as Sunset Highway) to Seaside or Cannon Beach.

If you're headed to the central or southern coast, several scenic highways connect I-5 to Highway 101: Highway 20 from Albany to Newport, Highway 126 from Eugene to Florence, Highway 42 from Roseburg to Bandon.

Highway 101 hugs the coastline the entire length of the state. Allow plenty of time for travel—this is an excellent two-lane highway but at almost every curve a magnificent vista, a trail leading off the highway, a quaint town, or an interesting attraction beckons you to make an unscheduled stop.

### REGIONAL RESOURCES

#### CENTRAL OREGON COAST ASSOCIATION
P.O. Box 2094, Newport, Oregon 97365
541/265-2064; 800/767-2064; www.coca@newportnet.com
"Coast Travel Pack" includes guide, calendar, brochures, maps, and tidebooks.

**BOOKS AND PUBLICATIONS**

*Best Hikes for Children in Central and Western Oregon*, by Bonnie Henderson. The Mountaineers, 1992. Includes several hikes along the coast.

*Oregon Coast Magazine*, published bimonthly, includes maps, in-depth stories, and descriptions of towns and attractions. P.O. Box 18000, Florence, Oregon 97439-0130
541/997-8401

*Oregon's North Coast in a Nutshell Tourmap* and *Oregon's South Coast in a Nutshell Tourmap* are travel guides and road maps combined. Send $8 ($5.95 plus $2.05 shipping and handling. P.O. Box 230998
Tigard, Oregon 97281-0998

*Oregon's Coast: A Guide to Best Family Attractions from Astoria to Brookings*, by David and Carolyn Gabbe. Johnston Associates International. Offers interesting historical background and useful details on the many events and attractions of interest to families along the coast.

# NORTHERN OREGON COAST

## ASTORIA

The history of Astoria is inextricably tied to its location at the mouth of the Columbia River. Founded as a fur trading post in 1811, it served as winter quarters for the surveyors Lewis and Clark in 1805, and as the first defense of the Columbia River during the Civil War and World Wars I and II. Astoria today is a pleasant mix of working fishing docks and restored Victorian mansions, accessible beaches, and historical sites. Although it's not right on the ocean, it's a 10-minute drive to the beach, and there are plenty of activities right in town to keep a family entertained for a weekend.

### PLACES TO STAY

**RED LION INN**
*400 Industry St., 97103*
*800/547-8010; www.travelweb.com*
*Rates: Moderate*
*FYI: Restaurants; small pets OK (fee)*

If you brought the family hound along (and who can resist bringing Fido to the seashore), this comfortable hotel is a good choice. There are 124 units, but only one has two bedrooms, so make reservations early if your family requires a more spacious room.

The inn's location, one mile west of the junction with Highway 30, provides a nice view of the Columbia River.

**❝❝ PARENT COMMENTS**

*"We enjoyed standing on our balcony and watching the river activity."*

*"The hotel restaurant had good seafood and pasta dishes."*

### ROSEBRIAR HOTEL

*636 14th St. (at Franklin), 97103*
*503/325-7427, 800/487-0224;*
*www.oregoncoastlodging.com/rosebriar*
*Rates: Moderate*
*FYI: Full breakfast and afternoon tea; smoke-free throughout*

Built in 1902 as a private residence, this spot went through many changes before becoming the lovely 11-room hotel it is today. The Rosebriar sits high on a hill overlooking Astoria and, despite phones and TVs in every room, has retained a good deal of its original charm. The rooms are small, but beautifully furnished, and the common areas are cozy and comfortable.

The ground-floor suite works well for a small family—it has a queen-sized bed, plus a sofa bed in the sitting room. If your family doesn't require separate sleeping areas, the new Carriage House is also a good choice. Located across the courtyard from the hotel, it has kitchen, sitting, and sleeping areas all in one large room.

**❝❝ PARENT COMMENTS**

*"Every last detail has been taken care of to make sure you have a relaxed and pleasant visit. I came to this elegant inn for a weekend getaway with my two daughters (ages six and nine). We explored Fort Stevens Park all day and returned in time to enjoy afternoon tea by the cozy fireplace in the parlor."*

*"Divine breakfasts!"*

## PLACES TO EAT

### SHIP INN

*One 2nd St.*
*503/325-0033*
*Hours: Lunch, dinner daily*

This quintessential coast restaurant is located on the waterfront, with a great view of boat activity on the Columbia River. They are renowned for their four-star (halibut) fish and chips, but also serve classic sandwiches and salads, and a few English specialties. The child's plate features fish and chips, toasted cheese, or pb&j.

## RIO CAFÉ
*125 9th St.*
*503/325-2409*
*Hours: Lunch Mon.-Sat., dinner Thurs.-Sat.*

This bustling café serves real Mexican fare, homemade with fresh, local ingredients. The sauces are tangy and tasty; you're not likely to go wrong with any of the sauced entrées. The children's menu includes a small enchilada, tostada, burrito, soup, and salad. Generally, the children's foods are less spicy; more tolerant kids can add hot sauce. Visual interest here is high; colorful knickknacks and banners abound. And the Mexican tunes keep the place jumping.

Rio means river, and this spot is just a block from the Columbia. Take a stroll down and work off some of that hearty meal.

## WHAT TO SEE & DO

**THE ASTORIA COLUMN.** This is a great place to begin your exploration of Astoria. Climb the 164-step spiral staircase, and you'll be rewarded with more than just an aerobic workout. From the top, you'll have spectacular panoramic views of the town, river, and distant mountain peaks. The outside of the column depicts 14 historical scenes commemorating important events in the history of Astoria. The earliest scenes are at the base, and the mural spirals upward around the 125-foot structure.

*Atop Coxcomb Hill, on Coxcomb Hill Road. 503/325-6311. Open daily, 8 a.m.-dusk; information booth daily, 11 a.m.-6 p.m. (summer). Free.*

**COLUMBIA RIVER MARITIME MUSEUM.** Beginning with the "discovery" of the mouth of the Columbia by Robert Gray in 1792, this fine museum celebrates the fascinating maritime history of Astoria. Even the building is shaped like a roaring wave. Visitors can view the most extensive maritime collection in the Northwest, including displays about lighthouses, navigation, and naval history. Climb aboard the lightship *Columbia River*, view the river through a submarine conning tower, and see the actual bridge of a ship. Kids will especially enjoy the whaling exhibits, and the photos of past shipwrecks. When in port, the Coast Guard ship *Resolute* is moored outside, at the 17th Street Pier, and is open for tours.

*1792 Marine Dr. 503/325-2323. Open daily, 9:30 a.m.-5 p.m. Cost: $5/adult, $4/senior, $2/youth 6-17, free/under 6.*

## Oregon Coast Lighthouses: Connecting Us with a Romantic Past

What is the connection we feel with lighthouses? Is it the sense of history or just the romance? Whatever it is, children seem to feel it innately. The lighthouses of the Oregon Coast, though unoccupied by lightkeepers since the dawn of modern technology, have been painstakingly preserved to ensure that modern-day visitors feel the connection with their seafaring past.

Set on headlands or near estuaries, most of the lighthouses along the Oregon Coast were built in the late 1800s. The nine still standing have been placed on the National Register of Historic Places; seven are open to the public. Don't feel that if you've seen one, you've seen them all; each has unique characteristics and fascinating stories to tell.

These lighthouses, listed north to south, are described in detail under their individual locations:
- Cape Meares Lighthouse (1890), at the entrance to Tillamook Bay.
- Yaquina Bay Lighthouse (1871), in Yaquina Bay State Park at the southern edge of Newport.
- Yaquina Head Lighthouse (1873), in the Yaquina Head Natural Area.
- Heceta Head Lighthouse (1894), 12 miles north of Florence.
- Umpqua River Lighthouse (1890), just south of Reedsport.
- Coquille River Lighthouse (1896), in Bullard Beach State Park, near Bandon.
- Cape Blanco Lighthouse (1870), in Cape Blanco State Park, near Port Orford.

**FORT CLATSOP NATIONAL MEMORIAL** is an authentic replica of the log fort where Lewis and Clark wintered in 1805-06. Also here is the historic canoe landing on the Lewis and Clark River (watch little ones closely on this slippery riverbank). The expedition's Salt Works, where salt was derived from seawater, is 15 miles south in Seaside (on Lewis and Clark Way near Beach Drive).

During the summer, employees dress in period costumes to demonstrate frontier survival skills that include carving dugout canoes, starting fires, loading flintlock muzzles, tanning hides, sewing clothes, making candles, and drawing maps to scale. The Visitor Center's bookstore offers historical, natural, and cultural resources.

*92343 Fort Clatsop Road (six miles southwest, off Hwy. 101). 503/861-2471. Open daily, 8 a.m.-6 p.m. (summer); 8 a.m.-5 p.m. (winter). Cost: $2/person or $4/car.*

**FORT STEVENS STATE PARK** sits right at the mouth of the Columbia River. The fort was built by the Union Army during the Civil War, to keep Confederate frigates from entering the river. Though never needed for that purpose, the fort was fired on in 1942 by a Japanese submarine (thereby becoming the only U.S. fort to be fired on since the War of 1812, though the attack lasted about 10 minutes). School-age children will be interested in the old artillery installations (the noise you hear is not an invasion, merely youngsters testing the acoustics beneath the bunkers) and an Interpretive Center that displays old weapons, maps, and other war relics. At low tide, look for the hull of the British schooner *Peter Iredale*, which foundered here in 1906.

The largest state park in Oregon, Fort Stevens encompasses 4,000 acres, miles of hiking and biking trails, and two large picnic areas. The flat, paved bike paths are perfect for little peddlers; the family can bike the entire area in less than an hour. Other park recreation includes boating, fishing, and swimming at Coffenbury Lake.

*Ten miles west of Astoria, off Hwy. 101. 503/861-2000. Interpretive Center open daily, 10 a.m.-6 p.m. (summer); 8 a.m.-5 p.m.(remainder of year). Cost: parking $3/car.*

## CALENDAR

**MAY**
Maritime Week, Astoria.

### RESOURCES

##### ASTORIA CHAMBER OF COMMERCE
111 W. Marine Dr., P.O. Box 176, Astoria 97103
503/325-6311

## SEASIDE

Oregon's largest and oldest ocean resort town is on Highway 101, 16 miles south of Astoria. Seaside is at the western end of the Lewis and Clark Trail, and apparently many modern-day travelers also consider it the end of the trail—the town is crammed with hotels, game arcades, fast-food restaurants, cotton candy, and throngs of vacationers looking for a good time. Many families give Seaside a thumbs-down review because of this unleashed development and prefer to drive on to more scenic and restful spots. However, some of our reviewers loved the carnival atmosphere of this lively town. We have included their recommendations here.

### GETTING THERE

Seaside is about 12 miles south of Astoria on Highway 101.

### PLACES TO STAY

##### SHILO OCEANFRONT RESORT
*30 N. Prom, 97138*
*Rates: Moderate*
*FYI: Restaurant; kitchens (some units); indoor pool; fitness center; game room*

The two-mile promenade on the beachfront is crowded with places to stay. There's so little space between the various establishments that from behind them you're hard-pressed to catch a glimpse of the ocean. Once you're in Seaside, though, you might as well adopt the attitude that crowds and a "Coney Island" atmosphere are fine, in which case you won't mind accommodations along this strip.

This five-story Shilo Inn on "hotel row" is actually very comfortable. The rooms are clean and spacious, and the common areas are large and comfortable. It's nice to have such easy access to the beach.

### 66 PARENT COMMENTS

*"On our last visit here, we had quite a bit of rain. We were thankful for the indoor pool, which is exceptionally nice and*

*overlooks the ocean. We ended up reading books and maga-
zines in the lobby area, which is warm and comfortable."*

*"We loved the Shilo, and we loved the town of Seaside. The
Arcade on Broadway really wowed our kids—bumper cars,
video games, cotton candy—you name it! And it's an easy
shot to Cannon Beach."*

*"Just don't imagine a cozy beach cabin on a lonely beach-
you'll be sorely disappointed."*

## PLACES TO EAT

### DOOGER'S SEAFOOD AND GRILL

*505 Broadway
503/738-3773
Hours: Lunch, dinner daily*

Dooger's has a well-deserved reputation for offering a wide
selection of good, fresh seafood: halibut, scallops, squid, rock
shrimp, salmon, petrale sole, and, on occasion, razor clams.
You choose the preparation—lightly coated and fried, sautéed,
Cajun style, or poached. If seafood's not your first choice, you
can get a good sandwich, veggie or regular burger, fettucini, or
steak. Be prepared to wait for a table, especially in summer;
once you're seated, the service is quick.

## WHAT TO SEE & DO

**FUN ON WHEELS.** Biking of any kind is popular in Seaside.
Several shops rent bikes, trikes, quads, and skates of all shapes and
sizes. The three-wheeled "fun cycles," designed to be ridden on the
beach, are loads of fun for all ages. They sit low to the ground and
are so easy to pedal that the littlest ones won't have to struggle to
keep up. At **Manzanita Fun Merchants** (503/368-6606; 200 Ave.
A), you'll find traditional bicycles and complimentary trailers, jogging strollers, tandem and recumbent bicycles, and the ubiquitous
"fun cycles." **Prom Bike Shop** (503/738-8251; 622 12th) has bikes,
all-terrain bikes, "fun cycles," training bikes, tandems, and skates.

**MILLION DOLLAR WALK.** Chances are your kids will zero in
on this half-mile stretch of Broadway between Roosevelt
Drive and the beach. Good luck getting past the bumper cars,
miniature golf, skee-ball, video games, pinball, and sweets—
might as well dole out the quarters and resolve yourselves to
some people-watching.

## CANNON BEACH/TOLOVANA PARK

Cannon Beach was named for the cannon that washed ashore from a schooner shipwrecked in 1846. Seven miles down the coast from Seaside, it's a picturesque coastal town, full of interesting shops and art galleries, white-washed cottages, and good restaurants. Its seven miles of beach are marked by hulking Haystack Rock and the accompanying rock formations, The Needles. This is a great place to be if you enjoy mixing the fun of the beach with the diversions of a small business and art district.

Tolovana Park, just south of Cannon Beach, is a much smaller town and may feel more accessible. The drive into Cannon Beach (or even the bike ride) is short and relaxing. Finding parking in Cannon Beach is the trick, at least in summer.

### PLACES TO STAY

**HALLMARK RESORT**
*1400 S. Hemlock, 97110*
*503/436-1566, 800/345-5676*
*Rates: Expensive*
*FYI: Kitchens; fireplaces (most units); indoor pool; exercise room; pets OK (fee)*

This attractive, cedar-shake resort sits on a bluff just opposite Haystack Rock. Accommodations are available in different sizes and sleeping configurations. Typical accommodations for four would include living room with fireplace and pull-down Murphy bed, and a separate bedroom with queen bed or two twin beds. Fireplace wood and morning paper are delivered daily.

Pool facilities here are particularly convenient for families. There is a separate wading pool for little ones, two hot tubs of varying temperatures, and a sauna.

Beach access is via a wooden staircase that takes you down the bluff. The beach is lovely and wide, and the tide pools at Haystack Rock—right in front of the resort—are replete with starfish and sea anemones.

**❝ PARENT COMMENTS**

*"The wall bed in the living room is such a good idea. We housed the kids in the bedroom, and then were able to enjoy the ocean and fireplace from the living room after they'd gone to sleep. Hate to admit it, but it was great having two TVs."*

*"The long stairs to the beach can be a nuisance for families with very young children."*

*"In my opinion, this is the nicest place to stay with kids on the northern Oregon coast. The panoramic vista of the ocean, beach, and Haystack Rock is magnificent (splurge and get an oceanfront room). The indoor pool facilities were as nice as I've seen at a hotel, and Cannon Beach is a great little town to explore."*

*"Lovely, but very upscale for a beach vacation."*

**THE SEA SPRITE**

*280 Nebesna, Tolovana Park 97145*
*503/436-2266*
*Rates: Moderate*
*FYI: Kitchens; woodstoves; laundry*

The Sea Sprite is a lovely spot right on the beach, a 10-minute walk south of Haystack Rock. It is located on a dead-end street, so there is no traffic noise and kids can wander about the grounds safely. The décor is comfortable and homey. There are six units, each sleeping from two to eight people (one is a two-bedroom unit). Parents in charge of sand control will appreciate the free use of motel beach towels and blankets and the washer and dryer on premises.

**❝ PARENT COMMENTS**

*"It is very hard to find a funky but clean and comfortable little place right on the beach that welcomes children. The Sea Sprite is perfect—quiet and away from it all but an easy walk or drive into the charming diversions of Cannon Beach."*

**SURFSAND RESORT**

*1080 Ecola Ct., 97110*
*503/436-2274; www.surfsand.com*
*Rates: Moderate to expensive*
*FYI: Kitchens (some units); fireplaces (some units); indoor pool; pets OK (fee)*

This 174-unit motel is right on the ocean, just a few blocks from the center of town. The joys of being right on the beach are many—enjoying a cup of coffee on your balcony while watching the kids in the sand below, and taking the beach route into town, to name two. The beach is wide and good for flying kites and exploring tide pools. Understandably, it can be difficult to get reservations here, particularly in the summer.

Rooms at the Surfsand are spacious and comfortable. If you choose one with a kitchen, you may want to shop in Seaside; options for groceries are limited in Cannon Beach. Saturdays in summer, the resort hosts a wiener roast over a beach fire.

**❝❝ PARENT COMMENTS**

*"It's fun for little kids to feed seagulls from the balcony."*

*"At the Surfsand, the ocean is on your doorstep. In fact, the ocean is your doorstep! We love this place."*

### TOLOVANA INN
*3400 S. Hemlock, Tolovana Park, 97145*
*503/436-2211; www.v-a.com*
*Rates: Moderate to expensive*
*FYI: Kitchens; indoor pool; small playground, game room; pets OK (fee)*

The Tolovana Inn is right on the ocean, two miles south of Cannon Beach. The condominium-style units, built in the late '60s and early '70s, are functional if not particularly attractive. Each unit above the ground floor has a lanai, a fireplace, and a view. The two-bedroom units have two TVs, which is convenient for a larger group. The staff delivers a fireplace log and a morning paper, daily.

Less expensive than other motels on the beach, Tolovana Inn also has an indoor pool. All in all, it's a good bargain for this part of the coast.

**❝❝ PARENT COMMENTS**

*"We highly recommend the Tolovana Inn. We visited with our six-month-old baby and twin three-year-old boys. We were relieved it was not too fancy—we didn't have to worry about the kids damaging the place (green shag rug is very forgiving). It's less pretentious than the fancier places in Cannon Beach."*

*"We rented "fun cycles" in Cannon Beach and rode on the beach. All of us—kids ages 14, 10, and eight months—had a ball. The baby fell asleep in the trailer right away, and got her nap while the rest of the family got some exercise."*

### THE WAVES
*188 W. 2nd St., 97110*
*800/822-2468; www.thewavesmotel.com*

*Rates: Expensive*
*FYI: Kitchens (most units); fireplaces (most units)*

This new, upscale resort has four clusters of beautifully designed buildings, offering a variety of accommodations suitable for families. Units are new and nicely furnished. You can't beat the location—next to the beach and just a block from town.

**❝❝ PARENT COMMENTS**

*"The Craftsman-style buildings are lovely; units are tastefully furnished and offer every convenience. The beach is about ten feet away. It's pricey, but a worthwhile splurge for a couple of nights."*

*"Considering the cost, we were disappointed that there was no pool."*

**HOUSE RENTALS.** Oceanfront accommodations in Cannon Beach are quite expensive. Ask some of the hotels and resorts whether they rent houses or units in town, farther from the beach. The Chamber of Commerce may also be of assistance in finding less expensive accommodations.

**Cannon Beach Property Management** (503/436-2021) has more than 20 properties for rent to families. While not necessarily a cost saver, staying in a private home is a nice option if you are a mid- to large-size group. A one-week minimum stay is required in July and August.

## PLACES TO EAT

### DOOGER'S SEAFOOD AND GRILL

*1371 S. Hemlock*
*503/436-2225*
*Hours: Breakfast, lunch, dinner daily*

Dooger's has a well-deserved reputation for good, fresh seafood and friendly service. What's more, they serve a wide selection, including halibut, scallops, squid, rock shrimp, salmon, petrale sole, and, on occasion, razor clams. You choose the preparation—lightly coated and fried, sautéed, Cajun style, or poached. Seafood's your best bet, but you can get a good sandwich, veggie or regular burger, fettucini or steak. Breakfasts include some seaside favorites—fresh oysters and eggs, and Hangtown Fry, a tasty concoction of eggs, oysters, bacon, onions, and bay shrimp.

There is a kids' menu, but it pales beside the regular fare. Prices are moderate and, though you may wait for a table, the service is quick.

### MIDTOWN CAFÉ
*1235 S. Hemlock*
*541/436-1016*
*Hours: Breakfast, lunch daily*

You might feel a bit cramped for space, but kids will likely love this hole-in-the-wall spot. The décor is random—everything from wind-up toys to ceramic figurines—but in general the Midtown can easily accommodate families. Don't be surprised if there's a line, though; this is a favorite hangout for locals and visitors alike.

The food here is healthy—burritos, tofu egg scramble, corn-cheddar pancakes, oat scones—and the servings are generous. Lunches include hearty soups and sandwiches. Accompany your choice of entrée with a fresh-fruit smoothie, and you won't be disappointed.

### LAZY SUSAN CAFÉ
*126 N. Hemlock*
*503/436-2816*
*Hours: Breakfast, lunch daily; dinner Thurs.-Sun.*

This sunny little restaurant is where you'll find a large share of the locals on any given morning. The smell of fresh baked goods wafts out the door, and the customers wander in. Breakfasts here are delicious—waffles with fresh fruit, homemade granola, omelets to order. Lunch choices include hearty sandwiches, quiches, and soups (their seafood stew is very tasty). There's not much room to wait for your table inside the restaurant; put your name on the list and window-shop for a bit.

### MO'S RESTAURANT
*3400 S. Hemlock, Tolovana Park*
*503/436-1111*
*Hours: Breakfast, lunch, dinner daily*

More than a place to eat, Mo's is an institution that has become part of the experience of visiting the Oregon coast. Food reviews are mixed—some say the seafood is just so-so; others swear the clam chowder and oyster stew are to die for. Or try a dinner salad (sprinkled with tiny bay shrimp). If you arrive extra-hungry, start with a couple of orders of the cheese bread. (It won't win a heart-healthy competition, but it's a buttery favorite with kids.)

Mo's has a lengthy kids' menu, so those who turn their noses up at seafood can choose burgers, hotdogs, grilled cheese, and the like. All the Mo's Restaurants are busy, noisy places that work well for families.

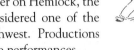

## WHAT TO SEE & DO

**THE COASTER THEATER** offers year-round live entertainment for a family audience in a rustic theater on Hemlock, the main street in Cannon Beach. It is considered one of the finest community theaters in the Northwest. Productions include plays, musicals, comedy, and dance performances.

*108 N. Hemlock. 503/436-1242. Schedules and ticket prices vary; call for details.*

**HAYSTACK ROCK.** This 235-foot monolith, looming just offshore at the south end of Cannon Beach, fascinates young and old alike. At low tide, the pools at the base of the rock teem with intertidal creatures. During low tide on summer weekends, volunteers from the Haystack Rock Interpretive Program offer on-site talks about the tide pools and their resident creatures.

**HEMLOCK STREET.** The main street of town, running parallel to the beach and two blocks away, is one long, entertaining stroll. To open your eyes of a morning, **Hane's Bakerie** (1064 S. Hemlock; 503/436-0120) has croissants worth getting out of bed for, as well as tasty muffins and breads. To fashion a quick picnic for the beach, grab a slice of pizza from **Pizza á Fetta** (231 N. Hemlock; 503/436-0333), or hit **Osborn's Ice Creamery & Deli** (240 N. Hemlock; 503/436-2234) for thick sandwiches and accoutrements. If the kiddos fancy a touch of the sweet, **Bruce's Candy Kitchen** (256 N. Hemlock; 503/436-2641) has delicious homemade saltwater taffy and buttery-good caramel corn.

There are art galleries galore along Hemlock Street; one of the nicest is **White Bird** (251 N. Hemlock; 503/436-2681). There's lots of glass here, though, so families with toddlers will want to stick with window shopping.

### PARKS

**ECOLA STATE PARK.** A short, pretty drive through a canopied forest brings you to the parking area overlooking Crescent Beach. Here are a number of picnic areas, but be sure to prepare for the ubiquitous coastal breezes. The beach itself, a short trek down the bluff, is better protected from the wind. The walk down to the beach can be difficult in parts, such as navigating large driftwood logs and stones, so little ones should be carried or closely supervised. It's a two-mile drive or hike from the parking lot to Indian Beach, an equally beautiful (and often less crowded) spot.

*Off Hwy. 101 just north of town.*

**OSWALD WEST PARK.** One of the first parks developed in Oregon, Oswald West encompasses nearly 2,500 acres, most of which are undeveloped. The recreational opportunities here are nearly endless, including surfing, kayaking, clam digging, photography, camping, and hiking.

Nearby **Neahkahnie Mountain** may well provide the best view on the northern coast. The two-mile hike that climbs Neahkahnie is steep, however, and not recommended for hikers under age five. It leads to a magnificent mountain-top view of the sea from 1,800 feet, an excellent place to watch for migrating gray whales. On the way up, depending on the season, you may cross meadows of vividly colored wildflowers, or spot some of the abundant wildlife.

*9500 Sandpiper Lane (off Hwy. 101, 8 miles south of Cannon Beach). 503/368-5154.*

### THE GREAT OUTDOORS

**BIKING.** On the wide beach, with no traffic or hills, what's not to like about biking? Especially good for young peddlers are the three-wheeled "fun cycles." They sit low to the ground and are easy to pedal, so even a child who hasn't learned to ride a two-wheeler can join in. These "fun cycles," as well as traditional bikes and trailers, are available at **Manzanita Fun Merchants** (503/436-1880; 1180 S. Hemlock). **Mike's Bike Shop** (503/436-1266; 800/492-1266; 248 N. Spruce) rents "fun cycles," mountain bikes, and single-speed beach cruisers. Trailers to carry toddlers are also available.

**HORSEBACK RIDING** on the beach or through coastal forest is a favorite Cannon Beach pastime (watch out for the evidence when you walk the beach). Horses to suit all ages and skill levels are available for guided rides through **Sea Ranch Stables** (north end of Cannon Beach; 503/436-1268). Reservations are advised.

**KITE FLYING.** Is any sight more joyful than a child flying a kite at the ocean? Practical, too, as there are steady winds, no trees, and no electical wires. There are eight **Catch the Wind** kite shops on the coast (Seaside, Cannon Beach, Lincoln City, Rockaway Beach, Depoe Bay, Agate Beach, Newport, and Florence). They'll dazzle the whole family with their selection of windsocks and kites of every size, shape, and color!

# Do You Speak "Whale Watching"?

California gray whales are magnificent animals that can be spotted off the coast of Oregon during their 6,000-mile migration between Baja California and the Arctic. The best times to spot these giant mammals are mid-December to February and March to June. In the spring, it's possible to see mothers with their calves, as well as courting behavior among adults.

Toward the end of March, volunteers hang out at various viewpoints along the coast, answering questions and helping visitors spot whales. Look for the "Whale Watching Spoken Here" signs. Be sure to dress warmly, bring a rain jacket (if the rain doesn't find you, the surf will), and, of course, your binoculars.

Early morning before the whitecaps appear is the easiest time to see the whales' spouts (although volunteer whale watchers are out from 10 a.m. to 1 p.m.). Gray days are better than bright ones, because the whales swim closer to the land when the sky is overcast.

Here are some of the more popular whale-watching spots (listed north to south):

- Neahkahnie Mountain Historic Marker, near Manzanita
- Cape Foulweather, north of Depoe Bay
- Depoe Bay State Park and the Observatory Lookout
- Devil's Punchbowl, south of Depoe Bay
- Yaquina Bay, Newport
- Yachats State Park
- Umpqua Lighthouse, near Reedsport
- Devil's Churn/Cape Perpetua, near Yachats
- Face Rock Wayside State Scenic Viewpoint, Bandon
- Cape Blanco Lighthouse, north of Port Orford
- Harris Beach State Park, Brookings

If you're seeking the thrill of viewing these leviathans up close and personal, look into a whale-watching cruise. They're offered by many tour companies, especially around Newport and Depoe Bay. Some run cruises as often as once an hour during peak migration.

## CALENDAR

### APRIL

Puffin Kite Festival: Competition includes the highest kite, ugliest kite, relay races, and much more, 541/436-2623.

### JUNE

Sandcastle Day: More than 1,000 participants produce imaginative sand sculptures in this renowned event.

## RESOURCES

### CANNON BEACH CHAMBER OF COMMERCE

2nd & Spruce, Cannon Beach 97110
503/436-2623

### THE HAYSTACK PROGRAM IN THE ARTS AND SCIENCES

Portland State University, P.O. Box 1491, Portland, OR, 97207
503/725-4081; 800/547-8887, ext. 4027 (outside Oregon)
Run by Portland State University, the program operates July through August, offering a variety of enrichment courses in music, art, writing, theater arts, and the environment.

### ON THE ROAD AGAIN

As you head south on Highway 101, you face a choice: to stay on 101, or to take the **Three Capes Scenic Loop.** Just north of Tillamook, 101 jogs inland for a stretch; soon after, you'll see signs for the scenic loop, a 20-mile road that heads westward to skirt the ocean, passing three ocean capes and reconnecting with Highway 101 just south of Pacific City. If you're up for more scenery, take it; it's one of the most beautiful stretches of road in the Northwest. Along the way, there are many places to stroll and appreciate the wonders of ocean power.

You'll first encounter **Cape Meares State Park,** a day-use area with viewpoints, trails, and interesting natural attractions. Check out the *Octopus Tree*, a large, gnarled Sitka spruce, 10 feet in diameter at its base. Trails from the parking area lead to the historic **Cape Meares Lighthouse** (503/842-4981). Built in 1890, it has the dubious distinction of being the shortest lighthouse on the coast—a mere 38 feet tall. Atop a towering, 200-foot cliff, however, the lighthouse illuminated the night for many years. After it was decommissioned, the light was badly vandalized, and parts of its first-order fresnel lens were stolen. Most have now been returned, and though the lens is not completely restored, it's still quite a sight. Visitors can climb into the lantern and inspect the lens up close. It's open daily, May through September, and weekends in October, March, and April, 11 a.m.- 4 p.m. Continue on the trail to spy offshore islets inhabited by Steller sea lions and nesting seabirds. Adjacent to the park, the 138-acre **Cape Meares National Wildlife Refuge** is home to common murres, tufted puffins, and pelagic cormorants, which nest on the cliff faces. Take your binoculars and see who can spot each of the species.

Driving south past Oceanside and Netarts, you'll soon pass **Cape Lookout State Park.** There are camping facilities here, including four yurts, an open picnic area, and restrooms. A quarter-mile self-guided nature trail, beginning near the registration booth, has 16 stations showing typical coastal rain forest vegetation. The cape trail, a 2.5-mile trek to the tip of Cape Lookout, leads through a stand of Sitka spruce. At the viewpoint you'll have a stunning view from Tillamook Head, 42 miles north, to Cape Foulweather, 39 miles south.

A bit farther south is Cape Kiwanda State Park, with its beautiful, haunting landscapes. The action of wind and waves on the cape sandstone has created an interesting headland to explore.

If you choose to stay on 101 rather than take the scenic route, you'll not necessarily be disappointed. This is dairy country, and the drive is as scenic in its way as that along the ocean. Even if you're just driving through to get back to the shoreline, several attractions are worth checking out.

Near Tillamook, there are three spots that may interest your family. The **Tillamook Cheese Factory,** just north of Tillamook, is a popular tourist attraction. The self-guided tour is informative, but a bit dry. The cheese samples are tasty, but just big enough to remind the kids they're hungry.

*Hwy. 101, two miles north of Tillamook. 503/842-4481. Open daily, 8 a.m.-8 p.m. Free.*

What better use for the old county courthouse (built in 1905) than to house a museum? The **Tillamook County Pioneer Museum** offers three floors of exhibits, including a remarkable natural history display on the second floor. Don't miss the basement; the kids will enjoy seeing the old Tillamook-to-Yamhill stagecoach and the jail!

*2106 2nd St. 503/842-4553. Mon.-Sat., 8 a.m.-5 p.m.; Sun., 11 a.m.-5 p.m. Cost: $2/adult, $1.50/ senior over 62 & $0.50/youth 12-17.*

The **Tillamook Naval Air Station Museum** is really fascinating, even for those who didn't think they were interested in aircraft. Here you can view vintage planes, especially from the World War II era; kids can climb up and look into the cockpits, which is quite a thrill. If you don't want to pay the cost of admission to view old airplanes, do take the five-minute detour off Highway 101 to show the kids the huge building that houses the exhibits. It's a former blimp hangar, and the largest wooden building in the world.

*6030 Hangar Rd. (two miles south of Tillamook on Hwy. 101). 503/842-1130. Open daily, 9 a.m.-5 p.m. (summer); 10 a.m.-5 p.m. (remainder of year). Cost: $8/adult, $7/senior 65 and older, $4.50/youth 13-17, free/under 13.*

Fifteen miles southwest of Tillamook on Hwy. 101, one parent reviewer found a great spot called **Sand Beach.** "It's an excellent beach—long and sandy with several sand hills that people hike up and slide down. Atop the hills are trails with spectacular views of the ocean. On the beach there are also rocky tide pools with caves. Just don't get caught in one when the tide comes in!"

## NESKOWIN

This tiny coastal town, approximately 33 miles south of Tillamook, combines charm and small size with big recreational opportunities. Its residents, who number fewer than 1,000, are committed to keeping it small, and amenities are limited. Neskowin is largely residential; the business district consists of a grocery store, post office, café, and two small resorts.

The town is bordered by a golf course and creek to the east, and the ocean on the west. Streets are short and narrow; a multitude of colorful hand-painted traffic signs remind visitors that the speed limit is 15 mph.

### PLACES TO STAY

**THE CHELAN**
*48750 Breakers Blvd., 97149*
*503/392-3270*
*FYI: Kitchens; fireplaces*

This pretty adobe hotel has nine condominium units, and each has an ocean view. Only the downstairs units are available to families. All have a living room with picture window, brick fireplace, and kitchen; most have two bedrooms. Outside the private back entrance is a small, enclosed yard.

### RENTAL HOMES AND COTTAGES

Many families prefer to rent a home or cottage, and Neskowin is a good place to exercise this option. Before making calls, decide which amenities are most important to your family, for example, spaciousness, beach access, deck, ocean view (expect to pay more for beachfront or view locations). In the small town of Neskowin, no home is far from the beach.

Most homes are furnished, with bedding, towels, fully stocked kitchens, as well as laundry facilities and cleaning supplies. Guests are expected to leave the premises as they found them. Often, you can find rentals through the vacation section of your local newspaper. Otherwise, try **Grey Fox, Inc. Vacation Rentals** (503/392-4355) or **Sea View Vacation Rentals** (503/965-7888).

## PLACES TO EAT

### THE HAWK CREEK CAFÉ
*4505 Salem Ave.*
*503/392-3838*
*Hours: Breakfast, lunch, dinner daily*

The Café offers sophisticated, moderately priced family fare. The gourmet pizzas are particularly popular. Eat here, or take food "to go" and head to the beach or back to your cottage.

### NESKOWIN MARKETPLACE
*Off Hwy. 101 in Neskowin*
*503/392-3035*
*Hours: 8 a.m.-6 p.m. Sun.-Thurs.; 8 a.m.-8 p.m. Fri.-Sat.*

In addition to selling groceries, the market rents videos and serves fast kid food, such as hotdogs. This is also the place to get your morning paper and eye-opener; they make a pretty good espresso!

## THE CENTRAL COAST

## LINCOLN CITY

This is a popular resort town that was once five little towns. Not only did they all grow together, but they also grew up; traffic here may remind you of a large metropolitan area. There are many attractions, not the least of which are the seven miles of sandy beach, three-mile long Devil's Lake, and the Siletz River. (Resident sea lions are sometimes visible at the mouth of the Siletz.)

## PLACES TO STAY

### HIDEAWAY MOTEL

*810 SW 10th, 97367*
*541/994-8874*
*Rates: Moderate*
*FYI: Fireplaces (some units); pets OK (fee)*

This pleasant little motel sits on a bluff, just west of the busiest section of Lincoln City. The six units are just what one looks for in a reasonably priced beach motel—clean and comfortable, but not fancy. The largest unit has two bedrooms, a knotty-pine living room, kitchen, and a dining area with a bay window. All units have a lovely view of the ocean.

A trail leads to the beach, and there's a lake and park nearby where kids can run and tumble.

### 66 PARENT COMMENTS

*"We love the Lincoln City area, and this is our favorite place to stay. Pleasant, but not so fancy we have to worry about every move the kids make."*

## PLACES TO EAT

### OTIS CAFÉ

*Hwy. 18 at Otis Junction, Otis*
*541/994-2813*
*Hours: Breakfast, lunch daily; dinner Fri.-Sun.*

The Otis Café, two miles off Highway 101 near Lincoln City, is a real blast from the past. An old-fashioned diner in size and décor, it is best known for generous breakfasts (including a bear-shaped pancake for kids). At lunch and dinner you'll enjoy surprisingly complex soups, juicy burgers (there's a three-ounce version for little ones), and a variety of country-style specials such as chicken-fried steak. Be sure to have some of the delicious brown bread (and some to go, it'll be ages before you get a loaf this good again). The fresh berry shakes and pies are heaven.

Space is at a premium here, but the place is so delightfully informal that even an active toddler won't ruffle any feathers.

### ROAD'S END DORY COVE

*5819 N. Logan Road*
*Hours: Lunch, dinner daily*

Dory Cove is an excellent place to satisfy diverse tastes: the seafood and chowder are satisfying, the 20 kinds of burgers are the answer to a child's dream. The fresh pie à la mode, the dessert of choice, will suit most anyone's taste.

There's almost always a line here. Put your name on the list, then walk the beach at the state park next door. Once seated, you'll find the restaurant a tad crowded. The ambiance is typical of a small coastal restaurant, but it may not be practical for families with active toddlers.

## WHAT TO SEE & DO

**CASCADE HEAD SCENIC AREA,** the first scenic/research area designated in the United States, offers diversity of landform, as well as animal and plant life. Several different environments are represented here—estuary and flood plain, river system, ocean, headland, and rain forest. The area is open to the public and hiking trails allow closer examination of some of these natural attractions.

*West off Hwy. 101, just north of Lincoln City. 541/392-3161.*

**DEVIL'S LAKE** is a good-sized freshwater lake located just east of Lincoln City. Boating here provides a fun change from the ocean beach. At **Blue Heron Landing** (541/994-4708; 4006 Devil's Lake Road) you can rent most anything that floats, including canoes, bumper boats, paddle boats, aqua bikes, and motor boats.

There are several fun spots for families on Devil's Lake. Drive the road that loops around the lake (Devil's Lake Road, off Hwy. 101), and stop when you feel the urge. At **Regatta Grounds Park,** there's the creative sandcastle playground (on West Devil's Lake Road). On East Devil's Lake Road is **Sand Point,** which offers a swimming area, picnic tables, and restrooms.

Flowing from Devil's Lake is "D" River. Renowned as the world's shortest river, it reaches its ocean destination in 120 feet.

**DRIFT CREEK COVERED BRIDGE.** Built in 1914, this is the oldest covered bridge in the state. Drive three miles south on Highway 101 to Drift Creek Road, then two miles east. Turn right and drive a half-mile to the bridge.

**KITE FLYING** is made easy thanks to **Catch the Wind** (503/996-9500; 266 SE Hwy. 101), the kite shop with eight locations on the Oregon Coast. You'll find every imaginable size, shape, and color of kite or windsock, and the staff is happy to offer tips on flying. One favorite place for kite flying is the "D" River Wayside, off Highway 101 on the south bank of "D" River.

## RESOURCES

**LINCOLN CITY CHAMBER OF COMMERCE**
3939 NW Hwy. 101, Lincoln City 97367
541/994-3070

**LINCOLN CITY VISITOR AND CONVENTION BUREAU**
801 SW Hwy. 101, Lincoln City 97367
541/994-8378; 800/452-2151

**SITKA CENTER FOR ART AND ECOLOGY**
541/994-5485
Dedicated to exploring the relationship between art and nature, the center offers classes June to September, including some for children.

## CALENDAR

**SEPTEMBER**
International Fall Kite Festival: Kite flyers from around the world participate in a number of events, including kite fights, team-kite choreography, and a lighted night kite fly, Lincoln City.

## GLENEDEN

Gleneden is a quiet, upscale coastal town put on the map by Salishan Lodge, the major resort in the area. The extensive tidal flats here are both aesthetically pleasing and great places to watch for wildlife, especially waterfowl.

### PLACES TO STAY

**SALISHAN LODGE**
P.O. Box 118, 97388
*541/764-2371, 800/452-2300; www.salishan.com*
*Rates: Expensive*
*FYI: Restaurant; indoor pool; fitness center; golf (18-hole), tennis; playground, video game arcade; nature trails, private beach; childcare; pets OK (fee)*

One of Oregon's largest and oldest resorts, Salishan was totally renovated in 1997 and continues to attract not only conventions but families who want to relax and recreate on its beautifully landscaped grounds. Covering more than 1,000 acres (including a 750-acre forest), and located on a beautiful stretch of the coast, it is an easy place in which to forget the rest of the world for a few days. Don't expect a beachfront resort, though; Salishan's private beach is a half mile away.

The units are large and comfortably furnished, with brick fireplaces, balconies, and carports. They are arranged in eight-plexes and scattered across a hillside overlooking the grounds. The wooden lodge has many comfortable common areas, including a library. The covered pool and fitness center are lovely.

**❝❝ PARENT COMMENTS**

*"The resort is spread out, so specify where you'd like your room. Some units are quite isolated. We ended up near the golf course, which didn't make sense for a family of non-golfers."*

*"The restaurant is pricey, but has good food and good views. Our teenagers enjoyed the nice meal out; I don't know that I'd go there with young ones."*

## DEPOE BAY

The harbor in Depoe Bay is the smallest in the world, but it's deep and sheltered. It's put to good use by the U.S. Coast Guard base and commercial and charter fishing boats. The beautiful stretch of coast near Depoe Bay boasts five state parks with woods, creeks, whale watching, and magnificent tide pools. Not surprisingly, this picturesque town fills up fast during the summer.

### PLACES TO STAY

**INN AT OTTER CREST**
*Otter Rock, 97369*
*541/765-2111; www.ottercrest.com*
*Rates: Expensive*
*FYI: Restaurant; kitchens; fireplaces; outdoor pool; tennis; playground, game room; laundry; smoke-free throughout*

Don't let the Inn's location on Cape Foulweather discourage you—the weather here is subject to the same foibles as at any other coastal resort. Set in 100 acres of beautifully landscaped grounds, this is a place to relax and soak up the magnificent scenery.

The suites are comfortable and include kitchens and fireplaces. The multiplexes are surrounded by greenery and quiet, not roads (on arrival, visitors park their cars and are shuttled to their suites). A tram takes you up and down the steep slope between accommodations and recreation.

In addition to swimming and court sports, there are organized activities for kids—including nature walks and arts and crafts—during the summer. Nearby are a lake and stream, golf course, and deep-sea fishing and crabbing in the ocean.

The Inn is 17 miles south of Lincoln City on Highway 101. Take the Otter Crest Scenic Loop off 101.

### 66 PARENT COMMENTS

*"The calm, quiet surroundings were very relaxing. Our children loved riding the tram back and forth, and the pool was great."*

*"This is a beautiful but expensive way to enjoy the Oregon Coast. We had a good time, but decided we prefer the funkier, on-the-beach kind of place when we travel with the kids."*

*"It was foggy during much of our visit, and we felt too far away from the ocean. The organized activities for kids were a nice feature, but overall we thought this spot better suited to conventions than family vacations."*

### PLACES TO EAT

### THE SPOUTING HORN
*110 NE Hwy. 101*
*541/765-2261*
*Hours: Breakfast, lunch, dinner Wed.-Mon.*

The Spouting Horn is famous for its deep-dish apple pie, known locally as deep-dish agony since it usually tops an already abundant meal (they also have good berry and cream pies). The variety of foods is tremendous and a real boon to families whose members each want something different to eat. Best known for its seafood dishes, The Spouting Horn includes steak, hamburgers, soups, sandwiches, and salads. The section of the menu reserved "for smaller appetites" offers a nice variety as well. On Thursday and Saturday nights, a buffet includes additional dishes, such as roast beef and potatoes. All this, and a view of the harbor, too!

### WHAT TO SEE & DO

**ALDER BEACH II** is a glass blowers' studio where visitors can watch molten glass being transformed into vases, bowls, paperweights, and goblets.

*On Immomen Road. 541/996-2483. Open daily, 10 a.m.-5 p.m.*

**OTTER CREST LOOP.** This five-mile loop drive between Depoe Bay and Newport climbs nearly 500 feet above the sea to the summit at Cape Foulweather. If the weather is clear, you'll have a panoramic view for 40 miles. During winter storms, gales often reach 50 miles per hour at the Cape.

A word of warning: This winding road is on a cliff, with many a precipitous drop to the ocean below. It might give kids a thrill, but some drivers will find it too harrowing.

**THE UNITED STATES COAST GUARD STATION** plays an important role in ensuring the safety of ocean swimmers and boaters. Tours of the station are available; if you're lucky, you'll see Coast Guard personnel practicing their rescue drills. *East side of harbor, Depoe Bay. Open daily until 9 p.m.*

## CALENDAR

### SEPTEMBER
Indian Salmon Bake, Depoe Bay.

## RESOURCES

### DEPOE BAY CHAMBER OF COMMERCE
663 SE Hwy. 101, P.O. Box 21, Depoe Bay 97369
541/765-2889

## NEWPORT

Situated on wide, wonderful Yaquina Bay, Newport is the most popular resort town on the coast. If you are looking for a quiet coastal retreat, this isn't your stop. But even if you don't stay here, it's worth a visit while you are on the Oregon Coast.

## PLACES TO STAY

### EMBARCADERO RESORT
*1000 SE Bay Blvd., 97365*
*541/265-8521, 800/547-4779; www.embarcadero-resort.com*
*Rates: Moderate*
*FYI: Restaurant; kitchens (most suites); fireplaces; indoor pool*

This is a quiet, comfortable resort, offering both hotel rooms and condominiums. Every room has a private patio with a view of Yaquina Bay and the ocean beyond. The one- and two-bedroom suites have a comfortable living room, dining area, and fireplace; most have kitchens.

The wide boardwalk takes you around the end of the bay, past moored boats (for rent), a small grocery and souvenir shop, and the resort's seafood restaurant.

**❝ PARENT COMMENTS**

*"We stayed in a very comfortable, modern, cheerful condo with nautical decorations. It was nice being able to stroll around Yaquina Bay (about 1.5 miles) to the Bay Front— somewhat touristy but fun, with quaint shops and eateries."*

*"Our kids enjoyed watching the steady stream of boat traffic from our patio."*

*"Don't miss the Oregon Coast Aquarium!"*

## HALLMARK RESORT
*744 SW Elizabeth St., 97365*
*541/265-2600, 800/982-8668*
*Rates: Moderate*
*FYI: Indoor pool; fitness center; laundry; pets OK (fee)*

This Hallmark Resort, a Best Western motel, works well for families. The 156 oceanfront rooms are spacious, and each has a gas fireplace, kitchenette, sitting area, private balcony, and spectacular ocean view. Each morning, visitors are greeted with complimentary newspaper and coffee.

When the kids have had enough beach time, enjoy family time with the collection of games and puzzles in the library.

**❝ PARENT COMMENTS**

*"After getting exhausted and chilled on the beach one morning, we came back and hopped into the fitness center spa. It was a dream come true."*

## PLACES TO EAT

### MO'S RESTAURANT
*622 SW Bay Blvd.*
*541/265-2979*
*Hours: Breakfast, lunch, dinner daily*

Eating at Mo's has become an integral part of a visit to the coast. The Newport restaurant was the first in the chain, and it has that oceanside ambiance. The problem is that it's quite small, and hence there can be quite a line outside (asking to share a table is quite acceptable at Mo's). All the Mo's Restaurants are busy, noisy places that work well for families.

Food reviews are mixed—some say the seafood is just so-so, others swear the clam chowder and oyster stew are to die for. Or try a dinner salad (sprinkled with tiny bay shrimp). If you arrive extra hungry, start with a couple orders of the cheese bread. (It won't win a heart-healthy competition, but it's a buttery favorite with kids.)

Mo's has a lengthy kids' menu, so those who turn their noses up at seafood can choose burgers, hotdogs, grilled cheese, and the like.

**WHALE'S TALE**
*452 SW Bay Blvd.*
*541/265-8660*
*Hours: Breakfast, lunch, dinner daily*
Located on the main drag in Old Town, "the Whale" can be trusted for an informal, upbeat atmosphere and a thoroughly satisfying meal. Large, fluffy omelets are breakfast favorites; kids will enjoy the poppyseed pancakes, French toast (breads are homemade), or homemade granola. Lunch and dinner feature thick, tasty soups, fresh pastas (including a lasagna from heaven), and creative seafood specials. The children's menu offers the requisite hamburger and grilled cheese, but also a tasty fish sandwich and—here's a winner—a peanut butter-and-banana sandwich. No fat-fried food is served here.

## WHAT TO SEE & DO

**HATFIELD MARINE SCIENCE CENTER.** Located south of Newport across the Yaquina Bay Bridge, this center is a coastal research facility of Oregon State University. It has a small but excellent collection of exhibits, including underwater viewing chambers in a natural aquarium and a touch-tank that includes a friendly octopus.
*2030 Marine Science Dr. 541/867-0271. Open daily, 10 a.m.-5 p.m. (summer); 10 a.m.-4 p.m. (remainder of year). Free; donations suggested.*

**OLD TOWN** by Yaquina Bay is a great place to take a stroll. Big shellfish steamers are operating right on the sidewalk, and there's a dock from which you can watch the fishing boats bring in and dump their catches. Listen for barking sea lions, and follow the sound to the dock that's teeming (almost sinking) with the comic mammals.
*SW Bay Blvd., along Yaquina Bay.*

**OREGON COAST AQUARIUM** is a small but well-designed collection of indoor and outdoor marine exhibits. The four outdoor acres include an aviary of seabirds, an underwater cave that houses an octopus, a rocky pool with sea lions and seals, otter caves, and a big, fascinating jellyfish tank. Keiko, the orca of Free Willy fame, lived here temporarily before going to his permanent home in Iceland.

*2820 SE Ferry Slip Road. 541/867-3474. Open daily, 9 a.m.-8 p.m. (mid-March to mid-Oct.); 10 a.m.-5 p.m. (rest of year). Cost: $8.75/adult, $7.75/senior 65 and over, $4.50/ youth 4-13, free/under 4.*

**THE WAX WORKS, UNDERSEA GARDENS** and **RIPLEY'S BELIEVE IT OR NOT** are all in Newport; this is the touristy side of town. Kids are easily attracted to these spots, but our parent reviewers called them "overpriced tourist attractions not worth the price of admission."

**YAQUINA BAY LIGHTHOUSE** was built in 1871, but replaced just three years later by the larger Yaquina Head Lighthouse. The original lens is gone, but the structure has been meticulously restored and the light was reactivated in 1996. Today the lighthouse is furnished with period pieces, and open for tours, providing kids a chance to see first-hand a fascinating part of coastal history. There's a nice gift shop in the basement.

*Yaquina Bay State Park, southern edge of Newport. 541/867-7451. Open daily, 11 a.m.-5 p.m. (Memorial Day-Labor Day); Sat.-Sun., noon-4 p.m. (remainder of year). Free: donations suggested.*

**YAQUINA HEAD LIGHTHOUSE.** The rocky outcropping of Yaquina Head and its 93-foot lighthouse are visible for several miles along Highway 101. Completed in 1873, the lantern here is a 12-foot-high fresnel lens. Set in the Yaquina Head Natural Area, this is one of the most-visited lighthouses on the West Coast.

*Yaquina Head Natural Area. 541/265-2863. Open daily, June 15-Sept. 15.*

## CALENDAR

**JULY**
Lincoln County Fair and Rodeo, Newport.

## RESOURCES

**NEWPORT CHAMBER OF COMMERCE**
555 SW Coast Hwy., Newport 97365
503/265-8801

# WALDPORT

This sleepy little fishing town, situated on the Alsea River estuary, calls itself the "Salmon Fishing Capital of the World."

(You'd look for a claim to fame, too, if you were sandwiched between resort towns like Yachats and Newport.) Those who tarry will discover there's more than salmon to recommend Waldport, including long, secluded beaches, a town center unspoiled by rampant development, and an abundance of Dungeness crabs and clams in the bay.

## PLACES TO STAY

### CAPE COD COTTAGES

*4150 SW Pacific Coast Hwy., 97394*
*541/563-2106*
*Rates: Moderate*
*FYI: Kitchens; fireplaces*

Between Waldport and Yachats, on a stretch of coast that is generally less traveled, sit these home-style cottages. Located on a low bank above the beach, each of the 10 tidy one- and two-bedroom cottages has a fireplace, kitchen deck, and picture window; some have adjoining garages. Larger cottages sleep up to eight people.

### ❝ PARENT COMMENTS

*"We love this quiet little town—away from the tourist hustle and bustle of Newport. The kids can frolic on the beach while we sit on our deck and read."*

### EDGEWATER COTTAGES

*3978 SW Pacific Coast Hwy., 97394*
*541/563-2240*
*Rates: Inexpensive to moderate*
*FYI: Kitchens; pets OK (fee); baby-sitting*

This Oregon Coast lodging books up early, especially in the summer and on holidays. Accommodations here include a four-plex, a duplex, and several individual cabins. All are comfortable, with fireplaces, kitchens, and decent beds.

The Edgewater is situated on a wonderful expanse of beach; though it's close to the highway, the focus is definitely toward the ocean. There's a grassy area for playing Frisbee or soccer and good access to the beach via stairs. Driftwood on the beach is perfect for building ships or forts.

### ❝ PARENT COMMENTS

*"Edgewater Cottages satisfied the whole family, ages eight months to 10 years and up."*

*"This is a comfortable place with easy access to a great beach. We like to go to Fudge in Waldport for a sweet treat."*

*"We recommend buying a fresh, live crab at the harbor in Newport—a delicious treat that you can cook in your Edgewater cabin, or even on the beach."*

### WHAT TO SEE & DO

**ALSEA BAY BRIDGE HISTORICAL INTERPRETIVE CENTER** contains exhibits about Oregon coastal travel dating back to the early 19th century. In the summer, the Center is the base camp for the Oregon Parks Department Junior Ranger Program, which teaches kids about marine life.

*620 NW Spring St. (south end of Alsea Bay Bridge). 541/563-2133. Open Tues.-Sat., 9 a.m.-5 p.m. (summer); 9 a.m.-4 p.m. (remainder of year).*

**HIKING.** Just seven miles from the ocean, the nine-square-mile **Drift Creek Wilderness** area, part of the Siuslaw National Forest, is a magnificent place to explore. Talk to the Waldport Ranger Station at 541/563-3211 for information about the three trails through the area.

### RESOURCES

**WALDPORT CHAMBER OF COMMERCE**
Hwy. 101 (south end of Alsea Bay Bridge), P.O. Box 669, Waldport 97394
541/563-2133

## YACHATS

This quiet seaside town on the Yachats River is the favorite of several of our parent reviewers, drawn by the combination of breathtaking natural beauty, good restaurants and lodging, and distance from the crowds. The town has an arty, counterculture feel.

### PLACES TO STAY

**THE ADOBE**
*1555 Hwy. 101, P.O. Box 219, 97498*
*541/547-3141, 800/522-3623*
*Rates: Moderate*
*FYI: Restaurant; refrigerator; pets OK*

Well off the highway, The Adobe sits on a spectacular shoreline, where breakers crash at high tide. Many rooms have fireplaces and ocean views. The pool is small, but parents can drink coffee in the lobby while viewing little swimmers through a large window.

The restaurant is a bit pricey, but the food is good, and every table has a view of the churning sea below.

**❝ PARENT COMMENTS**
*"We appreciated that the resort allowed us to have our family dog along."*

*"Sitting by the fireplace, we watched a winter storm and played a family game of monopoly. We have fond memories of The Adobe."*

### FIRESIDE MOTEL
*1881 Hwy. 101 N., 97498*
*541/547-3636*
*Rates: Inexpensive*
*FYI: Refrigerator; fireplaces (some units); pets OK (fee)*

This is a no-frills spot, but it offers nice amenities for families, especially if one family member is of the canine persuasion. The 43-unit motel is set well back from the highway, partially secluded by landscaping. Request a unit with a deck overlooking the ocean, as these provide extra space and privacy. There's a lovely walking trail along the beach, where families can picnic, enjoy beach fires, or in late summer, harvest berries.

**❝ PARENT COMMENTS**
*"The folks who run the place have kids of their own, and really made us feel comfortable. They also knew good places to take kids in the area."*

*"Sitting out on the deck for my morning coffee, I was only aware of the ocean. No noise from the highway or adjoining rooms. . .very peaceful."*

### SHAMROCK LODGETTES
*105 Hwy. 101 S., 97498*
*541/547-3312; www.o-tb.com\shamrock.html*
*Rates: Moderate*
*FYI: Kitchens (some units); fireplaces; exercise room; pets OK (fee)*

The Shamrock is beautifully set at the southern end of town, where the Yachats River meets the ocean. Modern motel units and cottages are available and both offer lovely ocean and/or river views. The motel units are nicely appointed, each with fireplace and deck.

But the rustic cottages, with adjoining carports, offer an ambiance more befitting a visit to the coast. They are situated to afford privacy, have separate bedrooms and well-equipped kitchens. The grounds are nicely landscaped and maintained. A large indoor hot tub, sauna, and exercise room are centrally located.

**❝❝ PARENT COMMENTS**

*"My husband and I felt comfortable letting our kids go back and forth to the beach without much supervision. The owners seemed genuinely pleased to have them around."*

*"Sometimes it's the little things that count. We appreciated the morning paper at our doorstep each day."*

### PLACES TO EAT

#### LA SERRE RESTAURANT
*160 W. 2nd*
*541/547-3420*
*Hours: Dinner daily (closed Tues. in winter); hours vary*

"La Serre" means "the greenhouse," and this light, airy restaurant lives up to the name. It's a good bet for fresh seafood prepared with imagination (their mussels are supurb), and for specialty Italian fare (including a particularly tasty cioppino). The chef is health-conscious in all offerings and willing to prepare special dishes for vegetarians. But the best trick in their book is the "children's corner" menu: a "baby distraction plate" of crackers, fresh fruit, and cookie, and a choice of catch-of-the-day or pasta meal for kids under 12.

#### TRAVELERS COVE CAFÉ
*373 Hwy. 101*
*541/547-3831*
*Hours: Breakfast, lunch, dinner daily (summer); lunch daily (remainder of year)*

This cozy little café is all wood and light during the day, bathed in firelight at night. The upper dining area overlooks the blue Pacific, and in summer there's an outside dining area as well.

The food here is good, though it can get pricey when the whole family sets to ordering. The espresso is a great way to start the day, no matter what accompanies it. Visitors partial to seafood may want the fresh crab or bay shrimp, or the crab and veggie quiche; locals swear by the black-bean chicken chili and garlic-laden Caesar salad.

## WHAT TO SEE & DO

**CAPE PERPETUA.** Before you go up this gorgeous cape, stop in at the Interpretive Center. You needn't be a geologist to find yourself fascinated by *Discovery at the Edge*, a 15-minute film describing the natural forces that formed the coastline.

Then hike or drive the easy, winding road to the top of the 800-foot cape, the highest point on the coast. One of our parent reviewers called this "our favorite place on the coast. We drive to the top, stopping to read the interpretive signs about weather—wind, rain, and so on. At the top, take a moment to appreciate the jutting coastline to the south; cape upon cape, as far as you can see. Next we always walk the short nature trail that circles the cape, alternating between ocean view and coastal forest. Along the way, there's a stone-and-wood lookout the kids like to watch for."

Down below again, stop at nearby **Devil's Churn** and take the short walk down to the rocky observation point. It's especially magnificent on a stormy day. Several hiking trails begin here, and the tide pools are spectacular at low tide.

*Three miles south of Yachats on Hwy. 101. 541/547-3289. Interpretive Center open daily, 9 a.m.-5 p.m. (Memorial Day-Labor Day).*

## RESOURCES

### YACHATS CHAMBER OF COMMERCE
441 Hwy. 101, P.O. Box 174, Yachats 97498
541/547-3530

## FLORENCE

Dunes, dunes, and more dunes are what lure most families to the Florence area. From here south for 50 miles, the rugged northern coastline is replaced by rolling sand dunes, some 300 feet high. Along with the sand dunes comes an abundance of freshwater lakes, offering a nice alternative to saltwater beaches. If you can coerce the kids out of the sand, stroll through charming Old Town.

## PLACES TO STAY

### DRIFTWOOD SHORES
*88416 First Ave., 97439*
*541/997-8263; www.driftwoodshores.com*
*Rates: Moderate to expensive*
*FYI: Restaurant; kitchens; indoor pool; laundry*
This oceanfront resort motel, four miles north of Florence and

west of Highway 101, is exceptional for its location right on the beach. It has 136 units—25 have three bedrooms, and 21 have two. Units are comfortable and clean, but not fancy. Most have kitchens; many have fireplaces and decks overlooking the beach (which is long and lovely). In rainy or wet weather, guests appreciate both the indoor pool and the laundry for drying wet suits.

The restaurant at Driftwood Shores has satisfactory food at moderate prices, and a spectacular view.

**66 PARENT COMMENTS**

*"This was a relaxing place with just enough diversion to keep everyone from getting tired of the beach. We did spend hours and hours on the long stretches of sandy, driftwood-strewn beach and loved it."*

*"The staff was friendly and accommodating. It was wonderful to be able to walk out the door onto the beach."*

## PLACES TO EAT

### BLUE HEN CAFÉ

*1675 Hwy. 101 N.*
*541/997-3907*
*Hours: Breakfast, lunch, dinner daily*

It's tough to beat the fried chicken and mashed potatoes they serve here, but there are pasta and burgers for those who'd like to try. Whatever the entrée, top it off with a piece of homemade pie. The Hen offers cheerful service, generous portions, and reasonable prices. Besides, the kids will be entertained just looking at all the blue plastic and glass chickens (hens, to be precise).

### MORGAN'S COUNTRY KITCHEN

*85020 Hwy. 101 S.*
*541/997-6991*
*Hours: Breakfast, lunch daily (year-round); dinner daily (May-Oct.)*

Specialties here include Oklahoma gravy and biscuits, pecan waffles, delicious omelets, and one of the newest treats: a real "buffalo burger." Also, they serve great clam chowder. Dinners feature tasty homemade Italian dishes, as well as the exceptionally good American dinner menu items.

### WINDWARD INN

*3757 Hwy. 101 N.*
*541/997-8243*
*Hours: Breakfast, lunch, dinner daily*

Serving locals and visitors since 1932, this restaurant teeters on the brink of "institution" status. The selection of fresh seafood is outstanding, as are the homemade desserts. Soups and sandwiches here are likely to please little ones, or they can order from the children's menu. In summer, you can opt for dining in the courtyard lounge.

## WHAT TO SEE & DO

**HECETA HEAD LIGHTHOUSE.** Twelve miles north of Florence, the Heceta Head Lighthouse is still in operation, sending out the strongest light on the Oregon Coast. If you're driving from Florence, be sure to pull out at the viewpoint just south of the lighthouse. From here, you have a lovely view of the lighthouse, perched on rocky Heceta Head. (You'll recognize this view from many a scenic calendar of the coast.)

The lighthouse and lightkeeper's house were built in 1894. The lighthouse itself is open to the public only occasionally, but the Victorian-style lightkeeper's house (**Heceta House**) has been restored, and serves as an interpretive museum and bed-and-breakfast.

*Twelve miles north of Florence. 541/547-3596. Grounds and Heceta House open daily, year round; lighthouse open every third weekend in summer.*

**JESSIE M. HONEYMAN STATE PARK.** This is a great park for camping or for day use. The day-use parking area provides instant access to the dunes. For a great view, not to mention an aerobic workout, climb to the top and wander about. (If there's a strong wind, save this hike for another time. The whipping sands will sting the eyes and ruin the fun.)

When you're hot and tired from your sandy hike, jump into adjacent **Cleawox Lake.** It's small and stays quite warm all summer long (sometimes it feels warmer than the fog-laden air). Take a drive around the lake to the park lodge, where you can get fast food such as hot dogs, large pretzels, and pizza. There's a supervised swimming area and a spot to rent paddleboats. The paddleboats are really fun for kids; because the lake is so small, they can paddle across to the dunes and back in a jiffy.

*84505 Hwy. 101 S. (3 miles south of Florence). 541/997-9143.*

**OREGON DUNES NATIONAL RECREATION AREA,** operated by the U.S. Forest Service, encompasses a 50-mile stretch of sand dunes, some of which are 300 feet tall. Here, visitors are treated to some of the most scenic stretches of coastline in the world.

The **Oregon Dunes Overlook,** located 11 miles south of Florence, is one of the few places where you can get a good look at these giant sand piles without detouring off the main drag. The overlook consists of a series of observation platforms built right on the dunes and is fully accessible to the handicapped.

**SANDLAND ADVENTURES** offers dune buggy-rides to the top of the South Jetty Dunes near the Siuslaw River. Four-wheelers are also available. Individuals under 16 must be accompanied by an adult. Drivers under 18 are not permitted on four-wheelers. Guided dune-buggy tours are available.

There's also a go-kart track and bumper boats here.

*85366 Hwy. 101. 503/997-8087. Open daily, 9 a.m.-7:30 p.m. (June-Labor Day); 9 a.m.-5 p.m. (remainder of year). Cost: rentals, $30-35; tours, $10-25.*

**SEAHORSE STAGECOACH** transports riders back to the mode of coast travel most common in the early part of this century—along the beach. Riders climb in the 16-passenger coach (heated during the winter with a wood stove) and are whisked away by three Percheron draft horses. The trip along the packed, wet sand lasts about an hour.

*541/999-0319. Sea coach rides by reservation only. Cost: $5/adult; $3/under 14.*

**SEA LION CAVES.** Eleven miles north of Florence, this is the only year-round home for wild Steller sea lions on the mainland. The huge mammals are not captive here; they are wild, and they choose this giant grotto as their home. Visitors descend by elevator to the 1500-foot-long cavern, fairly exploding with barking, roaring sea lions. Even the greatest skeptic will be entertained by the antics of these slippery, frolicking fellows.

*91560 Hwy. 101. 541/547-3111. Open daily, 9 a.m. to dusk. Cost: $6.50/adult, $4.50 /youth 6-15, free/under 6.*

## RESOURCES

### FLORENCE CHAMBER OF COMMERCE
270 Hwy. 101, P.O. Box 26000, Florence 97439
541/997-3128

### ON THE ROAD AGAIN
There's nothing quite as tiring as playing in the dunes, and the family will probably welcome the chance to climb back in the

car and drive for awhile. Twenty-one miles south of Florence is the **Reedsport/Winchester Bay** area. If the cry from the backseat is one of hunger, stop by **Don's Diner & Ice Cream Parlor** (2115 Hwy. 101, Reedsport; 541/271-2032). You can choose a "world famous burger" or a bowl of their locally famous soup or chowder. Good luck getting out the door without a round of homemade pie, topped with delicious Umpqua ice cream.

Reedsport is the south entrance to the **Oregon Dunes National Recreation Area.** If you haven't yet taken the opportunity to cavort in these huge sandpiles, now is your chance. For information about specific spots to visit in this giant playground, stop by the **Dune Recreation Area Headquarters** on Highway 101. They also have information about nature programs available during the summer.

*On Hwy. 101, just south of the Umpqua Bridge. 541/271-3611. Open daily, 8 a.m.-4:30 p.m. (summer); Mon.-Fri., 8 a.m.-4:30 p.m. (remainder of year).*

The **Umpqua Discovery Center,** located on the historic Umpqua River waterfront, is chock-full of wonders related to life on the river and sea. Check out the 35-foot periscope that gives a broad view of the estuary. In the Community room, you'll find antique sea treasures such as ship models, an old ship's bell and a fascinating old diver's helmet. A working Weather Station describes maritime climate. Throughout the museum are interesting displays on the birds, mammals, and shellfish of the region, including an attractive gray whale exhibit. Stop by Cannery Row, which tells the story of early settlers dependent upon the sea for their livelihood.

*409 Riverfront Way. 541/271-4816. Open daily, 9 a.m.-5 p.m., (June-Oct.); 10 a.m.-4 p.m. (remainder of year). Cost: $3/adult & youth, $1.50/child 5-12.*

As you travel south from Reedsport, watch for signs to the **Umpqua Lighthouse State Park,** offering access to ocean beaches, the mouth of the Umpqua River, sand dunes up to 500 feet high (including some of the highest in the nation), and a small lake (good for swimming). The **Umpqua River Lighthouse** (503/271-4631) is located west of the park, above the entrance to Winchester Bay. Built in 1890, the lighthouse still uses its original lens—a red-and-white fresnel, visible for 16 miles—to guide ships through the difficult spot where the Umpqua River meets the ocean. Visit the museum and, if the season's right, watch for migrating gray whales offshore. Tours are available May through September.

*Six miles south of Reedsport, off Hwy. 101. Park open daily, dawn-dusk; lighthouse open May-Sept., Wed.-Sat., 9-11:30 a.m. and 1-3:30 p.m.; Sun., 1-4:30 p.m. (May-Sept.). Free.*

If you decide to stop awhile in the area, or want to plan a return trip, there's more information available at the **Reedsport/Winchester Bay Chamber of Commerce,** at the junction of Highways 101 and 38 in Reedsport, 541/271-3495.

## THE SOUTHERN COAST

### BANDON

Bandon is an important harbor town and an increasingly popular vacation spot. It's a chief producer of cranberries, and bogs are visible along the highway outside town. Rockhunting and beachcombing are popular activities on Bandon's many beaches.

### PLACES TO STAY

**THE INN AT FACE ROCK**
*3232 Beach Loop Road, 97441*
*541/347-9441, 800/638-3092*
*Rates: Moderate*
*FYI: Restaurant; continental breakfast; kitchens (some units); refrigerators/microwaves; fireplaces (some units); indoor pool; laundry; pets OK (fee)*

The 55 units here include standard rooms and suites with kitchens and fireplaces. If possible, request an ocean-view suite. A trail across the road leads to a lovely, uncrowded beach.

**❝❝ PARENT COMMENTS**

*"We stayed here when the inn was very new, and there was no landscaping around our unit. But the rest of the grounds were quite nice, the pool is lovely, and there's a short trail to a beautiful little beach."*

*"Folks at the inn were most accommodating, welcoming both children and family dog with equal grace."*

**SEA STAR HOSTEL AND GUEST HOUSE**
*375 2nd St., 97411*
*541/347-9632*
*Rates: Inexpensive to moderate*
That's right, this spot was once an American Youth Hostel.

Today, visitors have a choice of accommodations—including a four-room Guest House that is several steps above the dormitory-style main building. A good choice for families is the second-floor suite; it's light and airy and has a deck with a view of the harbor.

**❝❝ PARENT COMMENTS**

*"We liked this location, near the harbor and Old Town. It's different from being on the ocean, but we found it a refreshing difference."*

## PLACES TO EAT

### BANDON BOATWORKS

*275 Lincoln Ave. SW*
*541/347-2111*
*Hours: Lunch, dinner daily (June-Oct.); closed Mon., dinner daily (Nov.-May)*

This cozy restaurant has arranged all its tables against the front windows, from which diners have a lovely view of the south jetty. The menu has something pleasing for everyone in the family—fresh seafood and beef, hearty soups and sandwiches, and a creative salad bar. The children's menu has the standard fare, and servers are happy to substitute if it will put smiles on little faces.

### THE WHEELHOUSE RESTAURANT

*125 Chicago, 97411*
*541/347-9331*
*Hours: Lunch, dinner daily*

This Old Town restaurant serves complex, pleasing entrées, focusing on fresh seafood and tasty pastas. Upon entering, children are handed their own brightly colored menus: their choices include deep-fried snapper or shrimp, hamburger, grilled cheese, and the ubiquitous p.b.&j. If the fog clears, this is a fun place to sit and watch people peruse the waterfront shops.

## WHAT TO SEE & DO

**OLD TOWN.** It's great fun to stroll in Old Town Bandon, amid art galleries, craft shops, and cafés. The area is often fogged-in, which adds a mysterious air to the stroll. For a bite to eat, our parent reviewers spoke highly of **Bandon Fisheries** (250 1st SW; 541/347-4282) for its good, fresh fish and chips. Once the kids have eaten a "good lunch," stop by **Cranberry Sweets** (21st & Chicago; 541/347-9475) for handmade candies once touted in *The New York Times*. There are lots of samples; unless you try them, you'll never imagine how many delicious candies can be made with cranberries. Also generous with the samples is **Bandon Cheese** (680 2nd; 541/347-2456), home of world-renowned cheddar cheeses.

**BULLARDS BEACH STATE PARK.** This park offers much in the way of hiking and biking trails (many of which lead to uncrowded beaches), wildlife viewing areas, and interpretive programs in summer. Face Rock Wayside, on Beach Loop Road, is a good place to try to spot migrating gray whales.

At the end of the main road you'll find the **Coquille Lighthouse,** built in 1896 to help guide seafarers across the bar at the mouth of the Coquille River (a junction known as the "navigator's nightmare"). The lighthouse, a rare example of the style of architecture called Victorian Italianate, was restored in 1979 as an interpretive center. Tours of the tower watch room are available on request.

*541/347-2209. Park open daily, daylight hours, year round. Lighthouse open summer only.*

**WEST COAST GAME PARK.** This 20-acre, walk-through safari has more than 75 species from around the world. While all the animals are on view, a selected number of youngsters are also available to pet.

*Seven miles south on Hwy. 101. 541/347-3106. Open daily, 9 a.m.-dusk (March-Nov.); 9 a.m.-5 p.m. (remainder of year). Cost: $7/adult, $6/senior over 60, $5.75/youth 7-12, $4.25/child 2-6, free/under 2.*

## CALENDAR

**JULY**

Old-fashioned Fourth, Coquille Lighthouse.

**SEPTEMBER**

Cranberry Festival: Celebrating "the marvelous flexibility of the cranberry."

**DECEMBER**

Festival of Lights: Businesses, homes, and boats go all-out to brighten the holiday season.

## RESOURCES

**BANDON CHAMBER OF COMMERCE**
300 SE 2nd; P.O. Box 1515, Bandon 97411
541/347-9616

**ON THE ROAD AGAIN**

Located 40 miles south of Bandon, **Port Orford** is one of the state's oldest incorporated towns. Its high bluffs were first noted and named by Captain Vancouver in 1792. Today, you'll find Port Orford a lot less tourist-ridden than most coastal towns and the life here dominated by sheep ranching and cranberry farming.

At the northern tip of what is rumored to be a coastal "banana belt" stretching to the California border, Port Orford is hopping with surfers and sailboarders who come from all over to catch wind and waves on the ocean and area lakes. It's also a great place to watch for gray whales; they often stop to rest in quiet coves during their spring and fall migrations.

**Cape Blanco State Park,** originally a privately owned ranch, has large campsites, picnic areas, and eight miles of trails highlighting both ocean and forest. Near the park entrance is the historic **Hughes House.** Built in 1898, this Victorian ranch house is open for viewing. Nearby **Cape Blanco Lighthouse,** built in 1870, is Oregon's oldest continuously operating light. Perched atop a 245-foot cliff, the one million-candlepower beacon at Cape Blanco is seen for 22 miles and protects a particularly treacherous stretch of the coast. As an interesting aside, Oregon's first woman lightkeeper kept the Cape Blanco Lighthouse, beginning in 1903.

*Located six miles west of Hwy. 101. 541/332-6774; 541/332-0248 (during open hours). Hughes House and Lighthouse open Thurs.-Mon., 10 a.m.-4 p.m. (April-Oct.). Free.*

## GOLD BEACH

Named for a placer mine swept to sea in 1871, Gold Beach is renowned for its location at the mouth of the "wild and scenic" Rogue River. Most visitors come to fish, jet boat, and raft the river, but Gold Beach also provides access to beautiful, secluded hiking trails in the Kalmiopsis Wilderness and Siskiyou National Forest.

### PLACES TO STAY

**TU TU TUN LODGE**
*96550 North Bank Rogue, 97444*
*541/247-6664; www.tututun.com*
*Rates: Expensive*
*FYI: Dining room; outdoor lap pool; 4-hole pitch-and-putt course*

Tu Tu Tun Lodge is not an ocean resort. It sits on the Rogue River, seven miles from the coastal town of Gold Beach. Two houses—the Garden House, with three bedrooms, and the new River House with two bedrooms—are ideal for families. The less expensive River View room—with two queen beds, a soaking tub, and a patio—is also very nice. The suites are more spacious and deluxe.

Three meals a day are available in the dining room by reservation only. Before dinner there is a get-together with all the guests. Appetizers and drinks are served. Kids are welcome, and soft drinks are available. The meals are excellent but expensive. At dinner, the kids are seated at a separate table and offered their own kid friendly menu.

**❝ PARENT COMMENTS**

*"There is nothing negative to say about the Lodge. The owners greet you by name, make sure the children feel at home by providing games and letting them play on the Par-3 golf course. The "cocktail hour" every night before dinner includes kids and is a great way to meet other families."*

**GOLD BEACH RESORT AND CONDOMINIUMS**
*1330 S. Ellensburg Ave., 97444*
*541/247-7066, 800/541-0947*
*Rates: Inexpensive to moderate*
*FYI: Refrigerators; indoor pool*

Gold Beach Resort has 39 units, all on the ocean, and all with balconies. Although it is right on Highway 101, it's easy to focus on the beach, and forget about the traffic. Here you

## Tips: "Doing Your Own Thing" Along the Rogue River

Water traffic along the popular lower Rogue River is carefully controlled, so those who want to go it alone must sign up for an annual lottery. During the first six weeks of the year, the Forest Service (1225 S. Ellensburg; 541/247-3600) draws names of those who will be approved to take solo trips.

If you're interested in planning your own hike, especially deep in the wilderness areas, you can get help from area jet-boat companies. A jet boat can drop you off upriver, where you can access some of the less-traveled trails.

have the advantage of being in town, while enjoying excellent beach access (from the resort, a private trail leads across the dunes to the ocean).

## WHAT TO SEE & DO

**HIKING.** The Siskiyou National Forest, covering 1.1 million acres of the southern coastal region, is a hiker's wonderland. The popular 40-mile **Rogue River Trail** allows exploration of the tortuous river and the area known as "Botanist's Paradise," forests that abound with large numbers of plant species. Obviously, it's too long a trek for the shortest legs, but it's quite doable with pre-teens and teenagers.

The National Forest also encompasses the 180,000-acre **Kalmiopsis Wilderness,** accessible only by horse or by foot. There are many backcountry adventures to be had here. If you're hiking with kids, though, plan to go in the fall or spring. Summer temperatures routinely climb into the 90s, and can spoil the adventure altogether. For more information about hikes in these areas, contact the Gold Beach Ranger District, 1225 S. Ellensburg, Gold Beach, 97444; 541/247-6651.

**JET BOAT TRIPS** into the nationally recognized "wild and scenic" section of the Rogue River are an unforgettable experience that will thrill all ages. Guides will whisk you upriver, while providing information about the area's rich natural history and pointing out the abundant wildlife. They'll even stop frequently to let you get those hard-to-shoot photographs. Be sure to pack the sunscreen; most of the jet boats are open, and visitors can wind up with nasty burns.

**Rogue-Pacific Adventure Center** (541/247-6504; 800/525-2161) is a central booking agent for jet boat and rafting trips on the Rogue River. One of the oldest jet boat companies in the area, **Jerry's Rogue Jets** (541/247-4571; 800/451-3645), leads four different guided trips, ranging in length from 64 to 104 miles. Children of all ages are welcome.

## RESOURCES

**GOLD BEACH CHAMBER OF COMMERCE**
29279 Ellensburg Ave., #3, Gold Beach 97444
541/247-7526; 800/525-2334

## ON THE ROAD AGAIN

Driving the 31-mile stretch between Gold Beach and

Brookings, you'll see some of the nicest scenery along the coast. **Cape Sebastian State Scenic Viewpoint** (seven miles south of Gold Beach) encompasses 1,104 acres of land, including 700-foot Cape Sebastian. There are scenic views and hiking trails throughout the park.

At **Samuel Boardman State Park,** located at the base of the Siskiyou Mountains, you'll find nine miles of rocky coastline and quiet beaches. The *North Hiking Trail* is an easy walk that gains 600 feet of elevation in the first 2.8 miles. This segment of the trail provides a good family trek, with views of rocky coastline, sea stacks and, in season, perhaps a pod of gray whales.

## BROOKINGS

Situated six miles north of the California border, Brookings enjoys mild weather and has the only ancient redwood groves in Oregon.

### PLACES TO STAY

#### BEACHFRONT INN

*16008 Boat Basin Road, 97415*
*541/469-7779, 800/468-4081*
*Rates: Moderate to expensive*
*FYI: Restaurants; continental breakfast; kitchens (some units); refrigerator/microwave; indoor pool; pets OK*

Beautifully set where the Chetco River meets the ocean, Beachfront Inn makes the most of both waterways. It is the only oceanfront motel in Brookings, and each of its 78 units has a private balcony.

**❝ PARENT COMMENTS**
*"These folks were most welcoming of both kids and dog. We also appreciated their suggestions about activities for families in the area, and on up the coast."*

### PLACES TO EAT

#### BEACHCOMBERS DELI & SEAFOOD

*800 Chetco Ave.*
*541/469-0739*
*Hours: Breakfast, lunch, dinner daily*

This is the place you'll hear recommended for fish and chips, but they also specialize in prawns and scallops with chips. For the heart-healthy crowd, there's a lovely baked halibut. If your little one is averse to seafood, the children's menu includes corndogs, hotdogs, chicken, and fettucine.

### WILD RIVER PIZZA COMPANY
*16279 Hwy. 101 S., Harbor*
*541/469-7454*
*Hours: Lunch, dinner daily*
   When family members have seafood coming out their ears, you know it's time for pizza! These folks offer a wide variety of ready-made pizzas, but you're welcome to come up with your own combinations as well. There's chicken and chips, deli-style sandwiches, and a nice salad bar. Eat in or grab it and run to the beach.

### WHAT TO SEE & DO

   **ALFRED A. LOEB STATE PARK.** Ten miles from Brookings, Loeb State Park is set in a beautiful stand of old-growth Oregon-myrtle trees (a tree that grows only in Oregon State and in the country of Lebanon). There are numerous hiking trails, one of which connects with the *Redwood Tree Nature Trail.* This well-maintained trail—a mile-long loop, with a few steep sections— affords access to the largest coast redwood trees in Oregon. These majestic trees range from 300 to 800 years old. (If conditions remain favorable, they could live for another 1,000 years.)
   *Take North Bank Road (off Hwy. 101 just south of Brookings) for 7.5 miles along the Chetco River.*

   **AZALEA PARK.** Sure, there are more than 1,000 wild azaleas here that bloom magnificently each late spring and early fall. But don't expect your kids to see them. They'll be too busy playing at Kid Town, a large, all-wood climbing structure featuring forts and bridges, ramps and ladders. This is a great place to stop for a picnic (tables available) and let the kids run, climb, and jump.
   *From Hwy. 101, drive east on Constitution Ave. to North Bank Chetco River Road. Turn left and watch for park on the right.*

### CALENDAR

**MAY**
Azalea Festival.
Southern Oregon Kite Festival.

## RESOURCES

**BROOKINGS-HARBOR CHAMBER OF COMMERCE**
16330 Lower Harbor Road, Brookings 97415
541/469-3181; 800/535-9469

**CHETCO RANGER STATION**
555 5th St., Brookings 97415
541/469-2133

# THE WILLAMETTE VALLEY

The Willamette Valley was understandably a popular stopping place for pioneers on the Oregon Trail, and many of the first Northwest settlements grew up here. The rich valley soil makes this one of the most productive agricultural areas in the country, producing a wide variety of fruits, berries, vegetables, and flowers. Locals have a favorite saying: "If it doesn't grow here, you can probably get along without it. If it does grow here, it's probably celebrated with a festival and sold at roadside stands."

The valley is very accessible to travelers, with easy stops off I-5, the main north-south freeway. A visit here affords families an opportunity to investigate both the history and the roadside stands, without a great deal of driving. Veering off the main drag can be quite rewarding, though, especially if you care to introduce the kids to the concept of covered bridges.

## REGIONAL RESOURCES

**WILLAMETTE VALLEY VISITORS ASSOCIATION**
P.O. Box 965, Albany 97321
800/526-2256; www.albanyvisitors.com

## SALEM

Although it's the state capital, Salem tends to be overlooked as a vacation destination. There are some fun and educational experiences to be had here, both indoors and out. Besides, while the many wonders of the area remain a "state secret," families can still travel here for bargain prices.

Settled by fur trappers who turned to farming in the early 1800s, Salem is one of Oregon's oldest communities. Methodist missionaries encouraged further settlement of the area, known at the time as Mill Creek, beginning in 1834. Missionary leader

Jason Lee moved his mission to Mill Creek in 1840 and soon thereafter founded the first institution of higher learning west of Missouri. First known as the Oregon Institute, it was later renamed Willamette University. The town that grew up around it was called Salem, an anglicized version of the Hebrew word *shalom*, meaning "peace." When the Territory of Oregon gained statehood in 1859, Salem became its official capital.

## GETTING THERE

From Portland, take I-5 south 47 miles. From Eugene, take I-5 north 64 miles.

Southwest of Portland, near Newberg, consider a stop at **Champoeg State Park,** originally the site of a Calapooya Indian village. The first American provisional government in the Pacific Northwest was formed here in 1843. The park is situated on the south bank of the scenic Willamette River and offers campsites (including eight yurts), picnic areas, amphitheater, and 10 miles of trails through acres of forest, fields, and wetlands. Bring your binoculars; it's easy for kids to spot wildlife while hiking. You can also take a guided walk to learn what happened to the pioneer town of Champoeg and how the Donald Manson Barn was built.

If you have a history buff in the family, you'll enjoy visiting the historical sites: Newell House, Pioneer Mother's Log Cabin, and the jail. Exhibits and artifacts demonstrate the lifestyle of early pioneers.

*8089 Champoeg Road NE, St. Paul (off Hwy. 99W, 7 miles east of Newberg). Open Feb.-Nov., Wed.-Sun., noon-5 p.m. Cost: $2/adult, $0.75/child.*

## PLACES TO STAY

### PHOENIX INN

*Phoenix Inn North Salem*
*1590 Weston Ct. NE, 97301*
*503/581-7004, 888/239-9593*
*Phoenix Inn South Salem*
*4370 Commercial St. SE, 97302*
*503/588-9220, 800/445-4498; www.phoenixinn.com*
*FYI: Complimentary continental breakfast; refrigerators/microwaves; indoor pool; fitness center; laundry; pets OK (south only)*
The Phoenix Inn chain is a small but up-and-coming addi-

tion to the Oregon vacation scene. The mini-suites are large and comfortable, with separate living and sleeping areas. The continental breakfast is more extensive than the name suggests, including hot and cold cereals, baked goodies, juice, and fruit.

Pools are warm, and most stay open late. Both Salem hotels are conveniently located near downtown and area attractions.

**❝❝ PARENT COMMENTS**

*"We learned that the rooms here are quite soundproof. There was a group of teens partying next door, but our family slept soundly."*

*"Families that tend to get a late start, as ours does, will appreciate that the pool is open when they arrive. There's nothing like a quick swim after a long day of driving or sightseeing."*

## PLACES TO EAT

### S'GHETTI'S

*695 Orchard Heights NW*
*503/378-1780*
*Hours: Dinner daily*

This is one of Salem's more attractive restaurants, a "cloth tablecloth" kind of place. However, the dining rooms are spacious and charming, and families will feel quite comfortable here. In spring and summer, the family can request dining on the open-air patio. The children's menu includes pasta favorites, such as macaroni and cheese, along with applesauce and choice of drink. For adult tastes, there's a wide variety of entrées, including Veal Marsala, stuffed shrimp, and chicken Parmesan.

## WHAT TO SEE & DO

### STROLL & BROWSE

**CAPITOL GROUNDS.** The **Oregon State Capitol Building,** built in 1938, is a majestic Vermont marble structure of modern design, topped by a gilded statue, *The Oregon Pioneer.* Inside the building are a number of impressive murals depicting historical events. The extensive capitol grounds give little ones an opportunity to run the wiggles out.

*Take State Capitol Exit and follow signs. Visitor Service Center, 503/986-1388. Building open Mon.-Fri., 8 a.m.-5 p.m.; Sat., 9 a.m.-4 p.m.; Sun, noon-4 p.m. Free.*

*Free guided tours available on the hour, during summer (daily, mid-June-Labor Day, Mon.-Sat., 9 a.m.-noon and 1-4 p.m.; Sun., noon- 4 p.m.)*

**WILLAMETTE UNIVERSITY.** Located just behind the capitol grounds, the Willamette University campus is a nice place to stroll, amid brick buildings (old and new) and along the nearby stream. If you're into flora, stop by the small botanical garden on the eastern edge of the campus. Tours can be arranged through the admission department.

*900 State St. 503/370-6300.*

## PARKS

**BUSH HOUSE AND BUSH'S PASTURE PARK.** Salem residents are fortunate to have this beautiful 89-acre urban park, located just south of the central business district. Pringle Creek winds through a section of the park, surrounded by shrubs, ferns, and wildflowers. These were originally the private grounds of Asahel Bush, an influential pioneer who built his Victorian-style home here in 1877 (for $5,000). In 1954, the city acquired the Bush House and restored it as a museum and art gallery. Tours are available; the last one begins at 4:30 p.m.

*600 Mission St. SE. 503/363-4714. Open Tues.-Sun., 2-5 p.m. (Oct.-April); Tues.-Sun., noon-5 p.m. (May-Sept.). Cost: $3/adult, $2.50/senior & student, $1.50/child 6-12, free/under 6.*

**MISSION MILL VILLAGE** is a 5.5-acre historic park featuring 19th-century buildings, a top-quality museum store, a café, and unique shops. It is the former site of the Thomas Kay Woolen Mill, founded in 1889, that includes the Jason Lee House and Parsonage (the oldest frame buildings still standing in the Pacific Northwest) and the Pleasant Grove Church. Technically inclined youngsters will enjoy seeing the restored, water-powered turbine and loom, which demonstrate the process of turning fleece to wool. Exhibits and tours are available. If the weather's fine, plan a picnic on the grounds, or feed the ducks by the "old mill stream."

*1313 Mill St. SE (From I-5, take Exit 253, west on Hwy. 22/Mission St., follow signs). 503/585-7012; 800/874-7012. Open Tues.-Sat., 10 a.m.-4:30 p.m. (year round); Sun., 11 a.m.-4:30 p.m. (June-Sept.).*

## MUSEUMS

**A.C. GILBERT DISCOVERY VILLAGE.** There's something for every family member here, and they're adding new attractions all the time. The focal point is the Gilbert Room, which features working American Flyer Trains and memorabilia of A.C.

Gilbert (inventor of the Erector Set and many other educational toys). Gilbert is remembered as "the man who saved Christmas," because he convinced Congress not to turn his toy plant into a munitions factory during World War I. Exhibits include Physics in Motion, Construction Zone, do-it-yourself Children's Theater, and Cave of Wonders.

*116 Marion St. NE. 503/371-3631; 800/208-9514; www.oregonlink.com/gilbert_house. Open Mon.-Sat., 10 a.m.-5 p.m.; Sun., noon-5 p.m.(Feb. 2-Labor Day); Tues.-Sat., 10 a.m.-5 p.m.; Sun., noon-5 p.m. (day after Labor Day-Feb. 1). Cost: $4/person 3-59, $3/senior 60 & over, free/under 3, $1.75/family on public assistance. Call for special economy times.*

## EXCURSIONS

**ENCHANTED FOREST.** Located on a wooded hillside south of Salem, Enchanted Forest is a dream come true for little kids. It features storybook characters in a wooded setting and a clever re-creation of an early mining town. The most recent additions include English Village and the Big Timber Log Ride.

For preschoolers, it's enough to romp along the twisted trails, peering into cottages, wriggling into bunny holes, and slipping down the bumpy slide at the Old Woman's Shoe. The trick here is to keep school-age children amused. (The scary haunted house, log ride, and bobsled roller coaster may suffice.) The whole family can enjoy Fantasy Fountains, a charming water-and-light show at English Village. The dense trees keep things cool, even in midsummer. Bring a picnic, or purchase snacks and lunch foods here.

*Take I-5 south to Exit 248 in Turner. 503/363-3060. Open March 15-Sept., daily 9:30 a.m.-6 p.m. Cost: $6.50/adult, $4.95/senior, $5.75/child 3-12, free/under 3. Some rides are extra.*

**SILVER FALLS STATE PARK.** The largest of Oregon's state parks, Silver Falls encompasses almost 9,000 acres of dense forest and 10 spectacular waterfalls (six are more than 100 feet tall). There are countless hikes of the "surprise at every turn" variety; most gain altitude, but some are short and quite manageable by little legs.

*20024 Silver Falls Hwy. SE, Sublimity (Twenty-six miles east of Salem on Hwy. 214. From I-5, take exit to Hwy. 22, and follow signs to park). 503/873-8681. Cost: $3/vehicle.*

## CALENDAR

### JULY

July 4th Celebration: Artists and fireworks, Mission Mill Village.

Salem Art Fair and Festival: Craftspeople, performing arts, children's activities, and food; Bush's Pasture Park.

## RESOURCES

### SALEM CONVENTION AND VISITORS ASSOCIATION

1313 Mill St. SE, Salem 97301

503/581-4325; 800/874-7012; www.stateoforegon.com

## EUGENE

As anyone who's raising a family here will attest, Eugene is a wonderful place to explore with children. It's small enough to feel safe and manageable, yet large enough to offer plenty of entertainment opportunities. For outdoor activity, it simply can't be beat—whether you stay close in or venture farther out. Eugene boasts 49 city parks covering nearly 2,000 acres, easy access to three national forests, and innumerable hiking trails, both inside and just outside the city. An hour west is the unsurpassable coastline (see "Oregon Coast"). To the east are the beautiful drives up the McKenzie River and into the Cascades (see "Willamette Valley: McKenzie River").

Eugene is located where the Willamette and McKenzie rivers meet, amid forests, farmland, and mountains. It is the second largest city in Oregon and home of the University of Oregon. Eugene's role as a college town lends it an air of sophistication, but at the same time it is an earthy, "counter-culture" kind of place.

The town was named after pioneer Eugene Skinner, whose wife was the first white woman in the area. Incorporated in 1862, Eugene still has a lively pioneer atmosphere, but it's also a great place for kids to get a taste of more recent history. Refreshingly, the '60s and '70s are still alive and well here.

Eugene suffered during the decline of the forest industry in Oregon in the late '70s and '80s. Real estate values crashed, and many people were forced by circumstances to leave the area. Due in part to the constancy of the University, Eugene has made a slow, steady recovery. Today, the city has a population of 126,000 and has managed to attract new industry to fill the gap left by logging.

## GETTING THERE

Eugene is located just off I-5, 108 miles south of Portland. Plan on a 2 1/4-hour trip, including a short rest stop. This stretch of I-5 is fairly monotonous, so you might plan a meal or activity break along the way (see "Salem").

## PLACES TO STAY

### BEST WESTERN NEW OREGON MOTEL

*1655 Franklin Blvd., 97440*
*541/683-3669*
*Rates: Inexpensive to moderate*
*FYI: Covered outdoor pool; racquetball court; laundry; pets OK (deposit)*

At first glance, this spot seems like a basic, two-story motel. The rooms are comfortable, but small (there are also eight two-bedroom units), and many rooms have adjoining covered parking. Best of all for families, the small but clean pool is under cover and stays open from 6 a.m. until midnight.

Despite being on a busy street, the location across from the University is very handy. Just west of the motel, a walkway leads across the Mill Race, past the Duck Pond and Urban Garden, and down to the banks of the Willamette River. It's a great place to bike, as long as kids are old enough to watch for occasional bike and pedestrian traffic.

### ❝❝ PARENT COMMENTS

*"We were able to bike most everywhere, although it was a first road experience for our seven year old. In Eugene, they make it easy to get around by bike, even to cross the river. Skinner's Butte Park was pure joy!"*

### HILTON HOTEL

*66 E. 6th (at Oak), 97401*
*541/342-2000; www.hilton.eugene.com*
*Rates: Moderate to expensive*
*FYI: Restaurant, lobby bar; refrigerators (suites); indoor pool; exercise facility; pets OK*

The biggest selling point of the Hilton is its great location: downtown, adjacent to the Hult Center for the Performing Arts and a short walk from the 5th Street Market and Eugene Saturday Market. Rooms are nicely appointed but on the small side. If budget allows, opt for one of the six suites; each has a separate bedroom and a refrigerator.

The restaurant here is quite good and affords the best view in town (short of hiking Spencer's Butte, of course). Children are welcome, but it's a "best behavior" kind of place. For a more relaxed atmosphere, the café on the lobby level serves three meals a day, plus special buffets, and has a salad bar. The children's menu offers standard choices, and the place mats come with crayons.

**❝❝ PARENT COMMENTS**
*"In a small city like Eugene, we enjoy being at the heart of things. We can walk to all the city events, and it's a short drive to take advantage of recreational opportunities. Our kids like the pool here."*

### PHOENIX INN
*850 Franklin Blvd., 97403*
*541/344-0001, 800/344-0131; www.phoenixinn.com*
*Rates: Moderate*
*FYI: Complimentary breakfast; indoor pool; refrigerators/ microwaves; laundry*

One of a growing number of "mini-suite" hotels, the Phoenix Inn provides comfortable two-room accommodations. This one has a small indoor pool and Jacuzzi, along with the added advantage of proximity to the university campus. The free continental breakfast offers a variety of fresh foods, including cereals and breakfast rolls to suit younger tastes.

**❝❝ PARENT COMMENTS**
*"When you're headed out for a full day of activities, as we were, it's really convenient to get breakfast before you leave the motel. And our picky eaters always found something appetizing."*

### THE VALLEY RIVER INN
*1000 Valley River Way, 97401*
*541/687-0123, 800/543-8266; www.valleyriverin.com*
*Rates: Moderate to expensive*
*FYI: Restaurant; outdoor pool (seasonal); bike/walking trail; pets OK*

If peace and quiet are more important to you than convenience, this is a great choice. (Nothing is really inconvenient in Eugene; the Inn is only a five-minute car ride from downtown and university districts.) Located near a large regional mall of the same name, the Inn sits right on the Willamette River. A paved bike path passes in front of the inn and continues along the river for several miles through two area parks.

The rooms are spacious, and many overlook the river or face onto grassy courtyards. If you're visiting in the spring or summer, the large outdoor swimming pool (with small toddler area) and hot tub will be huge hits with the kids. If you get some liquid sun, send the kids to the lobby to choose a game (board or video).

**❝❝ PARENT COMMENTS**

*"We love the easy access to the river and parks. We rented bikes from the Inn and took the river path to the campus, Alton Baker, and Skinner's Butte. There are stops along the way where older kids can wade safely."*

*"Be sure to ask about the Family Package. We got a room with two queen beds, breakfast for four, plus free rental of bikes, helmets, and videos. When we checked in, the kids got a "fun pack," and we got a "childproof kit," which actually was handy."*

## PLACES TO EAT

### GLENWOOD CAFÉ

*2588 Willamette St.*
*541/687-8201*
*Hours: Breakfast, lunch, dinner daily*

If you're looking for creative Northwest cuisine, this isn't your stop. Glenwood Café is an old standby for well-prepared food at a very reasonable price. Breakfast is especially popular here, and they serve it until 5 p.m. The extensive menu provides all the choice you can imagine, and then some: eggs any style, pancakes, French toast, organic granola, and fruit. At lunch and dinner, you'll find a selection of burritos, sandwiches, salads, and soups, as well as (we are, after all, in Eugene) tofu dishes. There's a basic kids' menu and plenty of crayons and paper.

### JAMIE'S GREAT HAMBURGERS

*24th & Hilyard St.*
*541/342-2206*
*1810 Chambers*
*541/343-0485*
*Hours: Lunch, dinner daily*

The whole family will get a kick out of Jamie's. This colorful version of a '50s soda fountain features an antique red Vespa, jukebox, and pinball machine, not to mention great burgers. There are 12 varieties of burger here, as well as assorted sandwiches; all are served in old-fashioned burger baskets surrounded by mounds of French fries. To complete your return to a decade past, splurge on a thick shake or traditional ice cream soda (one may be enough to satisfy two kids).

Parent reviewers checked out the Jamie's at 24th and Hilyard. Chances are their new restaurant is equally tasty and entertaining.

## MAZZI'S ITALIAN FOOD

*3377 E. Amazon Pkwy.*
*541/687-2252*
*Hours: Lunch Mon.-Fri., dinner daily*

When Eugenians think "family restaurant," they're likely to think of Mazzi's. It didn't start out that way; in fact, the restaurant was started by two university students fresh out of entertainment. But this spot has grown, created a pleasing Mediterranean atmosphere, and developed a reputation for catering to particular tastes.

Kids' meals at Mazzi's include an entrée (pizza, spaghetti with a choice of butter or sauce, or ravioli with meat or tomato sauce), drink, and ice cream. For grown-up tastes, dinner choices include pizza (ready-made or choose-your-own) and pastas, or special veal and chicken dishes. In case you're equivocating, the eggplant Parmesan is a winner.

## NAPOLI RESTAURANT AND BAKERY

*686 E. 13th (13th & Hilyard)*
*541/485-4552*
*Hours: Lunch, dinner Mon.-Sat.*

This is a "nicer" restaurant, but perfectly comfortable with kids of any age. Black-and-white checked floor and marble tables may look daunting, but take a closer look—the tabletops are easy-wipe "faux marble" and the floor is none the worse for a spill or two.

Though it's located only a few blocks from campus, you can shut your eyes and believe you're in an upscale café in Italy. Best of all, Napoli serves food that's equally convincing. There is a nice selection of Italian appetizers and lighter fare such as soups and salads. But the fresh pastas are the strong suit here, and you can choose from a tasty array. The servers bend over backward to accommodate families, taking special requests from fussy eaters and happily splitting orders. If you've got the room, check out the dessert tray.

Our parent reviewer reported their order was a little slow in coming, but the focaccia starter helped the kids wait patiently.

**THE ORIGINAL PANCAKE HOUSE**
*782 E. Broadway*
*541/343-7523*
*Hours: Breakfast, lunch daily*

This Eugene institution is still one of the best breakfast spots in town. Though frequented by a cadre of "old timers," the atmosphere is great for families. The extensive list of pancakes is an experience in itself. (The apple and German pancakes are specialties of the house, but be forewarned: they take 20 minutes to prepare.) For kids, the Pancake House offers junior plates of popular dishes such as "pigs in a blanket" and dollar pancakes. For that rare little one who doesn't much like pancakes, try the crisp waffles or cereal (cooked or cold).

This is a specialty restaurant, serving the same great breakfast fare through lunchtime (daily until 2 p.m.).

## WHAT TO SEE & DO

### STROLL & BROWSE

**FIFTH STREET PUBLIC MARKET.** Located by the train tracks and a few blocks from beautiful Skinner's Butte Park (see "Parks"), the Public Market features a variety of intriguing shops and restaurants built around a three-story courtyard. Plan on spending some time perusing the high-quality array of local arts and crafts. The food here is upscale and most likely to appeal to adult tastes. To stave off hunger, little ones might choose something from the **Metropol Bakery** (541/687-9370), which enjoys a deserved reputation as one of the finest bakeries on the West Coast. Pick up one of their fabulous, fresh-baked baguettes and stage an impromptu picnic!

While mom and dad sip an espresso next to the fountain, little kids will enjoy riding the "bubble" elevator; it climbs only three levels, but it's a fun ride, and there's a nice view from the top. There are occasionally special events for kids, such as face painting, mime, and live music.

At the 5th Street entrance, you'll find **Wonderland** (541/683-8464), a video arcade with all the bells and whistles. The arcade is open daily, noon to midnight. If you lose track of your kids at the Market, this is where you're likely to find them!

*296 E. 5th (corner of 5th & High St.). 541/484-0383. Open daily, 10 a.m.-6 p.m.*

**SATURDAY MARKET.** Saturday Market is a local tradition and a great place to get a true taste of Eugene. The oldest weekly open-air crafts fair in the United States (since 1969), it occupies four square blocks among the tall trees and fountains of downtown. Stroll and admire the fine collection of local crafts while munching a falafel or sipping fresh-squeezed lemonade. Or sit a spell while you eat, and enjoy the entertainment.

The family may want to make a "pit stop" before going to the market; the only restrooms are Sani-cans that can be unpleasant in hot weather. Free car and bicycle parking is available.

*Downtown Eugene at 8th & Pearl St. 541/686-8885. Sat., 10 a.m.-5 p.m. ("rain or shine"). Free.*

**UNIVERSITY OF OREGON.** One of the prettiest campuses on the West Coast, the University of Oregon was selected as the setting for the movie *Animal House* because it reminded producers of a small East Coast college. It's a fun place to stroll amid grassy quads, old-growth oaks, and intriguing sculptures. (Kids love to be photographed with *Pioneer Mother*, a sculpture located on the grass in front of the graceful University Library). Near here are two University museums older kids will enjoy—the Museum of Art and the Museum of Natural History (see "Museums").

*E. 13th & Kincaid St. 541/346-3201. Guided tours depart Oregon Hall, Mon.-Sat., 10 a.m. and Mon.-Fri., 2 p.m. Free.*

**PARKS**

**ALTON BAKER COUNTY PARK.** This is a beautifully tended urban park, located adjacent to the Willamette River. The small man-made lake is a favorite; kids love to explore the island at its center and feed the resident ducks. There are acres of grass for running and tumbling. From here, the riverside bike trail heads east to the university or west to Valley River Mall.

*On Country Club Road, just east of Ferry St. Bridge. 541/682-4800.*

**HENDRICKS PARK RHODODENDRON GARDEN.** Of course, not every child is an admirer of rhododendrons, but this is also a lovely spot for running and tumbling. Perched atop the forested ridgeline of southeast Eugene, Hendricks Park overlooks the Willamette River, the University of Oregon, and the city. The 77 acres of forested park contain stands of trees more than 200 years old and hiking trails that wander through a rich forest flora.

The Rhododendron Garden, situated beneath a canopy of Oregon white oaks, is a woodland garden of 5,000 rhododendrons and other ornamental plants, walkways, and secluded seating areas. The rhodies blossom February through July, peaking in April and May.

*Take Walnut St. to Fairmount Blvd., then east on Summit Ave. 541/687-5324. Open daily. Free.*

**MOUNT PISGAH ARBORETUM** affords a good opportunity to feel you're out in the wild without traveling far from the city center. The arboretum encompasses 208 acres of wooded hill-sides and seven miles of all-season trails. The Visitor Center features a "touch-me" nature exhibit, natural history displays, gift shop, and trail guides.

*33735 Seavey Loop Road. (5 miles southeast. Drive east on 30th Ave. to Seavey Loop Road.) 541/741-4110. Open daily, dawn-dusk. Free.*

**SKINNER BUTTE PARK.** This graceful little park is on the Willamette River near downtown Eugene. A bike/stroll path winds through the park, hugging the riverbank. At the west end of the park are the beautiful Owen Memorial Rose Gardens, at their peak May through July. There are a nice play area and a few scattered picnic tables.

*From downtown, drive north on High St. to park entrance. 541/682-5318.*

## MUSEUMS

**UNIVERSITY OF OREGON MUSEUM OF ART** leans toward Asian and contemporary American art and photography. Exhibits change frequently, though, so call or stop in to see what's current.

*1430 Johnson Lane (near the Library). 541/346-3027. Open Wed., noon-8 p.m.; Thurs.-Sun., noon-5 p.m. Cost: donation.*

**UNIVERSITY OF OREGON MUSEUM OF NATURAL HISTORY** focuses on the archeology, anthropology, and natural sciences of the Pacific Northwest. Throughout the year, the museum displays an interesting variety of traveling exhibits, featuring everything from human cultures to ancient tools.

*1680 E. 15th. 541/346-3024; www.uoregon.edu/~mnh/. Open Wed.-Sun., noon-5 p.m. Cost: suggested donation $1-2/person, additional fee for special exhibits.*

**WILLAMETTE SCIENCE AND TECHNOLOGY CENTER (WIS-TEC).** This small museum makes a good rainy-day excursion for families. It offers interactive displays that change every eight to ten weeks and an impressive planetarium.

*2300 Leo Harris Pkwy. (near Autzen Stadium). 541/682-7888. Open Wed.-Fri., noon-5 p.m.; Sat.-Sun., 11 a.m.-5 p.m. Cost: $4/adult, $3/child 4-16, free/under 4.*

## KID CULTURE

**HULT CENTER FOR THE PERFORMING ARTS.** This world-class concert facility, noted for its architectural and acoustical design, is home to a number of local arts organizations, including the Eugene Symphony, Eugene Opera, Oregon Bach Festival, Eugene Festival of Musical Theatre, and Eugene Ballet Company. It also features national acts, Broadway musicals, and premier children's theater.

Free, guided one-hour tours of the center are offered Thursdays and Saturdays at 1 p.m.

*6th & Willamette St. 541/342-5746 (recorded message); 503/682-5000 (tickets); 541/682-5733 (tour information). Lobby open Tues.-Sat., 11 a.m.-3 p.m. and one hour prior to performances.*

## EXCURSIONS

**DORRIS RANCH** is a 250-acre farm that operates as a non-profit organization, giving families an opportunity to experience early Oregon history firsthand. Guided year-round walking tours emphasize early farming, trapping, and Native American activities. Purchased by the Park and Recreation District in 1972, the farm has expanded to include new interpretive and living history exhibits.

Don't worry if your kids aren't big history buffs—this place has a way of making history "come alive" for the greatest skeptics. Then there are the acres of land to enjoy: orchards, lush forests, pastures, and wetlands. Self-guided tours follow a flat, two-mile trail.

*Located on S. 2nd St., Springfield. (Take Franklin Blvd. east until it becomes Main St. Continue east; turn right on S. 2nd.) 541/746-1669.*

**SPENCER BUTTE PARK.** Those who do nothing else in Eugene will want to hike one of the two relatively easy (but sometimes muddy) trails up 2,065-foot Spencer's Butte, the highest point in the region. Along the way, enjoy wildlife sightings, and sneak peeks at the surrounding terrain; at the top you're rewarded with an incredible bird's-eye view of surrounding urban and pastoral areas. (Take care toward the top: the trail requires some scrambling over large rocks, and there is poison oak growing in the area.)

The Butte is surrounded by acres of coniferous forest through which threads the South Hills Ridgeline Trail.

*Drive south on Ridgeline Road to Fox Hollow Road, south on Fox Hollow to S. Willamette St. Watch for sign and small parking area.*

### THE GREAT OUTDOORS

**BIKING.** Visitors are thrilled to discover Eugene's interlacing series of bicycle paths; there are more than 25 miles of off-street cycling and 300 miles of striped streets in the area. Especially nice for families is the bike path that meanders along the Willamette River, connecting the university and downtown with several of the city's nicest parks. A fun afternoon may be had here, as long as kids are old enough to watch for occasional traffic. Ride around campus, then cross Franklin Boulevard and the bike path over the river. From here, you can make a loop trip that includes Skinner Butte Park and Alton Baker County Park (see "Parks"). Along the path are plenty of quiet spots to stop and rest or wade.

If you really want to leave the car behind, bring bikes from home and explore the entire area on two wheels. Otherwise, you can rent bikes for the whole family at **Blue Heron Bicycles** (877 E. 13th; 541/343-2488) or **High Street Bicycles** (535 High St.; 541/687-1775). Both have smaller-frame bikes and tagalong trailers, but call in advance to make sure they can meet your particular needs.

**BOATING.** Eugene is loaded with great spots to raft and sail. Local river guides conduct rafting trips on the McKenzie, Willamette, and Deschutes rivers. To rent a raft or arrange a guided river trip, try **Justus Outfitters and Guide Service** (1090 Snell St.; 541/342-3587).

Fern Ridge Reservoir, located 15 miles west of Eugene, is especially popular for sailing; Dexter Lake, 20 miles east, is a favorite spot for canoeing. To rent sailboats, call **Sailing Center Oregon** (1475 Railroad Blvd.; 541/683-0818).

**ICE SKATING.** Eugene's state-of-the-art ice skating facility, **Lane County Ice** (796 W. 13th, at Lane County Fairgrounds; 541/682-3615), has a regulation-size floor and offers a Cheap Skate Night and Family Night.

### CALENDAR

**JUNE/JULY**

Oregon Bach Festival: Schedule of performances includes a family concert.

**JULY**

Oregon Country Fair: Arts and crafts, food and entertainment in a lovely, wooded setting, Veneta.

**JULY/AUGUST**

Concerts in the Parks, Tuesdays.

Eugene Festival of Musical Theatre.

**AUGUST**

Lane County Fair, Eugene.

**SEPTEMBER**

Oregon Festival of American Music: Eclectic festival celebrates all types of American music, Eugene.

Eugene Celebration: Festival features local food, crafts, and entertainment.

## RESOURCES

**CONVENTION AND VISITORS ASSOCIATION OF LANE COUNTY**

115 W. 8th Avenue, Ste. 190, Eugene 97440

541/484-5307; 800/547-5445; www.cvalco.com

*EUGENE WEEKLY*

1251 Lincoln, Eugene 97440

541/484-0519; www.eugeneweekly.com

Free newspaper featuring local arts, events, and entertainment.

## McKENZIE RIVER

The McKenzie River, which winds westward from high in the Cascades, is a favorite of anglers, rafters, and vacationers. Although it is a wild river and does not provide much access for swimming, there are many other joys to be had here. For those who wish only to relax and contemplate, it is a picturesque waterway, with many stopping points along its banks.

Highway 126 parallels the McKenzie River through the Willamette National Forest, then crosses the Cascades into the ponderosa-pine country of central Oregon. The Old McKenzie Pass Highway 242 is open only in summer, but it is a lovely alternate route over the mountains (see "Excursions").

## PLACES TO STAY

**BELKNAP SPRINGS RESORT**

*59296 Belknap Springs Road, McKenzie Bridge 97413*

*541/822-3512*

*Rates: Inexpensive to moderate*

*FYI: Kitchens (cabins only); two outdoor pools*

This rustic, charming resort has been around for decades, but was recently remodeled. Accommodations here are quite comfortable—simply furnished lodge rooms, and cabins set along the river.

There's a large camping and RV area, but the old hotel on the river is where the action is. Kids will love the two swimming pools, one at the RV area and one next to the river; both are open daily, 9 a.m. to 9 p.m. Fed by hot springs, these pools are bathtub temperature; too warm for the serious swimmer, but perfect for beginners and splashers. Neither pool is huge, but they're normally not crowded, either. Non-guests are welcome to swim, too, for a nominal charge, and towels and dressing rooms are available.

❝ **PARENT COMMENTS**

*"I learned to swim at the lodge pool, and—30 years later—so did my kids. The best time to come to the pool is after dinner and a dusty day of hiking. As sunset approaches and the steam rises off the water, you jump in, and it's pure bliss."*

*"We stayed once during the winter and had a dandy time skiing at HooDoo Bowl, about 45 minutes away."*

**LOG CABIN INN**
*56483 McKenzie Hwy., McKenzie Bridge 97413*
*541/822-3432, 800/355-3432*
*Rates: Moderate*
*FYI: Restaurant; kitchen (some units); wood stoves (some units); basketball, volleyball courts*

This historic, three-story inn was originally built in 1886, then rebuilt following a fire in 1906. Eight cabins are situated on a bluff, overlooking the rough and wild McKenzie River. Here you have a tough choice between two charming options—cabins and teepees—located along the banks. All eight cabins offer fireplaces, porches, and views of the river; beyond these amenities, you'll want to think carefully about your family's preferences. There's one cabin with two bedrooms and a kitchen, which costs a little more than the others. One cabin has a kitchenette and wood stove.

For a glorified camping experience, the six riverfront teepees are nice options (summer only). Nestled in the meadow along the river, they are near bathroom facilities, barbecues, and a campfire pit. The meadow has large open spaces and includes a horseshoe pit, basketball court, and volleyball court.

**❝ PARENT COMMENTS**

*"The sense of history in this place is really something. The guest books has the signatures of Clark Gable and the Duke of Windsor!"*

*"The restaurant here has an inviting menu, but it's pricey for a family."*

*"We had a fun vacation in one of the teepees, though we found we hadn't brought along enough food. There really are no great restaurants close by. Do walk the nature trail that takes off from the meadow."*

## PLACES TO EAT

### THE RUSTIC SKILLET CAFÉ
*54771 McKenzie Hwy., Blue River*
*541/822-3400*
*Hours: Breakfast, lunch, dinner daily*

The food here is just what you'd expect, given the name of the restaurant: if it can't be made in a skillet, they don't make it. That said, the meals are hearty and satisfying, and somehow appropriate to the setting.

## WHAT TO SEE & DO

### EXCURSIONS

**McKENZIE RIVER SCENIC LOOP.** Okay, scenery isn't always priority one with kids, but this drive affords opportunities to stop and swim, picnic, or hike. The first leg, Highway 242 through McKenzie Pass, is an Oregon classic. Normally open June through October, this narrow, twisty road is not recommended for trailers or RVs. Combine 242 with the more modern, year-round Highway 20 and Highway 126, and you have a lovely 85-mile loop through two mountain passes, past lakes and lava fields, and alongside the turbulent river.

There are a number of child-sized hikes in the area. Stop at the Ranger Station just east of McKenzie Bridge on Highway 126 for suggestions and maps. One family favorite is at **Proxy Falls,** along Highway 242; on a one-mile loop hike, you can catch spectacular views of both the upper and lower falls. At **Clear Lake,** off Highway 126, there's a five-mile loop trail that circles the lake, over lava beds and through deep forest; its gentle terrain is great for kids. **Koosah and Sahalie Falls,** both off Highway 126 near Clear Lake, are worthy of a stop. There's a trail along the river if you need to stretch your legs and want to see the falls from different vantage points.

The circle tour also takes you through the town of **Sisters,** in lodgepole-pine country. This small Western-style town offers a number of interesting boutiques and cafés (see "Central Oregon: Sisters"). It's a fun stop if your family likes to browse.

**THE DEE WRIGHT OBSERVATORY.** Located at the summit of the pass (5,324 feet), this Observatory affords a great view of one of the largest, most recent volcanic flows in the continental United States. Don't miss the stunning views of Mount Hood and other Cascade peaks, as well as nearby buttes and craters.

There are restrooms and plenty of parking spaces here. Take the short, very informative walk through the lava beds. Budding young geologists will learn as much as they wanted to know about lava and see good examples of the two principal types. Have binoculars handy, and you may get a glimpse of the Dusky Cony, a small animal found only in and around these lava flows.

### THE GREAT OUTDOORS

**RAFTING.** The McKenzie is a wild and wonderful river, and there are a number of excellent rafting guides in the area. For names, you can contact the **McKenzie River Guides Association** (P.O. Box 401, Walterville, 97489; 541/896-3348).

**SKIING.** HooDoo Ski Bowl (Box 20, Hwy. 20; 541/822-3799) is easily accessible off Highway 20, southwest of Santiam Pass. Here you will find opportunities for Nordic and alpine skiing and snowboarding. There are four lifts. You can rent equipment and sign up for ski school. Snow bunnies who tire early can hang out in the café or lounge, or order something from the deli.

### RESOURCES

**BLUE RIVER RANGER STATION**
P.O. Box 199, Blue River 97413
541/822-3317

**MCKENZIE RANGER STATION**
Milepost 53, McKenzie Hwy., McKenzie Bridge 97413
541/822-3381

**MCKENZIE RIVER CHAMBER OF COMMERCE**
P.O. Box 1117, Leaburg 97489
541/896-3330

# SOUTHERN OREGON

In many ways more like California than the rest of Oregon, the southern Oregon region stretches from the Coast Range over the Cascades to the Klamath Basin. Here are two major river systems, the Rogue and the Umpqua, and more recreational possibilities than most families will exhaust in a lifetime of vacations.

As in the Willamette Valley, I-5 is the major north-south corridor, traversing the Rogue and Umpqua Valleys. Several major highways branch off I-5: Highway 199, the Redwood Highway, passes southwest from Grants Pass into California; Highway 62, northeast from Medford to Crater Lake; Highway 66, east from Ashland to the Klamath basin; and Highway 140, east from Medford to Klamath Falls and beyond.

## REGIONAL RESOURCES

### SOUTHERN OREGON VISITORS ASSOCIATION
548 Business Park Dr., Medford 97504
541/779-4691; 800/448-4856; www.sova.org

## CRATER LAKE NATIONAL PARK

The deepest lake in the United States, and fifth deepest in the world, Crater Lake was formed by the massive explosion and collapse of 12,000-foot Mount Mazama. The explosion occurred some 7,700 years ago and was witnessed by the native Klamath and Modoc tribes, who felt sure their gods were engaged in battle. Today, geologists have a different theory about how Crater Lake was formed, but modern-day visitors are no less awed than their predecessors by the incredible beauty of it.

Crater Lake is particularly accessible to visitors. Catch the spectacular view from various perspectives: by car, boat, or on foot. During summer, families can choose to navigate the 31-mile Rim Drive, hike some of the trails, or take a boat tour of the lake. Park facilities are mostly closed during winter, when the area normally gets heavy snowfall, but visitors still come for winter views, or to enjoy cross-country skiing and snowshoe hikes.

### GETTING THERE

In summer, the park can be entered from the north, via Highway 138, or from the south, via Highway 62. The northern entry opens mid-June and closes with the first snowfall (generally October). It's often possible to include an excursion to Crater

Lake on your way from one region to another, such as between Bend and Ashland. It makes a long day of driving, so make sure you have accommodations prearranged on both ends of the drive.

### PLACES TO STAY

Although accessible from several directions, Crater Lake National Park is in a somewhat isolated position. There's not much lodging available close to the park, though you might find a spot in one of the small towns along your route. There are two park lodgings, listed below. Camping is available at Mazama Campground or 12 miles north at Diamond Lake.

### CRATER LAKE LODGE
*365 Rim Village Dr., Crater Lake 97604*
*P.O. Box 2704, White City 97503*
*541/830-8700*
*Rates: Moderate to expensive*
*FYI: Dining room*

This historic lodge was built in 1915 and completely restored in 1995. The restoration was painstaking, and the new lodge is very similar to the old, down to the rough-hewn Ponderosa trunks and the huge, basalt fireplace (the hearthstones were numbered, then returned to their original positions). With its setting on the rim of the crater, the lodge offers sweeping views of the piercing blue of Crater Lake.

The rustic lodge has 71 rooms, including four two-bedroom units. Twenty-six rooms face the lake, but all the rooms have pleasant, forested views. The dining room prepares three ranch-style meals daily; alternatively, food is available at nearby Mazama Village.

### ❝ PARENT COMMENTS

*"The sense of history here is tremendous; for our family, it really added to the Crater Lake experience."*

*"We did quite a bit of hiking and were glad to have a meal and a room waiting for us nearby at the end of the day. Our one-bedroom unit was pretty small, but then all we did in it was shower and sleep!"*

### DIAMOND LAKE RESORT
*HC 30 Box 1, Diamond Lake OR 97731*
*541/793-3333, 800/733-7593*
*Rates: Inexpensive to moderate*
*FYI: Two restaurants, pizza parlor; grocery store; kitchens (in cab-*

*ins); boating, biking, swimming; laundry*

Located five miles north of the northern park boundary, the resort is a relatively inexpensive way to spend a few days near Crater Lake. The spot gets crowded and somewhat claustrophobic at the height of the summer season.

Families can choose one of the two-bedroom cabins with kitchens, or a motel unit. Neither is fancy, but they are clean, and the cabins are reasonably roomy. The lake is warm and inviting during the summer months; kids will enjoy renting bumper boats, paddleboats, or canoes. Mountain bikes are also available.

**❝❝ PARENT COMMENTS**

*"If you don't mind the company of other families, this is a good place to vacation. We liked being removed from the Crater Lake area. It's beautiful there, but we didn't want it to be the only focus of our visit to the area."*

*"This is an inexpensive getaway, but buy the bulk of your groceries before you come into the area."*

**MAZAMA VILLAGE MOTOR INN**
*Mazama Village*
*P.O. Box 2704, 1211 Ave. C, White City 97503*
*Rates: Inexpensive*

The 40 units here are basic motel rooms—adequate, given that you'll be out touring the lake by day. The location makes it possible to be reasonably close to the lake without breaking the budget. We haven't had parent reviewers check it out, but this spot seems to have basic accommodations at a basic price.

**WHAT TO SEE & DO**

**RIM DRIVE.** This 33-mile scenic drive circles the lake on the rim of the caldera, passing Vidae Falls and countless overlooks along the way. If the kids are tired of the car, stop and picnic, or take a hike; little ones will love slipping a little something to the furry creatures that come out to beg.

The **Steel Information Center,** located at park headquarters on the south side of the park, is open year round. This is a good first stop, where you can gather information, get assistance planning your visit, and apply for a backcountry camping permit. An 18-minute video, *The Crater Lake Story,* will provide some background for your tour of the park.

**Sinnott Memorial Overlook,** located just below the Rim Village Visitor Center, is another great introduction to the park. An exhibit building houses maps, paintings, and displays that detail the geology and natural history of the area. It's open late-June through early September.

Kids tend to be fascinated by the **Phantom Ship Overlook,** located eight miles east of park headquarters on Rim Drive. A lava dike rising 160 feet above the lake creates the image of a phantom ship.

If you have time to take the spur road off Rim Drive, the

## Take a Look at Oregon's "Other Trail"

Nearly every child has heard stories of the Oregon Trail, but what about the lesser-known Applegate Trail? A group of dedicated southern Oregonians is offering visitors an opportunity to learn about this "other trail," an alternate wagon route between eastern Idaho and Oregon. Opened in 1998, the APPLEGATE TRAIL INTERPRETIVE CENTER is dedicated to telling that trail's dramatic story.

After losing two young sons on a treacherous stretch of the Oregon Trail, brothers Jesse and Lindsay Applegate set out in 1846 to blaze a safer, alternative route. At Fort Hall, Idaho, they recruited Oregon-bound pioneers to join them on the new trail. Unfortunately, the Applegate Trail proved to have perils of its own, and up to 20 pioneers died on that first trek. Among them was a 15-year-old girl credited with urging discouraged pioneers to keep striving, before she herself succumbed to diphtheria. At Grave Creek, close to her burial site, the Applegate Trail Interpretive Center offers a thoughtfully designed collection of artifacts and legends about the pioneers who passed this way. In addition, it devotes exhibits to the Gold Rush, the Indian Wars, and the coming of stagecoach and railroad to the area. What a great way to introduce youngsters to the history of the Pacific Northwest.

To get there, take Exit 71 from I-5, and drive two blocks east toward the covered bridge. Look for the Interpretive Center on the right. It's open Wednesday through Sunday, 10 a.m. to 5 p.m. The cost of admission is $5.95, $4.95 for youth 13-18. Children under 12 are free. For information, phone 888/411-1846, or visit the Web site at www.rogueweb.com/interpretive.

family will enjoy seeing the **Pinnacles Overlook.** Columns and spires—some as tall as 200 feet—were formed by the erosion of soft volcanic material.

When the family's ready for a climb, stop at **The Watchman,** a peak near the rim and just west of Wizard Island. A one-mile trail affords a panoramic view of the park, 1,800 feet above the lake. The kids may also enjoy seeing the fire lookout station at the top.

**CRATER LAKE BOAT TOURS.** No matter how you approach the rim drive and its many viewpoints, there's nothing quite like cruising this beautiful lake by boat. On these 1½-hour tours, park naturalists explain the geology and natural history of the area. Tours stop on Wizard Island, a cinder cone that rises 760 feet above the lake. Before you get the kids excited about this trip, however, check out the trail from the parking lot (off Rim Drive) to the boat launch—it's quite steep, and some family members may find it daunting.

*Cleetwood Cove Dock. 541/830-8700. Tours daily, 10 a.m.-4 p.m., mid-June-early Sept. Cost: $12/adult & youth; $7/under 12.*

### RESOURCES

**CRATER LAKE NATIONAL PARK**
P.O. Box 128, Crater Lake 97604
541/594-2511; 541/830-8700

## ASHLAND

Once a sleepy little cow town, Ashland has become a busy crossroad for culture and outdoor recreation. The Oregon Shakespeare Festival began in 1935 with a three-day summer festival of Shakespearean plays. Today, the season of 11 plays runs for nine months, and this little town of 17,000 plays host to 350,000 visitors each season. While it is often the theater that brings visitors here, many families stay to enjoy the beautiful Rogue River area that provides hiking, swimming, and rafting opportunities.

### GETTING THERE

Ashland is right off I-5, approximately five hours south of Portland and just 30 minutes north of the California border. From the east, it is easily reached via Highway 66 from Klamath Falls.

**ROADSIDE ATTRACTIONS.** Between Eugene and Ashland on I-5 you'll find a lot of hills and a smattering of small towns. For a sweet treat, try **K and R's Drive Inn** (541/849-2570), 20 miles north of Roseburg at the Rice Hill Exit. This spot serves fast food, which you can top off with mounds of delicious Umpqua ice cream. The **Wolf Creek Tavern** (100 Railroad Ave.; 503/866-2474), off Exit 76 at Wolf Creek, offers good, inexpensive fare. It's located in a historic inn—a stagecoach stop in the 1850s—purchased and restored by the state.

Off I-5 near Medford, the dusty little town of Central Point offers a detour worth taking. **Dogs for the Deaf, Inc.** (10175 Wheeler Road; 800/990-3647) is an organization that trains "hearing dogs," dogs who alert their deaf owners to certain sounds (e.g. doorbell, oven timer, smoke alarm). How the trainers choose these dogs, train them, and introduce them to new owners is a fascinating and heartwarming story. Families are invited to stop in, view a video, and observe a hearing dog at work. It's also possible to tour the facility and meet some of the dogs in training.

Tours are available Monday through Friday, 10 a.m. to 2 p.m. (May through September) and at 10 a.m. and 2 p.m. during the remainder of year. It's helpful to call in advance and let them know you're coming.

## PLACES TO STAY

### ARDEN FOREST INN
*261 W. Hersey, 97520*
*541/488-1496*
*Rates: Expensive*
*FYI: Complimentary breakfast*

The Arden Forest Inn is one of a few B&Bs that welcome children (in this case, ages 10 and older). Located in a quiet neighborhood within easy walking distance of the theaters, this light, airy inn is an updated turn-of-the-century farmhouse. For families, there are a couple of good options: the two-bedroom suite in the main house; or the adjoining rooms in the carriage house—one with a king bed and the other with twin beds. With separate entrances, the cottage rooms are more private, and parents won't have to worry about their kids thumping about and bothering guests staying below. All rooms have private baths.

**❝ PARENT COMMENTS**
*"This a wonderful place to stay. Hosts Art and Audrey*

*Sochor are very gracious about accommodating older children. There are no TVs, radios, VCRs—just lots of books and games and chances for stimulating discussion."*

## THE ASHLAND HOSTEL

*150 N. Main, 97520*
*541/482-9217*
*Rates: Inexpensive*

These dormitory-style rooms are open to all ages, and they are the best deal in town if you don't mind sharing a kitchen and common space with other guests. The hostel is located just a few blocks from the Shakespeare Festival theaters.

**66** **PARENT COMMENTS**

*"It is expensive to take a family to the Shakespeare Festival, so we go low-budget on accommodations by either camping or staying at the Ashland Hostel. It's clean and comfortable and the clientele is nice—fellow theater buffs."*

## CALLAHAN'S

*7100 Old Hwy. 99 S., 97520*
*541/482-1299, 800/286-0507; www.callahanslodge.com*
*Rates: Inexpensive to moderate*
*FYI: Restaurant; fireplaces (some units); Jacuzzis (some units)*

Long a popular restaurant, Callahan's has remodeled and opened lodge-style accommodations. There are 15 units, eight with fireplaces and Jacuzzis. Set in the woods six miles south of Ashland, this spot combines some of the finest points of a Southern Oregon vacation. On any given day, you can choose: grab a ticket and head for the theater or grab a raft and head for the river. (Some days, it can be a very tough choice.)

## HILLSIDE INN

*1520 Siskiyou Blvd., 97520*
*541/482-2626, 800/326-9903*
*Rates: Inexpensive*
*FYI: Kitchens; outdoor pool*

This is a low-budget option, and in some ways it looks like one. The 31 rooms are simple, but they're nice and clean, equipped with all you need to enjoy time in Ashland without breaking the bank. There's a small barbecue and picnic area, and a swing set for the small fry (parents need to supervise, as the busy road is not far from here). The outdoor pool is small and not far from the road, but it's good for a splash when the heat gets you down.

**❝ PARENT COMMENTS**

*"This spot more than meets our family's needs. The rooms aren't fancy, but by using the kitchens and outdoor barbecue, we're able to save money for the plays and other activities."*

*"We go in summer, so we appreciate the air-conditioned rooms and small pool. The rooms are back from the main road, but small children need to be watched."*

## OAK STREET COTTAGES

*171 Oak St., 97520*
*541/488-3778*
*Rates: Expensive*
*FYI: Kitchens; fireplaces; Jacuzzis*

This spot offers two- and three-bedroom cottages just one block from the theaters. The cottage that accommodates 10 is specially set up for kids, with bunks, highchair, and cribs. The location—across the street from lovely Lithia Park and within walking distance to theaters—is a plus. We didn't get a chance to send a family to review this spot, but if you can share the cost with another family, it sounds like a good option.

## QUALITY INN FLAGSHIP

*2520 Ashland St., 97520*
*800/334-2330; www.flaginn.com*
*Rates: Moderate*
*FYI: Continental breakfast; refrigerators/microwaves, stovetops (suites); fireplaces; outdoor pool; shuttle to theaters; pets OK (fee)*

Rooms are comfortably furnished and well kept. The outdoor pool is a nice bonus—it's hot in Ashland in the summer. The inn is located three miles from the theaters and has a shuttle service to get you there.

**❝ PARENT COMMENTS**

*"We were relieved to find a comfortable, affordable motel in Ashland that would take pets and had an outdoor pool. We didn't mind not being right near the theaters, because that wasn't our only focus—we spent several days exploring the wonderful Rogue River area."*

## WINDMILL'S ASHLAND HILLS INN

*2525 Ashland St., 97520*
*541/482-8310, 800/547-4747*
*Rates: Moderate to expensive*
*FYI: Complimentary continental breakfast; refrigerators/*

*microwaves (suites); outdoor pool, exercise room, tennis, bikes;*
*shuttle service; pets OK*

The 158 rooms are spacious and comfortably furnished;
the one-bedroom suites are downright luxurious (there's a
TV in the bedroom and another in the living area). All
the suites have decks overlooking the foothills. The
attractive grounds surround a pleasant central courtyard
and large outdoor pool.

**❝ PARENT COMMENTS**

*"This is a very comfortable, pleasant place to stay with*
*kids—probably the nicest motel in Ashland."*

*"This spot has just about every amenity you can hope for,*
*including continental breakfast brought to your room."*

*"They have bikes to borrow, but there really aren't very good*
*places for kids to ride. The main drag into town has too much*
*traffic, and many of the smaller side streets are dead ends."*

**HOUSE RENTALS.** If you are traveling to Ashland with
another family or two, consider renting a home in the area.
For information about house rentals available by the night or
the week, as well as helpful advice about B&Bs and motels in
the area, call the Ashland Clearinghouse at 541/488-0338.

## PLACES TO EAT

**AZTECA**
*2345 Ashland St., Ste. 205*
*541/488-5249*
*Hours: Lunch, dinner daily*

This franchise restaurant does an especially good job of
welcoming kids. The kids' menu offers the standard
Mexican options and also has some simple Spanish-lan-
guage word games and puzzles. Parents won't be disappointed by the food—it's not all that authentic, but it's fresh and
tasty. Try the fajitas for two; the sizzling ingredients come on
a large tray, and you can assemble them according to your
individual preferences.

**CALLAHAN'S**
*7100 Old Hwy. 99 S.*
*541/482-1299*
*Hours: Breakfast, lunch, dinner daily*

This rustic dining room/lounge is set among the beautiful

Siskiyou Mountains six miles south of Ashland (Exit 6 off I-5). It's a "nice" family restaurant—kids are more than welcome, but you'll hope they're on reasonably good behavior. The specialty is Italian cuisine, but there are a number of other choices as well (try one of their seafood specials).

Although there is no children's menu, most of the dinners are available at half price for kids under 12. Or consider sharing a meal; each entrée here is generous and comes with a side dish of spaghetti. If Italian doesn't appeal, kids can choose hamburgers, sandwiches, poultry, or seafood. Courses are generally well timed, but there are color books and crayons just in case.

### GREENLEAF RESTAURANT
*49 N. Main*
*541/482-2808*
*Hours: Breakfast, lunch, dinner daily*

Located across the street from the entrance to Lithia Park, this is the perfect place to grab a quick meal or picnic goodies before the show. Anything you see on the menu is available "to go." The well-prepared fare leans toward the Mediterranean, including such specials as spanakopita and pollo picatta. The kids can go with fish or chicken and chips, or any of a number of burgers and deli sandwiches. In case you're afraid of nodding off mid-play, the Greenleaf makes a nice, strong espresso.

### OMAR'S FRESH FISH AND STEAKS
*1380 Siskiyou Blvd.*
*503/482-1281*
*Hours: Lunch, dinner daily*

At first glance, this may seem a strange recommendation in a town where intimate Continental restaurants abound. But Omar's offers a lot that families can't get at those intimate little spots—such as food their kids will eat. There is no children's menu, but kids may order smaller portions of any of the meals. Known for steak and seafood, Omar's has a menu that's extensive enough to provide for the preferences of younger palates.

### WHAT TO SEE & DO

**LITHIA PARK.** Ashland's lovely central park comprises 100 acres along Ashland Creek, offering picnic areas, playgrounds, nature trails, tennis and volleyball courts, beautiful landscapes, and a Japanese Garden. Just behind the beautiful Elizabethan Theater is a small pond known for its beauty and its swans. (The water here is rich in lithium, hence the park name. You can taste a sample of the waters at the fountain across the street, next to the Visitor Information booth. But be warned: the sulphurous, rotten-egg smell is a turn-off for most kids.)

The park plays host to the annual *Feast of the Tribe of Will*, a celebration heralding the beginning of the summer theater season in June. On Monday evenings in summer, the State Ballet of Oregon offers free performances at the park amphitheater.

**MAIN STREET.** The main drag of Ashland is designed to be strolled. Beginning near the theaters and heading south, you will find every manner of boutique and art gallery. Kids enjoy **Paddington Station** (125 E. Main; 541/482-1343), for its stuffed animals, books, and kids' collectibles. Family members past the toddler stage will enjoy having a look at **American Trails** (27 N. Main; 541/488-2731), a lovely collection of Native American, Western, and wildlife jewelry, sculpture, and folk art.

**OREGON SHAKESPEARE FESTIVAL.** Among the oldest and largest regional theater companies in the United States, the Oregon Shakespeare Festival presents an ambitious program mid-February through October. This is an excellent place to bring a school-age child. The season includes 11 plays, four by Shakespeare and seven by classic or contemporary playwrights, presented on an authentic outdoor Elizabethan stage and in two superb indoor theaters. To determine which plays are appropriate for older children, read descriptions carefully. The box office can provide guidance regarding appropriateness of certain productions for children.

A word of warning to those who remember the good old days of last-minute "rush" tickets: These days, audience attendance routinely exceeds 90 percent, making "rush" tickets very hard to come by.

Parents of very young children face a challenge when including the Festival in vacation plans, as children under five are not admitted to the theaters or related events. However, theater and hotel staff can usually assist in locating reliable baby-sitting services.

Families will enjoy taking the **Backstage Tour**, a behind-the-scenes look at the Festival. It includes admission to the exhibit center, which can also be visited independently from the tour. This small museum features set pieces and designs, properties, and costumes from past productions (some are available for dress-up). The video presentations about the Festival's history and techniques are quite good.

*At 15 S. Pioneer St.; P.O. Box 158, 97520. 541/482-4331; www.orshakes.org. Open Tues.-Sun., mid-Feb.-Oct. Cost: $17.50-$49/adult, 25% discount/youth 5-17. Backstage Tours: daily except Mon., 10-11:45 a.m., reservations required. Cost: $9-10/adult, $6.75-7.50/youth 5-17. Separate admission to the Exhibit Center: $3/adult, $1.50/youth 5-17.*

### EXCURSIONS

**JACKSONVILLE.** A town born in the Gold Rush of 1851, Jacksonville provides an opportunity for families to step backward in time. Pioneer-era buildings have been beautifully preserved—more than 80 have historical markers. Take a self-guided tour of the historic downtown area; walking maps are available at the **Rogue River Valley Railway Depot** (Oregon & C St.; 541/899-8118).

There are two spots of particular interest to families. The **Children's Museum** (5th & D St.; 541/773-6536), housed in the historic county jail, portrays the life of Native Americans and pioneers from 1850 to 1930. Many of the artifacts here can be handled. Next door is the historic **Jacksonville Museum of Southern Oregon History** (5th & C St.; 541/773-6536), built in 1884 to serve as a courthouse.

*Located 14 miles northwest of Ashland on Hwy. 99. 541/899-8118; www.jacksonvilleoregon.com.*

### THE GREAT OUTDOORS

**MOUNT ASHLAND.** Eighteen miles south in the Siskiyou Mountains, Mount Ashland offers unusual hiking opportunities along the Pacific Crest Trail, in summer, and cross-country and alpine skiing in winter. The **Mount Ashland Ski Area,** with a 1,150-foot vertical drop and four chair lifts, offers 23 separate runs for all levels of skier and snowboarder. A lodge with café and bar is located at the summit.

*Located 18 miles south of Ashland; 541/482-2897.*

**WHITE-WATER RAFTING.** The Rogue and the Klamath rivers provide thrills for rafters. Companies offering river trips out of Ashland include **Noah's World of Water** (53 N. Main; 541/488-2811; 800/858-2811; www.noahsrafting.com) and

**Adventure Center and Eagle Sun** (40 N. Main; 541/488-2819; 800/444-2819). Both offer trips of various lengths (a half-day to several days), March through October.

## CALENDAR

**MID-FEBRUARY-OCTOBER**
Oregon Shakespeare Festival, Ashland.
**JUNE**
Feast of the Tribe of Will: Parade and opening ceremonies for summer theater season, Ashland.
**JUNE-SEPTEMBER**
Britt Music Festival: Showcases classical, jazz, and contemporary music, Jacksonville.

## RESOURCES

**ASHLAND CHAMBER OF COMMERCE**
110 E. Main, P.O. Box 1360, Ashland 97520
541/482-3486; www.ohwy.com

## OREGON CAVES NATIONAL MONUMENT

Oregon Caves National Monument may be small on land (at 488 acres, it's the smallest natural area administered by the National Park Service), but it's big on interest. Above ground, the monument includes old-growth forest, a wide array of native plants, and one of the best-known Douglas-fir trees in Oregon. Underground, there's another whole world to explore—a spectacular marble cave, created by groundwater dissolving bedrock, with narrow passageways and magnificent rooms of stalagmites, stalactites, and other formations. Not to mention a surprising diversity of microscopic creatures that have acclimated to the cold darkness.

This is a fun and educational place to visit with kids, but very young children will not be allowed on the cave tour. (Children must be at least 42 inches tall and able to negotiate stairs without assistance.)

### GETTING THERE

The monument is remote. From I-5 at Grants Pass, drive south on I-199 to Cave Junction. Turn east onto Highway 46 and continue on 19 miles to reach the National Monument. The last eight miles of 46 are narrow, steep, and winding.

## PLACES TO STAY

There's not a lot of choice for those who want to spend a full day at the Monument. Kids will be tired after the cave tour, and you'll be glad if you've booked a spot nearby.

### OREGON CAVES CHATEAU

*20000 Caves Hwy., Cave Junction 97523*
*541/592-3400*
*Rates: Moderate*
*FYI: Dining room*

Built of wood in the Swiss alpine style, the Oregon Caves Chateau is listed in the National Registry of Historic Places. Built in 1934, it's a nice example of buildings designed to blend with their natural surroundings. The six-story lodging has 22 rooms, a dining room, a 1930s-style soda fountain, and a coffee shop.

The Chateau operates from mid-June to early September.

**66 PARENT COMMENTS**

*"We were dirty and exhausted after a big day in the caves and on the trails. We were so thankful we had made plans to stay here."*

*"The lodge is beautiful, and the kids had fun at the old-fashioned soda fountain. Mom actually had some 'alone time.'"*

## WHAT TO SEE & DO

**BIG TREE TRAIL.** Among the many hikes for families, *Big Tree Trail* is one of the nicest. The highlight of the trail, not surprisingly, is Big Tree. This specimen is the largest Douglas fir tree in the state of Oregon. Estimated to be between 1,200 and 1,500 years old, it has a circumference of 41 feet, 3 inches; a diameter of 13 feet, 1 inch; and a height of 160 feet. (Hiking at this elevation can be more tiring than you expect. Check with park rangers before setting out.)

**OREGON CAVES TOUR.** A tour through the Oregon Caves is an adventure in geology and underground life, presenting lots of new information—but kids love it anyway! The darkness, the constant drip, drip, drip of water—it all adds up to a real adventure for youngsters (and, to a large extent, for parents). As you walk through the caves, tour guides tell entertaining stories of their discovery and exploration, and point out interesting formations and cave life.

All six of the world's major rock types decorate the cave. Eerie sculptures of calcite, flowstone like little parachutes, cave "popcorn," moon milk (calcite crystals that look and feel like cottage cheese), a passage that resembles the ribs of a whale (from the inside): there's much here to explore.

The tour route is about a half-mile long, with many low, narrow passages and more than 500 steps. The cave is cool (low 40s) and damp, and paths can be slippery in places. Best to wear rubber-soled, laced shoes and warm clothes. The temptation to touch the rocks can be overwhelming; please supervise kids so they don't add to the untimely erosion of this phenomenal natural site.

*Open daily, 9 a.m.-7 p.m. (summer); daily, 9 a.m.-5 p.m. (fall and spring); closed winter. Cost: $6.25/adult & youth, $4/child 6-11.*

# MOUNT HOOD / COLUMBIA RIVER GORGE

At 11,239 feet, majestic Mount Hood is the tallest point in Oregon. It towers above the Portland skyline and can be seen clearly from many points along the Columbia River to the east, providing both aesthetic enjoyment and year-round recreational opportunity. Standing in the middle of a large national forest, Mount Hood offers cross-country and downhill skiing in winter. In summer, hikers enjoy the many trails that honeycomb the area.

Alongside the mountain flows the mighty Columbia River, carving a spectacular canyon through the volcanic rock of the Cascade mountain range. As the only sea-level river flowing through the Cascades, the Columbia is both a natural wonder and an important transportation corridor. Recognizing the importance of the region, the federal government established the 292,000-acre Columbia River Gorge National Scenic Area in 1986.

## MOUNT HOOD

### GETTING THERE

From Portland, drive east on Interstate 84. Take the Wood Village Exit; turn right onto 238th to Burnside Street. Follow Burnside to Highway 26; turn left. The highway proceeds up the mountain, through the small towns of Welches, Zig Zag, and Government Camp.

From Central Oregon, drive northwest on Highway 26 to the mountain.

From points east, make your way to either Highway 14 in Washington, or I-84 in Oregon, both of which follow the Columbia toward Portland. At White Salmon, Washington, or Hood River, Oregon, catch Highway 35 south to Mount Hood.

**REFUELING.** Refueling on Highway 35 can be great fun. Consider a stop at **Santacroce** (4780 Hwy. 35; 541/354-2511), five miles south of Hood River. This is a comfortable, come-as-you-are kind of place—neither the décor nor the prices are fancy. You'll find the standard Italian entrées, including pizza, calzone, and a variety of Parmesan dishes. The food is a notch above the usual, and families are very welcome, even in their ski togs.

## PLACES TO STAY

### INN AT COOPER SPUR
*10755 Cooper Spur Road, Parkdale 97041*
*541/352-6692*
*Rates: Moderate to expensive*
*FYI: Restaurant; kitchens (some units)*

Located 80 miles from Portland at the 4,000-foot level of Mount Hood, the Inn is just minutes from area ski resorts, including Cooper Spur, Mount Hood Meadows, and Timberline. This spot is lovely in summer, too, and the area is popular for hiking, rafting, and mountain biking.

The Inn at Cooper Spur offers cozy log cabins with two bedrooms and a loft (accessed by spiral staircase). All these units have full kitchens and will sleep up to seven people. If you don't need this much space, ask about the small "sleeper units," each with a queen bed and bath.

**❝ PARENT COMMENTS**
*"If you have a young child, the smaller units may be your best bet; the cabin staircases were not designed with adventurous toddlers in mind!"*

### THE RESORT AT THE MOUNTAIN
*68010 E. Fairway Ave., Welches 97067*
*503/622-3101, 800/669-7666; www.theresort.com*
*Rates: Moderate to expensive*
*FYI: Two restaurants; kitchens (some units); fireplaces; outdoor pool; four tennis courts, bicycle rentals, golf; baby-sitting, orga-*

*nized activities for children (summers)*

This 400-acre resort, located on the western slope of Mount Hood, has 160 rooms and suites (one and two bedrooms). The suites, each with a private patio, are good choices for families.

The grounds here are spacious and wooded, and the feeling is one of quiet relaxation. Older sections of the facility are nicely maintained; new sections feature modern Northwest architecture. Activities revolve around golf, swimming, and tennis, but there are also bike and jogging paths. For young children, there's a wading pool alongside the large swimming pool. Older kids will enjoy the game room.

**❝ PARENT COMMENTS**

*"The suites have kitchens, but when you don't feel like cooking, you have two options right at the resort. The dining room-style restaurant is good, but the coffee shop is more relaxed and has an outdoor eating area. Both spots have highchairs."*

*"It's a country-club atmosphere in a beautiful part of Oregon."*

*"The indoor pool was fabulous for our young children, ages two and five."*

**TIMBERLINE LODGE**
*Hwy. 26, Timberline 97028*
*503/272-3311, 800/547-1406; www.timberline.com*
*Rates: Moderate to expensive*
*FYI: Restaurant; outdoor pool; skiing, hiking; baby-sitting; smoke-free throughout*

Timberline Lodge is one of the great western mountain lodges, with characteristic stone fireplaces, heavy timbers, and large leaded-glass windows. The lodge, built by the WPA in 1937, is located 6,000 feet up the slope of Mount Hood. It's a real showplace for local arts and crafts, including handmade furniture, fabrics, hand-hooked rugs, mosaics, and paintings.

The lodge rooms are quite attractive. In winter, you might want to spend the extra to get a room with a fireplace.

Skiing is offered year round at Timberline; lifts are right outside the door. You can rent all your gear here. There are lessons for all age levels; the Skiwee program (ages three to 12) is fully supervised and available seven days a week. There are also excellent cross-country trails in this area. The outdoor pool is kept at 86 degrees and is open all year, so you can swim while it snows!

### WHAT TO SEE & DO

#### OUTDOOR ACTIVE FUN

**SKIING.** With more than 60 trails and a vertical drop of 2,777 feet, **Mount Hood Meadows** (503/337-2222) is the largest ski resort on the mountain. Mount Hood Meadows Day Care opened in late 1999 with an outstanding facility and state-of-the art program for ages six weeks to four years old. Call for reservations, they often fill to capacity 503-337-2222 ext. 74. **Timberline Ski Area** (503/231-7979) is less extensive (and less expensive), and it's a good area for beginning and intermediate skiers. At **Mount Hood Skibowl** (503/272-3206), there's a 1,500-foot vertical drop; Skibowl has good expert runs, but it's not great for younger, less experienced skiers.

Cross-country ski trails on Mount Hood offer a full range of difficulty. For information, call the Mount Hood Visitor Information Center (503/622-4822) or Timberline Lodge (503/272-3311; 800/547-1406). Parking at the trailheads requires a Sno-Park permit; they're available at most sporting-goods stores throughout the state.

**HIKING.** During the summer, U.S. Forest Service Guides lead hikes and alpine wildflower walks from Timberline Lodge. A free booklet, *Day Hikes Around Mount Hood*, provides details on hikes in the area. You can pick one up at the Mount Hood Visitor Information Center (65000 E. Hwy. 26, Welches; 503/622-4822).

### CALENDAR

#### AUGUST

Mount Hood Jazz Festival: Nationally acclaimed festival attracts big-name jazz artists and thousands of jazz enthusiasts, Mount Hood Community College, Gresham.

### RESOURCES

#### MOUNT HOOD VISITOR INFORMATION CENTER
65000 E. Hwy. 26, Welches 97067
503/622-4822; 888/622-4822
Open daily, 8 a.m.-6 p.m. (summer); 8 a.m.-4:30 p.m. (winter)

## COLUMBIA RIVER GORGE

### GETTING THERE

From Portland, travel east on I-84: 20 miles to Troutdale, 62 miles to Hood River, 83 miles to The Dalles. For a more scenic route, you can exit I-84 at Troutdale (Exit 17) and travel east on Highway 30 until it rejoins I-84 at Ainsworth Park. Both highways parallel the river, but at different elevations. Highway 30 (also called the Columbia River Scenic Highway) is the upper road and, therefore, offers better viewpoints than does the modern I-84, built at sea level. (See sidebar).

**ROADSIDE ATTRACTIONS.** Along I-84, at Cascade Locks (named for a series of locks built on the Columbia River in 1986), you'll find roadside attractions and good refueling options. Visit the **Bridge of the Gods,** built across the Columbia River in 1926, then raised in 1938 to accommodate the back flow from the Bonneville Dam.

This town marks the starting point of the **Pacific Crest National Scenic Trail,** which extends 2,638 miles through Canada, the United States, and Mexico. The trail passes through 24 National Forests, one National Recreation Area, 33 Wildernesses, and six State/Provincial Parks.

For a made-to-order hamburger with all the fixings, stop at the **Char Burger** (745 NW Wanapa St.; 541/374-8477). The gift shop sells yummy home-baked cookies for snack time. Another option, just down the street, is the **East Wind Drive-In** (395 NW Wanapa St.; 541/374-8380), where you can get a skyscraper of soft ice cream without breaking the bank.

### REGIONAL RESOURCES

**COLUMBIA RIVER GORGE NATIONAL SCENIC AREA**
902 Wasco Ave., Ste. 200, Hood River 97031
541/386-2333

**COLUMBIA RIVER GORGE VISITORS ASSOCIATION**
404 W. 2nd St., The Dalles 97058
800/98-GORGE

**NORTH CENTRAL OREGON TOURISM PROMOTION COMMITTEE**
404 W 2nd St., The Dalles  97058
541/296-2231; 800/255-3385

## A Road for All Seasons:
## The Columbia River Scenic Highway

If you've got time and the backseat is relatively peaceful, get off I-84 at Troutdale (Exit 17) and take Highway 30, the Columbia River Scenic Highway. This 22-mile detour between Troutdale and Ainsworth Park affords breathtaking views of the Gorge and Cascade peaks. A masterpiece of engineering when it was built in 1915, the road winds along a high bluff, past a dozen waterfalls and six state parks. There are a number of spectacular vistas and winding wooded trails along the way.

If refueling is in order, get off I-84 at Exit 18, and stop at **TAD'S CHICKEN 'N DUMPLINGS** (943 Crown Point; 503/666-5337), a local favorite for down-home cooking at budget prices. After you eat, it's easy to get onto Highway 30 for the scenic detour.

One of the best viewpoints is at **CROWN POINT STATE PARK** (503/695-2230), five miles east of Corbett and 730 feet above sea level. From the park's Vista House—a two-story stone tower with marble floors—a breathtaking, 30-mile panorama of the gorge, including several serpentine bends of the mighty Columbia, lies below. The gift shop offers local crafts, books, and miscellaneous goodies. The park is open daily, dawn to dusk. Vista House is open daily, 9 a.m. to 6 p.m., mid-April to mid-October.

Six miles east of the park, stop at magnificent **MULTNOMAH FALLS**, the second highest waterfall in the country at 620 feet. Here little ones can paddle in the stream, and older children may want to hike to the top of the falls. However, take the steep, 1.25-mile trail at your own risk; there are several pronounced drop-offs, and no railings. (Note: This trail is occasionally closed due to adverse weather or soil conditions.) The historic lodge, built in 1925, features a cozy restaurant, restrooms, and a snack bar.

The Columbia River Scenic Highway disappears at Hood River, then reappears for a short but lovely stretch between Mosier and The Dalles. This winding road takes you through cherry and apple orchards to the **Tom McCall Preserve,** on a high plateau overlooking the river, then back onto I-84.

## HOOD RIVER

Apple and pear orchards line the roads around this lovely little town on the Columbia River. Mount Hood towers just 30 miles south. In recent years, the area has become a haven for sailboarders; a strong wind in the opposite direction of the river current creates ideal boarding conditions. Families will find plenty to enjoy on a weekend getaway here, including skiing, hiking, and several fun local attractions.

Don't limit your visits to winter or summer. Spring is beautiful for the raging waterfalls and fruit blossoms. In fall, enjoy crisp, cool weather and spectacular autumn leaves.

### PLACES TO STAY

#### BEST WESTERN HOOD RIVER INN
*1108 E. Marina Road*
*541/386-2200*
*Rates: Moderate*
*FYI: Refrigerators/microwaves; fireplaces (some units); outdoor pool; small pets OK (fee)*

This motel sits well back from the highway, with lovely views of the Columbia River. The 64 rooms are clean, comfortable, and roomy, and there's a small reading area on each floor. To add to the coziness, each two-bedroom unit has a Jacuzzi and a fireplace. All suites overlook the river and have either a deck or a patio.

The grounds include a large, grassy area, a playground, and a heated pool. The restaurant attached to the motel has an area for formal dining and a café for lighter, more casual dining. The service is quick, and children are treated attentively. Weather permitting, families might enjoy eating outdoors, overlooking the river. The motel gift shop has limited picnic supplies, wine, and local food specialties.

**❝ PARENT COMMENTS**

*"There is no fence between the grassy area and the river, so younger children will need supervision."*

*"We visited Hood River for a long weekend in the spring with our boys, four and six. We took the Fruit Blossom Train Trip and hiked to Multnomah Falls. It was great fun."*

*"This is windsurfing country. There's a marina down the road where you can rent equipment."*

## PLACES TO EAT

### ANDREW'S PIZZA AND BAKERY
*107 Oak St.*
*541/386-1448*
*Hours: Breakfast, lunch, dinner daily*

Andrew's is well known for its great New York-style pizza, basic or gourmet, available by the slice. It's a comfortable, upscale spot, with barstool seating downstairs and a loft with tables above. The small bakery here is divine, offering fresh-baked coffee cakes, croissants, and breads (not to mention giant cinnamon rolls to die for).

For parents, there's a pub in back that offers regional micro-brews and wine. The attached cinemas allow food and drink. Kids are allowed to attend the first showing alone; after that, they must be accompanied by an adult (due to the presence of alcoholic beverages on the premises).

### HOLSTEIN'S COFFEE COMPANY
*12 Oak St.*
*541/386-4115*
*Hours: Breakfast, lunch daily*

This spot has gone through several reincarnations and seems now to have found itself. This is the place for your morning caffeine hit, to be sure, but come back for lunch, too. They serve a variety of fine sandwiches, accompanied by soup or salad, at very reasonable prices.

Decorated with big, overstuffed chairs, Holstein's is full of friendly, Generation-X energy.

## WHAT TO SEE & DO

### STROLL & BROWSE

**OAK STREET/DOWNTOWN.** Hood River is a sailboarder's mecca, as a walk down Oak Street will quickly reveal. Shops here hawk every device necessary for outfitting a sailboarder. But you'll also find some fun restaurants, the requisite souvenir spots, and some nice, upscale shops. **Artifacts** (202 Cascade; 541/387-2482) offers kid kitsch—offbeat toys, books, and art. In the same build-ing is **Ikote** (541/387-3786), an import shop older kids will enjoy, offering beads, jewelry, musical instruments, and more.

The whole family is likely to enjoy the new **International Museum of Carousel Art** (3rd & Oak St.; 541/352-6820). The owners, world-renowned refurbishers of antique carousel animals, have remodeled an old bank building in which to display their handicraft.

When the little ones have had enough of window shopping, walk the four blocks to **Children's Park,** or take the central city overpass to **Port Marina State Park** (see "Parks").

## PARKS

**CHILDREN'S PARK,** about four blocks from downtown, was constructed by the local community to provide active fun for the smaller fry (under eight or so). It offers room to run, plus all kinds of swings and climbing structures.

*8th & Eugene St.*

**JACKSON PARK.** This family-friendly spot has play equipment, tennis courts, and a softball field. On Thursday evenings in August, the *Families in the Park* series offers free performances here.

Nearby is the **Hood River Aquatic Center** (1601 May St.; 541/386-1303), a public swimming pool with a removable roof for sunny weather.

*13th & May. 541/386-1303.*

**PORT MARINA PARK.** When the wind is up, you'll have a front-row seat for the windsurfing activity for which the area is known. Here you'll see the full range—from beginners learning the sport in the protected marina, to experts (called "loopers") flying and catching air on their colorful boards. Nearby is a roped-off swimming area.

Here also is the **Hood River County Historical Museum** (541/386-6772), offering exhibits on area history and a nice collection of pioneer artifacts. This free museum is open April through October, Wednesday through Saturday, 10 a.m. to 4 p.m., and Sunday, noon to 4 p.m.

## EXCURSIONS

**THE BONNEVILLE DAM** spans the Columbia River, 18 miles west of Hood River. It's the longest—and fourth largest—dam in the United States. The **Bradford Island Visitor Center,** off I-84, offers an observation deck, displays about salmon migration, and information about the dam's operation. There's an underwater viewing room here, from which families can watch the migrating fish (September through November is the best time for viewing salmon). Take a self-guided tour of the hatchery, and walk along the waterway to see the boats and barges.

*Forty-four miles east of Hood River on I-84 (Exit 40). 541/374-8820. Open daily, 9 a.m.-5 p.m. Free.*

**MOUNT HOOD RAILROAD,** departing from the Hood River Depot with a stop in Parkdale, provides a two- or a four-hour scenic trip through the orchards of the Hood River Valley. Also offered are a Saturday evening dinner train and a Sunday morning brunch train. Built in 1906, the railroad takes you alongside Hood River and up the mountain. (The locomotive actually pushes the train for the first three miles to more easily negotiate the steady incline.) You'll have views of Mount Hood and Mount Adams (on the Washington side of the river).

All excursions depart and return to the Mount Hood Railroad Depot in Hood River, located on the south side of Interstate 84. *110 Railroad Ave. (south side of I-84). 541/386-3556. Cost: Tour, $22.95/adult, $14.95/child 2-12, free/under 2; Dinner Train, $67.50 /person; Brunch Train, $55/person.*

**M.V. COLUMBIA GORGE** is a 599-passenger sternwheeler that plies the Columbia three times daily, June through September. You can begin the two-hour excursion at Cascade Locks Marine Park (in Cascade Locks), Bonneville Dam, or on the Washington side of the river, at Stevenson. During the cruise, visitors will learn about local history, points of interest, and Native American lore. A snack bar and lounge are available. *503/223-3928. $11.95/adult, reduced fare/child 4-11, free/ under 4.*

**SCENIC FRUIT LOOPS.** The Hood River Valley is home to acres and acres of orchards—mostly Anjou and Bartlett pears and Pippin apples. Pick up a copy of the *Fruit Loop Guide to Local Farm Stands* (available at shops and restaurants in town). **River Bend Organic Farm & Country Store** (2363 Tucker Rd.; 541/386-8766) sells homemade jams from its cozy country store. Kids can feed goats and burros and get within spitting distance of llamas.

### THE GREAT OUTDOORS

**WINDSURFING.** Sailboarders who come to Hood River are convinced they've achieved Nirvana. Due to some interesting wind and river patterns, the windsurfing here is unparalleled in the Pacific Northwest. Unless you have some experience, though, it's not advisable to rent equipment and head out. A wiser choice is to consult one of the windsurfing schools; the best known is **Rhonda Smith Windsurfing Center** (Port Marina Park; 541/386-9463).

If you have windsurfing experience and need to rent equipment, try **Gorge Surf House Inc.** (13 Oak St.; 541/386-1699).

Boards of many different sizes are available, including small inflatable boards designed for young children.

### CALENDAR

**APRIL**

Hood River Blossom Festival: Garden shows, local foods, and orchard tours.

**JULY**

Gorge Games: Lots of outside activity (extreme sports competitions, mountain biking, kayaking, windsurfing) and music.

**OCTOBER**

Harvest Fest: Small-town fun includes arts and crafts, local produce and food products, and kiddie rides, at Port Marina Park.

### RESOURCES

**HOOD RIVER COUNTY CHAMBER OF COMMERCE**

405 Portway Ave. (at Port Marina Park), Hood River 97031
541/386-2000; 800/366-3530

## THE DALLES

The Dalles lies on a large bend of the Columbia River, where the river narrows and, in days past, spilled over a series of rapids (now submerged by back flow from The Dalles Dam). The French named the area *les dalles*, meaning "the trough." This "trough" once marked a fork in the Oregon Trail for emigrants heading west. Those who chose the overland route around Mount Hood turned south here; others continued to follow the river. This was an obvious place for travelers to stop and regroup, and it became a popular place to trade with Native American tribes. Lewis and Clark called this spot "the great Indian mart."

The area has gone through rough times in the past couple of decades, but has managed to preserve and accentuate its pioneer history. There are a number of interesting, well-maintained 19th-century homes and churches around town.

### PLACES TO STAY

**QUALITY INN**

*2114 W. 6th, P.O. Box 723, 97058*
*541/298-5161*
Rates: Inexpensive
FYI: Restaurant; refrigerators; outdoor pool; laundry; pets OK (fee)

This two-story motel has 85 rooms, many of which are adequate for families. Particularly nice for families are the four suites, each with fireplace and kitchen. The restaurant serves breakfast, lunch, and dinner; the kids may get a kick out of its farm theme.

**❝ PARENT COMMENTS**

*"The outdoor pool is nothing special, until the temperature begins to soar. Our kids were mighty glad to have it!"*

## PLACES TO EAT

**COUSINS' RESTAURANT**
*2116 W. 6th St.*
*541/298-2771*
*Hours: Breakfast, lunch, dinner daily*
This is a friendly spot, with home-style cooking you might even write home about. The restaurant is best known for its tender, flavorful pot roast. Also noteworthy are the cinnamon rolls. The kids won't fuss when they see where you're headed; Cousins' is decorated with tractors, plastic cows, and other agricultural paraphernalia the little ones will enjoy.

## WHAT TO SEE & DO

**CRATE'S POINT INTERPRETIVE COMPLEX.** This is the official interpretive center for the Columbia River Gorge National Scenic Area, created by a five-way public/private partnership. The facility is home to the **Columbia Gorge Discovery Center,** with exhibits showing the natural and human history of the area. Exhibits are well designed for kids—many are large models and hands-on displays. Check out the working model of the Columbia River! Interpreters in period dress add a realistic feel to the setting.

Also here is the **Wasco County Historical Museum,** which displays the artifacts and heritage of a county which once stretched eastward to the Continental Divide. Get a map and visit some of the Native American petroglyphs in the area.

*5000 Discovey Dr.(approximately three miles west of The Dalles). 541/296-8660; 800/255-3385. Open daily, 10 a.m.-6 p.m. Cost (both museums): $6.50/adult, $5.50/senior, $3/youth 6-16.*

## RESOURCES

**THE DALLES CHAMBER OF COMMERCE**
404 W. 2nd St., The Dalles 97058
541/296-2231; 800/255-3385

901 E. 2nd St., The Dalles 97058
541/296-6616

## CENTRAL OREGON

The Central Oregon desert is a recreational haven for families. The summers are hot and dry and smell of sage and Ponderosa pine—ideal for camping and hiking, or kicking back at a resort. Winters are cold, with crystal-clear skies and enough snow to satisfy any ski bum.

Central Oregon encompasses the forested eastern slopes of the Cascades to the west, and the foothills of the Blue Mountains to the east. The rest of the area is one great plateau, referred to locally as the "high desert," marked by juniper and sagebrush and interrupted at intervals by volcanic buttes and lava fields. The primary north-south artery, Highway 97, traverses the region, following the Little Deschutes River through Deschutes National Forest. Traveling the less beaten track can be highly rewarding here, but check local road conditions before venturing far afield.

### GETTING THERE

**BY CAR.** From Portland, via Mount Hood, take Highway 26 over the mountain to Madras, where it connects with Highway 97, the major north-south highway. On Highway 26, 24 miles southeast of Portland, are a couple of intriguing stops. **Oral Hull Park** (43233 SE Oral Hull Road; 503/668-6195), 2.4 miles east of Sandy, provides more than just a chance to get out and run around. Designed especially for the vision-impaired, this park offers the Gardens of Enchantment, which have five sections dedicated to the five senses. Open May through September, Oral Hull Park provides food for thought and family discussion about physical challenges.

Five miles east of Sandy is the **Oregon Candy Farm** (48620 SE Hwy. 26; 503/668-5066), where master candy makers create hand-dipped chocolates, truffles, caramels, and other sweets. Kids can watch the whole process and, parents willing, try a sample. It's open Monday through Friday, 9 a.m. to 5 p.m., and Saturday and Sunday, noon to 5 p.m.

Sixty miles east of Portland on Highway 26 is beautiful **Timberline Lodge** (see "Mount Hood and Columbia Gorge"), which makes a nice stop, approximately halfway between Portland and Bend, to view peaks, stretch legs, and satisfy hungers.

From Portland, via the Columbia Gorge, take I-84 east to The Dalles, then Highway 197 south to connect with Highway 97. I-84 follows the Columbia River, and there are many scenic stops along the way (see "Mount Hood and Columbia Gorge").

From Salem, take Highway 22 east to Highway 20, then east on 20 to connect with Highway 97.

From Eugene, Highway 126 follows the McKenzie River eastward, then heads north to connect with Highway 20. Take 20 east to Sisters. Stay on 20 (south) or take Highway 126 (east) to join Highway 97. (During summer, you may prefer to take Highway 126 from Eugene, then connect with Highway 242, the Old McKenzie Pass Highway, to Sisters.) Along Highway 126, which runs parallel to the McKenzie River, are a number of spots to stop, stretch, and admire the wild river (see "Willamette Valley: McKenzie River").

## *Make a Day of It:*
## *Combine Excursions on Scenic Drive*

**THE CASCADE LAKES HIGHWAY** is an 87-mile National Scenic Byway; along the way are countless attractions that may be woven together into one long day of fun. For details on some of these attractions, see "Bend: Excursions."

Assuming Bend as a start point, your first stop is at Mount Bachelor. Ride the lift up the mountain to gain dramatic views from the summit. Then drive into the alpine country, where dozens of lakes offer fishing, hiking, resorts, and sightseeing. (Snowfall closes the road beyond Mount Bachelor from November through May.) Continuing on, pass North and South Twin lakes, Wickiup Reservoir, Pringle Falls, and the Experimental Forest. Then head south to Newberry National Volcanic Monument. Or turn north to Sunriver Resort, Lava River Cave, and the Lava Cast Forest. Finally, head back to Bend on Highway 97, with stops at Lava Lands Visitor Center and The High Desert Museum.

If you decide to take Highway 242, the Old McKenzie Pass Highway (open summer only), note the amazing change of scenery—from evergreen coastal forest to Ponderosa pines. Stop and admire the landscape at **Cold Spring Park and Campground**—off Highway 242, a few miles west of Sisters. This park is rarely crowded—for day use or for camping—so it's a good spot to break open the picnic basket. (There are few bees here, but more than enough scavenging chipmunks. The kids will love seeing them up close.) You'll also find running water and outhouses.

The **AMTRAK** (800/872-7245) train from Seattle-Portland stops 65 miles south of Bend at Chemult Station.

The **BEND/REDMOND AIRPORT** (541/382-1687) is about 16 miles north of Bend, off Highway 97. Horizon and United airlines fly here from Portland and Seattle.

## REGIONAL CALENDAR

### FEBRUARY
Sisters-Hoodoo Winter Carnival, Hoodoo Ski Bowl.

### JUNE
Festival of Cascade Music, Bend.
Sisters Rodeo: Attracts upwards of 50,000 fans annually, Sisters.

### JULY
Cascade Children's Festival, Bend.
Old-fashioned Fourth: Features a Pet Parade and fireworks from Pilot Butte, Drake Park, Bend.
Outdoor Quilt Show: Features 800 quilts hung from roofs and balconies, Sisters.
Jefferson County Fair & Rodeo, Madras.
Cook County Fair, Prineville.

### AUGUST
Summer Music Festival at Sunriver: Several days of classical concerts, Sunriver.
Deschutes County Fair, Redmond.
Cascade Festival of Music: Eight days of classical music and jazz, Bend.

## REGIONAL RESOURCES

**CENTRAL OREGON VISITOR'S ASSOCIATION**
63085 N. Hwy. 97, Ste. 104, Bend 97701
541/382-8334; 800/800-8334; www.covisitors.com

## WARM SPRINGS

Warm Springs itself is just a jog in Highway 26, on the high desert, halfway between Mount Hood and Bend. Still, there are at least two good reasons to stop here, briefly or for the duration: The Museum at Warm Springs (see "Central Oregon: Excursions") and Kah-Nee-Ta Resort. As added incentive, remember that there are more than 300 days of sunshine a year in this part of the state.

Warm Springs Reservation is the homeland for more than 3,400 tribal members, most of whom live in the community of Warm Springs. The Confederated Indian Tribes comprise 14 tribal groups, including Warm Springs, Umatilla, Wasco, and Northern Paiute. The tribal economy depends upon natural resources—primarily hydropower, forest products and ranching—as well as tourism and recreation. Visitors are welcome at many of the annual festivals, feasts, and pow-wows.

### PLACES TO STAY

#### KAH-NEE-TA RESORT
*P.O. Box K, 97761*
*503/553-1112, 800/554-4SUN; www.kah-nee-taresort.com*
*Rates: Inexpensive to expensive*
*FYI: Restaurants; kitchens (some units); outdoor pools; horseback riding, tennis and basketball courts, golf and miniature golf, bicycle rentals, fishing; casino; pets OK (village only)*

Kah-Nee-Ta is owned and operated by the Confederated Indian Tribes of Warm Springs. It is the centerpiece of a half-million-acre Native American reservation, complete with working ranch and wild horses. The resort has two sections—the Lodge and the Village—and an array of accommodations that will fit any budget. At the low (and fun) end of the accommodation scale are authentic teepees. Also in the Village are one- and two-bedroom cottages, some with kitchens.

More elaborate quarters can be found at the Lodge, along with several restaurants. The Juniper Room, a formal dining room with an impressive view, serves buffalo steak and venison among many other dishes. Make reservations early. The informal Appaloosa Room serves breakfast and lunch and offers the option of eating poolside. In the Village, the River Room is very informal and well suited to families. The food is only okay; the best part of the meal is feeding the bread scraps to the hungry trout from the deck.

The frequent sunshine and the warmth of the mineral pools

allow swimming year round. The pool, larger than Olympic-size, is heated by the hot springs, and there's a 140-foot slide the kids will love.

**❝❝ PARENT COMMENTS**

*"The kids were enthralled by the Native American dances performed regularly at the resort. We enjoyed horseback riding in the desert and lazing in the pool."*

*"Service was excellent. The only drawback to this resort is the lack of good restaurants, which can be easily resolved by securing a cabin with a kitchen at the Village. Anticipate all your needs in advance as Kah-Nee-Ta is very isolated and the nearest town for supplies or gas is 11 miles away."*

## WHAT TO SEE & DO

**THE MUSEUM AT WARM SPRINGS,** 50 miles north of Bend on Highway 26, is a small but magnificent museum the whole family will enjoy. Built in 1993 by the Confederated Indian Tribes to preserve their local history and culture, the museum houses treasured tribal heirlooms in a lovely building designed to blend in with the landscape. The kids may move quickly through the beaded artifacts and woven basket exhibits, but they'll slow down for a multimedia presentation that allows them to participate in a traditional hoop dance. And they'll enjoy exploring the traditional dwellings (examples include a tule mat lodge, wickiup, and plankhouse) constructed to show the tribal life of the past.

*52189 Hwy. 26; 541/553-3331. Open daily, 10 a.m.-5 p.m. Cost: $6/adult, $5/senior 60 and over, $3/child 5-12, free/4 and under.*

## BEND

Bend was founded in 1900 and originally named "Farewell Bend." In 1904, when the town was incorporated, the post office opted for the shorter moniker. For decades, Bend residents were largely ranchers and farmers. Today, these "old timers" seem to coexist fairly peacefully with the "new generation" of writers, outdoor enthusiasts, and real estate investors who have moved into the area. Even Hollywood has discovered Bend and covets it as a movie-making location because of its dependable four-season climate and rugged beauty.

As the seat of Deschutes County, Bend has a decidedly upscale air. At the same time, it doesn't take much imagination to sense the Old West in the region. For kids, Bend can provide a wonderful introduction to the history, geology, and Native American lore of Central Oregon.

### PLACES TO STAY

#### INN OF THE SEVENTH MOUNTAIN
*18575 SW Century Dr., 97702*
*541/382-8711, 800/452-6810; www.7thmtn.com*
*Rates: Moderate to expensive*
*FYI: Restaurants; kitchens (some units); fireplaces (some units); two outdoor pools (seasonal); ice/roller skating rink (seasonal), tennis, biking, golf, horseback riding, rafting, sleigh rides (seasonal); organized program for children (summer and holidays)*

Located seven miles west of Bend, this condominium facility offers accommodations close to Mount Bachelor. The location and the wide range of activities offered at the resort make it a popular place for families. When making reservations, ask to be in a building situated close to the resort center and in an apartment, so you have a kitchen. If you'd rather not cook, there are two good restaurants here. The Poppy Seed Café serves a hearty breakfast at a reasonable cost; Josiah's is pricey, but the meals are excellent.

**66 PARENT COMMENTS**
    *"We go off-season when the rates go way down. Our kids love the pool with the water slide and the busy schedule of activities offered by the resort."*
    *"The staff is very helpful about planning activities for the kids."*

#### THE RIVERHOUSE
*3075 N. Hwy. 97, 97701*
*541/389-3111, 800/452-6878 (Oregon), 800/547-3928; www.riverhouse.com*
*Rates: Moderate*
*FYI: Three restaurants; kitchens (some units), microwaves/refrigerators (some units); fireplaces (some units); indoor and outdoor heated pools; exercise room; jogging trails; pets OK*

To describe this spot as a motel may be technically correct, but it doesn't tell the whole story. With its great location straddling the Deschutes River, The Riverhouse has a more refined atmosphere than that description suggests. Although it's located on the main drag, it doesn't feel like it; the river provides a calm and beautiful setting. Little ones will enjoy scampering along the large, flat river rocks and watching folks fishing right on the grounds.

The wide variety of units includes luxury suites, river-view rooms, and rooms with a spa. Consider a living room suite, which offers a common space with Murphy bed and separate bedroom with queen bed. The kitchen suites (two rooms, three queen beds, and kitchen) are a bit more expensive, but will save the family some bucks on food. Unless you're calling at the last minute, request a river-view room (small additional fee). You might get lucky.

**66 PARENT COMMENTS**

*"Be sure to take advantage of the lovely deck overlooking the river. Although it's adjacent to the bar, kids are allowed to sit there and enjoy a "kiddie cocktail." There's a delicious complimentary shrimp cocktail with each room."*

*"There were actually current, good movies for rent in the lobby."*

## BEST WESTERN ENTRADA LODGE
*19221 Century Dr., 97702*
*541/382-4080*
*Rates: Inexpensive*
*FYI: Complimentary continental breakfast; outdoor pool (seasonal); laundry; pets OK (fee)*

Location is a big plus here, if you plan to spend any time on Mount Bachelor. The Entrada Lodge is 17 miles east of Mount Bachelor Ski Resort, and just four miles west of Bend. This is an attractive motel, offering 79 rooms in several separate buildings, set among the pine trees. Rooms are comfortable, but not spacious. Parking is available just outside each room.

Although it has obvious advantages for skiers, don't hesitate to consider the Entrada Lodge as a summer spot. The outdoor pool is small, but clean. A lovely nature trail winds among the rock and sagebrush and ends with a sweeping view of the river (the viewpoint is high on a bluff, so keep an eye on small children and dogs).

**66 PARENT COMMENTS**

*"The whole family enjoyed the nature trail, several times a day."*

*"This spot is far enough from Bend to allow peace and quiet, but close enough to make the trip into town convenient."*

## ROCK SPRINGS GUEST RANCH
*64201 Tyler Road, 97701*
*541/382-1957; www.rocksprings.com*
*Rates: Expensive (weekly only)*
*FYI: All meals included; outdoor pool; horseback riding; youth*

*program; baby-sitting; no smoke-free units*

Nine miles northwest of Bend, on 2,000 acres adjacent to the Deschutes National Forest, Rock Springs Guest Ranch is truly a family vacation spot. The 26 knotty-pine cabins are comfortable and nicely furnished. They sleep two to eight people and generally include kitchens and fireplaces. The dining room, open to guests of the ranch only, serves good, basic food; the cost is included in the room rate. Also included in the one weekly rate: snacks, riding, children's programs, and special events. Special rates are available for baby-sitters accompanying the family.

From the end of June until Labor Day, there's a daily program for kids five to 12, which operates 9 a.m. to 1 p.m. and 5 to 9 p.m. Children meet each morning with a wrangler/counselor to plan their day; options include an excellent riding program, hiking, swimming, and arts-and-crafts.

A free-form whirlpool includes a 15-foot waterfall, and there's a sand volleyball court and two stocked fishing ponds (bring your own gear). For teens, there are special outings. Parents can ride, swim, play tennis, or just enjoy the natural beauty and sunshine. At night there are hayrides, talent shows, and movies.

**❝ PARENT COMMENTS**

*"The staff makes a big effort to make families feel welcome and it shows. The children's program was excellent."*

*"Unlike some ranches, you can go here and not ride and still have a great vacation. I don't ride, but my husband and children do. I was perfectly content to loaf by the pool."*

### SUNRIVER LODGE AND RESORT

*One Center Dr., P.O. Box 3609, Sunriver 97707*
*541/393-1246, 800/547-3922; www.sunriver-resort.com*
*Rates: Moderate to expensive*
*FYI: Restaurant; kitchens; two outdoor pools; horseback riding, 22 tennis courts, bicycle rentals, golf, skiing, fishing, rafting; playgrounds; organized activities for kids; baby-sitting*

Sunriver is a 3,000-acre resort and residential community located 15 miles south of Bend. It's designed for those who like the wildness of the high desert, but also like all the amenities. There are 360 units here, including houses, housekeeping suites, and two- and three-bedroom condos. The motel-like condos are very reasonably priced, have a good central location, and are perfectly adequate for the amount of time a family will spend indoors. Or cut the cost dramatically by sharing a nice house with another family. In the spring or fall, you may find special offers that are a real bargain.

The scenery on this sagebrush-studded plateau is spectacular, and there is no shortage of activity. There are two very different swimming areas: one with a lap pool for serious swimmers and a large wading pool with lawn for sunning. The other has a large, round pool of uniform depth with a diving area and a separate wading pool. The riding program offers pony rides for kids from age two and a half.

There are 25 miles of paved trails and all kinds of bikes to rent, including tandems, and bikes with kid trailers or kid seats. The Nature Lodge, with staff naturalist, is a fun place for kids to visit recovering wildlife and learn about the high desert.

For winter skiing, there are cross-country trails on the resort grounds, and part of Sunriver Mall is frozen into a small skating rink with skate rentals available. Mount Bachelor is just 18 miles away. On the grounds are several restaurants. For the treat of the day, Goody's is a dazzling old-fashioned creamery/candy store with espresso for the grown-ups.

**❝❝ PARENT COMMENTS**

*"Unfortunately we chose the most formal of the lodge eateries in which to have our one restaurant meal. The staff tolerated us but the place didn't have that good old family ambiance."*

*"Because the resort is so expansive, it's difficult to meet other families. Consider sharing a large house with friends from home."*

*"Any self-respecting hedonist would love Sunriver."*

## PLACES TO EAT

### CAFÉ PARADISO
*945 NW Bond St.*
*541/385-5931*
*Hours: Breakfast, lunch, dinner daily*

This is the place to go for your morning eye-opener. This old-style coffeehouse, located in an historic downtown building, offers a good, strong espresso and a tasty collection of pastry. Stop back later in the day for a light meal or one of their delicious homemade desserts.

### CAFÉ SANTÉ
*718 NW Franklin*
*541/383-3530*
*Hours: Breakfast, lunch daily*

Here's your chance to introduce the kids to health food they'll love. The café serves creative natural cuisine, concentrating on low-fat and low-cholesterol meals. What's more, they truly cater to children, with a healthy and imaginative kids' menu (including tofu scramble, tofu hotdog, and black beans and rice). If your kids won't go for the health foods, the ubiquitous pancakes, grilled cheese, and peanut butter and jelly are also available. Adults choose from a wide range of hearty and heart-healthy selections. Don't be put off by the healthiness of these offerings; there is no sacrifice of good taste.

### DESCHUTES BREWERY AND PUBLIC HOUSE
*1044 NW Bond (at Greenwood)*
*541/382-9242*
*Hours: Lunch, dinner daily*
Who'd think of taking the family to a brewery for dinner? You'll be surprised! The small restaurant area is separate from the bar, and children are more than welcome. (Plan to dine fairly early, though, as state law requires children be off premises by 8:30 p.m.) The quarters are close and the energy is high, so families with toddlers might want to stroll by and see if it looks "do-able."

The core menu here is standard, but tasty, pub food—sandwiches, soups, and salads. Also take a close look at the blackboard, which lists seven specials during the day and seven different ones in the evening. The kids' menu offers some fun variations on the usual themes, such as chicken nuggets shaped like dinosaurs.

### PINE TAVERN RESTAURANT
*967 NW Brooks St.*
*541/382-5581*
*Hours: Lunch, dinner daily*
You'll hear this spot described as a first choice of Bend residents looking for a fine-dining experience. Don't let that dissuade you from taking the whole family. The cozy dining area is informal (there's a large 200-year-old Ponderosa pine tree growing through the roof) and easily accommodates children. If you have toddlers, you might prefer a booth. When weather permits, the family can dine outside on a stunning garden patio overlooking Mirror Pond.

The hearty, home-style fare is terrific; lighter eaters might consider one of the petite menu items. Prime rib is the forte here, but the chef works miracles with pork and seafood as well. The children's menu has several standard offerings, but the more adventurous might choose the salad bar or prime rib au jus. If you have room, top off your meal with one of the restaurant's award-winning desserts.

## WESTSIDE BAKERY AND CAFÉ
*1050 NW Galveston*
*541/382-3426*
*Hours: Breakfast, lunch daily*

This is just a great place for families. The meals are wholesome and delicious, and the attitude of the servers seems to be, "the more the merrier." Here you will find everything from dad-sized omelettes to kid-sized pigs-in-blanket (and most everything in between). Other favorite breakfast selections include hearty croissant scramble, spicy huevos rancheros, and homemade granola. For lunch, the Westside serves sandwiches chock full of meat or cheese on their delicious homemade breads.

There are four rooms of tables, and still you will likely have a wait. Bring books for the whole family!

## WHAT TO SEE & DO

### PARKS

**DRAKE PARK** winds along the banks of the Deschutes River as it passes through downtown Bend. It's named after A.M. Drake, the city founder, though many people assume it's a reference to the hordes of ducks residing here. Kids will enjoy feeding these feathered friends, but you'll want to wipe everyone's shoes before you get back in the car.
*Borders Riverside Blvd. near downtown.*

**JUNIPER PARK** has large, grassy areas with picnic tables, tennis courts, ball field, walking path, and terrific playground. The Juniper Swim and Fitness Center has an indoor and a seasonal outdoor pool.
*800 N.E. 6th St. 541/389-POOL.*

**PILOT BUTTE.** As you gaze east from the center of town, you can't miss Pilot Butte, a 511-foot-high cinder cone surrounded by 101 acres of park. There's a good road to the top that offers a magnificent panoramic view of the Cascade Mountains. The observation area has arrows that identify which Cascade peaks are which, so this is a great first stop to orient the family to Bend and the surrounding landscape.
*Just east of town on Hwy. 20. Open daily, dawn-dusk.*

**TUMELO STATE PARK.** This popular camping area is nestled amid the juniper, Ponderosa pine, and sagebrush along the Deschutes River. Most campsites are small and fairly close together, but they are well maintained. Larger sites are located on a cul-de-sac near the river. There is a pleasant, though dusty, playground area that kids will enjoy. Local fauna, especially ground squirrels and lizards, inspire "hunting" expeditions. For day use, a shady picnic area is located across the highway from the campground. A swimming area is situated at the far end of the trail through the campground.

*62976 OB Riley Road (5.5 miles northeast of Bend, off Hwy. 20). 541/388-6055.*

### EXCURSIONS

**DESCHUTES NATIONAL FOREST.** The entrance to Deschutes National Forest, the third-largest national forest in Oregon, is six miles south of Bend. It encompasses 1.6 million acres of dense forest, alpine meadows, and volcanic landscape. Mount Jefferson, Mount Washington, Diamond Peak, and the Three Sisters afford endless opportunities for hikers, campers, and climbers.

A large section of the National Forest, extending 30 miles south of Bend, has been set aside as a showcase for the many volcanic sights in the area (see "Newberry National Volcanic Monument"). Even if you have no budding young geologists along, the family can't help but be fascinated by the sheer immensity of the lava flows, buttes, and cinder cones in this area.

*Closest entrance is six miles south of Bend on Hwy. 97. 541/388-2715.*

**HIGH DESERT MUSEUM.** This participatory museum is manageably sized and beautifully conceived; it is a must-do for families. Located six miles south of Bend on Highway 97, the museum offers indoor and outdoor exhibits on history, geology, and science.

Don't hurry past the dioramas on the history of the American west; they are fascinating. Also allow plenty of time for the trailside exhibits on forestry settlement. Kids love these real-life exhibits; from time to time, real people demonstrate the huge saws and other logging machinery.

The live animal exhibits house a variety of desert animals living in natural enclosures. Highlights include the raptors, porcupines, and otters. Daily presentations provide answers to all those little "whys?"

*59800 S. Hwy. 97. 541/382-4754. Open daily, 9 a.m.-5 p.m. Cost: $6.25/adult, $5.75/senior & youth 13-18, $3/child 5-12, free/under 5.*

**MOUNT BACHELOR.** Towering over the countryside southwest of Bend is beautiful Mount Bachelor, offering year-round entertainment. In winter there's Nordic and Alpine skiing and snowboarding on Bachelor's renowned powder snow (see "Outdoor Active Fun: Skiing"). In summer, the summit chair lift operates daily for sightseers, hikers, and mountain bikers. Other services on the mountain include a café, picnic sites, and bike rentals.

*Twenty-two miles west of Bend on the Cascade Lake Hwy. 800/829-2442; www.mtbachelor.com.*

**NEWBERRY NATIONAL VOLCANIC MONUMENT.** The 30 miles south of Bend on Highway 97 are replete with opportunities to view the effects of volcano flows on the geology of the area. Even if you have no little geologists along, family members can't help but be interested by the many volcanic wonders. The best of these sites are listed below:

The **Lava River Cave** (on Hwy. 97, 11 miles south of Bend) is a fascinating mile-long tunnel formed by lava flows. It's cold, damp, and dark inside; be sure everyone has a warm jacket and sturdy shoes. Even a large flashlight will not provide adequate light inside the cave; lanterns can be rented for a small fee. The walk will likely inspire a hunger; picnicking is allowed on the grounds, but no drinking water is available.

The nearby **Lava Butte Area** is named for, and dominated by, a 500-foot-high volcanic cinder cone. At the top is an observation/fire lookout and a quarter-mile trail that circles the peak. It's worth the small fee to take the shuttle to the top; it runs daily, departing each half hour, 10 a.m.-4:30 p.m. Kids with a fascination for things volcanic will want to take a quick look in the Lava Lands Visitor Center (541/593-2421) at the base of the butte, offering dioramas and other displays. It's open daily, 9:30 a.m. to 5 p.m.

**Lava Cast Forest Geological Area** (from Bend, three miles south and 11 miles east on FR 9720) offers a paved, 1.1-mile nature trail that winds among the casts of trees incinerated by lava thousands of years ago. Yes, it's a lesson in history and geology, but it's also a nice walk. Choose morning hours during the summer, as there is precious little shade along the way.

Some of the casts are large enough for kids to crawl into, so keep a close eye on the younger ones.

**Newberry Crater** (from Bend, 22 miles south and 13 miles east on CR 21), is a popular area for camping and hiking. Families can drive or hike the 7,686 feet up **Paulina Peak** for a panoramic view of the Oregon high desert. Here, Paulina and East lakes are separated by a large obsidian (black glass) lava flow; make sure that small fry resist the temptation to pocket some of the shiny material. The Visitor Center is open daily, 10 a.m. to 4 p.m. during the summer.

*The Monument encompasses a large area that extends 30 miles south of Bend, along Hwy. 97.*

**PINE MOUNTAIN OBSERVATORY.** If you have little stargazers along, you might want to visit Pine Mountain Observatory, the University of Oregon's astronomical research facility. It's the only major observatory in the northwestern United States; one of its three telescopes is the largest in the Northwest.

Visitors must call first, then may visit on Friday or Saturday evenings (or by appointment) May through September.

*Thirty miles southeast of Bend on Hwy. 20. 541/382-8331 (after 3 p.m.). Cost: suggested donation, $2/adult.*

**RIMROCK SPRINGS WILDLIFE MANAGEMENT AREA.** This wetland environment of ponds and springs, dotted with oases of juniper-sagebrush steppe, is home to a wide variety of wildlife, including songbirds, waterfowl, raptors, and aquatic mammals. With luck and careful timing, you may spot land mammals such as deer, antelope, and coyote. Take the easy 1.5-mile trail to two observation decks; one is barrier-free. Past the observation deck, the trail loops around the hilltop, affording 180-degree views of the Cascades.

*Adjacent to Hwy. 26, 54 miles northeast of Bend. Drive north on Hwy. 97 to Redmond, east on Hwy. 126 to Prineville, then northwest on Hwy. 26 for 19 miles. 503/447-9640. Free.*

**SMITH ROCK STATE PARK,** a stunning 641-acre area, is a haven for rock climbers, mountain bikers, and those who seek majestic viewpoints. The state has taken pains to preserve the rocky spires of the Crooked River Canyon; shifting shadows change the look of these spires regularly throughout the day. For families, a short hike from the main parking lot provides a panoramic view of the canyon floor. If the kids are fairly seasoned hikers, take the two-mile developed trail to the top of Misery Ridge; the view is tremendous, and the whole family will enjoy watching climbers scale the vertical rock walls (be sure to bring binoculars and camera). Wildlife is abundant in the area, including golden eagles, prairie falcons, mule deer, river otter, and beaver. Due to the unique and fragile nature of the park, rangers enforce the animal leash law and strongly encourage all visitors to stay on trails.

*Off Hwy. 97, 22 miles north of Bend. 541/548-7501; 800/551-6949. Cost: $3/car for day use.*

**SUNRIVER NATURE CENTER.** Most families will appreciate the mission of this Center, "to create and maintain a community in which man and nature can coexist." It's a lofty goal, but the Center is doing its part to see it become a reality. In keeping with the philosophy, Sunriver Nature Center offers a relaxed schedule of interpretive programs including an astronomical observatory, a self-guided geology trail, and a botanical garden. Particularly intriguing to young visitors is the bird-rehabilitation program, which cares for sick and injured wildlife and encourages people to recognize how their actions directly affect creatures in the wild.

*Located at Sunriver, 15 miles south of Bend. 541/593-4394. Open Tues.-Sat., 10 a.m.-4 p.m. Cost: $2/adult, $1/child under 13.*

### THE GREAT OUTDOORS

**RAFTING.** The Deschutes is Oregon's second longest river, renowned for its spectacular canyons. It is particularly popular with families, because it offers both scenic flat water and stretches of reasonably gentle white water-rapids. A multitude of guides offer trips here; gather information from several, and choose the one that best fits your family's needs.

The **Bend Outdoor Center, Inc.** (413 NW Hill St.; 541/389-7191) offers canoe and kayak outings as well as half- and whole-day raft trips. Alternatively, you can rent boats from them; they'll help you plan your trip and provide a shuttle service up-river. Long-time operators in the Bend area include **Sun Country Tours and Cascade River Adventures** (541/389-8379; www.suncountrytours.com) and **Fantastic Adventures Whitewater Rafting Trips** (541/389-5460; 800/524-1918).

**SKIING.** Bend is one of a few rare cities that can boast a ski resort within one half hour of downtown. If that's not convenient enough, you can acquire accommodations partway up the mountain (see "Places to Stay"). For alpine skiers,

Mount Bachelor's 17 lifts (including seven high-speed quads) provide access to 54 downhill runs. At high season, parents can choose from several options for their children: ski school, Mountain Masters Program or, for pre-skiers, day care. Nearby, Nordic skiers will find a 60-km system of machine-groomed trails. When it's time to take a break, stop into one of the six day lodges, each with a restaurant. (They all serve unexpectedly good food.) Ski school and general information is available at 800/829-2442. For an up-to-date snow report, phone 541/382-7888. Or check out the Web site at www.mtbachelor.com.

Equipment may be rented on the mountain. If you have means of transporting it, though, the equipment choices may be best in town. There are several spots right on SW Century Drive, as you approach the ski resort, including **Powder House** (541/389-6234), **Skjersaa's Ski Shop** (541/382-2154), and **Stone Ski & Sport** (541/389-0890).

### RESOURCES

**BEND CHAMBER OF COMMERCE**
63085 N. Hwy. 97, Bend 97701
541/382-3221; www.bendchamber.com

**DESCHUTES NATIONAL FOREST INFORMATION**
1645 Hwy. 20 E., Bend 97701
541/388-2715; www.empnet.com/dnf/

**MOUNT BACHELOR INFORMATION**
800/829-2442

## SISTERS

Sisters is an Old West town of stagecoach rides and western storefronts. A plethora of shopping areas and restaurants has grown up here, burying what was once a quiet, laid-back little town. The new Sisters does attract crowds, but the weather is pleasant and the terrain is gorgeous; all in all, no one thinks to complain.

### PLACES TO STAY

**BLACK BUTTE RANCH**
*P.O. Box 8000, Hwy. 20, Black Butte Ranch, 97759*
*541/595-6211, 800/452-7455; www.blackbutteranch.com*
*Rates: Expensive*

FYI: *Restaurant; kitchens; four outdoor pools; horseback riding, tennis courts, bicycle and canoe rentals, two golf courses; organized activities for children; baby-sitting list*

The setting of this 1,800-acre resort is quite spectacular, with a large meadow dominating the central area and snow-capped peaks on the horizon. Black Butte was a family-owned cattle ranch from the late 1800s until 1970 and is still a working cattle operation. In the summer the climate is warm and dry, and in winter you can usually count on snow for skiing at nearby HooDoo Ski Bowl or Mount Bachelor.

The units at Black Butte are individually owned homes and condos, so furnishings vary. But they are well designed and geared to accommodate families. Several units have a third bedroom that can be included with the rental if needed or closed off, reducing the rate. All units have kitchens.

The range of things to do at Black Butte is impressive, including catch-and-release fly-fishing and white water rafting. The Recreation Barn is a good place to send the kids when you need a break.

The dining room is excellent; you will need reservations for dinner. The setting is stylish and may not be comfortable for families with young children. The snack shops by the main pool and the golf clubhouses are good for lunch. Or venture into Bend and Sisters to test the fare there.

**66 PARENT COMMENTS**

*"There is so much to do at Black Butte that I can't imagine wanting to leave it, with the possible exception of skiing in the winter or going into Bend or Sisters, seven miles away."*

*"This is a well-planned resort in a breath-taking setting. We shared a house with friends who have children too, and it worked very well. The ranch is so spread out it might have been hard to get to know other families."*

## LAKE CREEK LODGE
*Star Route, 97759*
*541/595-6331; www.lakecreeklodge.com*
*Rates: Moderate to expensive (No credit cards)*
FYI: *Rates include dinner during summer; restaurant; outdoor pool; tennis, lawn games, fishing; playground; organized children's activities; baby-sitting*

It is hard to get reservations in July and August at Lake Creek Lodge, since returning guests have first choice and some families have been coming for 20 years. This is a charming place, with pine cottages and houses in a wooded setting overlooking a small lake. Each cottage has a refrigerator and two bedrooms joined by a bathroom; each house has a full kitchen and a living room, some with fireplaces. There is a lodge with shuffleboard, Ping-Pong, and pool table.

Kids aged 12 and under can fish in the stocked trout stream—be sure to bring your own poles.

Breakfast and dinner are served at the lodge, but not lunch. Food is simple family fare, served buffet style. Children go first and are seated with other kids; adults can bring their own wine.

### 66 PARENT COMMENTS

*"The rooms in the lodge may sound romantic, but they're too cramped for a family."*

*"A great place to vacation. I read a 1,500-page book by the pool, my husband climbed mountains, my six year old fished, rode horses and swam. The baby napped and swam and rode around in the backpack."*

## PLACES TO EAT

### PAPANDREA'S PIZZA
*E. Cascade St.*
*541/549-6081*
*Hours: Lunch, dinner daily*

Long a favorite of visitors to Sisters, Papandrea's is one of a chain of pizza spots in the state. The ingredients are fresh, and the combinations are appealing. Don't expect "fast food," however; these Western folk take their time to get it right. While you're waiting, you can window shop along the main drag. Or, if your lodging includes a kitchen, try a take-out pizza from the You-Bake line.

### HOTEL SISTERS RESTAURANT
*105 Cascade St. (at Fir)*
*541/549-RIBS*
*Hours: Lunch, dinner daily (summer); lunch Mon.-Fri, dinner daily (winter)*

If you're out to rub elbows with the local cowboys, this is the place to go. Here they serve up tasty ranch-style meals, including tender ribs and juicy burgers. There's no need to go with the red meat, though; they cook up a fine seafood or chicken meal as well.

This spot was designed to resemble a Western hotel, circa 1900, with a large, comfortable deck and private dining rooms upstairs.

## WHAT TO SEE & DO

### STROLL & BROWSE

**CASCADE STREET.** In the real Old West it would have been called Main Street. The central drag in Sisters offers more boutiques, shops, and restaurants, per capita, than most big cities. Many have a Western flavor, and the antique and quilt stores add a dash of country. Kids whose allowances are burning holes in their pockets can check out **Sisters Bakery** (251 E. Cascade; 541/549-0361), purveyors of sweets and more sweets. There are also several novelty stores where children can while away their time while mom and dad hit **Sisters Coffee Company** (342 Hood St.; 541/549-0527; 800/524-JAVA) for a tall one.

### RESOURCES

**SISTERS AREA CHAMBER OF COMMERCE**
352 E. Hood St., Sisters 97759
541/549-0251

# EASTERN OREGON

Roughly speaking, the western border of this region follows Highway 395, the major north-south corridor east of Highway 97 in central Oregon. On the east, the region is defined by the border between Oregon and Idaho, which follows the Snake River through the continent's deepest gorge, Hells Canyon. Though probably more heavily populated with cattle than with people, the region offers gorgeous landscapes, geologic wonders, and history lessons for the whole family. Here are the remnants of mining towns, the ruts of wagon wheels that once rolled along the Oregon Trail, and the story of a multitude of cultures coming together to settle a region.

Much of eastern Oregon remains vast, almost unpopulated wilderness; as such, it demands respect from visitors. Before setting out, be sure to check weather conditions and identify which towns offer services, such as gasoline stations. If your children tolerate long car rides and miles of landscapes, go for it; otherwise, stick to the main roads and the more developed parts of the region.

### GETTING THERE

From Portland, travel east on Interstate 84, the new Columbia Gorge Highway. I-84 departs the river at Boardman and heads southeast through Pendleton, La Grande, and Baker City. You can catch Highway 395, the major north-south road through eastern Oregon, at Pendleton; or via Highway 244 west from La Grande; or via Highway 7 west from Baker City.

From Central Oregon, both Highway 26 (from Redmond) and Highway 20 (from Bend) traverse the eastern region.

From Southern Oregon, take Highway 140 east from Klamath Falls to intersect Highway 395 at Lakeview.

**ROADSIDE ATTRACTIONS.** If you're coming by car from the southwest, you'll find some intriguing geological attractions off Highway 395, in the Lakeview area. South of Lakeview, near the California border, is **Abert Rim,** a 31-mile-long escarpment (a cliff created by a shifting fault). At 2,000 feet high, it's one of the highest exposed faults in North America. Two miles north of Lakeview on Highway 395, across from the Ranger Station, the family can see the only spouting geyser in Oregon. The **Old Perpetual Geyser** erupts every 30 seconds or so, shooting 75 feet into the air.

## NORTHEASTERN OREGON

## PENDLETON

Traveling southeast on I-84, the first eastern Oregon town you will encounter is Pendleton (at the junction with Highway 395). If you're looking for what's left of the Wild West, you'll likely find it here. Tell the kids to keep their eyes open, and they're sure to see some "real live cowboys." The town has taken advantage of its western reputation, and its heritage, to develop attractions and events that are worthy of further investigation by families. Alternatively, your family can use Pendleton as a jumping-off spot for exploration of the less-traveled northeastern corner of the state.

### PLACES TO STAY

**BEST WESTERN PENDLETON INN**
*400 SE Nye Ave., 97801*
*541/276-2135*
*Rates: Inexpensive to moderate*
*FYI: Complimentary continental breakfast; refrigerators/microwaves (some units); outdoor pool; fitness center; laundry*

This two-story motel has 69 units, including five two-bedroom units. Nineteen of the units have been enlarged and nicely redecorated. Kids will enjoy the outdoor pool.

**66** **PARENT COMMENTS**

> *"If you're traveling in summer, don't try to do without a pool. Pendleton is hot and dry, and kids who've spent hours in the car will be begging for a chance to get wet."*

### DOUBLETREE HOTEL PENDLETON

*304 SE Nye. Ave., 97801*
*541/276-6111, 800/222-TREE (reservations)*
*Rates: Inexpensive to moderate*
*FYI: Dining room, coffee shop; outdoor pool*

This Doubletree Hotel offers the amenities and service one expects from a large, upscale franchise, and the price is right. It's conveniently located a mile from downtown, and most of the sights you'll want to see. The pool/hot tub area is especially nice, and definitely welcome in this climate. The hotel eateries offer standard fare; you'll do as well to explore restaurants in town.

## WHAT TO SEE & DO

### STROLL & BROWSE

**DOWNTOWN.** To get a feel for the Old West, take a stroll in downtown Pendleton. Stop by the Umatilla County Courthouse (Court Ave. & SE 4th) to see the restored 1880 **Seth Thomas Clock Tower.** The 57-foot tower, symbolizing the prosperity of the gold-mining era, has clockworks that can be viewed at eye level. Then saunter down to **Hamley's and Company** (30 SE Court; 541/276-2321). This purveyor of western wear and custom-made tack has been a Pendleton institution since 1883.

**PENDLETON UNDERGROUND TOURS** offers an interesting 1¹/₂-hour tour through tunnels built by Chinese immigrants in the late 1800s. The tour includes a card room, laundry, meat market, and jail. If you'd rather avoid defining historical terms such as "bordello" and "opium den," you might want to give this one a miss until the kids are a bit older.

*37 SW Emigrant. 541/276-0730; 800/226-6398. Open Mon.-Sat., 10 a.m.-4 p.m. (reservations recommended). Cost: $10/adult & youth, $5/child under 13.*

**PENDLETON WOOLEN MILLS.** For more than 80 years, these mills have turned out thick, handsome woolens, and they're happy to show you how they do it. Visitors are welcome to tour the mills (sturdy footwear required) and to visit the mill store.

*1307 SE Court Pl. 541/276-6911; 800/568-3156. Tours Mon.-Fri., 9 and 11 a.m., 1:30 and 3 p.m. Store open Mon.-Sat., 8 a.m.-5 p.m.*

### EXCURSIONS

**TAMASTSLIKT CULTURAL INSTITUTE.** This large, beautifully designed museum opened to high praise in the summer of 1997. Unique among the several museums that tell the history of the Oregon Trail, the Tamastslikt Cultural Institute portrays that same history from the perspectives of the Cayuse, Umatilla, and Walla Walla tribes. (Tamastslikt means "interpret" in the Walla Walla language.)

Visitors enter the building via a pathway along the base of the Blue Mountains. Inside, attractive exhibits tell the story of the tribes in three parts: "We Were," "We Are," and "We Will Be." There's also an art gallery that hosts changing exhibits. If all this history fosters an appetite for less abstract nourishment, there's a nice café on the premises. The museum store sells local tribal arts and crafts.

*Seven miles east of Pendleton, on the Umatilla Indian Reservation. 541/966-9748; www.umatilla.nsn.us/. Open daily, 9 a.m.-5 p.m. Cost: $6/adult, $4/senior over 55 & student, free/under 5.*

**WALLOWA-WHITMAN NATIONAL FOREST.** Pendleton provides the northernmost access to the Wallowa-Whitman National Forest (for details about the area, see "Joseph: Excursions"). Though longer than other possible routes, the trip to the Wallowas from Pendleton is scenic and rewarding.

*Take Hwy. 11 northeast from Pendleton to connect with Hwy. 204. Follow 204 to Elgin. At Elgin, catch Highway 82 east, through Lostine and Enterprise, to Joseph.*

### CALENDAR

#### SEPTEMBER

Pendleton Round-Up: More than 50,000 visitors attend this four-day event, featuring bronco riding, horse races, Indian feasts and war dances, a greased-pig contest, sack races, and fireworks, Pendleton.

### RESOURCES

#### PENDLETON CHAMBER OF COMMERCE
501 S. Main St., Pendleton 97801
541/276-7411; 800/547-8911

**ON THE ROAD AGAIN**

The drive between Pendleton and Baker City is a particularly nice stretch of I-84. Forty miles south of Pendleton, near the small town of La Grande, the highway dips into the Grande Ronde Valley, with its rolling hills and sagebrush. If you're continuing on, but need a stop to refresh and refuel, La Grande is a good place to do it.

If you have time and the urge to see some real scenery, La Grande is the veering-off point for a fantastically scenic day trip into the Wallowa-Whitman National Forest (see "Joseph: Excursions"). The drive to **Hells Canyon Overlook at Hat Point** is a great way to see the most scenic features of the area all in one day. Be forewarned, however: this is a long drive, only to be undertaken with emergency supplies, several picnics, and plenty of books or car games on board.

*From La Grande, take Hwy. 82 east to Joseph (approximately 75 miles), the paved road to Imnaha, then the gravel road for 24 miles to Hat Point (allow a full hour to drive this last 24 miles).*

**REFUELING.** As you explore the Wallowa area, you'll find plenty of places to rest and refuel. Sixty-six miles east of La Grande on Highway 82, you'll pass through **Enterprise,** the county seat and largest town in Wallowa County. If you're looking for your morning eye-opener, stop into **The Book Loft** (107 E. Main; 541/426-3351), which combines bookstore and art gallery with espresso and pastry. For an all-natural meal, you'll enjoy **The Common Good** (100 W. Main; 541/426-4125). This spot offers good, healthy entrées; or you can buy munchies from the health-food section and take them on the road.

Perhaps the greatest find in town is actually three finds that share one space: **Terminal Gravity, Wildflower Bakery,** and **Blue Willow Sausage** (803 School St.; 541/426-0158). Wildflower Bakery offers breakfast, lunch, and pastries until 3 p.m. The Terminal Gravity Brew Pub serves tasty pub food at lunch and dinner. Kids are more than welcome—in fact, there's a play space just for them—but they need to eat and clear out by about 9 p.m., when the brew really starts flowing. During the summer, Blue Willow Sausage offers incredibly tasty homemade sausage, mesquite-barbecued on the porch.

## JOSEPH

The town of Joseph was incorporated in 1887. This is the ancestral land of the Nez Percé tribe, and the town is named after Chief Joseph, their venerable leader during the mid-1800s. The tribe originally occupied the Snake and Salmon river canyons; during summer months, they grazed their animals and caught salmon with special traps called "wallowas."

In a treaty signed during the 1850s, the U.S. government guaranteed the Nez Percé continued ownership of the heart of their homeland, in return for several million acres of surrounding lands. After gold was discovered in 1877, the government renegotiated the treaty, stripping the tribe of large portions of land they had previously been promised. Several Nez Percé chiefs refused to sign the treaty.

In ensuing years, the non-treaty Nez Percé were increasingly pressured to move onto a reservation. Finally this portion of the tribe took flight, attempting to move into Montana. They were met with resistance from settlers, and fought many battles before surrendering near the Canadian border. Upon surrender, Chief Joseph made an impassioned speech, declaring "I shall fight no more forever."

### PLACES TO STAY

**EAGLE CAP CHALETS**
*59879 Wallowa Lake Hwy., 97846*
*541/432-4704*
*Rates: Inexpensive*
*FYI: Kitchens; fireplaces (some units); indoor pool*

Cabins and condos at Eagle Cap offer a variety of accommodations. All cabins have kitchens; some have fireplaces as well. Families will want to investigate the condos, however—they're more spacious, and many have two bedrooms. The indoor pool is not large, but it provides a nice distraction when lake swimming is out of the question.

**❝ PARENT COMMENTS**

*"The area offers a nice mix of gorgeous scenery and outdoor fun, together with small towns that are fun to explore."*

*"The Wallowas are spectacular, but rain is not unheard of here. Be sure to bring indoor diversions—games and such."*

**WALLOWA LAKE LODGE**
*60060 Wallowa Lake Hwy., 97846*
*541/432-9821*
*Rates: Moderate*
*FYI: Kitchens (some units); fireplaces (some units)*

Surrounded by tall pines, Wallowa Lake Lodge sits on eight acres at the northern end of the lake. Built in 1923, the lodge is cozy and comfortable, with accommodations large enough for families; ask about the two suites and eight two-bedroom units. All lodge units have individual baths. More private—and perhaps more comfortable—are the one- and two-bedroom cabins, each with kitchen and fireplace. The walls are still lined with the original knotty pine, but kitchens and baths have been tastefully updated.

**66 PARENT COMMENTS**

*"We liked the atmosphere here a lot; the kids wished there were a pool."*

*"The proximity to the Tramway and other area attractions is a real plus."*

## PLACES TO EAT

**OLD TOWN CAFÉ**
*8 S. Main*
*541/432-9898*
*Hours: Breakfast, lunch, dinner daily (summer); breakfast, lunch Fri.-Wed. (winter)*

The owner of the Old Town has a commitment to good food and good prices, and so far she has upheld it faithfully. The hearty soups are made from scratch, and according to the weather (cold soups, such as cucumber soup and gazpacho, are served in summer). Year round, the café serves good, healthy breakfast and lunch entrées. Dinner is served during the summer, featuring a different specialty pizza each night, Sunday through Thursday. On Friday and Saturday nights, an "international dinner" is offered, highlighting a specialty cuisine such as Thai or Cajun. (These are very popular among locals and visitors alike. Arrive early and prepare to wait a bit.) If the kids don't like the international cuisine, ask the chef to whip up a cheese sandwich or two.

**VALI'S ALPINE DELI AND RESTAURANT**
*59811 Wallowa Lake Hwy.*
*503/432-5691*
*Hours: Breakfast, dinner Tues.-Sun. (Memorial Day-Labor Day)*
This Hungarian-German restaurant serves a different imaginative dinner special each night of the week (Memorial Day through Labor Day), and they all tend to be delicious. On nice evenings, the family will enjoy dining out on the enclosed porch. Although you might not expect it in the little town of Joseph, reservations are recommended.

## WHAT TO SEE & DO

**WALLOWA COUNTY MUSEUM** details interesting aspects of the area's history, including the ill-fated exodus of the Nez Percé from the area, which ended in a standoff near the Canadian border (see description under "Joseph").
*On Hwy. 82, in Joseph. 541/426-3811. Open Memorial Day-mid-Sept., 10 a.m. to 5 p.m. Cost: donation.*

**WALLOWA LAKE STATE PARK.** You'd be hard-pressed to find a prettier setting for a state park than this one, on the shores of Wallowa Lake, amid the tall peaks of the Wallowa Mountains. For day use, there's a boat ramp and marina, grassy picnic area, and swimming beach (protected by buoys, but unsupervised). Boats, motors, and water sports equipment are available for rent at the marina. The camping area has 90 tent campsites.
The remote, unspoiled **Eagle Cap Wilderness** is accessible from the park, via trails leading up the Wallowa River from the south picnic area (the climb is quite steep in parts).
*Upper Power House Road. 541/432-8855.*

**WALLOWA LAKE TRAMWAY.** Kids generally love tram rides, and this is an extraordinary one. The 15-minute ride takes visitors to the top of 8,200-foot Mount Howard. Parents with weak stomachs should be forewarned—this is the steepest vertical lift for a four-passenger gondola in North America. At the summit is a two-mile system of trails with spectacular views. If you haven't left your stomach below, the restaurant at the summit serves hamburgers, sandwiches, soups, and salads.
*On Upper Power House Road, across from the Wallowa Lake State Park. 541/432-5331. Open daily, 10 a.m.-4 p.m., mid-May-Sept. Cost: $12/adult & youth, $10/senior over 62, $6/under 11.*

**EXCURSIONS**

**HELLS CANYON NATIONAL RECREATION AREA.** From Joseph, it's just a hop and a skip (on some pretty narrow, undeveloped roads) to the scenic Snake River and Hells Canyon. The National Recreation Area encompasses more than 650,000 acres, a third of which has been designated as wilderness. The surging Snake River has carved out the continent's deepest gorge here—8,000 feet deep. Along the 70 miles of gorge, the river alternates between foaming white water and deep, quiet pools. You're likely to spot wildlife along the gorge, so be sure to have those binoculars handy. The area is home to bears, bobcats, bighorn sheep, cougars, and mountain goats, among many other species.

**WALLOWA-WHITMAN NATIONAL FOREST** encompasses two million acres in two large sections (separated by I-84). The national forest is subdivided into regions, including the Wallowa Mountains, Eagle Cap Wilderness, and Hells Canyon National Recreation Area. This is a good choice for families, whether you're planning a day's excursion or a month-long vacation. Enjoyed for its aesthetics and its recreational opportunities, the region is dotted by small towns, most of which can provide accommodations, food, and gasoline. In addition, there are lodges and campgrounds throughout the area.

The 216,000-acre **Eagle Cap Wilderness** offers alpine lakes and meadows surrounded by the rugged peaks of the Wallowa Mountains (also known as the "little Swiss Alps"). Mountain climbing and nature study are popular here. If you'd like to explore the area on horseback, contact **Eagle Cap Wilderness Pack Station** (59761 Wallowa Lake Hwy.; 541/432-4145; 800/681-6222). These folks offer anything from a one-hour ride to a 10-day pack trip.

**CALENDAR**

**SEPTEMBER**
Alpenfest: Music, dancing, and Bavarian feasts.

**RESOURCES**

**JOSEPH CHAMBER OF COMMERCE**
P.O. Box 13, Joseph 97846
541/432-1015
Open Mon., Wed., Fri., 11 a.m.-2 p.m.

**WALLOWA COUNTY CHAMBER OF COMMERCE**
P.O. Box 427, 107 SW 1st, Enterprise 97828
541/426-4622; 800/585-4121

**WALLOWA-WHITMAN NATIONAL FOREST**
1550 Dewey Ave., P.O. Box, Baker City 97814
541/523-6391

## BAKER CITY

Back on I-84, the next stop to the south is Baker City, nestled amid the stunning Elkhorn Range of the Blue Mountains. In the 1860s, the area surrounding this town was teeming with prospectors looking for gold. Today, you can visit a number of the abandoned mines, scattered throughout the adjacent mountain areas.

### PLACES TO STAY

**BEST WESTERN SUNRIDGE INN**
*One Sunridge Lane, 97814*
*541/523-6444*
*Rates: Inexpensive to moderate*
*FYI: Two restaurants; microwaves/refrigerators (some units); outdoor pool; laundry*

The 156 guestrooms include a number of different configurations, including one- and two-bedroom suites; they're clean and neat, if not inspired. The grounds are nicely maintained, and the large outdoor pool is surrounded by an inviting courtyard area. There are three restaurants: a casual daytime spot, evening dining, and a seasonal patio grill.

**❝ PARENT COMMENTS**

*"Of the Inn's three restaurants, our family was most comfortable at The Sunridge. This café had lots of the kids' favorite foods, and the atmosphere was very informal and congenial."*

### PLACES TO EAT

**THE PHONE COMPANY RESTAURANT**
*1926 1st St.*
*541/523-7997*
*Hours: Lunch Tues.-Fri., dinner Tues.-Sat.*

Yes, it really is housed in the old phone exchange, dating from 1910. It's a roomy, nicely designed restaurant, featuring fresh Northwest cuisine (in fact, this may be one of the only restaurants in town with fresh offerings). Some choices may be a bit too chi-chi for kids, but there are less complex options available.

## WHAT TO SEE & DO

### STROLL & BROWSE

**BAKER CITY.** The horse-drawn Oregon Trail Trolley is a thrill for kids, as it clops through downtown Baker City, and tours turn-of-the-century Victorian buildings. Designated a National Historic District, the area features more than 100 examples of Victorian architecture.

Stop in at the **U.S. Bank** (2000 Main St.; 541/523-7791), home of the largest display of gold in the state (including a nugget that weighs in at more than 80 ounces).

### EXCURSIONS

**ELKHORN SCENIC BYWAY,** also known as the "Ghost Town Tour," follows Highway 7 and various forest service roads to complete a 106-mile loop from Baker City. Check out the steam train in the restored ghost town of Sumpter (see description below). If you have older kids, or young ones who are easily entertained in the car, you'll find this trip well worth the price of gasoline. The road passes a number of old mining and logging towns, including Granite, Bonanza, and Whitney, as well as the Anthony Lakes Recreation Area. Self-guided tour maps of the area are available at the Baker County Visitors Center (490 Campbell St.; 541/523-3356; 800/523-1235).

**HELLS CANYON NATIONAL RECREATION AREA.** The southernmost access to this recreation area is via Highway 86 east from Baker City. The road traverses farm land and plateaus, and passes through old mining towns such as Pine and Halfway. Early Oregon Trail pioneers took this route on their way to the Willamette Valley.

You'll be rewarded with a good view of Hells Canyon and the surging Snake River from **Hells Canyon Overlook.** Take Highway 86 east from Baker City, approximately 55 miles along the foothills of the Wallowa Mountains. After you pass Halfway, watch for signs to Hells Canyon. For a description of the area, see "Joseph: Excursions."

**OREGON TRAIL INTERPRETIVE CENTER.** Located at the summit of Flagstaff Hill, where many Oregon Trail travelers caught first sight of the Promised Land, this center succeeds in bringing to life both the trials and joys of life on the journey. Permanent and changing exhibits are complemented by volunteers in period costumes, who demonstrate pioneer arts and skills.

Consider hiking the 4.2-mile interpretive trail that takes you past scenic overlooks and historic sites. Older kids will appreciate seeing the actual ruts left by thousands of wagon wheels.

*Four miles east of I-84 on Highway 86. 541/523-1843; 800/523-1235; www.or.blm.gov/nhotic. Open daily, 9 a.m.-6 p.m. (April-Oct.); daily, 9 a.m.-4 p.m. (Nov.-March). Cost: $5/adult, $3.50/senior over 62 & youth 6-17.*

**SKIING.** Located in the majestic Elkhorn Range of the Blue Mountains, **Anthony Lakes Mountain Resort** has a 7,100-foot base, the highest in Oregon. There are runs of every level of difficulty here; beginners access the mountain via Poma lift, while more experienced skiers ride the double chair. Snowboarders have a snow park of their own, though they're also allowed on any of the main trails. About nine miles of groomed cross-country trails, some of which border the John Day Wilderness Area, round out the options.

The day lodge has been recently remodeled. In addition to food service, the lodge is the place to go for ski school registration and ski rentals.

*Nineteen miles west of the North Powder Exit from I-84. 541/963-4599 (information); 541/856-3277 (snow report).*

**SUMPTER VALLEY RAILROAD** offers tours through the historic gold-mining district around Baker City. The train ride is fun for kids and a nice break from driving for road-weary parents. The train passes through a wildlife refuge established after mining operations left the land unsuitable for agriculture.

Both one-way and round trips are available; the best bet for families is to board at McEwen Station and take the round trip.

*Located 22 miles southwest of Baker City on Hwy. 7. 541/894-2268. Tours depart Sat.-Sun., 10 a.m., 12:30 and 3 p.m. (Memorial Day-Sept.). Cost: round trip, $9/adult, $6.50/youth 6-16; one-way, $6/adult, $4.50/youth 6-16.*

## RESOURCES

### BAKER COUNTY VISITOR AND CONVENTION BUREAU
490 Campbell St., Baker City, OR 97814
541/523-3356; 800/523-1235
Mon.-Fri., 8 a.m.-6 p.m.; Sat. 8 a.m.-4 p.m.; Sun., 9 a.m.-2 p.m.
Offers self-guiding maps and brochures of the historic district, gold-mining region, and Elkhorn Scenic Byway.

**ON THE ROAD AGAIN**

**ONTARIO/VALE.** On I-84, 72 miles southeast of Baker City, is an area of special historical interest. It can be visited as a day trip from nearby towns, a stop-off on the way into Idaho, or a destination in and of itself. Our parent reviewers didn't stay in this area, but we did hear tell of a good eating spot, a Mexican restaurant called **Casa Jaramillo** (157 SE 2nd St., Ontario; 541/889-9258).

**FOUR RIVERS CULTURAL CENTER AND MUSEUM.** The name refers to four rivers that converge in the western Treasure Valley, where Oregon borders Idaho. It's meant to be a reminder of the constant flow of people of varied ancestry—Native American, Basque, northern European, Hispanic, and Japanese—who settled the region and gave it a diverse culture. Be sure to visit the Japanese garden, designed by world-renowned landscape artist Hoichi Kurisu.
*676 SW 5th Ave. (off I-84 in downtown Ontario). 541/889-8191; 888/211-1222. Open daily, 10 am.-6 p.m. Cost: $4/adult, $3/senior over 65 & child 3-12.*

Looking for a longer excursion? The town of **Vale,** 12 miles west of Ontario, makes a fun and educational destination. In and around this small town are reminders of the many settlers who passed this way on the Oregon Trail. Throughout town, you'll encounter 17 murals depicting the daily lives and progress of the early settlers. Tour the **Rinehart Stone House** (283 S. Main St.; 541/473-2070), built in 1872 as a way station on the Oregon Trail. The collection includes Oregon Trail memorabilia and Indian artifacts. This free museum is open March through November, daily, 12:30 to 4 p.m. Ten miles from Vale is **Keeney Pass,** one of the best places to view deep wagon ruts left by Oregon Trail travelers. A kiosk at the pass describes and illustrates a day's journey on the trail.

For more information on all these historic attractions, contact the **Ontario Visitors & Convention Bureau** (541/889-8012; 888/889-8012).

**JOHN DAY.** In the 1860s, John Day and the surrounding area were "gold country," a heritage that is commemorated here still. At the geographic center of the eastern Oregon region, John Day marks the junction of two major highways: interstates 26 and 395.

**KAM WAH CHUNG MUSEUM,** a turn-of-the-century Chinese doctor's office and herbal store, gives visitors an opportunity to gain an interesting perspective on the transplanted Chinese culture. The museum building served as a center for the Chinese community in eastern Oregon until the early 1940s.

*One block north of Highway 26, adjacent to the city park. 541/575-0028. Open May-Oct., Mon.-Thurs., 9 a.m.-noon, and 1-5 p.m.; Sat.-Sun., 1-5 p.m. Cost: $2/adult, $1.50/senior over 65 & youth 13-18, $.50/under 13.*

**JOHN DAY FOSSIL BEDS NATIONAL MONUMEN**t lies between 40 and 120 miles west of John Day on Highway 26. Family members don't have to be rock hounds to appreciate the geologic history represented at this site. It's a rare opportunity to see a 50-million-year record of the plant and animal life that inhabited the region. Fossilized bones, shells, teeth, tracks, and plants create a mosaic that tells the fascinating story of the Age of Mammals—the time between extinction of the dinosaurs and the Ice Age. Some of the greatest finds on the continent are on display here.

The monument consists of three separate units. **Sheep Rock Unit** (on Hwy. 19 near Dayville) has a visitor center that provides information about the site, as well as a lovely, shaded picnic area. Once the family has picnicked, follow the half-mile *Island In Time* interpretive trail into blue-green canyons. The fossil beds are an area of ongoing scientific research; visitors can view a laboratory where specimens are prepared for study. **Clarno Unit** (off Hwy. 218, 20 miles west of Fossil) features The Palisades—cliffs formed by a succession of ash-laden mudflows. The quarter-mile, self-guided *Trail of the Fossils* features 10 numbered stops that afford youngsters a close look at a variety of fossils. At **Painted Hills Unit** (off Hwy. 26, 9 miles northwest of Mitchell), the colorful landscape demonstrates the effect of weathering on volcanic ash. The short *Painted Cove Trail* permits a close view of the clay stone that distinguishes the area.

A word of warning: rattlesnakes abound among the large rocks in this area. Be sure to stay on established trails.

*Located north of Hwy. 26, between Hwy. 97 and Hwy. 395. 541/987-2333. Call for Visitor Center hours. Free.*

## SOUTHEASTERN OREGON

### BURNS

Delineated by east-west Highway 20, southeastern Oregon is sparsely populated and well-nigh devoid of manmade attractions for families. However, this region is a treasure trove of rare geological sites and wildlife. If the terrain here looks familiar, it probably is—the region has been used for the shooting of countless Westerns in recent decades.

### PLACES TO STAY

#### BEST WESTERN PONDEROSA

*577 W. Monroe, 97720*
*541/573-2047, 800/528-1234*
*Rates: Inexpensive*
*FYI: Refrigerators (some units); outdoor pool; pets OK*

If you're visiting here in the summer, a swimming pool will never be more welcome. The rooms are comfortable; if you have a large group, ask about the two-bedroom units. Nearby Pine Room Café (Monroe & Egan St.) has a children's menu and is touted by locals as one of the best restaurants in town.

### 66 PARENT COMMENTS

*"The area around Burns is beautiful. But we went in the summer and couldn't believe how hot and dusty it was. When we saw the pool at the motel, we were convinced it was a mirage!"*

### WHAT TO SEE & DO

#### MALHEUR NATIONAL FOREST AND WILDLIFE REFUGE.

This 1.5 million-acre national forest is a place of dramatic beauty. On more than 200 miles of trails, families can experience a changing terrain of timbered slopes, alpine lakes and meadows, and sage grasslands.

Probably the greatest area attraction for families, the refuge extends approximately 40 miles by 40 miles and includes the high desert area watered each spring by mountain snowmelt (sometimes heavily enough to turn Malheur and Harney lakes into one big lake). The best times to spot wildlife—early morning and late afternoon—are not necessarily the easiest times for families to be on the road, but your extra effort is likely to be rewarded.

If you've got birders in the car, have binoculars at the ready; you'll find a spectacular variety inhabiting the refuge's wetlands. Critical to bird migration, the refuge hosts migrating geese, pintails, and curlews in the spring, and tundra swans and great sandhill cranes in the fall. You may also spy cormorants, herons, egrets, ibis, and a variety of hawk and owl species.

As you head south on the automobile tour route, you'll come first to **Buena Vista Overlook,** where there is an exceptional view of the Blitzen River Valley and Steens Mountain, one of the largest fault-block mountains on the continent. (A fault-block mountain is created by a combination of volcanic and glacial forces.) The visitor center here has interpretive exhibits, restrooms, maps, and information to help guide your trip through the area.

At **Benson Pond,** stop to see which water birds are around, and watch for animals in the stand of cottonwoods around the periphery.

*The Refuge headquarters is 6 miles east of Hwy. 205, just off the Narrows-Princeton Road, at the southern edge of Malheur Lake. 541/493-2612.*

**ROME.** Rockhounds will want to put the area around Rome at the top of their lists. Located approximately 100 miles southeast of Burns, the region is rich in thunder eggs—volcanic geodes (hollow rocks containing opal and agate). Nearby are the **Pillars of Rome,** the dramatically sheer, layered sides of a dry canyon.

*Off Hwy. 95, approximately 15 miles east of Burns Junction.*

## FRENCHGLEN

This pretty little town hasn't changed much since Pete French and his fellow cattle barons ruled the area in the late 1800s. At the junction of highways 20 and 395, Frenchglen has become a transportation hub in this widespread region. The Paiute Indian reservation is located on the northern edge of town.

### FRENCHGLEN HOTEL
*Hwy. 205, 97736*
*541/493-2825*
*Rates: Inexpensive*
*FYI: Dining room*

It's an adventure to stay in this 1916 hotel, now registered as a state historic landmark. The rooms are small, and the baths are shared, but that's all part of the experience. On the main floor is the dining room and a large, screened porch. The cook whips up hearty, ranch-style dinners nightly; reservations are required.

Southeastern Oregon can be snowbound throughout much of the winter, so the hotel is closed during that season.

**❝❝ PARENT COMMENTS**

*"As the single parent of two little ones, I felt pretty adventurous heading into the Oregon outback. But the people were welcoming and accommodating, and we all three ended up having a great time and learning a lot about state history."*

*"With the small rooms and shared bathrooms, I probably wouldn't stay here with babies or toddlers."*

**EXCURSIONS**

**HART MOUNTAIN NATIONAL ANTELOPE REFUGE.** Thirty-six miles southwest of Frenchglen is an isolated 251,000-acre refuge populated by pronghorn antelope, bighorn sheep, mule deer, and sage grouse, among many other species. The headquarters is located 13 miles inside the refuge. There's no electric service here, and it's 50 miles to the closest town, so to call it isolated is an understatement. Still, thousands of visitors flock to the refuge each year.

Before 1936, the year in which President Franklin D. Roosevelt established the refuge, antelopes in the area had nearly been hunted to extinction. Today that species numbers about 1,900.

*Head south on Hwy. 205 and watch for signs. No phone.*

**STEENS MOUNTAIN.** Rising to 9,670 feet, this is one of the largest fault-block mountains (created by a combination of volcanic and glacial forces) on the continent. An unimproved road climbs the mountain and is generally passable from July through October. Nevertheless, the climate on the mountain is subject to change without warning; it's a good idea to call the Bureau of Land Management in Hines (541/573-4400) for current weather and road information before setting out.

*Located just east of Frenchglen*

## WASHINGTON STATE

Incorporating history, scenery, and adventure, Washington has much in common with its Northwest neighbors. From sea level to the top of Mount Rainier, the Evergreen State has it all—mountains and foothills, plateaus and wheatlands, basalt deserts and alpine regions. All in all, the state has plenty of amazement and amusement for any family.

**HISTORY.** Native American heritage in Washington dates back thousands of years, and has profoundly affected the state's history. Coastal tribes were instrumental in the survival of the "Corps of Discovery," the Lewis and Clark expedition that wintered near the mouth of the Columbia River. Eastern Washington tribes traded goods and information with missionaries and pioneers who ventured across the mountains. (In many instances, those relationships grew rocky over the years, but early settlers would likely not have survived in the new territory without the assistance of Native Americans.)

Washington became the 42nd state of the Union in 1887, but its growth can be marked from the gold rush in the Klondike, beginning in 1897. During this era, the region served as gateway to the north for thousands of prospectors, and many a local fortune was made. Many prospectors returned to settle in the state.

Families interested in providing an out-of-school history experience for their younger members will find the history here accessible and fascinating. From the National Historic Site that celebrating the Whitman Mission (Walla Walla) to the Underground Tour and Pioneer Square in old Seattle, you'll find lots of fun, and education, in Washington.

**GEOGRAPHY.** The geography of Washington State is nothing if not dramatic. A bird's eye view underscores the enormous effect of the Cascades, which divide the wet and sometimes "wild" western region from the drier, more sedate eastern state.

The largest city in Washington, Seattle "anchors" the Puget Sound region, which includes the lowlands along Interstate 5 from Olympia to Bellingham. This narrow strip of land, between Puget Sound and the Cascades, is home to more than half of the total population of the state. Off shore are the beautiful San Juan Islands, hosts to thousands of visitors— many on foot or bike—each year.

Just west of the sound, the Olympic Peninsula offers terrain that ranges from the "sun belt" near Sequim to the constantly soaked rainforests of Olympic National Park, and every kind of recreational pursuit for families. Farther south are the coastal havens of Ocean Shores, Kalaloch, and the Long Beach Peninsula.

The Cascades stretch from the Canadian to the Oregon border, and includes Interstate-90, the major east-west throughway from Seattle. Here, families will find year-round adventure: skiing, hiking, rafting and other recreational pursuits, as well as sight-seeing at majestic Mount Rainier and awe-inspiring Mount St. Helen's.

The central portion of Washington encompasses a varied terrain, including Cascade foothills, grasslands, and vast orchards, interrupted periodically by raging rivers and pristine lakes. Here are outdoor pursuits aplenty, as well as fun family excursions into the unique regional towns of Winthrop, Leavenworth, Chelan, and others.

Due south, along the Columbia River at the Washington-Oregon border, is the Columbia Gorge. Dramatically carved by wind and water, the gorge provides a show place for nature, tastefully enhanced by man-made visitor centers and viewpoints.

In Eastern Washington, families will find a slower-paced region, replete with geographic nuance and drier climates. With lots of time for recreational and historical exploration, visitors here can look forward to a unique experience in a unique part of the State.

The nine sections of this chapter roughly correspond to these geographic divisions, and appear in this order: Seattle, Anacortes and San Juan Islands, The Puget Lowlands, Olympic Peninsula, Washington Coast, Washington Cascades, Central Washington and the Columbia Gorge, and Eastern Washington.

**SPECIAL FEATURES.** A progressive state from the get-go, Washington has a number of firsts among its accomplishments. The state granted suffrage to women in 1909, a decade earlier than the rest of the nation. In 1942, the state completed construction of the Grand Coulee Dam, one of the greatest engineering feats of the century.

In 1962, Seattle burst into the limelight with the Century 21 World's Fair. This highly successful event ignited the region and set the stage for the steady growth that (despite occasional lapses) has brought high technology and a booming economy to the region.

## STATEWIDE RESOURCES

### WASHINGTON STATE PARKS AND RECREATION COMMISSION
7150 Clearwater Lane
Olympia, Washington 98504
360/902-8500, 800/233-0321


### WASHINGTON TRAVEL DEVELOPMENT DIVISION
General Administration Building
Olympia, Washington 98504
360/586-2088, 360/586-2102; www.tourism.wa.gov


### WWW.TRAVEL-IN-WA.COM
Designed for the first-time visitor, this Web site provides a quick overview of the Evergreen State, including accommodations, activities, and events.

# SEATTLE

There's no question—Seattle is one of the best cities in the country to visit with kids. Lying between saltwater Puget Sound and freshwater Lake Washington, framed by the Olympic Mountains to the west and the Cascades to the east, and enjoying the benefit of a booming local economy, it is a city that offers visiting families a fabulous assortment of things to see and do.

Come to explore Pike Place Market, with its cornucopia of cultures; to experience the world-class zoo; or to attend the award-winning Seattle Children's Theater. Scale a pretend wall or a real mountain, ride a ferry, or hike, bike, sail, and ski the great outdoors. Whatever you choose to do in this wonderfully situated metropolitan center, you will never lack the ingredients for a memorable family vacation.

## GETTING THERE

**BY CAR.** Interstate 5 is the main route into Seattle from the north and south (3 1/2 hours from Portland; three hours from Vancouver, British Columbia, barring a long wait at the U.S./Canadian border.) From the east, you can reach Seattle via Highway 520 or Interstate 90.

**BY TRAIN.** The Amtrak station (800/USA-RAIL) is at 3rd Avenue and Jackson Street, at the southern edge of downtown. Amtrak operates six trains a week along the Seattle-Portland corridor, as well as trains north to Vancouver and east over the Cascades and beyond.

**BY PLANE.** Seattle-Tacoma International Airport is about 16 miles south of the city center.

## GETTING AROUND

**METRO BUS.** Getting there can be half the fun if you let Metro (206/553-3000) do the driving while visiting Greater Seattle. For bus information, just tell the Metro representative where you are, where you want to go, and when.

While exploring the city center, take advantage of the Metro Free Zone: There is no charge to ride buses in the downtown district, including Pioneer Square, the International District, Pike Place Market, the downtown shopping core, and the waterfront. A 1.3-mile transit tunnel runs beneath Pine Street and Third Avenue, with several stops at underground stations along the way.

Metro also runs **WATERFRONT STREETCARS** (206/553-3000) that travel from Pier 70 on the waterfront to the International District and back again, with nine stops along the way. Streetcars run approximately every 20 minutes.

**SEATTLE MONORAIL** (206/684-7200) runs between Westlake Center (in the downtown shopping district) and the Seattle Center. Constructed for the 1962 World's Fair, the Monorail offers a thrilling elevated ride that runs about every 15 minutes and takes less than two minutes.

**WASHINGTON STATE FERRIES** (206/464-6400) operates the largest ferry system in the United States and links island and peninsula communities throughout the Puget Sound region. Boats vary from the passenger-only vessel that carries 250 people to the jumbo ferries that carry 2,000 people (and 206 cars). Walking onto a ferry for a round-trip ride is one of the most entertaining and least expensive activities you can find here, and one usually enjoyed by all ages. From downtown Seattle you can catch a ferry to Bremerton (on Kitsap Peninsula), Bainbridge Island, and Vashon Island (passenger only, limited schedule). If you want to take a car to Vashon, you'll need to drive to West Seattle to catch the Fauntleroy ferry.

**WATER TAXI.** During the summer, an 80-passenger water taxi ferries people between Pier 54 and West Seattle's Seacrest Marina. It's a fun ride, ideal for commuters, cyclists, and visitors who'd like to visit Alki Point for some fish and chips or a stroll along the beach. The taxi operates weekdays 7 a.m. to 11 p.m., Saturday 9 a.m. to 11 p.m., and Sunday 9 a.m. to 8 p.m. The cost is $3 one-way, $2 for seniors and children.

## PLACES TO STAY

### CITY CENTER

### CAVANAUGH'S ON FIFTH AVENUE

*1415 5th Ave., 98101*
*206/971-8000, 800/325-4000; www.cavanaughs.com*
*Rates: Moderate to expensive*
*FYI: Restaurant; fitness center; Nintendo*

Cavanaugh's is a good choice for families who want to stay right in the middle of the downtown shopping district without paying for a luxury hotel. If your kids threaten an uprising when they figure out the hotel doesn't have a swimming pool, remind them you chose it because of its proximity to Game Works and F.A.O. Schwartz (one block north).

Need a refueling spot nearby? Try Desert Fire at Pacific Place (see "Places to Eat").

**❝ PARENT COMMENTS**

*"We came to Seattle to see a show at the Fifth Avenue Theater (right across the street from Cavanaugh's) and to shop. Since we spend almost no time in the room, we didn't want to pay for deluxe accommodations, but we wanted to be in the middle of downtown. I told my kids they could add the money we would have spent getting a place with a pool to their shopping budget."*

**COMFORT SUITES-DOWNTOWN**
*601 Roy St., 98109*
*206/282-2600, 800/228-5150*
*Rates: Moderate*
*FYI: Complimentary breakfast buffet; refrigerators/microwaves; exercise room; complimentary parking*

Until recently it was impossible to find moderately priced, clean, and comfortable accommodations close to downtown Seattle. Within a year, two such places will have opened near the Seattle Center. (The second is the Hampton Inn, reviewed below.) Comfort Suites opened after this book went to press, but it promises to be very similar to the Hampton Inn—no frills, but comfortable and well situated at the base of Queen Anne hill, with easy access to most Seattle attractions. Two-room deluxe suites are available.

Recommended places to eat nearby include the Thai Restaurant (see "Places to Eat").

**COURTYARD BY MARRIOTT/LAKE UNION**
*925 Westlake Ave. N., 98109*
*206/213-0100, 800/321-2211; www.courtyard.com*
*Rates: Moderate to expensive*
*FYI: Restaurant; refrigerators; indoor pool, exercise room; baby-sitting; shuttle to attractions, shopping*

**RESIDENCE INN BY MARRIOTT/LAKE UNION**
*800 Fairview Ave. N., 98109*
*206/624-6000, 800/331-3131; www.residenceinn.com*
*Rates: Moderate to expensive*
*FYI: Complimentary continental breakfast, dinner delivery from*

*local restaurants, kitchens; indoor pool, exercise room; laundry; pets OK (fee); baby-sitting; shuttle to attractions, shopping*

It's good news for families that over the last five years two family-friendly Marriotts have sprung up around the south end of Lake Union. The newest, the Courtyard Marriott, is situated at the southwest end of the lake and is a close relative of the Marriott Residence Inn, located less than a mile away at the southeast margin of the lake.

Both hotels are situated across busy streets from the water, but the views are nice and the neighborhoods are more scenic and relaxed than downtown. To get you where you want to go, all three provide free shuttle service, so in five minutes you can be at the Seattle Center, the waterfront, Pike Place Market, or the downtown shopping district. Access to I-5 is also right outside the door. If you want just a room with two beds and value a restaurant on the premises, the Courtyard will do the job. On the other hand, if you prefer (and are willing to pay the extra dollars) to stay in a more spacious two-room suite with a kitchen and free breakfast, head over to the Residence Inn. The Inn is geared to the business traveler who has to stay awhile, but works exceptionally well for families. The rooms are spacious and kitchens are fully equipped. The free continental buffet breakfast includes lots of choices for picky eaters. Both hotels have indoor pools but the pooch is welcome only at the Residence Inn.

Recommended places to eat nearby: Cucina! Cucina! (see "Places to Eat").

### HOTEL EDGEWATER
*Pier 67, 2411 Alaskan Way, 98121*
*206/728-7000*
*Rates: Expensive*
*FYI: Restaurant; exercise room*

The Edgewater's location can't be beat. It's right on the water and within easy walking distance of the Seattle Aquarium, ferry terminals, Bell Street Pier (Pier 66), Victoria Clipper terminal, and Pike Place Market.

The Northwest décor is comfy, but not too fragile. The only down side, and it's a big one, is the high rates you pay for the location. At these prices you should have a swimming pool on the premises, but instead (for a small fee) you can use the Seattle Club. It is an excellent facility for families, but it's located a ten-minute walk uphill, near the Pike Place Market.

**❝ PARENT COMMENTS**

*"Our kids loved sitting in our waterside room and watching the constant boat traffic. One day we walked onto the Bainbridge ferry and had breakfast at the Streamliner Diner in Winslow. Delicious breakfast and the ferry ride was great, inexpensive fun for our three year old. He could run around on the outside decks and be as noisy as he wanted, while we enjoyed the ride and the fabulous views."*

## FOUR SEASONS OLYMPIC
*411 University St., 98101*
*206/621-1700*
*Rates: Expensive*
*FYI: Restaurants; indoor pool, exercise room; baby-sitting; strollers, toys; pets OK*

If you want to go first-class in the heart of downtown Seattle, rest assured your family will be well cared for at the grand old Olympic. When you make a reservation, tell them the ages of your children; they'll have suitable toys waiting when you arrive. Whatever child-related paraphernalia you need—bibs, strollers, playpens, car seats, kids' videos, even Nintendo—will be provided. The children receive a fun gift when they arrive, and cookies and milk at check-out. Even the family pet is welcome!

The pool and large Jacuzzi are as lovely as you'll find in a hotel and the dressing rooms are wonderful for small kids—warm and comfy with an endless supply of big, soft towels. The food and service at the three restaurants are also four-star and they all have a children's menu. The Garden Court, an enormous, skylighted room with massive potted plants, serves an elegant High Tea and a special Children's Tea.

**❝ PARENT COMMENTS**

*"We live in Seattle, but we have taken several "vacations" at the Four Seasons. We catch a bus downtown with our three children and check in for a night of relaxation and indulgence."*

*"Amazing! A four-star hotel that treats children as well as they treat adults!"*

## HAMPTON INN
*700 5th Ave. N., 98109*
*206/282-7700*
*Rates: Moderate*
*FYI: Free breakfast buffet, refrigerators; fireplaces (some rooms);*

*fitness center; baby-sitting; free parking*

Newly constructed in the Queen Anne area, this attractive and moderately priced motel gives families who want to avoid paying top rates a comfortable place to stay within easy walking distance of the Seattle Center and a monorail ride from downtown. Jacuzzi and deluxe two-room suites with fireplaces are available.

### HOMEWOOD SUITES HOTEL

*206 Western Ave. W., 98119*
*206/281-9393*
*Rates: Moderate to expensive*
*FYI: Complimentary breakfast; full kitchens; exercise room; laundry, pets OK ($20 fee); free transportation in the downtown area; free grocery-shopping service*

The location of the Homewood Suites is a little strange—neither downtown nor on the waterfront, but the free shuttle service takes visitors to main attractions and shopping areas. It's about five blocks from the Seattle Center, and five blocks to the north end of the waterfront (lovely Myrtle Edwards Park).

Other than that, this hotel offers families an excellent place to settle in and explore the Greater Seattle area. Everything here feels spacious, from the lobby to the rooms, and if you have energetic kids you'll appreciate the extra space. The tiny store shows they have families in mind—the limited stock includes frozen kid meals, canned noodle soup and spaghetti, baby food, and diapers.

If you have kids under the age of six, don't miss the Cotton Caboodle Factory Outlet store (203 W. Thomas, open 10 a.m.-5 p.m., Tues.-Fri.) offering great deals on adorable, all-cotton, brightly colored clothing for infants through early school-age.

Recommended restaurants nearby: The Old Spaghetti Factory (see "Places to Eat").

**66 PARENT COMMENTS**

*"The view in our spacious suite was fantastic, far better than anything we would have found in a downtown hotel. We had plenty of room to relax and with full place settings and an eating area, so we ordered take-out from Culinary Couriers (443-TO GO) a delivery service connected to many area restaurants."*

### INN AT HARBOR STEPS

*1221 1st Ave., 98101*
*888/728-8910; www.foursisters.com/innat.html*
*Rates: Expensive*

FYI: *Free breakfast, afternoon tea, hors d'oeuvres, refrigerators; fireplaces; access to pool, exercise facility*

The Inn is located on the bottom floor of the Harbor Steps Apartments, an impressive downtown high-rise with lots of glass and terraced gardens. It's a central location for exploring downtown attractions, and a nice place for families who prefer quiet and privacy in beautiful surroundings. It's just a short walk down the Harbor Steps (about 100 steps, depending on which route you take) to the waterfront attractions. Just across the street, Hammering Man pounds away in front of the Seattle Art Museum, and Pike Place Market is a few blocks north. If you're up to a challenging walk, head steeply uphill to enjoy shopping and entertainment activities.

Rooms are suite-sized, with separate sitting areas. They're classy but comfortable—no antiques to break. Toddlers or preschoolers will need to be watched around the balcony and its full-length door, which opens both vertically and horizontally.

Using the pool is only slightly inconvenient—guests are issued a special pass to enter the apartment building where the fitness center, pool, and Jacuzzi are located.

The afternoon tea in the library includes hors d'oeuvres and desserts, and the hotel's lobby has a stash of tasty chocolate chip cookies. The gourmet breakfast is served buffet style and includes items such as freshly made quiche.

Recommended restaurants nearby: Anthony's Homeport, Chef Wang (see "Places to Eat").

**❝ PARENT COMMENTS**

*"Beware the strategically placed teddy bear on the bed! The hotel's signature bear has a hefty $60 price tag so you may want to hide it or explain immediately to Junior that it lives there and will stay behind when you go."*

*"While I have never stayed at the Four Seasons Olympic, I have been in the rooms and found the Inn at the Harbor's rooms more impressive, both in size and comfort. And, there's the lovely view. The pool here isn't great and you don't get the elegant and extraordinary service, but for the price Harbor Steps is really impressive!"*

*"The complimentary breakfast was delicious and a money-saver. The chef was on hand in the adjacent kitchen and even offered to make something special for my picky eater."*

### PACIFIC COAST SUITES
*Multiple locations*
*800/962-6620*

As any parent who has been in a hotel room knows, it's easy to feel cramped in the company of kids. Renting a condo rather than staying in a hotel will typically give you more space and the convenience of your own kitchen. Pacific Coast Suites has 20 properties in Greater Seattle (and a three-night minimum stay). The staff is very helpful about recommending a location that suits your particular needs. All have kitchen facilities; many have pools, VCRs, and other conveniences. Even if you want to give yourself a vacation and eat dinner out, you can save money and stress by eating lunch and breakfast in your condo.

### RAMADA INN SEATTLE AT NORTHGATE
*2140 N. Northgate Way, 98133*
*206/365-0700, 206/272-6232; www.ramadainnseattle.com*
*Rates: Moderate*
*FYI: Complimentary continental breakfast; outdoor swimming pool, exercise facility; laundry; shuttle to downtown*

If you are looking for a basic motel close in, the Ramada is a good choice. A $2 million renovation in 1996 spruced things up and the location, right off I-5 and less than five miles from the heart of downtown, is very convenient. The courtesy shuttle service will take you to points of interest and downtown, a great way to spare yourself hassle and save some parking change.

For a quick meal close by, try Seattle Crab Co. (see "Places to Eat").

### 66 PARENT COMMENTS
*"We don't like to blow the vacation budget on the hotel room, so the Ramada suits our family perfectly. In the summer the outdoor pool is a great way to end a long day of sightseeing, and the new Food Court at the Northgate Mall is a perfect way to feed the troops. (It has an unusually good assortment of fast food and we all find something we enjoy."*

### SUMMERFIELD SUITES (FORMERLY PARK PLAZA SUITES)
*1011 Pike St., 98101*
*206/682-8282, 800/833-4353; www.plazaparksuites.com*
*Rates: Expensive*
*FYI: Complimentary continental breakfast, kitchens; outdoor pool, exercise facility; fireplaces and Jacuzzis (some rooms); pets OK; exercise facility; free van service in downtown area*

Located just east of the Convention & Trade Center, this is a good choice if you want a spacious room close to the downtown shopping and business core. The one-bedroom suites have living room with a sleeper sofa, comfortable bedroom with a second TV, and fully equipped kitchen. Some have fireplaces and Jacuzzis. While clearly aimed at the business traveler, the comforts of home at the Plaza Park are nice for traveling families as well.

66 **PARENT COMMENTS**

*"The family stayed here while on a business trip with my spouse. It was expensive, but we saved by eating meals in our room and getting around via public transportation It worked fine for us!"*

### SHERATON SEATTLE HOTEL & TOWERS

*1400 6th Ave., 98101*
*206/621-9000, 800/325-3535*
*Rates: Moderate to expensive*
*FYI: Restaurants; indoor swimming pool, fitness center*

You know what they say: location, location, location. The Sheraton is right in the center of things, including Gameworks, Planet Hollywood, F.A.O. Schwartz, and a huge, 16-screen movie theater.

However, this spot fills the vast majority of its rooms with business conventions. They don't claim to cater to parents traveling with kids, though they do have a good room-service children's menu and a nice pool.

If hunger strikes, consider Desert Fire at Pacific Place (see "Places to Eat").

66 **PARENT COMMENTS**

*"I took two preschoolers and two teens for a night out at a downtown hotel (we live ten minutes away). Even though kids don't seem to be frequent customers, the staff went out of their way to be helpful and friendly. There is no convenient place to buy snack food in the area, so bring your own unless you want to spend a fortune at the mini-bar."*

### SILVER CLOUD INNS

*206/526-5200; 5036 25th Ave. NE, Seattle 98015*
*425/775-7600; 19332 36th Ave. W, Lynnwood, 98036*
*425/637-7000; 10621 NE 12th Bellevue 98004*
*206/447-9500; 1150 Fairview Ave. N, Seattle*

*And other locations*

*Rates: Moderate*

*FYI: Free continental breakfast, kitchens (most units); swimming pool (most locations), fitness centers; laundry*

Silver Cloud Inns are well suited to families. All locations except Redmond have an indoor or outdoor swimming pool (the Lake Union location has both). All have refrigerators in the rooms, and most have the option of either a kitchenette (microwave, wet bar, refrigerator) or a full kitchen. Best of all, they are moderately priced.

The Silver Cloud near the University Village Shopping Mall and the main campus of the University of Washington is an excellent location if you are traveling by car. It's right next to the outstanding Burke-Gilman trail, a 10-minute drive from downtown and Woodland Park Zoo.

The Silver Cloud at the southern end of Lake Union is the newest in the region and an excellent choice for families who want to be close to downtown and I-5. The indoor and outdoor swimming pools are both attractive, and the spacious communal breakfast area has a fabulous view of Lake Union.

**❝❝ PARENT COMMENTS**

*"The new Silver Cloud on Lake Union is the best hotel in Seattle for parents traveling with their kids. It is well situated, and the rooms are comfortable and attractive (ask for a view of Lake Union). The indoor pool has natural light and the outdoor pool has a gorgeous view."*

*"We save the big hotel splurges for when we travel without the youngsters. Silver Cloud is our favorite in-city hotel for families."*

**THE WESTIN HOTEL**

*1900 5th Ave., 98101*

*206/728-1000, 800/WESTIN-1*

*Rates: Expensive*

*FYI: Restaurants, refrigerators; indoor pool, exercise room; pets OK; Westin Kids' Club*

Like many other hotel chains, the Westin recognizes that catering to families is good business. Since 1994 they have offered the Westin Kids' Club to make your stay with kids hassle-free. An in-room Sony Playstation, children's movies, strollers, stepstools, and potty seats are yours for the asking. The newest addition to the program is the Story Line. Dial K-I-D-S and hear pre-recorded children's stories. Upon arrival, children receive a laundry bag with special pricing and parents get family activity information and a safety kit.

Recommended restaurants in the area: Desert Fire, Chef Wang (see "Places to Eat").

**❝❝ PARENT COMMENTS**

*"The staff was very good about providing the little touches that make it easier to travel with a baby."*

### TO THE NORTH
#### EDMONDS HARBOR INN

*130 W. Dayton, Edmonds 98020*
*425/771-5021, 800/441-8033;*
*www.NWCountryInns.com/Harbor*
*Rates: Inexpensive to moderate*
*FYI: Complimentary continental breakfast, kitchenettes; access to health club ($10/family)*

Edmonds is a pretty little town that sits right on Puget Sound. By staying in this peaceful, waterside suburb, you will pay very reasonable rates and have access to beach walks and ferry rides (the Kingston Ferry terminal is nearby), with all the big-city fun just 20 minutes away. The rooms are spacious, clean, and comfortable, and the health club next door has an indoor pool.

Recommended restaurants nearby: brusseau's (see "Places to Eat").

**❝❝ PARENT COMMENTS**

*"I had a great holiday with my two preschoolers when we took the Amtrak train from Seattle to Edmonds and stayed at this lovely little hotel. We combed the beach, browsed in the little shops in town, and enjoyed the swimming pool at the club next door. Even though we were only a half hour from home, it felt like a big break from the daily routine."*

#### RESIDENCE INN BY MARRIOTT SEATTLE-NORTH

*18200 Alderwood Mall Pkwy. Lynnwood 98037*
*425/771-1100, 800/331-3131*
*Rates: Moderate to expensive*
*FYI: Free continental breakfast buffet, kitchens; outdoor pool (seasonal); pets OK (deposit and fee)*

The hotel is located next to Alderwood Mall, about 20 minutes north of downtown Seattle. Rooms are spacious and comfortable, with full kitchens. You may choose a studio with a queen bed and hide-a-bed, a one-bedroom unit, or a two-bedroom/two-bath suite. The breakfast buffet is served in the lobby, and can be eaten there or taken back to the room.

Recommended restaurants nearby: Anthony's Homeport, Azteca, and Red Robin (see "Places to Eat").

## EAST OF LAKE WASHINGTON
### BEST WESTERN BELLEVUE INN
*11211 Main St., Bellevue 98004*
*425/455-5240, 800/421-8193; www.bestwestern.com*
*Rates: Moderate*
*FYI: Restaurant; outdoor swimming pool*

Nothing fancy here, which is why this is a good bet for families staying in Bellevue. The two-story, clean, and comfortable motel is arranged around a lawn and outdoor heated pool. The location—just off Highway 405 on "Hotel Row"—provides easy access to the freeway and across the bridge to Seattle.

**66 PARENT COMMENTS**

*"We spent one day in Seattle at the Pike Place Market and one day school-shopping on the Eastside (be aware that the sales tax is slightly higher in Bellevue than in Seattle). The kids loved cooling off in the pool at the end of the day."*

### EMBASSY SUITES
*3225 158th Ave. SE, Bellevue 98008*
*425/644-2500*
*Rates: Expensive*
*FYI: Complimentary breakfast buffet; refrigerators/microwaves; indoor swimming pool, fitness center; pets OK*

If you want a place to stay that's near I-90 or Bellevue Community College, this is a good choice. The two-room suites are especially comfortable for families, and the complimentary "cook-to-order" breakfast buffet includes a number of kid favorites.

**66 PARENT COMMENTS**

*"We liked the location because we wanted to spend some time in Seattle and some time hiking at Snoqualmie. The indoor swimming pool area was very pleasant for sitting and watching kids swim."*

### LA RESIDENCE SUITE HOTEL
*475 100th Ave. NE, Bellevue 98004*
*425/455-1475, 800/800-1993; www.laresidencehotel.com*

*Rates: Moderate*
*FYI: Kitchens; laundry; dogs OK (fee)*

The rooms here have complete kitchens (including oven and dishwasher) and separate bedrooms, so they work well for families who can use some extra space and don't want to eat every meal out. The location—across the street from Bellevue Square, one of the best shopping centers in the region—offers easy entertainment and several reasonably priced eating options. Downtown Seattle is an easy 15-minute drive away.

**66 PARENT COMMENTS**

*"The rooms are spacious and worked well for our family of two adults and two kids, 11 and 14. The kids were in heaven because we let them go wander Bellevue Square alone while we stayed at the hotel and read."*

**COURTYARD BY MARRIOTT**
*14615 NE 29th Pl., Bellevue 98007*
*425/869-5300, 800/321-2211*
*Rates: Moderate*
*FYI: Restaurant, refrigerators; indoor pool*

**RESIDENCE INN BY MARRIOTT-BELLEVUE**
*14455 NE 29th Place, Bellevue 98007*
*425/882-1222, 800/331-3131*
*Rates: Expensive*
*FYI: Complimentary continental breakfast buffet; kitchens; fireplaces; outdoor pool; sport court, access to three nearby health clubs; pets OK (fee); grocery service*

Located just off Highway 520 in east Bellevue, the Residence Inn and Courtyard are next-door neighbors and both offer families excellent accommodations. At the Residence Inn, suites are clustered about the quiet grounds, and the outdoor pool and sport court guarantee kids will find fun. The buffet breakfast is excellent, and the fully equipped kitchens with comfortable eating space allow you to cook in your suite if you choose.

The Courtyard has basic hotel rooms but also offers an indoor pool and a restaurant (breakfast and dinner). Rates are easier on your wallet than those at the Residence Inn. However, Fido is welcome at the Residence Inn and not at the Courtyard.

Recommended restaurants nearby: Anthony's Homeport, Cucina! Cucina! (see "Places to Eat").

**RESIDENCE INN BY MARRIOT-REDMOND**
*7575 164th Ave. N.E., Redmond 98052*
*425/497-9226*
*Rates: Expensive*
*FYI: Complimentary continental breakfast; kitchens; outdoor pool,
fitness center; shuttle service; pets OK*

The Residence Inns are always a good choice for families. Located right in the Redmond Town Center, this new inn is close to shops (check out Zany Brainy) and family-friendly restaurants. Studios and two-bedrooms suites are available, and both offer kitchens, dining space, and separate sitting areas.

Recommended restaurants in the area: Cucina! Cucina! and Desert Fire (see "Places to Eat").

See Also: Silver Cloud Inns, under "Places to Stay: City Center."

## PLACES TO EAT

**THE 5 SPOT**
*1502 Queen Anne Ave. N.*
*206/285-7768*
*Hours: Breakfast, lunch, dinner daily*

This cheery eatery, perched at the summit of Queen Anne Hill, welcomes children and adults in equal proportion. The 5 Spot, a relative of Coastal Kitchen on Capitol Hill, Jitterbug in Wallingford, and the new Atlas in the University Village, features a permanent menu of eclectic dishes and a rotating menu based on a culinary theme (also reflected in the décor). When the theme was "Baja Border Grill," for example, an array of dishes from that region of Mexico was offered; decorations included piñatas hung from the ceilings and walls festooned with chili-pepper lights.

The children's menu offers the usual finicky-eater standbys: a foot-long hot dog, peanut-butter sandwich, fish and chips, charcoal-broiled chicken breast, and quesadillas. The fresh lemonade arrives in frosty mason jars. For dessert, a parade of ice cream treats is offered, along with other goodies. For adults, the permanent menu features entrées from five U.S. regions. Small and entrée-size salads are available, as well as a respectable variety of vegetarian entrées.

The 5 Spot's child-friendliness extends to the restrooms. Both men's and women's feature baby-changing tables. After your meal, walk off some calories in the inviting urban neighborhood. Stroll along Queen Anne Avenue, past the bistros, bakeries, and bookstores, or stop at the playground on 1st Avenue West at Blaine.

### ANTHONY'S BELL STREET DINER/ANTHONY'S FISH BAR
*Pier 66, 2201 Alaskan Way (downtown, on the waterfront)*
*206/448-6688*
*Hours: Lunch, dinner daily*

Located at the newly renovated Bell Street Pier (Pier 66), this place is three restaurants in one, all run by Seattle's leading seafood restaurant chain. Anthony's Pier 66 serves dinner only and has excellent food, but you'll pay for the beautiful view. The first-floor café (Bell Street Diner) or the sidewalk fish bar, with indoor or outdoor seating, are the best choices if you're dining with young kids.

At the diner, seafood dishes are simple and well prepared. You'll also find fish tacos, pastas, clam chowder, burgers, and salads. If you have room, try Anthony's Northwest classic dessert, a warm cobbler of tart native blackberries.

The menu at the sidewalk fish bar is more limited, but each option is outstanding. You'll find fish and chips and fish tacos (made with blackened rockfish or char-grilled mahi mahi), Caesar salad with shrimp, and red or white clam chowder. Don't overlook a chocolate-chip cookie to finish off the meal.

### ATHENIAN INN
*1517 Pike St. (at Pike Place Market)*
*206/624-7166*
*Hours: Breakfast, lunch, early dinner (until 6 p.m.) Mon.-Sat.;*
*closed Sun.*

This Seattle institution, tucked away at the western end of Pike Place Market, is an increasingly rare find—great view, friendly service, tasty home cooking, and low prices. Exploring the Market is stimulating and exhausting for young kids; as tempting as it is to grab a quick snack, you might be wise to sit down for a real meal. With hundreds of items on the vast and varied menu, chances are good that even finicky eaters will find something of interest at the Athenian. If it's not too crowded, ask to sit upstairs at a window table and enjoy the spectacular view of Elliott Bay.

### AZTECA
*5025-25th NE, near University Village, Seattle*
*206/5242987*

150-112th NE, Bellevue
425/453-9087
*And other locations.*
*Hours: Lunch, dinner daily*

Azteca serves plentiful, filling Mexican food quickly and at reasonable prices. Children are made to feel welcome by the gracious attitude of the staff, an excellent children's menu, crayons, and balloons. The prices are good every day. Sundays are an even better deal for families; a child's meal is only 95 cents! Though the quality of the food can be uneven from an adult perspective, it's generally well liked by the young ones.

## BILLY McHALE'S

4065 128th SE, Bellevue
425/746-1138
1800 S. 320th, Federal Way
253/927-4450
*And other locations.*
*Hours: Lunch, dinner daily*

The big hit at this restaurant is the miniature train running on a track just below the ceiling. Many a preschooler has been entertained by watching it chug circles around the dining area. Some restaurants also have play areas set off from the waiting area so parents don't have to strain to amuse kids before and after they're seated. Kids' meals are a little pricier, but they are served with French fries, carrot sticks, applesauce, and a packet of cookies. Drinks cost extra. On Sundays, any kids' entrée is half price for those 12 and under. There are free refills on pop and "bottomless" fries.

## CARMELITA

7314 Greenwood Ave. (near Woodland Park Zoo)
206/706-7703
*Hours: Dinner Tues.-Sun.; closed Mon. Reservations recommended.*

Taking a kid to a vegetarian restaurant is a little like giving a cat a bath—they sense trouble coming and plot their escape as you approach the place. But if you prefer to go meatless, you owe yourself a meal at this bright star in the Greenwood area. (Even if you're a proud carnivore, eating here is a treat.)

Luckily for families, this place has a super kids' menu, with noodles and cheese, cheese pizza, and other goodies (just don't mention the ravioli is made of squash).

The menu is Mediterranean-Mexican, but that description

doesn't do justice to the marvelous marriage of ingredients here. Try a bowl of Mediterranean Mélange, an exotic relative of minestrone soup, or the Poblano Relleno, mildly spicy chilés stuffed with potatoes, onions, olives, and fresh mozzarella.

### CHEF WANG

*2230 1st Ave. (north of Pike Place Market)*
*206/448-5407*
*Hours: Lunch Mon.-Fri.; dinner daily*

Don't be put off by the hip, Belltown location of this spot. It's true that Chef Wang (pronounced "Wong") has opened a sleek and attractive restaurant, with wooden booths, live jazz weekends, and counter seating that faces an open kitchen. Nevertheless, Chef Wang is kid-friendly, and the food is excellent.

Here you will find the usual assortment of dishes. (Our parent reviewers liked everything they tried, but especially recommend the General's Chicken.) One featured menu item that might be ideal for a finicky child is the chef's classic dinner: mix and match from a list of meat, shrimp, chicken, veggies, and sauce.

### CHANG'S MONGOLIAN GRILL

*1827 Broadway (Capitol Hill)*
*206/325-6160*
*Hours: Lunch, dinner daily*

This place has a gimmick and, like most restaurants with a gimmick, it is successful in entertaining the kids. (The food is only so-so, and parents might not otherwise choose to eat here.) Diners at Chang's fill their bowls from a long buffet: pieces of beef, chicken, fish, and shrimp; noodles; and vegetables. They then top their selections with a number of flavorings, such as garlic and soy sauce. The cooks empty each bowl onto a large, round grill, and kids love to watch their dinners being fried. (Meat juices often spark a blaze, which is always an attention-getter.)

Chang's is a good place to get children to eat their vegetables, as they'll likely think even carrots taste good after they watch chefs stir-fry their mixture. Servers bring rice to accompany the meal, or rice pancakes that can be filled and rolled. Meals include soup and a dish of ice cream.

### CHINOOK'S AT SALMON BAY

*1900 W. Nickerson St. (Fisherman's Terminal, in Ballard)*
*206/283-4665*

*Hours: Lunch, dinner daily; breakfast Sat.-Sun.*

Chinook's is a good place to observe a working marina and eat well-prepared seafood without emptying your wallet. As part of the Anthony's Homeport restaurant empire, Chinook's success rests on the same formula of high-quality seafood at moderate prices. Kids will find plenty to see through the large windows that enclose this attractive, bustling restaurant at Fishermen's Terminal, about 10 minutes by car from downtown. Choose from more than 125 items on the dinner menu, as well as fresh daily specials. There's also a decent children's menu.

There may be a short wait for breakfast on the weekends, but once you are seated, a basket of scrumptious fresh-baked scones with orange butter will arrive at your table. If you want to work off your meal afterwards, drive a few blocks west to Discovery Park, the largest park in the city (see "What to See & Do: Parks").

### COASTAL KITCHEN
*429 15th Ave. E. (Capitol Hill)*
*206/322-1145*
*Hours: Breakfast, lunch, dinner daily*

Coastal Kitchen is a cheerful and lively mix of delicious food served swiftly in colorful and fun surroundings. There's a regular menu and a separate regional menu that changes quarterly (Provençal, Indonesian, or Spanish, for example), locally created art that reflects the regional theme, even foreign-language tapes playing in the restrooms. But the fun never overshadows the seriously good food. Best of all, the quality has rubbed off on the kids' menu—you'll be fighting the kids for bites of their macaroni and cheese! Also recommended: Atlas Cafe in the University Village. Same excellent food and family-friendly scene.

### CUCINA! CUCINA!
*901 Fairview (south end of Lake Union)*
*206/447-2782*
*800 Bellevue Way, Bellevue*
*425/637-1177*
*Southcenter Pkwy., Tukwila*
*206/575-0520*
*Hours: Lunch, dinner daily*

At Cucina! Cucina! you'll find good Italian food at moderate prices and a lively staff that will show you and your kids a good time. It's an excellent choice if you want to take the kids out for a special meal that they will actually eat. The restaurant on Lake Union in Seattle is located near several motels and overlooks a pretty little marina. It's fun to poke along the docks after your meal.

If there's a wait, the hostess will give you a pager so you can explore the waterfront while your table is made ready. Then your kids are offered balloons and crayons (the tables are covered with white butcher paper, so kids can scribble without worrying about staying in the lines). You can even request a ball of raw pizza dough, which kids can shape and play with while they wait.

The children's menu offers individual pizzas and a good selection of pasta dishes, such as buttered pasta and spaghetti with meatballs. But be forewarned, a basket of bread will cost you several bucks. (Complimentary bread is sorely missed when you are a parent with a kid on the verge of a breakdown, and a surprising oversight for a restaurant that caters to families.)

For quicker and less expensive versions of the same, check out Cucina Presto.

### CUCINA PRESTO
*10002 Aurora Ave. N.*
*206/524-5110*
*7807 SE 27th, Mercer Island*
*206/236-6888*
*And other locations.*
*Hours: Lunch, dinner daily*

An offshoot of the highly successful Cucina!Cucina! chain, Cucina Presto has proven to be especially popular with families. Many of the same wood-fired pizzas, specialty pastas, and salads are on the menu, but the prices are lower, the service is (usually) faster, and the atmosphere is more casual. Kids' meals, such as mini pizzas, are a real bargain. Pasta lovers can "mix and match" from a selection of pastas and sauces.

Hand-tossed pizzas, featuring adult-oriented ingredients such as goat cheese, artichokes, pesto, and pine nuts, are reasonably priced. If you're watching your fat intake, pizzas can be ordered with low-fat mozzarella or no cheese at all, and a few of the pastas are also designated as heart-healthy.

### DESERT FIRE CAFÉ
*6th & Pine St. (Pacific Place, downtown)*
*425/895-1500*

*Hours: Lunch, dinner daily*
*Other locations: Redmond Town Center*

This latest Desert Fire (the first opened in 1998 in Redmond Town Center, east of Lake Washington) is on the top floor of elegant new Pacific Place mall, just across from the 11-screen Pacific Place movie theaters. Both restaurant locations are packed with parents who want to enjoy a good meal with their kids.

The décor is rustic (that is to say, forgiving) and the cuisine includes ingredients and spices of the Southwest. Chicken predominates in appetizers, soups, salads, pasta, tacos, and quesadillas. Non-chicken choices include an excellent grilled salmon with chipotle barbecue sauce and a fine pot roast. For dessert, try the tortilla-wrapped banana with caramel and chocolate.

There is often a wait, but once you get on the list you will be given a pager so you are free to wander around the shopping center until your table is ready.

### THE FRANKFURTER

*Seattle Center House*
*206/728-7243*
*1023 Alaskan Way*
*206/622-1748*
*Bellevue Square, Bellevue*
*425/455-4492*
*And other locations.*

You'll find these excellent local landmarks scattered across malls, in the Seattle Center, and at sundry locations around the Seattle area. Serving up a small, but good, assortment of hot dogs and more exotic relatives, along with a salad or two, fresh baked cookies, and its signature freshly squeezed lemonade, the Frankfurter is a great choice for a quick meal when time and money are short. Kids' dogs are offered, along with the traditional Old Fashioneds, Italian hots, and kielbasa. A couple of recent, and delicious, yuppie additions, such as a dog made of chicken sausage and sundried tomatoes, offer lower-fat options.

### GREEN VILLAGE

*721 S. King St. (International District)*
*206/624-3634*
*Hours: Lunch, dinner Tues.-Sun; closed Mon.*

At Green Village, your toughest moment will be choosing from the menu of more than 100 items. Don't agonize too much: we haven't found a bad choice yet. The style is mostly

Szechuan, so you will need to determine the level of spiciness acceptable to younger palates. For a tasty thrill, order sizzling rice soup—the server brings a big bowl of broth, vegetables, and shrimp to your table, ceremoniously dumps in hot fried rice, and it does sizzle! All the noodle dishes are wonderful; seafood dishes are exceptional, but pricier. Several round tables, with spinning trays in the middle to accommodate sharing, can comfortably seat a large group.

### IRON HORSE
*311 3rd Ave. S. (near Pioneer Square)*
*206/223-9506*
*Hours: Lunch, dinner daily; stops seating one half-hour before closing*
   We break a few of our own rules by including this restaurant, even rule number one: the food must be good. Go for lunch anyway, because every child deserves to have the experience of getting his or her hamburger delivered by a model train. The fare is standard—salads, burgers, sandwiches—and the service can be slow. But when your little one's face lights up as the train pulls up with the food, you'll be glad you came. Special arrangements can be made for birthday celebrations.

### IVAR'S SALMON HOUSE
*401 Northlake Way NE (northern end of Lake Union)*
*206/632-0767*
*Hours: Lunch Mon.-Fri.; dinner Mon.-Sat.; brunch Sun.*
   With a children's menu that doubles as a colorful Native American mask, friendly servers who go out of their way to make kids feel welcome, and decent food (such as salmon, cornbread, and slaw) at reasonable prices, Ivar's makes a great destination.
   The Salmon House occupies a replica of a longhouse, with magnificent canoes, masks, and photographs decorating the dining area. Cod and salmon are prepared over a smoky alder fire, a process kids will enjoy watching. If you want fish and chips only and the weather is decent, you can order at the fish bar outside and eat on the deck that overlooks the water, with a great view of boat traffic and frequent openings of the University Bridge.

### MEDITERRANEAN KITCHEN
*366 Roy St. (near Seattle Center)*
*206/285-6713*
*103 Bellevue Way NE (Bellevue)*
*425/462-9422*

*Hours: Dinner daily; lunch Mon.-Sat.*

The décor got fancier when the Mediterranean moved to its current location, one block north of the Seattle Center. Luckily, the food is just as marvelous. This friendly, noisy place is a good choice for families staying in the area. The Farmer's Dish, with its many chicken wings marinated in spices for 24 hours, charbroiled, and served in lemon garlic sauce, is alone worth a visit. Kafta kabob, skewered ground beef mixed with spices, and chicken shawarma, marinated strips of chicken or beef grilled with red cabbage, onions, and tahini sauce, are also highly recommended. Most kids like this kind of food, but the plainest, safest choice for a kid who's hesitant is the shish tawook, a skewer of marinated, charbroiled chicken.

There is a second location in Bellevue with the same good food and family-friendly service.

### THE OLD SPAGHETTI FACTORY

*2801 Elliott Ave. (near the Waterfront)*
*206/624-3634*
*Hours: Lunch, dinner daily*

The first clue that this place is good for families is its name: "factory" is not a word usually associated with elegant dining. Even so, the Old Spaghetti Factory has managed to create a festive atmosphere, with Victorian style décor, a beautiful old weighing scale (only kids like to weigh themselves before and after dinner), and a real caboose that sits in the middle of the main dining area. The food is good and very reasonably priced. All dinners include salad, a loaf of sourdough bread, and spumoni ice cream for dessert. A typical kid meal includes spaghetti, applesauce, beverage, dinosaur cookie, and frozen treat. A junior meal, for bigger or hungrier children, costs slightly more and includes spaghetti, salad, bread, beverage, and ice cream. Since you aren't the only parent looking for good food and fast service at great prices in a fun setting, plan to go early (before 5:30 p.m.) if you want to avoid a wait. Reservations are not accepted.

### PAGLIACCI PIZZA

*Seattle Delivery*
*206/726-1717*
*Eastside Delivery*
*425/453-1717*
*And other Seattle locations.*

Thin, chewy crust, covered with a light tomato sauce and a healthy portion of mozzarella cheese, delivered with speed and good humor to an ever-widening area of Seattle—what more can you ask? Pagliacci is the year-after-year winner in the "best delivered food" category in local contests, serving up pizza and salad that can't be beat. Order a basic pizza for the tots, but go for the primo pizzas for the adults—how about asparagus, Walla Walla sweet onions, roasted garlic, sun-dried tomato, and goat cheese?

### PALISADE WATERFRONT RESTAURANT

*2601 W. Marina Pl.*
*206/285-1000*
*Hours: Lunch, dinner daily; brunch Sun.*

Although it's not your typical "family restaurant," Palisade nevertheless offers one meal with great appeal for kids and adults alike: Sunday brunch. Offerings include fresh-squeezed orange juice (mimosas available for the grown-ups), berry muffins, fruit bar, and a buffet that features the brunch's signature item—banana-macadamia nut-sourdough griddlecakes served with pineapple butter and maple-rum syrup.

If the all-you-can-eat offerings aren't enough to fill the kids, try a "wacky waffle" (bearing a striking resemblance to Mickey Mouse, complete with a strawberry nose) or scrambled eggs with cheese and apple sausages.

In addition to tasty food, the Polynesian-theme Palisade has a grand piano above the bar that plays all by itself, ponds filled with live tropical fish, an ice sculpture that tempts little hands (despite parental admonitions), and views of boats in the marina and the city skyline beyond.

### PASTA YA GOTCHA

*823 3rd Seattle*
*206/223-4788*
*11025 NE 8th, Bellevue*
*425/637-7019*
*And other locations.*
*Lunch, dinner daily (lunch only, downtown)*

Pasta Ya Gotcha's quick service (under three minutes), casual dining atmosphere (food is served on paper plates, even if you're eating in), and goofy name might lead you to expect uninspired dishes. However, you'll actually find a pleasant balance between standards (spaghetti with red sauce) and more unusual offerings such as BBQ pasta, Thai peanut noodles, and Caesar salad linguini. Kids' meals are inexpensive, and include spaghetti with red sauce or circle noodles with Alfredo sauce or butter and cheese.

### RAY'S BOATHOUSE RESTAURANT AND CAFÉ
*6049 Seaview N.W.*
*206/789-3770*
*Hours: Lunch, dinner daily*

Ray's Boathouse is arguably the most popular place in town to take an out-of-town visitor for a good view and great seafood. Sitting on the shore of Shilshole Bay, beyond the Ballard Locks, Ray's offers a lovely view across Puget Sound to the Olympic Mountains.

As with any upscale restaurant, the pleasure of the setting is destroyed by having to keep the kids under control. So unless your children are exceptional, or old enough to be civilized, save yourself stress by eating upstairs in the café. The menu is similar to downstairs, though less expensive, and the atmosphere is more relaxed. Combine your meal with a trip to the Ballard Locks (see "What to See & Do: Parks") for a great Seattle outing with kids.

### RED MILL BURGERS
*312 N. 67th St. (Phinney Ridge)*
*206/783-6362*
*1613 W. Dravus St. (Magnolia)*
*206/284-6363*
*Hours: Lunch, dinner Tues.-Sun.*

As school kids, Babe and John Shepherd often hung out at the Red Mill, a diner-style restaurant on Capitol Hill. Now, many years later, the brother-and-sister team have opened two Red Mill Burger diners, in Phinney Ridge and Magnolia. This is not a fast-food joint, but the wait is worth it—as you'll find out when you sink your teeth into a burger that reminds you just how good a burger can be.

After some initial grumbling about the lack of a toy prize, the four-year-old eating with our parent reviewer took a few bites and yelled, "This is the best burger I've ever had!"

### RED ROBIN
*1100 4th Ave. Seattle*
*206/447-1909*
*138 Northgate Plaza, at Northgate Mall*
*206/365-0933*

*11021 NE 8th, Bellevue*
*phone number*
*And other locations.*
*Lunch, dinner daily; breakfast Sun. (some locations)*

You'll find "mocktails" (sweet fruit and ice cream drinks) for the kids, more than a dozen burger selections, and a wide assortment of tasty salads at Red Robin. The food is good and the place caters to the needs of kids. Locations are handy for visiting families, especially downtown Seattle, the waterfront, and several shopping malls.

### ROY'S RESTAURANT

*1900 5th Ave., in the Westin Hotel*
*206/256-7697*
*Hours: Breakfast, lunch, dinner daily*

It is surprisingly difficult to find a meal in downtown Seattle that will satisfy both adults and children without breaking the budget; you'll find it at Roy's. This cheery café, located off the main lobby of the Westin (close to the Monorail station), offers a wide variety of healthy and delicious choices and a kitchen willing to accommodate the picky eater. Crayons are provided, and service is excellent. There is a children's menu, which features delicious and affordable homemade pizzas; if you're lucky, the chef might take you in the back and let your kids ball their own dough! This is a good place to take a child before a night out at the theater.

### SEATTLE CRAB CO.

*1000 NE Northgate Way*
*206/366-9225*
*Hours: Lunch, dinner daily*

This offshoot of Skipper's is a good choice for families in search of something more interesting and wholesome than fast food, yet pleasing to young diners. The décor alone is guaranteed to amuse: crab shells sporting painted faces with dried-seaweed tresses or beards line the walls. There's an interesting picture of the Kalakala, a streamlined, Art Deco ferryboat turned fish processor that's attempting to stage a comeback as a sightseeing attraction in Seattle. Other quirky items decorate the premises, so if you have a wait (weekends are busy), there's plenty to check out before you're seated.

While the emphasis here is on seafood and steak, pasta entrées are also available. Most dishes will pass muster with children; there's also a kids' menu with the expected items. Prices are low to moderate, portions are large, and overall quality is quite good.

### THAI RESTAURANT
*101 John St.*
*206/285-9000*
*Hours: Lunch Mon.-Fri.; dinner Mon.-Sat.; closed Sun.*

There may be as many Thai restaurants as hamburger joints in Seattle, but this one was one of the first and remains one of the best. Located near the Seattle Center, Thai Restaurant serves foods usually acceptable to kids—noodles, rice, chicken, and tofu are the basis of 99 percent of the dishes here. Just be sure to emphasize that you want no (that is, zero) hot spice on the dishes you intend to offer the kids, or you'll spend mealtime putting out the fire in your child's mouth.

### WORLD WRAPPS
*7900 E. Green Lake Dr. N.*
*206/524-9727*
*University Village*
*206/522-7873*
*Westlake Center*
*206/628-6868*
*And other locations.*

You will walk away from the meal with a good conscience, for feeding the family such healthy chow and for paying such reasonable prices. There are rice bowls and tortilla wraps, embellished with all kinds of wonderful fresh ingredients, and kids will find a great selection that caters to their taste for simple food (quesadillas, fruit smoothies, plain rice). The University Village and REI locations have small playgrounds nearby.

### ZOOPA
*Northgate Mall*
*206/440-8136*
*Bellevue Mall, Bellevue*
*425/453-7887*
*Hours: Lunch, dinner daily*

The problem with most buffet-style restaurants is that they sacrifice quality for quantity. (Sure, you can eat your fill, but who would want to?) Zoopa rises above. It offers a full meal, from salad to dessert, focusing on pasta and soups. Besides the huge salad bar, diners can choose among three kinds of pasta sauce, four kinds of soup, several styles of baked potato, and a variety of fresh breads. Kids have all the adult options, plus a special bar just for them, with favorites such as fruit, crackers, and Jell-O. After-dinner treats include low-fat, soft-serve ice cream, toppings, and several tempting desserts.

### TO THE NORTH
#### ALEXA'S CAFÉ
*10115 Main St., Bothell*
*425/483-6275*
*Hours: Breakfast, lunch daily*

If you want to take a little more time to enjoy lunch than it takes for your child to scarf down a sandwich, try this friendly café in downtown Bothell. A giant Barney doll sits near the entrance, and a dollhouse, books, crayons, and a basket full of toys occupy a section of this otherwise grown-up place. A cozy couch invites little ones to curl up and read, and just beyond are tables where parents can enjoy lunch while perusing local artwork and sculptures. All sandwiches are made on inch-thick homemade bread, and the soups are hearty and delicious. (The only drawback is that the kids' sandwiches come on the same bread and are too cumbersome for little mouths without a lot of extra cutting. The result can be a mess.) The desserts, such as fresh pies and brownies, are also wonderful.

#### ANTHONY'S BEACH CAFÉ
*456 Admiral Way, Edmonds*
*425/771-4400*
*Hours: Lunch, dinner daily*

Located in the same building as its more upscale relative, Anthony's Home Port, the café is fairly large, with ample seating outdoors overlooking the Edmonds Marina and the comings and goings of the Edmonds-Kingston ferries. The menu is the same as the Anthony's Fish Bar on the Seattle waterfront: four-star fish tacos, fish and chips, and chowder along with other basic seafood dishes. The atmosphere is more relaxed and the prices less expensive than at the fancier Anthony's restaurants.

Parents will be glad to know the restaurant area is well fenced. While it would be theoretically possible to tumble into the water, it would take a fair bit of effort. The pièce de résistance, from the toddler and preschooler perspective, is the sandbox and digging utensils right outside the restaurant and adjacent to the outdoor tables. This is a fabulous place for a meal with the kids on a warm night, but even on a cool spring night there was a 25-minute wait. Try to get there early.

### BRUSSEAU'S SIDEWALK CAFÉ AND BAKERY
*117 5th Ave. S., Edmonds*
*425/774-4166*
*Hours: 7 a.m.-4 p.m. Mon.-Fri.; 8 a.m.-5 p.m. Sat.-Sun.*

This Edmonds institution offers delicious, wholesome bakery goods, along with quiches, salads, sandwiches, and soups. It's all served cafeteria style, and in warm weather diners can enjoy a meal on the flower-filled patio as well as inside the café. The pace is unhurried and friendly.

### CANYONS
*6003 244th St. SW (Exit 177 off I-5), Mountlake Terrace*
*425/744-1525*
*22010 17th Ave. SE (Exit 26 off I-405, in the Canyon Business Park), Bothell*
*425/485-3288*
*Hours: Lunch, dinner daily*

A toy box filled with playthings, crayons and a children's menu set the kid-friendly tone at this close relative of the Desert Fire restaurant chain out of California. While the décor is decidedly Southwestern, the food selections are diverse. Salads include two that are Asian-inspired, three types of Caesar, and two Tex-Mex. Try the chicken wraps (grilled Caesar, Thai peanut, and sweet-and-sour), smoked ribs, or choose from among several "Southwest Favorites" that include fajitas, burritos, and enchiladas. Our parent reviewer liked the Portabella Quesadilla—marinated portobello mushrooms, provolone and asiago cheese—an "unusual combination" she'd gladly eat again.

Besides the tasty food, reasonable prices, and warm Southwestern ambiance, the service is fast and decidedly friendly toward the younger set.

### KATHY'S COURTYARD CAFÉ
*515 Main St., Edmonds*
*425/778-8701*
*Hours: 10 a.m.-3 p.m. Tues.-Sat.; closed Sun.-Mon.*

This is literally a hole in the wall—from the outside. Inside, there's a charming open-air courtyard patio with a good-sized pond to investigate, invisible from the street. Diners select from a menu of sandwiches, salads, and other light fare. There's a very affordable children's menu, too. This is a good place for a special mother-small daughter luncheon.

## EAST OF LAKE WASHINGTON
### BROWN BAG CAFÉ
*12217 NE 116th, Kirkland*
*425/822-9462*
*8412 164th Ave. NE, Redmond*
*425/861-4099*
*Hours: Breakfast, lunch daily*

This casual restaurant wins rave reviews from parents as a choice for breakfast out with the kids. Omelets stuffed with fresh veggies, toast from "homemade" sourdough bread, and hash browns from thickly cut and grilled potatoes are typical fare. In addition to fresh food, the Brown Bag specializes in big portions. The restaurant's slogan warns, "Not for sissies," which apparently included the mom in our review group, who ate only half her omelet and less than half the enormous serving of hash browns. Her husband, who was greatly cheered by the promise of large portions, took the "sissy" challenge personally and polished off his lunch plus the rest of his wife's.

The breakfast menu offers all kinds of omelets, and French toast (a homemade cinnamon roll split in half and coated in egg batter).

For lunch, options include salads, burgers, and sandwiches. The Cactus Burger features fresh jalapeños, onions, bell peppers, and melted cheddar cheese; the Brown Bag Salad offers mixed salad greens, shredded cheddar, tomato, bacon bits, mushrooms, scallions, black olives, bell pepper, and egg.

Brown Bag offers no special gimmicks to entertain kids—no crayons or balloons—but the atmosphere is casual, the tables are covered with vinyl tablecloths, and the wooden chairs are sturdy.

### THE EATING FACTORY
*10630 NE 8th St., Bellevue*
*425/688-8202*
*Hours: Lunch, dinner daily*

Trust Bellevue to be the place where even smorgasbords are yuppified. The Eating Factory offers a Japanese buffet with all-you-can-eat sushi. And you'd better eat all you take, because the restaurant charges $1 for any leftover pieces of sushi that your eyes thought your stomach could accommodate. Even those who aren't big on raw fish and rice wrapped in seaweed can enjoy noodle, chicken, and seafood dishes; miso soup; tempura; fresh fruit; and a Japanese salad bar. It's a great place to sample different sushis without having to tally the cost up in your head each time you (or your kids) take one. The décor is bright, clean, and colorful. A television playing Japanese music videos makes for a sort of multi-cultural pop experience. Children under 4 feet, 2 inches tall eat for half price; those under 3 feet, 2 inches eat free.

See also, "Seattle: Places to Eat." Many of the restaurants listed there have multiple locations, including Cucina!Cucina!, Desert Fire, Mediterranean Kitchen, and Zoopa.

## WHAT TO SEE & DO

**CITYPASS.** Visitors to Seattle can save 50 percent on some of the city's top attractions with the Seattle CityPass visitor program. This package includes half-price tickets to the Space Needle, Museum of Flight, Woodland Park Zoo, Pacific Science Center, Seattle Art Museum, and Seattle Aquarium. Ticket booklets may be purchased at the main entrance of any of these six participating attractions. For more information, call any of the attractions directly or visit www.citypass.net/seattle.

### STROLL & BROWSE

There are many areas worth exploring with kids in Seattle, but five really stand out: the waterfront, the downtown core, Pioneer Square, Pike Place Market, and Seattle Center. While the areas all adjoin, traveling among them can be tiring, especially given Seattle's famous (and steep) hills! Try to take advantage of the **METRO BUS RIDE FREE ZONE** (206/553-3000). The zone extends north and south from Jackson Street—near Safeco Field on the edge of the International District—to Battery Street at the northern end of downtown. East-west parameters are I-5 to the waterfront. The bus trip through the tunnel in downtown Seattle is an adventure for kids, and the underground stations are full of colorful murals. Inquire about Metro's Family Pass (weekends only).

There are other means of saving little legs and avoiding a meltdown during your Seattle visit. A ride on the **MONORAIL,** elevated above the street level, will thrill the kids and provide convenient transport between downtown and the Seattle Center. The monorail departs downtown's Westlake Mall about every 15 minutes, whisking riders to the Center (home of popular attractions such as the Space Needle, Pacific Science Center, and Seattle Children's Museum).

Old-fashioned **STREETCARS** (206/553-3000) run frequently along the waterfront, from the northern end of Myrtle Edwards Park to Pioneer Square and the International District. It's fun and inexpensive ($1/person; $1.25 during rush hour). The ride may even include entertainment—streetcar drivers have been known to burst into song on occasion! The trolleys meet the bus tunnel at its southern terminus.

**THE DOWNTOWN WATERFRONT** is a helter-skelter mix of magnificent views, schlocky tourist shops, a first-class aquarium, historical landmarks, fountains, and colorful maritime traffic. It is a splendid place to spend a day with the kids.

If you are driving, look for a meter beneath the monstrous Alaskan Way Viaduct that runs parallel to the waterfront. If you want to walk from Pier 50 to the new Pier 66, a reasonable goal if your kids are in strollers or willing walkers, park near the Pike Place Hillclimb, across from the aquarium, and take the southbound trolley to the Washington Street station. You can then stroll back along the water and return to your car. If you are still feeling energetic after touring the waterfront, you can climb steps or take an elevator to the north end of the Pike Place Market and continue your adventure at this colorful spot.

If you are approaching on foot from the downtown core, take the new, park-like Harbor Steps between 1st and Western avenues at University Street. They provide a playful and scenic route down to the waterfront. The eight waterfall fountains and inviting seating areas provide an ideal place to relax and regroup.

Another fun approach is to walk north from Pike Place Market to Lenora Street (about one block). Turn left and walk toward the water and you'll see a walkway leading to an elevator and steps that will take you down to the waterfront. When you reach the waterfront, keep your eye on the kids: the trolley speeds along here, and guardrails next to the water are not childproof.

Pier 50 marks the beginning of Colman Dock, the terminal for ferries to Bremerton (Kitsap Peninsula), Winslow (Bainbridge Island), and Vashon Island (passenger only). Just north of the terminal on Pier 53 sits Fire Station #5, home port for two splendid fireboats, the *Alki* and the *Duwamish*. You might get lucky and see the boats in the bay, testing their hoses by spraying them sky-high.

Further north, at Pier 54, don't miss **YE OLDE CURIOSITY SHOP**. Since 1889, this one-of-a-kind spot has been a Seattle fixture. Look for the fully dressed fleas, two shrunken heads, two real mummies and a navy bean that holds 10 ivory elephants. When stomachs begin to growl, there's good fast food at **IVAR'S FISH AND CHIPS**, **RED ROBIN EXPRESS**, or **THE FRANKFURTER** at Piers 54 and 55.

Tucked inside The Pavilion at Pier 57, you'll find a grand old carousel. It's at the end of the pier, overlooking the water. Next door on Pier 59, **WATERFRONT PARK** offers an unparalleled view of the water and Olympic Mountains. Just north of the park sits the outstanding **SEATTLE AQUARIUM** (see "Animals, Animals").

At Pier 66 (Bell Street Pier), there's a marina, an international conference center, several restaurants, shops, a fun fountain for kids, and **ODYSSEY: THE MARITIME DISCOVERY CENTER** (see "Museums"). If you're lucky, a gigantic cruise ship will be moored at the pier, a sight certain to thrill all ages. For tummy-rumbles, the Pier has three related options, all run by the same folks: **ANTHONY'S**, which offers a classy sit-down dinner; takeout fish and chips at **ANTHONY'S FISH BAR**; or a lunch of clam chowder and sandwiches at **BELL STREET DINER** (see "Places to Eat").

If you continue walking or hop in the car for the short drive, you'll come to the dock from which the Victoria Clipper departs (see "Victoria, B.C.: Getting There") and, last but not least, **MYRTLE EDWARDS PARK**. This excellent little park has paths for biking, rollerblading, walking, and running (about eight miles round-trip), and offers unparalleled views of the Sound and mountains. If the family needs to refuel, **THE OLD SPAGHETTI FACTORY** is nearby (see "Places to Eat").

If walking along the waterfront just isn't enough, you might extend your adventure by hopping on one of the ferries or tour boats that depart from various piers. You can walk aboard the **WINSLOW FERRY** (206/464-6400) at Pier 50 for the half-hour ride to Bainbridge Island, a fine way to view the Seattle skyline and enjoy a ride. Consider taking a morning boat, then walk into the small town of Winslow for a scrumptious breakfast at the **STREAMLINER DINER** (397 Winslow Way E.; 206/842-8595).

Kids and adults alike will enjoy a boat tour offered by **ARGOSY TOURS** (206/623-1445), departing from Piers 55 and 57. The 2 1/2-hour tour aboard *Cruise the Locks* is the most interesting: It includes the Chittenden Locks, Lake Union, and Elliott Bay, as well as an informative and lively narrative.

If you're really up for adventure, try a speedboat ride. **PIER 54 ADVENTURES** (206/623-6364) offers a trip on the bright yellow, turbo-powered *Seattle Rocket*, at speeds up to 40 knots. Available May to September, the boat departs from Pier 54.

**LET'S GO SAILING** (206/624-3931; at Pier 56) offers tours on the 70-foot sloop *Obsession*. Operating May to mid-October, the company runs three one-hour trips around Elliott Bay daily, and a two-hour Sunset Sail, which may include a run to Bainbridge Island. With a 49-passenger maximum, this custom-built ocean racer can accommodate wedding receptions, birthdays, and other celebrations.

Finally, there's the loading dock for the **VICTORIA CLIPPER** (448-5000; at Pier 69), a hydrofoil craft that carries passengers to Victoria, British Columbia. This makes a great day trip for families (children ages eight and older only). See "Victoria, B.C." for details and suggested attractions.

**PIONEER SQUARE.** One block off the waterfront at the southern end of the downtown core, Pioneer Square offers a glimpse of Seattle's rich history, along with a number of first-class galleries and shops. During the summer months, an information booth (Occidental S. & S. Main St.) is open from 10 a.m. to 4 p.m., Monday through Saturday, to provide directions and tips about the area.

Until the late 1880s, Pioneer Square was a thriving business district where most of Seattle's 40,000 residents lived and worked. Then, in June of 1889, a furniture maker left a pot of glue unattended on a hot stove, and the fire that resulted left the young city in ashes. Here's the good news: Your family can still visit what remains of the original Seattle on a 1 1/2-hour **SEATTLE UNDERGROUND TOUR** (206/682-4646). Lively guides are full of historical trivia and corny jokes, but the tour is geared toward adults; kids under 12 may be bored. The tour route is not accessible to wheelchairs or strollers.

More regional history is available in the area. Drop by the **KLONDIKE GOLD RUSH NATIONAL HISTORICAL PARK** (117 Main St.; 206/553-7220). This little museum uses maps, photos, slides, and films to tell the dramatic story of the Alaska Gold Rush and its enormous impact on the City of Seattle.

If a little shopping spree is on the agenda, there are many choices in the area. **THE ELLIOTT BAY BOOK COMPANY** (1st

Ave. S. & S. Main; 206/624-6600) is a favorite bookstore among the locals. It boasts an expansive and outstanding children's section and a two-story castle where kids can relax and read their selections. Downstairs, the café makes a nice stop for lunch or a snack. The **GREAT WINDS KITE SHOP** (402 Occidental S.; 206/624-6886) has a dandy selection for flying or decorating, and **MAGIC MOUSE TOYS** (603 1st Ave.; 206/682-8097) is a top-of-the-line toy store. In addition to the usual gadgets, gizmos, dolls, and balls, they carry an exceptionally good selection of books and art supplies.

For a snack in the Pioneer Square area, try **WALTER'S WAFFLES** (106 James St., a block uphill from Magic Mouse Toys; 206/382-2692). If you want to enjoy your food in a relaxed atmosphere, make your way to the **WATERFALL GARDEN** (2nd Ave. S. & S. Main St.). This tiny enclosed park, with its waterfall and benches, is a soothing island of calm in the midst of urban hustle and bustle.

**PIKE PLACE MARKET**, located at Pike Street and 1st Avenue, doesn't attract the nine million shoppers who flock here each year for its farm-fresh goods alone, although the bountiful produce and wide variety of foods are certainly a major draw. Open continuously since 1907, the market has grown to encompass a wide variety of merchants and wares, plus numerous ethnic groceries and bakeries, restaurants, and novelty shops. It's an ideal place for a family outing, with something to interest everyone.

Parking can be frustrating in the market area, especially on sunny summer days. Whatever you do, don't get stuck driving on Pike Place, the street closest to the market and invariably packed with shoppers and tourists. (Though you may find a parking space, you will surely lose your sanity.) Take a bus to the area or opt for parking in one of the many garages or lots along Western Avenue below the market.

For most kids (and adults), canvassing both the market and the waterfront in one day will be too much. It is possible, though, to visit each briefly, and you can travel between the two via the elevator from the Public Market Parking Garage. Or use the long, steep stairs at the southern end of the market (the Pike Place Hillclimb) to get down to the waterfront.

The market itself is a hodgepodge of stairways and halls, so we recommend you make your first stop the **MARKET INFORMATION BOOTH** (1st Ave. & Pike St.). Open daily, 10 a.m. to 6 p.m., it offers shopping and restaurant brochures, maps, tour information, and discount theater tickets.

The **MAIN ARCADE** is the heart of the market: locate it by listening for the shouts of fishmongers and the wet slap of fish being tossed around. You'll also find rows of meticulously arranged fruits and veggies, handmade children's clothing and toys, dried or seasonal fresh-cut flowers, handcrafted jewelry, and pottery. If that isn't enough of a sensory feast, there is always a variety of musicians, balloon sculptors, puppeteers, and magicians offering entertainment to all who stop to watch. Point out to the kids that each of the 46,500 tiles that make up the floor bears the name of someone who gave money to replace the old wooden floor back in the 1980s.

Don't forget to explore the shops tucked away on the floors below the Main Arcade. The places likely to interest kids include the **CRAFT EMPORIUM** (Pike Place Market; 206/622-2219), selling beads, feathers, sequins, and other paraphernalia, and **SILLY OLD BEAR** (Pike Place Market; 206/623-2325), carrying stuffed bears, gnomes, and other creatures. Always entertaining is the **SEATTLE PARROT MARKET** (1500 Western; 206/467-6133), where a 50-cent "browsing fee" will get you a close look at exotic birds, iguanas, lizards, snakes, pythons, a Fuzzy Baboon Tarantula, and a Tomato Toad.

If all this exploring whets appetites, take advantage of the bountiful eating opportunities at the Market. Some of the tastiest food and best bargains are found here. For breakfast, **THE CRUMPET SHOP** (Pike Place Market; 206/682-1598) offers fresh-baked crumpets with various delicious toppings. At lunch, the **BIRINGER FARM AND BAKERY** (1530 Post Alley; 206/467-0383) offers yummy soup and sandwich, topped off by fresh berry pie and shortcake for dessert. Nearby, there's pizza by the slice at **DELAURENTI'S PIZZA WINDOW** (1435 1st Ave., 206/622-0141), or homestyle Mexican fare at bargain prices at **EL PUERCO LLORON** (1501 Western; 206/624-0541).

**DOWNTOWN SHOPPING DISTRICT.** As recently as four years ago, Seattle's downtown retail core appeared to be gasping its last breath, trampled by the shopping malls that sucked shoppers into the suburbs. That has all changed, and if you enjoy browsing, especially with older kids, a visit to the downtown shopping core will be one of the highlights of your trip to Seattle. Within a four-square-block area, between Pine and Union streets, and 4th and 6th avenues, you'll find Old Navy,

GAP, Nordstrom's, and Banana Republic. As in so many cities, **F.A.O Schwartz** (1420 5th Ave.; 206/442-9500) is the place to go to watch little eyes widen, to purchase a special toy or stuffed animal, or just to wander aimlessly. Nearby is **Gameworks** (1511 7th Ave.; 206/521-0952), featuring virtual reality games, real-time Net interactive games, and gourmet foods. Mom and Dad, don't despair—there's fun here for everyone, not to mention the on-site microbrewery.

When hunger strikes, you'll find many options for a quick bite in the immediate area. For a quick stop, there's pizza by the slice at **Joey's Jet City Bistro** (515 Olive Way; 206/343-0877). The gourmet pizza is great, but there's not always a place to sit. An option is the top floor of the Westlake Center (5th Ave. & Olive St.), where you'll find a wide selection of fast foods.

**Seattle Center.** On the northern edge of downtown, near the foot of Queen Anne Hill, sprawls this 74-acre funfest. Constructed for the 1962 World's Fair, its vast expanse offers a multitude of indoor and outdoor activities, along with numerous fine arts (Seattle Opera, Seattle Repertory Theatre, Pacific Northwest Ballet) and sports facilities (Seattle Supersonics basketball).

The Center is home to several outstanding spots for families: the **Pacific Science Center** and the renowned **Seattle Children's Museum** (see "Museums"); the **Seattle Children's Theatre** (see "Kid Culture"); and, coming soon, the **Experience Music Project**, built by Microsoft multibillionaire Paul Allen to honor rock guitarist Jimi Hendrix and other rock musicians. Also at the Center is the landmark **Space Needle**, still one of the best viewpoints in the city. Visitors ride the elevator 518 feet to the Observation Deck for a panoramic view of city, Sound, mountains, islands, and beyond.

Not that you'll need more to do, but it may be difficult to steer the young ones past the **Fun Forest** without stopping to take a ride or two. There are attractions here for pint-sized riders and full-grown thrill seekers alike. Tickets can be purchased individually or in books.

If your kids get hungry while you are visiting, head for the **Center House**, one of the world's first food courts, offering a collection of take-out restaurants, including some of the familiar fast-food standbys we all know, if not love. This spot works especially well for families who can't agree on what to eat—there's something here for everyone. For a more substantial meal in the area, try the nearby **MEDITERRANEAN KITCHEN** or **THAI RESTAURANT** (see "Places to Eat").

## PARKS

Thanks to early city planners dedicated to preserving open spaces for public enjoyment, Seattle parks are numerous and well maintained.

**DISCOVERY PARK** is the largest and most diverse park in Seattle, including 534 acres of forest, meadows, cliffs and beaches, self-guided interpretive loops, short hiking trails, man-made ponds, and a thriving population of birds and animals. (There are even bald eagles living here.) Located at the northern end of the Magnolia neighborhood, the park is about 10 minutes from downtown Seattle. Enter at the west entrance (W. Government Way & 36th Ave. W.) and drive straight ahead to the Visitors Center to get the lay of the land. Excellent drop-in nature walks, free of charge, depart the Visitors Center each Saturday at 2 p.m. Or walk some of the seven miles of nature trails on your own.

A definite highlight of the park is the **DAYBREAK STAR CENTER**, a Native American cultural/education center located in the park's northwest corner. Twelve Native American artists were commissioned to create artworks for this beautiful building and most of the pieces are large murals and carvings depicting legends and traditions children will find interesting. Daybreak Star's gift shop features a variety of Native American beadwork, baskets, and dolls.

*3810 W Government Way. 206/386-4236, 206/285-4425 (Daybreak Star Center). Open Mon.-Sat., 10 a.m.-5 p.m.; Sun., noon-5 p.m. Free.*

**GASWORKS PARK.** When park designers first presented the idea of integrating the old gasworks plant (operational until the mid-50s) into a new park on Lake Union, there were plenty of noisy critics. Today, the grotesque remnants are a familiar part of the cityscape—so ugly they're almost pretty. There's a large picnic shelter, a children's play barn, a working sundial, and a grassy hill that's great for kite-flying and offers an unobstructed view of the city skyline. Note: The playground at the park is quite challenging—best for ages six and up. Because there's lots of boat traffic and commercial activity on this stretch of Lake Union, swimming is not recommended.

*3300 Meridian Avenue N. (northern end of Lake Union, accessible from downtown via the Fremont Bridge). 206/684-4075. Open 4 a.m.-11:30 p.m.*

**GREEN LAKE.** Many Seattleites exercise religiously, and Green Lake has become their Mecca. Situated just east of the Woodland Park Zoo (about 15 minutes from downtown) the 2.8-mile paved trail that circles the lake is ideal for running, walking, skating, and biking. There's also a good playground (at the east main entrance), beaches with lifeguards mid-June through Labor Day, a big wading pool (northwest corner), a community center with an indoor public swimming pool, and boat rentals. Across Greenlake Way N. are shops for renting bikes and skates, and plenty of spots to snack or enjoy a cup of java.

*On Greenlake Way N., in northeast Seattle.*

### HIRAM M. CHITTENDEN GOVERNMENT (BALLARD) LOCKS.

The locks allow boats to negotiate the waterway from the higher (clear water) level of Lake Union to the lower (saltwater) level of Puget Sound. The operation of the locks is fascinating, and can be viewed at close range. On a warm day, bring a picnic to enjoy on the grassy knoll above the locks while you sit and watch the boat traffic. Pleasure craft and big ships alike use the locks, and while it's fun to watch assorted boaters paying out line as the water level drops and boats drop with it, it's possible for kids to get too fascinated; vigilant supervision is recommended. There are also fish ladders with underwater viewing (although, with the salmon shortage, it is sometimes hard to spot a fish) and a lovely botanical garden.

*3015 NW 54th, in Ballard. 206/783-7059; www.nps.usace.army.m:/opsdiv/lwsc/lakewsc.htm. Open daily, (June-Sept.); Sat.-Sun. (rest of year).*

**MAGNUSON PARK.** This is currently one of the wildest, most natural of the large Seattle parks, but all that is slated to change in the next few years. The old Sand Point Naval Station is being integrated into the park to establish a 365-acre park with a mile-long shoreline, open spaces, sport fields, and numerous large building spaces for community programs.

One of the changes has already been made, and it's one families will love. The Seattle Junior League has built a large playground, with many climbing structures, slides, tunnels, and playhouses. It's a place where imaginations soar and "boredom" is eliminated from the vocabulary. Adjacent to the playground is one of several entrances to the fenced, off-leash dog area.

Much of Magnuson Park remains wetland, so careful observers can spot lots of urban wildlife, especially various bird and frog species. A long, paved path follows the lake, and it's a lovely stroll past the public swim area (with restrooms), picnic sites, various displays of public art, a wonderfully tall kite-flying knoll, and a good deal of natural area (much of which turns into blackberries, come August). At the northern end of the path is the entrance to the National Oceanographic and Atmospheric Association (NOAA). Keep going through the turnstile and over the little bridge walk that takes you through public art displays emphasizing the relationship between man and nature. Take the path to the left to visit the **SOUND GARDEN**, a sculpture of steel towers and aluminum pipes that create eerie sounds as the wind blows.

*Enter off Sand Point Way NE, at NE 65th or NE 74th.*

**VOLUNTEER PARK**, one of the "grand old parks" of Seattle, includes 44 acres of beautiful gardens and expansive lawns. The conservatory (near the park entrance at 15th Ave. & Galer St) has an impressive collection of orchids and subtropical plants, and a koi pool that kids tend to love. There's a small playground near the conservatory. Be sure to take the time to walk to the top of the water tower at the southern end of the park; the view from here is glorious. Don't miss the Seattle Asian Art Museum here (see "Museums").

*Enter at 15th Ave. E. & E. Galer St. 206/684-4743. Open daily dawn-dusk; conservatory open daily, 10 a.m.-7 p.m. (May-mid-Sept.), 10 a.m.-4 p.m. (rest of year). Free.*

## MUSEUMS

**THE BURKE MUSEUM**, located on the northern edge of the beautiful University of Washington campus, is the state museum of natural history and anthropology. A recent renovation and new exhibits allow visitors to tour millions of years of Northwest history. There are hands-on exhibits for kids, including spectacular dinosaur displays, and a glowing, walk-through volcano.

*NE 45th St. & 17th Ave. NE, on the University of Washington Campus. 206/543-5590. Open daily, 10 a.m.-5 p.m., Thurs. until 8 p.m. Suggested donation: $5.50/adult, $4/senior, $2.50/student, free/ under 6.*

**CENTER FOR WOODEN BOATS.** This floating museum and shop, located at the south end of Lake Union, features approximately 60 wooden boats, ranging from the smallest dinghy to a tall, three-masted schooner. Many of the boats are moored along the docks; children can climb aboard the *Paesano*, a Monterey Bay fishing boat. The museum staff builds and restores watercraft of many sizes, so there is always interesting activity. During the summer you can rent skiffs, sailboats, canoes, and kayaks. Over the Fourth of July weekend, the annual Wooden Boat Festival includes small-boat races, music, food, contests, and exhibits for kids.

*1010 Valley St. 206/382-2628. Open Wed.-Mon., noon-6 p.m. Free.*

**MUSEUM OF FLIGHT.** Boeing's first manufacturing plant has been transformed into a spectacular museum that tracks the history of flight from the earliest aircraft to the space stations of the future, spanning an era that extends from the 13th century through the 1930s.

The Great Gallery is the hangar exhibit, which features more than 40 aircraft, many suspended dramatically from the ceiling. Displays include a restored World War II Corsair, an Apollo command module, and the first presidential jet. Interactive exhibits allow children to work with equipment and learn about the design and maintenance of aircraft. Tours are offered daily.

*9404 E. Marginal Way S, near Boeing Field. 206/764-5720. Open daily, 10 a.m.-5 p.m.; Thurs. eve. until 9 p.m. Cost: $8/adult 18-64, $7/senior, $4/child 5-17, free/under 5.*

**THE MUSEUM OF HISTORY AND INDUSTRY**, located just south of the Montlake Bridge near the University of Washington, focuses on Seattle and Northwest history. It is a small, well-designed museum that is well suited to children. Displays include historic clothes and toys, local inventions, and nautical and aviation artifacts. Don't miss the exhibits on the Great Seattle Fire of 1889 and the full-scale model of a section of First Avenue in the 1880s.

After visiting the museum, take the scenic walk on the *Foster Island Trail*, which begins in the northeast corner of the museum parking lot. The trail leads over footbridges, across boardwalks, and through marshes to a section of the University of Washington Arboretum.

*2700 24th Ave. E. 206/324-1126; www.historymuse-nw.org.*
*Open Tues.-Fri., 11 a.m.-5 p.m.; Sat.-Sun., 10 a.m.-5 p.m.*
*Suggested donation: $5.50/adult, $3/child 6-12, $1/child 2-5,*
*free/under 2.*

**ODYSSEY: THE MARITIME DISCOVERY CENTER.** A contemporary interactive museum, The Discovery Center explores Seattle's working relationship with Puget Sound and the North Pacific—from commercial fishing and shipping to trade, recreation, and marine protection. The hands-on exhibits include virtual kayak rides, a "Kid Skiff," and Harborwatch, huge windows that overlook the Sound while audio broadcasts let visitors eavesdrop on real-time Coast Guard communications. Try your hand at simulated tugboat navigation or pedal a 10-foot propeller into motion. Note: Odyssey is financed by shipping and fishing conglomerates, so you may want to balance your kids' experience with information about the environmental challenges we all face.

*2205 Alaska Way (Pier 66, on the Seattle Waterfront at Wall*
*St.) 206/374-4001; www.discoverodyssey.com. Open Thurs.-*
*Sat., 10 a.m.-5 p.m.; Sun.-Wed., 10 a.m.-9 p.m. Cost:*
*$6.50/adult, $4/senior, student & child 5-18, free/under 5.*

**PACIFIC SCIENCE CENTER** makes science a hands-on experience, through a rich assortment of permanent and traveling exhibits. Favorite permanent exhibits include: WaterWorks, an outdoor maze of pumps and water wheels and TechZone, which features experiments in virtual reality and robotics. All exhibits at the Science Center are stroller and wheelchair accessible; choose a stroller instead of a backpack if your little one is old enough to want to run and touch.

A recent retooling of the Center resulted in stunning new additions: a lovely Tropical Butterfly House and Insect Village are housed in the new **ACKERLY FAMILY EXHIBIT GALLERY**. But the pièce de résistance is bound to be the new **BOEING IMAX THEATER**. Both additions were designed by French architect Denis Laming, a prominent European architect. Once you've explored the exhibits, old and new, spend some relaxed time at the new IMAX Theater. The theater's screen is six stories tall (twice that of the old theater). You'll pay extra for the IMAX movie, but it's well worth it. Arrive early: popular movies sell out fast on busy days.

**LASER FANTASY**, another theater within the Science Center complex, provides good evening entertainment for teenagers. Viewers lie back in comfy chairs or stretch out on the carpeted floor to watch a laser light show accompanied by music. Evening shows feature music popular with teens; the daytime show is a space odyssey set to classical and popular music and provides a soothing break from museum exploration.

*At the Seattle Center. 206/443-2001; www.pacsi.org. Open daily, 10 a.m.-6 p.m. (mid-June-Labor Day); Mon.-Fri., 10 a.m.-5 p.m.; Sat.-Sun. & Holidays, 10 a.m.-6 p.m. (rest of year). Cost: $7.50/adult, $5.50/senior & child 6-13, $3.50/child 2-5 years, free/under 2. Combination exhibits plus either IMAX or Fantasy Laser: $9.50/adult, $7.50/senior & child 6-13, $5.50/child 2-5. (Call the Laser HotLine, 206/443-2850, for movie information.)*

**ROSALIE WHYEL MUSEUM OF DOLL ART.** What's big and pink and full of dolls? The Rosalie Whyel Museum of Doll Art, a 13,000-square-foot Victorian-style mansion that tells the history, technology, and artistry of doll making. The museum, which cost Rosalie Whyel $3.5 million to build, houses more than 1,000 dolls, ranging from Egyptian tomb dolls to modern-day Barbies (and a lot of fascinating dolls in between). Dolls occupy a hospital and show off the latest Paris fashions à la 1880. Children will enjoy pulling out the drawers, located beneath the glass exhibit cases, that contain doll trousseaus and all kinds of elegant accessories.

*1116 108th Ave. NE, Bellevue. 425/455-1116. Open Mon.-Sat., 10 a.m.-5 p.m.; Sun., 1-5 p.m. Cost: $6/ adult, $5.50/senior,$4/child 5-17, free/under 5.*

**SEATTLE ART MUSEUM** opened its state-of-the-art downtown building in 1991, one block south of Pike Place Market. Kids will appreciate the art before they even step inside; the famous 48-foot, 10-ton sculpture, *Hammering Man*, guards the front entrance. The museum interior is spacious and bright, and the collection includes Native American art, European works, African art, modern art, and photographs. There's also an extensive collection of Asian art. Exhibits are fully accessible to strollers but there are none available for rent.

*100 University St. 206/654-3100; www.seattleartmuseum.org. Open Tues.-Sun., 10 a.m.-5 p.m.; Thurs., 10 a.m.-9 p.m. Cost: $7/adult, $5/senior & student, free/under 12 (with adult), free/ first Thursday of every month, free/senior on first Friday of every month.*

**THE SEATTLE ASIAN ART MUSEUM** sits majestically like a jewel in Volunteer Park's crown, with one of the best Asian art collections in the country. Formerly the site of the entire Seattle Art Museum collection, the Volunteer Park site is now an adjunct of SAM, dedicated to showing off works rarely seen in the formerly overcrowded museum. Thanks to SAM's expansion downtown, these breathtaking works of art now have Volunteer Park to themselves. Along with frequent temporary exhibits, the museum presents performances and a variety of art activities, many for children. A recent exhibit included Chinese shadow puppets.

*1400 E. Prospect St. Enter Volunteer Park at 14th Ave. E. & E. Prospect St. or at 15th Ave. E. & E. Galer St. 206/654-3100; 206/654-3255 (information desk); www.seattleartmuseum.org. Open Tue.-Sun. 10 a.m.-5 p.m.; open Thurs. until 9 p.m.; closed Mon. Cost: $6/adult, $4/senior & student, free/under 12 & members. Free first Thursday and first Saturday of every month.*

**SEATTLE CHILDREN'S MUSEUM**, one of the best hands-on museums in the country, offers room after room of child-sized exhibits that will keep your kids entertained (and educated) for hours. Allow plenty of time—kids should not feel rushed here. There is a multitude of opportunity for creative play: a store, a restaurant, a doctor's office, and much more. Parents can sit and relax while keeping an eye on the little ones.

If you have time, check out the Museum Shop, offering a small but well-chosen selection of toys, games, and art materials.

*Seattle Center House. 206/441-1768. Open Mon.-Fri., 10 a.m.-5 p.m.; Sat.-Sun., 10 a.m.-6 p.m. Cost: $4/adult, $5.50/child 1-12, free/under 1.*

**WING LUKE MUSEUM.** This small storefront museum is named in honor of the son of a Chinese immigrant who became the first Asian-American elected to the Seattle City Council (1962). The museum focuses on "One Song, Many Voices," an exhibit that highlights the story of Asian immigration to the region, and includes an early Asian barber shop, laundry, and pharmacy.

*407 7th Ave. S. 206/623-5124. Open Tues.-Fri., 11 a.m.-4:30 p.m.; Sat.-Sun., noon-4 p.m. Cost: $2.50/adult, $1.50/senior & student; $0.75/child 5-12, free/under 5.*

### ANIMALS, ANIMALS

**THE SEATTLE AQUARIUM,** at Pier 59 on the downtown waterfront, is well designed to optimize viewing and learning. It's an ideal outing for folks of all ages. Strollers are allowed, but backpacks will give small children a better view of the action.

Your visit will begin with tanks of exotic species, including seahorses, leaffish and lionfish, followed by the local invertebrates. If you can get the kids past the life-size, great white shark model hanging overhead (Puget Sound is home to seven varieties of shark), they'll be rewarded with an exceptionally good "touch tank."

One of the most popular features of the Aquarium is the 400,000-gallon underwater dome, a glassed-in area where families can relax on comfortable benches and watch sea life circle overhead and all around. Even an infant will be mesmerized by the action in this "inside-out" aquarium. Don't let the group tire out ahead of schedule, because one of the last exhibits will be a child favorite: underwater and above-water views of playful marine mammals. The sea otters, as usual, take first place honors in the cuteness sweepstakes.

Adjacent to the Aquarium is the **OMNIDOME THEATRE,** featuring films that put you so close to the action, you're sure to feel a part of it.

*1483 Alaskan Way, at Pier 59 on the waterfront. 206/386-4300; www.seattleaquarium.org. Omnidome: 206/622-1868. Open daily, year round: 10 a.m.-5 p.m. (Labor Day-Memorial Day); 10 a.m.- 7 p.m. (Memorial Day-Labor Day). Cost: Very complex; several fee structures apply depending on visitors' residence and which attractions are seen; please call for fee schedule. Tickets available for: Aquarium Only, Aquarium & Omnidome, Omnidome Only.*

**WOODLAND PARK ZOO.** Frequently numbered among the 10 best zoos in the United States, the Woodland Park Zoo is an outstanding example of how zoos can incorporate natural habitats and allow animals to roam free. Located just 10 minutes from downtown Seattle, the 92-acre zoo features an extensive collection of animals: giraffes, zebras, and hippos roam the African Savannah; pachyderms plod through the Asian elephant exhibit; gorillas go native in their jungle home. The Tropical Rain Forest makes a vivid impression, with an exhibit that leads visitors from the floor of the forest high up into the canopy. A kid favorite is the Nocturnal House, where bats, raccoons, lizards, and others live in a nighttime environment, visible with infrared light. It is linked to the Reptile House, equally popular with kids and likely to draw "oohs," "ahhs," and "eeks." In July and August the zoo presents an outdoor evening concert series on the north meadow, free for kids 12 and under when accompanied by an adult.

*5500 Phinney Ave. N. 206/684-4800. Open daily, 9:30 a.m., closing time varies with the season. Cost: $8.50/adult, $7.75/student/senior, $6/child 7-17, $3.75/child 3-5, free/under 3. Parking is $3.50.*

## KID CULTURE

**DANCE.** The 50-member **PACIFIC NORTHWEST BALLET** (206/441-9411) offers productions of classical and contemporary works at the Seattle Opera House (Seattle Center), September through June. In November and December, PNB presents "The Nutcracker," with acclaimed sets and costumes by Maurice Sendak. Older children will appreciate the sophisticated **DANCE AT MEANY THEATRE** (206/543-4880; 206/685-2742) offering a season of visiting performances by top professional companies such as the Dance Theatre of Harlem. Meany Theatre is located on the campus of the University of Washington.

**MUSIC.** Each year, the **SEATTLE SYMPHONY** (206/215-4747; www.seattlesymphony.org) presents its popular Discover Music! series for children ages six to 10. Concerts are on Saturday mornings, at the beautiful new Benaroya Hall (3rd Ave. & Union St., downtown). Older children, and those of any age with a penchant for classical music, will enjoy the regular concert series as well.

The largest youth symphony in the country, **SEATTLE YOUTH SYMPHONY ORCHESTRAS** (206/362-2300; www.syso.org) include nearly 600 young musicians in five different orchestras. Each orchestra offers three weekend concerts per season, November through June. These concerts are invariably first-rate, and tailor-made to inspire your young musician. There are several very good youth vocal groups in Seattle. **THE SEATTLE GIRLS' CHOIR** (425/656-9229) is internationally renowned; its advanced choir, Prime Voci, is one of the best in the world. Annual public performances include concerts in December, February or March, and May. **NORTHWEST GIRLCHOIR** (206/329-6225) and **NORTHWEST BOYCHOIR** (206/524-3234) are also popular choices in the Seattle area.

**THEATER.** Rated one of the top children's theaters in the country, **SEATTLE CHILDREN'S THEATRE** (206/443-0807; at the Seattle Center) presents some of the best family entertainment around for ages four and up. Each sterling production gives special attention to the young theater audience, without losing its appeal to teens and adults. The season runs late September through May, with performances in two theaters at the lovely new Charlotte Martin Theatre at the Seattle Center. A question-and-answer period is held after the show, during which the audience has a chance to talk with the actors, always a big hit with the younger set. Of the two theaters, the smaller tends to offer more plays for younger children. (Note that not all subject matter is appropriate for all ages; call first for details.)

Broadway musicals, still popular with kids, are the main attraction at the **FIFTH AVENUE THEATRE** (1308 5th Ave., 206/625-1900). The **PARAMOUNT THEATRE** (911 Pine St.; 206/682-1414) also offers some Broadway shows. Ticket office staff at both theaters can advise parents about the suitability of a given show for children. **NORTHWEST PUPPET CENTER** (9123 15th NE; 206/523-2579; www.nwpuppet.org) the Pacific Northwest's only puppet theater, offers puppet performances and houses a museum, store, and research library.

## SPECTATOR SPORTS
### Baseball

If major league baseball is your passion, you'll want to check out the **SEATTLE MARINERS** (206/622-4487; www.mariners.org), who play baseball at the new Safeco Field (1250 1st Ave. S.), south of Pioneer Square. It seats more than 46,000 fans, and its retractable roof allows kids an open-air experience when the rains don't threaten. The club prices tickets with families in mind (discount for kids in selected seats) and offers family fun, including a fireworks display when the Mariners hit a home run.

Minor league baseball is just as fun and a lot easier on the family wallet. For many baseball lovers, minor league ball is closest in spirit to the great national sport of times past, generating an infectious love of the game for its own sake. The Seattle area sports two minor league teams affiliated with the Mariners. Each hosts special events and activities galore for children.

**THE EVERETT AQUASOX** (425/258-3673; www.aquasox.com), the Mariners' Class A farm team, play at Memorial Stadium (38th & Broadway) in Everett, about 35 minutes north of Seattle. The stadium is one of the most family-friendly spectator sport facilities in the region. There's a children's play field where kids can play catch or wait for a foul ball, and Homer Porch, where fans can walk behind right field and try to catch a homerun ball. All in all, the Aquasox provide the baseball-watching experience nostalgic parents hope to find for their kids, at cut-rate prices.

**THE TACOMA RAINIERS** (253/752-7700, 800/281-3834; www.rainiers.com), members of the AAA Pacific Coast League, perform their magic at Cheney Stadium (2502 S. Tyler) in Tacoma, 33 miles south of Seattle. It's a fun, affordable outing for the whole family.

**THE SEATTLE SEAHAWKS**, a National Football League franchise, have a local owner (Microsoft billionaire Paul Allen) and a new stadium on the way (due to open in 2002). While the new stadium is under construction, the team will play at Husky Stadium, on the University of Washington campus. A limited number of less-expensive tickets are available for each game; be sure to call as early as possible. (Remember that professional football can be a mystery, and therefore a bore, to young ones who aren't familiar with the game.) The season runs August through December.

*206/515-4791; www.seahawks.org. Cost: $10-$48.*

**THE SEATTLE SUPERSONICS** play basketball September through May at the updated Key Arena (Seattle Center). Due to the popularity, and sometimes notoriety, of National Basketball Association players, your kids may beg for basketball tickets above all others. It's pricey to take the whole family to Key Arena, but if you can swing it, the SuperSonics will guarantee a fast-paced competition. Other diversions include the Sasquatch mascot, a dance team, and a small blimp that cruises the stands, dropping prizes and treats.

*Key Arena, 1st Ave. N. at Republican (Seattle Center). 206/281-5850, 206/628-0888 (tickets); www.nba.com/sonics. Cost: $7-$100. Family Night first Saturday of each month: $7/under 18.*

**SEATTLE THUNDERBIRDS** play hockey at the Key Arena (Seattle Center) September through March. This Western Hockey League team plays hard and provides non-stop action, so kids tend to be well entertained.

*Key Arena, 1st Ave. N. at Republican (Seattle Center). 206/448-PUCK. Cost: $10-$20/adult, $8-$12/child.*

**THE UNIVERSITY OF WASHINGTON** offers a host of sporting events featuring talented athletes and great competition at a fraction of the cost of the professional games. The Husky football team (September through December) is often strong, and always good entertainment. The UW Women's basketball team (November-March) is a top contender, and one of the most popular sporting events in town. Both men and womens' soccer teams are also a good bet.

*Husky Stadium and Hec Edmondson Pavilion, University of Washington campus. 206/543-2200.*

### OUTDOOR ACTIVE FUN

Many Seattle locals seize every opportunity to enjoy the great outdoors. Let the kids burn off excess energy while you explore the city and its scenic environs.

**RECREATIONAL EQUIPMENT, INC.** is one of the best retailers in the country for outdoor equipment and clothing. REI's flagship store near downtown Seattle (222 Yale Ave. N.; 206/470-4020) sells and rents an amazing variety of outdoor goods. With its climbing rock and wet, shower-like jacket-testing system, it is worth a visit even if you don't plan to scale any mountains in the near future.

### BIKING

Despite the hilly terrain, bicycling is very popular in Seattle. The city and county have worked with the area's many avid bicyclists to develop an impressive network of trails. From May to September, on the third Sunday of every month, the Seattle Parks Department sponsors **BICYCLE SUNDAY**, when all auto traffic is stopped on scenic Lake Washington Boulevard. The road is flat, with plenty of places to stop and explore, making it an ideal bike route for families. Other routes recommended for youngsters are noted below. There are bicycle rental shops located near these trails, but be sure to call first to make sure they have the size of bike you need. Helmets are required, and are typically provided by the rental shop.

**ALKI.** Alki Beach is a popular 2.5-mile strip of saltwater beach in West Seattle with a spectacular view of the downtown skyline. The trail is safe, about 10 feet wide, and features a separate six-foot path for pedestrians. While you're here, visit the **ALKI POINT LIGHT STATION**, maintained by the Coast Guard. If you bike beyond the beach to the south, the path continues to Lincoln Park—a large, wooded park adjacent to the Fauntleroy ferry dock.

Nearby, bike rentals are available at **ALKI BICYCLE COMPANY** (2611 California SW, 206/938-3322). If your ride results in a hunger, try **PEGASUS PIZZA AND PASTA** (2758 Alki Ave. SW, 206/932-4849) or **SUNFISH** (2800 Alki Ave. SW, 206/938-4112) for fish and chips.

**BURKE-GILMAN TRAIL & SAMMAMISH RIVER TRAIL.** Thanks to the recent connecting of the Burke-Gilman Trail in Seattle with the Sammamish River Trail on the Eastside, bicyclists can now enjoy a level, scenic trail from Gas Works Park past the University of Washington, around the north end of Lake Washington to Marymoor Park in Redmond. The 25-mile route is too long for most kids (and some adults), but there are numerous short stretches that are ideal. Families will enjoy the 2.5-mile stretch from the University of Washington to Gas Works Park. Or head in the other direction from the University, and ride several miles to Matthews Beach, where there's a nice playground and lake access. Further north a few miles is Logboom Park, at the far north of the lake, with picnic tables, restrooms, a tiny beach and playground. The ducks and geese here enjoy being fed. If you find yourself here, you're likely hungry. Head a half-mile south to **LAKE FOREST PARK TOWNE CENTRE** (Bothell Way NE & Ballinger Way NE). At **THIRD PLACE BOOKS** you can browse among books while you nosh on a pastry from the **HONEYBEAR BAKERY**; ice cream, espresso and all the other necessities of life are also provided. On the Eastside, try the 3.5-mile stretch from Marymoor Park to the lovely Chateau Ste. Michelle Winery (tours and tastings: 425/488-3300).

Bike rentals are available near the trail in Seattle at **AL YOUNG BIKE AND SKI** (3615 NE 45th, 524-2642) or **THE BICYCLE CENTER** (4529 Sand Point Way NE, 523-8300). On the Eastside, you can find rentals at **REDMOND CYCLE** (16205 Redmond Way; 425/885-6363).

**ELLIOTT BAY BICYCLE PATH.** This trail is rarely crowded, except at noon on weekdays, when it attracts a large number of downtown workers trying to get some exercise and fresh air during their lunch breaks. Even then, the runners are on a separate path, so it doesn't get too busy for bicyclists or skaters. The three-mile route begins at Myrtle Edwards Park and winds past grain elevators and other interesting port activities. The views are spectacular.

*3130 Alaskan Way W., near Pier 70.*

**GREEN LAKE.** The 2.8-mile trail around the lake is flat and paved, and there are endless good places to stop along the way. On sunny days, the loop gets crowded with cyclists, runners, skaters, walkers, and other folks having a good time, so try going on a weekday or get started early on a weekend.

Rentals are available at **GREGG'S GREENLAKE CYCLE** (7007 Woodlawn NE, 523-1822).

*On Greenlake Way N., in northeast Seattle.*

### BOATING

Seattle is replete with avid boaters, who take advantage of the many waterways in the region. If you're interested in renting a small craft, there are several good choices.

**THE CENTER FOR WOODEN BOATS,** located at the southern end of Lake Union (five minutes from downtown) rents rowboats, paddleboats, canoes, and sailboats. With houseboats lining much of the shore and seaplanes coming and going, Lake Union is a fun place to explore by boat. Before being allowed to rent a sailing craft, your boat-handling skills will be checked out. The cost begins at $12.50 per hour; rowing and paddling craft are $10–$15 per hour.

*1010 Valley St; 206/382-BOAT; www.eskimo.com/~cwboats. Open Wed.-Mon., noon-6 p.m.*

**GREENLAKE BOAT RENTALS,** located on the eastern edge of the lake near the community center, offers rowboats, paddleboats, canoes, and sailboards for rent, mid-April through September. Reservations are recommended during busy summer months.

*7351 E. Green Lake Dr. N. 206/527-0171.*

**MOSS BAY ROWING & KAYAKING CENTER.** Located minutes from downtown at the southern end of Lake Union, Moss Bay aims to provide water activities for enthusiasts of all ages, sizes, and abilities. Out of town guests can schedule same-day lessons or participate in a 90-minute Mini-Lesson/Tour. Boats may be rented by the half-hour, day, or multiple days. Children under 18 must be accompanied by an adult; very young children may go with a parent, provided they wear a life jacket.

*1001 Fairview N. 206/682-2031. Open daily, 8 a.m.-dusk (April-Nov.), 10 a.m.-4 p.m. (rest of year).*

**NORTHWEST OUTDOOR CENTER.** Renting a kayak from Northwest Outdoor Center is a great way to see Lake Union from a new perspective. Paddle to Gas Works Park, Ballard Locks, and among the communities of houseboats. Several models are available, seating one, two, or three people. Kids sit in front, adults in the rear (steering) position. Rentals are available by the hour, half day, full day, and longer. No experience is necessary.

*2100 Westlake Ave. N. 206/281-9694. Cost: Single, $10/hour; double, $15/hour.*

**UNIVERSITY OF WASHINGTON WATERFRONT ACTIVITY CENTER.** Enjoy a leisurely paddle through the University of Washington Arboretum in a canoe or rowboat. The Foster Island area is full of byways and footbridges to navigate around, a multitude of interesting birds to observe, and unlimited places to hop ashore and enjoy a picnic. Canoes seat up to three people and rowboats up to four. Life vests are available for children as small as 25 pounds. Boats are available on a first-come, first-served basis; on a sunny weekend, they're in high demand. You'll be asked to leave a driver's license at the rental shop.

*Off Montlake Ave. NE, at the northern end of the Montlake Bridge. 206/543-9433. Open daily, 10 a.m.-dusk (Feb.-Oct.). Cost: $5/hour per boat.*

## HIKING

When you think of hiking with the kids, do you picture the family in lederhosen, yodeling together up the mountain? Or do you imagine yourself dropping a trail of jelly beans just to get your kids up the hill? If the second scenario is closer to the truth, don't be discouraged. There are hundreds of easy day hikes within a short drive of Seattle that will likely convert your couch potato to an avid fan of Mother Nature. Just remember to be generous with praise and snacks, and set a realistic pace and goal.

**ISSAQUAH ALPS TRAIL CLUB** (206/328-0480) sponsors free hikes for all ages and skill levels, year round, on the mountains and plateaus in the greater Issaquah area. No reservations are necessary, and no special gear is required. Each hike is rated by length and climbing difficulty. Hikers meet at the Issaquah City Hall (about 30 minutes from downtown Seattle) at a preset time, and carpool to the trailhead.

**THE MOUNTAINEERS** (206/284-6310) is the largest outdoor organization in the region, currently comprising 14,000 members. The club is dedicated to offering a wide range of outdoor activities for all ages, including hiking, skiing, backpacking, kayaking, and more. Mountaineer Books publishes two excellent books for families (see "Resources").

### EXCURSIONS

**BOEING TOUR CENTER.** Free tours of the Boeing Everett Plant are offered for ages 10 and up, weekdays, on a first-come, first-served basis. The tour begins with a half-hour video presentation in the plant's theater, and continues at a moderate pace through the factory, covering about one-third mile, including some steep stairs. Tours are very popular, so arrive at least one hour prior to the start time. (The 9 a.m. and 1 p.m. tours accommodate up to 90 people; the others are limited to 45.)

*Drive north on I-5 to Exit 189. 206/342-4801. Tours Mon.-Fri. at 9, 10 & 11 a.m., 1, 2, & 3 p.m. Free.*

**EDMONDS.** A 20-minute drive from downtown Seattle, Edmonds is an ideal destination for a less urban experience with kids. Unlike many of Seattle's suburban communities, Edmonds is not a sprawl of shopping centers. It has a charming collection of small shops that can easily be perused in an hour, even when strolling with young kids.

Right in the downtown area, you'll find the Edmonds-Kingston Ferry (206/464-6400) and a lovely stretch of beach. The ferry travels from Edmonds to Kingston, on the northern end of the Kitsap Peninsula. The crossing takes one half-hour; for a fun outing, walk onto the boat and enjoy the round-trip ride. Or disembark and explore Kingston before catching a return ferry. There's a nice beach with picnic tables and a restaurant at the ferry landing, and a few craft shops in town.

**ENCHANTED VILLAGE AND WILD WAVES WATER PARK.** Pack a picnic and spend the day enjoying 50 acres of family fun. The price of admission is steep and there's plenty to keep kids busy, so plan to get there early to get your money's worth. Enchanted Village is a magical place for young children. It is a quiet, forested setting—a pleasant switch from the carnival atmosphere of most amusement parks. It has attractions likely to drive any kid to delirium, including 14 amusement rides, a double-corkscrew looping rollercoaster, a giant wading pool, bumper boats, and a tiny zoo. Best of all, the price of admission covers all the rides, so parents can relax and let the kids enjoy the same ride over and over (and over).

There are a few rides that will thrill older kids, but this place is ideally suited for children under age 8. Older kids will likely gravitate next-door to Wild Waves, the Northwest's largest water park. Here they will find 20 acres of watermania, including giant water slides and a 24,500-square-foot wave pool.

*36201 Enchanted Pkwy. S., Federal Way (south of Seattle off I-5). 253/661-8001. Open mid-April–Labor Day; seasonal hours vary. Cost: Enchanted Village only, $9/child under 4 feet tall, $11/person over 4 feet tall; Enchanted Village & Wild Waves, $17.95/under 4 feet, $19.95/over 4 feet.*

**FUNTASIA.** This seven-acre amusement center has go-karts, bumper cars, electric bumper boats, an outdoor batting cage, miniature golf, and Laser Tag. Many of the rides are restricted to kids at least 42 inches tall, so the center is most popular for ages five and up.

*7212 220th St. SW, Edmonds. 425/774-GAME. Open Sun.-Thurs., 10 a.m.– 11 p.m.; Fri.-Sat., 10 a.m.-1 p.m. Cost: Admission is free. There is a separate fee for each game and ride.*

**MOUNT RAINIER SCENIC RAILWAY.** The railway's vintage steam locomotive departs Elbe for 90-minute excursions through the foothills of Mt. Rainier to Mineral Lake (14 miles). If the extraordinary scenery doesn't keep your kids entertained, the live music will. No reservations are required for this ride. If you want to treat an older child, the Cascadian Dinner Train offers a complete five-course prime rib dinner during a four-hour train ride from Elbe to the logging town of Morton. At year's end, Santa makes an appearance on each trip. Arrive early. Parents who rise at the crack of dawn to bring their kids on this adventure will appreciate the excellent espresso stand adjacent to the station. In addition to the noble bean, it carries a wide assortment of Italian sodas and sundry other child pleasers.

*Located about 40 miles south of Tacoma on Hwy. 7, in Elbe. 360/569-2588. Departs daily, mid-June–Labor Day, 3 times per day on weekends, Memorial Day–Sept. Prices: $8.50/adult, $5.50/child 2-11, free/under 2. Call for Santa Train details.*

**NORTHWEST TREK AND WILDLIFE PARK.** This unique park offers tram tours, led by expert naturalists, through 435 acres of habitat. For details, see "Tacoma: Excursions."

**PUGET SOUND AND SNOQUALMIE VALLEY RAILWAY.** Travel aboard this historic steam train for a 75-minute tour of the scenic Snoqualmie Valley. The train departs from the small town of Snoqualmie, and runs every weekend from Memorial Day through Labor Day, as well as select days during the spring and fall. No reservations are necessary.

*Departs from Snoqualmie, about 35 miles east of Seattle on I-90. 425/888-3030, 425/746-4025. Departs Sat.-Sun. (April-Oct.) Call to confirm departure times. Cost: $6/adult, $4/child, free/under 3.*

**SNOQUALMIE FALLS PARK,** located in the foothills of the Cascade Mountains, is a scenic place to get out in the woods and view a waterfall. Just outside the town of Snoqualmie (35 miles east of Seattle on I-90), the Snoqualmie River plunges 270 feet into a rock gorge. The grounds feature observation platforms to view the falls, picnic areas, a gift shop, and a café. For the ambitious, the half-mile *River Trail* leads down to the river's edge, for an up-close view of the cascading falls. The trail is steep, though, so be prepared to help little ones on the way back up. The falls are especially impressive in late spring, heavy with snowmelt.

*Take I-90 east from Seattle 25 miles to Exit 27. Open year-round. Free.*

**TILLICUM VILLAGE.** For a boat ride and a firsthand look at local Native American culture, consider the popular four-hour Tillicum Village Tour (206/443-1244; at piers 55 and 56). The tour travels eight miles across Puget Sound to Blake Island, a Washington State Park with nearly 500 acres of forest and beachfront. On the island, you'll visit Tillicum Village, with its huge cedar longhouse and alderwood fire. Following a complete salmon dinner, visitors are treated to a Native American production, including traditional music, dance, and storytelling.

## CALENDAR

**JANUARY**
Science Circus, Pacific Science Center.
**MARCH**
St. Patrick's Day Parade.
Whirligig, Seattle Center.

**MAY**

Bicycle Saturdays & Sundays (through September).

Northwest Folklife Festival, Memorial Day Weekend, Seattle
  Center.

Opening day of boating season.

Pike Place Market Festival.

Seattle International Children's Festival, Seattle Center.

**JUNE**

Edmonds Art Festival.

KidsDay.

Seattle Maritime Week.

**JULY**

Bellevue Jazz Festival.

Edmonds Art Festival.

Flight Festival & Air Show.

Marymoor Heritage Festival, Marymoor Park.

Paine Field International Air Fair, Everett.

**AUGUST**

KOMO Kidsfair, Seattle Center.

Seafair.

Taste of Edmonds, third week.

**SEPTEMBER**

Bumbershoot, Labor Day Weekend, Seattle Center.

**OCTOBER**

Issaquah Salmon Days, Issaquah.

**NOVEMBER**

Model Railroad Show, Pacific Science Center, Seattle Center.

"The Nutcracker," Pacific Northwest Ballet, Opera House,
  Seattle Center.

"Peter Pan," Intiman Theater.

**DECEMBER**

Festivals of Light, Seattle Children's Museum, Seattle Center.

KING-5 Winterfest, Seattle Center.

Seattle Civic Christmas Ship, various locations.


## RESOURCES

### CHILDREN'S RESOURCE LINE

206/526-2500

Nurses at Children's Hospital answer questions 24 hours a day.


### SEATTLE-KING COUNTY CONVENTION & VISITOR'S BUREAU

520 Pike St., Ste. 1300, Seattle  98101

206/461-5840; www.seeseattle.org

Mon.-Fri., 8:30 a.m.-5 p.m., Sat.-Sun. 10 a.m.-4 p.m. (Memorial Day-Labor Day); Mon.-Fri., 8:30 a.m.-5 p.m. (rest of year)

## BOOKS AND PUBLICATIONS

*Best Hikes with Children in Western Washington & the Cascades, Volume 1 and 2*, published by Mountaineer Books, available at local bookstores.

*Out and About Seattle with Kids,* by Ann Bergman and Stephanie Dunnewind.
The ultimate family guide for fun and learning is available at local bookstores.

*Seattle's Child and Eastside Parent*
Monthly newsmagazines offering feature articles and calendar of family activities.

## WEBSITES

**SEATTLESIDEWALK.COM**
Features attractions, events, shopping, and accommodations.

**WWW.SEATTLEONLINE.COM**
Includes attractions, shopping, and entertainment.

**WWW.PAN.CI.SEATTLE.WA.US**
Visitor information, parks directory, and other attractions.

**WWW.CI.BELLEVUE.WA.US**
Visitor information and directory of attractions for Bellevue (east of Seattle, across Lake Washington).

# ANACORTES AND SAN JUAN ISLANDS

This magnificent archipelago is a wonderful place for families to vacation. Estimates vary, depending on what you call an island and what you call a rock, but there are about 450 islands at low tide and 172 at high tide; 40 are populated. Four islands—Orcas, San Juan, Lopez, and Shaw—share two-thirds of the total population and are served by state ferries.

Unless you plan to camp, Shaw Island is not an overnight

option. Members of a local order of nuns have been operating the ferry landing at Shaw Island for more than 15 years. Aside from a tiny grocery store at the landing, and a small county park at Indian Cove that has limited camping and picnicking facilities, Shaw has no amenities to offer.

The ferries are both a highlight and a hindrance. The winding voyage and spectacular scenery provide a fine transition from the world left behind to a slower pace ahead. However, the ferry lines are long, and the wait to board can be frustrating—except mid-week during the off-season. Once on the islands, you will find the makings of a well-rounded vacation—plenty of outdoor activity along with the comforts of good food and lodging. As if the natural beauty and abundant recreational opportunities weren't enough, these islands lie in a "rain shadow" created by the Olympic Mountains, and they receive about half as much rain as Seattle does.

The fact that the islands are accessible only by boat or airplane has done little to keep crowds away during the summer. If you plan to visit June through August, expect plenty of company and make reservations well in advance.

## GETTING THERE

When planning your route to the San Juans, be sure to call for the most current information. Boat and plane schedules and rates change season to season and year to year.

**BY BOAT.** The least expensive, most popular way to get to the San Juans is by **Washington State Ferry** (206/464-6400; 800/843-3779). Ferries sail from Anacortes (90 miles northwest of Seattle) through the San Juans to Sidney, British Columbia. To reach the ferry terminal, drive north on I-5 about 85 miles from Seattle or south 90 miles from Vancouver, British Columbia. Just north of Mount Vernon, take Highway 20 west to the Anacortes-Sydney ferry terminal.

The time spent riding the ferry through the San Juans will likely be a vacation highlight for the kids: They'll have fun just watching the ferry load and unload its assortment of trucks, cars, bicyclists, and pedestrians. Cars and trucks traveling between islands often have to back onto the ferry—a sight that amuses the on-lookers (if not the drivers). Cafeteria food service is available on all the boats. Between islands, keep an eye out for bald eagles, seals and, if you're lucky, a pod of black-and-white orcas.

The ride to Lopez takes about 45 minutes, to Orcas about 1 1/4 hours and to San Juan about 1 1/2 hours. But none of these estimated travel times include the long ferry wait you will typically encounter during the summer months and on three-day holiday weekends throughout the year. During these busy periods, you may need to queue up at the dock in Anacortes as much as three hours before sailing time to get on the boat. To avoid a before-dawn drive to the ferry, consider spending the night in Anacortes.

If the thought of long ferry lines is already giving you a headache, consider boarding the ferry on foot or with bikes. Be careful, however, if you are tempted by the thought of leaving the car behind. Getting from your parked vehicle to the ferry with suitcases, paraphernalia, and kids in tow, plus the inconvenience of no car once you reach your destination, might be worse than a long wait for the boat.

As you've no doubt gathered by now, parking and overcrowded ferries are a perennial problem for the San Juan ferries—boats simply are not big or numerous enough to meet demand. (Bremerton and commuters in Seattle have gotten first pick of the big ferries that used to run on this route.) The best place to leave your car overnight, should you walk or bike onto the ferry, is in the lot adjacent to the terminal. There's another lot close to the ticket booths (a long walk from the terminal) and a third on the hill above the terminal—also a long walk if you've got small kids and baggage. During the summer months, all these lots fill early.

A few years ago, a Park & Ride lot was created for use during the high season. Unfortunately, it's quite a bit east, next to the oil refinery you pass on your way to Anacortes (the lot is opposite the Texaco Station, on the north side of Hwy. 20). Park here and wait for the free shuttle to take you, kids, and belongings to the ferry. It takes 20 minutes to go from this lot to the ferry terminal, one way. Add unloading and loading and, if you don't get on the first shuttle, a wait of 45 to 60 minutes. Picture it with several kids in torrential rain or blazing sun. . .

One of our parent researchers, who's been traveling to San Juan Island for 15 summers, describes the family ferry strategy as follows:

"Sometimes we split into two groups, so that one member of our party goes early and gets on the boat with a car; the rest of our group comes later, parks, then walks onto the ferry. Needless to say, the luggage goes with the car. What we've come to do in summer, if we can't do the two-car maneuver, is to aim for the 8:45 p.m. (or thereabouts, schedule changes each summer) Friday evening ferry to San Juan Island. If that ferry is full, another ferry is added. (You'd have to check whether this applies to Orcas and Lopez as well.) It may get you to Friday Harbor late—midnight or so—but you're there, and you have the rest of the weekend. Kids sometimes fall asleep on the way."

When you are preparing to return to the mainland, keep in mind that each island is allotted only a certain number of car slots on the return trip to Anacortes. Plan to catch your ferry before noon if you are traveling on Sunday or wait until Monday to come home. On the morning of your departure, call the local ferry dock on the island where you are staying for advice on when to get in line for your boat. Be sure to pack games, snacks, and books for the waiting times.

**REFUELING ON THE WAY TO THE FERRY.** In the Anacortes ferry terminal is a small store that is usually open daily (but there are no guarantees; it is staffed by one person and sometimes closes inexplicably). It sells espresso, a few juices and bottled drinks, and a small selection of muffins, pastries, and snacks. It also has books, a few toys, and ferry memorabilia. A café at the terminal is open daily during the summer, but only on Friday and Saturday for limited hours during the off-season. Quality and price are equivalent to what you pay on the ferry.

There are two restaurants within walking distance of the terminal: **Charlie's** (360/293-7377; lunch, dinner daily) and **Compass Rose** (360/293-6600; breakfast Sat. & Sun., lunch, dinner Tues.-Sun., closed Mon.). Both are located right above the terminal; Charlie's on the left as you face the ferry and Compass Rose on the right. You can leave your car parked in line and walk to either restaurant in five minutes. Whether you dine inside or out on the deck, the view at both places is fabulous and, perhaps more to the point, you can see your ferry coming and dash off if need be. Orders can be, and frequently are, packed up to go. Charlie's is a good steak and seafood restaurant, moderate to high in price, but with quite reasonable specials. They have a senior's and children's menu with The Usual (fish and chips, burgers, grilled cheese, meatballs, chicken strips), as well as charbroiled chicken breasts and prawns. Prices on that list top out at $6.95.

Compass Rose is fairly new and we didn't get a chance to review it. Staff says they welcome families and the menu shows a yummy-sounding tapas bar and other Spanish dishes. On a nice Friday evening in summer, both places will fill up, often with young adults who sip wine until the ferry comes. Don't count on being able to get a meal here without reservations. See "Anacortes: Places to Eat" for several restaurants in town that pack delicious take-out meals that can be toted to the ferry.

If you want to go by boat without a car, there are other alternatives to walking onto the ferry. The **Victoria Clipper** hydrofoil boat (206/448-5000; www.victoriaclipper.com) departs Seattle once a day at 7:30 a.m. and arrives in Friday Harbor on San Juan Island around 10:30 a.m., with a stop at Rosario Resort on Orcas Island. If you'd like to take a day trip to Canada during your stay in the San Juans, the Clipper also goes to Victoria, British Columbia twice a day from Friday Harbor. Passenger-only service throughout the San Juans is also provided by **Island Shuttle Express** (360/671-1137) from Bellingham, May to September.

**BY PLANE:** If you can afford it, flying to the islands is quick and spectacularly scenic. **Harbor Air** (800/359-3220) departs from the Seattle-Tacoma airport and flies to San Juan Island. From there, you can catch a West Isle Air flight to the other islands or opt for ferry travel. **West Isle Air** (360/293-4691) has six flights per day departing Anacortes and hopping among the San Juan Islands. **Kenmore Air** (425/486-8400; www.kenmore-air.com) flies seaplanes from Lake Union in Seattle, and from Kenmore (north of Seattle) to the islands, four times daily.

You'll pay for the pleasure and convenience of flying: A round-trip flight to Orcas via Kenmore Air costs about $118 per adult (mid-week) and $148 on weekends; children two years and older (accompanied by an adult) fly round-trip for $108. Flying time between Orcas Island and Seattle is approximately 45 minutes.

If you fly into Seattle and are planning to walk onto the ferry, ground transportation to the Anacortes Ferry Terminal is available from Seattle/Tacoma airport and the Bellingham airport. Call **Airporter Shuttle** (800/235-5247, WA, AK, B.C.; 800/423-4219, all other states).

**BY TRAIN:** Unfortunately the **Amtrak train** (800/872-7245) running between Seattle and Vancouver, British Columbia doesn't stop in Anacortes, but if you are determined to get there by rail, you can ride the train to Mt. Vernon. From there, catch a Skagit County Bus (360/757-4433) to the ferry terminal.

### THE GREAT OUTDOORS ON THE ISLANDS

The following activities are some of the best reasons for a visit to the San Juan Islands. Check **What to See & Do** under each island for details about specific rental and guided-tour options.

**BICYCLING** in the San Juans is very popular, so much so that in the summer there may be a ferry line just for cyclists. Lopez and San Juan are most suitable for young cyclists: Lopez is almost flat and has a very scenic 30-mile route that circles the island. San Juan Island has about 95 miles of mostly flat, scenic roads. The roads on Orcas Island are generally too hilly and winding for young kids. Shaw Island is a fine place to spend a day with small fry on bikes: road traffic is almost nonexistent.

If your family likes to bike together, consider joining an organized bicycle tour group. You'll get to leave the logistics to someone else, so you can truly join in the fun. **Backroads** (800/462-2848; www.backroads.com) an active-travel company based in Berkeley, California, offers family-oriented bike tours in the San Juans. Accommodations and meals are pre-arranged at carefully selected inns and restaurants in the region. Backroads has a long-standing reputation for well-run tours that accommodate a wide range of skill and endurance.

**SEA KAYAKING** allows you to explore the nooks and crannies of the islands by water. If your child is old enough to stay put in the boat, he or she can enjoy learning to paddle and the fun of sitting close to the water: adults sit in the rear steering position in a double kayak, with the child in front. Don't be discouraged from giving it a try, even if family members are novices: all the rental places offer instruction and guided tours, and kayaking is easy to learn.

**WHALE WATCHING.** There are at least three pods of orcas (approximately 90 whales) living in the San Juans, and sightings are common. You may get lucky and have a pod cavorting next to your ferry, but if you want to be more certain that you'll get a good view of these magnificent creatures, there are a number of commercial whale-watching companies offering tours in this region. Most are based in Friday Harbor on San Juan Island but there are also tours from Orcas Island, Bellingham, and even

Seattle, on the **Victoria Clipper** (206/448-5000; www.victoria clipper.com). Contact the San Juan Island Visitors Information Center (360/468-3663) for information about operators. The **Seattle Aquarium** (206/386-4353) also offers summer whale tours, including transportation to Anacortes from Seattle.

## REGIONAL RESOURCES

### SAN JUAN ISLANDS VISITOR INFORMATION SERVICE
P.O. Box 65, Lopez 98261
360/468-3663, 888/468-3701; www.guidetosanjuans.com

### BOOKS
*Best Hikes with Children, Vol. 2*, by Joan Burton. The Mountaineers, 1992. This second volume of family-friendly hikes includes several on the San Juan Islands.

*The Curve of Time*, by M. Wylie Blanchet. Seal Press, 1993. A delightful, first-person account of a mother's exploration of the coastal waters of British Columbia with her five children in a 25-foot boat during the 1920s and 1930s. It's intended for adults but makes a captivating vacation read-aloud for school-age kids, especially while you are visiting the San Juans.

*Let's Discover the San Juans*, by Diamond & Mueller. The Mountaineers, 1988. A child's activity book that teaches about area wildlife, history, and environmental responsibility. Full of games, puzzles, projects and pictures to color for ages six through 11.

*Orcas in Our Midst: The Whales that Share Our Inland Waters*, by Howard Garrett. Center for Whale Research, 1995. An excellent read about the orcas that populate the San Juans.

*See also  B.C.: Central and North Vancouver Resources for more suggested titles about whale watching.*

## ANACORTES

If you spend time in Anacortes, it will most likely be because you're waiting to get on the ferry to head out to the San Juans or Vancouver Island in Canada. You may be pleasantly surprised, however, by what this little town has to offer a family stopping through. Keep your eyes open for the life-size cutouts of pioneers scattered throughout town.

## PLACES TO STAY

### FIDALGO COUNTRY INN
*250 Hwy. 20, 98221*
*360/293-3494*
*Rates: Inexpensive to moderate*
*FYI: Complimentary continental breakfast; refrigerators/microwaves (suites); outdoor pool (seasonal); pets OK (fee)*

Don't let the name fool you; this spot is not really an inn, and not really in the country. However, it is a comfortable, clean motel offering 50 rooms and suites. Most important, it's a 10-minute drive from the Anacortes Ferry Dock, so it's very convenient if you're catching an early-morning ferry (to San Juan Islands; Victoria, B.C.; Canadian Gulf Islands).

The small grounds are nicely maintained, and there's an adequate noise buffer between the motel and the highway. Although the pool is seasonal, the spa is open year-round.

### 66 PARENT COMMENTS
*"We were taking the early-morning ferry to the Gulf Islands. The management was nice enough to have the continental breakfast ready for us very early, so we could eat before we had to rush off."*

## PLACES TO EAT

### CALICO CUPBOARD
*901 Commercial Ave.*
*360/293-7315*
*Hours: Breakfast, lunch daily*

There are three Calico Cupboards: in La Conner, in Mount Vernon, and in Anacortes. They specialize in freshly baked goods, which are delectable and quite reasonably priced. All grains are organically grown; many heart-healthy choices are offered. You can dine in or take out; travelers to the San Juans frequently exercise the latter option. Quiches, soups, muffins, pies, and breads can be purchased whole and taken with you. If you're in a hurry, the plethora of good choices can slow you down; close your eyes and pick.

There's an excellent and, for once, original children's menu, too. A typical offering is "Ants on a Log" (celery sticks with peanut butter and raisins), with a garnish of parched corn (better than popcorn) and fresh fruit. They also offer soup (a hard-to-find selection on kids' menus), pb&j, and other standbys.

Each kids' lunch entrée comes with a generous-sized gingerbread boy cookie.

### GERE-A-DELI
*502 Commercial Ave.*
*360/293-7383*
*Hours: Breakfast, lunch Mon.-Sat.; dinner Fri.; closed Sun.*

This large, airy cafeteria is always busy, but lines move fast. It's a top choice if you're running late for the ferry. Baked goods are fabulous—sandwiches, quiches, cinnamon rolls, muffins, cobblers—along with a selection of salads. You can eat in or take out.

### LA VIE EN ROSE
*418 Commercial Ave.*
*360/299-9546*
*Hours: Breakfast, lunch daily*

This small bakery/café has a few tables, but it's probably best to buy and take out. As the name suggests, this is a French bakery, and offerings are a rare combination of delicious and child-friendly. Quiches, tarts—both savory and sweet—cookies, cheesecakes, muffins, rolls, and bread are on the menu; loaves of bread can be purchased to take along. An assortment of drinks and juices is also offered. All are moderately priced.

### VILLAGE PIZZA
*807 Commercial Ave.*
*360/293-7847*
*Hours: Lunch, dinner daily*

You can dine in, take out, or have it delivered. They cater to families with mini-pizzas and small portions of pasta for kids, not to mention the—somebody had to do it—pb&j pizza.

### WHAT TO SEE & DO

**GUEMES ISLAND FERRY.** This tiny ferry with a flatbed holds up to 12 cars and shuttles passengers from Anacortes to Guemes Island in five minutes. Stay on for the ride, or get out and explore the beach next to the ferry landing.

*Off 6th St. 360/293-6356. Cost: $1.25/adult; $.50/child under 6.*

**THE *W.T. PRESTON,*** a steam-wheeler snagboat, is moored right next door at James Rice Civic Park. Free, self-guided tours are available all summer and offer a quick education on this interesting piece of marine transportation history in Puget Sound.

**WASHINGTON PARK** is located less than one mile west of the ferry terminal. This 220-acre waterfront park has a lovely beach and boat launch. The *Loop Trail* is an easy, 3.5-mile hike, offering fine vistas of the San Juans and Guemes Channel.

## LOPEZ ISLAND

Lopez is the first ferry stop, about 45 minutes into the voyage. The moment you drive off the ferry, you'll notice the pastoral calm that envelops the island. With sheep, goats, and cows grazing in rolling pastures, a single sleepy village, and scant car traffic off the main road, a visit to Lopez truly takes you out of the fast lane. The few hills (there is one long one as you leave the ferry), light traffic, and pleasant scenery have earned Lopez a reputation as the best island for bicycling— many cyclists leave their cars in Anacortes and take their bikes to the island for the day.

### PLACES TO STAY

#### EDENWILD INN B&B

*P.O. Box 271, Lopez 98261*
*360/468-3238*
*Rates: Moderate to expensive*
*FYI: Restaurant, complimentary breakfast; fireplaces (some rooms)*

Designed by owner and architect Susan Aran, this elegant Victorian-style inn, built in 1990, has eight rooms, each with a private bath. It sits on a lovely two-acre yard at the edge of the tiny village of Lopez (the largest town on the island); the grounds can be explored on foot in about five minutes.

Rooms 2 and 8 are best suited to parents traveling with children. Room 2 has spacious accommodation with fireplace, queen bed and convertible couch, a sitting area, and garden view. Room 8 is the largest room, with king and queen beds and a sitting area. Dinner is served Wednesday through Saturday, but there are less formal places to eat on the island, better suited to small children.

❝ **PARENT COMMENTS**
*"This is a lovely place—beautifully decorated and well run. But as with most B&Bs, I wouldn't be comfortable here with*

*a noisy young child, because it is so peaceful and quiet. It worked well when I brought my ten year old for an overnight stay and a day of biking."*

### ISLANDER LOPEZ

*P.O. Box 459, Lopez 98261*
*360/468-2233, 800/736-3434*
*Rates: Inexpensive to moderate*
*FYI: Restaurant, kitchens (some units); outdoor pool (seasonal); boat rentals; fishing charters; 50-slip marina*

The Islander offers 28 units (two are three-bedroom units). The motel sits right on the main road, so even though traffic is light and noise is minimal, it's not a pastoral setting.

Located on Fisherman's Bay, the Islander offers moorage for those traveling by boat. There's also a beach where the kids can dig and wade. If you go during the summer, you'll appreciate the pool, which has a nice sundeck and offers a welcome alternative to swimming in chilly Puget Sound. The beach and the restaurant are across the main road from most of the units, so young children will need careful supervision.

For those who come to Lopez to bike along the quiet country roads—as so many do—the Islander Lopez is a good place to rest overnight. There is a bicycle rental shop located right next door.

**❝❝ PARENT COMMENTS**

*"The Islander is a comfortable, basic motel. It worked well for us when we wanted to spend a weekend on Lopez biking with our school-age kids. We took our bikes on the ferry to avoid the ferry line."*

**VACATION RENTAL PROPERTIES.** If you want to look into renting a private cabin on Lopez, contact **Lopez Island Vacation Rentals** (360/468-3401; 800/781-2882).

### PLACES TO EAT

### BAY CAFÉ

*Lopez Village*
*360/468-3700*
*Hours: Breakfast Sat.-Sun., year-round; dinner daily, summer; winter hours vary*

The Bay Café is not really a family restaurant, but the atmosphere is laid-back and friendly, and the food is too good for parents to miss. The menu is imaginative and ever-changing—ethnic dishes are popular and there is always at least one outstanding seafood and vegetarian selection. Considering that soup and salad come with every dinner, prices are quite reasonable. Reservations are a must. The space was recently remodeled to include a fabulous view of the water and an outdoor deck, which should be ideal if you bring along noisy or wriggling kids.

### FAERIES LANDING
*In a trailer next to the ferry landing*

On your way home, you'll likely spend some time waiting for the ferry, and this cheerful little snack bar could make your wait a bit more tolerable, especially if the kids are running on empty. The food is surprisingly good.

### GAIL'S
*Lopez Village*
*360/468-2150*
*Hours: Breakfast, lunch daily; dinner seasonal*

Offering delicious baked desserts, hearty breakfasts, tasty burgers, sandwiches, salads, and pasta, this is a good place to put together a picnic. Prices are moderate and the food is reliably good.

### THE ISLANDER LOPEZ RESTAURANT
*Fisherman Bay Road*
*360/468-2234*

Located right on the water, across the street from the Islander Lopez Motel, this family-friendly restaurant has a wonderful view and an excellent seafood selection that changes daily. The clam chowder is outstanding. The rest of the menu is standard American fare. During the summer months there is an outdoor dining area and often a long wait for dinner.

### LOPEZ ISLAND PHARMACY
*Lopez Village*
*360/468-2644*
*Hours: Lunch daily, except Sun.*

Sit on the counter stools at this old-fashioned, pink-and-gray soda fountain and treat the kids to shakes, malts, or phosphates to wash down their burgers or sandwiches. This is good food, at low prices—and a fun, '50s-style lunch.

## WHAT TO SEE & DO

### PARKS

**SPENCER SPIT STATE PARK** is an ideal place to spend a sunny afternoon playing on the beach. Next to the parking lot, you'll find a 100-yard trail leading to the park's mile-long, sandy beach bordering a saltwater lagoon. Butter clams, mussels, horse clams, and geoducks are abundant here, so bring along a shovel and bucket (always call the Red Tide Hotline, 800/562-5632, to make sure shellfishing is safe). This is a great spot for beach fires and picnics and the campground at the park is very popular. (A sign is posted at the Anacortes ferry if the campground is full, so campers can make other plans.)

When the tide rolls in over the long, hot beach, the water temperature is usually warm enough for frolicking and it's sufficiently shallow for young kids. At the tip of the spit sits a one-room log cabin—a replica of the original Spencer family guesthouse from the 1800s. The new cabin has a picnic table inside and makes a first-class playhouse.

*From the ferry landing, drive 1.1 miles on Ferry Road to the first junction and turn left on Port Stanley Road. After 2.5 miles, go left again on Baker View Road and continue a half-mile to the park. 360/468-2251.*

**SHARK'S REEF PARK** is a fun destination for a bike ride or car outing. Park your vehicles in the small parking area and take a half-mile hike through the forest to the rock promontory that overlooks a large kelp bed, enormous rocks, and the channel to San Juan Island. You'll likely see sea lions and seals snoozing and frolicking near the rocks just offshore, so take binoculars. There are high cliffs here; keep an eye on the youngsters.

*Follow Fisherman's Bay Road, about 3 miles past the Islander Lopez Resort (up one very long hill). When you reach Airport Road, turn right and continue about one-half mile to Shark Reef Road. Turn left and drive about 2 miles to the park.*

### THE GREAT OUTDOORS

**BICYCLING** is a popular sport on Lopez because of the pleasant country scenery and relatively flat roads. There aren't any separate bike trails, but the light traffic poses little danger to young riders, providing they are steady enough on wheels to steer a straight course.

You can rent bikes at **Lopez Bicycle Works** (360/468-2847) or **Bike Shop on Lopez** (360/468-3497). Both shops will deliver to your lodging or the ferry dock and provide helmets as well as advice on a suitable bike route.

**SEA KAYAKING.** Tours are offered by **Lopez Kayaks** (360/468-2847) in MacKaye Harbor. Kayaks are also available without guides to experienced kayakers. Open summers only.

**MUSEUMS**

**LOPEZ HISTORICAL MUSEUM** is tiny, but it houses an interesting collection of artifacts, sure to be appreciated by those who want to learn more about the island's history. The exhibits include some nifty ship models and a "please touch" table for the kids. While you are there, ask for the island map that includes a tour of historical landmarks.

*Lopez Village. 360/468-2049. Open May to September, Fri.-Sun., noon-4 p.m. Donations accepted.*

## RESOURCES

**LOPEZ ISLAND CHAMBER OF COMMERCE**
P.O. Box 103, Lopez 98261
360/468-3663; www.lopezisland.com

**LOPEZ FERRY TERMINAL**
360/468-2252

## ORCAS ISLAND

Orcas is the largest of the islands with ferry service and it is often called the most beautiful. The highest point in the San Juans, 2,400-foot Mount Constitution, tops this horseshoe-shaped island. From the mountaintop on a clear day, you can see the San Juans, Mount Baker, Vancouver, British Columbia, and the Canadian Gulf Islands. Orcas is busier than sleepy Lopez, but has many secluded nooks and crannies for escaping the hustle and bustle. The island has recently become a popular choice for posh vacation property, but ferries have been running there since the 1890s.

## PLACES TO STAY

**BEACH HAVEN RESORT**
*Rte. 1, P.O. Box 12, Eastsound 98245*
*360/376-2288*

*Rates: Moderate*

*FYI: Kitchens; wood stoves; boat rentals; mooring buoys; playground; Ping Pong, horseshoe pit, tetherball; no phones or TVs; no smoke-free units (patrons asked to smoke outside); seven-day minimum stay in summer, three-night minimum during holidays, two-night minimum other times*

Beach Haven sits on a long, pebbled beach and the cabins are nestled in the woods nearby. Cabins are quite rustic, but clean and comfortable; they all have a nice view of the water and an airtight wood stove to take off the morning or evening chill. Two of the cabins are large enough to accommodate two small families or one large one. These larger cabins have space to spare and a wonderful view of the water.

As you leave the resort, a sign reads "Leaving Beach Haven. Entering the world." Indeed, this is how the vacation is likely to feel. Bring your swimsuits and consider renting a rowboat or canoe, or taking a hike in the forest. Since the cabins don't have phones, TVs, videos, and other distractions, remember to bring some of your own entertainment, such as playing cards, books, art supplies, and games (and lots of popcorn) to pass the evenings. It is some distance to dine out, so you'll probably want to cook most of your meals.

**❝ PARENT COMMENTS**

*"This is a place for parents to relax and for kids to run free."*

*" Since there are no grocery stores nearby, it is nice to bring your groceries with you when you arrive so you don't have to immediately jump back in the car to shop for your first meal."*

*"The seven-day minimum stay worried us when we first got there, but we really unwound by about the fifth day and wished we could stay another week."*

**CASCADE HARBOR INN**

*HC 1, P.O. Box 195, Eastsound 98245*
*360/376-6350, 800/201-2120*
*Rates: Expensive*
*FYI: Complimentary continental breakfast; kitchens; fireplaces*

Located just east of Rosario's along the shore of Cascade Bay, this lovely, 48-unit inn is well-suited to families. Accommodations vary from studios with Murphy beds to multi-room suites with fully equipped kitchens. All have decks and water views. Families planning to stay on the island for several days will appreciate the comfort and spaciousness of either the Cascade Suite or the Island Hearth Suite. Amenities in both include fully equipped kitchen, dining area, living room with fireplace, and a comfortable Murphy bed in the living room. The Cascade Suite has two bedrooms, each with either one or two queen beds and three full bathrooms. Three private waterfront balconies overlook Cascade Bay. The Island Hearth suite has a bedroom with either one or two queen beds, two full bathrooms, and two waterfront balconies.

**❝ PARENT COMMENTS**

*"This place is a neighbor of, and used to be owned by, Rosario's. We prefer it to Rosario's because the kitchens are a great convenience and cost-saver, and the comfort and attractiveness of the accommodations are far superior."*

**ISLAND INSTITUTE**

*Orcas Hotel, Orcas Ferry Landing*
*Write to: Island Institute, 4004 58th Pl. S.W, Seattle, 98116*
*360/376-6720; www.Orca@islandinstitute.com*
*Rates: Moderate*
*FYI: Price includes lodging, meals, boat tours, guides, and all activities. Bathrooms are shared. All ages welcome, best suited to ages 9 and older. 4 day/3 night package: June-September. Program starts on Sunday and ends on Wednesday. Also available: three-night extension for a full-week program, including a trip to Victoria, British Columbia.*

Island Institute, in its tenth year, operates fully guided adventure programs. It is not your usual vacation resort—more like an educational summer camp for the whole family—but if you and your school-age kids would like to learn more about the remarkably unspoiled and wild maritime territory of the San Juan Islands, Island Institute provides a rare opportunity. Started by Jane O. Howard, an environmental and science educator, the Institute is a small entrepreneurial company based on Orcas Island providing active learning vacations for all ages.

Accommodations are in the Orcas Hotel, a charming, converted 12-room B&B located within easy walking distance of the ferry landing and within 20 minutes of restaurants and shopping in the village of Eastsound. Delicious, home-style meals include an abundance of local delights: Oysters, salmon, and fresh baked bread, to name a few.

Expert guides, friendly staff, and knowledgeable naturalists facilitate a unique vacation experience in a spectacularly beautiful setting. Activities include: Whale watching aboard the Institute's 32-passenger, Coast Guard-certified vessel, the *Navigator*; sea kayaking in stable two-person sea kayaks to explore marine life close up; hiking through Orcas Island forests and to the top of Mount Constitution; guided bicycle treks; outer island explorations to some of the San Juans' most fascinating places and remote wildlife habitats.

**66 PARENT COMMENTS**

*"The staff was uniformly fun and knowledgeable and the activities were fabulous. The "camp director" kept the activity level just right. Our teenagers were starting to make noises about not wanting to go on family vacations, but this proved to be the perfect place for us to get away together."*

### NORTH BEACH INN

*P.O. Box 80, Eastsound 98245*
*360/376-2660*
*Rates: Moderate; no credit cards*
*FYI: Kitchens; fireplaces; boat rentals; pets OK; no smoke-free units; one-week minimum July-August, two-night minimum other months*

If you feel that little changes at the North Beach Inn, you're right. The Gibson family has operated this peaceful resort since 1932. The 11 cottages are in a wooded setting along a 1.3-mile stretch of pebble beach. There are also 90 acres of woods and fields, and lovely views of the Canadian San Juans and sunsets. Cottages are simple and clean. The Shamrock cabin has a loft that would be dangerous for toddlers, but older kids love it. In addition to kitchen and fireplace, each cabin has a grill, a great view and comfortable chairs for the beach.

Bring your own entertainment; this is a no-frills vacation spot where you'll have plenty of time for beachcombing, games of charades and cards, and that 500-page novel you've been trying to read for months.

**66 PARENT COMMENTS**

*"The real fun is in building a fire on the beach at night. But beware—with all the fires over the years, playing in the sand can result in some pretty dirty legs and hands."*

*"When we got restless we drove to Moran State Park and climbed to the top of Mount Constitution. Our children, ages seven and 10, did not find the hike too difficult, and the view at the top was spectacular."*

### YMCA ORKILA FAMILY CAMP

*For reservations: 909 Fourth Ave., Seattle, 98104*
*206/382-5009*
*Rates: Inexpensive*
*FYI: Rate includes all meals and activities, plus transportation from the ferry landing; outdoor pool (summer only); boating; crafts, archery and gun range; rock climbing*

Five weekends each year, the YMCA of Greater Seattle opens this popular summer camp to families. Families stay in the 40 cabins—mostly rustic, open-air buildings located on the beach or nearby in the woods. Sometimes two or more families will share a large cabin. Bathroom facilities are located nearby. Except the few "winterized" cabins sometimes available upon request, the accommodations are primitive—think of it as camping with a roof over your head. If possible, get one of the three-sided cabins right on the beach and wake each day to a spectacular view of the water and nearby islands. The kids can scamper right out the door to the beach. Meals are served in Norman Lodge (typical camp food—reasonably nourishing but not inspired).

Orkila Farm offers a chance to meet pigs, cows, turkeys, llamas, and rabbits. For sports activities, enjoy the ball fields, basketball court, or swimming pool, or boat to small islands nearby. The strong of heart will enjoy the challenge of the simulated rock-climbing wall, archery area, or BB gun range. For the artistically inclined, the Craft and Pottery Shop usually has several craft projects in progress.

**❝❝ PARENT COMMENTS**
*"This is a totally relaxing, fun way to vacation. Not first-class comfort but great fun being a camper right alongside your kids in a gorgeous natural setting."*

**VACATION RENTAL PROPERTIES.** For information on rental property, call **Cherie Lindholm Real Estate** at 360/376-2204.

## PLACES TO EAT

### BILBO'S FESTIVO

*North Beach Rd. and A St., Eastsound*
*360/376-4728*
*Hours: Dinner daily; lunch seasonally*

This spot offers good Mexican food served in an intimate, charming setting—Mexican tiles and weavings, a large fireplace, mud walls and colorful courtyard flowers in summer, small playground, indoor fireplace and outdoor firepit. The generous portions are reasonably priced, but the service can be slow. Reservations are strongly advised.

### La Famaglia
*Eastsound*
*360/376-2335*
*Hours: Lunch Mon.-Sat., dinner daily, breakfast Sun. (summer); dinner Tues.-Sun. (remainder of year)*

Outstanding Italian food, cheerful décor, friendly service, and reasonable prices. The smoke-free environment and outdoor patio make it an especially good place for young ones. The menu includes fresh pastas, calzones, pizza, and other kid-friendly fare.

### Rose's Bakery Café
*Eastsound*
*360/376-4220*
*Hours: Breakfast, lunch daily*

This is delicious, simple food in a relaxed setting. The outdoor patio is a fine place to have a meal with the kids when the sun is out.

## What to See & Do

### PARKS

**Madrona Point** is a lovely, quiet madrona-forested water-side park saved from development by the Lummi Indian Tribe. Pick up food at Island Market in Eastsound and enjoy a picnic.

*Located at the end of the unmarked road just past Christina's Restaurant in Eastsound.*

**Moran State Park** is one of the best reasons for visiting Orcas Island. The fourth largest state park in Washington, it offers more than 30 miles of hiking trails, five lakes (the two largest have swimming, fishing, and boat rentals), and four campgrounds (reservations required). Topping it all is Mount Constitution—the highest peak in the San Juans, accessible by foot or car. Although the park borders the Strait of Georgia, the saltwater frontage is a rocky cliff with no beach access. For families, the park has several highlights: **Cascade Falls** are a spectacular and popular destination at the park. To get there, either walk one-quarter mile from the road, or take the *Cascade Falls Trail* (2.7 miles) from the south end of Mountain Lake to the falls, and on to the South End Campground at Cascade Lake.

**Cascade Lake** has a large day-use area with a pleasant picnic spot, swimming beach, dock, and short nature trail (in the trees west of the picnic area). Paddle boats and rowboats are available for rent. Both Cascade and Mountain lakes have a boat launch and provide excellent trout fishing (outboard motors are prohibited on all park lakes). The 2.5-mile *Cascade Lake Loop Trail* is a mostly level circuit of the lake, where you may spot muskrat, otter, and great blue heron. The Environmental Learning Center at the south end of Cascade Lake has nine cabins, a fully equipped kitchen and mess hall, infirmary, swimming beach, and dock. It is available for rental.

**Mountain Lake** also has rowboat rentals. *Around-the-Lake Trail* (four miles) is fairly easy and includes a variety of sights and sounds to keep young hikers intrigued, including deserted log cabins, a dam, and a foot bridge (south end of the lake).

# Whale of a Good Time

### BY MARIE SHERLOCK

"Whoa! Did you see that? It was a double spyhop! Look—over there! It's a double breach! I can't believe this!"

Tom Averna is excited, and his enthusiasm is contagious. He's describing the antics of the orca whales that are cavorting alongside the *Squito,* Averna's 43-foot boat. Breaches are full-body jumps; "spyhopping" is what a whale does when it thrusts its majestic head out of the water—to keep an eye on what's happening topside.

Averna is the owner of Deer Harbor Charters, a whale-watching company located on Orcas Island. My husband and I and our two sons, eight and six, are on his afternoon cruise, which departs from Rosario's Resort. Tom's wife, Jean, and their twin 10 year olds have joined us, and on this particular day we've hit the proverbial whale-watching jackpot: We're being entertained by a "super-pod." As many as 88 whales from three separate pods have converged and are putting on a show not more than 30 feet away.

The first hour or so of the trip was spent motoring to the west side of San Juan Island, where most Orcas congregate. The waters are pretty choppy, and I am having a hard time relaxing, even though we're all suited up in life preservers. Elizabeth Petras, the on-board naturalist, diverts my attention by offering information about the whales that we're hoping to see.

### SUPER-POD ENCOUNTER

As Petras talks to us, we have no idea that within minutes we will see orcas for ourselves, nor can we imagine the impact the experience will have on us. While our "orca encounter" lasts no more than an hour, we will undoubtedly remember it for the rest of our lives.

We are treated to dozens of breaches, spyhops, and tail-lobs—several times in tandem. Due to the sheer numbers of whales present, it is difficult to take it all in. As Petras points to a breach on the right, we are busy "oohing" over a spyhop on the left. Several times, after witnessing a particularly impressive series of gymnastic moves, the passengers spontaneously burst into applause.

At least a dozen other whale-watching boats are also in the audience. Tom comments that all the boats are behaving in accordance with the "100-yard rule." (Federal law dictates that when boats come within 100 yards of an orca, they must cut their engines. If the orca then swims closer, that's great—but boats are not allowed to approach them.)

The grand finale comes when a sub-pod of about six orcas blesses us with a "swim by" and comes within five feet of the port side of the Squito. I was the one who had been chanting mantras to calm myself as we rode the choppy seas at the outset of our journey. Now I find myself hanging over the side of the boat, snapping photos. Had I reached out, I could have touched the whales. As the orcas breach, my boys and I are splashed!

Not all whale watchers are so lucky. Averna is quick to point out that he can't guarantee that his passengers will

To get to the trail, go to the Mountain Lake Landing and park near the ranger cabins. Take the loop counter-clockwise and stay left on the lake trail. At the north end of the lake there is easy access to the water; have the kids wear bathing suits under their clothes so they are ready for a quick dip.

**Mount Constitution** offers sweeping vistas and numerous

see whales on any given day. But he is able to give his customers a good prognostication by using the services of a whale-spotting concern that operates out of Victoria, British Columbia. Averna estimates that throughout the entire whale-watching season (May through September), he probably has a 70 percent sighting record. In June, however, the chances of an orca encounter rise to more than 90 percent.

### DWINDLING NUMBERS

On the trip home, eight-year-old Ben and I sit with Petras to learn more. She notes that while Orcas are neither an endangered nor a threatened species, this particular group of pods has seen its population diminish in recent years from 95 to 88. The popular explanation among whale experts, she says, is that the dwindling numbers of king salmon—the killer whale's primary food source—has meant a decrease in the Orcas' numbers.

When Ben hears this, he tells Petras about his school's project. Students are growing salmon fry and then releasing them into Johnson Creek. Petras congratulates him on his efforts, and Ben lights up when he realizes that his actions may actually help these majestic creatures.

An encounter with orcas can leave a profound impact. The day of the super-pod party, we weren't the only witnesses to be spellbound. Comments by our fellow passengers, as recorded in the ship diary, reflect this: "Such a wonderful, spiritual afternoon." "I'm not sure how, but seeing these creatures changed us." "We loved every magical moment of the trip!"

My family felt the same way. We're planning another family trip to visit our whale friends next summer.

hikes. Mount Constitution Road is a narrow, steep and winding trip to the top (travelers prone to carsickness, beware). Once you get to the summit, you'll find a magnificent 50-foot stone lookout tower built in 1936 by the Civilian Conservation Corps and modeled after a 12th-century Caucasian mountain fortress. The climb up the tower stairs is fun, even for preschoolers, and the view at the top provides ample reward.

*To reach Moran Park from the ferry terminal, travel north on Horseshoe Hwy. to Eastsound, then continue east and south to the park entrance (13 miles). 360/378-2326.*

### MUSEUMS

**ORCAS ISLAND HISTORICAL MUSEUM** is a fine local museum—well worth a visit. Exhibits of pioneer and Native American artifacts are displayed in four interconnected log cabins. Ethan Allen, San Juan Island's school superintendent, gathered much of the valuable Indian collection at the turn of the century. The hand-built boat he used to row between the islands is on display at the museum. The lawn next door has picnic tables—a good spot to have a bite after a journey through history.

*Located in Eastsound. Turn north off Main St. onto North Beach Rd.; two blocks to museum. 360/376-4849. Open Weds.-Sun.*

### THE GREAT OUTDOORS

**SEA KAYAKING.** East Sound, a large bay on the side of Orcas Island, is one of the most popular places in the San Juans for newcomers to learn to paddle, as well as the launching point for many multiday trips. **Crescent Beach Kayaks** (360/376-2464) and **Shearwater Adventures** (360/376-4699) offer rentals, lessons, and guided tours at East Sound and **Island Kayak Guides** (360/376-4755) has the same services at Doe Bay. If you really want a thrill, ask about the kayak whale-watching tours.

**WHALE WATCHING.** Summer is the best time to spot these graceful giants, when pods follow migrating salmon close to shore, but an organized network of whale spotters keeps track of the pods and sightings occur throughout the year. Most whale-watching companies operate out of Friday Harbor on San Juan Island, however, there are a few companies on Orcas, including **Deer Harbor Charters** (800/544-5758), featured in "Whale of a Good Time" on page below and **Orcas Island Eclipse Charters** (360/376-4663; 800/376-6566).

### RESOURCES

**ORCAS ISLAND CHAMBER OF COMMERCE**
P.O. Box 252, Eastsound 98245
360/376-2273; www.orcasisland.org

**ORCAS FERRY TERMINAL**
360/376-2134

**TRAVEL INFOCENTER**
Located adjacent to the Historical Museum on North Beach Road in Eastsound, this unstaffed kiosk has free maps and brochures.

## SAN JUAN ISLAND

San Juan is the most populated of the islands and has the greatest number of visitor attractions. The island's historical claim to fame is The Pig War—aptly named for its one and only casualty. This 1859 boundary dispute began when a British pig dug up some potatoes planted by an American settler. An argument ensued between Britain and the United States about whose land the pig was on while committing the offense. Troops built two separate camps, but the "war" was conducted cordially—the troops even entertained one another socially. In 1872, the ruler of Germany was asked to decide the boundary issue, and he decreed the islands belonged to America. There are now two parks that pay tribute to the war: The British Camp on the northwest side of the island and the American Camp on the southwest side.

Not surprisingly, it is the noble black-and-white orca, not the historical pig, that attracts most visitors to San Juan Island. Here you'll find the first whale museum and the first whale-watching park in the nation. Above all, San Juan Island is a place to explore the outdoors. Let the little ones get wet surveying tide pools. Fly a kite at American Camp or watch a bald eagle soar overhead. When you tire of outside endeavors—and of emptying the sand from little tennis shoes—Friday Harbor is a fun town to explore.

### PLACES TO STAY

**HARRISON HOUSE SUITES**
*235 C St., Friday Harbor 98250*
*360/378-3587; 800/407-7933*
*Rates: Moderate*
*FYI: Kitchens, free breakfast; hot tub, whirlpool baths*
Located up the hill from downtown Friday Harbor, only a block and a half from the ferry terminal, Harrison House Suites

offer fully furnished, private suites with all the amenities of home, including private baths and well-stocked kitchens. The main building is a 1905 Craftsman. The cottage next door is a "Roche Harbor House" from the thirties. Both are beautifully restored and furnished. Suite One is spacious (1,650-sq.-ft.), with two-plus bedrooms, two baths, hardwood floors, formal dining area, piano, and wood stove. It sleeps at least 10 and is probably too "nice" for rambunctious children. The 35-foot private deck is accessed through the sunroom and offers all-day sunny exposure, with partial views of town, the port, and the harbor. Suite Two has about 800 square feet of living space and a deck with spectacular views; it sleeps two to eight. The cottage is smaller, and comfortably sleeps at least four. The yard is beautifully landscaped: The sun porch on the south side of the cottage faces a wildflower and winter annuals garden. Sumptuous breakfasts include fresh harvests from the kitchen garden.

**❝ PARENT COMMENTS**

*"The suites are elegantly furnished, including French doors, antiques, and a piano in the largest. If you have a destructive toddler, you won't be able to fully relax. The cottage is the best choice for families, unless your kids are very civilized."*

### INN AT FRIDAY HARBOR/SUITES INN AT FRIDAY HARBOR

*P.O. Box 339, Friday Harbor 98250*
*360/378-3031*
*Rates: Moderate to expensive*
*FYI: Restaurant (Suites Inn); kitchens (Suites Inn); refrigerators/microwaves; indoor pool; exercise room (Inn at Friday Harbor); shuttle service; pets OK (Inn at Friday Harbor only)*

The Inn at Friday Harbor and Suites Inn at Friday Harbor are sister establishments, located within two blocks of one another. All guests may use facilities at either accommodation. The Suites is the newer of the two. Previously a retirement center, it offers spacious one- and two-bedroom suites and kitchenettes with microwaves. Though older, the Inn at Friday Harbor has been remodeled and offers a nice indoor pool and exercise room.

**❝ PARENT COMMENTS**

*"We chose not to take our car to the islands, so the free shuttle was a real lifesaver. We visited in the fall when there were less crowds and the indoor pool was a nice treat in the evening, after we had spent a busy day exploring."*

## LAKEDALE RESORT

*2627 Roche Harbor Road, Friday Harbor 98250*
*360/378-2350, 800/617-CAMP*
*Rates: Moderate*
*FYI: Complimentary continental breakfast, kitchens; fireplaces;*
*hot tub; fishing; boat rentals; grocery store*

If the family enjoys fishing and lake swimming, this is the place. This family-friendly resort used to have just a campground and park with three stocked lakes, but they recently added attractive log cabins. The lakeside cabins have two bedrooms and two full baths (linens provided) and will sleep five or six comfortably. Each offers a fully stocked kitchen with service for six, pots and pans, microwave, a full-size stove, oven and refrigerator, and a dining nook.

A fireplace and large, lakefront deck add to the all-around comfort. A continental breakfast is delivered to your door each morning. Outside, each cabin has a fire ring with a grill for cooking.

The three lakes are large, private, and stocked annually with more than 5,000 rainbow trout and resident bass. Cabin guests can fish free and also receive two hours of free boat rental per day. Fishing poles, canoes, and paddleboats can be rented at regular rates. There is no lifeguard on duty. The small store stocks basic food items and fishing supplies.

**❝❝ PARENT COMMENTS**

*"My kids love to fish so they were in heaven. The log cabins are super comfortable and the staff very friendly and helpful."*
*"You will need a car to explore the island."*

## LONESOME COVE RESORT

*5810 Lonesome Cove Road, Friday Harbor 98250*
*360/378-4477*
*Rates: Moderate*
*FYI: Kitchens; fireplaces; five-night minimum stay in summer,*
*two-night minimum other seasons*

The six charming cabins that sit in the trees on the water's edge are small (the largest sleeps six), but you probably won't care because you'll want to spend your time outside on the lovely beach or lounging on the well-kept lawn. Kids will enjoy spotting the domesticated deer that roam the 75-acre woods.

**66 PARENT COMMENTS**

*"Lonesome Cove looks like every island resort should—minimal but immaculate. I escaped for a weekend of "special time" with my seven year old in late May and the only bad part was pulling ourselves away and heading back to the ferry on Sunday."*

### MARIELLA INN AND COTTAGES

*630 Turn Point Road, Friday Harbor 98250*
*360/378-6868*
*Rates: Expensive*
*FYI: Complimentary continental breakfast, kitchens; bikes, kayaks for rent; yacht charters*

The Mariella is physically close to Friday Harbor, yet far from the hubbub of downtown activity. Children are not allowed to stay in the Inn, but they are welcome in the 11 romantic, but small, waterfront cottages; these range in size and amenities, so be sure to ask for specifics when making reservations. A breakfast basket with juice, fresh muffins, and croissants is delivered each morning. There are nine acres to roam or bike, and the waterfront is nice for sunbathing or boating (kayaks and sailboats for rent). A volleyball net is always up in the summer. A 65-foot yacht, the *Arequipa*, is available for day charters.

**66 PARENT COMMENTS**

*"The location was lovely—our cottage was perched right next to the water. But it was an expensive weekend. Next time we visit San Juan with the kids we will go someplace more funky and save this lovely place for a mom-and-dad getaway."*

### ROCHE HARBOR RESORT

*Roche Harbor Road, P.O. Box 4001, Roche Harbor 98250*
*360/378-2155*
*Rates: Moderate*
*FYI: Restaurant, snack bars, kitchens (condos and cottages); outdoor pool; paddle boats, canoes, kayaks; whale-watching, fishing; tennis courts, playground; grocery store, gift shop*

Located on the northern tip of the island, Roche Harbor Resort manages to be both romantic and family-oriented. If you are trying for romance on this family getaway, try a dinner reservation at the restaurant overlooking the marina and a saunter in the well-kept gardens. For the family, there's a heated Olympic-size swimming pool (with a snack bar nearby), boat rentals, tennis courts, and a small, old-fashioned playground. But don't expect a fancy resort or you will be disappointed.

Nine former workers' cabins have been converted to two-bedroom cabins: They are the closest accommodations to the swimming pool and the best bet for families. Furnishings in the cottages are "Salvation Army," perfect if you want to relax and not worry about the kids damaging fancy décor. Condos are a bit nicer, but farther from the pool and the beach. The hotel restaurant is nothing special, but convenient if you don't want to cook or drive to town.

Located near what was once the largest lime mine and kiln west of the Mississippi, Roche Harbor Resort was originally a company town. Industrialist John McMillan, who owned the town, built the Hotel De Haro, at the center of the resort. It is historically interesting but rooms are small and slightly dank—not a good choice for most families.

Afterglow Vista, the bizarre mausoleum McMillan built on the premises, will most likely fascinate school-age kids. The ashes of family members are contained in stone chairs set around a concrete dining table.

**❝ PARENT COMMENTS**

*"This is an 'old-time' resort, in good repair if somewhat saggy. It feels like a summer camp, including a delightful sunset flag ceremony."*

*"Not fancy—has somewhat the feel of a place that has seen better days. But we had a very pleasant three-day summer weekend with our kids, six and eight. Parents of younger kids, beware: It's a long walk from the condos to the pool!"*

*"The mausoleum is set in the middle of old-growth forest, so the dining table and chairs are a short hike into the forest. Truly spooky; our kids love it and no trip to the island is complete without a visit here. You can get a map to the mausoleum from the front desk at the hotel."*

*"At the end of the pier at Roche Harbor is a small café. It's a good value for a quick meal. Also, the snack bar makes a good root beer float. On a hot day, we like to come here, get ice cream or a float and stroll the grounds."*

**VACATION RENTAL PROPERTY.** For information on rental of private cabins, call **San Juan Island Vacation Rentals** (360/378-5060; 800/992-1904).

## PLACES TO EAT

### BELLA LUNA
*175 Front St. S., Friday Harbor*
*360/378-4118*
*Hours: Breakfast, lunch, dinner daily (open later on weekends)*

Bella Luna is housed in the building that was once home to the adult-oriented Electric Company bistro. Now reincarnated as a pleasant Italian family restaurant, it welcomes diners of all ages. Along with a good assortment of pizza options, half portions of straightforward pasta dishes are available for child-size appetites, with prices to match. Adults can enjoy traditional Italian favorites, such as eggplant Parmesan, at reasonable prices. Service is pleasant and accommodating to family needs and small-fry preferences.

### THE BISTRO
*35 First St., Friday Harbor*
*360/378-3076*
*Hours: Lunch, dinner daily*

Head here for your pizza fix. A selection of pastas and lasagna is available, too. Local families dine here regularly, taking advantage of the moderate prices and laid-back (even for the islands) atmosphere.

### BLUE DOLPHIN
*185 1st St., Friday Harbor*
*360/378-6116*
*Hours: Breakfast, lunch daily*

The Blue Dolphin is a no-frills diner serving generous portions of delicious, home-cooked favorites for breakfast and lunch, at budget prices. It opens very early for those taking the super-early ferry back to the mainland.

### THE CANNERY HOUSE RESTAURANT
*174 N. First St., Friday Harbor*
*360/378-2500*
*Hours: Lunch daily (year-round); dinner daily (summer)*

This small restaurant with a big view overlooks the Port of Friday Harbor marina; kids will enjoy watching the ferries come and go. A deck with tables and umbrellas is open in the summer, and that's the place to be unless the yellow jackets beat you to it.

The Cannery House is known for its thick, tasty sandwiches

(named for islands and usually served hot), melted cheese sandwich, and the ever-popular pb&j. If there's a picnic in your plans, this is also a good spot to order take-out sandwiches.

### FRIDAY'S CRABHOUSE
*65 Front St., Friday Harbor*
*360/378-8801*
*Hours: Lunch, dinner daily (seasonal)*
   This outdoor café is open during the high season only; it's closed from early fall to spring. Near the Front Street Café and just north of the lot where cars park waiting for the ferry, Friday's serves all kinds of fresh seafood (mostly deep-fried) and a few salads. What's offered depends on the local catch: There's usually salmon, scallops, prawns, oysters, and calamari. Crab is the exception to the frying rule; it's boiled and cracked. Diners order and pay at the gazebo, and servers bring food to the outdoor tables (some have sun umbrellas).
   There's no children's menu here, but an order of fish and chips can be divided between two little ones. A selection of drinks, including beer and wine, is available. The lovely view to the east extends to Mount Baker. You can see the ferry coming in time to hustle back to your car with the remains of your dinner boxed up for you.

### FRONT STREET CAFÉ
*7 Front St., Friday Harbor*
*360/378-2245; no credit cards*
*Hours: Breakfast, lunch, dinner daily; shorter hours in winter; pick-up and delivery*
   If it's scrumptious eggs and breads you seek, try this café across from the ferry dock. Front Street Café offers great breakfasts, baked goods (try the beer bread), and espresso. If breakfast time has come and gone, opt for a homemade soup or head straight for the homemade ice cream and Italian ices. There's a great view of the ferry landing and cars unloading and loading.

### MI CASITA
*75 Nichol St., Friday Harbor*
*360/378-6103*
*Hours: Lunch, dinner daily*
   Another newcomer to Friday Harbor, Mi Casita features a wide variety of Mexican favorites at family-friendly prices. A kid menu offers the tried-and-true. Our parent reviewers— anxious to dine quickly, in order to fit in a visit to the wild

bunny rabbits at American Camp before sunset—were fed promptly even though the restaurant was quite busy. Service is pleasant and efficient.

### ROBERTO'S
*1st & A St., Friday Harbor*
*360/378-6333*
*Hours: Dinner daily*

This lovely little restaurant is perched above street level and serves up delicious, authentic Italian dishes, with an emphasis on pasta and seafood. Plenty of offerings appeal to kids and the staff is welcoming to young diners. However, it gets crowded on warm summer nights, and waits can be long. Your best bet is to arrive early or make reservations.

### VIC'S DRIVE-IN
*25 2nd St., Friday Harbor*
*360/378-8427*
*Hours: Breakfast, lunch, dinner Mon.-Fri.; breakfast, lunch Sat.; closed Sun.*

Located across from the county courthouse, Vic's offers a great selection of burgers, fries, and shakes, as well as lattés and veggie burgers. If your child doesn't find the books and art supplies behind the back counter, owner Mike Sharkey will likely bring a selection to you.

This place is old-fashioned and child-friendly. But don't be misled by the name; Vic's hasn't been a drive-in for years. In fact, if your child lives for the next stop at MacDonald's or Taco Time, the San Juans are a great place to go "cold turkey." There are no franchise restaurants on the islands. Local teens haunt Vic's; it's where they head after school and sometimes at lunchtime. It's a good place to meet other kids, if yours are social.

## WHAT TO SEE & DO
### STROLL & BROWSE

If you want to stroll the streets of Friday Harbor, do some leg stretches first. This charming old fishing village is built on a hillside and the only way to get to the town center is to go up. It can be a real chore with a stroller or a youngster that wants to be carried. Parking is at a premium. Take the signs seriously; the local authorities don't hesitate to ticket tourists.

A good first stop is the **San Juan Roasting Chocolate Company** (formerly San Juan Chocolate Company) in the

Cannery Landing. This spot offers coffee fresh-roasted daily, a selection of fine chocolates, ice cream cones, and sandwiches. Baby strollers need to go behind the building for wheeled access. **The Toy Box** (also in Cannery Landing) is about the size of a big toy box, but it's packed with a variety of small treasures.

### PARKS

**SAN JUAN HISTORICAL PARK** preserves the American and British camps from the Pig War of 1859.

**AMERICAN CAMP** is located at the south end of the island. It includes the officers' quarters and a laundress' building. A trail leading from an interpretive shelter to an earthen redoubt provides an interesting opportunity to discuss defensive warfare strategy. On several Saturdays, June through August, there are historical reenactments depicting camp life in the 1860s and a guided walk. (Call 360/378-2902 for schedule of events.)

The park also boasts the longest public beach on the island. It's a great place to picnic and watch for whales, shorebirds, and bald eagles. **Fourth of July Beach,** located on the northeastern edge of American Camp Park, is secluded and sandy. The shallow bay is good for wading.

*From ferry terminal, drive up Spring St. to Mullis. Turn left, drive 6 miles (Mullis will become Cattle Point Road) and follow the signs. 360/378-2240.*

**BRITISH CAMP,** located 12 miles away near the northern end of the island, preserves the log blockhouse, a barracks, a commissary, and a small formal garden. This is a lovely place to picnic. There is a small, rocky beach for wading, but bring extra shoes or sandals that can get wet; the rocks are hard on little feet. Take the trail up the mountain—note that it crosses a busy road—for an unsurpassed view of the islands.

*Follow Cattle Point Road to Bailer Hill Road, which becomes West Side Road. You'll pass Lime Kiln State Park. Continue to Mitchell Road, turn right, then left onto West Valley Road and the park. 360/378-2240.*

**LAKEDALE PARK.** If the kids want to swim, but don't enjoy the chilly salt water of the Sound, this is a great place to swim on a hot summer day. There are three lakes on 82 acres and canoe, paddleboat, and rowboat rentals as well as good trout fishing. There is no lifeguard, however, and while it's tempting to trust the little ones in the shallow water, it's good to keep a close eye. There's also a small grocery store, a campground, and six new log cabins (see "Places to Stay").

*Four-and-one-half miles from Friday Harbor on Roche Harbor Road. 360/378-2350.*

**LIME KILN POINT STATE PARK.** On Haro Strait, on the western side of the island facing Victoria, British Columbia, sits the nation's first, if not only, whale-watching park. There are three resident pods of whales, most frequently seen June through August. Even if the whales don't show, enjoy the rocky cliffs and wildflowers at this former limestone quarry. Be sure to bring binoculars. No running water or flush toilets.

*The park is approximately 7 miles from the ferry dock. From Spring St., turn right on San Juan Valley Road, then left on Douglas Road. In 1 mile, turn right on Bailer Hill Road, which becomes West Side Road. Stay on West Side Road to the park.*

## THE GREAT OUTDOORS

**KAYAKING.** Whether you want to take your child for a short ride in a double kayak in protected waters, join a group searching for orcas, or take an overnight, guided wildlife tour, check out the following rental and tour spots: **Crescent Beach Kayaks** (360/376-2464), **Osprey Tours** (360/376-3677), **Shearwater Sea Kayak Tours** (360/376-4699), **Spring Bay Kayaking** (360/376-5531), and **Sea Quest Expeditions** (360/378-5767).

**WHALE WATCHING.** San Juan Island is the hub of whale-watching activity in the San Juans so, not surprisingly, there are many tour companies. Here are a few: **Western Prince Cruises** (360/378-5315; 800/757-ORCA), **San Juan Excursions** (360/378-6636; 800/80904253), **San Juan Boat Tours** (360/378-3499; 800/232-6722), **Grey Eagle Charters** (360/378-6403), and **Roche Harbor Marine Activities Center** (360/378-2155, ext. 505; 800/451-8910).

**WESTCOTT BAY SEA FARMS.** Kids can harvest oysters and clams from saltwater bins at bargain prices and parents can enjoy a shellfish feast. When choosing the quantity to buy, though, don't assume your youngster will not eat these slippery, slimy, weird-looking critters. It might be something to do with the fun of plucking the little morsels from the shell, but defying all kid culinary rules, many super-picky eaters have been known to devour huge numbers of steamed clams and even oysters.

*4071 Westcott Dr. (Off Roche Harbor Road, 2 miles south of Roche Harbor Resort.) 360/378-2489.*

### MUSEUMS

**THE WHALE MUSEUM.** This little spot is reputed to be the first whale museum in the nation. You'll find yourself immersed (excuse the pun) in the world of sea-going leviathans—from the large mural on the building exterior to the whale songs that greet you and the museum store that's replete with whale paraphernalia. Located three blocks northwest of the ferry dock in Friday Harbor, the museum also features complete skeletons of a gray whale calf and an adult killer whale, a children's room, and a short movie about whale parenting that will be enjoyed by all ages.

*62 1st St. N. 360/378-4710; www.whale-museum.org. Open daily, 10 a.m.-6 p.m. Cost: $5/adult, $2/child 5-18, free/under 5.*

## CALENDAR

### JULY

San Juan Dixieland Jazz Festival: Three days of jazz, mid- to late-July, Friday Harbor, 360/378-5509.

### AUGUST

San Juan County Fair.

## RESOURCES

### CHAMBER OF COMMERCE

P.O. Box 98, Friday Harbor 98250
360/378-5240; www.sanjuan.com

### FRIDAY HARBOR FERRY TERMINAL

360/378-4777

### THE NATIONAL PARK SERVICE

125 Spring St., P.O. Box 429, Friday Harbor 98250
360/378-2240

# THE PUGET LOWLANDS

With such attractive and well-known neighbors—the North Cascades to the east, Vancouver, B.C. to the north, and

Seattle just south—this region of Washington State is easy to overlook when planning a vacation. Running from the Canadian border to King County and the mountains to the sound (including Whidbey Island), it is a fine place to visit. For the most part, the region is uncrowded and unhurried, presenting fewer hassles and more opportunity for family fun.

## BIRCH BAY/BLAINE

The town of Blaine is located on the U.S.-Canada border; Birch Bay is located nearby. Each is well situated for day trips to Bellingham, Mount Baker, or even Vancouver, B. C. (45 minutes north). Birch Bay, a popular beach community, is on a shallow bay on the Georgia Strait. The water temperature in the bay is uncharacteristically warm for Northwest salt water, and the tidal beach is great for water play. There are also a number of other family activities here.

### GETTING THERE

**BY CAR.** Birch Bay is approximately 110 miles north of Seattle, just off Interstate 5. Blaine is a few miles farther north, at the border.

**REFUELING.** If you're heading north on I-5, Mount Vernon is a good rest stop. There are numerous fast-food establishments at Exit 230, on the northern edge of town. If you want a more relaxed break, **PACIONI'S PIZZA** (606 S. 1st St.; 360/336-3314) and **CHUCKWAGON DRIVE-IN** (800 N. 4th; 360/336-2732) come highly recommended (see "Mount Vernon: Places to Eat").

If you want to break up the drive and do more than just fill stomachs, check "Things to See & Do" in the Skagit Valley and Bellingham chapters.

### PLACES TO STAY

#### INN AT SEMIAHMOO
*9596 Semiahmoo Pkwy., Blaine 98230*
*360/371-2000, 800/-770-7992; www.inn-at-semi-ah-moo.com*
*Rates: Expensive*
*FYI: Three restaurants; fireplaces (some units); indoor/outdoor pool; steam rooms; weight room; tanning booths; bike rentals; indoor and outdoor tennis courts, squash and racquetball courts, indoor track; golf (including putting area for kids); cruises; gift shop and galleries; baby-sitting*

For a weekend getaway, or if you happen to have a meeting here and want to bring the family along, the Inn at Semiahmoo is a lovely place to play and rest, with or without kids. It is an attractive, Cape Cod-style resort sitting at the tip of a spit, across the harbor from Blaine. Operated by Wyndham Resorts, it is tastefully decorated and service is good.

The rooms are spacious and nicely furnished in rattan and pine. The first-floor rooms with a view of the bay may be worth the extra expense for families; they look out on the beach and sand play area, so you can supervise children from your room. There's a small sundry and snack store, as well as laundry facilities, at the marina next to the resort.

A main attraction for families is the deluxe health club with every imaginable convenience. In addition to the first-class indoor athletic facilities, there are outdoor tennis courts, a pool that is both indoor and outdoor, and an Arnold Palmer-designed golf course nearby. Tennis, racquetball, and golf lessons are available for adults and kids at extra cost. There are also cruises on a resort boat to the San Juan Islands (early May through October) and sportfishing expeditions. The large, well-maintained sandy areas between hotel and beach are intended for horseshoes and volleyball, but they wind up being used as giant sandboxes. (Be sure to bring the sand toys.) Jogging, biking, and hiking paths are just outside the door of the resort, and clamming permits are available if you want a clambake on the beach.

The inn has three restaurants: the gourmet, most expensive option; the more casual place with the best view and a tasty grill-and-pasta menu; and a lounge and oyster bar that serves lunch outside on the deck in nice weather.

The best idea for breakfast is room service. The children's breakfast menu for room service is very reasonably priced, and kids can stay in their pajamas to eat.

**❝ PARENTS COMMENTS**

*"This is an ideal place to escape to if the rain is getting to you and you want to give the kids a place to burn off excess energy. We went on a rainy three-day weekend. The athletic club was a big treat for us (we got massages, sat in the steam room) and our school-age kids, who played indoor tennis and swam in the indoor/outdoor pool."*

*"This resort is expensive (we got a good deal by using a coupon book), but we returned to Seattle feeling completely refreshed."*

*"There are no refrigerators in the rooms so bring non-perishable snacks and drinks, unless you want to sell your soul to room service."*

**BIRCH BAY CONDO RENTALS**
*7824 Birch Bay Dr., Blaine 98230*
*360/371-7633*
*Rates: Moderate to expensive (two-night minimum)*
*FYI: Kitchens; fireplaces; washers/dryers (in units); indoor pool; indoor racquetball courts; outdoor tennis courts (bring your own equipment)*

Formerly Jacobs Landing Rentals, this condo development has a pleasant architectural style and a good location—across the road from the beach and two miles from the state park in Birch Bay. Not all units have views, but each has a deck, living room, dining area, fireplace (not always wood-burning), fully equipped kitchen, and laundry facilities. One-, two- and three-bedroom units are available; two-bedroom units have a queen bed in one room, twins in the other, plus a sofa bed in the living room. Good insulation between the units keeps the atmosphere restful.

The beach near the condos is rocky and not particularly inviting. Although the bay is warm enough for swimming in the summer, the indoor pool is a nice alternative.

**❝❝ PARENT COMMENTS**
*"It was the rainy season and we needed a quick escape to a place with an indoor pool. I wouldn't recommend Birch Bay for longer than a couple of days, but for a weekend getaway with our kids (ages nine and 12) it did the job."*

*"In the summer Birch Bay is a lively beach town. Not the place to go if you are trying to escape the crowds. But with the waterslides, go-karts, and all, it was a big hit with our eight and 11 year olds."*

**WHAT TO SEE & DO**

**BIRCH BAY** is one of the oldest resort towns in Washington State and offers a number of fun-in-the-sun activities that make it very popular during summer months. If the family tires of the beach, you can try out the go-karts, 18-hole miniature golf course, game arcades, and miniature train ride at **BIRCH BAY FAMILY FUN CENTER** (4620 Birch Bay/Lynden Road; 360/371-7700). There's also a 36-hole all-weather putting course at **BORDERLAND MINI-GOLF AND FAMILY ENTERTAINMENT CENTER** (4815 Alderson Road; 360/371-3330) and **WILD 'N WET WATERSLIDES** (4874 Birch Bay/Lynden Road; 360/371-7500), a huge water park.

**BIRCH BAY STATE PARK.** With more than two miles of outstanding sandy beach along the Strait of Georgia, kite-flying, clam digging, an excellent swimming area, and good sites for picnicking and overnight camping, Birch Bay State Park is a popular destination for both Canadians and Americans. Numerous short interpretive trails wind through the 192 acres of forest, marshland and beach grass—home to beavers, muskrats, opossums, and great blue herons. The occasional minus tides reveal not only a large section of the gently sloping beach but many intertidal creatures for kids to inspect. If you are visiting during the summer, ask about the park's outstanding Junior Ranger program.

*5105 Helwig Road (Take Exit 270 off I-5, head west on Birch Bay/Lynden Road for 3 miles, then turn south on Blaine Road. Continue through town about 1 mile, watching for the park gate on Birch Bay Dr.) 360/371-2800.*

**PEACE ARCH PARK,** at the U.S.-Canada border in Blaine, has lovely formal gardens and wide, sweeping lawns. The arch that straddles the border, engraved with the mottoes "Children of A Common Mother" and "Brethren Dwelling Together In Unity," is a magnificent sight. Peace Arch Park and the companion park on the Canadian side were developed in 1920 to commemorate 100 years of an undefended border between the two countries and to acknowledge the countries' shared origins. Displays tell the history of the park.

North of the large parking lot there is a long, tree-bordered lawn with picnic tables and an enclosed kitchen shelter. Above the northbound lanes of the highway, more picnic tables are scattered around a tree-shaded lawn among beautiful flower gardens.

*Follow the signs to the park off I-5. 360/332-8221.*

**SEMIAHMOO COUNTY PARK.** Combine 200 acres of beach and tideland with a small but excellent museum that captures the history of the spit (once the site of the largest salmon-canning operations in the world) and you have a great spot for families. Located across Drayton Harbor from Blaine, at the

south end of Semihamoo Spit, the park is worth a visit.
Consult a tide table to schedule your visit: The ultra-low tides
of shallow Drayton Harbor allow the beach to warm in the sun;
when the tides return, kids have a perfect place to wade and
swim. The Raven-Salmon Women Totem Pole is a reminder of
the Semiahmoo Indians for whom the park is named.

*9261 Semiahmoo Pkwy. 360/371-5513.*

**SHELLFISH HARVESTING** is popular in Birch Bay and on
Semiahmoo Spit. Low tides expose miles of tidal flats, making
this one of the best areas on the Washington coast for digging
butter clams and the hefty horseneck clams (good for chow-
der). To determine the low-tide schedule for Birch Bay, use the
Port Townsend tide table with a correction for Cherry Point.
Before you dig, though, make sure the shellfish are safe to eat
(*Red Tide Hotline, 800/562-5632*).

See also: "Bellingham: What to See & Do."

## CALENDAR

### JUNE

Hands Across the Border: Celebrate relations between the
   U.S. and Canada, second Sunday, 800/624-3555, Blaine.
   (This celebration shuts down the border for a few hours
   mid-day, so either steer clear or join the fun.)

### JULY

Birch Bay Discovery Days, 360/371-5004.

## RESOURCES

### BIRCH BAY CHAMBER OF COMMERCE

7806 Birch Bay Dr., Birch Bay 98230
360/371-5004

### BLAINE VISITORS INFORMATION CENTER

215 Marine Dr., Blaine 98231
800/624-3555

## BELLINGHAM

Bordered on the west by Bellingham Bay and on the east by
Mount Baker, Bellingham encompasses an interesting mix of
historical architecture, modern commercial districts, and

urban and semi-rural residential areas. The area was "discovered" in 1792 by Capt. George Vancouver, and the early settlement was bolstered by the discovery of coal in 1852. Coal mining, lumber milling, and connection with the trans-Canada railroad kept the area booming into the late 1800s.

Four small settlements originally clustered along the bay were consolidated in 1903 to form the town of Bellingham (the rather jumbled downtown area still shows signs of this consolidation). Today, Bellingham Bay supports an active waterfront port: the marina here is the second largest in the state and home to the Bellingham Cruise Terminal, the southern terminus of the **ALASKA MARINE HIGHWAY SYSTEM** (800/642-0066). Both the city proper and rural surroundings offer much for a family to explore.

## GETTING THERE

**BY CAR.** Bellingham is the last major town before the Canadian border. From Seattle it's 89 miles north on I-5. Mount Vernon is a good place to stop on the way to stretch legs and eat, see "Mount Vernon: Places to Eat."

**BY TRAIN.** The train that runs between Vancouver, B.C. and Seattle stops in Bellingham twice a day. For schedules, phone Amtrak (800/USA-RAIL).

## PLACES TO STAY

### BEST WESTERN LAKEWAY INN
*714 Lakeway Dr., 98226*
*360/671-1011, 800/528-1234*
*Rates: Moderate*
*FYI: Restaurants; indoor pool with children's pool, game room; laundry facilities; small pets OK (fee)*

This is an older hotel, but clean and well maintained. Though also popular with business people, The Lakeway is known for its family atmosphere. The game room and indoor pools offer diversion for travel-weary little ones. There are no rooms with kitchens, but the Lobby Café is casual and serves all three meals.

### HOLIDAY INN EXPRESS
*4160 Guide Meridian, 98226*
*360/671-4800, 800-HOLIDAY*

*Rates: Moderate*
*FYI: Free breakfast buffet; free in-room movies; kitchens (some units); indoor heated pool; baby-sitting; small pets OK*

The locals are proud of this 101-room hotel, the newest of five built in the last two years. It offers great amenities for families—kitchens, indoor pool, and free movies—at very reasonable prices.

### QUALITY INN BARON SUITES

*100 E. Kellogg Road, 98226*
*360/647-8000*
*Rates: Moderate*
*FYI: Free breakfast buffet; VCR (some units); kitchens (some units), refrigerators (most units); outdoor heated pool; whirlpool suites available; exercise room; free shuttle service; pets OK (some rooms—limited availability)*

This is a new hotel, with bright, clean rooms and a lovely outdoor pool that's a big hit with kids. Traveling families will appreciate the rooms with kitchens. The location is convenient to I-5 and restaurants. Visitors who want to explore may use the free shuttle service.

**❝❝ PARENT COMMENTS**

*"We took full advantage of the free shuttle service. How refreshing not to hassle driving in a strange town with all the kids in the car!"*

## PLACES TO EAT

### THE COLOPHON CAFÉ AND VILLAGE BOOKS

*1208 11th St., Fairhaven*
*360/647-0092*
*Hours: Lunch, dinner daily*

This trendy little spot in Fairhaven is two joys wrapped into one—the café is located downstairs beneath Village Books (360/671-2626), a great bookshop for browsers and buyers alike. Delicious offerings include hearty, homemade soups, quiches, and salads. Fancy desserts and coffee drinks are a specialty. In summer. You might enjoy dining on the patio, from which you'll enjoy a view of the bay.

### LA FIAMMA

*200 E. Chestnut (at Railroad Ave.)*
*360/647-0060*

*Hours: 11 a.m.-11 p.m. daily*

These delicious pizzas are wood-fired in an open oven, with tasty toppings and hand-thrown crust (which adds to the entertainment value as well). A hot item for kids is the rosemary lemonade—both sweet and refreshing. After your spicy pizza, walk across the street to **BAY CITY ICE CREAM COMPANY** (1135 Railroad Ave.; 360/676-5156) for the best homemade frozen delights in town.

### STANELLO'S
*1514 12th St., Fairhaven*
*360/676-1304*
*Hours: Dinner daily*

This casual, family-oriented Italian restaurant, located in the Fairhaven historical district, has been the place to go for pizza since the mid-70s. They've developed a gourmet pizza that works well for families with finicky eaters: Diners choose a combination of toppings from an incredibly long list of possibilities.

But don't pass on this one if you're not in a pizza mood; the menu features a wide range of tasty Italian entrées, steak dinners, and soup/salad combinations. Though there's no kids' menu, the staff is happy to accommodate families with half-orders for smaller appetites and free spaghetti for those under five.

## WHAT TO SEE & DO

### STROLL & BROWSE

**HISTORIC FAIRHAVEN DISTRICT.** When Fairhaven, one of the original towns incorporated into Bellingham, was believed the natural choice for a terminus for a transcontinental railroad, speculators made big bucks on land sales and development. That boom ended when Great Northern chose to terminate the tracks in Seattle, but many of the interesting old buildings and homes remain. It's a lively place to stroll, with businesses, restaurants and galleries, some still clinging to a historic theme. Ask for a Walking Tour guide to public buildings and nearby Victorian homes.
*12th St. & Harris Ave.*

**SQUALICUM HARBOR.** Once host to sailing ships carrying timber and coal, today Squalicum Harbor bustles with industry, shipping, pleasure boats and commercial fishing vessels. A two-mile promenade along the inner basin affords sweeping views of the city and close-up views of marine activities. Be sure to bring along a kite; this is a favorite kite-flying spot. The Marine Life Center, located at the Harbor, has a touch tank and several aquariums (see "Animals, Animals").

*1801 Roeder Ave. (one mile northwest). 360/676-2500. Open daily, dawn-dusk. Free.*

### PARKS

Thanks to founding mothers and fathers with foresight, Bellingham is an absolute paradise of parks. For a complete list, contact Bellingham Parks & Recreation, 360/676-6985.

**BOULEVARD PARK.** With one-half mile of saltwater shoreline on Bellingham Bay, Boulevard Park is a popular place for fishing, crabbing, and windsurfing. There is a fun play structure and a large, grassy area for flying Frisbees and kites.

At S. State & Bayview Dr. 360/676-6985.

**FAIRHAVEN PARK.** Developed early this century, Fairhaven Park includes a test garden for the American Rose Society as well as hiking trails, picnic shelters, barbecues, a playground and wading in a toddler pool during the summer or anytime of the year in Whatcom Creek.

*107 Chuckanut Dr. 360/676-6985. Toddler pools open noon-6:30 p.m. summers only.*

**LAKE PADDEN PARK.** The 2.6-mile gravel trail around scenic Lake Padden is just about right for most parents— long enough to provide exercise and entertainment, short enough to avoid complaints. The trail is partially wooded, and there are bridle trails through the woods as well. Or if hiking's not your pleasure, take a swim, enjoy the playground, or rent a paddleboat.

*4882 Samish Way. 360/676-6985.*

**SAMISH PARK.** Located on Lake Samish, this 39-acre park was formerly a log rafting site and fishing resort. During the summer you'll find a lifeguarded swimming area, boat rentals, fishing dock and children's play area. Terraced picnic sites provide a pleasant place for the family to refuel. The Day lodge can be reserved for parties.

*673 N Lake Samish Dr. 360/733-2362.*

**WHATCOM FALLS PARK.** Occupying 241 acres on Whatcom Creek, this park has hiking trails, waterfalls, picnic shelters, tennis courts and a basketball hoop. The juvenile fishing Pond and fish hatchery are especially popular with kids.

*1401 Electric Ave. 360/676-6985.*

## MUSEUMS

**WHATCOM CHILDREN'S MUSEUM** has hands-on exhibits to touch, climb and explore, including Our Town, a pirate ship, human body systems and a newly remodeled Toddler area. Recommended for ages 1 to 8.

*227 Prospect St. 360/733-8769. Open Sun.-Weds., noon-5 p.m.; Thurs.-Sat., 10 a.m.-5 p.m. Closed Mon. Cost: $2/person.*

**WHATCOM MUSEUM AND SYRE EDUCATION CENTER.** One of the largest museums in the state, the Whatcom's three-building complex offers exhibits of historical significance, including Eskimo and Indian artifacts, indigenous birds, and logging memorabilia. For budding young artists, there is a changing collection of contemporary art.

*121 Prospect St. 360/676-6981. Open Tues.-Sun., noon-5 p.m. Free.*

## ANIMALS, ANIMALS

**MARINE LIFE CENTER,** located at Squalicum Harbor, is a cost-free opportunity for families to observe sea life in semi-natural habitats—a small marine life tank and various aquariums. There's even a Touch Pool for those kids (OK, you big kids, too) who can't resist the urge to feel the slimy, squishy creatures and an Observation Pool, where the more delicate species are kept.

*1801 Roeder Ave., at Harbor Center Mall. 360/671-2431. Open daily, 8 a.m.-dusk. Donations.*

**MARITIME HERITAGE CENTER.** Here you'll learn as much as you ever wanted to know about the spawning, hatching and rearing of salmon. This interpretive center has informative displays and a self-guided tour (pick up a brochure). The time to see the hatchling salmon released is in the spring; in the fall (mid-Sept. to mid-Dec.), the adult fish return to spawn.

*1600 C St. 360/676-6806. Open Mon.-Fri., 10 a.m.-3 p.m. Free.*

### THE GREAT OUTDOORS

**BOATING.** With saltwater coastline and several beautiful lakes in the vicinity, you'll find plenty of boating opportunities in Bellingham. **Fairhaven Boatworks** (360/647-2469) rents sailboats and rowboats. Kayaks are available at **The Great Adventure** (360/671-4615).

**HIKING.** Short, easy hikes abound in area parks and neighborhoods. Two are noteworthy: *Lake Padden Park Trail* (see Lake Padden Park, under "Parks") and the *Interurban Trail*, a 5.6-mile hike from Old Fairhaven Parkway through Arroyo Park to Larrabee State Park. This flat trail follows a former railroad bed, and offers some scenic views. It's best for older kids; the trail becomes a bit steep as it traverses Arroyo Park Canyon.

### EXCURSIONS

**HOVANDER HOMESTEAD PARK.** An old farmhouse, a big red barn with real farm animals and a mile of riverbank—what else does any kid need to spend an afternoon exploring? As a National Historic Home, Hovander has been restored to its turn-of-the-century elegance, surrounded by gardens and orchards. Near the barn are farm animals and displays of antique farm implements. Families who explore these 200 acres will find walking trails, fishing facilities, a treehouse, picnic tables and a water tower with a lookout.

Next door to the park is **TENANT LAKE NATURAL INTERPRETIVE CENTER**, where the old Neilsen Homestead has been transformed into an interpretive center for the environment. A one-half mile system of trails and a bird-watching tower tie interpretive displays to the 200 acres of marshy habitat. Be sure to bring the rubber boots. Next to the Interpretive Center is the Fragrance Garden, which allows sight-impaired visitors to explore by fragrance and Braille and provides a sensory treat for visitors with normal sight also.

*5299 Nielsen Road. To get there, take the Ferndale turnoff (Exit 262) off I-5 (about ten minutes north) and drive west to the railroad underpass. Turn left to park. 360/384-3444. Tours May-Sept. Cost: $3/person for the park; $1/person for the house.*

**LAKE WHATCOM RAILWAY.** Since you're in the area, why not give the kids the thrill of a ride on a train pulled by an old steam engine that dates back to the late 1800s. The Lake

Whatcom Railway provides a one-hour trip through woods, a tunnel and past a lake. Passengers may work the handcar at the end of the line. The road at the train site is unpaved, so be sure to take boots if the weather is wet.

*Take I-5 north to Exit 232 (Cook Road) and turn right on Cook Road, left at Sedro Woolley, left at traffic light (Hwy. 9). Proceed north 10 miles, turn right on NP Road. 360/595-2218. Train runs mid-June-Aug., Sat. & Tues., 11 a.m. & 1 p.m. Cost: $10/adult, $5/child 1-17 years, free/under 1. Special seasonal trains: Valentine Train is the Saturday before Valentine's Day; Easter Train is the Saturday before Easter; Independence Day Train is the Saturday before July 4; Christmas Trains are each Saturday in December.*

**PIONEER PARK** is a remarkable collection of pioneer homes, reconstructed from those originally in the area. In addition to the homesteads, there are a general store, a schoolhouse, a printer's shop, and a church. Buildings are crammed with objects from the past.

*First & Cherry sts., Ferndale. 360/384-6461. Tours May-Sept., 11:30 a.m.-4 p.m., or by special arrangement.*

## CALENDAR

### JUNE

Scottish Highland Games, Ferndale first Saturday, 360/384-3444.

### AUGUST

Northwest Washington Fair, Lynden, third weekend, 360/354-4111.

### LATE AUGUST/SEPTEMBER

Bellingham Festival of Music, 360/676-5997.

### OCTOBER

Nooksack Valley Fall Festival and Farm Tours, first weekend, 360/9666-2531.

## RESOURCES

### CONVENTION AND VISITORS BUREAU

904 Potter St., Bellingham, 98226
360/671-3990; 800/487-2032

### WHATCOM TRANSPORTATION AUTHORITY

360/676-RIDE

## SKAGIT VALLEY

The Skagit Valley is wonderfully situated between mountains to the northeast (Mount Baker and the North Cascades) and the salt waters of Puget Sound. It is a region of contrasting terrain: farmland and mud flats, and contrasting seasons: stark winter, when bald eagles flock to the area, and spring, when an explosion of vivid color bursts forth in the fields. An easy one-hour drive from Seattle, it's close enough for a one-day excursion and interesting enough for a week's vacation.

### GETTING THERE

**BY CAR.** On I-5, approximately 60 miles north of Seattle.

### PLACES TO STAY

#### BENSON FARMSTEAD B&B

*1009 Avon-Allen Road, Bow 98232 (northeast of Burlington)*
*360/757-0578; www.bbhost.com\bensonbnb*
*Rates: Moderate*
*FYI: Complimentary breakfast; hot tub; accommodations daily April-Sept., weekends only remainder of year*

The Benson Farmstead is a rarity—a B&B that welcomes kids. Owned by Jerry and Sharon Benson, the 17-room Scandinavian farmhouse was once a working dairy farm, and has extensive grounds which guests are welcome to explore. These include an English garden, an antique machinery garden, and a restored granary, which is now a private preschool run by Sharon.

A homemade dessert is served in the evening and a delicious farm-style breakfast in the morning.

There are four guest bedrooms available on the second floor, as well as an extra foldout bed in the den on the first floor that can be used by families.

The Bensons make available a second vacation rental, the **BAKKE FARMHOUSE**, located on the banks of the Nooksack River, 25 miles northeast of the Benson Farmstead. This three-bedroom, fully furnished farmhouse is situated in a beautiful, secluded valley at the foot of the Twin Sisters mountains. Jerry and Sharon recently restored the house, originally built by Sharon's great-grandparents in 1906. The fields and hills around it are home to elk, deer, and other wildlife. It's a great retreat for hiking, fishing, river tubing, horseback riding, and skiing. A nearby log cabin helps accommodate large groups, retreats, and family reunions.

**❝ PARENT COMMENTS**

*"Too bad there aren't more B&Bs that welcome kids—it's a relaxing way to travel. The Bensons were very hospitable and their familiarity with the region was helpful when planning our weekend. It was our kids' only experience with a B&B and they loved it."*

### LA CONNER COUNTRY INN

*2nd & Morris, P.O. Box 573, La Conner 98257*
*360/466-3101*
*Rates: Moderate*
*FYI: Complimentary continental breakfast; fireplaces (gas); pets OK (fee)*

This is an older, rather nondescript hotel located in downtown La Conner, within easy walking distance of shops, restaurants, and the Swinomish Channel. Not as elegant or expensive as its companion hotel, the La Conner Channel Inn, it is nevertheless a spacious, convenient, and comfortable place for families.

Adjacent to the front deck is a pleasant sitting area with a rock fireplace and plenty of comfortable chairs and tables—nice for families who need some space for reading or games. A breakfast of tasty baked goods, granola, and beverages is served in this room.

**❝ PARENT COMMENTS**

*"We had a room with two double beds and it was so great to have it be spacious (even a table and chairs). We didn't have the usual 'cramped into a tiny room' feeling that we often get when we stay in a motel with the kids. The location was excellent."*

## PLACES TO EAT

### CALICO CUPBOARD

*1720 S. 1st, La Conner*
*360/466-4451*
*120 N. 1st, Mount Vernon*
*360/336-3107*
*Hours: Breakfast, lunch daily; early dinner Thurs.-Sat.*

There are three Calico Cupboards: in La Conner, in Mount

Vernon, and in Anacortes. They specialize in freshly baked goods, which are delectable and quite reasonably priced. All grains used are organically grown; many heart-healthy choices are offered. You can dine in or take out. There's an excellent and, for once, original children's menu. They offer hearty soup, a hard-to-find selection on kid menus, as well as pb&j and other standbys.

Not surprisingly, there are long lines on busy weekends. Put your name on the waiting list (they don't take reservations) and take a stroll to distract the kids from their rumbling bellies. Or buy pastries at the take-out window and have a picnic. Even at busy times, service is speedy once you're seated.

### CHUCK WAGON DRIVE-IN
*800 N. 4th (also known as River Side Dr.), Mount Vernon*
*360/336-2732*
*Hours: Sun.-Thurs., 10 a.m.-10:30 p.m.; Fri.-Sat. until 11:30 p.m.*

Where do you take the crew to eat after a day of wandering through muddy tulip fields and admiring spring displays? For many families the answer is easy: the Chuckwagon in Mount Vernon. Operated since 1947, this local landmark is easy to spot, with its covered wagon entrance flanked by a bench on which a sculpted prospector sits. Inside, three small dining rooms are populated with wildlife and cowboy statues and—best of all—electric trains traversing the ceilings.

Menu options are diverse and imaginative, including at least 55 variations on a hamburger and a full spectrum of desserts, including the Cookie Monster—ice cream with cookies for arms and legs.

### LA CONNER SEAFOOD & PRIME RIB HOUSE
*614 S. 1st St., La Conner*
*360/466-4014*
*Hours: Lunch, dinner daily*

Located on the Swinomish Channel in the middle of town, this restaurant boasts a great view of boating activity. It's the place to go if you want a nice atmosphere and good food—steak, seafood, pasta, and sandwiches—without spending the kind of money you'd spend at some of the more gourmet restaurants in town. Though there is no child's menu per se, most kids will be happy with the chicken strips off the appetizer menu or the fish and chips. Outdoor dining is available in the summer. On a busy weekend, make sure to get your name on the waiting list early and plan on about a half-hour of strolling the town before you are seated.

### PACIONI'S PIZZERIA
*606 S. 1st St., Mount Vernon*
*360/336-3314*
*Hours: Tues.-Sat., 11 a.m.-9 p.m.; Mon., 4:30-9 p.m.; closed Sun.*

If your kids think pizza only comes from a box delivered to the door, treat them to the real thing. Owner Dave Albert tosses the pizza dough gleefully into the air, providing the live entertainment. Red-and-white checkered tablecloths and friendly, amenable servers set the family-friendly ambiance; the pizza will make you a loyal customer, with or without kids.

## WHAT TO SEE & DO

### STROLL & BROWSE
**LA CONNER** is a quaint waterside town on the Swinomish Channel. With its fine restaurants, comfortable B&Bs, and abundance of shops filled with fragile items, You might think it a place to avoid taking the kids. But don't scratch it off your list: This tiny town will interest many youngsters, especially those who like to frequent stores loaded with super-cute and furry items.

A stroll along 1st Street reveals La Conner's charm. The road sits partially on wooden piers over the Swinomish Channel, a narrow waterway loaded with small boats. If shopping is on the agenda, you may want to check out **CASEY JONES TOYS** (610 S. 1st St.; 360/466-2116), which specializes in small stuffed items, baby clothes, and tin toys. **BUNNIES BY THE BAY** (617 E. Morris St.; 360/466-5040; www.bunnies-bythebay.com) is also worth visiting; this Bloomsbury-inspired shop is overflowing with exquisite handmade bunnies, cats, dogs, and bears. (These creations are often fragile, however, so you may be better off window shopping if you have a rambunctious child in tow.) Next door is the **TILLINGHAST SEED COMPANY**, the oldest seed company in the Northwest and also fun to check out. Finally, the **O'LEARY BUILDING** (609 1st St.) combines two kid favorites: candy and books.

Any parent who has frantically searched for a restroom for a desperate child will appreciate the efforts of former mayor Bud Moore to have one built smack in the middle of downtown La Conner. One Moore Outhouse sits next to the Volunteer Firemen's Museum. Look for "The Outhouse Poem," written by Seattle Post-Intelligencer columnist Jon Hahn, posted on the restroom wall.

*Exit 221 off I-5. If you have trouble finding street parking, there are small lots at both ends of the main drag.*

**TULIP AND DAFFODIL FIELDS** surrounding La Conner positively explode with color each spring, and the region celebrates with the Skagit Valley Tulip Festival in late March or

---

## Tiptoe Through the Tulips (But bring bikes and boots!)

**BY CHERYL MURFIN BOND**

The Skagit Valley Tulip Festival, held annually in late March or early April, welcomes the advent of spring with a dazzling display of flower color. A visit to the festival is a fine family outing, but viewing the fields by bus or by bicycle will be far more enjoyable for kids and adults than the miles-long car caravans that congest roads along the fields during festival weekends and several weekends before and after. If possible, plan your visit for midweek to avoid the weekend crowds altogether.

For a day trip to the fields, bring the basics: a lunch, lots of fluids and snacks, boots, bikes, and a bike repair kit. Head to the Park & Ride lot just off I-5 at Exit 226 in Mount Vernon. (Information booths, with maps, are at Exits 221 and 226; restrooms are located at Park & Ride lots.)

Here are directions to some of the sights you can take in on bikes, beginning at the Park & Ride lot:

Pedal west on McLean and before you know it you'll be in the heart of bloom country. You'll see a field of daffodils and, soon after, the Roosengaarde display garden and store. If you take a right at Beaver Marsh Road, don't miss the Art Bash, which features original artwork of the valley and surrounding area by local artists. The display is open daily, 10 a.m.-6 p.m.

Continue straight on Beaver Marsh Road to the Washington State University Discovery Garden, then turn left on Young to visit the Museum of Tulip History. A left on Brashaw circles you back toward McLean, past the Skagit Valley Bulb Farm and its popular "Tulip Town," loaded with beautiful flowers, crafts, food, and fun. Take a right when you get back to McClean and start looking for Christianson's Nursery on your left. It features a large selection of roses. Enjoy a leisurely lunch; by the time you get back to the parking lot for the ride home, little ones are sure to be tired out.

As an alternative to driving or cycling, consider the festival's "Tulip Transit" program. During the week, buses leave from the Prime Outlet Centers at Burlington (Exit 229 from I-5) and go to various spots on the tulip map. The two-hour bus tour includes stops at bulb and flower shops, display gardens, and art displays. Cost for the weekday tour is $8 per adult, $4 per child, and it's free for kids under three. On Saturdays and Sundays, several color-coded bus tours take visitors to various locations to view the flowers. Board buses between 9 a.m. and 3:30 p.m. in La Conner at Kokomo Joe's, in Mount Vernon at Skagit River Brewing Company, in Burlington at the Prime Outlet Centers or Fred Meyer, and in Conway at Skagit Valley Gardens. The cost is $3 per person or $5 for the entire family.

You can avoid the road altogether by cruising to La Conner on the Victoria Clipper III (206/448-5000). The cruise, which departs Pier 69 on the Seattle waterfront, is 2 1/2 hours each way and includes a 2 1/2-hour guided bus tour of the fields.

The tulip festival offers families several other attractions in addition to flowers, including the Annual Salmon Barbecue; the Tulip Picnic, with music and a pet parade; the Farm and Floral Parade, with a fireworks grand finale; the Mount Vernon Street Fair; and the Tulip 10K and three-mile Slug Run. There's also the Great Skagit Duck Race, a race of approximately 6,000 rubber ducks on the Skagit River, and the "tulip pedal," a noncompetitive bike tour starting in Mount Vernon.

If it has been a wet spring, be sure to bring along the rubber boots. Also, don't underestimate the popularity of this festival: On a sunny weekend when the flowers are in bloom, it will look like there are as many people as there are flowers.

early April (see "Tiptoe Through the Tulips," below).

For more information or to obtain a booklet with maps, tips, and event information, call the festival office at 360/428-5959 or visit the festival Web site at www.tulipfestival.org.

**THE GREAT OUTDOORS**

**BIKING** is very popular in the Skagit area, because the terrain is flat and the scenery picturesque. But if you want to two-wheel it with the little ones, be prepared: Few paths are designated solely for cyclists, so most riding is done on wide, well-marked shoulders off the main roads. Also be sure to bring along a bike-tire repair kit (and know how to use it): You are a long way from a bike shop.

Biking is an excellent way to get a good view of the tulip and daffodil fields in the spring but be extra careful: traffic is heavy and motorists are preoccupied with looking at the flowers. Bird watching on bikes is even better than flower watching: There's much less traffic on a winter weekend.

One fun bike ride takes you from La Conner on the La Conner-Whitney Road (riding on the wide shoulder of a fairly busy road) to Highway 20. About a quarter-mile after crossing Highway 20 (road name changes to Bayview-Edison Road), you'll come to the *Padilla Bay Shore Trail*, a delightful 2.2-mile ride. If the group has the energy, you can continue another 4.4 miles to the Interpretive Center. (The ride from La Conner to the Interpretive Center is 8.2 miles one way.) In the winter, the bird watching is wonderful on the Shore Trail.

**BIRD WATCHING.** The fertile Skagit Valley is one of North America's great wintering bird migration areas—more than 180 species of birds have been recorded. Even the child who never wants to feed the ducks may show some interest in the magnificent creatures that grace this area; the kid who hyperventilates every time he sees a pigeon will probably need an oxygen tank. The names alone sound like they're out of a kid's book: black brant, dunlins, black-bellied plovers, mergansers, great blue herons, and canvasbacks. The suggestion of birdwatching may not excite your child much: Consider looking at a bird book before you take this excursion, making the search for the birds a game, and buying junior a pair of small binoculars.

The **PADILLA BAY ESTUARINE RESEARCH RESERVE** (on Bay-Edison Road, three miles north of Highway 20; 360/428-

1558) includes the Interpretive Center and the *Padilla Bay Shore Trail*. It's an ideal place to take kids for their first bird-watching foray. There are viewing blinds and boardwalks, and the center provides a good place to warm up on a chilly day.

Snow geese begin arriving in early October, but peak view-ing follows hunting season—mid-January through mid-April. It's not unusual to spot a flock of 5,000 geese, as well as the large, graceful tundra swans. The **SKAGIT WILDLIFE AREA**, at the river's mouth, is the optimum place to see both the geese and the swans. To get there, exit I-5 at Conway, drive west and follow the binocular signs. Stop at the Wildlife Area head-quarters (360/775-1311) near Conway for viewing advice.

**BOAT TOURS.** Narrated nature and bird-watching cruises from La Conner are offered by **VIKING CRUISES**. Bring binoc-ulars and keep your eyes open for bald eagles, great blue heron, grebes, loons, mergansers, harbor seals, sea lions, otters, and thousands of ducks.

The *Viking Star* is a fully enclosed, heated cruising boat with 31 large windows for great viewing in any weather. The boat is big enough to hold up to 49 passengers but is built to maneuver in areas where larger boats can't go. Up to a dozen people at a time may join the skipper in the large wheelhouse. There are spacious outside decks; field guides, binoculars, and knowledgeable naturalists are on hand. Other programs offered by Viking Cruises during the summer include a three-day/two-night stay in the San Juans.

*Viking Cruises: P.O Box 327, 109 N. 1st St., La Conner 98257. 360/466-2639; FAX: 360/466-2124.*

**DECEPTION PASS AND DECEPTION PASS STATE PARK** are "must-sees" if you are in the area. Located at the northern tip of Whidbey Island, the park is easily accessed from the Skagit Valley (see "Whidbey Island: What to See & Do").

**KAYAK POINT PARK.** This popular park in Stanwood, about 15 miles south of La Conner, has 3,300 feet of saltwater beach, with mussels and clams to harvest, a 300-foot pier ideal for fishing, and 40 acres to explore along the shores of picturesque Port Susan. From shoreline to evergreen forests, Kayak Point Park offers a rich setting for a variety of outdoor activities, including hiking trails and an 18-hole golf course. And if you hanker for more, Wenberg State Park is just four miles away, on a warm-water lake. We picked this place as a destination not only for its beauty, but because of the furry huts, "yurts," clustered in one corner of the park.

**YURT CAMPING** is a favorite family activity at Kayak Point (see "Yurt Camping," below). For reservations, phone 360/652-7992, 11 a.m. to 3 p.m. There are picnic tables with fire pits in front of each cabin, and grills in a common area. If

## One Step Up: Yurt Camping Works Well for Families

We haven't met a kid yet who doesn't love camping. Many parents, on the other hand, prefer sleeping on a comfortable mattress under a roof and, as a result, never quite get around to buying camping equipment and heading to the woods. The yurt-camping areas that have sprung up in the Northwest offer a great compromise.

Though there are some individual differences among the various yurts set up at selected state parks, the facilities are quite similar. All have tents with wooden floors, heat (the wall heater really heats the place), electricity, and a lock on the door. The combination of futons and bunk beds normally sleeps five people. (Bring your own sleeping bags.)

At most locations, a caretaker lives nearby and keeps an eye on the entire area. Don't expect that you will necessarily be in the woods; many yurts are set up in clearings or near the beach.

Our parent reviewers had this to say about the yurt camping adventure: "This was the perfect escape when we all desperately needed an adventure, but not too big an adventure, and something really low-budget. It's great to drive into a beautiful park and know you have a place to stay, protected from the elements. I'm glad we didn't know in advance that there was a restaurant nearby, because cooking on the open fire was the highlight for the kids. Our menu: hot dogs, s'mores, corn on the cob wrapped in foil for dinner, and sausage and eggs in the morning. My kids were in heaven."

For ideas about where to camp in yurts, see the Quick Index.

you don't want to cook out, there's a restaurant at the 18-hole golf course (360/652-9676 for tee times) across from the park.

*15610 Marine Dr. N.E., Stanwood. (From I-5, take Exit 199 at Marysville and turn west on 4th Street, which becomes Marine Dr. NE. The park entrance is 13 miles ahead on the left.)*

**LANG'S PONY AND HORSE RIDES.** Trail rides are available for individuals and families. Rides are by reservation only. There are covered picnic facilities on the premises. Lang's also offers birthday parties, lessons, and therapeutic riding.

*4565 Farm Mountain Road, Mount Vernon. (North on I-5 to Exit 225; turn on Anderson Road, then an immediate left on Cedardale Road. Go right on Blackburn Road, which becomes Farm Mountain Road.) 360/424-7630. Open year-round; call for schedule.*

**PADILLA BAY NATIONAL ESTUARINE RESEARCH RESERVE** provides a great opportunity to view local wildlife and gain a better understanding of the plant and animal life that flourishes when the fresh water from the Skagit River meets the salt water of the bay. Start your visit to the Reserve at **BREAZEALE-PADILLA BAY INTERPRETIVE CENTER**, just north of Bay View State Park. It's the headquarters for the Reserve and houses an outstanding interpretive museum with exhibits, saltwater aquariums, and an excellent hands-on room for children. Every Saturday at 10:30 a.m., staff members feed the fish and tell tales about saltwater creatures.

There's also access to outdoor observation decks and the beach (except in the winter months, to protect wildlife). From 1-2:30 p.m. on Saturdays, kids can participate in a Junior Ecologists program. When planning a visit to the Center, be sure to inquire about bird-watching classes, storytelling, Sunday movies, and other activities that may occur during your stay. Write for a calendar of Padilla Bay Events.

After visiting the Interpretive Center, head out to the *Padilla Bay Shore Trail*, a level, 2.2-mile trail along the shoreline of Padilla Bay. If the boat traffic doesn't keep your young walker entertained, the ducks and gulls will. Keep your eyes open for raccoons, harbor seals, muskrats, otters, blue herons, and eagles.    Advance arrangements can be made at the Interpretive Center for stroller and wheelchair access.

*10441 Bayview-Edison Rd, Mount Vernon (Approximately 8 miles north of La Conner on the Bayview-Edison Road. Or take*

*Hwy. 20 off I-5, west toward Anacortes and turn right at the stoplight at Bayview-Edison Road.) 360/428-1558; http://inlet.geol.sc.edu./PDB/home.html. Open Wed.-Sun., 10 a.m.-5 p.m. Cost: donations accepted.*

### MUSEUMS

**SKAGIT COUNTY HISTORICAL MUSEUM**, which sits on a hill two blocks from downtown La Conner, offers a good view of the Skagit Flats. In the north wing, kids can get a sense of what domestic life was like in early Skagit County— what kinds of toys were popular and what utensils would have been found in a typical farmhouse kitchen. In the south wing, they will learn about the Swinomish Indian tribe and find out how early settlers made a living. The museum occasionally offers excellent family programs; consult the schedule when you get to town.

*501 4th St. 360/466-3365. Open Tues.-Sun., noon-5 p.m. (daily during the Tulip Festival). Cost: $1/adult, senior & child 5-12, free/under 5.*

## CALENDAR

**JANUARY**
Peak time for viewing snow geese, trumpeter swans, eagles.
**FEBRUARY**
Smelt Derby, first Saturday, La Conner.
**MARCH-APRIL**
Skagit Valley Tulip Festival, 360/428-5959.
**JUNE**
Strawberry Harvest Month, 360/428-8547, Mount Vernon.
**JULY**
Highland Games and Scottish Fair: A weekend celebration of the culture and pageantry of Scotland, 360/416-7611, Mount Vernon.
**AUGUST**
Skagit County Fair, 360/336-9453, Mount Vernon.
**DECEMBER**
Christmas Boat Parade, 360/466-4902, La Conner.

## RESOURCES

**LA CONNER CHAMBER OF COMMERCE**
P.O. Box 1610, La Conner 98257
360/466-4778

**MOUNT VERNON CHAMBER OF COMMERCE**
117 N. 1st, Ste. 4, Mount Vernon 98273
360/428-8547

**TULIP FESTIVAL INFORMATION**
360/428-5959

**WASHINGTON DEPARTMENT OF WILDLIFE**
16018 Mill Creek Blvd., Mill Creek 98012
425/775-1311
Information about the snow geese and other wildlife in the
Skagit wildlife area.


## WHIDBEY ISLAND

The longest of all the saltwater-surrounded islands in the
continental United States, Whidbey Island marks the northern edge of Puget Sound. The island is connected to the mainland by the Highway 20 bridge across Deception Pass and by
Washington State Ferries, with a ferry route connecting
Clinton at the south end of the island with Mukilteo on the
mainland. There are three good-sized towns: Langley, at the
south end closest to the ferry; Coupeville, approximately 25
miles up the island; and Oak Harbor in the north.

Oak Harbor is home to the Whidbey Naval Air Station
and has by far the largest concentration of population and
commercial development. Coupeville is a picturesque little
town on the edge of Penn Cove. It's well worth visiting,
both for its historic charm and because it is located close to
two exceptional outdoor attractions: Ebey's Landing and
Fort Casey Park. Langley, a 15-minute drive from the ferry,
has the best restaurants and shops, and draws the most
tourists. But the towns are not the most important reason to
visit this long, skinny island with kids. Young explorers will
no doubt prefer to skip the clusters of civilization and head
straight for the forests, beaches, wildlife, and history the
island has to offer.


### GETTING THERE

One of our parent reviewers had this to say about getting to
Whidbey Island: "It's so easily accessible from Seattle that it is
a perfect place to escape for a weekend of R&R with your kids.
Even getting there, with the short time on the freeway and the

short ferry ride, is relaxing. During one visit, our ferry was escorted by a pod of Orca whales!"

**BY FERRY.** Whidbey Island is served by **WASHINGTON STATE FERRIES** (800/843-3779). From Seattle, head north on I-5 to Exit 182, Mukilteo-Whidbey Island Ferry. Drive west on Highway 525 to the ferry terminal. Travel time to the ferry from Seattle is about 35 minutes (except during the weekday commute—4-6 p.m.). Ferries depart on the hour and the half-hour; the crossing takes 20 minutes.

During summer months, it is not unusual to encounter a wait of one to two hours at Mukilteo, especially on Friday after 2 p.m. and on Saturday mornings, and at Clinton anytime on Sunday (or Monday if it's a long weekend). If you travel during these high-traffic periods, be sure to bring car entertainment for the kids or plan to explore the area near the ferry dock. The pier at the Mukilteo ferry dock is a very popular fishing spot and young kids will enjoy watching the activity.

**REFUELING.** Speaking of fish, **IVAR'S** has a restaurant and take-out counter at the ferry dock (excellent fish and chips and chowder) and there are several other small eateries with take-out food windows within easy walking distance. The Mukilteo Historical Society maintains the 30-foot octagonal lighthouse located off Front Street just west of the ferry landing. It's open to the public April through September, on Saturdays, Sundays, and holidays, noon to 4 p.m.

From the Olympic Peninsula, you can take the Port Townsend-Keystone ferry to Whidbey Island. The ferry sailing takes about 45 minutes but, due to adverse tides and winds, this ferry run is subject to frequent cancellations.

**BY CAR.** If waiting for ferries isn't your idea of vacation, a good alternative is to drive to Whidbey via Deception Pass, across the bridge that connects the mainland to Fidalgo Island and to the northern tip of Whidbey Island. If you opt for this route, take I-5 north to the Anacortes-Whidbey Exit (Exit 230). Head west on Highway 20 and follow the signs to Whidbey. Once you get off I-5, this is a very scenic drive, but it takes $1 1/2$ to 2 hours from Seattle, depending on where you are going on the island (if you are staying in Coupeville or farther north, driving is the faster route during busy ferry periods).

**ROADSIDE ATTRACTIONS.** The **BOEING EVERETT PLANT**

(Exit 189 from Hwy. 525; 206/544-1264; www.boeing.com) straddles the highway as you approach the Mukilteo ferry terminal. Just a glimpse of the awesome metal birds under construction will thrill the kids. Public tours for anyone 4'2" or taller are offered weekdays on a first-come, first-served basis. During the summer, the 90-minute tours are very popular, so expect a wait. If you'd rather make a quick visit, you can browse in the lobby and gift shop, open week-days 8 a.m. to 4 p.m.

If you are driving onto Whidbey Island, allow time for a stop at **DECEPTION PASS STATE PARK**, the most frequently visit-ed state park in Washington (see "Things to See & Do"). Here you'll find spectacular scenery, good beach access, and, if the tides are low, excellent tidepools.

## PLACES TO STAY

### BOATYARD INN
*200 Wharf St., Langley 98260*
*360/221-5120; Boatyard@whidbey.com*
*Rates: Moderate to expensive*
*FYI: Kitchens; gas fireplaces; dock; futons for extra beds*
The location of this attractive inn is delightful, tucked on the beach next to a fishing pier and a five-minute walk from the center of the picturesque town of Langley. The galley kitchens have a cook-top stove, microwave, dishwasher, and refrigerator. Each room has a private balcony overlooking Puget Sound and the beds sit up extra-high so you can soak up the view while you lie in bed.

The only downside for parents is that there are no units with separate bedrooms—even when you get the larger accommodations with a loft you won't be separated from the kids by a wall. Also, if your child is not yet a strong swimmer, the fact that at high tide the water comes right up to the Inn might make you too nervous to enjoy your visit.

**❝ PARENT COMMENTS**
*"The combination of the beautiful setting for the Inn and the close proximity to the fabulous restaurants and fun little shops made this a great choice for our family when we spent a week-end exploring Whidbey. By the way, the bookstore in Langley, the Moonraker, has a great selection of children's books!"*

### COUPEVILLE INN
*P.O. Box 370, Coupeville 98239*
*360/678-6668, 800/247-6162*
*Rate: Inexpensive*
*FYI: Free continental breakfast*

This is a spiffy blue motel that gives you just what you need and nothing more. Located at the entrance to the pretty town of Coupeville, this is the place to stay if you don't need scenery or fancy—just a clean room ideally situated for exploring one of the most interesting areas on Whidbey Island. Rooms have private baths with tub and shower, queen beds, and most have private balconies.

**❝ PARENT COMMENTS**

*"Hooray! A low-budget, attractive motel on Whidbey! We never spend much time in our room when we travel with the kids so we hate to spend big dollars on our accommodations. We love staying in Coupeville because it is has several good restaurants and an interesting history. We ate several delicious meals at the Penn Cove Restaurant, spent our days at Fort Casey and Ebey's Landing. Inexpensive, clean, and comfortable places to stay with kids such as this are surprisingly hard to find."*

### FORT CASEY INN
*1124 S. Engle Road, Coupeville 98239*
*360/678-8792*
*Rates: Expensive*
*FYI: Complimentary continental breakfast; wood stoves*

Originally built in 1909 for the then-active defensive installation at Fort Casey, this inn is located next door to Fort Casey State Park. The inn has several houses, each with two bedrooms and a good-sized bath upstairs, and a living room and large kitchen downstairs. They are beautifully decorated with comfortable furnishings from the World War I era (romantically patriotic). Although relatively expensive, this inn feels like a good value because families have an entire "home" to themselves, with plenty of space. This is a good place for a family reunion or for vacationing with another family.

There are no cribs or highchairs available; families traveling with infants or young toddlers should also bring along a safety gate (the stairs in the houses are steep and long). Also, during winter visits, parents will need to be concerned about keeping toddlers away from the wood stove, which, though not the only source of heat, keep things cozy.

The inn is located amid pastures in an isolated, sparsely populated area. The kids will probably think they've reached the end of the earth when they learn there are no television sets here, but they'll soon discover that the outside world has much to offer. Tell them to look for the pretty little hiking trail that begins behind the houses and goes through the woods to the beach, or take them to Fort Casey State Park (less than a mile away), where they'll find bunkers, a light-house, beaches, and trails to explore.

If you want a change of scenery and more activity, hop in the car and visit one of the nearby towns. It's only 4.5 miles (a pretty drive) to Coupeville and a 27-mile trip to Langley. Less than a mile from the inn, you can catch the Port Townsend/Keystone ferry for a fun day in Port Townsend.

### 66 PARENT COMMENTS

*"Our city girls (three and six) loved the country feel of this charming spot. Each night we went to sleep hearing owls in the woods and awoke to deer grazing on our lawn."*

*"The best place to stay on Whidbey, if you bring the kids. (Inn at Langley is a fun splurge if you left the kids at home!). The area around the Fort Casey Inn is ideal for exploration: We had several good meals in Coupeville, spent one glorious afternoon at Ebey's Landing and flew kites at Fort Casey. Not bad for a weekend!"*

### THE VICTORIAN BED AND BREAKFAST

*602 N. Main, P.O. Box 761, Coupeville 98239*
*360/678-5305; www.whidbey.net/~asasso/*
*Rates: Moderate*
*FYI: Complimentary breakfast; children allowed in cottage only; pets OK (with restrictions)*

Guests at this 100-year-old home in the charming town of Coupeville may choose one of the upstairs bedrooms (each with private bath) or the Cottage Hideaway. The cottage is the place to stay if you have kids along. It is a small cabin behind and across a courtyard from the house, featuring four nicely appointed rooms: a master bedroom with TV/VCR, a day room with a trundle bed (which can sleep two children), a full kitchen, and a bath.

This is a space for families who can coexist peacefully in

close proximity—spacious it is not. The bathroom is small and not suited for diaper changing. But there is a courtyard to spill into, weather permitting, as well as common areas in the main house. Overall, the Victorian's cottage is a nice choice if you want to stay in the lovely town of Coupeville.

**❝ PARENT COMMENTS**

*"The cottage worked well for us for a weekend although more than that we would have been too crowded. We visited with our two preschoolers. They loved the "cozy" accommodations; we enjoyed the warm hospitality and the chance to explore charming Coupeville."*

**VACATION RENTAL PROPERTY.** While there has been a big increase in overnight accommodations on Whidbey in the last few years, unfortunately most of the new places to stay are "romantic escapes" (in other words, "no kids allowed"). You may want to consider renting a house. **Tara Vacation Rentals** (221 2nd St., Langley 98260; 360/331-7100) arranges daily, weekly, and monthly rentals of private waterfront and view homes, as well as condos and cabins—completely furnished.

## PLACES TO EAT

**THE DOG HOUSE**
*230 1st St., Langley*
*360/221-9825*
*Hours: Lunch, dinner daily; no credit cards*

The Dog House is a local institution with a long and colorful history. It is a funky, comfortable sort of place, where generations of locals have gone for good talk, good service, and decent food. This is also an easy place to take kids—they are more than welcome, as is evidenced by the sign outside stating "Family entrance—kids welcome," and the crayons and paper that arrive once you are seated.

Though the kitchen doesn't offer a kid's menu, there are plenty of choices to please young palettes—mini-burgers, fish and chips, grilled cheese sandwiches, tacos—at very reasonable prices

**ISLAND BAKERY**
*1675 E. Main St., Freeland*
*360/331-6282*
*Hours: 11 a.m.-3:30 p.m. daily*

Freeland is about 10 miles from the ferry landing, just off the main highway. This bakery/deli, on your right as you enter the tiny town, is a good place to stop if you are driving to Coupeville from the ferry and need to feed the kids. There is always a good assortment of healthy and delightful soups, sandwiches, salads, and quiches, plus magnificent baked goodies.

## KNEAD AND FEED
*4 Front St. (downstairs), Coupeville*
*360/678-5431*
*Hours: 10:30 a.m.-3 p.m. Mon.-Fri.; until 9 p.m. Sat.-Sun.*

This small, informal spot on the water has a great view and scrumptious baked goods, sandwiches, soups, and salads. The people here go out of their way to accommodate families and make kids feel welcome, though children's menus and highchairs aren't offered (booster seats are available). The only real drawback is that the seating is rather tight—not good for a fussy infant or super-active toddler.

## PENN COVE RESTAURANT
*11 NW Coveland, Coupeville*
*360/678-5474*
*Hours: Breakfast Sat.-Sun.; lunch, dinner daily*

This restaurant bills itself as a "fine family restaurant" and definitely meets our criteria. It's highly recommended by our parent reviewers (for all three meals) if you are staying in the Coupeville area. The food (steaks, seafood, Penn Cove mussels, chowder) is well prepared and moderately priced; the service is fast. Grown-ups will appreciate the family-sized booths.

## STAR BISTRO
*201 1/2 1st St., Langley*
*360/221-2627*
*Hours: Lunch daily (sometimes closed Mon. in winter); dinner Tues.-Sun.*

Sitting above the Star Store, this cafe has it all: outstanding food, great view, and reasonable prices. Don't be put off by the trendy appearance; kids are graciously welcomed. The kids' menu shows an appreciation for child preferences, and includes word games and puzzles to distract impatient, hungry young diners. Service is prompt. The outside eating area is divine on a summer night and even has heaters so you can dine in the open air year round.

## WHAT TO SEE & DO

### STROLL & BROWSE

**COUPEVILLE.** Founded in 1852 by Captain Thomas Coupe, Coupeville is the second oldest town in Washington and was home to many of the Northwest's sea captains during the late-19th and early-20th centuries. In addition to many well preserved Victorian homes, visitors will find historic blockhouses, the Island County Historical Museum, and Ebey's Landing National Historic Reserve. The historic wharf extends 400 feet into the cove. More than 50 homes and stores here appear on the National Register of Historic Places.

This charming seaside town is a delightful place to browse and learn about the region's history. Don't worry if you've forgotten the umbrella—located smack in the rain shadow of the Olympic Peninsula, this area has only 18.64 inches of precipitation annually, compared with 25 inches at the south end of Whidbey and 36 inches in Seattle.

You can pick up a walking-tour map (available at most stores along Front St.) to help you identify the most interesting historic landmarks, including the **ALEXANDER BLOCKHOUSE** on Front Street, part of an 1855 fort. A visit to the **ISLAND COUNTY HISTORICAL SOCIETY MUSEUM** (see "Museums") is a fun way to get a quick overview of the history of the town. (Ask about their historic walking tours, offered during the summer). For a self-guided historical tour of the greater region, stop by the **NATIONAL PARK SERVICE OFFICE** (in Mariner's Court on Front Street) and pick up a free brochure about the Ebey's Landing National Historical Reserve.

**LANGLEY** is a six-mile drive from the Mukilteo-Clinton ferry, on Langley Road off Highway 525. Over the last 20 years, it has been transformed from a sleepy haven for big-city dropouts to a popular tourist destination, replete with art galleries and a wide assortment of restaurants. Sitting on a bluff overlooking Saratoga Passage, it is a pretty little town that is fun to stroll with an espresso or ice cream cone in hand. The **MOONRAKER BOOKSHOP** (209 1st St.; 360/221-6962) has an excellent selection of children's books. Also, be sure to check out the exceptional toy and children's clothing departments at the **STAR STORE** (201 1st St.; 360/221-5222).

### PARKS

**COUPEVILLE TOWN PARK** has a decent playground, a covered community kitchen area, tennis courts, and a lovely walking trail along the bluff overlooking the cove. Both kids and adults will be impressed by the cross-section of a gigantic old tree that dates back to Columbus' time.

*Located one block west of the wharf on Coveland St. in Coupeville.*

**DECEPTION PASS** is the beautiful and tumultuous waterway between Whidbey and Fidalgo islands. From the lofty bridge above, your family will enjoy a breathtaking view of this deep gorge and the smaller neighboring passage, Canoe Pass. **DECEPTION PASS STATE PARK**, which blankets both sides of the pass with 2,300 acres of forest and beach, is the most popular State Park in Washington, with lake and saltwater fishing and an abundance of campsites, swimming beaches, and hiking trails.

Two short two-mile hikes that are especially good for kids, *Cranberry Lake* and *West Point*, begin at the large parking lot at West Beach (on the western side of the pass), near Deception Pass Park headquarters.

*Follow Hwy. 20 west to Fidalgo Island; then follow signs to Deception Pass. 360/675-2417.*

**EBEY'S LANDING NATIONAL HISTORICAL RESERVE.** Established by Congress in 1980, this is the first and one of the largest historical reserves in the nation. Unlike many, it encompasses a mixture of federal, state, county, and private property, all managed to preserve historic integrity. The area appears to today's visitor much as it did a century ago, when New England sea captains were first drawn to Penn Cove. The farms are still farmed, forests still harvested, and century-old buildings still serve as homes and offices.

The 17,000-acre reserve encompasses Fort Ebey State Park and Fort Casey State Park, as well as beaches, trails, farmlands, the town of Coupeville, and 91 nationally registered historic structures. This preserved and protected portion of central Whidbey Island provides an unbroken historic record of this rural community, from 19th-century exploration and settlement to the present. It includes: the first exploration of Puget Sound by Captain George Vancouver in 1792; early settlement by Colonel Ebey, an important figure in Washington Territory; growth and settlement resulting from the Oregon Trail and the westward migration; the Donation Land Laws

(1850-1855); and the continued growth and settlement of the Puget Sound area.

Though 90 percent of the territory is privately owned, there is public access. A free self-guided driving/bicycling tour highlights the reserve's scenery, introduces you to its recreational opportunities, and helps you learn about its history. Pick up a tour brochure at the Island County Historical Museum, Admiralty Head Lighthouse, or by writing or calling the reserve office (P.O. Box 774, Coupeville, WA 98239-0774; 360/678-6084). The tour takes anywhere from 1 1/2 hours to a full day, depending on your pace and level of interest.

Interpretive waysides are located throughout the reserve. The sites touch on a wide variety of issues related to history and natural resources. Guided interpretive walks offered at Sunnyside Cemetery, Ebey's Prairie, and Fort Casey are free of charge on weekends during the summer. Evening slide shows are provided free of charge during the summer months at Fort Casey State Park and occasionally in Coupeville.

One of the nicest hikes on Whidbey Island can be found on the ridge trail that crosses Ebey's Prairie. To reach the trailhead, turn south on Shurman Road, and bear right to the parking pullout across from the cemetery. The trail takes walkers along the fence line between the original land owned by Isaac Ebey and the property his brother owned. If you decide

## TIPS: When Visiting Ebey's Landing National Historical Reserve

- Some hiking trails in the Reserve cross private property. Please respect the fields and crops of local farmers by staying on trails and keeping pets on a leash.
- High tides can be dangerous to beach hikers. Use extreme caution to avoid being trapped on headlands and watch carefully for beach logs moved by sudden high waves.
- Scenic waysides are located on public land, and visitors have unlimited visual access to surrounding farmland and other scenic areas—look all you like, but please don't trespass.
- Use wayside pullouts; do not stop in the middle of the highway or paved roads.

to stroll through the cemetery as well, you'll not only see Ebey's grave, but an old blockhouse—one of the few log forts remaining from the time of the Indian wars.

*P.O. Box 774, Coupeville, WA 98239-0774. 360/678-6084.*

**FORT CASEY STATE PARK** is one of the finest parks in the state for kids—plenty of wide-open spaces for games and kites and great nooks and crannies to explore. Located on the site of Fort Casey, one of the coast artillery posts established during the late 1890s for the defense of Puget Sound, it is one of two state parks within the Ebey's Landing National Historic Reserve. The park is also home to the **ADMIRALTY HEAD LIGHTHOUSE**, built in 1860 and now housing interpretive displays and a gift shop.

The emplacements, fortifications, and underground bunkers from the old fort are still in place, offering venturesome kids endless possibilities for hide-and-go-seek (flashlights will make it safer and more fun). The cannons now on display at the park are not the originals; the U.S. Navy brought them here from the Philippines in 1968. In the bunker area, there are surprisingly few fences and "Do Not Climb" signs, so supervise young kids closely. The parade grounds behind the bunkers are ideal for kite flyers, and the numerous short, easy hiking trails in the area are perfect for short legs.

There are also 35 campsites at the park that sit very close to the water. These are very popular but unfortunately cannot be reserved in advance.

*Located 3 miles south of Coupeville on Hwy. 20, near the Port Townsend/Keystone ferry landing. Open all year. 360/678-4519.*

**FORT EBEY STATE PARK.** Put this park on your "must do" list when visiting Whidbey Island. The views are spectacular: On a clear day, hike out on the bluff and take in the panorama of the San Juan Islands, the Strait of Juan de Fuca, and the Olympic Mountains.

The fort was constructed in 1942 and named after Colonel Isaac Ebey, the pioneer commander of the 1855 Militia stationed on an island in the nearby slough. The Colonel homesteaded land on a bluff above the fort, and held several commands before being slain by Native Americans seeking revenge for the death of their chief. The park is the site of a World War II gun battery, which sported two six-inch guns during wartime. Following the war, the guns were removed and dismantled for scrap. In addition to the gun battery, the original fort had observation stations, storage rooms, residences, and other facilities.

The beach section of Ebey's property later became the State Park, with campsites and picnic areas. If you're up for a hike, take the easy one-mile trail from the parking area to Lake Pondilla. The tiny lake, less than a quarter-mile around, is stocked with bass and teeming with wildlife activity. Look for bald eagles nesting in nearby snags, as well as visiting deer, coyotes, raccoons, pheasants, and foxes.

Near the south entrance to the park, notice the **COUPEVILLE OUTLYING LANDING FIELD**, which was built during WW II to train Navy pilots and is still in use today. You may get lucky and see a jet landing or taking off.

*The park is located six miles northwest of Coupeville. 360/678-4636. The landing field is 3 miles west of Coupeville on Ebey Landing Road.*

**JOSEPH WHIDBEY STATE PARK**, named after the explorer accompanying Captain Vancouver on an exploration of north Puget Sound in 1792, has 3,100 feet of beach and 20 excellent picnic sites.

*Three miles west of Oak Harbor, at Swantown Road & West Beach Road. 800/233-0321. Open summer only.*

**KETTLE TRAIL PARK.** Island County's newest trail connects the town of Coupeville and Fort Ebey State Park via unusual Ice Age geologic formations known as "kettles." Wonderful for biking, horseback riding, or just a scenic stroll.

**KEYSTONE STATE PARK** is home to one of the two scuba-diving sites in Washington and is an excellent place to comb beaches and observe marine animals in their natural habitats.

*Located next to Fort Casey State Park, 3 miles south of Coupeville near the Keystone ferry landing.*

**MEERKERK RHODODENDRON GARDEN** is a 53-acre, beautifully maintained garden with many well-groomed paths for easy strolling. In early August, Meerkerk hosts the Whidbey Folk Festival, a weekend of acoustic folk music on the lawn, surrounded by a natural amphitheater of towering trees. Top musicians from the Puget Sound area are featured. Refreshments are available; no pets are allowed. The cost is $5 per adult; children under 12 are free when accompanied by an adult.

*3531 Meerkerk Lane. (Take Hwy. 525 to Resort Road, then right one-half mile to Meerkerk Lane. Follow signs.) 360/678-1912. Open daily, 9 a.m.-4 p.m. Cost: $3/person ($5/person during Folk Festival); free/ under 12 accompanied by an adult.*

SOUTH WHIDBEY STATE PARK comprises 85 acres, including 2.5 miles of hiking trails and two miles of shoreline. The forest contains some of the last old-growth trees on the island. A network of short, easy trails allows you to walk among ancient Douglas fir, grand fir, moss-covered alders, and large maples. The educational, self-guided *Forest Discovery Trail* offers the greatest variety of trees; pick up a trail brochure at the parking lot. On the Harry Wilbert Trail, across Smuggler's Cove Road, hikers pass the oldest trees on the island. One cedar, estimated to be 500 years old, is 40 feet in circumference. The *Beach Trail* and the *Hobbit Trail* wind through beautiful forests to the pebbled beach.

*Located 4 miles northwest of Freeland on Smuggler's Cover Road. Open daily, dawn to dusk (mid-Feb.-mid-Nov.); weekends and holidays (remainder of year)*

## MUSEUMS

ISLAND COUNTY HISTORICAL SOCIETY MUSEUM houses Native American artifacts, various items from the homes of local pioneer families, personal histories of some of Whidbey's earliest settlers, and a doll collection. Next door, you'll find the Alexander blockhouse (built in 1855) and an exhibit of Indian dugout canoes. While you're here, pick up a self-guiding driving tour map.

*Alexander & Front St. 360/678-3310. Open daily, 11 a.m.-5 p.m. (summer); Fri.-Mon., 11 a.m.-4 p.m. (winter). Cost: $2/person, $1.50 child & senior, free/under 6, $4.50/family.*

## KID CULTURE

BLUE FOX DRI-VIN MOVIE THEATER. Remember how thrilled you were when your parents took you to a drive-in movie? Put the kids in their jammies, grab some blankets and pillows, and seize this endangered opportunity! Prices are from the good old days, too: $4.50 for a double feature!

*Corner of Hwy. 20 & Monroe Landing Road, 2 miles south of Oak Harbor. 360/675-5667. Cost: $4.50/person, free/under 12.*

### ACTIVE FUN

**BRATTLAND GO-KARTS.** Just a spin around the track in one of these high-powered, low-ridin' machines may be your youngster's rite of passage from big-wheels and bumper cars to driver's education.

*On the corner of Hwy. 20 & Monroe Landing Road, 2 miles south of Oak Harbor. 360/675-5667. Open Sat.-Sun., hours vary.*

**JOHN VANDERZICHT MEMORIAL POOL** is a first-class facility in Oak Harbor. Consider splashing about here if the rain ruins your beach plans.

*2299 20th NW, Oak Harbor. 360/675-7665. Open daily, Mon.-Fri., 6 a.m.-8:30 p.m.; Sat.-Sun., 2-8 p.m. Cost: $2.75/adult, $2.50 youth & senior, free/under 4.*

**SHELLFISHING** is a popular activity on the beaches and in the shallow waters of Whidbey Island—soft and hard-shelled crabs, Pacific oysters, and mussels are abundant. Mussels are especially easy to harvest, if you can get locals to direct you to the right beach.

You must obtain a license to gather shellfish on any Washington beach. Licenses are readily available at local stores. For up-to-date information regarding shellfishing, phone the Washington State Department of Fisheries, 360/249-6522.

There is a danger of shellfish poisoning from a microscopic organism that can turn the water red (called "red tide"). It is highly toxic to humans and cooking doesn't destroy it. Be sure to call the Red Tide Hotline (800/562-5632) before venturing forth with buckets and shovels.

### CALENDAR

**MAY**
Penn Cove Water Festival, Coupeville.
**JULY**
Choochokum Arts and Crafts Fair: A hodge-podge of street entertainment, good food, and arts and crafts, Langley.
**AUGUST**
Whidbey Island Folk Festival, see "Parks, Meerkerk Rhododendron Garden."
Dixieland Jazz Festival, Oak Harbor.
Arts and Crafts Festival, Coupeville.
Island County Fair, Langley.

## RESOURCES

### ISLAND TRANSIT
360/678-7771, 360/321-6688
The bus system on Whidbey is extensive and free; schedules are available at businesses across the island. Buses run Monday through Saturday among many stops: Clinton ferry dock, Langley, Freeland, Greenback, Keystone ferry dock, Coupeville , Deception Pass, and Oak Harbor.

### CENTRAL WHIDBEY CHAMBER OF COMMERCE
P.O. Box 152, 302 N Main St., Coupeville 98239
360/678-5434

### LANGLEY CHAMBER OF COMMERCE
124 ¹/₂ 2nd St., P.O. Box 403, Langley 98260
360/221-6765

### OAK HARBOR CHAMBER OF COMMERCE
5506 Hwy 20, Oak Harbor 98277
360/675-3535

# SOUTH PUGET SOUND

The region due south of Seattle on I-5 includes two cities worth a visit when you are in the region. Tacoma, just one half-hour south, boasts close looks at Mount Rainier and the Olympics, as well as a number of fine new museums and a world-class zoo. Farther south is Olympia, the state capital, where families can enjoy lovely scenery and also learn about political systems and Washington State history.

## GETTING THERE

**BY CAR.** South of Seattle are the cities of Tacoma (33 miles south) and Olympia (60 miles south). The driving times vary according to the time of day; if you travel during the commute, plan to share the road and bide your time. The stretch between Tacoma and Olympia is likely to have lighter traffic, any time of day.

**BY TRAIN.** Four Amtrak (800/USA-RAIL) trains depart Seattle daily for points south, including Tacoma and Olympia.

## TACOMA

Dramatically situated between Commencement Bay to the west and Mount Rainier to the southeast, Tacoma (the name derives from *Tahoma*, the Puyallup Tribe's word for Mount Rainier) offers easy access to a wide range of recreational opportunities.

The city's early growth was founded on the lumber industry, beginning with the first sawmill in 1852. Today, Tacoma continues to depend on lumber and shipping for its livelihood, but has made a successful effort to shed the "mill town" image in favor of a more upscale and multidimensional one. With plentiful cultural opportunities to offer vacationing families, Tacomans refuse to consider their city Seattle's "little sister," and rightly so.

### PLACES TO STAY

#### SHERATON TACOMA HOTEL
*1320 Broadway Plaza, 98402*
*253/572-3200, 800/845-9466*
*Rates: Moderate to expensive*
*FYI: Restaurant; refrigerators (some rooms); exercise facility*

Conveniently located downtown, adjacent to the convention center, the Sheraton Tacoma provides probably the nicest accommodations in town. (This is due in part to a notable lack of hotels in the area.) The rooms are clean and comfortable, if not inspired, and most have lovely views.

The Altezzo restaurant, on the top floor, serves good Italian cuisine. The atmosphere here is inviting, but best for families with children over six or so.

### PLACES TO EAT

#### THE ANTIQUE SANDWICH CO.
*5102 N. Pearl*
*253/752-4069*
*Breakfast, lunch, dinner daily*

Located just two blocks south of Point Defiance Park, this relaxing coffeehouse makes a perfect stop after an outing at the zoo. Choose from a long list of deli sandwiches or quiche, among other entrées, then top it off with a home-style dessert.

In the summer, you can dine in the "Garden of Eatin'," which gives the kids a little more flexibility in terms of noise level. A large collection of toys will keep little ones busy while parents linger over their free coffee refill.

## THE CLIFF HOUSE

*6300 Marine View Dr.*
*253/927-0400, 800/961-0401*
*Hours: Lunch, dinner daily*

It's of a certain age and a bit frayed at the edges, but the Cliff House still has the best view in Tacoma, a city with a lot of good ones. Don't be misled by the "fine dining" atmosphere here. The ambiance is relaxed and welcoming to kids. While you gaze out the window over Commencement Bay, your kids can enjoy pasta and other "old reliables." The quality of food can be uneven, but the Cliff House is a draw in its own right.

## FREIGHTHOUSE SQUARE

*2501 E. D St.*
*253/305-0678*
*Hours: Mon.-Sat., 10 a.m.-7 p.m.; Sun., noon-5 p.m.*

When you crave a touch of the ethnic, this food court just north of the Tacoma Dome may be just the place. A dozen locally owned eateries offer cuisine from around the globe, including Mexican, Vietnamese, and Greek. There's also an espresso stop, a bakery, and an ice cream shop to round out your meal.

## HARMON PUB AND BREWERY

*1938 Pacific Ave.*
*253/383-2739*
*Lunch, dinner daily*

At first glance, the Harmon doesn't really look like a family restaurant, but come on in! While parents sample the "Brew Ski" and classic pub grub, kids can choose from one of the more interesting kids' menus in Tacoma, including bratwurst with garlic mashed potatoes and rainbow pasta with cheese sauce. (These are scaled-down versions of adult offerings; the mild garlic-herb flavoring may be surprising, or even distressing, for less adventurous eaters).

You can't beat the Harmon for convenience—it's located across the street from the lovely new Washington State History Museum.

## LUCIANO'S WATERFRONT RISTORANTE

*3311 Rushton Way*
*253/756-5611*
*Hours: 11 a.m.-10 p.m. daily, Sat.-Sun. until 11 p.m.*

If you can disregard the adjacent casino, Luciano's makes a good meal stop on Tacoma's waterfront, handy to Old Town and downtown. Although there's no kids' menu, the staff is very welcoming and accommodating to children. Parent reviewers report that the staff hauled out the more child-friendly lunch menu when the dinner menu failed to appeal to their young food critics. Pizza, pasta, and other familiar Italian dishes are offered.

### THE OLD SPAGHETTI FACTORY
*1735 Jefferson St.*
*253/383-2214*
*Hours: Lunch, dinner daily*

Located two blocks west of Union Station, this restaurant bears a close resemblance to its "mother" restaurant in Seattle (see "Seattle: Places to Eat").

### ROCK PASTA BRICK OVEN PIZZA AND BREWERY
*1920 Jefferson St.*
*253/272-1221*
*Hours: Lunch, dinner daily*

If you're hungry for something you wouldn't prepare at home, you'll find a number of elegant options here. Try the Elvis Sighting (sun-dried tomato and ricotta filling in ravioli with a rich pesto sauce) or perhaps the Philadelphia Freedom pizza (shaved sirloin and caramelized onions topped with cheeses and a horseradish-sour cream sauce). Don't worry: the kids can enjoy a meal here, too. There's a plain cheese or peanut butter and jelly pizza, for example, or buttered noodles.

If there's a wait for your meal, the staff will bring a blob of pizza dough that kids can knead and sculpt while they wait. Be sure to check out the bear skeleton near the entry: it's Jessie, a relic from the TV series Northern Exposure.

### WHAT TO SEE & DO

**CHILDREN'S MUSEUM OF TACOMA** offers interactive displays about science and the arts. Here you are greeted with colorful, oversized flowers and a fish motif that's bound to put a smile on your face. Exhibits include: Curiosity Corner, with a collection of creative "make and take" projects; Becca's Studio, where kids can satisfy their artistic urges; Grubby Gardeners, where small green thumbs get put to imaginary use; and Music Box, with a large variety of musical instruments for strumming and humming. There's also a Toddler Area and a Theatre. Interactive exhibits come and go, so kids who've been here before will continue to find new areas to explore. The target age range is one to nine, but we've seen older kids find some fun as well.

*936 Broadway. 253/627-6031. Open Tues.-Sat., 10 a.m.-5 p.m. (also open Sun., noon-5 p.m., Sept.-mid-June). Cost: $4.25/person, free/under 2.*

**NORTHWEST TREK AND WILDLIFE PARK.** In 1971, Dr. and Mrs. David T. Hellyer donated 600 acres of beautiful forest, lake, and meadowland to the Metropolitan Park District of Tacoma to create a protected place where Northwest wildlife could roam free. The result of their generosity is a unique park ideally suited to children. Tram tours, led by expert naturalists depart hourly, taking visitors through 435 acres of habitat—home to bison, bighorn sheep, elk, caribou, water fowl, moose, mountain goats, and blacktail deer, among others. Don't be surprised to see a curious caribou walking alongside the tram or a herd of bison calmly grazing in the thicket—so close that your child can almost reach out and pat their heads! Allow at least three hours for your visit.

*From I-5 south, take Exit 142B; travel south on Hwy. 161 to Northwest Trek, 17 miles south of Puyallup. 800/433-TREK. Open year-round; seasonal hours vary. Cost: $8.25/adult, $7.75/senior, $5.75/youth 5-17, $3.75/child 3-4, free/under 3.*

**POINT DEFIANCE PARK,** on the western side of the city, offers 500 acres of pristine forest and miles of woodland trails and waterfront. There's a picnic area here, and rental boats and fishing gear at the boathouse. Even if you don't have time to drive around the point and stop to ogle the views, you might grant your youngsters a peek at this large and diverse habitat for animals of land and sea.

Especially attractive for families is the **POINT DEFIANCE ZOO AND AQUARIUM,** where you'll find an impressive array of animals from a variety of Pacific Rim habitats. The zoo's 29 acres house more than 5,000 animals. Visitors make their way from the parking lot through zoo exhibits to the aquarium. On the way, you'll pass a well-stocked farm (where little city slickers love to feed the goats), discover how a variety of animals are adapting to an increasingly inhospitable world, and visit with three Asian elephants. The shark exhibit is sure to engage your young biologist; a variety of marine mammals and birds are on display, too.

The Discovery Reef Aquarium features exotic tropical marine life, and carefully designed exhibits allow visitors an optimal view of some wildlife, from both above and below the water line. The jellyfish are especially mesmerizing. But the aquarium's star is the 160,000-gallon tank filled with some of Puget Sound's watery residents. People food is available—typical zoo fare, but it goes down well with the small fry.

In November and December, Point Defiance offers its popular "Zoolights" display. The zoo is festooned with 500,000 lights, arranged in life-size animal shapes, and is open to visitors after dark. It's fun to wander through a zoo at night! Stop for cocoa or hot cider to warm your fingers as you make the rounds.

*5400 N. Pearl St. (I-5 south to Exit 132, follow signs to Hwy. 16. Turn right onto Pearl St. and follow signs). 253/591-5337; www.pdza/org. Open daily, 10 a.m.-7 p.m. (Memorial Day-Labor Day); 10 a.m.-4 p.m. (rest of year). Cost: $7.25/adult, $6.75/senior, $5.50/youth 4-13, free/under 4.*

**TACOMA ART MUSEUM.** For a small museum, TAM packs in a lot of art and has attracted some excellent traveling exhibits. The permanent collection focuses on paintings of the 19th and 20th centuries, and Northwest and Asian art, but many visitors head straight for the fine collection of glass works by Tacoma native Dale Chihuly.

It seems as if just about every cultural institution in Tacoma is expanding and TAM is no exception. It will move into a new 50,000-square-foot facility next to Union Station in 2001.

TAM offers a variety of exceptional educational programs for families and children of all ages. There's a good museum store, too.

*1123 Pacific Ave. (12th & Pacific). 253/272-4258; www.tacomaartmuseum.org. Open Tues.-Sat., 10 a.m.-5 p.m.; Thurs., 10 a.m.-7 p.m.; Sun., noon-5 p.m. (Later hours may apply during special exhibits; call for details.) Cost: $5/adult, $4/senior & student, free/under 6, third Thurs.*

**WASHINGTON STATE HISTORY MUSEUM.** When it comes to museums, Tacoma may well have the best in the state. Visitors to WSHM can explore Washington's rich natural and human history in a 106,000-square-foot building located next to Union Station and designed to blend in with that historic Tacoma landmark.

On arrival, children are given a treasure map with items scattered about the museum for them to locate. Some are fairly well hidden, but several parent reviewers have reported that their children, who usually give up on this sort of educational activity, have risen to the challenge. Meanwhile, on the way, they've learned about Washington's true natives, explored a petroglyph, investigated a covered wagon, read how apples are grown and harvested, and discovered some little-known elements of the state's past (such as its dynamic early labor movement). Dramatic exhibits incorporate hands-on elements that keep even very young children entertained.

The Great Hall of Washington History allows visitors to walk through the history of the state, while listening to personal commentary. In a Seattle Hooverville shack, for example, two residents discuss the Depression; the Coast Salish plank house features a conversation between an elderly basket maker and her granddaughter. History becomes something that visitors experience, whether they sit aboard the replica of a covered wagon or explore a coal mine. Don't miss the opportunity to take a ride down the Columbia River via large-screen video. Of special interest to many children will be the 1,800-square-foot model train exhibit. Indoor and outdoor theatres offer live presentations and films.

A well-appointed museum store rounds out the attractions. A small café offers a limited assortment of snack and lunch items.

Be sure to check out **UNION STATION** (800/272-2662) next door. The 1911 building is impressive in its own right. No longer a working train station, it's now a federal courthouse. It also houses some of Dale Chihuly's most breathtaking installations. Even the most art-weary children will be impressed when they gaze up at the dome at the deep-blue chandelier composed of 2,500 shells.

*1911 Pacific Ave. 253/272-WSHS, 888/238-4373; www.wshs.org. Open Mon.-Sat., 10 a.m.-5 p.m.; Sun., 11 a.m.-5 p.m. Closed Mon., fall & winter. Thursdays are free from 5-8 p.m. year round. Cost: $7/adult, $6.25/senior, $5/child, free/under 6, $20/family, Thurs. free 5-8 p.m.*

## OLYMPIA

Many people regard Olympia as a stop-off along I-5 on the way to someplace else, but the state capital deserves consideration as a final destination. Nestled at the southern tip of Puget Sound, Olympia is a pretty little city that might get sleepy if it weren't for the stimulation that comes from being the hub of the state government and the home of a state college. To see democracy in action, visit Olympia at least once with your school-age kids when the legislature is in session, usually January through April. Your children may study civics, but the classroom can't match the experience of seeing the legislative system first-hand.

## PLACES TO STAY

### CAVENAUGH'S AT CAPITAL LAKE (FORMERLY HOLIDAY INN)
*2300 Evergreen Park Dr., 98802*
*360/943-4000*
*Rates: Moderate*
*FYI: Restaurant with kids' menu; refrigerators (suites); outdoor pool (seasonal); year-round Jacuzzi; baby-sitting; shuttle service to capital buildings; laundry*

This is a large motel (191 units) in an exceptionally attractive setting overlooking Capital Lake. The building has been remodeled, with nicely appointed rooms. To avoid a noisy room and to take advantage of the fabulous view of the lake and the State Capitol dome, request a room on the water side.

**❝ PARENT COMMENTS**
*"Definitely request a remodeled room, preferably with a view. Our five year old enjoyed the pool and the grounds."*

### COMFORT INN OF LACEY
*4700 Park Center Ave. NE, Lacey 98516*
*360/456-6300*
*Rates: Inexpensive*
*FYI: Complimentary continental breakfast; refrigerators/microwaves (suites); indoor pool*

The Comfort Inn is located near I-5, shopping, parks, theaters, and St. Martin's College. Despite its proximity to the freeway, it enjoys a wooded setting. Most of the rooms are designated non-smoking, and eight suites have microwaves and refrigerators.

**❝ PARENT COMMENTS**
*"My preschooler and I stayed here while looking for a house to buy. The staff was friendly and the pool was great. For convenience, you can't beat the location."*

### PUGET VIEW GUESTHOUSE B&B
*6924 61st NE, 98516*
*360/459-1676*
*Rates: Inexpensive to moderate*

*FYI: Free continental breakfast; microwaves/refrigerators; barbecue; pets OK (prior approval)*

Though known as a romantic getaway, this B&B works well for families. The private, wooded grounds are adjacent to Tolmie State Park and provide views of the Olympic Mountains and Puget Sound.

The guesthouse has a bedroom with a queen bed, as well as a living room with a sofa sleeper, so it can comfortably accommodate a family of four. The refrigerator comes in handy for snacks or restaurant leftovers, and there's a microwave and a barbecue. A continental breakfast is served.

With a tree house on the grounds and a private trail to the beach, the kids won't have to look far for entertainment. If weather interferes with outdoor play, Olympia is just a short drive away.

**❝ PARENT COMMENTS**

*"The owners are exceptionally nice. Our kids loved the beaches, opportunities to explore tide pools and other marine life. The only drawback was the lack of a full kitchen."*

### RAMADA INN GOVERNOR HOUSE

*621 S. Capitol Way 98501*
*360/352-7700*
*Rates: Moderate*
*FYI: Restaurant with kids' menu; kitchenettes (some rooms); outdoor pool (seasonal); exercise room; shuttle service; pets OK ($50 deposit)*

Located downtown, this hotel offers easy access to shopping and the capital. There are view rooms on both sides of the motel; request one that's newly remodeled. Families looking to save money on meals may prefer one of the five mini-suites with kitchenettes.

**❝ PARENT COMMENTS**

*"The motel is located across the street from Sylvester Park and within easy walking distance of Capital Lake—we found both helpful for burning off excess energy."*

## PLACES TO EAT

### FALLS TERRACE

*106 S. Deschutes Way, Tumwater*
*360/943-7830*
*Hours: Lunch Mon.-Sat., dinner daily*

This Tumwater restaurant has become an institution. Not only does it have a gorgeous setting overlooking the Tumwater Falls of the Deschutes River, it also serves a fine American/Northwest cuisine at reasonable prices. The limited children's menu (grilled cheese, burgers, steak, fish and chips) is moderately priced.

Reservations are advised. By dining early, you can avoid the crowd and take advantage of the "early bird" specials. Request a window seat so children can watch the tumbling waterfalls.

### JoMamas
*120 N. Pear*
*360/943-9849*
*Hours: Lunch, dinner Mon.-Sat., dinner Sun.*

This is a non-traditional pizza place with delicious custom pizzas. At first glance the pizzas may seem expensive, but they're so loaded with goodies that a little goes a long way. For non-pizza eaters (are there any?), JoMamas serves sandwiches, soups, and salads at lunch and a few pasta dishes at dinner.

Located in an old house with spacious wooden booths and an upstairs area, this is an informal, kid-friendly restaurant. The service is attentive, but not necessarily fast, so you'll be grateful that crayons are supplied.

### URBAN ONION
*116 Legion Way SE*
*360/943-9242*
*Hours: Breakfast, lunch, dinner daily*

Located downtown in the old Olympian Hotel, the Urban Onion serves healthy Northwest food and pasta dishes. There is a low-priced kids' menu. This is a popular spot and service sometimes is slow; request some crayons and drawing paper to help youngsters pass the time.

### WAGNER'S EUROPEAN BAKERY AND CAFÉ
*1013 Capitol Way S.*
*360/357-7268*
*Hours: Breakfast, lunch daily*

This full-scale bakery and café, walking distance from the capital, is an Olympia landmark. Wagner's serves up pastries (not a full breakfast menu), sandwiches, and salads. Or order a box lunches to take out (one will feed two children).

### THE WHALE'S TAIL
*501 N. Columbia, on Percival Landing boardwalk*
*360/956-1928*

*Hours: Breakfast, lunch daily (until 6 p.m.)*

This is a good place for breakfast, lunch, or snacks while exploring the Olympia waterfront (walk-up or bike-up service available). The menu is simple and kid-friendly (soups, salads, sandwiches). The proximity to the water, marvelous whale décor and outdoor tables make it a fun, relaxed place for kids.

## WHAT TO SEE & DO

### STROLL & BROWSE

**CAPITOL AND GROUNDS.** Chances are good you came here to show your kids democracy in action. Even if you are just driving by Olympia on your way to someplace else, it's well worth your time to stop for a visit and lesson in civics. If at all possible, come when the legislature is in session, but any time of year the buildings and grounds are impressive. Don't worry if your recall of the legislative process is rusty; the free tours present a very informative and entertaining crash course in state government—one that you and your school-aged children can enjoy.

Even preschoolers will appreciate the grandeur and spaciousness (good for echoes) of the **CAPITOL BUILDING**, the capital's centerpiece, spiffed up for the state centennial in 1987-88. Free guided tours depart daily (except holidays) on the hour, 10 a.m. to 4 p.m. Reservations are required for groups of 15 or more. Tours visit the House and Senate chambers; if the legislature is in session (January through early spring), visitors can observe the process from balconies. There is no age minimum for the tour, but children must be at least 10 to attempt the 262-step climb to the top of the Capitol Dome.

Just opposite the capitol building stands the **TEMPLE OF JUSTICE**, seat of the Washington State Supreme Court. The **GOVERNOR'S MANSION**, within easy walking distance of the Capitol Building, is open to visitors on Wednesdays, 1-2:45 p.m., by reservation (360/586-TOUR). Tours run every fifteen minutes and are confined to the library, sitting room, dining room, and ballroom. Not much is likely to hold the attention of a younger child on this one-hour tour, except perhaps the story of the governor and his wife finding a live bat in their baby's room!

The capitol campus is a lovely place to stroll. The greenhouse and conservatory are open Monday through Friday. Also worth a visit are the rose garden, Tivoli Fountain, and the Vietnam and Korean War Memorials. This is a great place to eat your picnic lunch, fly a kite, or just let the kids run loose. In spring, enjoy the abundant pink cherry blossoms. *Take I-5 to Exit 105 and follow signs west.*

**DOWNTOWN.** Olympia's town square, **SYLVESTER PARK** (7th between Washington and Capitol), is named for founding father Edmund Sylvester. Landscaped in 1893, its huge trees provide a park-like atmosphere. Nearby you will find renovated turn-of-the-century buildings, most notably the Old Capitol (7th & Washington), a magnificent, turreted structure built in 1892. It had a clock tower, which was removed after a 1949 earthquake left it unstable.

**WATERFRONT.** The waterfront park at **PERCIVAL LANDING** is a focal point for community activity in Olympia. The area features 1 1/2 miles of boardwalk, with moorage facilities and views of the Capitol, Port of Olympia, Budd Inlet, Mount Rainier, and the Olympics. The **OLYMPIA FARMERS MARKET**, second largest in the state, displays local produce, flowers, and crafts April through October, and is open for holiday buying of crafts only through December.

### MUSEUMS

**HANDS-ON CHILDREN'S MUSEUM.** Dedicated parents spent several years planning and raising funds to open this museum. Fun times abound for kids age one to 10: dress up as sea creatures and play on a fishing pier, explore a ship-building center, or splash in a water play area. Overnight slumber parties are available, with story times, snacks, science, art activities and breakfast (something to consider if you need overnight accommodations)!

*106 11th Ave. SW, downtown. 360/956-0818. Open Tues.-Sat., 10 a.m.-5 p.m.; Fri., 6-9 p.m.; Sun., noon- 5 p.m. Cost: $3.50/person over 1, free/under 1, free/first Friday of month.*

**STATE CAPITAL MUSEUM.** The museum houses a permanent collection of Native American and early pioneer artifacts and Northwest art exhibits. Housed in a California mission-style mansion, the 32-room museum has a permanent collection of Native American and early pioneer artifacts, and historic Washington State photographs and manuscripts. A gallery displays changing Northwest art exhibits.

If weather permits, stroll around the grounds, which include a pioneer herb garden.

*211 W. 21st Ave. (eight blocks south of the capitol campus). 360/753-2580. Cost: $2/adult, $1/youth 7-18, free/under 6, $5/family.*

## PARKS

**TUMWATER FALLS PARK**, near the Olympia Brewery, is a pleasant stop for families. A paved trail along the Deschutes River crosses the lower falls to form an easy, one-mile loop. (Be sure to hold young and/or impulsive children by the hand.) In the fall, children will learn a lesson in nature as they watch salmon swim up the fish ladders to their hatchery. The park has picnic areas and restrooms.

*Off Deschutes Pkwy., adjacent to the brewery.*

**CAPITOL LAKE PARK** offers 10 acres of waterfront along a man-made saltwater lake. Play equipment, a picnic area, ducks to feed, boat rentals, and restrooms are available here.

*5th &Water St., at the edge of downtown Olympia.*

**PRIEST POINT PARK** has 265 wooded acres, six miles of trails, sheltered picnic areas, a wading pool, and restrooms. Or walk the four-mile *Ellis Cove Trail* to the beach. The trail is hilly, but there are benches to rest on along the way.

*On East Bay Dr. between Mission and Flora Vista avenues.*

**TOLMIE STATE PARK.** The big attraction of this park is a man-made reef that attracts fish and other sea life—a great place to be during low tide! Families will enjoy the 105 acres of park offering 180 feet of Puget Sound waterfront, trails, picnic facilities, and restrooms.

*Take Exit 111 from I-5 and follow signs west (approx. 5 miles).*

**WOODARD BAY CONSERVATION AREA.** A State Department of Natural Resources conservancy area located on Henderson Inlet, Woodard Bay has four miles of marine shoreline and 450 acres of upland and tideland. This is a great place to observe marine animals, especially seals, and their habitats. A six-mile walking and biking trail offers exercise for energetic families.

*Take Libby Road north, turn right on Woodard Bay Road and continue to the bay.*

## EXCURSIONS

**MIMA MOUNDS.** Bizarre phenomena, the Mima Mounds are

six-foot-high, 30-foot-wide mounds of earth that have baffled scientists for years. Prevalent theories about the origin of the mounds range from Indian buffalo decoys to giant, prehistoric gophers. Whatever they are, they are intriguing any time of year. They're especially beautiful in the early summer, when they blossom with wildflowers. Self-guided tour instructions are available at the interpretive center.

*Take Exit 95 from I-5 and drive 4.5 miles on Hwy. 121. Open daily, 8 a.m.-dusk. Free.*

**NISQUALLY NATIONAL WILDLIFE REFUGE**, located in the Nisqually River delta, is home to nearly 400 wildlife species. The refuge offers more than 3,700 acres of grasslands, marshes, and meandering streams, as well as seven miles of trails and a visitor center. Families will enjoy the level, five-mile hiking trail that follows an old dike around the wetlands (bring binoculars). There is a rookery of great herons that provide an amusing sight—a bird condo.

*Take Exit 114 off I-5 and follow signs. 360/753-9467. Cost: $3/family.*

**WOLF HAVEN INTERNATIONAL**, a sanctuary for captive wolves from all over the country, is home to more than 35 wolves. "Howl-ins" (including a tour, storytelling, sing-along, campfire, and howling with the wolves) are available mid-May to mid-September; reservations are required. Tours are available year round.

*Off Lake Road in Tenino. 360/264-4695; 800/448-WOLF. Cost: tours, $5/adult, $2.50/child 5-12, free/under 5; "howl-ins," $6/adult, $4/child 5-12, $2.50/under 5.*

## CALENDAR

**JULY**
Capitol Lakefair.
**AUGUST**
Renaissance Faire.
**SEPTEMBER**
Harbor Days.

## RESOURCES

**OLYMPIA THURSTON CHAMBER OF COMMERCE**
521 Legion Way E., Olympia 98501
360/357-3362

**TACOMA-PIERCE COUNTY VISITORS AND
CONVENTION BUREAU**
1001 Pacific Ave., Ste. 400, Tacoma 98401-1754
253/627-2836, 800/272-2662

## BOOKS AND PUBLICATIONS

*Puget Sound Parent*, a monthly newsmagazine offering feature articles and a calendar of family activities, is available at local bookstores.

*South Puget Sound Afoot and Afloat*, by Marge Mueller, Mountaineers Publishing, offers hiking and boating suggestions for all ages.

## KITSAP PENINSULA

The Kitsap Peninsula is a crooked finger of mainland that rests in the middle of Puget Sound, between the Tacoma-Seattle-Everett corridor to the east and Hood Canal to the west. Urban sprawl is creeping into the region, but you can still find abundant local history and natural beauty to explore with the kids.

### GETTING THERE

Take the Seattle-Bremerton ferry from downtown, a one-hour ride.

### PLACES TO STAY

**SILVERDALE ON THE BAY HOTEL AND RESORT**
*3073 Bucklin Hill Road, Silverdale 98383*
*360/698-1000*
*Rates: Moderate to expensive*
*FYI: Restaurant; indoor pool; pool table, Ping-Pong, video game room; basketball hoop, tennis courts, horseshoe pit, shuffle board (indoor and outdoor); baby-sitting by arrangement*
This isn't the sort of place you go for a week's vacation, but it is well suited for a family weekend of R&R any time of the year. Rooms are spacious and comfortable (most have a majestic view of Dyles Inlet) and there is plenty to keep children busy. The ground-floor rooms on the waterside have sliding glass doors that lead out to the grass and down to the beach-nice for parents who

want to sit on the patio and keep an eye on the kids.

The Mariner restaurant at the resort is quite good and welcomes children with a friendly staff and a children's menu. Fish tanks next to the restaurant keep kids entertained while waiting for the food to arrive.

**❝ PARENT COMMENTS:**

*"We stayed in the mini-suite (two doubles and one Murphy bed), which was ideal for our family of five. The Sunday brunch at the hotel restaurant at the hotel was a big treat."*

*"I love to escape to this place on a dreary winter weekend. Just a pleasant ferry ride from Seattle, there's minimal travel hassle for a nice getaway. My kids spend most of their time in the pool, and I bring several books and kick back. There is a mall and movie theater nearby, in case the group gets restless."*

## PLACES TO EAT

### THE BOAT SHED

*101 Shore Dr., Bremerton*
*360/377-2600*
*Hours: Lunch, dinner daily, Sunday brunch*

Sitting just one mile from the ferry terminal, just across Manette Bridge, the delicious food, cheerful nautical decor (including a big aquarium) and reasonable prices make the Boat Shed an ideal family restaurant. All the food is fresh and tasty and there's a very good kid's menu.

### STREAMLINER DINER

*397 Winslow Way, Winslow*
*206/842-8595*
*Hours: Breakfast daily, lunch Mon.-Fri.; no credit cards*

This Bainbridge Island institution hums with contented diners enjoying delicious comfort food at reasonable prices. It is a nice place to stop at the start of your trip or well worth a special trip from Seattle-just walk onto the ferry some morning and enjoy a leisurely breakfast and browsing in the charming town of Winslow before catching the ferry back to the city.

### VICTORIA'S

*Hwy. 106, Union*
*360/898-4400*
*Hours: Dinner Wed.-Sun., lunch Sat.-Sun., breakfast Sun.*

The food is excellent, the prices are moderate, and the setting is charming in this Old English-style restaurant in the tiny town of Union. The grounds are lovely-including a mini-croquet course, a small brook, and towering firs. Outdoor dining is quite pleasant in the summer.

Pasta and seafood dishes are especially recommended. The staff is very accommodating about special orders for both adults and kids, and glad to split the generous portions.

## WHAT TO SEE & DO

**THE BREMERTON NAVAL MUSEUM** is located just a half-block from the Bremerton ferry terminal, near the Puget Sound Naval Shipyard. Although you might expect it to be dull for anyone without a passion for naval history, in fact all ages seem to find something of interest in the small but fascinating collection of ship models. And don't miss the world's oldest surviving cannon (dated 1377).

There is usually one of the big aircraft carriers moored at the docks which you can view from several side streets close to the ship yard or by taking the passenger-only ferry to Port Orchard from the Bremerton ferry dock.

*The museum is located on Washington Ave. 360/479-7447. Open Tues.-Sat., 10 a.m.-5 p.m., Sun. 1-5 p.m. (Memorial Day-Sept.) Free.*

**HOOD CANAL** dominates the southern end of the Kitsap Peninsula. Unlike other Pacific Northwest salt waters, the temperature of the canal reaches into the 70s in the summer, a boon for swimmers. Its shoreline is rich with shrimp, clams, oysters, and crabs. In season, seafood stands skirt the roads. Many public beaches near the northern end of the canal are good for clam and oyster gathering, a beach activity most children love. Farther north, there are several picturesque towns rich in Northwest history.

**POINT NO POINT,** just beyond Hansville, is home of the **POINT NO POINT LIGHTHOUSE** and several beautiful and easily accessible beaches. Tours of the lighthouse are offered each weekend, May to September, noon to 4 p.m. Take Hwy. 3 to Poulsbo exit (305 S) and go left at Bond Road (307N). Follow Bond Road to Hansville Hwy. and turn left. Travel 5 miles to Point No Point Country Road and turn right into a dead end parking area.

**PORT GAMBLE,** 23 miles north of Bremerton via Highway 3, is the oldest continually operating company town in the United States. Situated on a bluff at the intersection of Admiralty Inlet and Gamble Bay, it was founded by New Englanders in the mid-19th century and is still owned by the Pope and Talbot lumber firm. The town has been lovingly restored to its turn-of-the-century appearance and our parent reviewers put it on their "well worth a stop" list.

The **PORT GAMBLE HISTORICAL MUSEUM,** located behind the store, is one of the finest museums of its kind in the Northwest and worth coming all the way from Seattle to visit. Designed by Alec James, who designed the displays for the Royal Provincial Museum in Victoria, British Columbia, the life-size dioramas will hold the interest of all ages, while teaching the rich history of the region.

*360/297-8074. Open daily, 10:30 a.m.-5 p.m. (May-Oct.); by appointment (early Nov., March-April); closed mid-Nov.-Feb. Cost: $2/adult, $1/child & senior 65 and over, free/under 6.*

The **PORT GAMBLE COUNTRY STORE** is full of old-fashioned toys and also houses a good deli. On the second floor, the tiny **OF SEA AND SHORE MUSEUM** houses aquariums and, allegedly, the largest collection of seashells in the United States. This place is usually a big hit with the kids-for pennies they can take home a pocketful of shells.

*Port Gamble Country Store. Open daily, 8 a.m.-5 p.m. (Sept.-March); daily, 7 a.m.-7 p.m. (April-Aug.). 360/297-7636.*

*Of Sea and Shore Museum. 360/297-2426. Open Tues.-Sun., 11 a.m.-4 p.m. (June-Aug.); Sat.-Sun., 11 a.m.-4 p.m. (Sept.-May). Free.*

**PORT ORCHARD** is a scenic little town, a 15-minute drive from Bremerton and also accessible via passenger-only ferry across Sinclair Inlet from Bremerton. The ferry leaves each half-hour between about 6 a.m. and midnight, and the 10-minute ride offers a good view of the big ships in the shipyard as you leave Bremerton. The Port Orchard pier extends 150 yards into the water, with a floating dock winding around the marina. Fall is squid season, and the pier gets crowded with excited kids catching their limits in less than 30 minutes. This is a hit with even the very young, for patience and a long attention span are not needed. When squid run, they run by the thousands, and can be caught with a bare hook.

If it's raining, the covered sidewalks in the little shopping section of town will keep you dry. If you have a child fascinated with all things miniature, take them to **LITTLE HABITATS**, a collection of tiny toys, tiny pianos, and tiny everything else imaginable filling more than 2,600 square feet in a house located on the town outskirts.

*3238 Locker Road SE, Port Orchard. 360/871-1100. Open Mon.-Fri., 10 a.m.-5 p.m.; Sat., 10 a.m.-4 p.m. Cost: $1/adult & youth, free/under 5.*

**POULSBO,** known locally as " Little Norway," has had some of its Scandinavian charm obscured by rapid growth and development over the last 10 years, but once you get past the strip malls you'll find a charming little town with a fine view of Liberty Bay and the Olympic Mountains. If you are making this your lunch stop, assemble a picnic at one of the many delis along the boardwalk between the bluff and the water. Then take your picnic to **LIBERTY BAY PARK** where you can enjoy watching the boats come and go.

The **MARINE SCIENCE CENTER** in Poulsbo has aquariums, touch-tanks of marine life and other well-presented exhibits aimed at educating all ages about the biology and geology of Puget Sound.

*18743 Front St. NE, Poulsbo. 360/779-5549. Open daily, 11 a.m.-5 p.m. Cost: $4/adult, $3/senior & youth 13-17, $2/child 2-12, free/under 2. Free/third Tuesday of the month.*

**SUQUAMISH MUSEUM AND TRIBAL CENTER** is located just off Highway 305 on the Port Madison Indian Reservation. It's a good stop on your way to or from the Winslow ferry on Bainbridge Island. The excellent exhibits give a vivid account of life on Puget Sound for the thousands of years before white settlers arrived. There are also two short films about the tribe, narrated by tribal elders. Near the museum, on Suquamish Way off Highway 305, you can visit the grave of the famous Salish leader Chief Seattle (or Sealth). During Chief Seattle Days in August, the tribal center comes alive with traditional Indian dancing, games, canoe races, storytelling, and a salmon bake.

*Hwy. 305, Suquamish. 360/598-3311. Open daily, 10 a.m.-5 p.m. (summer); Fri.-Sun., 11 a.m.-4 p.m. (winter). Cost: $2.50 /adult, $2/senior 55 and over, $1/child under 12. Group tours, $15/hour.*

## CALENDAR

**MAY**
Viking Fest, Poulsbo.
**JUNE**
Skandia Midsommarfest, Poulsbo.
**AUGUST**
Chief Seattle Days, Suquamish.
**DECEMBER**
Yule Fest, Poulsbo.

## RESOURCES

**BREMERTON VISITORS BUREAU**
120 Washington Street
Bremerton, WA 98310
360/479-3579

**PORT ORCHARD CHAMBER OF COMMERCE**
839 Bay Street
Port Orchard, WA 98366
(360)876-3505

# THE OLYMPIC PENINSULA

The Olympic Peninsula is a 7,200-square-mile area stretching from the Kitsap Peninsula and Hood Canal out to the northern beaches of the Pacific Ocean, and encompassing nearly every kind of geography, wildlife, and climate to be found in the state. Rainfall varies from 15 inches annually (in the Sequim sunbelt, on the northern boundary) to a perpetually moist 200 inches in the rain forests of Olympic National Park. It is a richly endowed chunk of nature, too much to be digested at one time. Fortunately, the peninsula is reasonably close to the greater Seattle area. Depending on your destination, in less than an hour's driving time from Seattle, you can be nibbling away at it.

## GETTING THERE

There are many ways to reach the Olympia Peninsula, including several different routes that require ferry rides as well as routes that skip the ferry. The route you choose will depend on your preferred mode of travel, time of year, and your precise destination. When you reserve your accommodations, you might be wise to ask for the recommended route.

**BY FERRY.** From downtown Seattle, you can take the ferry to Winslow, on Bainbridge Island, or to Bremerton, on the Kitsap Peninsula. If you go to Winslow, you will then drive north 23 miles and cross the Hood Canal Floating Bridge onto the Olympic Peninsula. If you go to Bremerton, you will drive 20 miles northwest, across the Kitsap Peninsula, and cross the Hood Canal Floating Bridge.

A ferry crosses from Edmonds (about 20 miles north of Seattle) to Kingston, on the Kitsap Peninsula. From Kingston, it's an eight-mile drive to the Hood Canal Floating Bridge.

A two-ferry route takes you from Mukilteo (about 30 miles north of Seattle) to Whidbey Island. From here, drive 25 miles to Keystone and take the ferry to Port Townsend, on the Olympic Peninsula.

**BY CAR.** If you prefer to skip the ferry rides, you can take the Tacoma Narrows Bridge from Tacoma to the Kitsap Peninsula. From here it is about 45 miles to the Hood Canal Floating Bridge. Or, you can hook up with highways 302 and 106 west, which take you around the southern tip of Hood Canal and onto the Olympic Peninsula near Potlatch (about 45 miles from Tacoma).

If you are headed north toward the Port Townsend area, or points northwest of there, you will add about 60 miles of driving by taking the Tacoma Narrows Bridge route; at the same time, you'll avoid the huge summer ferry lines, and you may save your sanity. On the other hand, if your destination is along Hood Canal (Lilliwaup/Lake Cushman area), the southern route may be just as convenient.

If you are approaching from Portland, head northwest on Highway 30 along the Columbia River to Astoria. Take the toll bridge across the Columbia from Astoria to Megler, and follow Highway 101 to Aberdeen-Hoquiam. Continue north on 101 to circle the Olympic Peninsula.

**ROADSIDE ATTRACTIONS.** If you're on Highway 101 heading west to Sequim, the town of **GARDINER** is worth a short detour. Watch for signs to the boat launch at Gardiner, and turn onto the Old Gardiner Highway. Follow the road to the boat launch, then turn left and head uphill. Soon you'll notice carved fence posts and then trolls, castle-like houses, dragons, goblins, and other creatures. These homes are private, but you can walk up the road to give the kids a good view.

See also: "What to See & Do" under Port Townsend, Port Angeles, Sequim, Kitsap, Lake Crescent, and Lake Quinault.

## PORT LUDLOW

The Olympic Peninsula is dotted with ports this and ports that; Port Angeles, Port Townsend, Port Gamble, and Port Orchard, and all are worth visiting with the kids. Port Ludlow is dominated by the popular Resort at Port Ludlow, a condo community that is known for its golf course, but has plenty to offer non-golfers as well.

### PLACES TO STAY

#### THE RESORT AT PORT LUDLOW
*9483 Oak Bay Road, 98365*
*360/437-2222, 800/732-1239; www.portludlowresort.com*
*Rates: Expensive*
*FYI: Restaurant; kitchens; indoor and outdoor pools; boat and fishing rentals; bicycle rentals; golf, squash, tennis; sailing charters in summer; organized activities for kids*

The Resort at Port Ludlow consists of a large number of condos spread out through attractive grounds, among paths and lawns. (There are a few motel rooms but they aren't recommended; they're small and noisy.) It has an indoor and an outdoor swimming pool, a golf course, seven tennis courts, and a supervised outdoor program for kids. Condos, all privately owned, have twin or queen beds and private baths. Apartments have living room, fully equipped kitchen, dining room, fireplace, private deck, and view. Since the units are individually owned, the décor varies, but it's uniformly comfortable. Several families could easily share one of the larger units, thereby making the visit more affordable.

Grounds are large and well maintained, with lots of room for children to roam and explore. There are paved bicycle paths, nature hikes, and lots of water sports: boating, fishing, clam digging, and crabbing. During the summer, a recreation director arranges field games, water games on the lagoon, and trips to nearby attractions such as the Olympic Game Farm, Port Townsend, and Olympic National Park.

The resort restaurant, The Harbormaster, is moderately expensive and offers standard steak fare. A better alternative at the resort is the deli at the golf course, which serves hamburgers, hot dogs, and sandwiches. Port Townsend, 20 miles away, offers ample opportunity for diversion and meals (see "Places to Eat" and "What to See & Do").

**66 PARENT COMMENTS**

*"We left spouses at home and spent two nights here with four kids. The atmosphere was a little too golf-condo for the grown-ups, but the pool and beach were great for the kids, and the accommodations were very comfortable."*

*"Don't expect woods."*

*"We visited in the fall with our kids, ages five and nine. The indoor pool was nice, and we enjoyed exploring Port Townsend."*

*"We held a family reunion here in August, with about 30 people ranging in age from three months to 83 years. By making reservations several months in advance, we were able to get all our condos close to each other and several of the units were big enough to handle six people each, so we could put grandparents with younger families. It worked well. A group would play golf every day while some went to the pool or played tennis. One night, a foursome of twenty-somethings went into Port Townsend for some fun."*

## PLACES TO EAT

### AJAX CAFÉ
*271 Water St.*
*360/385-3450*
*Hours: Dinner Tues.-Sun.*

This charming place sits on the tiny and colorful waterfront of the tiny and colorful town of Port Hadlock, about a 15-minute drive from the Resort at Port Ludlow. The atmosphere is funky and relaxed, just right for a group of all ages, and the food is delicious. Most nights there's live jazz or folk music, and the youngsters will enjoy watching the musicians.

Ajax is most famous for a flavorful fisherman's stew, but there are a variety of other choices on the menu that will suit an eclectic collection of diners. If a kid gets restless, it's fun to walk on the little street along the water. It can get busy here; reservations are recommended.

## PORT TOWNSEND

Port Townsend, a National Historic Landmark at the northeastern tip of the peninsula, is sometimes called the "Victorian Seaport." It's about a one-hour drive from Winslow (on Bainbridge Island) and about 45 minutes from either Port Angeles or Kingston.

This charming town is an excellent destination for a quick

family getaway. Also, several of our parent reviewers named it their favorite place to take one child for a special trip with mom or dad.

### PLACES TO STAY

#### BAY COTTAGE
*4346 S. Discovery Road 98368*
*360/385-2035; www.oldconsulateinn.com*
*Rates: Moderate*
*FYI: Kitchens; no credit cards*

The well-kept cottages sit on the edge of Discovery Bay, just six miles from Port Townsend. The beach is fine for swimming, gathering sand dollars, digging for clams, and building bonfires. Furnishings include antiques and feather beds, so a rambunctious preschooler might not be a good idea here.

Fully equipped kitchens come stocked with the basics, including pancake mix and cereal and often fresh fruit and homemade cookies. Each cottage has its own picnic basket, binoculars, and library.

#### 66 PARENT COMMENTS
*"Owner Susan Atkins goes out of her way to make families feel welcome. Pure relaxation. The feather bed was a real treat!"*

#### BISHOP VICTORIAN
*714 Washington St. 98368*
*360/385-6122*
*Rates: Moderate to expensive*
*FYI: Free continental breakfast; kitchens; pets OK (fee and with prior approval)*

In a town awash with Victorian charm, Bishop Victorian is a rare and wonderful treat—a hotel that truly welcomes kids (games and playpens are available). The three-story brick building is well situated just a block from the waterfront.

There are kitchens in each room, so you don't have to go out for every meal. The two suites have ample room—two bedrooms with double or queen beds plus sofa beds. Every morning, fruit and pastries are served on the second-floor landing.

#### 66 PARENT COMMENTS
*"Both the kids and the parents were well taken care of. They gave our girls crayons and games and were very helpful about suggesting good restaurants and places of interest to visit."*

## THE ECOLOGIC PLACE
*10 Beach Dr., Nordland 98358*
*360/385-3077, 800/871-3077; www.olympus.net/ptchambr*
*Rates: Moderate*
*FYI: Kitchens; woodstoves*

The eight rustic cedar cabins, situated around a lodge in a meadow above the beach, vary in size and accommodate from two to six guests each. They have relatively new bathrooms, kitchens, and woodstoves and are equipped with linens, towels, dishes, and basic utensils. Cabins have views of Oak Bay and the Olympic Mountains to the west and Mount Rainier to the southeast.

The Ecologic Place sits on 10 acres and is a great place to relax, ride bikes, play, and explore on the three miles of driftwood-strewn beach and salt marsh. Since it is a wildlife refuge giving special attention to ground-nesting birds, no pets are allowed. Bird books, binoculars, and a telescope are available to guests. Indoors, the lodge has a supply of books, board games, and a piano.

### 66 PARENT COMMENTS

*"The Ecologic Place is very quiet and blends well in the beautiful natural surroundings. The idea is to make your own fun. We liked going into Port Townsend to browse and eat. The kids loved the beautiful beach."*

## FORT WORDEN STATE PARK OFFICERS' QUARTERS
*200 Battery Way 98368*
*360/385-4730; www.olympus.net/ftworden*
*Rates: Inexpensive to moderate*
*FYI: Kitchens; cafeteria; tennis courts; fishing; hiking/biking trails*

One mile north of Port Townsend is 448-acre Fort Worden State Park, perched on wooded hillsides overlooking the Strait of Juan de Fuca. Eighteen stately two-story houses, officers' quarters at the turn of the century, now house visitors. Most of the houses are completely refurbished, with carpeting and reproductions of Victorian furniture. The units that haven't been refurbished have wood and linoleum floors and less attractive furnishings, but are fully adequate. All accommodations are comfortable, and most have fireplaces. Bed linens and towels are provided, and the houses are heated to be comfortable year round. Most of the houses are large enough for two (or even three) families to share, which brings the cost well into the "inexpensive" range.

The kitchens are large and fully equipped. If you don't feel like cooking every meal, you can eat at the cafeteria with advance notice. Or take a short trip into Port Townsend, which offers several good dining possibilities.

Fort Worden is a fine place for a family to ride bikes. The beach is good for romping, but the water is too cold for all but the hardiest swimmers. The highlight is the old fort itself, complete with gun mounts, bunkers, and cliffs to explore.

These facilities fill up fast: plan to make reservations a year in advance. Cancellations also need to be made in advance; if you cancel less than three weeks prior to your scheduled date of arrival, your deposit will be forfeited (unless the unit is re-rented). There is a $10 fee for canceling.

**❝ PARENT COMMENTS**

*"We loved the spacious rooms. Two families with a total of five young children shared a refurbished six-bedroom house for four days in July and had a ball. Remember to bring flashlights for the kids—they are essential for hide-and-go-seek in the bunkers at the park. And bring kites to fly on the parade grounds."*

**HARBORSIDE INN**
*330 Benedict St. 98368*
*360/385-7909, 800/942-5960 (Washington only)*
*Rates: Inexpensive to moderate*
*FYI: Complimentary continental breakfast; refrigerators/ microwaves; outdoor pool (seasonal)*

The Harborside is a clean, comfortable, and reasonably priced motel with rooms overlooking a marina and a heated outdoor pool.

**❝ PARENT COMMENTS**

*"Although I can't give it too many points in the 'unique' category, the Harborside was a perfect choice for our night in Port Townsend with twin two-year-olds. They spent a full hour on the balcony watching the boats come and go at the marina."*

**MANRESA CASTLE**
*7th & Sheridan, P.O. Box 564, 98368*
*360/385-5750, 800/732-1281; www.olympus.net/manresa*
*Rates: Moderate to expensive*
*FYI: Complimentary buffet breakfast*

Built by a Prussian baker who amassed a fortune by supplying bread and crackers to ships that put into harbor in Port Townsend, and designed to resemble a medieval European edifice, Manresa Castle sits on a cliff overlooking the town. Since it looks like a castle, turret and all, it is a grand place to bring a child. (A door marked 'Dungeon' near the end of a dimly lit hall adds to the illusion.) Parents will appreciate the fine antique furnishings and the majestic view.

**❝ PARENT COMMENTS**
*"If you have a child who prefers castles to camping, this is your place. I spent one night here with my five-year-old daughter and it was perfect."*

## PLACES TO EAT

### BURRITO DEPOT
*609 Washington St.*
*360/385-5856*
*Hours: Lunch, dinner daily*
   Burritos, fajitas, nachos, quesadillas, tacos, and Southwestern specialties are heaped with fresh ingredients at the Burrito Depot. This is a friendly, very informal, and inexpensive place to eat—just right for kids.

### FERINO'S PIZZERIA
*846 Ness Corner Road, Port Hadlock*
*360/385-0840*
*Hours: Lunch, dinner Mon.-Sat.; dinner Sun.*
   If you are staying around Port Townsend or Port Ludlow, it is worth driving to Port Hadlock for this scrumptious pizza—a crisp, tasty crust, piled with fresh toppings.

### KHU LARB THAI
*225 Adams St.*
*360/385-5023*
*Hours: Lunch, dinner daily*
   Khu Larb Thai offers well-prepared Thai food served in a relaxed setting. The noodle dishes are especially popular with kids (be careful to order "no stars" if your kids want to avoid hot spices). Chicken Satay (marinated chicken pieces grilled on a stick) is also well liked by tykes. Grown-ups will appreciate the interesting soups.

### NIFTY FIFTYS
*817 Water St.*
*360/ 385-1931*
*Hours: Lunch, dinner Mon.-Sat.; closed Sun. (hours vary seasonally)*

Step back in time and enjoy all your favorites from sundaes, shakes, malts, and sodas to phosphates, lime rickeys, and cherry cokes. The authentic 1950s soda fountain and jukebox will cheer up the weariest sightseer.

### THE PUBLIC HOUSE GRILL
*1038 Water St.*
*360/385-9708*
*Hours: Lunch, dinner daily*

The spacious room works well with kids, and the food—seafood grill, steaks, and fresh pasta—is exceptionally well prepared. The prices are moderate, and there's a kids' menu offering the usual burger, fish and chips, and pb&j. Grown-ups who fancy a drink will appreciate the nice bar.

### SALAL CAFÉ
*634 Water St.*
*360/385-6532*
*Hours: Breakfast, lunch daily; dinner Thurs.-Mon.*

This light, cheerful deli caters to all tastes, including vegetarian. A typical kids' plate includes a grilled-cheese sandwich in the shape of a heart, yogurt for dessert, and fresh fruit. Breakfast here is excellent.

## WHAT TO SEE & DO

### STROLL AND BROWSE

If you're interested in the self-guided walking tour, you can pick up a map at the Visitor's Information Center. At the end of Water Street there are several attractions of interest to children. The **JOHN B. POPE MARINE PARK** (on the water across from City Hall, Water & Madison streets), which sits right on the beach, offers carved dolphins, a swing set, and picnic tables. Nearby at the **JEFFERSON COUNTY HISTORICAL SOCIETY MUSEUM** (210 Madison St.; 360/385-4730) kids will enjoy seeing the original jail cell on display and reading stories about how prisoners tried to escape. The museum is located across from City Hall and its collection of Northwest Indian artifacts is also excellent.

Don't miss the **CAROUSEL OF THE OLYMPIC SEA**, a fantastic, magical work-in-progress by William H. Dentzel, a fifth-generation carousel maker. The permanent location of the carousel has yet to be decided, but it's worth tracking down to give your child a rare chance to play the old-fashioned game, "grab the silver ring," while riding around. Dentzel's work is characterized by simple wooden animals with a hand- or foot-powered mechanism rather than an electrical motor. Installed in the summer of 1994, the figures on this carousel include a leaping orca whale, a grizzly bear, a salmon, and a sea cucumber.

**FORT FLAGLER STATE PARK** has a scenic beachfront campground with 116 sites; it's one of the most popular campgrounds in the state. Also on the park's 800 acres are a wonderful stretch of beach, a lighthouse, bunkers, a fishing pier, and hiking trails.

*Located eight miles northeast of Hadlock on Fort Flagler Road (follow "Marrowstone Island" signs from Hwy. 20). 360/385-1259; 800/233-0321.*

**FORT WORDEN STATE PARK**, just north of Port Townsend, has endless parade grounds for kite flying, picnicking, and playing, as well as gun mounts and bunkers for all kinds of hide-and-seek activities (bring flashlights). There are overnight accommodations in the Officers' Quarters (see "Places to Stay"). Between Fort Warden and Point Hudson, a pleasant mile-long beach walk beckons.

**THE CENTRUM CENTER FOR ARTS AND CREATIVE EDUCATION** (360/385-3102), located at the park, has educational programs and workshops for writers and musicians and a series of festivals and concerts throughout the year. Visitors can often watch artists-in-residence at work. The **CABLE HOUSE CANTEEN**, located across from the park and open only during the summer, is a good spot to grab a burger or fish and chips.

*One mile north of Port Townsend. 360/385-4730; www. parks.wa.gov.*

**OLYMPIC MUSIC FESTIVAL.** This popular summer festival offers a special "Concert in the Barn" series for families on weekends, June to September. What better way to expose your child to classical music than while sitting on a bale of hay in a barn? You can bring your own picnic to eat on the grounds before the concert, buy limited food (beverages, sandwiches) there, or reserve a gourmet lunch in advance. When kids get tired of listening to Mozart, they can wander around and pet the friendly farm animals. Advance reservations are strongly advised.

*Near Quilcene, 10 miles west of Hood Canal Floating Bridge. 206/527-8839. Concerts Sat.-Sun., 2 p.m. (June-Sept.) Cost: $11-$24; discounts for children.*

**PORT TOWNSEND MARINE SCIENCE CENTER.** The Marine Science Center does an exceptionally good job of showing kids what lies beneath the surface of the water. Outside, a live underwater video camera provides a view of what is under the pier; inside, you'll find "touch tanks." Interpretive programs are offered daily, along with day and overnight camps.

*At the end of the dock, in Fort Warden State Park. 360/385-5582; www.olympus.net/ptmsc/ Open Tues.-Sun., noon-6 p.m. (June 15-Labor Day); Tues.-Sun., noon-4 p.m. (Sept. 10-Oct., April-June 14). Cost: $2/adult & student, free/preschooler.*

## CALENDAR

**MAY**
Rhododendron Festival, Port Townsend.
**JUNE-AUGUST**
Olympic Music Festival, Port Townsend.
**JULY**
Jazz Festival, Port Townsend.
**SEPTEMBER**
Wooden Boat Festival, Port Townsend.

## RESOURCES

**VISITOR INFORMATION CENTER**
2437 E. Sims Way
Port Townsend  98368
360/385-2722; 888/ENJOY; www.ptchamber.org

## SEQUIM

Between Port Townsend and Port Angeles on Highway 101 lies the driest coastal area north of Southern California. This sunny oasis has grown rapidly as a retirement center in the last few years, and Sequim (pronounced "Skwim") is fast losing its farm-town identity. However, the frequent sightings of wild elk in the middle of town are reminders of the abundant wild beauty that surrounds the area.

## PLACES TO STAY

### JUAN DE FUCA COTTAGES

*182 Marine Dr., 98382*
*360/683-4433; www.dungeness.com/juandefuca*
*Rates: Moderate to expensive*
*FYI: Kitchens; whirlpool baths; fireplace in the two-room cottage; well-behaved pets ok with prior approval (no charge)*

Located seven miles north of Sequim on Dungeness Bay and the Strait of Juan de Fuca, these six well-kept cabins are comfortable and tastefully appointed. Each cottage has a fully equipped kitchen, a whirlpool bath, and a view of bay or mountains. The two-room cottage also has a lovely fireplace. There's a nice big yard in front for playing and reading, and nearby Dungeness Spit beckons to explorers.

**❝ PARENT COMMENTS**

*"First-class accommodations in a lovely setting. We brought bikes to explore the area."*

*"Our ten year old loved the Jacuzzi in our cottage!"*

## PLACES TO EAT

### HIWAY 101 DINER

*Hwy. 101*
*360/683-3388*
*Hours: Breakfast, lunch, dinner daily*

The '50s theme (neon and the back end of a '56 T-bird that now holds the CD player) and the hefty, juicy burgers and outstanding pizza will please every member of the family. Be forewarned, though: the service is sometimes slow.

### OAK TABLE CAFÉ

*292 W. Bell St.*
*360/683-2179*
*Hours: Lunch daily*

This spot offers moderate prices and generous servings of good, basic dishes. The service is fast and friendly.

### JEAN'S DELI & LITTLE TASTE OF HEAVEN

*134 S. 2nd*
*360/683-6727*
*Hours: Breakfast, lunch Mon.-Sat., 6 a.m.-3 p.m.*

Stop by for the marvelous homemade soups, delectable desserts, and generous sandwiches. In the morning, choose between fresh-out-of-the-oven muffins, cinnamon rolls, and pecan sticky buns. Yum.

### WHAT TO SEE & DO

**CEDARFIELD OSTRICH FARM.** Broaden your children's definition of a farm animal by taking them on a tour of a farm that raises the world's largest bird. Find out how farmers care for the birds, hatch eggs and even (prepare the kids) how they use the feathers and meat. While you are there, pick up some feather dusters. Individual, family, and group rates are offered for tours, but reservations are necessary.

*702 Kitchen Dick Road, Sequim. Call or e-mail in advance to schedule tour: 360/683-1837; cedarfieldfarm@tenforward.com.*

**LAVENDER FARMS.** The Sequim Dungeness Valley has weather conditions that are well loved by the fragrant, purple lavender plant. Many varieties of lavender are grown here. There's even a Sequim Lavender Festival, held at the height of the season in mid-July, with farm tours, craft workshops, and every lavender product imaginable offered for sale. Ask at the Sequim Visitor's Center for the location of farms that you can visit to pick your own and enjoy the visual and aromatic feast of purple haze.

**MUSEUM AND ARTS CENTER.** The Manis Mastodon Site, where a team of archaeologists from Washington State University is collecting evidence that early man hunted mastodons, is closed to the public. The massive bones can be seen at this fine museum, along with exhibits spanning 12,000 years of local history from Ice Age Man to the early Clallam Indians.

*175 W. Cedar St. 360/683-8110. Open Mon.-Sat., 9 a.m.-4 p.m.; Sun., 1 p.m.-4 p.m.(March-Oct.); closed Nov.-Feb.*

**THE OLYMPIC GAME FARM** near Sequim is worth a visit. This 90-acre preserve houses animals used in wildlife films and television shows. Two loop drives allow visitors to view 56 species including wolves, bison, and bears. Our parent reviewers reported an enthusiastic response from the kids and a so-so vote from the adults. You'll have the opportunity to purchase loaves of bread at the front gate, where you'll also be reminded to stay in your car. Kids will thrill at the sight of free-ranging llamas, zebras, and bison coming right up to slobber on the car windows.

*1423 Ward Road, Sequim. 360/683-4295. Open daily, 9 a.m.-7 p.m. (summer); 9 a.m.-4 p.m. (winter). Two tours: one dri-*

*ving, one walking.* Cost: $6/adult 13 and over, $5/ senior & youth 5-12, free/under 5 (summer); $4/adult & youth 5-12 (winter).

## CALENDAR

**JULY**
Sequim Lavender Festival.

## RESOURCES

**SEQUIM/DUNGENESS VALLEY VISITOR INFORMATION CENTER**
1192 E. Washington, P.O. Box 907, Sequim
360/683-6197; www.cityofsequim.com

## PORT ANGELES

While Port Townsend capitalizes on the past, Port Angeles offers visitors access to the northern (and most popular) edge of the vast and beautiful Olympic National Park. As a bonus, **BLACK BALL TRANSPORT** (206/622-2222; 360/457-4491) operates passenger and auto ferries from here across the strait to Victoria on Vancouver Island. (See "Victoria and Vicinity and Salt Spring Island" for details.)

### PLACES TO STAY

**DOUBLETREE INN**
*221 N. Lincoln St. 98362*
*360/452-9215*
*Rates: Moderate*
*FYI: Restaurant; refrigerators; outdoor pool (year round); pets OK*

Located at the ferry landing on westbound Highway 101, this two-story motel is well suited to families, whether stopping on their way to Victoria or spending several days exploring the Olympic Peninsula. There is only one two-bedroom unit, so if your group is large, make reservations early for the summer months. Request a room with a view and a balcony to take full advantage of the harborside location.

**❝❝ PARENT COMMENTS**
*"We have stayed here several times on our way to Victoria. The year-round outdoor pool is kept at 86 degrees and our kids love the fun of swimming outside on a cold, winter day."*

## PLACES TO EAT

### FIRST STREET HAVEN
*107 E. 1st St.*
*360/457-0352*
*Hours: Breakfast, lunch Mon.-Sat., brunch Sun.*

Fresh, generous salads and pasta dishes are the main attraction; the fajitas are good too. This spot offers reasonable prices and good service.

## WHAT TO SEE & DO

**THE ARTHUR D. FEIRO MARINE LABORATORY** educates visitors of all ages about the marine life of the Washington Coast. Situated on the City Pier, it displays more than 80 species, including sea slugs, wolf eels, and sculpins.

*On the City Pier. 360/417-6254. Open daily, 10 a.m.-6 p.m. (June-Sept.); Sat.-Sun., noon-4 p.m. (remainder of year). Cost: $2/adult, $1/child 6-12, free/under 6.*

**FERRY TO VICTORIA.** If you want to spend a day in Victoria (a 90-minute ferry ride away), you can walk onto the M.V. Coho ferry (cars are a nuisance on a day trip to this compact city). For ferry schedules call **BLACK BALL TRANSPORT** (360/457-4991; 206/622-2222). They do not take reservations. (See "Victoria and Vicinity and Salt Spring Island" for more details.) Another alternative is the faster (and more expensive) **VICTORIA EXPRESS** (360/452-8088, 800/633-1589) a foot-passenger ferry that runs two or three times daily during summer and early fall. Reservations are advised.

**HURRICANE RIDGE.** A fitting introduction to the majestic beauty of the area is a drive to Hurricane Ridge. Just 17 miles from Port Angeles, it's the most accessible region in Olympic National Park and among the most popular. During the half-hour drive, you'll gain one mile in elevation, rising from sea level to the top of the world. At the end of the road there's an easy 1.25-mile hike on an asphalt path that takes you to the top of the hill and a spectacular 360-degree view. Hurricane Ridge is 5,230 feet above sea level and on clear days offers some magnificent views. The best time to visit the top of the ridge is late July through October, unless you are looking for snow.

Open virtually year round (it is periodically inaccessible after a heavy snowfall), Hurricane Ridge is a popular winter destination offering snow-shoeing as well as cross-country and downhill skiing. Snowshoe rentals are available at the Hurricane Ridge Shelter. There are two sliding areas for kids: Sunrise Family Snow Play Area and Tiny Toys Snow Play Area. Bring your own sleds, snow saucers, and inner tubes. (No compressed air is available. No metal runner sleds, snowboards, or wooden toboggans are allowed in the sledding area.) The Visitor Center provides maps of cross-country ski trails. Be sure to call ahead for road conditions in the winter. *360/452-0330. Road conditions and weather: 360/452-0329. Cost: $10 per car (Fee covers park admission for 7 consecutive days).*

If you prefer not to drive up, **OLYMPIC VAN TOURS** (360/452-3858, 800/550-3858) offers three-hour tours that depart Port Angeles twice daily.

**OLYMPIC NATIONAL PARK VISITOR INFORMATION CENTER.** Pick up a list of recommended family hikes, and visit the **PIONEER MEMORIAL MUSEUM** and its Discovery Room, just for kids. There is a slide show and two nature trails that are easily accessible for all ages and abilities. Several books of interest to children visiting the area are on sale at the museum. Or call the Center for a complete travel information packet.

*3002 Mount Angeles Road (south of Hwy. 101 via Race St.), Port Angeles. 360/452-0330. Open daily, 8:30 a.m.-6 p.m. (July-Labor Day); 9 a.m.-4 p.m. (remainder of year).*

**SALT CREEK COUNTY PARK.** This is the site of Camp Hayden, a coastal fort used during World War II. Gun emplacements and bunkers remain, and make fun exploring for families. The park has campsites, facilities and playgrounds. There is easy access to the beach and, at low tide, to Tongue Point tide pools.

*Take Hwy. 112 west to Camp Hayden Road and proceed 2.5 miles to the park.*

## RESOURCES

**OLYMPIC NATIONAL PARK HEADQUARTERS**
600 E. Park Ave.
Port Angeles 98362-6798.
360/452-4501 (Visitors Center); 360/452-0300 (Wilderness Information).
The park entrance fee is $10.

**PORT ANGELES CHAMBER OF COMMERCE & VISITOR INFORMATION CENTER**
121 E. Railroad St.
Port Angeles 98362
360/452-2363

## ON THE ROAD AGAIN

**NEAH BAY AND CAPE FLATTERY.** The town of Neah Bay is located about 65 miles west of Port Angeles on Highway 112. Just beyond Neah Bay, Cape Flattery represents the northwest-ernmost point of land in the mainland United States. At the cape, there's a half-mile trail through the forest to a view of the ocean, Tatoosh Island, and the lighthouse that sits on the island.

**LAKE OZETTE CAMPGROUND** is the departure point for one of the most interesting and scenic hikes on the penin-sula. There are two trails, *Sand Point* and *Cape Alava*. *Sand Point* is preferable for kids, because it is shorter (6 miles round-trip), all on boardwalk, and there is a sandy beach at the end. Once on the beach you can hike another 1.5 miles north to see Indian petroglyphs located at the high-tide mark on the only rock outcropping. It is possible to hike far-ther north to Cape Alava and then return on the *Cape Alava Trail*, but that is an ambitious hike with kids. You need to be careful not to get caught on the beach by the tide. Camping is also popular along this stretch of beach.

*Drive west from Port Angeles on Hwy. 101; at 4.6 miles, turn right on Road No. 112, which takes you along the Strait of Juan de Fuca, past Sekiu. Turn left on the Ozette Lake Road and drive 21 miles to the ranger station, campground, and parking lot.*

**MAKAH CULTURAL AND RESEARCH CENTER.** Neah Bay is home to the Makah Indians, a tribe that traces its ances-try as far back as 1000 B.C. More than 500 years ago, a mud-slide buried five Makah houses at the village of Ozette, 12 miles south of Cape Flattery. By 1970, tides had washed away enough soil to expose the Makah artifacts. That year, a team of archeologists from Washington State University began a dig that lasted 11 years and uncovered more than 97 percent of all Northwest Coast Indian artifacts discov-ered to date. The best are on display at the outstanding Makah Cultural and Research Center, which includes arti-facts from the Ozette dig as well as other sites, full-scale reproductions of canoes, and a longhouse. A visit to the Center is highly recommended.

*Hwy. 112, Neah Bay. 360/645-2711. Open daily, 10 a.m.- 5 p.m., Memorial Day weekend-Labor Day; Wed.-Sun., 10 a.m.-5 p.m.(rest of year). Cost: $4/adult, $3/senior & student, free/under 5.*

## LAKE CRESCENT

At scenic Lake Crescent, the awe-inspiring beauty of this corner of the state is on full display. If you want to introduce your child to a 400-year-old fir tree, this is the place to come. Many of the legends passed on by the region's native people, the Quileutes and Clallams, are about the lake and the upper Soleduck Valley in which it sits. If your kids are fighting in the back seat of the car, tell them this creation legend: when an angry Storm King Mountain was so fed up with the constant fighting of the local tribes, he threw himself into the Lyre River Valley, creating Lake Crescent.

### OLYMPIC PARK INSTITUTE

*111 Barnes Point Road, Port Angeles 98363*
*360/928-3720*
*Rates: Moderate*
*FYI: All meals included; full educational program*

Do you like the idea of attending summer camp with your kids while learning about this magnificent part of the country? The award-winning Olympic Park Institute, a non-profit organization based at historic Rosemary Inn at Lake Crescent, offers educational vacations for families to learn about the park's intertidal life, rain forest, marine mammals, Native American culture, and history. Under a cooperative agreement with the National Park Service, the Institute teaches 5,000 people a year, including many school groups during the school year.

During the summer, some sessions are two days mid-week, some are one day, and several are weekend sessions intended for all ages. Topics include: Nature Photography, Birds and Bugs, Art in the Wilds, Seashore Safari, Critters and Creatures. The season runs from May to October.

The Institute recommends the family sessions for ages four and up, although they will allow younger ages if proper supervision is provided.

**❝❝ PARENT COMMENTS**

*"It was great fun to be learning alongside our kids and to meet other families with similar interests. The instructors were first-rate and the facilities excellent. This is a wonderful program in a breathtakingly beautiful setting."*

## LAKE CRESCENT LODGE

*416 Lake Crescent Road, Port Angeles 98362*
*360/928-3211*
*Rates: Moderate*
*FYI: Restaurant; fireplaces (in four cottages); rowboat rentals; pets OK in most cottages (fee)*

This Olympic National Park concession is open late April through October. With majestic peaks rising from the shores, and the color of the water in the 642-foot-deep lake varying from turquoise to green, Lake Crescent is extraordinarily lovely in the summer.

Located 25 miles west of Port Angeles on Highway 101, this lovely lodge was built in 1915. Children are not allowed to stay in the lodge, but it's too cramped for a family, anyway. The cottages and motel units are the best accommodations for families; they're clean and comfortable, but not fancy. There are no kitchens or refrigerators, but you'll have a fireplace. (It's rumored that President Franklin D. Roosevelt stayed in Cabin 34 in 1937 when he was debating whether or not to create Olympic National Park.)

There's a nice beach at the lodge, and swimming in the cold water can be fun for the hardy on hot summer days. For warmer swimming, it's a reasonable drive to the hot springs at Sol Duc. In addition to swimming, guests can boat, fish from the dock, take short hikes, attend evening nature programs, or just use the facility as a base for excursions into Olympic National Park.

**❝❝ PARENT COMMENTS**

*"After camping in the rain, Lake Crescent Lodge looked very nice for a couple of nights."*

*"We like to go here for a weekend in late September. We don't swim at that time of the year, but the weather is usually good, and we do lots of hiking."*

*"No TVs or telephones! Hurrah!"*

## LOG CABIN RESORT

*3183 E. Beach Road, Port Angeles 98363*
*360/928-3325*

*Rates: Inexpensive to moderate*
*FYI: Restaurant; kitchens (some cabins); small store; boat rentals; hiking trails; pets ok (some units)*

This is an old-fashioned family resort where the chief attractions are the natural beauty and the slow pace. The resort consists of a collection of cabins, motel rooms adjacent to the lodge, A-frame chalets, trailer sites, and walk-in camping sites. It sits on 17 acres on the northern (sunny) shore of Lake Crescent, inside Olympic National Park. The resort is open from late April to October 1.

Individual rustic cabins (built in 1928) are the best accommodations for a family. They have a lake view, double and single beds, and a front porch with chairs where you can read away the hours. Most have kitchens; bring your own cooking utensils.

There's a good swimming area that gets plenty of sun and a small play area. The restaurant in the lodge is very good but moderately expensive; you might want a kitchen in your cabin. The Sol Duc Hot Springs are only 12 miles away if you want to swim/soak in warmer waters (see Sol Duc Resort, this section).

❝❝ **PARENT COMMENTS**

*"Emphasize the word "rustic" when you describe this place."*

*"My husband and I thought the water was cold for swimming, but our two preschoolers spent all afternoon puttering in the lake."*

*"Service was warm and friendly, the setting beautiful. The kids fished, mom and dad read; we all relaxed."*

## SOL DUC HOT SPRINGS
*P.O. Box 2169, Port Angeles 98362*
*360/327-3583*
*Rates: Moderate*
*FYI: Kitchens (some cabins); three hot sulfur pools, freshwater pool; pets ok*

Located 12 miles off Highway 101 between Port Angeles and Forks, this was a famous resort in the days when it was popular to visit such spots for the beneficial effects of the waters. It lost its charm over the years and became downright dismal, prompting a welcome overhaul and facelift.

Unfortunately, the restoration was done with little imagination or harmony with the surroundings (if you expect natural springs in a sylvan, pristine setting, you'll be disappointed). The 32 cabins are minimal and we do not mean "charmingly rustic." They have thin walls and sit close together near the parking lot.

On the plus side, the hot pools are a novel experience. The

hot springs consist of three tiled sulfur pools (98 to 104 degrees). There's also a freshwater pool. The resort is located at the trailhead for several beautiful hikes. (Dogs are not allowed on trails in the National Park.)

The outdoor burger stand makes an easy meal and the dining room is quite good, with a fairly priced children's menu. Keep in mind, though, that several more appealing places to stay can be found within an easy drive of the springs and you do not have to be a guest to use the springs. Lodging is available weekends in April and daily from mid-May to the end of September.

**66 PARENT COMMENTS**

*"We like to visit in early summer when it's less crowded. Our eight-year-old son didn't like the hot springs, so he stayed in the cooler freshwater pool."*

*"We were shocked at the ugliness of the lodgings—a shame in such a spectacular setting. Prefab cabins are deposited military-fashion in a compound that is barren of trees. We were particularly offended that we had to pay just to get in the pool area to watch our children swim."*

## WHAT TO SEE & DO

**HOH RAIN FOREST.** A trip to this part of the state without venturing into the rain forest is unthinkable. The Hoh Rain Forest is easy to access, just 18 miles up the Hoh River from Highway 101. There is a Visitor Center with information about the trail through the Hall of Mosses and other remarkable sights. One of the largest Sitka spruces in the park (230 feet tall and 11 feet, 8 inches in diameter) is about two miles west of the Hoh River Campground.

*Follow 19-mile paved road of Hwy. 101, 13 miles south of Forks. 360/374-6925. Open daily, 9 a.m.-7 p.m., July-Labor Day. Free.*

**MARYMERE FALLS.** At Lake Crescent, there is a short, easy trail (2.5 miles round trip) through old-growth forest to 98-foot Marymere Falls.

*Turn right off Hwy. 101 at Lake Crescent. A large parking lot marks the start of the trail.*

**SHELLFISHING.** Oysters are bountiful on the peninsula; good beaches for digging include Twanoh State Park, Bywater Bay, and Potlatch State Park. But be sure to call the red tide hotline to learn whether it's safe to eat the shellfish before you go to the trouble of digging in: 800/562-5632.

**SOL DUC HOT SPRINGS** is up a 12-mile road from Highway 101, just west of Lake Crescent. There are overnight facilities (see "Places to Stay"), or you can go just to soak and swim.

## LAKE QUINAULT

Lake Quinault can serve as either a starting point or a final destination on the route that encircles Olympic National Park. Located at the southern tip of scenic Lake Quinault, adjacent to the park, the surrounding Quinault Valley is lush and serenely beautiful. The area is home to some of the best short hikes in the entire National Park, as well as many of the finest day treks.

### GETTING THERE

From I-5 at Olympia, take the "Ocean Beaches" exit, then head west on Highway 8, which becomes Highway 12. Travel about 15 miles on Highway 12 to Hoquiam, then head north on Highway 101 to Lake Quinalt. Or you can take any of the routes to the northern part of the peninsula, then follow Highway 101 all the way around Olympic National Park to Lake Quinault. From the Seattle area, the northern and the southern routes to Lake Quinault are about the same in terms of travel time, but taking ferries will add expense and, in the summer, time. And be forewarned: many stretches of forest along Highway 101 have been heavily clear-cut.

### PLACES TO STAY

**LAKE QUINAULT LODGE**
*South Shore Road, P.O. Box 7, Quinault 98575*
*360/288-2900, 800/562-6672; www.visitlakequinault.com*
*Rates: Moderate*
*FYI: Restaurant; indoor pool; game room, playground; hiking trails, bikes; 9-hole golf course; nature program year round; baby-sitting; pets OK (annex only, fee)*

The setting of this lodge, on a beautiful lake in the middle of the rain forest, is one of the nicest on the Olympic Peninsula. The lobby of the main lodge, with its huge fireplace, rustic décor and Indian art, is charming. The least expensive rooms, located in the main lodge, either share a bathroom between two rooms or have bathrooms down the hall. Some of these rooms have views of the parking lot rather than the lake. Lakeside inn rooms, built in 1923 and remodeled more recently, have private baths. Newer still are the "gas fireplace units," which offer a queen-size bed and a queen hide-a-bed. The lodge offers lots of special deals—mid-week and off-season—but there's a two-night minimum on weekends and a three-night minimum on holiday weekends and during school vacations.

Lake Quinault Lodge is obviously geared to families. Adjacent to the pool is a game room with equipment for horseshoes, volleyball, Frisbee, and badminton, as well as pinball, Ping Pong, video games, and pop and candy machines. Hiking trails of varying lengths (.5 mile, 1.5 miles and 3 miles) start at the lodge and wind through the rain forest. You can pick up maps, and puzzles at the front desk, as well as arrange babysitting. Nature programs and canoe and rowboat rentals are available in the summer. A bar offers carry-out sandwiches and drinks and is a good alternative to the restaurant. Nearby alternatives for food are very limited.

**❝❝ PARENT COMMENTS**

*"The service in the restaurant was incredibly pleasant and incredibly slow. Waiters and waitresses are very nice to kids, but the setting is difficult. The gift shop is located right with the restaurant: millions of breakables are begging to be broken by curious little hands."*

*"A nice place for kids—plenty to keep them busy, although we were sorry to see video games in such an otherwise tranquil setting."*

## WASHINGTON COAST

Many familiar images of the Pacific Northwest are found on the coast of Washington: soaring mountains and rain forest, mile-long stretches of wide, sandy beaches, and windblown little towns that cling to the dunes. The Washington coast stretches from Neah Bay, at the entrance to the Strait of Juan de Fuca (the passage to Puget Sound), south to Ilwaco, where the Columbia River empties into the Pacific Ocean. If you want to take in rugged coastline, mountains, and rain forest, your best destination is Kalaloch to the north. If wide-open beaches and the ocean "out of the cradle, endlessly rocking" are your desire, the resorts near Pacific Beach and Ocean Shores are a good choice. To witness the pure, brute force of nature, head to the Long Beach Peninsula at the southwestern tip of the state, where the mighty Columbia River meets the world's largest ocean.

## GETTING THERE

To get to the coast from Seattle, head south on I-5. Just past Olympia, take Exit 104 to Highway 101 west, then bear left onto Highway 8 (which becomes Highway 12) to the coast. The trip from Seattle to Aberdeen takes about two hours.

Once you're in Aberdeen: If you are going to Kalaloch, take Highway 101 north. Allow about 90 minutes for the trip. (A shorter route from Seattle to Kalaloch is to take the Winslow (Bainbridge Island) ferry from Seattle or the Kingston ferry from Edmonds, and follow signs to Port Gamble and the Hood Canal Floating Bridge on Highway 104. Follow 104 as it joins Highway 101 to Port Angeles and keep going to Kalaloch.) If you're headed for Ocean Shores, take Highway 109 west from Aberdeen, then Highway 115 south.

Again from Aberdeen: to reach the Pacific Beach/Moclips area, take Highway 109 west then north along the coast. If your destination is the Long Beach Peninsula, take I-5 south to Exit 104, then connect with Highway 8 west (at Elma it changes to Highway 12). Continue west on Highway 12 to Montesano, then follow signs to Highway 101 and Long Beach.

From Portland to the southern Washington coast, take Highway 26 to Seaside. Head north on Highway 101 to Astoria, cross the Columbia River Bridge, and follow signs to Highway 103 and Long Beach.

**REFUELING.** After you leave I-5 and head toward the ocean from Seattle, you'll find mostly farms, forest, and fields, with few opportunities for a quick bite. If the kids are hungry, you'll be wise to eat in the Olympia (see "Olympia: Places to Eat") before turning onto 101.

If you're headed for Long Beach and get a hunger attack halfway there, Savory Faire (135 S. Main St., 360/249-3701) a half block from the historic county courthouse in Montesano, is a charming and delicious spot for breakfast or lunch. There are also several fast food options in Montesano.

Also towards the Long Beach Peninsula, you might want to make a stop in South Bend, on Willapa Bay. Here you'll find **Boondock's Restaurant** (1015 W. Robert Bush Dr., 360/875-5155), a quintessential coastal eatery. Boondock's serves three meals daily, including tasty Willapa Bay oysters, fresh salads, hearty clam chowder, and fish and chips. At this family-run restaurant, they gladly accommodate special orders, split orders and substitutions. If you're not hungry, stop for a cup of coffee and watch the river meet the bay.

**ROADSIDE ATTRACTIONS.** The major point of interest on the way to the ocean is the state capital in Olympia. If you want to include a tour of the capitol grounds in your trip, see "Olympia: What to See and Do."

Traveling between Olympia and Aberdeen, you may notice some bizarre structures on the south side of the road; chances are you've spotted the gigantic cooling towers for the controversial, mothballed WPPSS nuclear power plants between Elma and Satsop.

## KALALOCH

From Cape Flattery (Neah Bay)—the northwesternmost point in the continental United States—south to Kalaloch, the ocean beach is either Native American reservation or national park land. At Kalaloch you'll find some of the wildest surf and best beachcombing on the entire Washington coast.

### PLACES TO STAY

#### KALALOCH LODGE
*157151 Hwy. 101, 98331*
*360/962-2271; www.kalaloch.com*
*Rates: Moderate to expensive*
*FYI: Restaurant; kitchenettes (in cabins); pets OK (in cabins)*

Kalaloch offers lodge, motel, duplex, and cabin accommodations. The lodge rooms are a bit noisy and too cramped for a family. The duplexes are perched on a bluff overlooking the ocean and have lovely views. The newer log cabins are more expensive and nicer than the funky, older cabins, but bring your own utensils, pots, and pans—the kitchenettes are poorly equipped. There's a small grocery store on the site, but no larger ones nearby; try to shop ahead.

Although the resort is perched above the beach, there is a short, easy trail connecting the two. The beach is beautiful—filled with craggy driftwood, rocks, sand, and seashells—but the water is too cold and too dangerous for swimming. There is a small, calm lagoon for paddling about in the summer, right in front of the lodge. Kalaloch is a popular place, despite the 3 1/2-hour drive from Seattle: make reservations several months in advance at any time of year; for holidays and the summer season you may need to book a full year ahead.

The lodge has a dining room and a coffee shop, both of which have the same menu, same high prices, and same so-so food (best bets are fish and oysters). If you want to take the kids to the dining room, go early. The service is faster in the coffee shop.

**❝❝ PARENT COMMENTS**
*"We like to go to Kalaloch in the winter, when it's stormy. We bring plenty of books and games as well as raincoats and boots so we can take beach walks in the wild weather."*

*"We always bring kites with us as, whatever the season, we can usually count on at least one day windy enough to allow even a poorly designed kite to soar effortlessly."*

## WHAT TO SEE & DO

Kalaloch is a good home base for excursions—explore the rain forest, follow a tree-lined boardwalk from Lake Ozette to remote beaches, or visit the Makah Indian Village at Neah Bay. (See "Olympic Peninsula: What to See & Do" for details.) Guided walks and talks are offered by the Kalaloch Ranger Station (360/962-2283).

## PACIFIC BEACH

Washington's most accessible, broad, and sandy beaches extend north from Ocean Shores for a stretch of about 29 miles to the end of the road at Taholah.

## PLACES TO STAY

### THE SANDPIPER BEACH RESORT
*P.O. Box A, 98571, Hwy. 109, 13 miles north of Ocean Shores*
*360/276-4580; www.sandpiper-resort.com*
*Rates: Moderate to expensive*
*Extras: Kitchens; playground; barbecues (some units); pets OK*

With no TVs, video games, or in-room telephones, this is a good place to get away from it all. The resort includes 29 units of various configurations—studios, suites and separate cabins—all of which have complete housekeeping services, as well as puzzles, magazines, and rocking chairs. All but one of the units have a full ocean view, and all but one have fireplaces. The older units in the northern complex are slightly larger, and all units above ground level have lanais with space for barbecuing, hanging out wet clothes, and displaying beach treasures. The grounds are beautifully landscaped and maintained.

You'll find a playground on the beach, as well as a fire pit, which is convenient for barbecues or fireworks. There is also a well-stocked gift shop that sells books, toys, and kites. Grocery shopping is available at nearby Copalis, but if you prefer to dine out, the restaurant at the Ocean Crest Resort (see below) is the best in the area.

If you hanker for an excursion, Olympic National Park and Quinault rain forest are just a 40-minute drive away.

**❝❝ PARENT COMMENTS**

*"The Sandpiper is very well-managed by the resident owners, and they make a big effort to help families feel welcome."*

**OCEAN CREST RESORT**
*Sunset Beach, Moclips 98562*
*360/276-4465*
*Rates: Moderate to expensive*
*FYI: Restaurant; kitchens (some units); fireplaces (some units); indoor pool; health club; playground; laundry; gift shop; pets OK (some units)*

The best thing about this resort is the health club: Washington Coast weather is typically wet all but the summer months, so this large, attractive facility is a wonderful feature. The bad news for families with small kids is that the resort sits on a bluff above the ocean, and while the location makes for beautiful views, it is a hike down several flights of stairs to the beach. Accommodation options include studio and two-bedroom units with full views of the ocean, a multiunit A-frame across the road, and a two-unit annex one-quarter mile down the road.

The A-frame units, although they sit across the road and have no views, are convenient for parents who don't want to worry about their kids crossing the road to use the playground and health club. The playground is small, but safe and well designed; the health club is an especially nice facility that houses a large pool, hot tub and sauna, as well as massage and exercise rooms.

If you are traveling with another family, the annex may be your best option because it has two completely separate units— each with two bedrooms, a deck, and a view of the sea—connected by an inside door. The disadvantage of the annex is that you have to walk or drive one-quarter mile on the fairly busy main road to access the pool, restaurant, and beach.

The restaurant used to be one of the main attractions at Ocean Crest, but recent reviews have been mixed. It has a lovely view of the wooded bluff overlooking the ocean, illuminated by floodlights at night. Tell the kids to keep an eye out for raccoons—the little masked bandits frequently appear outside the restaurant's windows in the evening.

Dining here with the family is convenient; there's a children's menu, and the service is friendly. Breakfasts are consistently good. Be sure to make reservations when you first arrive at the resort, or you can expect long waits. (If you prefer to eat in your room, you may place an order to go.)

Prices at the restaurant are moderately expensive; most families will want to cook many of their own meals. There is a small but well-stocked grocery store (fresh meat and vegetables) in the nearby town of Moclips, a five-minute drive away.

### ❝❝ PARENT COMMENTS

*"Ocean Crest has been a favorite getaway for our family for the last five years. We prefer to go in the winter—we love walking the beach on a stormy day, and then enjoying the pool and hot tub."*

*"The resort rents VCRs and tapes, so we rented a movie for the kids and went to dinner by ourselves."*

*"On our recent visit we were disappointed to see the rooms were looking rather dowdy—the place is still worth visiting but could use some new furnishings."*

## WHAT TO SEE & DO

**CLAM DIGGING.** The clam digging is especially good on this stretch of the coast—it's a fun family activity that typically yields tasty results. Most kids love the chance to get elbow-deep in the sand and dig for these bivalve mollusks. The open season is short for razor clams and varies from year to year. There are occasional alerts for red tide, when the clams are highly toxic to eat. Call the State Fisheries Information Line at 360/249-4628 for information on red tide and on how to obtain a license. Rental buckets and clam shovels are available from several stores in the area.

**SWIMMING** is not recommended here, or anywhere else on the Washington coast, because of the strong undertow and riptides. Even when the kids are just wading in the surf, you need to be vigilant about the random strong wave that can knock even adults off their feet. If you don't have access to a pool, consider swimming at the health club at Ocean Crest Lodge. It has a beautiful indoor pool and hot tub and is open to nonguests. The cost is $8.50 per day for adults and $5 for children.

### CALENDAR

**JULY**
Annual Sand Sculpture Contest, Copalis Beach.

## OCEAN SHORES

Sitting on a 6,000-acre peninsula between Grays Harbor and the Pacific, Ocean Shores is the closest destination for Seattle residents in search of an ocean beach. Don't expect a scenic seaside town: the area, which was a ranch prior to the 1960s, features mostly high-rise hotels and restaurant sprawl and is not particularly attractive.

Although the topography becomes wilder and more beautiful as you head north or south along the coast, the video-game parlors, horseback riding, bumper cars, and other diversions make Ocean Shores a kids' paradise. Some parents don't mind sacrificing a bit of beauty and a couple of rolls of quarters to spare themselves the "I'm bored" complaints.

### PLACES TO STAY

**BEST WESTERN LIGHTHOUSE SUITES INN**
*491 Damon Road, 98569*
*360/289-2311, 800/757-7873; www.bwlighthouse.com*

## Beachcombing Basics

The prospect of a pristine, sandy beach brings out the beachcomber in adult and child alike. And Washington's beaches—onto which the Japanese current deposits items familiar and exotic—make great scavenging. Best of all, unlike most oceanside activities, this one doesn't require sunshine. In fact, the worse the weather, the better the treasures you're likely to uncover!

The best time for beachcombing is winter or spring,

during or immediately following stormy weather. Seek out flat beaches with heavy surf. Periods of extreme (spring) tides—when the moon is full or new—offer the best opportunities. Check your local tide table (tourist publications often carry them) and try to choose a time shortly after high tide.

Because these beaches are relatively inaccessible, a longish drive (and sometimes a brisk hike) from urban areas, finds can be rewarding. Serious beachcombers consider just about anything fair game, from glass fishing floats to interesting pebbles. However, some items are off limits. Laws prohibit collecting certain kinds of shellfish (Check with the state Department of Fish and Wildlife for details 360/902-2207.)

Supervise young children carefully. In recent years, ships have been known to discharge garbage at sea, including medical waste, and items such as hypodermic needles occasionally wash ashore.

Shells feature on most small scavengers' most-wanted list. However, when pickings are slim, don't despair. You can always count on finding beach glass (bits of bottle glass, scoured by the sand into interesting shapes and translucent colors). These small treasures can be wrapped with thin wire from a bead-supply store and fashioned into pendants or mobiles.

Kids enjoy collecting pebbles of all sizes, shapes, textures, and colors. When dry, these often lose their luster; to preserve colors, wash pebbles, then rub lightly with mineral oil and place in a glass jar for display. Or, using permanent markers, cover them with interesting designs.

### BOOKS ON BEACHCOMBING

*The Beachcombing Book*, by Bernice Kohn, Viking. A guidebook for children that includes dozens of project ideas.

*Beachcombing the Pacific* by Amos L. Wood, Schiffer. A detailed adult guide to this fascinating art and science.

**—NANCY THALIA REYNOLDS**

*Rates: Moderate to expensive*

*FYI: Complimentary continental breakfast; refrigerators/microwaves; gas fireplaces; indoor pool; fitness center; VCR (video rentals at front desk)*

Lighthouse Suites was built in 1996, on the beach in a more secluded part of Ocean Shores, about a mile north of the main town. The location makes it a little inconvenient for walking to shops and restaurants, but a short drive will bring you to them. The rooms are pleasant, with partial to full ocean views. Sleeping areas are partially separated from the sitting areas. Rooms with either two queen beds or one king are available; both have a queen sleeper sofa as well.

A special feature of the hotel is the five-story lighthouse observation tower, which offers a 360-degree view of the surrounding land and sea. There's also a very pleasant oceanfront library with a large stone fireplace.

### 66 PARENT COMMENTS

*"The whole family enjoyed looking out from the observation deck of the lighthouse. When we visited one August, we also were delighted to watch a beach fireworks display right from our balcony. There are even horse rentals in-season, right on the beach near the hotel."*

### GREY GULL

*P.O. Box 1417, 98569*
*360/289-3381*
*Rates: Moderate to expensive*
*FYI: Refrigerators/microwaves/dishwashers; gas fireplaces; outdoor pool (year round); laundry; pets under 20 lbs. OK (some units)*

The Grey Gull sits among the dunes in a prime beach location, within walking distance of "downtown" Ocean Shores. It is modern, and the ocean views are great. The fact that they allow small dogs is a plus for those who can't imagine embarking on a family vacation without Spot.

### 66 PARENT COMMENTS

*"The units were nice, but the pool is outdoors which was fine for summer, but inconvenient when we stayed in the rainy spring. (My kids thought swimming in the rain was fun but I was not as enthusiastic about it.)"*

### POLYNESIAN CONDOMINIUM RESORT

*615 Ocean Shores Blvd., 98569*

*360/289-3361*
*Rates: Moderate to expensive*
*FYI: Restaurant; kitchens (most units); fireplaces; indoor pool; VCR; pets OK (with prior approval)*

At the end of the condo and hotel strip sits the Polynesian—a three-story condominium building (with a penthouse) that provides direct access to the beach. It's a pleasant place to stay during the quiet off-season, though the summer months are optimal. Rooms are nicely furnished with modern décor, and each unit is equipped with a microwave, dishwasher, refrigerator, stove, oven, and coffee maker (you'll find a large grocery store one-half mile away).

The Polynesian owns a private park just south of the condos, where kids can play basketball (on a half-size court), volleyball, tetherball, or horseshoes, and families can picnic and barbecue. Young children will enjoy the play structure and sandbox in the park; older kids will appreciate the indoor game room, with its video games, pool table, and Ping Pong.

Moriah's, the restaurant at the resort, has an extensive menu and kid-friendly service, but the food did not get good reviews from our visiting parents.

**❝ PARENT COMMENTS**

*"The staff was very helpful. They provided a list of six babysitters, with ages, and made specific recommendations for us. Our kids went to the front desk to ask for paper for an art project and came back with tape and ribbon as well."*

**SHILO INN**
*707 Ocean Shores Blvd. NW, 98569*
*360/289-4600, 800/222-2244*
*Rates: Expensive*
*FYI: Restaurant; refrigerators/microwaves; indoor pool; fitness center (24-hour);*

The newest Shilo Inn in the state dominates the strip of resort hotels that sit along the beach at Ocean Shores. The rooms are all "junior suites," which means no separate bedrooms. All rooms have a sleeper sofa in addition to a choice of two queen beds or a king.

The pool and fitness center is very nice. The restaurant has a good view of the beach, and the staff makes every effort to accommodate kids.

**❝ PARENT COMMENTS**

*"As long as you aren't looking for a cozy cottage by the sea, this place is great. Although we were initially put off by the large size and "convention center" ambiance, once we got settled we greatly enjoyed the location and comfortable accommodations. It was especially nice for our teenagers to have the 24-hour pool, so they could have late-night fun without disturbing mom and dad."*

**RENTAL PROPERTY.** When visiting Ocean Shores, renting a private beach house is sometimes the best option, especially if you are a big family or are traveling with another family. If you plan to visit in the summer, it is necessary to call months in advance to make reservations. General vacation rental information is available at 800/544-8887.

## PLACES TO EAT

### ALEC'S BY THE SEA
*Chance Ala Mer Blvd. NE*
*360/289-4026*
*Hours: Breakfast, lunch, dinner daily*

There is no ocean view at this family-oriented restaurant stuck in the corner of a grocery-store parking lot, but that doesn't dissuade the lines of loyal customers that form at every mealtime. There is almost always a short wait, especially at dinner or breakfast, but it's worth it. The food, including many seafood selections, is well prepared and swiftly served. Several parent reviewers chose Alec's as their favorite place to eat in town and, in addition to positive reports on the food, reported unfailingly patient and behavior toward the kids.

### HOMEPORT
*857 Point Brown Ave.*
*360/289-2600*
*Hours: Breakfast, lunch, dinner daily*

Our reviewers sampled only breakfast (which cost just over $20 for four people). The waffles and French toast were reported to be delicious; service was excellent. According to the locals, lunch and dinner are also first-rate.

## WHAT TO SEE & DO

**BIKING.** With miles of flat, hard sand and more miles of flat, paved, and infrequently traveled roads, Ocean Shores is a good place for kids to ride bikes. **THIS & THAT** (748 Ocean Shores

Blvd. NW; 360/289-0919), a bike rental shop located just across from the main entrance to the beach, has a fun assortment of giant tricycles, tandem bikes, and other self-propelled vehicles built for beach riding and suitable for all sizes and abilities.

**HORSEBACK RIDING** has always been a popular way to explore the trails and beaches of Ocean Shores. Most weekends during the off-season and all summer long, a local stable brings horses to the beach to be rented. If you don't see them there, give them a call: **NAN-SEA STABLES** (255 Hwy. 115; 360/289-0194).

**KITE-FLYING.** With a steady, strong breeze and no trees or wires to worry about, the beach is an ideal place to introduce your kids to the art of flying kites. Just be sure your string is strong and that your child is strong enough to "hold on tight."

Several shops in town offer a fabulous variety of kites, free advice about the type of kite that will best suit your family, and kite-flying lessons. Try **CLOUD NINE KITE SHOP** (380 Hwy. 115; 360/289-2221), **CUTTING EDGE KITES** (676 Ocean Shores Blvd.; 360/289-0667), and **OCEAN SHORES KITES** (172 W. Chance ala Mer NW; 360/289-4103).

**THE OCEAN SHORES ENVIRONMENTAL INTERPRETIVE CENTER** traces the natural and human history of the area. Visitors learn about native wildlife and the formation of the peninsula.

*1013 Catala Ave. SE. 360/289-4617. Open summers, Wed.-Sun., 11 a.m.-6 p.m. Free.*

**POLAR SURFING.** Don't think you've lost your mind when you spot surfers near Westport on the coldest day of winter. West Haven State Park is a good spot to observe these hardy fun-seekers. In mid-January, you can watch the Polar Surf Challenge, which includes long-board and short-board categories. Despite the possibility of freezing temperatures, the event typically attracts 150 competitors and 200 spectators. (The challenge's motto best describes the sensibility of polar surfing: "It's cold and wet on the beach. It's cold and wet in the water. You might as well be surfing.")

If you're interested in grabbing the board to show the kids your surfing moves, call the **Boarding Factory** (360/268-5371) for more information.

**WESTPORT MARITIME MUSEUM** features exhibits about the U.S. Coast Guard, whaling, and the fishing industry, as well as tours of the Grays Harbor Lighthouse, two miles southwest. The Maritime History Trail connects the museum and lighthouse and includes the 1.25-mile Dune Trail along the Pacific Ocean.

*2201 Westhaven Dr. 360/268-0078. Open daily, 10 a.m.-4 p.m. (summer); Wed.-Sun., noon-4 p.m. (remainder of year). Admission by donation.*

## CALENDAR

**JANUARY**
Polar Surf Challenge, Westport

**JUNE**
Ocean Shores International Kite Challenge: One of Washington's largest kite festivals.
Quinault LeëKmaltch Festival: races, cultural displays, local foods, Ocean Shores Marina.

**JULY**
Annual Chainsawing Competition, Westport.

**NOVEMBER**
Annual Dixieland Jazz Festival: Nearly 100 hours of fantastic jazz at four venues, Ocean Shores.

## RESOURCES

**OCEAN SHORES CHAMBER OF COMMERCE**
P.O. Box 382, Ocean Shores, 98569
800/762-3224

**OCEAN SHORES RESERVATIONS BUREAU**
800/562-8612

**BEACH FRONT VACATION RENTALS**
800/544-8887

## LONG BEACH PENINSULA

The Long Beach Peninsula, about a 3 1/2-hour drive from Seattle and 1 1/2 hours from Portland, stretches 28 miles from Cape Disappointment at the mouth of the Columbia River to Leadbetter Point, dividing Willapa Bay from the Pacific Ocean. The point at which a mighty river meets the sea is inevitably rich in natural beauty and history, so visiting families will find much to explore here.

If your clan tires of too much Mother Nature, Long Beach is a dandy coastal town, complete with a boardwalk, game arcades, and shops that sell saltwater taffy and cotton candy. While summer is the obvious time to visit, don't overlook the opportunities provide by an off-season visit to this region: the pleasures of viewing wild winter storms at the convergence of the river and the sea and exploring the hibernating resort town can add up to a relaxing and memorable family getaway.

## PLACES TO STAY

### THE BREAKERS

*Hwy. 103 & 26th St., Long Beach 98631*
*360/642-4414, 800/288-8890*
*Rates: Moderate to expensive*
*FYI: Kitchens; indoor pool and Jacuzzi; children's playground, volleyball, and sports court; VCR (movie rentals in lobby)*

A condominium resort affiliated with Vacation Villages of America (the Polynesian at Ocean Shores and Tolovana Inn at Cannon Beach are also affiliated), this is a 24-acre complex with many family-friendly features. It's about a mile out of town, giving it a secluded feel but also making it slightly less convenient for walking and exploring the town of Long Beach. The walk to the beach through the dunes is fun and the beach is generally not crowded.

There is a barbecue and gazebo, as well as lots of grassy areas where kids can run and play while parents watch from the balcony.

**❝**

### PARENT COMMENTS

*"Our second-floor, one-bedroom condo had a separate bedroom with queen-size bed, a hide-a-bed in the living room, and a complete kitchen including microwave. It felt very cozy and homey with its wood-burning fireplace and the balcony with a great ocean view. The kids loved finding a basket full of toys and games to play."*

*"A Tip: Don't drive on the beach unless you know what you're doing or don't mind paying to get towed out of the sand when you get stuck. . ."*

### FORT CANBY LIGHTHOUSE KEEPER'S HOUSE

*Fort Canby State Park*
*360/642-3078*
*Rates: Moderate*
*FYI: Kitchen; linens provided*

Cape Disappointment Lighthouse, at Fort Canby west of Ilwaco, began operating in 1856 and is the oldest lighthouse still operating on the West Coast. The lighthouse at North Head was built in 1898 to help guide ships that were unable to see the light from Cape Disappointment. For a century, the scenic beauty from the North Head Lighthouse keeper's house was viewed only by the family of the light keeper. Since 1998, the house has been available for vacation rental.

The century-old Victorian house sits on a bluff, several hundreds yards from the lighthouse. Upstairs are three bedrooms with two double and two single beds. The downstairs has been lovingly furnished, and the sofa bed will sleep another two. There is a standard kitchen with microwave and dishwasher, an attractive dining room, and a cozy living room with TV and VCR (but there is no television reception here, so you'll need to bring your own videos).

The Assistant Lighthouse Keeper's Residence, also at Fort Canby, is expected to be available beginning summer 1999. Both residences rent for $200 a night (two-night minimum). For those who reserve six nights, the seventh is free. The house is rented through Fort Canby State Park. The office is staffed on weekdays; on weekends, leave a message.

**FORT CANBY CAMPSITE, YURTS, AND CABINS**
*Fort Canby State Park*
*Rates: Inexpensive*
*800/452-5687*

The best family accommodations for the Long Beach area may be in a tent, a yurt, or a primitive cabin at magnificent Fort Canby State Park. Located at the mouth of the Columbia River, Fort Canby is one of the best (and busiest) camping facilities in the state park system.

You can rent a yurt (a furry, domed tent with electricity) with a bunk bed that sleeps three, a queen size futon, a floor lamp, a small end table, and a heater. Bathrooms and showers are nearby. There are also primitive cabins offering similar amenities. Either accommodation rents for $35/night.

The campground includes 190 standard sites; try to get a site close to the beach. Be sure to make reservations for a yurt, cabin, or campsite early by calling Reservations Northwest (800/452-5687) 8 a.m.-5 p.m., from two days to 11 months in advance of your visit. Campsites require a $6 reservation fee, plus the first night's rent (these may be charged to a credit card). If you will be sending a check, call at least three weeks in advance of the date you would like to reserve. No reservations are accepted through the mail.

### FORT COLUMBIA STEWARD'S HOUSE

*Fort Columbia State Park*
*360/642-3078*
*Rate: Moderate*
*FYI: Kitchen; linens provided*

Fort Columbia State Park is about 15 miles southeast of the Long Beach Peninsula, where the Columbia River meets the Pacific Ocean. Along with Fort Canby and Fort Stevens (on the Oregon side), Fort Columbia constituted the harbor defense of the Columbia River during the Spanish-American War. In an area so rich in history, it is great fun to stay in the house that used to belong to the fort steward. (Ghost stories, anyone?)

The Steward's House is a charming, two-story spot, with wall-to-wall carpeting and lovely furniture. The house sleeps four, with two bedrooms and a bathroom upstairs. Downstairs there is a standard kitchen with gas stove and microwave, dining room, and a cozy, nicely furnished living room, with a wood stove and cable TV.

### KLIPSAN BEACH COTTAGES

*22617 Pacific Hwy, Ocean Park 98640*
*360/665-4888*
*Rates: Inexpensive to moderate*
*FYI: Kitchens; fireplaces, woodstoves, free firewood*

Klipsan Beach Cottages offers nine comfortable, cedar-shingle cabins with fireplaces (or woodstoves) and west-facing decks. The expanse of dunes and sea visible from the cabins makes up for their close proximity to one another. Each cabin has either one, two, or three bedrooms, a hide-a-bed in the living room, and fully equipped kitchens.

This is a popular place for families, so there are usually many children around. Hide-and-seek enthusiasts will find plenty of hiding places in the small rhododendron forest and along the safe stretch of dunes between the cabins and the beach.

**❝ PARENT COMMENTS**
*"This is a classic 'cabins at the sea' sort of place. When we stayed here in mid-August there were plenty of kids; everyone had a fabulous time romping in the dunes. We traded childcare*

*with another family for one night and went into Seaview for a
lovely dinner."*

### OUR PLACE AT THE BEACH

*P.O. Box 266, 1309 S Boulevard, Long Beach WA 98631
360/642-3793; 800/538-5107;
www.ohwy.com/wa/o/ourplace.htm
Rates: Inexpensive
FYI: Kitchens (some rooms); refrigerators/microwaves; fitness
room with steam room, sauna, and 2 Jacuzzis; weight room*

This slightly funky hotel has been here forever, offering
roomy accommodations and handy, if not spectacular, access
to the beach.

### ❝❝ PARENT COMMENTS

*"It's nothing fancy, but there was plenty of room, and the
beach was a short, safe walk from the hotel."*

### PLACES TO EAT

### THE ARK

*273rd & Sandridge, at the docks in Nahcotta
360/665-4133
Hours: 5-10 p.m. Tues.-Sat., 11 a.m.-3 p.m. and 4-8 p.m. Sun.*

Out in the middle of nowhere sits this fine little restaurant
that enjoys a well-deserved national reputation for outstanding cuisine. At night, the lights illuminate the grassy marsh
of Willapa Bay, and the mood is casually elegant. The dinner
menu and ambiance is not child-oriented (although the staff
is said to welcome kids). During summer months, reservations are essential.

Our parent reviewers recommend Sunday brunch if you
want to take the whole family. Young eaters may not appreciate the heavy emphasis on local seafood benedict and frittata
dishes, but they'll surely relish the superb baked goods, including the warm muffins and cranberry butter.

If you don't want to stop for a sit-down meal but are headed out
to Leadbetter Pont or the historic town of Oysterville, treat yourself to the out-of-this-world cinnamon rolls, muffins, cookies, and
other treats, available to take out at the front of the restaurant.

### 42ND STREET CAFÉ

*42nd St. & Pacific Hwy., Seaview
360/642-2323*

*Hours: Breakfast, lunch, dinner daily*

The atmosphere is crowded and homey, and the food is scrumptious. Tables are so close together that a hungry toddler with a good reach could snatch bread off a neighbor's plate, so keep this in mind if you have a high-energy tyke.

The cuisine is basic American (i.e., kids will like it), servings are plentiful, and prices are very reasonable. If you have room for dessert, you won't be disappointed.

### LAURIE'S HOMESTEAD
*42nd & Pacific Hwy., Seaview*
*360/642-7171*
*Hours: Breakfast, lunch daily*

This small spot, located across the street from the 42nd Street Café, offers an extensive menu of family favorites, including pancakes, waffles, and huge, scrumptious omelets (have your kids split one, if they can agree on the filling). We're not talking delicate, gourmet meals here; these are home-cooked, farm-style entrées, and there's one to please every palate.

### THE LIGHTSHIP RESTAURANT
*409 S. 10th, Long Beach*
*360/642-3252*
*Hours: Lunch , dinner daily; breakfast Sat.-Sun.*

Just a look at the nondescript Edgewater Inn would not entice you to try out its top-floor restaurant, which just goes to show that looks can be deceiving. The fare at the Lightship is a delicious surprise: the creatively prepared seafood and pasta dishes at dinner are excellent; breakfasts are equally tasty. It's located on the beach in Long Beach, with a great ocean view.

### MY MOM'S PIE KITCHEN
*S. Pacific Hwy. & 44th Pl., Seaview*
*360/642-2342*
*Hours: Lunch Wed.-Sun.*

The pies are magnìfico—banana cream, rhubarb, marionberry, raspberry and so on, depending on the season—but don't overlook the rich crab quiche, steamy clam chowder, or chili dogs for the kids. The prices here are very reasonable.

### WHAT TO SEE & DO

The beach on the Long Beach peninsula is super-wide at low tide and ideal for walking, digging, kite flying, horseback riding and—unfortunately—driving. There is a short "no cars allowed" section from late spring through Labor Day on the beach in front of the towns of Seaview and Long Beach. Benson Beach, the lovely two-mile stretch of beach in Fort Canby, is closed to motor vehicles year round. There's parking for the Fort Canby beach by the North Jetty, a man-made breakwater near the mouth of the Columbia River.

**CAPE DISAPPOINTMENT AND NORTH HEAD LIGHTHOUSES.** Located on Washington's southwesternmost tip in Fort Canby State Park, the Cape Disappointment Lighthouse has been guarding the "Graveyard of the Pacific" since 1856. The first ship transporting materials to build the lighthouse sank in stormy waters two miles offshore. Sitting near the interpretive center on the edge of a sheer granite cliff, it's the oldest lighthouse still in use on the West Coast and is reached by a short but steep trail.

Ships coming from the north couldn't always see the Cape Disappointment Lighthouse, so 42 years later the U.S. Government built a second lighthouse, North Head. Cape Disappointment is not open to visitors, but North Head Lighthouse is open daily for tours in summer. Visitors can ascend the narrow staircase inside the tower to the glassed-in light room ($1/ person). Hold tight to the kids, North Head is the windiest lighthouse on the West Coast. In 1921, winds were unofficially clocked at 160 mph!

*At Fort Canby State Park. 360/642-3078.*

**CAPE DISAPPOINTMENT COAST GUARD STATION** is located near the mouth of the Columbia River, where the bar between the river and the ocean creates treacherous waters responsible for hundreds of shipwrecks. The Coast Guard Station conducts a one-of-a-kind Rescue Boat Handlers school that draws applicants from around the country. Occasionally visitors will witness boats being launched through the heavy surf to practice rescue missions.

*Located about 4 miles southwest of Ilwaco. Open Mon.-Fri. afternoons; Sat.-Sun. all day.*

**CRANBERRY MUSEUM.** In the late 1800's, cranberry vines were shipped from Massachusetts to Washington. Today, one-third of Washington's cranberries are grown on the Long Beach Peninsula. During October's harvest, "blooms" paint the flooded fields bright crimson. A former cranberry research station north of Long Beach now serves as the Cranberry Museum and Gift Shop. Visitors can take a look at implements used by cranberry farmers, view historic research records, and visit an adjacent bog.

*2904 Pioneer Road, north of Long Beach. 360/642-3638. Open May-mid-Dec., Fri.-Sun., 10 a.m.-3 p.m. Free.*

**FORT CANBY STATE PARK.** First armed during the Civil War, Fort Canby was dedicated as a state park in 1957. A trip to the Long Beach Peninsula would be incomplete without a visit here. The park's 1,881 acres include more than 42,000 feet of saltwater shoreline and 7,000 feet of freshwater shoreline along Lake O'Neil. There are walking trails through old-growth forests with outstanding vistas of the ocean and the Columbia River bar and a lovely two-mile stretch of beach. Overnight accommodations include historic housing, yurts, primitive cabins, and extensive campgrounds (see "Places to Stay").

It was here in 1805 that Lewis and Clark finally reached the Pacific, the primary objective of their monumental journey. The Lewis and Clark Interpretive Center at the park commemorates their trek. Fort Canby is also home to two historic lighthouses, North Head and Cape Disappointment. If sea storms are your pleasure, Fort Canby in winter is one of the windiest places on the Washington coast with some of the wildest waves.

*Located 2.5 miles southwest of Ilwaco off Hwy. 101. 360/642-3078. For information about accommodations, call 800/452-5687.*

**FORT COLUMBIA STATE PARK.** Built atop historic Chinook Point promontory, Fort Columbia is one of the few intact historic coastal defense sites left in the United States. Upon its completion in 1904, the fort joined Fort Canby and Fort Stevens in defending the coast during World Wars I and II. In 1950, the military post became Fort Columbia Historical State Park. This 554-acre park at the mouth of the Columbia River offers great views of the river, the Columbia Bar, and the Oregon shore. Families will enjoy visiting the historical museum and viewing the abandoned gun batteries and buildings.

The Fort's Interpretive Center includes displays of Chinook Indian culture, as well as military life at the fort.

Just below Cape Disappointment sits an abandoned military outpost from the Spanish-American War of 1898. The interpretive center occupies the former barracks. On the main floor, a guest register for returning veterans shows hundreds of people who have listed the dates they served here, their rank, detachment, and duties. You can also tour the 1902 Commanding Officer's house, furnished as it might have been in 1910.

*Located on Hwy. 101, 2 miles east of Chinook, west of the north end of the Astoria-Megler Bridge. 360/642-3078 (Park); 360/777-8221 (Interpretive Center). Park open daily, 8 a.m.-5 p.m. (year round). Interpretive Center (360/777-8221) open Wed.-Sun., 10 a.m.-5 p.m. (Memorial Day-Sept.).*

**ILWACO HERITAGE MUSEUM** is an outstanding four-room museum offering an overview of Native American history and white settlement of the peninsula. Kids will likely enjoy the Victorian dollhouses and exhibits of local Chinook Indians' dugout canoes and food-gathering. Be sure to point out the display on Gerard D'Aboville, a French adventurer who in 1991 rowed alone 6,300 miles across the Pacific from Japan to Ilwaco. There's a model of his kayak-like, 26-foot-long boat; photographs of him at sea; and a video with footage of his journey, including some of the frightening 36 capsizes he endured before he arrived at his destination.

Vintage buildings in the downtown region of this little fishing town are being renovated, and murals on the exteriors of some buildings show natives and early settlers.

*115 SE Lake St. 360/642-3446. Hours: Mon.-Sat., 9 a.m.-5 p.m.; Sun., noon-4 p.m. (summer); Mon.-Sat., 10 a.m.-4 p.m. (winter). Cost: $3/adult, $1/child 6-12, free/under 6.*

**KAYAKING** to Long Island, at the southern end of Willapa Bay, is a wonderful plan if you're in the mood for a family boating adventure. It's about a quarter-mile across the protected waters to the southern tip of the island from the boat launch at Willapa Wildlife Refuge headquarters on Highway 101.

Part of the Willapa National Wildlife Refuge, the island has five miles of trails, five primitive camp sites, and a 274-acre ancient cedar grove that has remained untouched for thousands of years. It can be reached by a 2.5-mile trail that runs northwest near the beach landing nearest the launch at the Wildlife Refuge.

*Kayak rentals available at* **WILLAPA BAY EXCURSIONS**, 270th & Sandridge Road, Nahcotta. 360/665-5557.

For more information about Long Island, contact the Willapa National Wildlife Refuge Headquarters, 8 miles northeast of Seaview on Hwy. 101. 360/484-3482.

**LEADBETTER POINT STATE PARK** is a day-use-only park at the peninsula's northern end. Several miles of trails wind through salt marshes and dense forest on the Willapa Bay side. A trail also leads north into the adjacent Willapa Bay National Wildlife Refuge.

*Three miles north of Oysterville on Stackpole Road (drive north along Sandridge Road from Nahcotta to Oysterville, turn left, west, at Oysterville and follow signs). Open daily, 6:30 a.m.-dusk (April-mid-Oct.); daily 8 a.m.-dusk (mid-Oct.-March). Call Fort Canby State Park (360-642-3078) for information.*

**LEWIS AND CLARK INTERPRETIVE CENTER,** located on Cape Disappointment at Fort Canby State Park, celebrates the journey of explorers Meriwether Lewis and William Clark who arrived here in November, 1805. It is a "must-see" museum that captures wonderfully the harrowing adventure of the Lewis and Clark expedition. Situated on a rocky headland, the museum has large picture windows looking out at spectacular views of the ships and fishing boats heading up and down the Columbia. A "time line" runs throughout the museum with diary quotations, maps, and pictures chronicling their journey. There also are displays on the park's military history and on the two lighthouses located at the park.

History buffs can now trace the footsteps of Lewis and Clark from the Cape Disappointment lighthouse to the town of Long Beach. Ask park rangers for exact directions.

*Fort Canby State Park. 360/642-3029. Open daily, 10 a.m. to 4 p.m. Free.*

**LONG BEACH** is a lively beach town in the summer and wonderfully sleepy in the off-season. The half-mile-long elevated boardwalk (with night lighting) that edges the beach offers interpretive displays, telescopes for the superb views, and picnic areas.

While strolling through this "kitsch capital," anticipate multiple temptations for your kids, including kites, candy, cookies, and souvenir shops. When you just can't take another request for cotton candy, head out to the new two-mile Dune Trail that meanders through the ocean-side dunes for two miles. It stretches from 17th Street South to 16th Street NW. Bike riders, runners, and walkers are welcome.

**SWIMMING** in the ocean and even deep wading are strongly discouraged on Long Beach Peninsula. There are treacherous undertows, cross currents, riptides, icy temperatures, and rogue waves up and down the shoreline—and an absence of lifeguards. Drownings, usually of strong, young people, are reported each year. Even cautious waders can plunge suddenly into a "crab-hole"—a deep, unseen pit—and then be pulled out to sea. Climbing on big logs is also very dangerous, as they can suddenly be uprooted by a rogue wave and trap a person underneath. Our parent reviewers reported letting preschoolers play at the very edge of the water, turning their eyes for a split second and looking back to see their child being pulled out to sea. They were less than a foot away, and able to grab their child. If you let your kids wade in the water, don't let them wander out to deeper water. Be sure a vigilant adult is standing nearby at all times.

**OYSTERVILLE**, a tiny town north of Long Beach, was established in 1854 and is now on the National Register of Historic Places. The **WILLAPA BAY INTERPRETIVE CENTER** in Nahcotta is open seasonally and includes exhibits on the oyster industry. Today, the oyster industry has almost disappeared, but the interpretive center does a good job of using wall displays and a film to depict "the way it was." Oysters made fortunes for many settlers until the 1880s when the oyster beds were depleted. The Center is also one of just two publicly owned spots (Leadbetter Point is the other) with access to the shores of Willapa Bay. Fresh oysters can be purchased at **OYSTERVILLE SEA FARMS** (360/665-6585), located on the water in the center of town at 1st and Clark streets.
*Open May-Sept., Fri.-Sun. and holidays, 10 a.m.-3 p.m.*

**THE WORLD KITE MUSEUM AND HALL OF FAME** in Long Beach showcases more than 1,300 kites. See a winged box kite introduced in St. Louis the year Wilbur and Orville Wright made their historic flight. Check out a replica of Ben Franklin's "key-kite." Enter the Dragon's Den, displaying kites from Asia that resemble huge dragons, plus military kites, stunt kites and just about every other kite ever built. One is more than 200 feet long and capped with a head the size of an armchair! Films feature kite-festival highlights, kite-making basics, and other kiting events. Kite-making workshops are often scheduled.
*112 3rd St. NW (3rd & Pacific Hwy.), Long Beach. 360/642-4020. Open daily, 11 a.m.-5 p.m. (summer); Sat.-Sun. (winter). Cost: $4/family, $1.50/adult, $1/child.*

**ASTORIA, OREGON.** Take the bridge across the Columbia River to Astoria, in the state of Oregon, if you have the time. The excellent Columbia River Maritime Museum is especially worth a visit (see "Astoria: What to See & Do").

## CALENDAR

**MARCH**
Whale Watching.

**APRIL**
Dixieland Jazz Festival, Long Beach, 360/642-2400.

**JUNE**
Northwest Garlic Festival, Ocean Park.

**JULY**
Sandsations Sand Sculpture Contest, Long Beach.

**AUGUST**
International Kite Festival, Long Beach.

**OCTOBER**
Cranberrian Fair, Ilwaco.

## RESOURCES

**LONG BEACH PENINSULA VISITORS BUREAU**
P.O. Box 562, Long Beach 98631
360/642-2400; 800/451-2542; www.funbeach.com

## BOOKS

*Umbrella Guide to Washington Lighthouses*, by Sharlene P, and Ted W. Nelson, Umbrella Books, Friday Harbor, Washington, includes a five-page, easy-to-read history of Cape Disappointment Lighthouse.

*Best Hike with Kids, Part 2*, by Joan Burton, Mountaineers Press, offers 86 more hikes in the Cascade and Olympic Mountains, including the Long Beach area.

# WASHINGTON CASCADES

The Cascades dominate the middle section of Washington State, stretching south from the rough and craggy terrain of the North Cascades to the major peaks of the lower range. Mount Baker, the northernmost of the Washington volcanoes, stands above the wild terrain of Mount Baker-Snoqualmie National Forest. Farther south are Mount Rainier and Mount St. Helens. These accessible portions of the Cascades offer an abundance of outdoor adventure in any season, as well as the promise of quiet and relaxation, far from the urban hustle.

## NORTH CASCADES

The western slope of the North Cascades is vast and largely unsettled. Accommodations are few and far between, but that just adds to the thrill of exploring this awe-inspiring region of the state. The rugged snow-capped mountains, glaciers, forests of tamarack and fir, alpine lakes, and waterfalls provide magnificent vistas and abundant opportunities for a variety of outdoor activities.

### GETTING THERE

From Seattle, head north on Interstate 5 to Exit 230, just north of Mount Vernon. Follow Highway 20, the North Cascades Highway, east. For an alternate route, take Exit 208 (Arlington) and follow Highway 530 through the logging community of Darrington; this road merges with Highway 20 at Rockport. The Highway 530 route is about one half-hour faster than exiting at Mount Vernon, but the road is more narrow and winding.

After you pass Marblemount, the drive along the North Cascades Highway is stunning. Heavy winter snowfalls close parts of the highway at higher elevations from late fall to spring.

### PLACES TO STAY

#### SKAGIT RIVER RESORT
*58468 Clark Cabin Road, Rockport 98283*
*360/873-2250; www.northcascades.com*
*Rates: Inexpensive to moderate*
*FYI: Restaurant; kitchens (full and partial); fireplaces (some cabins); laundry; pets OK; no smoke-free units*

The Skagit River Resort (formerly known as Clark's Skagit River Cabins) is ideally located—right on Highway 20, two miles west of Marblemount and six miles east of Rockport. Don't come here expecting a cozy cabin deep in the woods, though, or you'll be disappointed. The tidy cabins sit close together, about 100 feet from the highway and across the road from the beautiful Skagit River. Nevertheless, the resort provides an affordable and pleasant base for exploring one of the most beautiful regions in the Pacific Northwest.

The cabins, offering one, two, or three bedrooms, are fully furnished and neatly kept. One triplex consists of three adjoining units that can be rented together to accommodate up to 12 people. The restaurant offers a standard "drive-in" menu plus some fresh berry desserts.

One unique feature of the Skagit River Resort will delight young visitors—there are rabbits everywhere (at last count there were about 175!). Especially in the morning and evening, the rabbits can be found grazing on the lawns. Keep this in mind when deciding whether to include Fido in your vacation plans.

**❝ PARENT COMMENTS**

*"Skagit River Resort is ideally located if you want to explore the western side of the North Cascades. We hiked and took the Seattle City Light tour at Diablo. Our kids (ages 6 and 9) loved the tour, we were completely satisfied with our accommodations, and the little restaurant was very convenient. We'll be back next year."*

*"Our two year old was enchanted by the rabbits that roam freely on the grassy yard. They will often come close enough to be fed, but they are not tame enough to be picked up. We brought our dog and had to be careful to keep him on a leash—the bunnies almost drove him crazy."*

**ROSS LAKE RESORT**
*Rockport 98283*
*360/386-4437*
*Rates: Moderate*
*FYI: Kitchens (full and partial); woodstoves (some cabins); boat rentals, fishing; water taxi to trailheads*

If you are looking for adventure and accommodations that take full advantage of the beauty of the North Cascades, this is the place. Ross Lake Resort, operating since 1950, has 10 individual cabins and three bunkhouses built on log floats. It is located on the western side of Ross Lake, a breathtakingly beautiful (and cold) body of water just north of Ross Dam. Except for the many campgrounds that line the lake (accessible only by boat), Ross Lake Resort is the only place to sleep and it's fairly remote with no direct road access. Nevertheless, the resort is easily accessible—just a three-hour drive from Seattle to meet the tugboat and truck that deliver you to the

Resort less than an hour later.

Accommodations include cabins with full kitchens, private baths, and bunk beds to accommodate five; smaller rustic cabins with a small kitchen (stove top only and small refrigerator) and bunk beds to accommodate four; and a bunkhouse for parties of six or more. The bunkhouse has a large open area that encompasses kitchen, dining room, and bedroom, and supplies a wood-stove, electric stovetop, full-size refrigerator, and bunk beds.

The marina includes 50 motorboats with 9.9 horsepower motors and eight canoes available for rent by resort guests and campers. Canoe and small-boat portage is available at neighboring Diablo Lake.

**❝❝ PARENT COMMENTS**

*"We took our canoe and went camping on Ross Lake. We stayed at the resort the first night so we could get an early start the next morning. It would also work well to stay at the resort and take day hikes in the region. The cabins are clean and plain-nothing special, but the setting is magnificent. My son who loves to fish would like to have stayed a month."*

**PLACES TO EAT**

**BUFFALO RUN RESTAURANT**
*5860 Hwy. 20, Marblemount*
*360/873-2461*
*Hours: 11 a.m.-9 p.m. Thurs.-Sun.*

A local landmark, this was known for years as the Mountain Song Restaurant, but little else has changed—the food is still delicious and nutritious and the prices are very reasonable. This is a cafeteria-style restaurant, with many options for kids and adults alike, including excellent soups, sandwiches, quiches, and desserts. If you're headed east over the Cascades, this is your best stop in the vicinity.

**GOOD FOOD**
*Hwy. 20, just west of Marblemount*
*360/873-9309*
*Hours: Lunch, dinner daily*

This fast-food drive-in on Highway 20 is an excellent place to stop for a quick bite on your way over the mountains or if you are staying in the region. The food is fine (try the fresh blackberry shakes in season), but the location is extraordinary. Behind the restaurant is a long, grassy lawn that leads to the banks of the Skagit River, giving kids plenty of room to stretch and romp. You can eat at picnic tables outside or in the small indoor dining room.

## WHAT TO SEE & DO

**BALD EAGLES** are flocking in increasing numbers to the Upper Skagit River Valley. The stretch of river on the eastern side of I-5 is a popular area to spot them. The best viewing time is late January through mid-February, when the eagles feast on the chum salmon run. With more than 400 eagles in the area during these weeks, it is not uncommon to see 25 or 30 at a time.

With all those eagles, you'd expect there would be a festival, and indeed there is! On the first weekend in February, the towns of Concrete, Rockport, and Marblemount sponsor the Upper Skagit Bald Eagle Festival, which features Native American storytelling and dancing, captive raptors, volunteers situated at the best viewing points, and numerous displays and programs.

*For information about eagle watching and other festival activities, 360/853-7009.*

**CASCADIAN FARM ROADSIDE STAND.** Yummy homemade ice cream, shakes, and shortcake—loaded with organic berries—are sold at this cute little stand that sits at the edge of the Cascadian Farm. You can also buy fresh berries to take home, July through September, and sweet corn and pumpkins in September and October. There's a picnic area.

*On Hwy. 20 at Milepost 100, near Rockport. Look for roadside sign. 360/853-8629. Open daily, May-Oct.*

**HIKING.** There are more than 345 miles of trails in **NORTH CASCADES NATIONAL PARK**. The ranger stations (see "Resources") provide trail maps and backcountry permits (required if you plan to spend the night in a wilderness area). It's also a good safety measure to check in with a ranger station before you take off on a day hike. Many trailheads are just off Highway 20.

**NEWHALEM.** This odd little town makes a perfect pit stop on your journey to the North Cascades. The Seattle City Light Visitor Center has ample restrooms, and the parklike grounds on which the town's small, identical houses are set offer plenty of room for small visitors to run and stretch. Originally a company town for Seattle City Light, the town has housed workers providing electricity for Seattle and points south since the 1920s.

The Skagit General Store here is the last store you'll encounter until you reach Mazama, on the other side of the mountains. Stock up on snacks and drinks, while the kids climb on the adjacent Old Number Six, a retired steam engine from the early days of dam construction. If you have time, take the *Trail of Cedars*, which takes you across a suspension bridge on a short nature walk through the forest. From the historic Newhalem Powerhouse, a slightly more strenuous hike takes you to Ladder Creek Falls. The trail winds among beautifully landscaped gardens of native plants and quiet pools. At night, when the trail is lit up, it is especially enchanting.

**NORTH CASCADES INSTITUTE** offers outdoor enthusiasts of all ages a wide variety of courses and workshops showcasing the region. Most classes take place on weekends in settings that range from the North Cascades to the San Juan Islands. Experts share their knowledge of natural history. Some classes integrate the curriculum with active fun such as backpacking, kayaking, rafting, and sailing.

*2105 Hwy. 20, Sedro-Woolley 98284. 360/856-5700, ext. 209.*

**NORTH CASCADES VISITOR CENTER**, staffed by the National Park Service, offers daily programs, nature walks, interpretive displays, films, and slide shows. There's a ranger on hand to answer questions. With its massive stone fireplace, skylights, and giant open beams, the building is nicely integrated with its surroundings.

*Located south of Hwy. 20, across the Skagit River, just west of Newhalem. 360/856-5700. Open daily, 8:30 a.m.-5:30 p.m. (Memorial Day-Labor Day); weekends only (rest of year).*

**SEATTLE CITY LIGHT SKAGIT TOURS** make fun and educational outings with school-age kids. The main tour departs from the City Light Diablo tour center and lasts 4 1/2 hours. Highlights include a 560-foot mountain ascent and descent on a railway incline lift, a slide show, a boat cruise on Diablo Lake, and a tour of the massive generating facilities of Ross Powerhouse. There's also an optional, all-you-can-eat dinner. Ninety-minute tours, preferable for younger children, include a slide show, a tour of Diablo Powerhouse, and a ride on the incline.

*Skagit Tours Ticket Office, Seattle City Light, 500 Newhalem*

*St., Rockport, Washington 98283. 206/684-3030. Cost: main tour (including dinner), $25/adult, $22/senior, $10/child 6-11; main tour (without dinner), $18/adult, $16/senior, $5/child 6-11; 90-minute tour, $5/person, free/under 6 (reservations not required). Discount packages available for families on some tours.*

**SPAWNING SALMON** can be viewed from several stops along Highway 20. (Spawning is a gripping and sometimes bloody struggle, and one that might reduce a sensitive kid to tears.) **PUGET POWER VISITORS CENTER** (near Baker River Bridge; 360/853-8341) in Concrete has a facility where adult salmon are trapped and transported by truck to Baker Lake. Farther east, at the **MARBLEMOUNT SALMON HATCHERY** (5937 Fish Hatchery Lane; 360/873-4241), you can see coho spawning in the fall.

**WILDFLOWERS.** The myriad colors, shapes, and fragrances of the mountain wildflowers can be discovered on numerous trails that thread through forests and across alpine meadows. The U.S. Forest Service leads hikes to see the flowers as part of the "Celebrating Wildflowers" observation the agency conducts each summer to help promote the appreciation and conservation of native plants. Hikes begin mid-June and end in late summer.

Information is available at Mount Baker-Snoqualmie National Forest Service offices.

*2105 Hwy. 20, Sedro-Woolley. 360/856-5700. Backcountry Ranger Station, Marblemount. 360/873-4500.*

## RESOURCES

**NORTH CASCADES CHAMBER OF COMMERCE**
P.O. Box 175, Marblemount 98267
360/873-2250

**NORTH CASCADES NATIONAL PARK**
**HEADQUARTERS/VISITORS CENTER**
2105 Hwy. 20, Sedro-Woolley 98284
360/856-5700
Mon.-Fri., 8 a.m.-4:30 p.m.

**NORTH CASCADES NATIONAL PARK/MARBLEMOUNT**
**RANGER STATION**
360/873-4500
The Wilderness Information Center provides information about recreation in the area and issues backcountry permits.

## MOUNT BAKER

Mount Baker rises majestically 10,778 feet above sea level, surrounded by the Mount Baker-Snoqualmie National Forest; its neighboring peak, Mount Shuksan, rises 8,268 feet. Located just an hour's drive from Bellingham, Mount Baker has the state's longest ski and snowboarding season, November through May. In the winter of 1998-99, Mount Baker set the world record for snow accumulation.

In the summer, the area boasts an abundance of hiking trails with spectacular views of nearby mountain peaks. The biggest drawback for families is that there is no overnight lodging on the mountain: the closest accommodations are 17 miles down the road, in the tiny town of Glacier.

### GETTING THERE

Mount Baker is located 56 miles east of Bellingham on Highway 542. To get there, take Exit 255 off I-5. From Seattle, the drive takes three to four hours, depending upon the weather.

### PLACES TO STAY

#### THE LOGS RESORT
*9002 Mount Baker Hwy., Deming 98244*
*360/599-2711*
*Rates: Inexpensive to moderate (two-night minimum on weekends)*
*FYI: Kitchens; fireplaces; outdoor heated pool; pets OK by permission; no smoke-free units*

Situated where Canyon Creek runs into the Nooksack River, these five rustic log cabins are well suited to the needs of families. Each has a natural-rock fireplace, two bedrooms, full kitchen, and bath (there is a sofa bed in the living room). Depending on the season, guests might enjoy swimming in the solar-heated pool, hiking, fishing, badminton, horseshoes, or downhill and cross-country skiing at nearby Mount Baker. This place has loyal, repeat customers, so book early.

#### 66 PARENT COMMENTS
*"Rustic but comfy."*
*"While relaxing at the pool, we spied an eagle and were 'visited' by two deer. We were as excited as our daughter!"*

#### SILVER LAKE PARK CABINS
*9006 Silver Lake Road, Sumas 98295*

*360/599-2776*
*Rates: Inexpensive*
*FYI: Kitchens, food concession; fireplaces (some cabins); boat rentals, fishing*

Sumas is too far from the ski area to make this a good choice if you are planning to ski; otherwise, it's a fun place if you want a semi-rugged getaway. In the summer, there's great hiking nearby.

Consider it camping with a roof over your head, and you'll be satisfied with the rustic cabins. Each has a stove/oven, refrigerator, gas heater, sink, cold water, and two or three double beds. There is a central shower building with toilets, as well as outhouses near the cabins. Bring your own cooking utensils and bedding. Cabins operate year round. A larger, three-bedroom cabin has recently been added. It has a fireplace and kitchen, and it sleeps eight.

The cabins are close to the pretty little lake, which is fine for swimming, fishing, and boating (you can rent canoes, rowboats, and paddleboats), and in the 400-acre park are 100 campsites and plenty of hiking trails.

**❝❝ PARENT COMMENTS**

*"We like to come in September when the crowds have gone and it is getting a little too chilly at night to camp."*

*"We used these cabins when our kids were preschoolers and we thought they (we) were not brave enough to try camping. This proved to be just the right amount of "roughing" it for all of us."*

**PRIVATE CABINS**

If you are seeking overnight accommodations near Mount Baker, your best option may be to rent a private condo or cabin. There are numerous vacation homes in wooded locations with pools, tennis, hot tubs, and golf. Call **MOUNT BAKER LODGING** (360/599-2453; 800/709-7669) or **MOUNT BAKER CHALET** (360/599-2405).

**PLACES TO EAT**

**MILANO'S**
*9990 Mount Baker Hwy., Glacier*
*360/599-2863*
*Hours: Lunch, dinner daily; breakfast Sat.-Sun.*

A casual, café-style restaurant serving tasty soups, wonderful sandwiches, pastas, salads, and espresso. They have no kids' menu, but little ones can order half-size servings or pasta without sauce. The pasta is homemade and delicious; there are specials each evening. Only one highchair is available.

## WHAT TO SEE & DO

**HIKING.** Mount Baker and Mount Shuksan offer some of the most awesome hiking in the state, but much of the terrain is too steep for young kids (not to mention out-of-shape parents). There are, however, some trails with spectacular vistas that can be reached easily by road and short day hikes out of the parking lot. The Heathers Meadows, Austin Pass, and Artist Point areas offer the glory of alpine hiking minus the sweat and aching thighs. Snows melt late in spring in this region, so be sure to call Glacier Public Service Center (360/599-2714) for trail suggestions and conditions. And don't forget to bring along the bug juice: the black flies can be ferocious in August. Because the bugs usually die off by September, early fall is often a glorious time to hike at Baker.

**SKIING/SNOWBOARDING.** Fifty-six miles east of Bellingham, the **MOUNT BAKER SKI AREA** has been a long-time favorite of skiers who prefer deep powder, bumps, gullies, and cliffs. But since the early 1980s, it has gained an excellent reputation with snowboarders as well. (Mount Baker is the home of a world-renowned natural halfpipe). With two new quad chairs, lift lines are some of the shortest in the state.

The terrain here is largely intermediate and advanced (not recommended for novices). If you have a pre-skier in the group, childcare is available.

Also here is a rental shop, offering ski and snowboard equipment, and lessons. There are two lodges, each serving good food—including morning omelets and sweet rolls, flame-broiled hamburgers and hotdogs at lunch.

## RESOURCES

### GLACIER PUBLIC SERVICE CENTER
360/599-2714
Information about hiking and cross-country ski routes.

### MOUNT BAKER RANGER DISTRICT AND NORTH CASCADES NATIONAL PARK
360/856-5700 (weekdays)

Information about hiking and cross-country skiing.

**MOUNT BAKER RECREATION COMPANY**
360/734-6771
Information about downhill ski conditions, rentals, childcare, or family lift passes.

**MOUNT BAKER-SNOQUALMIE NATIONAL FOREST**
206/775-9702; 800/627-0062
Information on trails.

**MOUNT BAKER SNOW PHONE**
360/671-0211
Information about snow conditions.

## PUBLICATIONS

*Best Hikes with Children in Western Washington, Vol. 1*, by Joan Burton. The Mountaineers, 1998. Includes several good mountain hikes near the town of Glacier.

## SNOQUALMIE SUMMIT

Snoqualmie Summit lies 60 miles east of Seattle. For families living in the Seattle-Tacoma area, or visiting for an extended period of time, the area offers quick and easy access for a variety of activities: hiking, mountain biking, snowshoeing, and skiing. The terrain is suitable for all ages and abilities.

### GETTING THERE

**BY CAR.** Snoqualmie Summit is at Exit 52 off I-90 (at 3,100 feet). Don't be deceived by the proximity of the summit; conditions can get ugly very fast during the winter, and avalanches and winter storm conditions will sometimes close the road. Always carry chains and check the road report before departing. Carrying a cell phone that will work in the mountains is also a good idea.

**BY BUS.** Greyhound bus service (800/231-2222) runs to the pass several times daily from downtown Seattle, January through mid-March. The round-trip cost is $18 weekdays and $19 weekends. For reservations, call 206/ 236-7277, ext. 3242.

## PLACES TO STAY

### SNOQUALMIE SUMMIT INN

*On I-90 at Snoqualmie Summit; P.O. Box 163, Snoqualmie Summit 98068*
*425/434-6300*
*Rates: Moderate*
*FYI: Restaurant; outdoor heated pool; playground; pets OK (deposit)*

For years, there wasn't a place for families to stay at Snoqualmie Summit, unless you were lucky enough to own (or know someone who owned) a private cabin. In 1989, Best Western built the Summit Inn, giving travelers a place to stop over when headed over the mountains, and a home base for a weekend of outdoor fun. The pool is small, but it's outdoors and open year round, so anyone inclined to swim in the snow can do so.

The location is convenient—just a few minutes from all four ski areas or hiking trails galore. If you're in a hurry to hit the slopes, the Family Pancake House Restaurant attached to the inn does a good job of providing tasty food quickly.

**❝ PARENT COMMENTS**

*"My eight year old and four year old were just learning to ski, so we went to the Summit Inn for a Saturday night in January. Accommodations were nothing fancy but were comfortable. My kids loved swimming in the pool as the snow fell."*

*"I like to go away for a night with one kid at a time, at least once a year. We make these special trips low-budget and easy: the point is to spend time together having fun. My eight year old and I went to Summit Inn last time, leaving after work for the easy drive to the summit. It was fun waking up there the next morning. After breakfast we went to Denny Creek for a hike, stopped at the outlet stores in North Bend and bought shoes and then came home."*

*"I know families that go to the pass without chains in the car when the weather looks fine in Seattle. But I had the most frightening drive of my life when a major storm hit on the way back to Seattle (I had several young skiers in the car). Cars were sliding everywhere; eventually I-90 was closed. Do not underestimate a winter storm, do not EVER go to the mountains from October to April without chains, and do know how to put them on!"*

## WHAT TO SEE & DO

**CROSS-COUNTRY SKIING.** This sport grows more popular

with families each year, and it's easy to see why: it's less expensive and easier to learn than Alpine skiing, and it gets you away from the crowds and into the woods. **SUMMIT NORDIC CENTER** (formerly Ski Acres Cross-country Center) is an outstanding place for Nordic skiing, a mere 45 miles from the intersection of I-90 and Highway 405. Nordic enthusiasts can choose between the lower five-kilometer trail system, good for beginners, or 45 kilometers of intermediate and advanced, groomed trails 1,000 feet higher, served by the Silver Fir chair lift. You can rent equipment, take lessons, and go on guided treks. Three kilometers are lit for night skiing.

*Off I-90 on Exit 53, at Snoqualmie Summit. 425/434-7669. Open Weds., 9 a.m.-10 p.m.; Thurs.-Sun., 9 a.m.-4:30 p.m.*

**DOWNHILL SKIING/SNOWBOARDING.** Snow conditions are frequently less than ideal (more concrete than powder), but many avid skiers have gotten their start at Snoqualmie Summit. A new owner, Booth Creek Ski Holdings, purchased the ski areas in 1996 and has made substantial improvements. The names have been changed for the six areas; they are now called "Alpental at the Summit," "Summit West," "Summit Central," "Summit East," "Summit Nordic Center," and "Summit Tubing Center." The Summits have Magic Carpets (snow-level conveyer belts), which replace the primitive, arm-wrenching rope-tows of the past, making them a good choice for beginners. All but Alpental (which has the most challenging terrain) are linked by trails, and one ski ticket is good at all four Alpine ski areas.

*Forty-eight miles east of Seattle on I-90. 206/236-PASS. Night skiing daily except Sat. at Summit East.*

**HIKING.** There are hiking trails approaching and at the summit of Snoqualmie that suit all abilities and energy levels. The condition of trails varies wildly depending on the season and snowfall: generally, trails starting below 1000 feet will be free of snow year round. In a heavy-snowfall year, you may run into snow on the trail at the summit even in early summer. For specific trail suggestions and information about conditions, there are several options.

**SNOQUALMIE PASS VISITOR INFORMATION CENTER** (off I-90 at Exit 52; 425/434-6111), operated by the National Forest Service, has a wealth of good information about hiking in the area. The folks operating the center are very helpful about recommending specific hikes suited to your group.

The **Summit Biking and Hiking Center** (425/434-7669) replaces the Summit Nordic Center once the snow melts, with cross-country trails converted to hiking and biking. For five dollars per hiker, the Silver Fir chair lift provides access to pedestrian-only trails including Mount Catherine, Twin Lakes, and Pacific Crest. Some trails must be shared with bikes; get a map and helpful advice before starting out.

Members of the **Issaquah Alps Trail Club** (425/413-1122) lead free hikes for all ages and skill levels year round on the mountains and plateaus in the greater Issaquah area. No reservations are necessary and no special gear is required. Each hike is rated by length and climbing difficulty. Hikers meet at the Issaquah City Hall (about 30 minutes from downtown Seattle) at an appointed time, and carpool to the trailhead. Call for more information and a complete hike schedule.

**The Mountaineers** (300 Third W.; 206/284-6310) is the largest outdoor organization in the region, with 14,000 members. The club is dedicated to offering a wide range of outdoor activities for all ages, including hiking, cross-country skiing, backpacking, and kayaking. Family and child-oriented programs are offered. Their publishing offshoot, Mountaineers Books, is a terrific resource for books on outdoor adventure of all kinds in the Pacific Northwest.

**Snoqualmie Tunnel** (425/888-1421) links the west and east sections of the *John Wayne Trail*, which begins at Rattlesnake Lake near North Bend. It is the longest tunnel in the country that is open to hikers. A 2.3-mile hike in the dark may not sound like fun, but kids with no interest in the woods will often brighten at the thought a tunnel hike. Be sure to bring flashlights and warm jackets.

**Mountain Biking.** Taking a bike out on the mountain trails requires a tolerance for bumps and an adventurous spirit. It's a good way to draw an older child, who may scoff at hiking, into the woods. Once the snow melts, the trails at Summit Nordic Center turn into **The Summit Biking and Hiking Center** (425/434-7669). Strap your bike to the chair lift and ride to the top, where you can take the speedy route or the slow, scenic route back down, choosing among 35 miles of trails. Lessons and bike rentals are available. Helmets are required and can also be rented. The Trailside Café is also open for the season.

*Take Exit 53 off I-90. 206/232-8182. Open Fri.-Sun. (May 22-Sept. 7) Cost: chair lift, $9/biker, $7/biker with rental equipment; bike rental, $27/day, $18/half-day.*

**SNOQUALMIE VALLEY RAILROAD.** The Northwest Railway Museum operates an interpretive railway program called the Snoqualmie Valley Railroad. This five-mile railroad allows museum visitors to experience a train excursion aboard antique railroad coaches through the Upper Snoqualmie Valley. Visitors may depart from the depot in Snoqualmie or 30 minutes later from the depot in North Bend, for either a half-hour or one-hour ride. Holiday Santa Trains and field trips on School Trains are very popular.

*Snoqualmie is 25 miles east of Seattle via I-90; North Bend is approximately 7 miles farther east. 425/746-4025; www.trainmuseum.org. Trains operate Sun., 10 a.m.-4 p.m. (April-Oct.) & Sat., 10 a.m.-4 p.m., (Memorial Day-Sept., weekends in Dec.). Cost: $7/adult, $5/child 3-12, free/under 3. Call for directions to the depots and departure times.*

**SNOWSHOEING.** Forest Service volunteers lead 90-minute guided snowshoe walks in the Commonwealth Basin area. Snowshoes are provided.

*Check in at Snoqualmie Pass Visitor Center, in front of Summit West ski area, one half-hour before the trip. Reservations required. 425/434-6111. Walks Sat.-Sun., 10 a.m. & 1 p.m. Cost: $7-10 donation requested.*

**SLEDDING AND TUBING.** You can bring along your own sleds and tubes and find your own hill along the side roads off I-90, but it's probably safer, if more crowded, at **SUMMIT TUBING CENTER** (formerly Ski Acres Snowplay and Tubing Area). You can rent an inner tube ($5/day) or bring your own and fill it from air hoses on the eastern side of the lodge.

There's a rope tow to pull tubers up the hill after they slide down, and also a small area for sledding, though sleds are not available for rent. Admission is charged whether or not you supply your own tube. Whatever you bring to get down the hill, it can't be made of wood, metal, or movable parts. Inner tubes and hard plastic objects such as toboggans, plastic sleds, and lids are OK. The area is well supervised, but on a busy day it gets too crowded and rowdy for young kids. Fridays and Sunday mornings are likely to be the least busy.

*Exit 53, off I-90. 888/804-6404. Open Fri. & Sat., 9 a.m.-10 p.m.; Sun., 9 a.m.-5 p.m. Cost: $10/adult, $8/child.*

**SNOQUALMIE FALLS PARK.** This scenic park, located in the foothills of the Cascade Mountains, is a fine place to get out in the woods and enjoy a scenic waterfall. Just outside the town of Snoqualmie (about 35 minutes from Seattle via I-90) the Snoqualmie River plunges 270 feet over a rock gorge. The park has observation platforms from which to view the falls, picnic areas, a gift shop, and a café. The half-mile *River Trail* leads down to the river's edge, for an up-close view of the falls. The trail is steep, however, so be prepared to help the little ones on the way back up. The best time to visit is late spring when the snowmelt is greatest and the volume of water over the falls makes for a spectacular show.

*Located 25 miles east of Seattle; take Exit 27 from I-90.*

## RESOURCES

**SNOQUALMIE PASS VISITORS INFORMATION**
425/434-6111

**ROAD CONDITIONS**
888/SNO-INFO

**CASCADE WEATHER REPORT**
206/464-2000, ext. 9904

## PUBLICATIONS

*Best Hikes with Children in Western Washington & the Cascades, Vols. 1 and 2,* Mountaineers Books, 1988.

## MOUNT RAINIER

At 14,410 feet, Mount Rainier reigns majestically over the Cascades. Fortunately, you can get close enough to touch this enormous "ice cream cone in the sky" without becoming a mountain climber. This great peak and much of the surrounding foothills lie within the well-developed Mount Rainier National Park.

More than two million people visit this national park each year, with the majority visiting during the high season (May through October). During peak months, the best time to visit the park is weekdays, as large crowds arrive early on sunny summer weekends. Parking lots at the most popular areas, such as Paradise and Sunrise, are generally full before noon on weekends.

The park entrance fee (a seven-day permit) is $10 per vehicle or $5 per person entering on foot or bicycle. All locations and facilities are open July through Labor Day; most spots are accessible from Memorial Day into early October.

## GETTING THERE

Mount Rainier National Park has four entrances: **NISQUALLY**, off Highway 706 in the southwest, the closest to I-5 and the most popular; **CARBON RIVER**, on Carbon River Road in the northwest; **WHITE RIVER**, on White River Road off Highway 410 in the northeast (closest to Sunrise); and **STEVENS CANYON ROAD** in the southwest. Your entrance to the park will depend on the direction from which you approach, where you want to go at the park, and the time of year. Only the Nisqually entrance is open year round; other park roads close in late October or at first snowfall, whichever comes first, and reopen between late April and early June, depending upon how fast the winter snow melts. Regardless of which route you choose and when you visit, always check weather and road conditions before starting your trip (24-hour Park Information Service, 360/569-2211), and pack extra warm clothing and shoes.

**FROM SEATTLE:** If you're headed toward Paradise, drive south on I-5 to Tacoma. Exit onto Highway 7 and drive south to Highway 706. Head east on 706, through Elbe and Ashford to the Nisqually entrance, Longmire, and Paradise.

To visit Sunrise, take I-520 east from Seattle to Bellevue, then head south on I-405. Exit to Highway 169. At Enumclaw (approximately 33 miles southeast of Bellevue), take Highway 410 east to the White River entrance, White River, and the Sunrise turnoff (summer only).

**FROM PORTLAND:** For Paradise, drive north on I-5, east on Highway 12, and north on Highway 7. Then pick up Highway 706 to the Nisqually entrance, Longmire, and Paradise.

For Sunrise, drive north on I-5, east on Highway 12, then north on Highway 123 to the Ohanapecosh entrance, White River, and the Sunrise turnoff (summer only).

**ROADSIDE ATTRACTIONS.** However you get there, the journey to Mount Rainier is long and winding. Fortunately, there are a variety of good stops along the way. Coming from Portland, Mount St. Helens is the most interesting attraction (see "Mount St. Helens").

There are also interesting stops on the way from Seattle, but they're not places that allow you to take a quick look-see and jump back in the car. Allow several hours, perhaps on your way home after a night at the mountain, to visit Northwest Trek, Mt. Rainier Scenic Railway, or Pioneer Farm (see "Seattle: What to See & Do").

### PLACES TO STAY

There are no places to stay in or around Mount Rainier National Park that offer ideal accommodations for families. Still, this awesome peak is too much to explore in a day, so we recommend spending at least one night nearby.

If you enjoy camping, any one of the five National Park campgrounds is a good option. Campsite reservations are required at the Cougar Rock and Ohanapecosh campgrounds between June 28 and Labor Day, and can be made by telephone (800/365-CAMP) or online through the National Park Reservation Service (reservations may be made up to five months in advance). You may also reserve a site when you arrive, if space is available (though this is unlikely). All other campsites (including the off-season at Cougar Rock and Ohanapecosh) are available on a first-come, first-served basis.

### ALEXANDER'S COUNTRY INN
*37515 Highway 706, Ashford 98304*
*360/569-2300*
*Rates: Moderate*
*FYI: Restaurant; complimentary breakfast; hot tub*

This renovated 1912 country inn is located just one mile from the Nisqually entrance to Mount Rainier National Park. It's a good place to stay if you want comfort, a good meal, and proximity to the mountain. Most rooms have a shared bath, but facilities are immaculate and there is a large, pleasant shared space on the second floor that is a nice place for the kids to play board games. The Tower Suite is a fun choice if you are on a special trip with just one child: it has two floors, connected by steep stairs—the first floor is a sitting area, the second is a bedroom. The free breakfast includes pastry, cereal, and beverage of choice.

There are also two guesthouses available, one of which

sleeps up to eight people. The restaurant at the inn is particularly accommodating for families (see "Places to Eat").

**66 PARENT COMMENTS**

*"I went to Alexander's Country Inn with my eight-year-old daughter for a mother-daughter getaway. We visited Paradise and took a hike during the day, ate a fabulous meal in the restaurant at the inn, and spent the night in the Tower Suite. On the way home the next day we visited Northwest Trek."*

*"The quarters are too close if you have rowdy kids."*

## THE NISQUALLY LODGE
*31609 Hwy. 706, Ashford 98304*
*360/569-8804*
*Rates: Moderate*
*FYI: Complimentary continental breakfast; hot tub*

The name of this place suggests a grand mountain lodge in a breathtaking setting, so brace yourself for a basic two-story motel sitting just off the highway. Even though the location isn't scenic, it's just five miles from the south entrance to the park.

There's a nice stone fireplace in the lobby, a hot tub outdoors (great after a big day on the mountain), and a breakfast of pastries, juice, and coffee in the lobby each morning.

**66 PARENT COMMENTS**

*"It is tough to find a good place to stay near Mount Rainier, but the park is without question one of the finest areas in the state to explore with kids. We wanted to stay in a cozy log cabin in the woods with a fireplace. There are numerous accommodations in the area that tempted us when we read their brochures, but once we got there they were too "rustic" (unsafe and dilapidated) for our standards. So we were relieved to discover the comfortable Nisqually Lodge so close to the park entrance."*

## INN AT LONGMIRE
*Paradise Lodge*
*360/569-2275; www.guestservices.com/rainier*
*Rates: Moderate to expensive*
*FYI: Restaurants; snack bar (at Paradise)*

The Mount Rainier National Park Service maintains two places to stay inside the park: the Inn at Longmire and Paradise Lodge. Neither is great for families—they have small rooms, no kitchens, and relatively high prices—but in the morning you will be able to jump out of bed and hit the trail! Rainier is one of the most popular tourist attractions in the Northwest, and the summer season is short so it is difficult to get reservations in the summer unless you call early.

The Inn at Longmire sits at the base of the mountain, just inside the Nisqually entrance. A major renovation in 1990 added a side wing that expanded the inn from 16 to 25 rooms. Rooms are available with or without a private bath, and with a choice of two single beds, two double beds, or a queen bed. The most spacious option is the two-room unit with bath. The downstairs lounge, with its lovely river-rock fireplace, is small but comfy.

One of the inn's greatest attractions is the opportunity it affords to appreciate some of the history of the area. Most of the buildings at Longmire date from the early 1900s, including the tiny Longmire Museum. The first inn at the park was a log cabin built by the Longmire family in 1884—you'll see what remains when you walk the *Trail of the Shadows*, across the road.

Meals at the restaurant are basic—burgers, sandwiches, salads, and soups.

**PARADISE LODGE,** located 5,400 feet up the mountain, first opened in 1917 and has the feel of all such national park edifices, with the signature massive lobby framed by huge log beams and stone fireplaces at each end. This is a busy place during the day, as there are lots of daytime tourists. Accommodations are comfortable, but neither spacious nor fancy. A few board games can be checked out from the desk and there's a gift shop to browse, but the real entertainment is located just outside the door.

There is a small snack bar and dining room at the lodge. Food in the dining room is pricey and nothing special, but children are well tolerated. As an alternative, consider heading down the mountain to Alexander's (see "Places to Eat").

**66 PARENT COMMENTS**

*"The rooms at Paradise aren't very nice, but since we only used them to sleep in, it really didn't matter."*

*"Be sure to check the weather! One June we took a nephew who was visiting from the east coast to Paradise to show him the mountains of the West, and we couldn't see a thing through a blizzard."*

*"We wanted to stay at Paradise, but it was full, so we went to Longmire. We were glad we did, because it was less crowded with tourists and the rooms were nicer."*

## PLACES TO EAT

### ALEXANDER'S

*37515 Highway 706, Ashford (at Alexander's Country Inn)*
*360/569-2300*
*Hours: Breakfast, lunch, dinner daily (June-Oct.); lunch, dinner*
*Fri.; breakfast, lunch, dinner Sat.-Sun. (Nov.-May)*

The fine food here is fresh, well prepared, and moderately priced. Kids can order off the children's menu. Grown-ups will have many attractive options, but it's hard to pass up the pan-fried trout (caught on the premises, it couldn't be any fresher). There's outdoor seating when the weather is agreeable.

## WHAT TO SEE & DO

Visitors' centers at Paradise, Longmire, Ohanapecosh, and Sunrise can provide tips on trails, camping, and interpretive programs. The nature and interpretive hikes and evening programs, offered at each of the centers, are ideal for families.

**CARBON RIVER.** If you plan to camp in the National Park, don't overlook the northwestern corner. Although it is the least visited, this area offers excellent hiking and camping for families. To get there, you travel via Highway 165, through several picturesque, old coal-mining towns. At Carbon River, if you can steel your nerves to cross a 50-foot-high suspension bridge, you can walk almost to the terminus of a glacier. (Mount Rainier boasts the largest single-peak glacier system in the contiguous United States.)

**HIKING.** Many hikes at Mount Rainier National Park are recommended for families. Visitors can pick up a park map at any entrance; individual trail maps are available at visitors centers and ranger stations. Here are a few of the tried-and-true trail suggestions:

The *Ohanapecosh Nature Trail* is a flat, shady half-mile loop to Ohanapecosh Hot Springs. The most interesting part is the lush meadow that grows where the water trickles down. Along the *Trail of the Shadows* you'll encounter an early homestead cabin—James Longmire filed a mineral claim here because of the colorful soda springs. (The trailhead for this half-mile loop is across the road from the Inn at Longmire.)

*Sourdough Ridge Self-Guiding Trail* provides a gentle climb to the ridge top, with stunning views of Mount Rainier, as well as Mount Baker, Glacier Peak, and Mount Adams in the distance. Here you'll find the opportunity to study the fragile sub-alpine environment and the plants and animals that thrive within it. (Access this one-mile loop trail from the north side of the parking area at Sunrise.)

The *Lake George Trail* begins with a gradual one-mile climb to the lake. Stronger hikers can continue along the trail, which gains 1,500 feet in 1.5 miles, to a fire lookout and spectacular views of the mountain. (The trailhead is at Round Pass on the Westside Road.)

*Silver Falls Trail* follows the lovely Ohanapecosh River past the hot springs to the 75-foot-high falls. The trail can be hiked as a three-mile loop by crossing the bridge below the falls and returning to the campground on the other side of the river. (The trail starts at Ohanapecosh Campground's Loop B.)

The popular *Naches Peak Loop* leaves from Tipsoo Lake and affords breathtaking views of Mount Rainier, flowering fields in July and August, and abundant huckleberries in the fall. Half of the 3.5-mile round trip follows the Pacific Crest National Scenic Trail.

**LONGMIRE.** Here you can browse through the small Historical Museum and visit the Hikers' Center—an excellent source of information about hiking in the park. The small inn here has been recently renovated (see "Places to Stay"). During the winter, **RAINIER SKI TOURING** (360/569-2211, ext. 3314) provides rental equipment and trail maps for cross-country skiing and snowshoeing, but the trails for winter sports are too difficult for inexperienced skiers.

**PARADISE** is the most popular destination for park visitors. Located at 5,400 feet, the historic **PARADISE LODGE** is open late May through the first week in October (Sunday brunch is served all summer). The **HENRY M. JACKSON MEMORIAL VISITOR CENTER** offers a cafeteria, nature exhibits, slide shows, and guided hikes. It's open 10 a.m.-5 p.m. on weekends and holidays until mid-April, when it opens daily for extended hours.

Many trails are accessible from Paradise, including some suitable for school-age children (there is excellent wildflower viewing in July and August and spectacular fall foliage in September). In winter, Paradise offers cross-country skiing, innertubing, and snowshoeing. Park naturalists lead snowshoe hikes (participants must be 10 or older) to explore winter ecology on weekends from January through mid-April. (Snowshoe rental is available at Paradise, or at REI in Seattle.)

**OHANEPECOSH** is just east of Paradise, at the end of Stevens Canyon Road. The park's most impressive stands of old-growth trees are here. Two good hikes for young children in this area include the two-mile loop to *Silver Falls*, and *Grove of the Patriarchs*, a 1.5-mile stroll through massive 1,200-year-old Douglas firs, red cedars, and Western hemlocks.

**SUNRISE**, located 6,400 feet up the northeast flank of the mountain, is the highest point accessible by automobile and is open only during the summer months. On a 17-mile spur road off Highway 410, the **SUNRISE VISITOR CENTER** opens July 1 and has displays depicting the volcanic history of Mount Rainier and a sweeping view of the mountain and other volcanic peaks. This is a good place to watch climbers negotiate difficult terrain. There are also walk-in picnic sites, a ranger station, and a snack bar. A campground with 10 sites is one half-mile away. Surrounded by alpine meadows, Sunrise is also a good place for viewing the wildflowers.

*360/569-2211, ext. 2357. Open daily, 9 a.m.-5 p.m. (July-early Oct.).*

## RESOURCES

### MOUNT RAINIER GUEST SERVICES
360/365-2267
Information about lodging in the park.

### MOUNT RAINIER NATIONAL PARK INFORMATION
360/569-2211
Information about visitors centers; hiking, skiing, and snow shoeing; food and lodging; camping; weather and road conditions.

### MOUNT RAINIER NATIONAL PARK WEB SITE
www.nps.gov/mora/index.htm
An excellent source of detailed information about history, recreational activities, overnight lodgings, and camping.

### PARK RADIO INFORMATION
Approaching the Nisqually entrance, tune the radio to AM 1610 for useful park information.

### PUBLICATIONS

*Best Hikes with Children in Western Washington and The Cascades*, Vols. 1 and 2, The Mountaineers.

*A Field Guide to the Cascades & Olympics*, by Stephen R. Whitney. The Mountaineers, 1983.
Comprehensive, compact guide to mountain flora and fauna.

*Road Guide to Mount Rainier National Park*, by Barbara and Robert Decker, Double Decker Press, 1996
Points out interesting attractions along major park roads and includes maps of hiking trails.

Two newspapers—*Tahoma* in the summer and *Snowdrift* in the winter—give details on seasonal activities in the park. Available free at the visitors centers.

## MOUNT ST. HELENS

After lying dormant for 123 years, Mount St. Helens exploded on May 18, 1980, and blew 1,300 feet off the top and much of the north face. The explosion (estimated to have the force of 27,000 Hiroshima-sized atom bombs) blew rock and ash 500 miles high (ash covered parts of three states) and triggered the largest landslide in recorded history. Fifty-seven people died in the eruption.

Two years later, Congress created the Mount St. Helens National Volcanic Monument. Managed by the U.S. Forest Service, the monument offers families a rare opportunity to closely encounter an active volcano and to witness firsthand the amazing resurgence of life in the devastated region around it. Recreational and educational opportunities abound here, including visitors centers with exhibits, multimedia presentations, and expert rangers; superb viewpoints, most of which are accessible by car; roadside interpretive signs; and hiking trails, from which families can seek their own views of the devastation and rehabilitation.

A Monument Pass is required to visit most Mount St. Helens visitors centers, viewpoints, and observatories. The pass is sold per person, and is valid for three days. The cost of the Monument Pass is: $8 per adult (ages 16-61), $6 per adult in off-season (November through April), $4 per senior, free for youth (to age 15). The passes are available at many centers and sites within the monument (see various entries in "What to See & Do").

## GETTING THERE

There are three approaches to Mount St. Helens—from the north, the west, and the south. Though the northern and southern approaches are impassable during the winter, the western approach, via Spirit Lake Memorial Highway, is open year round (traction devices may be required). There are intriguing sights along each of these routes; see "What to See & Do" for descriptions.

Approaching from the west provides access to the National Volcanic Monument, and is by far the most popular route. Driving north or south on Interstate 5, take Exit 49 (Hwy. 504). Travel east on 504, also known as the Spirit Lake Memorial Highway, through the small town of Castle Rock. (If you need gas, be sure to get it here; there is no gas available within the monument.) After Castle Rock, the highway continues for 54 miles, then dead-ends five miles from the mountain. There are five recommended stops along the way (and you'll no doubt find some of your own).

If you are entering from the northern access route, take Highway 12 east from I-5 (or west from Hwy. 82 in central Washington) to the town of Randle. (Tank up; no gasoline is available beyond this point.) Driving south from Randle on Forest Road (FR) 25, you will encounter a number of potential stops, including Wood Creek Information Station, Meta Lake, and Harmony Falls. Entering from Randle provides the best overall view of the destruction.

Visitors entering from the south will likely be headed toward the Ape Cave Geological Site or Windy Ridge. Depending on where you are coming from, choose one of two routes. If you exit I-5 onto Highway 500, near Vancouver, head east six miles and connect with Highway 503, headed north. It is approximately 42 miles to the monument (this route passes through Amboy, allowing a stop at the monument headquarters there). The other route departs I-5 at Woodland (23 miles north of Vancouver). Take Highway 503 east about 34 miles past Cougar, where the road becomes FR 90.

**ROADSIDE ATTRACTIONS.** If you're entering from the west, via Castle Rock, you might want to stop at **MOUNT ST.**

**Helens Cinedome Theater** for a "preview of coming attractions." The Cinedome plays the 25-minute, Academy Award–nominated film, "The Eruption of Mount St. Helens" on a three-story-high, 55-foot-wide screen. Older kids will likely be enthralled by the film, but the roar can be overwhelming for little ones.

*Off I-5 at the Castle Rock exit. 360/274-8000. Film plays daily, 9 a.m.-6 p.m., every 45 min. (May-Oct.). Cost: $5/adult, $4/senior & child 6-12, free/under 6.*

## Places to Stay

Overnight accommodations are few and far between in the Mount St. Helens area. If you're within shooting distance, you might want to make it a day trip. On the other hand, it's easy to spend a long, tiring day visiting the mountain, and you might be glad to have prearranged accommodations nearby.

Places recommended below are along major roadways approaching turnoffs to Mount St. Helens. Be sure to consult a map and choose accommodations according to which approach (from the north, south, or west) you will be taking. If weather is cooperating, camping is another good option—some suggestions are listed at the end of the "Places to Stay" section.

### King Oscar Motel
*1049 Eckerson Road, Centralia 98531*
*360/736-1661; 888/254-KING*
*Rates: Inexpensive*
*FYI: Complimentary continental breakfast; kitchenettes (some rooms); outdoor pool (seasonal); laundry*

Whether you're headed straight down I-5 to the western approach to Mount St. Helens, or across Highway 12 to enter from the north, Centralia is a convenient place to stay. The two-story King Oscar Motel has 94 rooms, but no suites. For larger families, some rooms have two queen beds and a kitchenette (refrigerator, stovetop, microwave); the staff is happy to add rollaway beds if needed. If you can swing it, go with a kitchenette room; restaurant options are not great between here and the mountain.

**❝ Parent Comments**
*"We were glad to wake up Saturday morning and be within an hour of Mount St. Helens. The free breakfast got us off to a good start, with no need to seek out a local restaurant."*

*"After hiking all day at Mount St. Helens, it was great to be able to drop five sets of muddy clothes into the laundry at the King Oscar."*

### TIMBERLAND INN & SUITES

*1271 Mt. St. Helens Way, Castle Rock 98611*
*360/274-6002*
*Rates: Inexpensive to moderate*
*FYI: Refrigerators/microwaves (some rooms); laundry; pets OK*

The prices are right for families at this two-story motel, located near the western end of the most popular (western) approach to the volcanic area. Family suites are a good deal here; they have two queen beds in the main room, a queen sofa bed in a partitioned area, and kitchenette, and can accommodate up to six people.

As an added advantage, the inn is located next to the Cinedome Theater (see "Roadside Attractions"); it's interesting to see the film of the volcanic eruption before driving up to witness its widespread effect and evolving aftermath.

### THE WOODLANDER

*1500 Atlantic St., Woodland 98674*
*360/225-6540*
*Rates: Inexpensive*
*FYI: Refrigerators/microwaves (some rooms); indoor pool; pets OK*

In many ways this is your basic, no-frills motel: there are 61 small, but clean, rooms on two stories. Still, for families it has the advantages of affordability, a heated indoor pool (it's small, but the little ones can splash around), and easy access to Mount St. Helens (about 35 miles to the southern entrance).

### 66 PARENT COMMENTS

*"We got a room with a refrigerator, and we were glad we did. There weren't many restaurants nearby, and also we were able to prepare lunches and snacks for our trip to Mount St. Helens."*

### RESIDENCE INN BY MARRIOTT VANCOUVER

*8005 NE Parkway Dr., Vancouver 98662*
*360/256-4758*
*Rates: Moderate to expensive*
*FYI: Free continental breakfast; kitchens; fireplaces (most rooms); outdoor pool; sport court; pets OK (fee)*

About 23 miles south of the turnoff for the southern entrance to Mount St. Helens, staying at this comfortable spot allows an easy drive the next morning for those who've already come some distance to see the mountain. With 120 suites, including 30 two-bedroom units, the Residence Inn is particularly comfortable for families. It is designed for longer visits, such as business trips, so the rooms are fairly spacious, with particularly nice kitchens and extra closet space. If your family prefers to get by with a one-room suite, the staff is happy to bring in a large folding bed.

When you're ready to hit the mountain, you'll find easy access to Highway 500 east. In six miles, 500 intersects Highway 503, which heads north to Mount St. Helens.

### 66 PARENT COMMENTS

*"As always, we had the family dog along when we stayed at the Residence Inn. They give you a magnetized sign for the door, "Pet in Room," so the maid doesn't accidentally happen upon a wary Fido, and put you in a room that has easy access to the pet "relief" area."*

*"The kids liked helping themselves to breakfast almost as much as they liked the pool."*

### CAMPING

When the weather cooperates, camping near Mount St. Helens can be a real treat. Entering from the south, there are campgrounds at Battle Ground Lake (off Hwy. 503) and Paradise Point (off I-5, near La Center). From the north, you'll find the Lewis and Clark campground (off Hwy. 12) and Ike Kinswa, near the Mossyrock Dam. Seaquest campground is on the Spirit Lake Memorial Highway (as you enter from the west), a few miles east of Castle Rock.

For information about these and other camping facilities near Mount St. Helens, phone **FOREST SERVICE CAMPGROUND RESERVATIONS** (877/444-6777).

### PLACES TO EAT

#### MARY MCCRANK'S RESTAURANT
*2923 Jackson Hwy., Chehalis*
*360/748-3662*
*Hours: 11:30 a.m.-8:30 p.m. Mon.-Sat., noon-8 p.m. Sun.*

Chehalis is on I-5, just north of the exit onto Highway 12. It makes a convenient stop whether your family is taking the western or the northern access route to Mount St. Helens.

This historic restaurant was opened in 1935 in a large home, with fireplaces, warm lighting and cushy armchairs throughout. The country-style cuisine includes hearty favorites such as chicken and dumplings; for dessert, the pies are fabulous.

The set-up here accommodates children well. The restaurant's beautiful lawns and gardens border a stream, and impatient little ones can walk while they await their table. Once seated, the server will bring bread and jam to occupy little hands until the "real" food arrives.

## WHAT TO SEE & DO

### APPROACHING FROM THE WEST

(Sites are listed in geographical order based on which route you are taking to the mountain.)

**MOUNT ST. HELENS VISITORS CENTER** is a good place to get oriented to the mountain and help decide what you'd like to see along the way. It offers excellent exhibits, including a walk-through volcano, photos, and a timeline of events leading up to and through the eruption, and an interesting film documenting the eruption and rebirth. A .13-mile trail leads to a viewpoint overlooking Silver Lake.

*Five miles east of Castle Rock on Spirit Lake Memorial Hwy. 360/274-2100. Open daily, 10 a.m.-6 p.m. (May-Sept.); 9 a.m.-5 p.m. (rest of year). Monument passes available.*

**HOFFSTADT BLUFF REST AREA AND VIEWPOINT** is an alpine-style building with a panoramic view of the Toutle Valley. Exhibits explore the lives and deaths of those who were directly affected by the eruption. There's a full-service restaurant, a gift shop, and picnic facilities. For a fee, you can take a helicopter tour or covered wagon ride from here.

*At Milepost 27. 360/274-7750; 800/752-8439. Open daily, 10 a.m.-8 p.m. (May-Oct.); 10 a.m.-5 p.m. (rest of year).*

**WEYERHAUSER FOREST LEARNING CENTER** focuses on how the eruption affected the forest—and explores efforts tosalvage, reforest, and conserve what remains. The young ones will be eager to pull over when they see the "volcano" playground at the entrance. Kids can also kids sit in the cockpit of a helicopter and take a virtual (videotaped) tour of the mountain.

*At North Fork Ridge, Milepost 33.5. 360/414-3439. Open daily, 10 a.m.-6 p.m. (May-Oct.).*

**COLDWATER RIDGE** is a multimillion-dollar facility, just seven miles from the crater, offering views of the upper Toutle River Valley, Coldwater and Castle lakes, and the two-mile-wide crater itself. You'll find fun, interactive exhibits that focus on native flora and fauna and their recovery since the eruption. The guided walk along the *Winds of Change Trail* is a good one for families. Have your kids watch for *hummocks*—rocky mounds that were blasted from the volcano.

*At Milepost 43. 360/274-2131. Open daily, 10 a.m.-6 p.m. (May-Sept.); 9 a.m.-5 p.m. (rest of year).*

**JOHNSTON RIDGE OBSERVATORY** is named in honor of David A. Johnston, a USGS volcanologist who lost his life in the 1980 eruption. At the terminus of the Spirit Lake Memorial Highway, the observatory is located within five miles of the north side of the volcano and offers spectacular views of the steaming lava dome and crater. There's an information booth here, as well as well-informed staff who offer both formal talks and guided walks.

Your young geologist will enjoy learning about the eruption, and how geologists monitor volcanoes. There's a 15-minute computer-animated program that older children will enjoy.

*At Milepost 52. 360/274-2140. Open Thurs.-Sun., 10 a.m.-4:30 p.m. (May-Oct.)*

### APPROACHING FROM THE SOUTH

(Sites are listed in geographical order as you move north.)

#### MOUNT ST. HELENS NATIONAL VOLCANIC MONUMENT

**HEADQUARTERS** provides information on road conditions and permits (which must be obtained prior to gathering any forest products or minerals).

*42218 NE Yale Bridge Road, Amboy, 98601. 360/247-3900. Open daily, 9 a.m.-4 p.m. (May 15-Sept.); Mon-Fri., 8 a.m.-5 p.m. (rest of year). Monument passes available here.*

**APE CAVE GEOLOGICAL SITE** is one of the more popular stops. The 12,810-foot Ape Cave formed some 2,000 years ago when a stream of lava cooled quickly, forming a crust under which molten lava continued to flow out. The cave is believed to be the longest lava tube in the Western Hemisphere.

This is a fascinating place to take the family, but be sure to pack plenty of warm clothing (the cave is a chilly 42 degrees) and sturdy shoes. Guided 45-minute tours are offered during the summer. Lanterns can be rented at the site.

*On FR 8303, 1 mile west of FR 83. Open daily, 10 a.m.-5:30 p.m. (mid-May-Sept.) Tours: Sat.-Sun., 10:30 a.m.-3:30 p.m. (mid-May-late June); daily, 10:30 a.m.-3:30 p.m. (late June-Sept.) Lantern rental: $2.*

**LAHAR VIEWPOINT** provides an excellent look at how the south side of Mount St. Helens was affected by the 1980 eruption. Once scoured by the volcanic mudflow, the area is beginning to recover, offering a lesson in the resiliency of life.

*Located 10.5 miles east of the junction of FR 83 & FR 90.*

**PINE CREEK INFORMATION STATION.** This is a good place to stop and get your questions answered along the southern edge of the volcanic area. A short movie will help orient you to this corner of the monument, and staff members can offer advice on camping, hiking, and other activities in the area.

*About 18 miles east of Cougar on FR 90. Open daily, 9 a.m.-6 p.m. (mid-May-Sept.). Monument passes available.*

**WINDY RIDGE VIEWPOINT**, on the eastern edge of the monument, is accessible from either north or south via FR 25 and FR 90. It is an excellent viewpoint, accessible only in summer (see "What to See & Do: Approaching from the North").

**APPROACHING FROM THE NORTH**

(Sites are listed in geographical order as you move south.)

**COWLITZ VALLEY RANGER STATION.** The kids will know you're "almost there" when they see the ranger station; consider a quick stop to pick up information on trails and facilities within the monument.

*One mile east of Randle on Hwy. 12. 360/497-1100. Open daily, 8 a.m.-4:30 p.m. Monument Passes available.*

**WINDY RIDGE** is accessible (summer only) via either the northern or the southern approaches. It's one of the best places to get the "big picture," a look at the total area of devastation created by the 1980 eruption. From here you will see deposits left behind by the debris avalanche. You'll see a faint plume of gas rising above the lava dome and, especially in late summer, you might see a rockfall stir up ash clouds above the rim.

Take the uphill walk from the northern end of the parking lot for an excellent view of the area adjacent to Spirit Lake. (The 1980 debris avalanche, with its load of timber and rock, poured over the ridge above the lake and created a giant wave; you can still see the "slosh line" along the lakeshore.)

In the late spring and summer, forest interpreters give talks at the Windy Ridge outdoor amphitheater. Call the Visitors Center for information.

*At the western end of FR 99, accessible off FR 25.*

**WOODS CREEK WATCHABLE WILDLIFE SITE** (open Memorial Day through Labor Day), where you can picnic or take a hike. The 2.5-mile *Watchable Wildlife Trail* is flat and easy for all ages.

*Six miles south of Randle on FR 25, across from the Woods Creek Information Station.*

## RESOURCES

### WEB SITES
### MOUNT ST. HELENS NATIONAL VOLCANIC MONUMENT
www.fs.fed.us/gpnf/mshnvm
This official Web site offers general information about the monument, including guides to specific attractions, services, and activities.

### PUBLICATIONS

*Discovering Mount St. Helens: A guide to the National Monument,* by Scott Shane. University of Washington Press, 1985.

*Roadside Geology of Washington,* by David Alt and Donald Hyndman. Mountain Press, 1984.
Introduces readers to geology of the state, organized by region; easy to use field guide.

## CENTRAL WASHINGTON

Central Washington encompasses the middle section of the state, just east of the Cascades. Roughly north to south, there are several popular scenic and recreational areas here: Methow Valley, the Lake Chelan area, Leavenworth, and Ellensburg/Cle Elum. These areas enjoy cold, crisp winters and hot, dry summers; annual rainfall is minimal. Whether your family enjoys adventure in the great outdoors, or relaxed summer days by the pool, this part of the state is a wonderful place to vacation.

## METHOW VALLEY

Before the North Cascades Highway was built through rugged mountain country, in 1972, the Methow Valley was a dead-end destination accessible only by a lengthy southern route—an isolated paradise known mainly to miners, ranchers, and sportsmen. Today, the miners are gone, but ranches, old orchards, and horses occupy this alpine valley. Families are attracted by majestic mountains, crystal-clear rivers, outdoor sports of all kinds, and a unique mixture of pioneer nostalgia and modern comforts.

The valley has a four-season climate averaging 300 days of sunshine and about 16 inches of rain. Mean average summer temperature is 78 degrees; in winter, 19 degrees. The valley in almost completely surrounded by national forest and range lands.

Mountain biking, hiking, cross-country skiing, horseback riding, and river rafting are the most popular outdoor activities; visitors can also heli-ski, snowshoe, snowmobile, swim, fish, and golf.

Although there are several towns in the valley, Winthrop is the acknowledged hub. From Winthrop, you can drive to Slate Peak, the highest point in Washington that's accessible by car (7,440 feet). North of the Methow, the Okanogan Valley extends into Canada. While the Canadian side has become a popular resort area (see "British Columbia: Okanagan"), ranching and wilderness still prevail on the U.S. side.

### GETTING THERE

From Seattle there are two main routes to this part of the state: Highway 20 (the North Cascades Highway) and Highway 2. The North Cascades Highway, one of the most spectacular drives in the nation, is closed by winter weather from about mid-November to late April. To reach it, take Interstate 5 north to its junction with Highway 20, at Burlington. Follow 20 eastward to Mazama and Winthrop. Seattle to Winthrop is 192 miles, approximately a four-hour drive.

To reach the valley for a winter outing, take Highway 2 over Stevens Pass, then Highway 97 north through Chelan to

Highway 153. Follow 153 to its junction with Highway 20, then head northwest on 20 to Winthrop. An alternate route from Seattle is to take I-90 and Blewett Pass to Wenatchee. Follow signs to East Wenatchee/Okanogan, then take Highway 97 north to Highway 153.

From Portland, drive east on I-84 along the Columbia River to Highway 97 (at Biggs). Cross the river and stay on Highway 97 north through Goldendale, Yakima, Ellensburg, and Blewett Pass to Highway 2 and Wenatchee.

On any route, the drive takes three to five hours from Seattle, and seven from Portland, depending on weather conditions. If this seems long and your budget allows, you can fly to Wenatchee and rent a car for the drive to Winthrop or the Okanogan.

**ROADSIDE ATTRACTIONS.** If you travel via Highway 2 to the Methow Valley, see "Leavenworth: Places to Eat" and "Things to See & Do." If you're on I-90, check the "Snoqualmie Summit" section. For information about what to see along the North Cascades Highway, see "Washington Cascades: North Cascades."

## PLACES TO STAY

### FREESTONE INN
*17798 Hwy. 20, Mazama 98833*
*509/996-3906, 800/639-3809; www.freestoneinn.com*
*Rates: Expensive*
*FYI: Restaurant, complimentary breakfast (inn rooms only), back-packer lunches available; kitchens (lodges and cabins); swimming, mountain biking, fly-fishing, ice skating, cross-country skiing*

The area's newest lodge, Freestone Inn, is located two miles west of Mazama on what was formerly the Wilson Ranch. The lodge—the first phase in an ambitious development that will include a golf course and 450 private homes—opened in 1996. So far, the architecture of the resort does justice to the magnificent area: the lodge has a lovely river-rock fireplace in the "great room," and 12 beautifully outfitted rooms with stone fireplaces.

The best accommodations for families, though, are the two lakeside lodges and the cabins. Each attractive lodge has two or three bedrooms and a kitchen, and sits a short distance from the inn, right next to the lake. The six original Early Winter cabins, built in the 1940s, are more rustic (though tastefully refurbished), and less expensive. These range in size from studio to two-bedroom, have kitchens, and are a short walk from the inn and the lake.

The setting here is so scenic, one might be tempted to sit and gaze, but outdoor activities beckon year round. In the winter, there's cross-country skiing and snowshoeing right out the front door, and skating on Freestone Lake. In the summer, cross-country trails are ideal for biking, hiking, and horseback riding, and river rafting is available nearby. An outdoor hot tub between the lake and the inn gives aching bodies a lus-cious place to soak after an active day.

**JACK'S HUT** (509/996-2752) was established near the inn to serve as an outdoor resource center for guests of the Freestone Inn and visitors to the Methow Valley area. Jack's friendly staff of outdoor recreation specialists can outfit visi-tors for any type of activity with skis, skates, blades, bikes, and fishing poles, and arrange rafting, hiking, climbing, back-country, and horseback trips for all ages and abilities.

The restaurant at the Freestone Inn offers excellent Northwest cuisine (entrées include salmon and game birds), but is too elegant for a meal with the kids. If you're feeding the whole family, drive into Winthrop (15 minutes) or prepare a meal in your lodge or cabin.

**❝❝ PARENT COMMENTS**

*"It was expensive, but a huge treat for our family of four (two adults, one 13 year old and one 10 year old). Those of us who prefer to curl up with a good book rather than romp in the snow are sometimes stuck with an unattractive and uncomfortable place to relax—not so here! It was a lovely to sit by the fire, with a view of the frozen lake, and read while kids and spouse went cross-country skiing."*

**MAZAMA COUNTRY INN**
HCR 74 Box B9, Mazama 98833
509/996-2681, 800/843-7951; www.mazama.com
Rates: Moderate
FYI: Restaurant; kitchens (cabins); hot tub; cross-country skiing; mountain biking; tennis; pets OK (some cabins)

The tiny town of Mazama (one general store, one outdoor-clothing store) is 14 miles west of Winthrop. The Mazama Country Inn is a wonderful getaway in an idyllic location. Prices are reasonable and meals at the inn are well prepared. In the summer, there's tennis and mountain biking on the premises and horseback riding and hiking nearby. In the winter, cross-country trails begin at the front door. If you need a bigger thrill, a helicopter will whisk you off to a nearby peak to ski.

In the winter, children under 13 are not allowed at the Inn, but there are six cabins available for rent in the Mazama area, some as close as 200 yards, others as far away as six miles. All have kitchens. These cabins offer a range of conveniences and settings, and the innkeeper is very helpful in recommending a place suited to your needs.

During the winter, the Inn offers a variety of private residences (usually, these are summer homes) as accommodation;. many have welcome features such as washers and dryers.

### 66 PARENT COMMENTS

"We stole away to the Mazama Country Inn one weekend in the winter without the youngsters. When we walked into the lovely sitting room with the massive stone fireplace, we both heaved a big sigh and felt the tension of city life begin to slip away. It is a wonderful getaway—the atmosphere is informal yet attentive to your needs. We plan to return with the kids during the summer and rent a cabin on the premises."

"We rented a house that had three bedrooms, three baths, and a washer and dryer for the four of us (two adults and kids, ages 12 and 10). It was very simple in design but perfect; off by itself in the woods and very quiet. Mazama deserves high praise for being a family-friendly place to stay. They seem genuinely helpful to all ages. We rented skis, had a ski lesson, and got our cross-country trail passes all at the inn."

"Mazama is not a town. It is really more like the end of the road. But when you get there you are smack dab in paradise. In the winter, Hwy. 20 is closed. This means that all who come have put effort into the five hour drive over the passes and seem to be a hearty and kind breed of people. The cross-country ski trails (Methow Valley Community Trail system) are mostly easy trails that make a day with kids a joy."

### NORTH CASCADES BASE CAMP

255 Lost River Road, Mazama 98833
509/996-2334; www.methow.com\~roberts
Rates: Inexpensive to moderate
FYI: Meals included (breakfast only or all meals); ski trails, ice rink, playground, fishing pond; baby-sitting

The North Cascades Base Camp is 2.2 miles northwest of the Mazama Store, at the upper end of the Methow Valley.

Sue and Dick Roberts have established a welcoming and comfortable place for families to stay at a reasonable cost. Facilities in the lodge include six rooms, all with shared baths. A two-bedroom cabin that sleeps six is also available. (Two families of four can fit into the cabin reasonably well.) It's hard to get a reservation here in the winter—it's been discovered by families who love cross-country skiing in the Methow Valley. North Cascades Base Camp is closed in November.

The lodge also includes a children's playroom, a library, a cozy living room, and the dining room where meals are eaten together around big tables. Right outside the door are lawns, a hot tub, patios, and a sandbox play area (which turns into a skating rink in the winter). Guests can choose bed-and-breakfast or full board, which includes a delicious and healthy dinner in the evening, a hearty breakfast, and fixings for a packed lunch.

Parents themselves, the Roberts are welcoming to children. They have plenty of skates to lend in the winter, along with excellent advice on the cross-country trail system in the area. In the summer, there are swings, a playhouse, and a trout pond a short walk away. The Base Camp land borders the river; it's easily accessible, but not so close as to be a constant worry.

**❝ PARENT COMMENTS**

*"A perfect place for a family vacation to the "almost wilderness;" you get a bed, meals and all conveniences for a reasonable price. Kids are welcomed and enjoyed. We had no desire to get in our car during the four days we were there."*

*"The Roberts are very familiar with the area and offer excellent advice about hikes and cross-country skiing trails, with kids in mind."*

**RIVER RUN INN**
*27 Rader Road, Winthrop 98862*
*509/996-2173, 800/757-2709; www.riverrun-inn.com*
*Rates: Moderate*
*FYI: Kitchenettes (some units); microwaves/refrigerators; indoor swimming pool*

The River Run Inn is a smaller property one-half mile west of Winthrop—a motel with 11 new units overlooking the Methow River. The pleasant rooms have one or two beds, microwave and refrigerator (some have kitchenettes), and are nicely decorated with log furniture. The room that our parent reviewer stayed in had a queen bed, queen futon sofa, TV, refrigerator, and microwave. All rooms have decks or patios.

There's a large expanse of lawn between the motel and the river, with picnic tables, hammocks, and barbecues. Perhaps the nicest feature is the 30-foot free-form indoor pool, open year round.

Also available is a six-bedroom house with a queen bed in each bedroom, 4 1/2 bathrooms, full kitchen, living area, wood heat, and deck. There is also a two-bedroom cabin that sleeps two to seven people in two bedrooms and has a kitchen and two bathrooms.

A relatively new property, this motel is small but very comfortable. The location, less than a mile's walk into the town of Winthrop, is nice if you have older kids prone to cabin fever. There's less on-site here, in terms of recreational supplies and opportunities, than at some of the more "resort-like" accommodations in the area. But the popular outdoor activities (fishing, hiking, cross-country skiing, and biking trail systems) are easily accessible, and the motel owner is knowledgeable and helpful about options for outdoor fun. Many families will gladly forgo the convenience of "on-site recreation" for a lower room rate.

**66 PARENT COMMENTS**

*"This was a very peaceful place. The best part of the room was the patio leading to the grounds outside, where we sat and watched the river, walked down to the riverfront to collect rocks, and relaxed in the hammock."*

*"The pool was exceptionally nice for such a small motel and a huge hit after cross-country skiing all day."*

**SUN MOUNTAIN LODGE**
*P.O. Box 1000, Winthrop 98862*
*509/996-2211, 800/572-0493; www.sunmountainlodge.com*
*Rates: Expensive*
*FYI: Restaurants; refrigerators/microwaves (some units); two outdoor swimming pools; TV room (lodge); exercise room; pool tables, Ping Pong; boat, fishing rentals; horseback riding with lessons; tennis courts, hiking trail, mountain bike rentals, river rafting; ski trails, rentals, and lessons; sleigh rides, ice skating; organized activities for kids; baby-sitting*

This beautiful lodge, 12 miles from Winthrop, is set amid 3,000 acres on the top of Sun Mountain, with a spectacular view of the Methow Valley and surrounding Cascade Range. It offers a variety of accommodations, including 50 rooms in the main lodge and 28 rooms with refrigerators and fireplaces in the Gardner Building. The most spectacular rooms are in the new Mount Robinson building, with magnificent views, fireplaces, refrigerators and microwaves, private decks, and large sitting areas.

The lodge has seven fireplaces for informal gatherings and a charming library. A mile and a half down the road from the lodge, on Patterson Lake, Sun Mountain has 13 lakefront cabins with kitchens and fireplaces, each of which can accommodate four to six people.

Activities vary according to the season, and organized programs for kids are available upon request (24-hour notice). The swimming pools are located next to the main lodge and next to the Mount Robinson building. There are often movies. In summer, there are hiking trails, one-half to 2.5 miles in length; some are marked with placards that provide interesting nature information. Staff can guide you to other trails nearby, ranging from easy to technically challenging. Horseback riding, hayrides, and mountain-bike rentals are also available. Scenic and whitewater rafting are offered nearby.

In the winter, there is more than enough to keep the most active kids busy. Sun Mountain Lodge offers a highly-regarded ski school and rental shop (including kids' skis for ages two and up); 70 km of groomed trails begin right outside the lodge. Ice skating, and sleigh rides are other options. On Saturdays and holidays, Christmas through February, and during the summer months, parents can drop off kids (ages four to 10) at the Sun Mountaineers Program and enjoy time to themselves.

The main restaurant provides a breathtaking view of the Methow Valley, but the food has had mixed reviews and is quite expensive. The less formal cafeteria-style restaurant is a better choice when dining with the kids, or you can drive to nearby Twisp or Winthrop.

**❝ PARENT COMMENTS**

*"The setting is spectacular, and the activities are endless. If I could afford to, I'd spend all summer there."*

*"The most gorgeous resort in Washington state. It's hard to choose between a summer or winter visit—sleigh rides, ice skating, and cross-country skiing versus biking, horseback riding, and river rafting."*

*"The highlight for our kids was the horseback ride and the cowboy dinner—complete with Western music."*

*"It would be nice to see a special kids' menu in the dining room to cut the cost. The refrigerator in our room helped keep our food costs down because we bought yogurt and dry cereal in town and had breakfasts in the room."*

*"The Sun Mountaineer activities were great—nature walks, crafts, and games."*

### THE VIRGINIAN

*P.O. Box 237, Winthrop 98862*
*509/996-2535, 800/854-2834; www.methow.com\~virginian*
*Rates: Inexpensive to moderate*
*FYI: Restaurant; kitchens (some units); outdoor pool (seasonal); ski and bike trails; volleyball, basketball; pets OK (fee)*

The Virginian, located on Highway 20 just east of Winthrop, offers a variety of accommodations: cabins with small kitchens, eight-plexes with very large rooms, and a row of motel units with smaller rooms. The place is built of logs, which lends it a rustic, Western appeal. However, the rooms are new and modern. Two grocery stores are located right next door—a good place for kids to get treats.

The informal and friendly setting at The Virginian makes it an obvious choice for a family. Some cross-country ski trails begin behind the hotel and follow the Methow River; others begin across the street. In summer, the small outdoor pool gives relief from the heat.

### 66 PARENT COMMENTS

*"Our family goes to the Winthrop/Twisp area at least twice a year, and The Virginian is always the children's favorite place to stay."*

*"This is a great motel, but you aren't paying for a resort or inn and shouldn't expect one. It is located next to the main highway, right outside town. It's convenient, but doesn't give the feeling of getting away from it all. The accommodations are comfortable and reasonably priced, but the Methow is such a beautiful part of the state that the next time we come, we will stay in a place that offers a prettier setting."*

### WOLFRIDGE RESORT

*Rte. 2, Box 655, Winthrop 98862*
*509/996-2828, 800/237-2388; www.wolfridgeresort.com*
*Rates: Moderate to expensive*
*FYI: Kitchens (some units), refrigerators (all units), microwaves (some units); outdoor swimming pool; playground; ski and bike*

*trails; pets OK (fee)*

Located six miles northwest of Winthrop on Wolf Creek Road, this attractive resort is well suited to families. There is a variety of accommodations, varying in size from a hotel-style room to a complete cabin. The deluxe hotel room has a microwave and refrigerator; the one-bedroom suite, two-bedroom townhouse, and Wolf Hollow Cabin have full kitchens.

The 50-acre resort sits right on an extensive cross-country trail system. On the premises is a public warming hut for cross-country skiers, with a river-rock fire pit. Hot beverages and baked goods are served to skiers resting here.

**66 PARENT COMMENTS**

*"A great addition to the area. Very attractive "log- cabin" style and very comfortable."*

## PLACES TO EAT

### BOULDER CREEK DELI
*173 Riverside, Winthrop*
*509/996-3990*
*Hours: Lunch, dinner daily; closed Wed., Oct.-April*

This is the spot to pick when hunger strikes and you don't want to make a big production of feeding the family. With a selection of 15 specialty sandwiches, as well as homemade calzones, soups, chilis, and salads, each family member will find a satisfying meal here. Picky eaters can special-order a sandwich or salad; the young couple who runs this deli are happy to accommodate. There are three tables inside, or eat on the large deck in back, along the creek.

### DUCK BRAND CANTINA AND BAKERY
*248 Riverside Ave., Winthrop*
*509/996-2192*
*Hours: Breakfast, lunch, dinner daily*

The Duck Brand serves up plentiful helpings of pasta and Mexican dishes; big, thick sandwiches; and delicious fresh-baked goods. The food is both healthy and hearty. If your kids are young, expect to cart a doggie bag or two out of this spot.

### THE VIRGINIAN RESTAURANT
*808 N. Cascade Hwy., at the Virginian Inn, Winthrop*
*509/996-2535, 800/854-2834*

The Virginian is a nice place to stay in Winthrop, and the

restaurant here is a great place for families to eat. The atmosphere is casual, the food is excellent, and the prices are reasonable. If Dad usually saves up his red-meat points and spends them on an occasional steak, this might be the place to do it. The children's menu (for kids under 12) offers a choice of chicken, spaghetti, or fish, served with soup or salad. Ask for a table near the front, so the kids can be entertained by the action on the street.

## WHAT TO SEE & DO

**BIKING.** Mountain biking is almost as popular as cross-country skiing in this part of the state, and that is no surprise—the same extensive system of trails and logging roads that provide so many choice skiing options in the winter turn into biking routes when the snow melts.

*Methow Valley System Trail Association (for trail information). P.O. Box 147, Winthrop, 98862. 509/996-3287; 800/682-5787; mvsta@methow.com.*

**CROSS-COUNTRY SKIING.** Plan at least a two-night stay, so you can explore a trail or two on skis and experience other winter recreation options as well.

Operated by the **METHOW VALLEY SPORT TRAILS ASSOCIATION** (800/682-5787), this area boasts the second-longest system of cross-country trails in the United States. Six areas offer a variety of terrains and challenges for every skiing level: Mazama, Sun Mountain, Winthrop, Twisp, Loup Loup, and Rendezvous (featuring the European tradition of skiing from hut to hut). Huts are furnished with bunks, a woodstove, and a cookstove. They make a cozy place to warm up during the day, as well as a fun overnight stop.

The Mazama, Sun Mountain, and Rendezvous trail systems are connected by the *Methow Valley Community Trail*, a fairly flat 19-mile route through farmland and along the Methow River. The entire system includes some 200 miles of trails. Restrooms are available at all trailheads.

In Winthrop, you can buy tickets and maps, rent gear, and sign up for lessons at **WINTHROP MOUNTAIN SPORTS** (257 Riverside Ave.; 509/996-2886). In Mazama, the easiest place to get tickets and maps is **JACK'S HUT** (on Hwy. 20, next door to Freestone Inn; 509/996-2752).

*509/996-2148; 800/422-3048 (trail and hut information). Cost: daily pass, $14; half-day pass (after 1 p.m.), $11; 3-day* *pass, $33. Children under 12 ski free. (Proceeds go to Methow Valley Sports Trail Association (MVSTA), a nonprofit organization that maintains all of the trails.)*

**HIKING.** It's hard to imagine a better place to hike than the Methow Valley. There's the 1.7 million-acre Okanogan National Forest, which includes the Pasayten and Lake Chelan-Sawtooth Wildernesses. The western boundary of the forest borders North Cascades National Park and Ross Lake National Recreation Area (permits required if you stay overnight). To the south are Lake Chelan National Recreation Area and Wenatchee National Forest. To the north, in the Canadian Province of British Columbia, are Cathedral and Manning provincial parks.

You can choose between spectacular alpine trails bordered by 7,000-foot peaks or lush paths in the alpine valley. To take an overnight hike without the hassle of heavy packs, consider pack animals: **EARLY WINTERS OUTFITTING AND SADDLE COMPANY** (509/996-2659; 800/737-8750) offers trips with horses or, if llamas appeal, call **PASAYTEN LLAMA PACKING** (509/996-2326).

*For information, phone Methow Valley Visitor Center, at 509/996-4000, or Methow Valley Ranger Station, 509/997-2131.*

## *"Heads Up" When Hiking the Methow Valley*

■ Remember that much of the Methow Valley is open range; always give livestock the right-of-way.

■ Keep your eyes open for wild animals. There are rattlesnakes, bear, cougar, lynx, and other potentially dangerous critters in this region.

■ Don't rely on your cell phone throughout the county. In some areas, coverage is spotty or non-existent.

■ Learn to identify poison ivy, and watch for it.

■ Be sure you don't contribute to the spread of noxious weeds and milfoil. Check the underside of your vehicle and the propeller of your boat.

■ Report forest and range fires.

**HORSEBACK RIDING.** Horseback riding is big in the Methow Valley—after all, this is cowboy country. Day trips and extended pack trips are available (children must be at least six years old). On the overnights, you can cook for yourself or go luxury and have three meals prepared for you. For information, contact **EARLY WINTERS** (509/996-2659; 800/737-8750).

**RIVER RAFTING.** River rafting on the nearby Methow River, or farther away on the Columbia, is a wonderful way to enjoy the natural beauty while getting a good workout and having a great time. Outfitters restrict rafters to older children and adults. To pursue this particular delight, contact **OSPREY RIVER ADVENTURES** (509/997-4116).

**SKATING.** It's hard to imagine hanging out indoors during any season in Winthrop, but if the kids are looking for a great spot to skateboard or skate, try **THE SKATE BARN** (31 W. Chewuch Road; 509/996-3809; www.skatebarn.com). This fully equipped indoor skate park features a vert ramp, a six-foot mini-ramp, a five-foot fly box, several quarter pipes, and a huge suicide rail down an eight-foot start box (your kids can translate). There's also a rental shop and snack bar.

**SWIMMING.** Rivers in the Methow Valley tend to run swift and strong, especially in the spring when mountain runoff causes them to swell unpredictably. Older, river-wise youngsters might enjoy innertubing on the tamer sections of these rivers. For younger children, even wading should be closely supervised, and waders should wear life jackets at all times.

It's tough to find cool relief in this area on a hot afternoon. Families might enjoy a visit to **PATTERSON LAKE**, located just below Sun Mountain Lodge in Winthrop. Here, there's a public beach that offers good swimming and splashing for all ages.

**WINTHROP.** It may seem a little kitschy to the grown-ups, but kids will love this Western-style town, with its Old West storefronts and wooden walkways. You can take a leisurely stroll along "main street," checking out the stores as the spirit moves you. **VISITOR INFORMATION** (Hwy. 20 & Riverside Ave.; 509/9962125) and is one of the few places in town where you'll find a public restroom.

Across from Visitor Information, be sure to visit **SHERI' S SWEET SHOPPE** (207 Riverside Ave.; 509/996-3834), where the homemade ice cream alone is worth the trip over the mountains. They also have handmade chocolates, caramels, and fudge (kids can watch them pour the sweet confections into large metal trays to cool).

If your kids are at all interested in history, stop by the **SHAFER MUSEUM** (off Hwy. 20; 509/996-2712), open daily during the summer. There's a cabin built in 1897 by the town's founder, Guy Waring. (It was while visiting Waring in Winthrop in the early 1900s that Owen Wister gathered material for his novel, *The Virginian*.) Other period buildings include a print shop, a general store, a doctor's office, and a number of antique machines and appliances. There's a rare Rickenbacker car here, too—one of only 30 still in existence.

## CALENDAR

### MAY
Memorial Day Rodeo.
Packers Rendezvous and '49er Day Parade.

### JULY
Winthrop Rhythm and Blues Fest.

### AUGUST
Methow Music Festival, classical chamber music in the barns
  and meadows of Mazama.

### SEPTEMBER
Mule Days Rodeo.

## RESOURCES

### METHOW VALLEY CENTRAL RESERVATIONS
P.O. Box 505, Winthrop 98862
509/996-2148; 800/422-3048
Booking service for the entire valley.

### METHOW VALLEY SPORTS TRAIL ASSOCIATION
P.O. Box 327, Winthrop 98862
800/682-5787
Maintains and provides information regarding a vast system of cross-country trails.

### METHOW VALLEY VISITOR CENTER
509/996-4000

### WINTHROP CHAMBER OF COMMERCE
P.O. Box 39, Winthrop 98862
509/996-2125

## LAKE CHELAN

It is no surprise that Lake Chelan is one of the most popular family vacation spots in the state—the combination of fine weather, a lively little resort town, a beautiful lake, and access to some of the most spectacular wilderness in the country is nearly unbeatable.

It's not just Chamber of Commerce puffery that's established Lake Chelan as "a place in the sun." Whatever the weather may be west of the Cascades, it's a good bet that in spring, summer, and fall, your drive to Lake Chelan will be rewarded with sunny skies.

### GETTING THERE

From the Seattle area there are two main routes, each with a travel time of 3 1/2 to four hours.

The first route is via Stevens Pass. From Seattle, take I-5 north 27 miles to Exit 194 (Hwy. 2). Or take Hwy. 405, on the eastern side of Lake Washington, to connect with Highway 522 near Bothell. Follow 522 to the junction with Highway 2 at Monroe. Near Wenatchee, turn north on Highway 97 and follow it into Chelan.

The second route is over Snoqualmie Pass. From Seattle, take I-90 to Exit 85, near Cle Elum. Follow Hwy. 970, which merges with Hwy. 97 through Blewett Pass, and connects with Hwy. 2. Travel east on Hwy. 2, then north on Hwy. 97.

From Portland, take I-84 east along the Columbia River to meet Hwy. 97 at Biggs. Cross the Columbia River and follow Hwy. 97 north through Goldendale, Yakima, and Ellensburg. Continue over Blewett Pass to Hwy. 2. Travel east on Hwy. 2, then north on Hwy. 97.

**ROADSIDE ATTRACTIONS.** Both **STEVENS PASS** (I-90) and **SNOQUALMIE PASS** (Hwy. 2) are popular skiing developments with complete winter-sport facilities. At other times of the year, both areas offer good rest stops with trail walks, food service, and picnic spots.

If you take Hwy. 2, you'll pass through the Bavarian-style town of **LEAVENWORTH** (see "Leavenworth: What to See & Do").

Both routes merge just west of the town of Cashmere. This spic-and-span early American town celebrates apples and pioneers. A popular stop is the **APLETS & COTLETS CANDY KITCHEN** (509/782-2191) which offers continuous 15-minute tours and samples of their famous fruit-and-nut confections.

**REFUELING.** Several eateries along the way offer decent food, fast service and the possibility of an outdoor picnic.

If you're traveling I-90, exit at Cle Elum and drive through the main street of town. At the eastern outskirts, you'll find **MCKEAN'S QUICK STOP** (1011 E. First; 509/674-2254), purveyors of "the giant hamburger" and a number of other types of sandwiches. The **CLE ELUM BAKERY** (50 E. First; 509/674-2233) offers wonderful rolls, breads and breakfast muffins.

If you're on Hwy. 2, see the Leavenworth section for suggestions.

In the tiny town of Cashmere, 42 miles from Chelan, check out **RUSTY'S** (700 Cotlets; 509/782-2425), a classic burger-and-shake establishment the whole family can appreciate.

## PLACES TO STAY

Your choice of where to stay on Lake Chelan has a lot to do with how much peace and quiet you prefer. Generally, the farther uplake you go (away from the resort town of Chelan), the quieter it gets. Even if you stay uplake, though, the family will enjoy stopping into Chelan for a good meal out, a video rental, or a scenic stroll along the river.

### CAMPBELL'S
*104 W. Woodin Ave., Chelan 98816*
*509/682-2561, 800/553-8225; www.campbellsresort.com*
*Rates: Expensive*
*FYI: Restaurant, beach bar; kitchens (some units); fireplaces (some units); patios; two outdoor pools; beach, boat moorage*

Campbell's is the oldest establishment in Chelan (since 1901) and still a favorite of many vacationing families. There's no question it offers options, including 170 well-appointed guestrooms in five lodges. Situated on eight landscaped acres, Campbell's has two outdoor pools, 1,200 feet of beach and private boat moorage. All rooms have private patios and uplake views of the Cascades.

Campbell's location can be a plus or minus, depending upon your preferences. Located in the center of town, it is within walking distance of stores and restaurants and across the street from a scenic walkway that winds along the river. On the other hand, if you visit in summer, you will contend with scores of tourists seeking the same sun-and-water combination you are after.

**❝ PARENT COMMENTS**

*"It's fun to eat at the restaurant here, especially outside on the balcony, where you can watch all the activity on the street below. The food is good, but it's a bit pricey for everyday purposes. You can always get food at a nearby grocery store and picnic by the lake."*

### KELLY'S RESORT

*Rte. 1, P.O. Box 119, Chelan 98816*
*509/687-3220*
*Rates: Moderate to expensive*
*FYI: Kitchens; fireplaces; playground, swimming beach, boats; Ping Pong; pets OK (cabins); baby-sitting*

Operated by the Kelly family for more than 45 years, this is the kind of place where families return year after year and lifelong friendships are formed. Located 13 miles uplake from Chelan, Kelly's attracts a crowd that hopes to avoid the jet-ski atmosphere at the southern end of the lake. Summer reservations should be made at least six months in advance.

The pine-paneled cabins are located in the woods across the road from the lake, and there's a small playground nearby. Each cabin has a fireplace, deck, and full kitchen; larger cabins have a screened sleeping porch. There are also four lakeside units, all with full kitchens.

On the lakefront is a concrete-enclosed swimming area for younger kids and a roped swimming area and diving board for stronger swimmers. There's a little store in the office, and guests can borrow games and puzzles here.

Some of the accommodations are now open year round and offer a quiet, scenic place to stay while enjoying winter sports in the area.

**❝ PARENT COMMENTS**

*"We always take one night during our visit and drive five minutes to Lake Chelan State Park, play miniature golf, eat burgers at the drive-in across the street, and when it gets dark sit on the lawn and watch a movie and listen to a lecture about the geology of the area."*

*"It's a bit of a trek from the cabins down to the beach and store, including crossing a road, so you can't let young children run back and forth between the cabin and the beach."*

*"The beachfront units are lovely, but we were on the ground level and, even though my two-year-old wore a life jacket, I couldn't relax knowing he could be out the door and in the water so quickly."*

**WAPATO POINT**

*P.O. Box 426, Manson 98831*
*509/687-9511, 800/572-9531*
*Rates: Moderate to expensive*
*FYI: Restaurant, kitchens; indoor and outdoor swimming pools; tennis, basketball, miniature golf; two playgrounds; ice skating rink (seasonal); fishing; rentals: sports equipment, boats, bicycles, cross-country skis; organized activities for children; baby-sitting*

This is an extensive condo development located nine miles north of Chelan on a point of land that juts into the lake. The resort has two miles of private waterfront and well-designed indoor and outdoor swimming pools.

The condos all have different floor plans, although most have two floors. Units have kitchens with dishwashers, and each is equipped with a Weber grill. Organized activities for kids include arts-and-crafts and evening movies. During the winter, families can swim in the indoor pool, skate on the outdoor ice rink, and cross-country ski at the resort or at nearby Bear Mountain or Echo Valley.

The restaurant at Wapato Point has a good children's menu, good service, moderate prices, and better-than-average food.

**❝ PARENT COMMENTS**

*"We like to visit here in the late spring or early fall. The weather is not so hot, it is less crowded, and prices are lower."*

*"The one-bedroom unit we rented had a spiral staircase between living area and bedroom; not great for our toddler."*

*"For a family, I think this is a great place. It is completely furnished—all you need to bring is your food. And if you don't want to cook, the Wapato Café, at the entrance to Wapato Point, serves a good selection of favorites."*

*"There is a lot of room on the grounds of the resort for older kids to explore. Nearly all the visitors have families, so you have a real sense of safety and the children find playmates easily."*

## PLACES TO STAY

**DAGWOOD'S**

*246 W. Manson Way (in Chelan Plaza)*
*509/682-8630*
*Hours: Lunch , dinner daily (summer); lunch, dinner Mon.-Fri. (winter)*

This is a small restaurant, with soda-fountain seating and a few small tables. The menu tends toward the Asian, featuring a variety of stir-fry and vegetarian dishes and some excellent Thai choices. After your meal, cool your mouths off with ice cream, frozen yogurt, and other delectables.

### EL VAQUERO RESTAURANT
*75 W. Wapato Way, Manson*
*509/687-3179*
*Hours: Lunch, dinner daily*

About a ten-minute drive from Chelan, El Vaquero is a family-run business that serves down-home Mexican food. If you have a large family to feed, you'll love this place—the quantities are big and the prices are small!

### GOOCHI'S
*On E. Woodin, across from Campbell's Lodge*
*509/682-2561*
*Hours: Lunch, dinner*

When you long for a good fresh salad or a flavorful cup of soup, take a break at this casual restaurant around the corner from Riverfront Park. Kids who have overdosed on vacation fare of burgers and pizza will likely welcome the yummy pasta selections. Grown-ups can choose among several tempting dishes, including daily seafood and chicken specials, Chinese Joe's Special, and an oyster-loaf sandwich.

### YESTERDAY'S PIZZA & ICE CREAM PARLOR
*115 E. Woodin Ave.*
*509/682-4276*
*Hours: Lunch, dinner Mon.-Sat.*

This family oriented spot serves pizza, subs, and burgers, as well as old-fashioned ice cream treats. Order a coke and watch them concoct it with syrup and sparkling water, and serve it in an old-fashioned soda glass. If the kids require diversion, send them to the game room. Or, if the family's too pooped to leave the motel room, Yesterday's will deliver!

## WHAT TO SEE & DO

The friendly town of Chelan has more to offer families than fun in the sun. When you want a break from swimming and sunbathing, look into one of these other diversions.

### STROLL & BROWSE
**WOODIN AVENUE.** Along Woodin Avenue, Chelan's "Main

Street," you'll find restaurants, hardware stores, and the requisite tourist shops. This is the place to find whatever you've forgotten—from bathing suits and sunscreen to batteries and coolers. But there are also a couple of interesting historical stops along the avenue. Look for **ST. ANDREW'S EPISCOPAL CHURCH**, a little log structure at 120 E. Woodin. Designed by famed architect Stanford White, it's a beautiful example of vintage Northwest architecture. On the other side of the street is the historic **RUBY THEATRE** (135 E. Woodin; 509/682-5016), a building that will take mom and dad back to the "good old days." Best of all, it still plays movies, and first-run films at that!

**PARKS.** Two city parks provide access to various outdoor activities. The **DON MORSE MEMORIAL CITY PARK**, just past the Red Apple Market on Manson Highway, has an excellent swimming beach and good playground equipment, plus bumper boats, go-karts, and miniature golf. The **RIVERWALK PARK**, a grassy knoll that overlooks the river, is just a block off Woodin Avenue in downtown Chelan. At various times during the summer, the park is host to arts fairs and other community events.

**SLIDEWATERS.** One of the largest waterslide parks in the Northwest, Slidewaters offers nine major slides, a 60-person hot tub, a fabulous innertube river ride, and a large pool with slides and fountains for preschoolers. Though it's a popular spot, the waiting times are relatively short and visitors can enjoy a full day of sliding. Best of all, the staff-to-visitor ratio is high, and friendly employees give careful instructions to children before they zip down the slides. Parents can relax and have fun right alongside the small fry.

There is a snack bar inside, with limited selection; no other food or drink is allowed on the premises. Plan to feed the group before you go into the park, or budget some money for snacks.

Taking a whole family to Slidewaters can add up; prices are reduced after 5 p.m. (it's also less crowded then, and kids will appreciate more sliding and less waiting). Have a late lunch that day and go into town for pizza or Mexican food when the slides close at 8 p.m.

*102 Waterslide Dr. (off Hwy. 97A at southern end of town). 509/682-5751(summer); 206/821-1796 (winter). Open Memorial*

*Day-Labor Day, daily, 10 a.m.-8 p.m. (closes at 6 p.m. through mid-June). Cost: $13/adult, $10/child 3-7, free/under 3. Reduced cost (daily, 5 p.m.-8 p.m.): $10/adult, $7/child 3-7.*

### THE GREAT OUTDOORS

**BOATING.** Chances are that at some point you'll want to get out on the water. If you didn't bring your own boat, it's easy to rent one in Chelan. Motor boats, jet skis, fishing boats, Hobie cats, sailboards, canoes, rowboats, and paddle boats are available at one or both of these spots: **CHELAN BOAT RENTALS** (1210 W. Woodin Ave.; 509/682-4444) or **SHIP 'N SHORE DRIVE INN** (1230 W. Woodin Ave.; 509/682-5125).

**CROSS-COUNTRY SKIING.** If yours is a winter visit, Nordic skiing is available at nearby Bear Mountain. Although lack of snowfall can sometimes be a problem, there are 55 kilometers of trails as well as warming huts with picnic tables. The gently rolling terrain is good for beginners.
*Located 5 miles west of Chelan off Highway 97A; 509/682-5444.*

**HIKING.** The vast and varied wilderness that stretches out from the northern end of Lake Chelan is laced with hundreds of miles of trails that provide access to mountain glaciers, high country lakes, and alpine meadows. Including Wenatchee National Forest, the North Cascades National Park, Lake Chelan National Recreation Area, Okanogan National Forest, and Mount Baker-Snoqualmie National Forest, the best hiking terrain is uplake and accessible only by boat. For the visitor without a boat, the Lady of the Lake passenger boat will drop off and pick up campers and hikers, on request. For information about maps, trails, and guides in this region, contact: **CHELAN RANGER DISTRICT OFFICE** (428 W. Woodin Ave.; 509/682-2576).

### EXCURSIONS

**OHME GARDENS.** The whole family can enjoy a visit to these natural-style gardens, set on a rocky bluff overlooking the Columbia River and the Wenatchee Valley. The Ohme family developed this nine-acre showplace over a 50-year period; today, it's rated one of the outstanding gardens in the nation. Kids longing to stretch their legs after hours in the car will like exploring the stone pathways, a wishing well, numerous pools, and rustic shelters.
*Three miles north of Wenatchee on Hwy. 97A; 509/662-5785.*

*Open daily, April-Oct., 9 a.m.-7 p.m. (Memorial Day-Labor Day), 9 a.m.-6 p.m. (remainder of season). Cost: $6/adult, $3/youth 7-17, free/under 7.*

**ROCKY REACH DAM.** In the fish-ladder viewing room, you can observe at close range the salmon swimming upriver to return to their spawning grounds. There are also good geology exhibits and the story of electricity, complete with hands-on gadgets for kids to operate. With 15 acres of beautiful lawn and gardens and a good playground (not to mention a copse that's positively teeming with rabbits and guinea pigs), this is an ideal spot to picnic.

*Five miles north of Wenatchee on Hwy. 97A; 509/663-8121. Open daily, dawn-dusk. Free.*

## CALENDAR

**APRIL**
Salmon Derby.
**MAY**
Mountain Bike Festival.
**JULY**
Arts and Crafts Fair.
Chelan Rodeo.
Lake Chelan Bach Feste.

## RESOURCES

**CHAMBER OF COMMERCE**
P.O. Box 216, 102 E. Johnson, Chelan 98816
509/682-3503; 800/4-Chelan

## STEHEKIN

At the head of Lake Chelan sits the tiny community of Stehekin. Perched on the edge of magnificent North Cascades National Park, Stehekin is the starting point for the backpacking, mountain biking, boating, guided horseback, and fishing activities for which the area is renowned. The Park Service operates a $3 shuttle ride along the Stehekin River Road, linking the town with the joys of the national park. The lectures and guided nature walks provided by the Park Service are excellent.

## Getting There

Stehekin is accessible by boat or plane or on foot. For most people, experiencing the remote reaches of Lake Chelan means a scenic excursion on one of the locally run watercraft.

**By Boat.** The **Chelan Boat Company** has two passenger excursion boats: the 350-passenger *Lady of the Lake II* and the *Lady Express* provide round-trip service to Stehekin and the Lake Chelan Recreation Area. The dock is one mile south of Chelan on Hwy. 97, or you can board about 30 minutes later, uplake at Fields Point Landing. Both boats have snack bars and offer indoor and outdoor seating. No pets are allowed.

The *Lady of the Lake II* departs Chelan daily, May through mid-October, at 8:30 a.m., for the four-hour trip to Stehekin. The boat makes a 90-minute layover, then returns to Chelan by 6 p.m. Although it remains popular as a day trip, the ride can be tedious for kids. If you decide to do it in a day, pack the crayons, cards, and games.

The *Lady Express* is a smaller, faster boat. It departs daily at 8:30 a.m. and returns from Stehekin at 2 p.m. If you want more time in Stehekin, take the Express up the lake and return on the Lady of the Lake II (allowing a three-hour visit in Stehekin).

Reservations are not necessary for the *Lady of the Lake II* because of its large seating capacity; reservations are strongly advised for the *Lady Express*. The boats run less frequently during winter months; call for details.

*Lake Chelan Boat Company, P.O. Box 186, Chelan 98816. 509/682-2224. Cost: Lady of the Lake II round-trip, $21/adult, $10.50/child 6-11, free/under 6. Lady Express round-trip, $39/adult, $19.50/child, free/under 2 (mid-May-Sept.); $21/adult, $10.50/child 2-11 (Oct.-mid-May). It costs $38.50 round-trip to take the Express uplake and the Lady II back. Parking at the Boat Company parking lot is $4/day in Chelan or $3/day ($15/week) at Field's Point.*

**By Air.** For an unforgettable 30-minute ride from Chelan to the head of the lake, call **Chelan Airways**. Reservations are strongly recommended.

*P.O. Box W, Chelan; 509/682-5555. Call for schedule. Cost: round-trip, $100/adult, half-price/child 2-12, free/under 2.*

**By Foot.** The hike over the North Cascades into Stehekin is a wonderful two- or three-day hike for a family of reasonably fit walkers. For information, contact the **Chelan Ranger**

**DISTRICT OFFICE** (428 W. Woodin Ave.; 509/682-2576).

## PLACES TO STAY

### NORTH CASCADES LODGE

*Write: P.O. Box 457, Chelan 98816*
*509/682-4494*
*Rates: Moderate to expensive*
*FYI: Restaurant; kitchens; hot tub; fishing; bicycle, snowshoe, boat rentals*

The North Cascades Lodge is located down-valley (near the Stehekin dock). It isn't particularly fancy or imaginative, but the accommodations provide a "home base" for exploring the beautiful surroundings. There are lodge rooms and cabins; some units have housekeeping facilities. Maid service is prompt and the staff is friendly and helpful.

In winter, the lodge is open for cross-country skiing, which is excellent (average snowfall November to March is four feet), but during the off-season the boat goes up the lake only two or three times a week, so plan your trip carefully.

If you rent a housekeeping unit, be sure to bring your food with you, as groceries at Stehekin are limited. The restaurant at the lodge serves breakfast, lunch, and dinner.

**❝ PARENT COMMENTS**

*"Stehekin has a wonderful relaxed atmosphere. The Lodge isn't the focal point of the trip, but rather a starting point for some super wilderness experiences."*

*"We hiked into Stehekin from the western side of the mountains. Our party had five adults and seven kids, ranging in ages from nine to 16. We spent a night at the lodge, then took the boat down to Chelan where we had arranged to leave our cars. We all treasure the memories of that trip!"*

### SILVER BAY INN

*P.O. Box 43, Stehekin 98852*
*509/682-2212*
*Rates: Moderate; no credit cards*
*FYI: Continental breakfast; kitchens; woodstoves; bicycles, canoes, croquet*

No TV, no phone, and steps away from rugged wilderness—a vacation at the Silver Bay is a comfortable way to get away from it all. The Inn is heated by passive solar heat and sits on 700 feet of waterfront with a broad expanse of green lawn that stretches to the water. There are two lakeside cabins that can be rented by families (the main house is a B&B for adults only), as long as your children are eight or older. Both cabins have woodstoves, private decks, and a beach area, and come fully equipped with dishes and linens. Kitchens even have microwaves and dishwashers.

Kathy and Randle Dinwiddie are happy to suggest ways to explore the magnificent surroundings. The Inn will arrange transportation to and from Stehekin Landing for your arrival and departure.

**❝❝ PARENT COMMENTS**

*"The Inn and cabins are right on the lake. They are attractive and very comfortable. The setting is spectacular."*

**STEHEKIN VALLEY RANCH**
*P.O. Box 36, Stehekin 98852*
*509/682-4677*
*Rates: Inexpensive; no credit cards*
*FYI: Meals included; horseback riding; river rafting*

If roughing it in the boonies appeals to you, but you don't quite have the nerve or energy to take the kids on an overnight backpacking trip, you can compromise by staying in one of the 10 tent-cabins at this lovely ranch. Accommodations have concrete floors, wooden walls, and canvas roofs, and vary in size and number of beds. The cost includes transportation from the boat landing (nine miles), beds, a kerosene lamp, hot showers, and three meals a day in the outdoor dining room. The ranch is open summers only.

**❝❝ PARENT COMMENTS**

*"After a day in the saddle, we'd be ready for the huge, ranch-style meal they serve here. Meals are fun; everyone sits together at big, long tables and chows down. It's easy to get to know your fellow visitors. Oh, and be sure to try the pecan pie!"*

**PLACES TO EAT**

**STEHEKIN VALLEY RANCH**
*Nine miles outside Stehekin*
*509/682-4677*

If you're staying in Stehekin, you can give the family a fun trip and a hearty meal at the Stehekin Valley Ranch (also see "Places to Stay"). The ranch will provide van service out and back from town, or you can take a taxi. Dinner is served buffet-style, with a different entrée each night; hamburgers and steaks are always available as alternatives. Everything is cooked on a woodstove, including wonderful pie, and guests eat together at long log tables. The kitchen and dining room are covered, but with open-air walls and a view of the corrals and alfalfa fields. Coffee is available at the campfire. Kids are welcome, but there are no highchairs.

## WHAT TO SEE & DO

In the summer, good weather is almost guaranteed. The water is very cold for swimming, but horseback riding, hiking, and boating possibilities abound. The National Park Service offers many free programs, including slide shows, bus service to scenic points, and nature walks (some are designed with kids in mind—they are short, and include a stop at the one-room schoolhouse and apple juice at the Ranger's house).

If you seek larger-scale outdoor adventures, try **CASCADE CORRALS** (509/682-4677). Owned by the same family who owns Stehekin Valley Ranch, the company arranges horse-back riding and pack trips into surrounding wilderness areas.

In the winter, it gets very quiet in this remote part of the state, and the only way to explore is by ski or snowshoe. Boat service is limited, so plan your winter trip carefully.

Although there are myriad recreational opportunities here, many families come just to relax. It's an isolated spot, where parents and kids can get to know one another better, play old-fashioned board games, and enjoy the quiet.

## RESOURCES

### CHELAN RANGER STATION
509/682-2576
Information on hikes, mountain biking, and other activities in the area.

### LADY OF THE LAKE VACATION PLANNER
509/682-2224
Free information about Stehekin, accommodations, and tours.

### NATIONAL PARK SERVICE DISTRICT OFFICE
At the dock in Stehekin.
No phone service.
Information about routes and trail conditions.

## LEAVENWORTH

Parents who recoil from anything resembling a tourist trap might be inclined to put the pedal to the metal and move right on through this ersatz-Bavarian town, along Highway 2 on the eastern slope of the central Cascades. The fact is, though, that most kids love Leavenworth, and sacrifices are what parenting is all about, right? So strap on the lederhosen and dust off the accordion. We expect even parents will be pleasantly surprised at the fun they'll have in this colorful little town and the beautiful terrain surrounding it.

Once a booming mill and railroad town, Leavenworth made a successful transition to tourism in the early 60's. Believing the town's primary selling point to be its gorgeous alpine setting, boosters took advantage and pushed the point even farther by adding a Bavarian touch to virtually every structure (yes, even McDonald's has gone alpine).

Located just beyond the Seattle "rain zone," Leavenworth has a fine climate—cold, crisp winters and hot, dry summers, gloriously colorful autumns, and sweet alpine springs. The town is also exceedingly good at celebrating: there is at least one good festival to commemorate each of the seasons. With a festive, holiday atmosphere year round and easy accessibility to a wide assortment of outdoor activities, Leavenworth is one of the best family vacation spots in the Northwest.

### GETTING THERE

The direct route to Leavenworth from the western side of the mountains is via Stevens Pass, on Highway 2. An alternative route is to take I-90 over Snoqualmie Pass; then Exit 85 (near Cle Elum) to Highway 970 (which shortly becomes Hwy. 97) and over Blewett Pass. Highway 97 connects with Highway 2 just east of Leavenworth. Whichever route you choose, allow about 2 1/2 hours to make the trip.

**REFUELING.** If you travel via Stevens Pass, a good place to grab a bite is at the **BITTER CREEK BAKERY** (360/793-8867; 509 Main St.), a block off Highway 2 in Sultan. Salads, sandwiches, and cookies are all homemade and delicious.

**ROADSIDE ATTRACTIONS.** Both Stevens and Snoqualmie passes are popular winter-sports areas with complete facilities. At other times of the year, they offer limited food service, restrooms, and an opportunity to stretch legs.

## PLACES TO STAY

### ENZIAN MOTOR INN

*590 Hwy. 2, Leavenworth 98826*
*509/548-5269, 800/223-8511; www.enzianinn.com*
*Rates: Moderate to expensive*
*FYI: Complimentary breakfast buffet; fireplaces (some units); outdoor pool (May-Sept.), indoor pool; exercise facility; Ping Pong; racquetball, basketball, wallyball courts; golf; complimentary cross-country ski equipment; pets OK (some units, fee)*

Don't let the name fool you; this place is closer to a resort than a motel. From the generous complimentary breakfast buffet to the extensive recreational activities on the grounds, the Enzian is a fine place to settle in with kids.

The motel sits on the main highway, which is unfortunate given the spectacular natural setting of Leavenworth. On the other hand, though, it's just a short walk into the center of town, where restaurants and shops abound.

There are 104 units here, all with queen beds. Many rooms have sliding doors that close off the master bedroom from shared areas, making them ideal for families. The front lobby is large and comfortably furnished. The ample breakfast offers pastries, omelets, fruit, hot and cold cereal—perfect for kids, if not gourmet.

The new Enzian Falls championship putting course is nestled along the river, directly across the street from the Inn. It offers 18 holes of bent-grass greens—a nice outing for either the novice or the accomplished golfer.

**❝❝ PARENT COMMENTS**

*"The indoor pool is exquisite— large and very beautiful. The kids had a great time swimming and splashing in one part of the pool; my husband and I were in a whole different part. It was almost romantic!"*

*"We have a love/hate relationship with the Enzian because we stayed there longer than we expected when we were trapped in Leavenworth during a major winter storm. We were two families with a total of six kids, ranging in age from two to 14. We were frustrated not to make it to our destination, but the Enzian was a very comfortable, friendly place to be stuck. The free breakfast was hearty, and super-easy with the kids. We borrowed cross-country skis right at the motel, and the indoor sports courts and pool saved our sanity. With the snowy weather, we appreciated being able to walk to restaurants."*

### HAUS LORELEI INN
*347 Division St., 98826*
*509/548-5726, 800/514-8868; www.hauslorelei.com*
*Rates: Moderate to expensive*
*FYI: Complimentary breakfast; TV (common areas only); hot tub (adults only); sandy swimming area on river; tennis courts; sledding; pets sometimes OK (ask in advance)*

This is a rare find for families: a spacious, beautifully appointed B&B where children are truly welcome (except in the hot tub). Located on two acres overlooking the Icicle River, the inn feels secluded, though it is only a few blocks from the center of town.

Each of the six lovely rooms has a private bath; several are appropriate for families. A delicious homemade breakfast is served in a large, cheerful sunroom (complete with caged birds). Several common areas and two fireplaces give families room to move about without worrying about disturbing others.

**❝ PARENT COMMENTS**
*"We loved the River Room, which has gorgeous views from the master bedroom and two kids' alcoves adjoining the bath. The hosting family was really friendly toward our girls—they even loaned us a new-fangled sled to take to the sledding hill."*

### HAUS ROHRBACH PENSION
*12882 Ranger Road, Leavenworth 98826*
*509/548-7024, 800/548-4477; www.hausrohrbach.com*
*Rates: Moderate to expensive*
*FYI: Outdoor swimming pool (summer), hot tub; sledding hill (equipment available); game room; badminton, croquet*

This is a charming place, managed by friendly, helpful hosts who go out of their way to make kids feel welcome. A two-minute drive from downtown, the pension is located at the base of Tumwater Mountain and offers beautiful views of farms and pastures nestled in the valley. All in all, it has a very Tyrolian, Sound of Music feel to it.

Most of the rooms in the inn have private baths and balconies, and in fine weather the scrumptious breakfast can be enjoyed al fresco. But the real boons for families are the three suites, one in the main inn and two in a separate annex. Each has a king bed, gas fireplace, whirlpool tub, and private deck with a great view.

66 **PARENT COMMENTS**
> *"We had great fun at the sledding hill."*
> *"Our family enjoyed the Nordic custom of soaking in the hot tub, then rolling in the snow. The kids couldn't stop giggling."*

## MOUNTAIN SPRINGS LODGE
*19115 Chiwawa Loop, 98826*
*509/763-2713; www.mtsprings.com*
*Rates: Expensive*
*FYI: Kitchens (some units); woodstoves, free wood; outdoor hot tub; Jacuzzis (some units); VCR (videos on request); washer/dryer (some units); horseback riding; trout pond; cross country skiing; horse-drawn sleigh rides; snowmobile tours*

Mountain Springs Lodge is located on a homestead dating from the late 19th century. The main lodge—a remodel of the original farmhouse built of Douglas fir and ponderosa pine—offers cozy rooms, each with a private bath. But families are likely to be most comfortable in the guest lodges, which accommodate up to eight people and include a kitchen, washer/dryer, woodstove, sun deck, and private outdoor hot tub.

This is a wonderful place, owned and operated by a friendly, hospitable family. Located 20 minutes from Leavenworth, it offers a choice of secluded relaxation or in-town activity. For outdoor fun, there are acres of meadows and trails for skiing and hiking, a catch-and-release trout pond (bring your own pole), and guided tours on horseback.

66 **PARENT COMMENTS**
> *"A beautiful lodge in a gorgeous setting with top-notch hosts. The ideal mountain getaway!"*
> *"Our kids loved fishing, playing baseball and football on the playfield outside our front door, exploring wooded paths along the creek, and relaxing in our own hot tub after a long day."*

## NATAPOC LODGING
*12338 Bretz Road, Leavenworth 98826*
*509/763-3313, 888/NAT-APOC; www.natapoc.com*
*Rates: Expensive*
*FYI: Kitchens; fireplace or woodstove; hot tub (some houses); washer/dryer*

Natapoc consists of seven individual houses, each with two to five acres on the banks of the Wenatchee River about 15 miles northwest of Leavenworth (not far from Lake Wenatchee).

Each house (they call them lodges) is completely furnished and offers linen service and washer/dryer. The kitchens are spacious and fully equipped, with dishwashers, electric ranges, microwaves, small appliances, and dishes. The bedrooms are attractively decorated, with quilts and comforters.

Five lodges have their own hot springs hot tubs. All lodges have fireplaces, telephones, radio/cassette players, gas barbecues, TV/VCRs, and electric heat. The lodges range in size from Stuchin, which sleeps four snugly, to Mahsahwe, which accommodates up to 20 people (good for multiple families).

**❝ PARENT COMMENTS**
*"The Web site was very helpful in selecting the best lodge for our combined family."*

### SCOTTISH LAKES HIGH CAMP

*Write to:* High Country Adventures,
P.O. Box 2023, Snohomish 98291
425/844-2000, 888/9HI-CAMP; www.scottishlakes.com
*Rates: Inexpensive*
*FYI: Propane cooking stoves, dishes, cooking utensils, drinking water; evening snacks; hot tub (outdoor), sauna (indoor); wood-stoves; day lodge; fishing, hiking, cross-country and downhill skiing, snowboarding, snowshoeing, sledding*

The eight rustic cabins at Scottish Lakes, on the edge of the Alpine Lakes Wilderness, have neither electricity nor running water, but the gentle glow of kerosene lamps and the sweet taste of spring water are well suited to the pristine mountain setting. This place is about high-altitude cross-country skiing and snowshoeing in the winter, and hiking and scrambling during the summer months.

Scottish Lakes is a remote getaway, most appropriate for adventurous families. A private parking lot for guests is located just south of Highway 2, approximately halfway between Stevens Pass and Leavenworth. The scenic, eight-mile ride up the restricted Coulter Creek Road is provided by heated Sno-Cat or snowmobile; it takes as much as an hour to reach High Camp.

Our parent reviewers stayed in the Lupine cabin with their seven year old. They described the cabin as follows: "Two double bunk beds are at opposite walls with a woodstove between. Pillows are provided but you bring your own sleeping bag and towels. There's plenty of firewood under the beds. A small table with four chairs and two large kerosene lamps constitute the "sitting area." The "kitchen" has a taller table, with a two-burner stove (gas), dishes, and pots and pans. Two containers hold fresh drinking and cooking water. Guests bring their own food, and it must be stored carefully at night to avoid befriending the mice. All food must be brought by the guests and stored well at night, as the mice are busy checking your offerings. Lavatory options include standard outhouses and indoor composting toilets (clean and not smelly). With the woodstoves, kerosene lamps, and steep steps, the accommodations are not well suited to kids under five (except perhaps infants who are not yet mobile)."

Cross-country and telemark skiing are the main activities in winter, but High Camp also has snowshoes (in various sizes) and snowboards, both at no charge. Snowboarding is available on the relatively flat terrain in front of High Camp or on the steep slopes of nearby Wild Bill Hill. Downhill skiers can try the new two-mile intermediate run that starts at the top of Wild Bill Hill. A small day lodge is the setting for planning the next day's activities with staff and fellow guests, board games, and hot drinks.

Before booking your weekend, ask to see the Scottish Lakes calendar. A Winter Solstice Celebration includes torchlight skiing on Wild Bill Hill, information about full-moon weekends is provided for moonlight skiers, and Five Family Weekend Specials offer great deals for families (kids 5-14 free; kids 15-18 half-price).

66 **PARENT COMMENTS**

*"Scottish Lakes is wonderfully isolated and alpine. The new owners have done a wonderful job of continuing to run Scottish Lakes with the same philosophy as the founders, Bill and Peg Starks, legendary Northwest outdoors people who named most of the Enchantment lakes. In the winter, it is marvelous to ski the eight miles out and there are two excellent telemark hills en route. The sauna and hot tub are nice, but the true beauty lies in the wilderness and high altitude surroundings. This is a place for outdoor types to introduce their children to their particular outdoor passions. The chocolate mint on the bunks was a nice touch!"*

**SLEEPING LADY**
*7375 Icicle Road, Leavenworth 98826*
*509/548-6344, 800/574-2123;*
*http://www.sleepingladyresort.com/*

*Rates: Moderate to expensive*
*FYI: All meals included; outdoor pool (seasonal); sauna*

Sleeping Lady sits on 67 acres, just a few miles from Leavenworth. Its location—at the end of a back road, against the foot of a steep mountain range—gives it a delightfully isolated setting. So finely is the place attuned to its lovely surroundings that once you enter the grounds, the outside world is forgotten. Founder Harriet Bullitt is a long-time environmentalist, and her mission for Sleeping Lady is "...to provide a year-round retreat where nature, arts, outdoor recreation, and healthful dining inspire reverence for Earth's life-giving wellspring." (Don't let the lofty tone scare you off; although it's designed as a conference and retreat center, individual guests (including kids) are welcome.)

Everything at Sleeping Lady was built with the mission in mind, from the understated architecture, with its sophisticated heat-exchange system and decks and walkways made of Trex (a wood lookalike created from recycled plastic grocery bags and hardwood scraps) to the towels and sheets of unbleached cotton and the no-smoking policy. An organic garden supplies vegetables for the restaurant, where delicious, healthy food is serve buffet-style. Drought-tolerant plants native to eastern Washington are used for landscaping.

Most of the guestrooms are clustered in quadrangles of 10. They have minimal but tasteful furnishings, to encourage guests to get out and enjoy the natural surroundings or mingle with other guests in common areas. Many guests come to hike in the surrounding mountains or cross-country ski and snowshoe in the winter. Concerts and plays are presented year round in the theater on the grounds.

This place may seem a little pricey, but, considering that meals are included, a family will pay less than in a deluxe Seattle hotel (and the experience will be infinitely more relaxing). Reduced-rate, mid-week packages are available Sunday through Thursday in winter (except during the holiday season). These "Nordic Packages" include double-occupancy lodging, three meals, and a pass to ski the groomed Nordic trails or for the Stevens Pass cross-country trails on weekends. A similar downhill-ski package is available mid-week.

**❝ PARENT COMMENTS**

*"The weekend in May that we visited Sleeping Lady it was very quiet—if there were any conferences happening they were*

*small and low-key. The weather was gloriously hot and dry. Our room was tasteful but had no comfy chairs—if the weather had been wet we might have had serious cabin fever. Although Sleeping Lady does not bill itself as a "family resort," this was one of the easiest, most restful getaways we have had with our preschoolers. It helped enormously not to have to cook meals or even worry about which restaurant we were going to choose. We took one trip to Leavenworth but retreated quickly to this quiet oasis. The staff was very warm with our kids and the serenity and calm of the place put us all in a mellow mood. The beautiful swimming pool also helped."*

## PLACES TO EAT

### EDEL HAUS INN CAFÉ

*320 9th St.*
*509/548-4412*
*Hours: Lunch (seasonally), dinner daily*

Located in a classic old home overlooking the Wenatchee River (and the sledding hill), the Edel Haus serves fresh pasta, seafood, and several vegetarian entrées. The menu includes some traditional kid foods, such as hot dogs and half-portions of pasta, and there is a separate children's menu with such offerings as "oodles of noodles," cheeseburgers, and "smashed potatoes." Mom and dad might enjoy the chicken piccata or veggie lasagna, accompanied by a selection from the complete wine and beer list.

For a little extra privacy, request the "green room," which has three tables separate from the main dining area. In nice weather, meals are also served outdoors.

### THE GINGERBREAD FACTORY

*828 Commercial St.*
*509/548-6592*
*Hours: 7 a.m.-7 p.m. summer; 7 a.m.-6 p.m. winter*

This small, informal spot is a great place to enjoy a morning espresso, pick up deli foods for a picnic lunch, or relax with a drink and a sweet in the afternoon. Featured are authentic gingerbread cookies, assorted pastries, soups, and deli salads. If you like to browse, there are gingerbread houses and related utensils, books, cards, and tee-shirts. (The gingerbread houses are also sold by mail; ask for a catalogue.)

### KRISTALL'S RESTAURANT

*280 Hwy. 2*

*509/548-5267*
*Hours: Breakfast, lunch, dinner daily*

Kristall's is the quintessential "family" restaurant, with large, comfy booths and tolerant servers. The menu is extensive, with several selections just for kids; it's a rare child who won't find something to love. If you arrive with hungry, impatient little ones, order the cheese bread while you peruse the menu. Our reviewers found the food good, the service fast, and the server willing to split orders or adapt combinations to suit everyone's tastes.

### LOS CAMPEROS
*8th & The Alley*
*509/548-3314*
*Hours: Lunch, dinner daily*

It may seem somewhat out of place to be enjoying a Margarita and nachos in the midst of a Bavarian village, but after a few meals of wiener schnitzel, the kids (and perhaps the grown-ups as well) will be overjoyed to dine on tacos and fajitas. Service is kid-friendly and prices are reasonable. Be prepared for a wait on busy weekends.

### THE SOUP CELLAR
*725 Front St.*
*509/548-6300*
*Hours: Lunch, dinner daily*

For a quick, cafeteria-style meal, duck downstairs to The Soup Cellar, featuring a variety of sandwiches, salads, and soups (billed as the "home of famous white chili"). The décor features family-sized booths, spill-proof tablecloths, and a collection of dollar bills that paper the beams and provide quite a conversation piece!

### WHAT TO SEE & DO

Regardless of the season, the Leavenworth area offers an array of outdoor activities and beautiful scenery. In winter, it can be a wonderland or slushville, depending on the temperature. But don't let moderate temperatures stop you—a short drive will usually net a decent ski or sledding area. In summer, the weather tends to be hot and dry. When you've had enough of the great outdoors, you can always browse the shops and let kids ponder how to spend their souvenir money.

## STROLL & BROWSE

**AROUND TOWN.** Leavenworth is a small town, and the shopping district is contained within a few square blocks. Kids (and grown-ups) who delight in itty-bitty trinkets, holiday decorations, music boxes, and nutcrackers will be overjoyed. The less enthusiastic can be sent off for lemonade or hot chocolate and diverted to one of the several public benches for some people-watching. The shopping is unusually kid-friendly, with several toy and candy stores, a great hat shop, and at least two large, well-situated public restrooms.

Browsing works well here, because the shopping area is so small. **DIE MUSIK BOX** (837 Front St.) displays more than 2,500 music boxes from around the world and is a "must stop" (yes, they're breakable, but there are lots of clerks to help parents control those little hands). If you have an aspiring train engineer, stop by **THE TRAIN SHOP** (636 Front St., in Alpenhoff Mall). It has toy trains, drawings, and railroad memorabilia. For a great assortment of wooden toys, try **THE WOOD SHOP** (719 Front St.) and for teeny-tiny miniatures and dollhouse furniture stop by **ALPEN HAUS** (807 Front St., downstairs). **ROCKY MOUNTAIN CHOCOLATE FACTORY** (636 Front St., in the Brewery Building) is another popular stop for youngsters. Watch candy makers hand-fashion chocolates and try a sample of their yummy fudge.

**ICICLE JUNCTION.** You'll spot this amusement center on your right just as you drive into town from the west, so if you want to avoid being pestered by the kids, divert their attention to the other side of the street until you are safely past. It has a miniature-train ride, bumper boats, remote-control boats, and a miniature golf course.

*Hwy. 2 & Icicle Road, behind the Icicle Inn. 888/462-4242.*

**NUTCRACKER MUSEUM.** It's up a steep set of stairs, and there's a small admission fee, but how many times in your life will you get the chance to see 3,000 different nutcrackers and a video about nutcrackers to top it off? It's also a nice way to start your child thinking about collections in general.

*735 Front St. 509/548-6525; 800/272-9775. Open daily, 2-5 p.m. (closed weekdays Nov.-April). Cost: $2.50/person.*

### THE GREAT OUTDOORS

Internationally renowned skiing, hiking, fishing, and camping are right outside your door (or nearly so) in the Leavenworth area. Leavenworth Ranger Station (509/548-6977) and Lake Wenatchee Ranger Station (509/763-3103) can provide information on outdoor recreation, Sno-park permits, and trailhead permits. The Leavenworth station is also in charge of the Enchantment Wilderness Permit system (restricted overnight permits required June 15 until October 15).

**CROSS-COUNTRY SKIING** in Leavenworth is available on several trails designed specifically for families and beginning skiers. The 8-km *Icicle River Trail* meanders gently along the Icicle River and offers beautiful scenery and occasional glimpses of wildlife. At the Leavenworth Golf Course, skiers will find 12 km of groomed trails on gently rolling terrain, with breathtaking views of the Wenatchee River and Cascade Mountains.

For information about trails, conditions, and fees, or about Ski for Health Day, an annual cross-country ski event for families, call the **LEAVENWORTH WINTER SPORTS CLUB** (509/548-5115). There are several places in town to rent skis.

To get to either of the trails, drive west on Highway 2 and turn left onto Icicle Road (western end of town). The golf course is one-half mile on your left; the Icicle River Trail is two miles farther (there is a small parking area).

If you want to go up to Stevens Pass to cross-country ski, you'll find the **NORDIC SKI CENTER** five miles east of Stevens Pass Summit on Highway 2. It has 25 km of tracked trails, including a skating lane, along with rental equipment, lessons, and restrooms.

*Located 5 miles east of Stevens Pass Ski Area on Hwy. 2. 360/973-2441. Open Fri.-Sun./holidays, 9 a.m.-4 p.m. Cost: $7.50/adult.*

**DOWNHILL SKIING.** If you're just trying out the sport, check out the **LEAVENWORTH SKI HILL**, located at the top of Ski Hill Drive. It features an alpine ski area with rope tows and a light cross-country ski course.

If you're a more serious enthusiast, check out the **STEVENS PASS SKI AREA**, just 38 miles from Leavenworth. Always a popular area for families and intermediate skiers, Stevens Pass has now opened the "backside," with nearly 400 acres of new terrain, much of it advanced. Seven lifts are lighted for night skiing, seven nights a week.

At 4,200 feet, Stevens Pass has always enjoyed good snowfall. Its recently increased popularity stems from road improvements on Highway 2 and ski lift improvements by new owners, Harbor Properties. Ski schools are offered for skiers of all abilities. The Kid Zone, housed in the Pacific Crest Lodge (formerly the East Lodge) is a licensed childcare facility for kids three months and older. Indoor and outdoor activities are offered and lunch is available. Reservations are required for children under three (and recommended for others).

*On Hwy. 2, 38 miles west of Leavenworth. 360/973-2441; 206/812-4510. Open daily, 9 a.m.-10 p.m. Cost: Lift, weekend/holiday, $30-$35/adult 13-61, $21-$24/ child 7-12, $23-23/senior 62-69, $5/ under 7 and over 70. Weekdays, $18-$25/adult, $18-$24/child. First-time deal: Lesson, rentals and Daisy (beginner chair) lift ticket, $34-$42. Kid Zone: open daily (7 days/wk), 8:30 a.m.-5:30 p.m. Cost: $45/full day (3-8 hrs.), $25/3 hours.*

**HIKING.** A list of relatively short, easy hikes in the Leavenworth Ranger District is available from the Chamber of Commerce (Hwy. 2 & Sherbourne St.; 509/548-5807). If hiking companions are short-legged, don't miss the easy and scenic *Waterfront Park Interpretive Trail*, with two bridges and interpretive and historical signage, along the Wenatchee River in downtown Leavenworth.

The 1.5-mile *Old Pipeline Bed/Tumwater Canyon Trail* affords views of the cascading Tumwater River and access to small, sandy beaches perfect for wading. Drive 1.7 miles west on Highway 2 and turn left at the public fishing/picnic area. Cross the old footbridge and hike upstream.

For more ambitious family hikes, check out *Best Hikes with Children in Western Washington* (see "Resources").

**HORSEBACK RIDING/HAY RIDES.** Several stables around Leavenworth offer trail rides, from an hour to a half-day, as well as "high-country" pack trips, sleigh rides, and hay rides. The minimum age is usually six. To investigate these options, call **MOUNTAIN SPRINGS LODGE** (800/858-2276), **EAGLE CREEK RANCH** (800/221-7433), **ICICLE OUTFITTERS** (509/763-3647), or **RED TAIL CANYON FARM** (800/678-4512).

**RIVER RAFTING.** Some of Washington's most thrilling white-water rafting tours start at Leavenworth and take enthusiasts down the Wenatchee River (spring and early summer). Although most companies don't recommend (or permit) rafting for children under 10, older children just might have the ride of their lives. A list of river runners and outfitters is available from the Chamber of Commerce (Hwy. 2 & Sherbourne St.; 509/548-5807).

**SLED DOGS.** Rides and lessons are available in the Leavenworth area for those who want the experience of flying across the snow behind a pack of man's best friends. Half- and full-day tours are available, as well as custom tours for groups and overnight tours. In Leavenworth, try **ALASKA DREAMIN' SLED DOG COMPANY** (20103 Chiwawa Loop Road; 509/763-8017). Another company, **ENCHANTED MOUNTAIN TOURS** (P.O. Box 768, 98284; 800/521-1694) operates out of Sedro-Woolley.

**SLEDDING.** As long as snow is on the ground, you'll find kids sledding on a small but steep hill, on Front Street in the middle of town. There are several restaurants located within a few hundred feet of the hill, so if you are going to dinner and it looks like you might have a wait at the restaurant, bring along a sled so the kids can slide while you wait to be seated.

If you're up for a drive, the summer parking area at **LAKE WENATCHEE STATE PARK** is converted into a sledding hill during the winter. It's a nice tame slope, perfect for young kids (see "Excursions: Lake Wenatchee State Park").

If you are looking for bigger thrills, check out **STEVENS PASS TUBE CITY** at Stevens Pass Ski Area, where inner tubers enjoy a vertical drop of 80 feet and a horizontal run of 500 feet (and a tow to bring them back up the hill). Visitors must use the tubes provided: no personal sledding devices are allowed. Children must be three years old or taller than 42 inches to tube here.

*Stevens Pass Ski Area. 206/812-4510. Open Sat.-Sun., 10 a.m.-4 p.m. Cost: $8 includes tube rental.*

**SLEIGH RIDES.** Old-fashioned sleigh rides are a wintertime tradition in and around Leavenworth. Most go over pastures and through woods for 45–60 minutes, stopping along the way for a campfire and hot cider. Others return to a lodge area for a warm-up following the ride. Reservations are recommended.

Sleigh rides are offered by **EAGLE CREEK RANCH** (509/548-7798; 800/221-7433) and **RED TAIL CANYON FARMS** (509/548-4512; 800/678-4512).

## Keep Safety in Mind While Sledding

Sledding is great, inexpensive family fun, but keep in mind the following safety tips:

■ To minimize risk, choose a moderate slope with a run-out that flattens, with no trees or obstacles.

■ To reduce the risk of spinal injuries, use inner tubes rather than saucers or other hard-sliding devices.

■ Resist the temptation to pig-pile onto the inner tubes—only one person should ride at a time.

**SWIMMING.** Right in town, at Waterfront Park, there's a pleasant sandy beach for dipping in the cool waters of the Wenatchee River. Lake Wenatchee State Park (20 minutes west of Leavenworth) has a large swimming beach.

There's also a public pool at Lion's Club Park, on Highway 2 across from the main business district.

### EXCURSIONS

**LAKE WENATCHEE STATE PARK** has a very popular campsite and a pleasant—although often windy—public swimming beach. In winter, the area offers a maze of groomed Nordic trails and a popular sledding hill (at Nason Creek Campground).

*Located 20 miles northwest of Leavenworth (take Hwy. 2 west to Rte. 207 and head north, watching for park signs).*

**LEAVENWORTH NATIONAL FISH HATCHERY.** Established in 1940 to help preserve salmon in the Columbia River following construction of the Grand Coulee Dam, the hatchery features exhibits identifying the fish and describing their habitats and environmental needs. Pick up a trail guide and walk the one-mile interpretive trail that describes the history, environment, and wildlife of the area.

*Turn south from Hwy. 2 onto Icicle Road (west end of town) and continue 1.5 miles. Turn left at the sign. 509/548-7641. Open daily, 8 a.m.-4 p.m. Free.*

**LEAVENWORTH SNOW TRAIN.** These festive train trips offer a full day of fun during the first two weekends in December. In the morning, the train winds over the mountains from Seattle to Leavenworth, with a continental breakfast and entertainment by an OomPah band. On the return trip, dinner is served.

The trips are scheduled to coincide with holiday happenings in Leavenworth, including the Christmas Lighting Festival.

*Alki Tours. 800/895-2554. Trains depart Seattle at 8 a.m. and return about 10 p.m. (with additional stops in Edmonds and Everett). Cost: $119/person.*

**OHME GARDENS COUNTY PARK** includes nine acres of lush, mountain beauty on a rocky bluff overlooking the Wenatchee Valley (a 35-minute drive from Leavenworth). For details, see "Lake Chelan: Excursions."

**ROCKY REACH DAM.** When weather permits, this dam (five miles north of Wenatchee) makes an interesting outing. For details, see "Lake Chelan: Excursions."

## CALENDAR

**JANUARY**
Great Bavarian Ice Fest.
**MAY**
Maifest.
**JUNE**
Kinderfest: All for kids!
International Folk Dance Festival.
**SEPTEMBER**
Washington State Autumn Leaf Festival.
Leavenworth International Accordion Celebration.
**OCTOBER**
Wenatchee River Salmon Festival.
**DECEMBER**
Christmas Tree Lighting Festival.

## RESOURCES

**LEAVENWORTH CHAMBER OF COMMERCE**
Hwy. 2 & Sherbourne St., P.O. Box 327, Leavenworth  98826
509/548-5807; www.leavenworth.org

**LAKE WENATCHEE STATE PARK**
509/763-3101

**LEAVENWORTH RANGER DISTRICT**
509/548-6977

**LEAVENWORTH WINTER SPORTS CLUB**
P.O. Box 573, Leavenworth 98826
509/548-5115

**LINK** (509/662-1155; 800/851-LINK) is a free transit system serving Chelan and Douglas counties. Buses operate 6 a.m.-8 p.m. weekdays and 8 a.m.-8 p.m. Saturdays.

## CLE ELUM/ELLENSBURG

Cle Elum and Ellensburg are located in the eastern foothills of the Cascades. Cle Elum is gateway to a vast recreational area that encompasses two national forests and affords opportunities for the full range of outdoor activities, including fishing, camping, boating, horseback riding, bicycling, hiking, and skiing. Ellensburg is a charming Western town that successfully mixes college and cowboy ambiance. Cattle ranching prevails here, and area "dude" ranches are popular with families.

### GETTING THERE

Cle Elum and Ellensburg are located along I-90, approximately 82 miles and 102 miles east of Seattle, respectively.

**ROADSIDE ATTRACTIONS.** For more information about stops along the way, see "Snoqualmie Pass: What to See & Do."

### PLACES TO STAY

**HIDDEN VALLEY GUEST RANCH**
*3942 Hidden Valley Road, Cle Elum 98922*
*509/857-2344, 800/526-9269; www.ranchweb.com/hiddenvalley*
*Rates: Moderate to expensive*
*FYI: Meals and snacks included; outdoor pool; recreation room (books, piano, Ping Pong); sport court; horseback riding, hiking trails, cross-country skiing trails and instruction, fishing*

Hidden Valley is quite a spread—800 acres of field, river and gently rolling hills. The ranch house sits atop a hill, with a gorgeous vista from any side of the wraparound porch. There are hammocks for dreaming in, friendly ranch cats, and a ranch dog.

Cabins here are best described as "comfortably rustic"—all have propane heat and showers. Floor plans vary, so ask the manager to recommend the right accommodation for your group. Rates include hearty meals and all facilities and activities except trail rides, hay rides, and a few special services.

The trail-riding program is exceptionally good here. Children must be six years old and accompanied by an adult. Younger children seeking a thrill can be led around the corral on horseback. (Bring your own helmets.) The cost is $32.50 for a 90-minute ride. Trail rides are offered several times a day; childcare for ages two to five is available during the 9 a.m. ride.

Other outdoor activities include a heated outdoor pool and fishing in Swauk Creek. In the winter, the ranch offers Nordic skiing weekends, with skiing on the fields, meadows, and trails of the ranch or at nearby Blewett Pass.

During the high season (May through mid-Oct.), there is a two-night minimum. During the off-season the ranch operates as a B&B and is open weekends and certain holidays only.

**❝ PARENT COMMENTS**

*"Visiting here is like stumbling onto the set of a John Wayne movie."*

*"We like to visit in the spring. The days are sunny, and the hills are green and inviting."*

*"Our children were charmed. They loved watching the wranglers work the horses in the corral and feeding the horses apples through the fences. After dark, we had star-filled chats around the outdoor fireplace. Bring a star chart!"*

*"Except the space heater in the cabin, the rooms were fairly childproof. We left the heater off when our toddler was in the room."*

**STEWART LODGE**
*805 W. 1st St., Cle Elum 98922*
*509/674-4548*
*Rates: Inexpensive*
*Essentials: Refrigerators (some rooms); outdoor heated pool (seasonal); small pets OK*

If you're looking for a basic motel to serve as your home base so you can explore the great outdoors in this part of the state, the Stewart Lodge does the job. Located at the western end of Cle Elum, the lodge is a two-story building with outside corridors. Rooms have an attractive country motif.

**❝ PARENT COMMENTS**

*"We spent a night here when we came over from Seattle to*

*raft the Yakima River. It was very hot and the outdoor pool was a nice bonus."*

## PLACES TO EAT

### CLE ELUM BAKERY
*1st & Peoh, Cle Elum*
*509/674-2233*
*Hours: Mon.-Sat., 7:30 a.m.-5:30 p.m.*

At this local institution, they bake a variety of delectables in brick-hearth ovens. The kids will love their old-fashioned cake doughnuts.

### THE VALLEY CAFÉ
*105 W. 3rd St., Ellensburg*
*509/925-3050*
*Hours: Lunch, dinner daily; breakfast Sat.-Sun.*

Even if you are just passing through, it's worth taking the time to stop at this attractive restaurant. Here the salads are fresh and reasonably priced, and the sandwiches are hearty and delicious. Breakfast and dinner selections are also interesting and nicely prepared. If you don't have time for a full meal, pick up a picnic at the take-out counter next door.

## WHAT TO SEE & DO

### STROLL & BROWSE

**DICK AND JANE'S DRIVE-BY ART.** Give the family material for a lengthy car discussion by driving them past this remarkable "yard art." Even the preschooler will be impressed by 20,000 bottle caps, 15,000 bike reflectors, and tons of other random items assembled in what the creators describe as their attempt to "encourage peace through art."
*101 N. Pearl St, Ellensburg. 509/925-3224.*

**DOWNTOWN ELLENSBURG.** A walk around Ellensburg's downtown historic district (rebuilt of stone and brick following a fire in 1889) will give kids a chance to see *The Cowboy*, a sculpture by Dan Klennard—a lanky cowboy who stands with his six-guns at his side (corner of 5th Ave. & Pearl). While you're on Pearl Street, don't miss the droll *Ellensburg Bull* sculpture by Richard Beyer (this well-known doggie lounges on a bench, cowboy hat in lap). At **WINEGAR FAMILY DAIRY** (7th & Main; 509/933-1821), you can treat the kids to ice cream fresh from the farm. Parents will enjoy the eclectic mix of cowboy and espresso that characterizes this historic part of town.

### PARKS

**GINKGO PETRIFIED FOREST STATE PARK** is located close to the geographic center of the state, near the small town of Vantage. One of the most unusual fossil forests in the world is located here, in what was once a region of lakes and swamps (some 15–20 million years ago). The Heritage Center, which houses the park's Interpretive Center, has more than 50 varieties of petrified wood on display. There is also a .75-mile interpretive trail that follows an exposed prehistoric lakebed and a half-mile hiking trail through the sagebrush terrain.

*Located where I-90 crosses the Columbia River, near Vantage. Heritage Center open daily (May-Sept.), 10 a.m.-6 p.m. Free.*

**OLMSTEAD PLACE STATE PARK** is a heritage site celebrating the legacy of the family farm. The park includes the homestead of Sarah and Samuel Olmstead, who crossed the Cascade Mountains on horseback with their young family and settled here in 1875. In 1908, a red barn was constructed and a new residence was built. The Seaton Cabin Schoolhouse, built in the 1870s, was reconstructed at Olmstead Place in 1980.

*Located 4.5 miles southeast of Ellensburg at I-90 & Squaw Creek Trail Road. 509/925-1943. Free.*

### MUSEUMS

**CLE ELUM HISTORICAL TELEPHONE MUSEUM.** Perhaps not surprisingly, this is the only telephone museum west of the Mississippi. Kids who think nothing of a car phone will be interested in seeing the 1901 switchboard and collection of old, crank-style telephones on display here.

*221 E. 1st St, Cle Elum. 509/674-5702. Open Sat.-Mon., noon-4 p.m. Admission by donation.*

**THE CLYMER MUSEUM & GALLERY** in historic downtown Ellensburg features the work of Western artist John Clymer, known for the storytelling quality and fine detail of his work. Parents may recognize some of the 80 Saturday Evening Post covers on display, drawn by Clymer.

*416 N. Pearl St. 509/962-6416. Open Mon.-Fri., 10 a.m.-5 p.m., Sat.-Sun., noon-5 p.m. Free.*

**ELLENSBURG CHILDREN'S ACTIVITY MUSEUM** features a mini-city with bank, post office, and other important stops. Special events for children are staged throughout the year.

*400 N. Main. 509/925-6789. Open Wed.-Fri., 10 a.m.-3 p.m., Sat., 10 a.m.-4 p.m., Sun., 1-4 p.m. Cost: $2.50/person.*

**KITTITAS COUNTY HISTORICAL SOCIETY MUSEUM.** It's tough to get kids interested in history when there are horses to be ridden, but pick a rainy day and check out this museum. Housed in a building that dates from 1889, the museum has a display for everyone, including Native American artifacts, pioneer tools, dolls, petrified wood, rocks, and minerals.

*114 E. 3rd St., Ellensburg. 509/925-3778. Mon.-Sat., 10 a.m.-4 p.m. (May-Sept.); Tues.-Sat., 11 a.m.-3 p.m. (remainder of year). Admission by donation.*

### ANIMALS, ANIMALS

**CHIMPOSIUMS.** Central Washington University's Chimpanzee & Human Communication Institute offers one-hour, educational workshops showcasing their world-renowned signing chimpanzees. Located on the CWU campus in Ellensburg, the Institute is designed to facilitate research on primate communication. Washoe and four other signing chimps, who have acquired extensive American Sign Language vocabularies, are fascinating to behold. Visitors learn about the research being done at the Institute and observe the chimps conversing with one another and with their human teachers.

*Corner of Nicholson Blvd. & "D" St. 509/963-2244; www.cwu.edu/~cwuchci. Workshops Sat., 9:15 a.m. & 10:45 a.m., Sun. 12:30 & 2 p.m. Cost: $10/adult 18 & over, $7.50/under 18 & student.*

The **ELLENSBURG RODEO**, rated one of the top ten rodeos in the country, has been an annual event every Labor Day weekend since 1923. The **KITTITAS COUNTY FAIR** takes place on the same wild weekend, so Ellensburg is jam-packed with tourists and entertainment. Lodging and tickets go quickly, so make your plans early.

Every kid should see wild bronco riding and the magic of cow roping at least once, but you can opt for the Saturday-night rodeos in July and August instead of the huge Labor Day extravaganza. They are much smaller versions, but give families a chance to experience the thrill of the rodeo without the crowds and expense of the major event. (For information, phone the Chamber of Commerce, 509/925-3137.)

*Ellensburg Rodeo Arena, at Kittitas County Fairgrounds. Labor Day weekend. 509/962-7831, 800/637-2444. Cost: $10-$18/seat, family ticket (two adults & two children under 12) for Fri. & Mon. rodeos: $39.*

### THE GREAT OUTDOORS

**CROSS-COUNTRY SKIING.** Trails in Iron Horse State Park once used as railroad tracks are now used as paths for cross-country skiing and snow shoeing. The *John Wayne Pioneer Trail* winds through the forests of Easton to the rolling farm-land of the Upper Yakima River Valley. The Forest Service (803 W. 2nd St., Cle Elum; 509/674-4411;) provides maps of other ski trails in the area, as well as SnoPark permits.

*At the foot of 4th St., Cle Elum. 509/656-2230.*

**ELK FEEDING.** After the snow is deep enough to cover nat-ural forage, the Department of Wildlife feeds some 750 elk a day at Joe Watt Canyon, 15 miles northwest of Ellensburg. Be there by 8 a.m. to see these spectacular animals. Dress warmly!

*From Ellensburg travel west on I-90 to the Thorp Exit 102. Proceed left over the freeway approximately .25 mile to the top of the hill. Go right on Old Thorp Cemetery Road and continue to the Joe Watt Canyon Road. Turn left and proceed to the elk feeding station at the end of the road (approximately one mile).*

**HIKING.** For families who want to hike in this beautiful sec-tion of the state, an almost unlimited variety of wilderness set-tings await.

*For information about trails and campgrounds, contact the Cle Elum Ranger Station (509/674-4411; 803 W. 2nd St., Cle Elum 98922).*

**HORSEBACK RIDING.** Horseback riding is available at two area ranches for guests and non-guests alike. An hour's trail ride at **CIRCLE H RANCH** (810 Watt Canyon Road, Thorp; 509/964-2000) costs $15. It's $32.50 to ride for 1 1/2 hours at **HIDDEN VALLEY RANCH** (3942 Hidden Valley Road, Cle Elum; 509/857-2087).

**RIVER RAFTING** on the Yakima River is a do-it-yourself adven-ture that works well for families. The river is gentle, so you won't need previous rafting experience or a guide to have a successful trip. Most of the river's 40 miles from Cle Elum to Roza Dam can be floated. The trip is fun with a group; taking two or more cars allows you to shuttle from the finish back to the beginning. (For a half-day float, leave a car at Roza Dam, 21 miles south of Ellensburg on Highway 821, and drive nine miles north to Umtanum access area. For a shorter float, begin at the Squaw Creek access area, five miles south of Umtanum.) Be fore-warned: the only tourist facilities available on the river are the portable toilets at the Roza Dam and Umtanum access areas.

Equipment can be rented near Cle Elum at **RIVER RAFT RENTALS** (seven miles northwest of Ellensburg, off Hwy. 10; 509/964-2145). Be sure to ask for a map that provides river-access information. If you don't have your own life jackets, be sure to get them; they are included in the cost of the rental. Rafts come with pumps and can be transported inflated or deflated. The river is crowded on summer weekends, so reserve your rafts at least one day in advance. (Tips: Always wear a life jacket. The sun can be scorching beginning in May: bring sunscreen, sunglasses, and swimsuit cover-up. Wear old tennis shoes to protect your feet from the rocky bottom. Keep a dry change of clothes and food in large plastic bags.)

## CALENDAR

### SEPTEMBER
Ellensburg Rodeo, Labor Day weekend.
Threshing Bee, Olmstead Place Park, Ellensburg.
### NOVEMBER
Celebration of Lights, Ellensburg.

## RESOURCES

### CLE ELUM CHAMBER OF COMMERCE
401 W. 1st St., Cle Elum 98922
509/674-5958

### CLE ELUM RANGER STATION
803 W. 2nd St., Cle Elum 98922
509/674-4411

### ELLENSBURG CHAMBER OF COMMERCE
801 S. Ruby, Ellensburg 98926
509/925-3137

## YAKIMA VALLEY

Yakima grew up around a Northern Pacific Railroad depot built in 1884. Today it's a town of 60,000, with both cultural and recreational opportunities to offer families. Its location on the banks of the Yakima River make it a scenic spot, and the cold, snowy winters and hot, dry summers spell r-e-c-r-e-a-t-i-o-n. The Yakima Valley is a prime fruit- and grape-growing region now famous for fine wineries.

We also include here a spot in the Naches River area, near Chinook Pass, about 40 miles northeast of Yakima. We include it here because the pass is closed in winter, making the area most accessible from the east.

### GETTING THERE

Yakima is approximately 2 1/2 to three hours east of Seattle. Whether you are traveling east or west, take I-90 to I-82 south (near Ellensburg, marked as "Yakima"), then I-82 south for 32 miles. From Portland, head east on I-84 (along the Columbia Gorge) to connect with I-82. Follow 82 north for 110 miles. From eastern Oregon, take I-84 west to the junction with I-82, then north to Yakima.

The Naches River area is approximately 40 miles northeast of Yakima. Take Highway 12 east, then head northeast on Highway 410.

### REFUELING

See "Snoqualmie Pass" and "Cle Elum/Ellensburg" sections for restaurants along the way. If you're headed up from Portland, see "Columbia Gorge," in the Oregon chapter.

### ROADSIDE ATTRACTIONS

Ellensburg, located on I-90 near the junction with I-82, makes a good stop for families. If the kids need to run and jump, the Children's Museum is a good place to do it (see "Cle Elum/Ellensburg: Things to See & Do").

### PLACES TO STAY

**OXFORD SUITES**
*1701 Terrace Heights Dr., 98901*
*509/457-9000; 800/404-SUITE*
*Rates: Inexpensive to moderate*
*FYI: Complimentary breakfast; refrigerator/microwave; indoor*

*pool; pets OK*

The best thing about this newer, low-rise hotel is its location on the Yakima River. There's also a nice lobby with stone fireplace, and a pleasant lounge/library area. The suites are pleasant, but not a lot larger than hotel rooms (although they do have partial walls separating sleeping and sitting areas). All suites face the river. First-floor rooms have patios; on the second floor, they have decks.

**❝ PARENT COMMENTS**

*"The kids liked playing on the grassy area next to the patio, and directly beyond that is the Yakima Greenway for walking, biking, and rollerblading along the river."*

### WHISTLIN' JACK LODGE

*20800 Hwy. 410, Naches  98937*
*800/827-2299; www.yakima.net/wjl/*
*Rates: Moderate to expensive*
*FYI: Restaurant; kitchens (in cabins); fireplaces; hot tubs*

This mountain lodge on the Naches River offers a variety of accommodations, from motel units to cabins. Some of the cabins are right near the river; others are set farther back. All have hot tubs, except two that are across the highway. The Yakima Cottage's hot tub faces the parking lot, so is a little less private than the others. There's also a great restaurant, small gift shop, and small mini-market and gas station (expensive).

If you're happy with a cabin, a restaurant, and plenty of great outdoors, this is the lodge for you. Our parent reviewers had a cabin near the river, with high ceilings and lots of windows, a stone fireplace (gas), full kitchen, and two small bedrooms. The hot tub was on a deck looking out at the river.

**❝ PARENT COMMENTS**

*"We enjoyed being "away from it all" and sharing some quiet family time in front of the fireplace, some louder times splashing in the hot tub and walking along the river."*

*"Since cabins have fully equipped kitchens, we brought an ice chest of food and snacks, to save on the expense of eating out. You could also stop for groceries in Yakima, but don't plan on buying all you'll need at the small grocery store/deli—the choices are very limited!"*

## PLACES TO EAT

### BIRCHFIELD MANOR
*2018 Birchfield Road*
*509/452-1960*
*Hours: dinner Thurs.-Sat.*

This is an elegant, French-countryside kind of place, most appropriate for "parents night out," or a family outing with older children. Meals are served in the lovely living room of the owners' historic home. Each evening, diners choose among six entrée offerings, which often include a hearty soup. They specialize in Washington wines, and offer a lovely selection. Don't even think about feeling rushed; the table is yours for the evening.

### EL RANCHITO
*1319 E. 1st Ave., Zillah*
*509/829-5440*
*Hours: 8 a.m.-7 p.m. daily*

This is authentic Mexican food, freshly made and inexpensive. The menu features standards such as tacos, enchiladas, burritos, and tamales, as well as specialties like menudo, papitas (tater tots), barbacoa (shredded beef), carnitas, and lots more. The atmosphere here is great for families, but take-out is available if you prefer. While you wait for your food (and it can be a wait, this isn't fast food and the place is busy on weekends), check out the small gift shop with its inexpensive toys, food items, and jewelry. The bakery is another place where you can "get lost" among the goodies—Mexican rolls, cookies, cakes, and breads.

### MUSEUM SODA FOUNTAIN
*2105 Tieton Drive, at Yakima Valley Museum*
*509/248-0747*
*Hours: 10 a.m.-9 p.m. daily (summer); 10 a.m.-5 p.m. daily (rest of year)*

This wonderful circa-1930s soda fountain is considered a "working exhibit" of the museum. The antique equipment was purchased from a local drug store when it closed in 1994. The friendly "soda jerks" are happy to create old favorites like phosphates, soft drinks with syrup flavors, ice cream sodas, and lots of other ice cream specialties. Also on the menu are hot dogs, chili cheese dogs, soup, and chili. It's all tasty, full of nostalgia, and inexpensive.

### WHISTLIN' JACK LODGE DINING ROOM
*20800 Hwy. 410, Naches 98937*

*Phone: 800/827-2299*
*Hours: Breakfast, lunch, dinner daily*

If you're staying in Yakima, you probably won't want to drive 40 miles just for a great meal (though you wouldn't be the first). If you're in the Naches area, though, don't give this one a miss. Many people come here just to dine, especially on special occasions. The kids' menu includes popular breakfast options (cereal, french toast, or pancakes) and three lunch and dinner choices (grilled cheese, fish and chips, and chicken strips). For adults, there's seafood, fresh salads, piquant pasta dishes, and a variety of other entrées. Service can be uneven, but kids are well accommodated.

## WHAT TO SEE & DO

**DARIGOLD DAIRY FARM.** Here's the spot to learn all you want to know about how cheese is made. There's a self-guided tour of the cheese factory upstairs, which is a good length for families. Then check out the cow memorabilia and other gift items, and sample some cheese. If you've a sweet tooth, don't leave the premises without trying some of the hand-dipped ice cream!

*400 Alexander Road, Wapato (take Exit 67 from I-82). 509/837-4321. Open 8 a.m.-8 p.m.*

**DRIVE & BROWSE.** A driving tour of the area around Yakima can be a fun way to spend a day. Drive over to Granger to see the dinosaurs! It's not Jurassic Park, but it's the closest thing you'll find in the Yakima Valley: more than two dozen life-like dinosaur replicas. Kids can climb on the dinosaurs and have their pictures taken "up top." There's also a trout-stocked pond and lots of ducks. Located at Hisey Park (take I-82 to Exit 58. Drive south on Hwy. 223 to the third Granger exit.)

East of Yakima, the small town of Toppenish is home to more than 40 historical murals, depicting Western scenes, painted on the sides of buildings. The award-winning murals were painted by nationally known western and wildlife artists. (Take I-82 about 22 miles east of Yakima to Exit 50; 509/865-3262.)

Be prepared to make sudden stops: throughout the Yakima Valley, there are wineries and roadside produce stands in season. There is also the "Zillah Fruit Loop," which takes you past orchards, wineries, and fruit stands. (Take I-82 east to Exit 52 and follow the signs.)

**WASHINGTON'S FRUIT PLACE.** Here's the place to go to learn about the state's tree fruit industry, complete with exhibits and displays. There are free fruit samples and apple juice, and a gift shop where you can purchase fruit-related provisions to take with you.

*105 S. 18th (adjacent to the Yakima Greenway, next to Sarg Hubbard Park). 509/576-3090. Open Mon.-Fri., 9 a.m.-5 p.m. (year round); Sat.-Sun., noon-5 p.m. (summer). Free.*

**YAKAMA NATION MUSEUM.** This museum is part of the larger Native American Cultural Heritage Center, which has an RV park and teepees for rent, a restaurant, theater, library, and gift shop.

*100 Spilyiy Loop, Hwy. 97, Toppenish (off I-82 east of Yakima). 509/865-2800. Cost: $4/adult, $2/student over 10, $1/child 7-10, $.75/under 7, $10/family. www.wolfenet.com/!yingis/spilyay.*

**YAKIMA ELECTRIC RAILWAY MUSEUM** offers rides on vintage 1920s trolleys.

*S. 3rd Ave. & Pine St. 509/575-1700. Trolleys depart Sat.-Sun. & holidays, 10 a.m., noon, 2 & 4 p.m. (May-Sept.) Cost: $4/adult, $2.50/child 6-12, free/under 6, $12/family.*

**YAKIMA GREENWAY.** This paved path follows the Yakima River for 10 miles. Along the path is Sarg Hubbard Park, where families can enjoy free concerts on Tuesday evenings in July and August. The park has a big playground, and adjacent is the Washington Fruit Place. Other recreation opportunities include boating, fishing and hiking.

**YAKIMA VALLEY MUSEUM.** Local history exhibits here include "Yakima at Work" and "Yakima at Home," horse-drawn vehicles and farm equipment, and Native American art. Downstairs, the "Children's Underground" is a hands-on learning center downstairs. There is also a gift shop, and a large park (Franklin Park) adjacent to the museum.

*2105 Tieton Dr. 509/248-0747; yakimavalleymuseum.org/. Open Mon.-Fri., 10 a.m.-5 p.m., Sat.-Sun., noon-5 p.m.; Children's Underground open Weds.-Sun., 1-5 p.m. Cost: $3/adult, $1.50/senior & student, free/under 5, $7/family.*

## RESOURCES

**YAKIMA VALLEY VISITORS AND CONVENTION BUREAU**
10 N. 8th St., Yakima  98901
509/575-3010; 800/221-0751

## COLUMBIA GORGE

The Columbia River slices between the mountains and hills of southern Washington and northern Oregon, forming the dramatic and beautiful Columbia Gorge. It is one of the most scenic areas of the state, but is often overlooked by vacationers from outside the area.

Visitors tend to be more familiar with the Oregon side of the gorge, but there are lovely spots on the Washington side as well, with the added attraction of being less visited. Interested in a full-size replica of Stonehenge? A world-class museum literally in the middle of nowhere, chock-full of child-friendly and unusual exhibits? One of the nation's largest public telescopes and great weather conditions for looking through it? Seek no further than this lovely region that offers a surprising range of family activities and adventures.

### GETTING THERE

Highway 14 skirts the Columbia River in Washington State, passing through or near small towns such as Maryhill, White Salmon, and Stevenson.

From I-5 near Vancouver, take I-205 to Highway 14, then east along the gorge. From central Washington, travel south on I-82 to intersect Highway 14, and head west along the gorge. Or, take I-82 south to Highway 97 (south of Yakima) and continue south on 97 to intersect Highway 14 midway along the gorge (at Maryhill). In eastern Washington, many east-west highways intersect Highway 395. From 395, head south to the Tri-Cities, and across the Columbia River to connect with I-82. Head south to intersect Highway 14.

From Portland, there are several options. Head north on I-5 through Vancouver to connect with I-205, and then follow previous directions. Or, take I-84 east about 35 miles to the bridge at Cascade Locks. Cross over the Columbia River to Stevenson, on Highway 14. From eastern Oregon, I-84 heads northwest to intersect I-82. Travel north across the Columbia River to Highway 14.

**ROADSIDE ATTRACTIONS.** Off Highway 14, 16 miles east of Vancouver, sits the small town of Washougal. This is the home of the **PENDLETON WOOLEN MILL** (2 17th St.; 360/835-1118, 800/568-2480), purveyors of the popular, high-quality line of clothing and other woolens. The mill offers free one-hour tours, where kids can see for themselves how raw wool is processed.

There's a store here, too, where woolen fabrics and "seconds" of garments and blankets can be had at a fraction of their usual cost.

### PLACES TO STAY

#### FAR VUE MOTEL
*808 E. Simcoe Dr., Goldendale 98260*
*509/773-5881, 800/358-5881*
*Rates: Inexpensive*
*FYI: Restaurant on premises; kitchens (2 units), refrigerators (all units); heated outdoor pool (seasonal); RV parking*

Located at the intersection of Highway 97 and Simcoe Drive, the Far Vue is your basic motel. Its 48 simple but comfortable rooms have refrigerators and mountain views. Two suites offer full kitchen and separate living room and bedroom.

#### ❝❝ PARENT COMMENTS
*"We straggled in after a long hot day of exploring the gorge. We were so tired even our six year old happily watched an old black-and-white film on TV. It was peaceful and quiet. There was a pool, but we were too exhausted to try it out. Staff were friendly."*

#### LLAMA RANCH BED & BREAKFAST
*1980 Hwy. 141, Trout Lake 98672*
*509/395-2786*
*Rates: Inexpensive*
*FYI: Complimentary breakfast; playground; llamas; pets OK*

Located 20 miles north of White Salmon, at the base of Mount Adams, this is a comfortable, informal, and child-friendly place to stay. A visit in the spring, when the baby llamas are born, is especially fun.

In summer, there's rafting, horseback riding, and hiking nearby; in winter, cross-country skiing is popular.

Accommodations include a room with two queen beds; or a room with a king bed, a queen sofa bed, and a kitchen. The kitchen at the lodge is available for use by all guests.

#### ❝❝ PARENT COMMENTS
*"This friendly place is especially well suited to young children. The llamas and many peacocks are right outside, along with a playground and an area to run and play in without any cars around."*

### SKAMANIA LODGE
*1131 Skamania Lodge Dr., Stevenson  98648*
*800/221-7117*
*Rates: Expensive*
*FYI: Restaurant; indoor swimming pool; mountain biking, nature trails; tennis, golf*

Located just 45 minutes from Portland and about three hours from Seattle, the Skamania was opened in 1994 by the same people who own Salishan Lodge on the Oregon Coast and Salish Lodge at Snoqualmie Falls, near Seattle. With its gorgeous location overlooking some of the most beautiful sections of the gorge, and its first-rate accommodations, Skamania is a marvelous addition to the area. The lodge, designed in the mountain lodge tradition of America's national parks, is an impressive structure of 195 rooms sitting on 175 acres. The soothing décor features earth tones and first-class service, creating an atmosphere of woodsy luxury.

### 66 PARENT COMMENTS

*"Very deluxe—perhaps best as a splurge for the parents. But if you do bring the kids, there is plenty to keep them busy at the resort and in the surrounding area."*

## PLACES TO EAT

### THE HOMESTEAD RESTAURANT
*808 E. Simcoe Dr., Goldendale*
*509/773-6006*
*Hours: Breakfast, lunch, dinner daily*

Located at the Far Vue Motel, this bustling restaurant serves the usual in small-town family fare. While there is no children's menu per se, at least three meals are guaranteed child-pleasers: junior chicken strips, fish 'n chips, and burgers. Prices are low and portions large.

## WHAT TO SEE & DO

**COLUMBIA GORGE INTERPRETIVE CENTER.** This splendid $10.5-million interpretive museum depicts Native American lifestyles, the fur-trading era, and the harnessing of geologic forces along the gorge. Children will especially enjoy the full-scale, 38-foot replica of a fish wheel and the diorama of a Native American dip-net fisher. One of the highlights is the continuous showing of a stunning nine-projector show dramatizing the geologic forces that carved the Columbia River Gorge.

*990 S.W. Rock Creek Dr. (above Hwy. 14, adjacent to Skamania Lodge). 509/427-8211, 800/991-2338. Open daily, 10 a.m.-5 p.m. (Call to confirm hours.) Cost: $6/adult, $5/student, $4/child 5-12, free/under 5.*

**GOLDENDALE OBSERVATORY STATE PARK.** This state park and interpretive center houses an astronomical observatory with a Cassegrain telescope, which was built by four local residents and donated to the community on the condition that a public observatory be built to house it. At 24.5 inches, it is one of the nation's largest public telescopes.

Open year round, the observatory allows visitors large and small to watch the heavenly bodies dance across the heavens. The distance from city lights and east-of-the-mountains (hence, not rainy) location makes for great viewing conditions much of the time.

A secondary dome houses a smaller telescope; portable telescopes are also available for use, and there are some astronomical exhibits. Staff and volunteers offer observatory tours and interpretive programs to help visitors make sense of what they're seeing.

*1602 Observatory Dr. Located just north of Goldendale. From Hwy. 97, go west on Hwy. 142 (Broadway) to Columbus Ave.; go north (right) on Columbus and follow signs to Observatory. 509/773-3400; www.parks.wa.gov. Open Weds.-Sun., 2-5 p.m. & 8 p.m.-midnight (April-Sept.); Sat.-Sun., 11 a.m.-5 p.m., Sat. 7-9 p.m. (Oct.-March). Also open by appointment (call 509/773-3141 for details). Free.*

**MARYHILL ART MUSEUM.** Sam Hill, a Gilded Age entrepreneur and a Quaker, built this imposing building as his home. The project began in 1914, evolved into a museum, and was still incomplete at Hill's death in 1931. Hill's wide-ranging interests are reflected in the permanent collections. Exhibits include sculptures and watercolors by Auguste Rodin; an impressive assortment of American and European paintings; an extensive collection of Native American artifacts, including beads, basketry, and rock carvings; and artifacts, Russian icons, and royal regalia donated by Hill's friend Queen Marie of Romania.

What's to interest kids? you might ask. The answer is: plenty. Jewels, including some by Faberge, are intriguing, but the collection of over 250 chess sets is truly extraordinary. The tiny, intricately carved ivory chessmen are sure to fascinate kids. The nine sets of miniature Parisian mannequins dressed in the latest haute couture from the mid-20th century are irresistible.

Traveling exhibits pass through here, and the museum hosts a variety of special programs for children in partnership with schools. Exhibits of works by children are sometimes shown.

There is something enchanting and fairy-tale-like about this elegant and civilized spot carved out of the grand western wilderness. The building itself is lovely and also contains memorabilia documenting Hill's life. The pleasant museum café serves snacks and sandwiches. A small store sells interesting books, jewelry, posters, and gifts. The 26 acres of landscaped grounds are available for picnicking; there's an attractive sculpture garden.

*35 Maryhill Museum Drive. Located on Hwy. 14. 509/773-3733. www.maryhillmuseum.org. Open daily, 9 a.m.-5 p.m. March 15-Nov. 15. Café open 10 a.m.-4 p.m. Cost: $6.50/adult, $6/senior, $1.50/children 6-12, free/under 6. Special rates available; call for details. Free admission to picnic grounds, restrooms, outdoor sculpture garden.*

**STONEHENGE.** OK, so it's not *the* Stonehenge, but what it lacks in Druid ancestry it more than makes up for in dramatically beautiful scenery. Below its cliff-side perch runs the mighty Columbia River, framed by high cliffs and the golden Oregon wheat fields rising beyond it. The same Sam Hill who built the Maryhill Museum built this replica of the English site to serve as the first World War I memorial in the United States. Why Stonehenge? Hill believed the purpose of the original Stonehenge had been to sacrifice human beings to an ancient British god of war. In his pacifist view, soldiers killed in World War I had also been sacrificed. It is now known that Stonehenge was not used for the purpose Hill imagined.

Hill's Stonehenge is more accessible than the English version. Visitors can drive up and park, then walk the short distance to the memorial. The view is extensive, unfiltered by trees and shrubs. A short walk to the southwest is the crypt where Hill is buried.

*Located 4 miles east of Maryhill Museum off Hwy. 14; follow signs. 509/773-3733. Open daily, 7 a.m.-10 p.m. Free. Donations accepted.*

For more information about this area, see "Oregon: Columbia Gorge."

## EASTERN WASHINGTON

Eastern Washington is a vast expanse of changing land-scapes, interrupted only occasionally by anything resembling an urban enclave. Even the larger population centers of Spokane, Wenatchee, Walla Walla and Tri-cities continue to orient themselves around outdoor pursuits, whether they be farming or recreation.

The region, encompassing everything between the Okanogan Valley and the Idaho border, is a study in contrasts. The terrain includes: the Okanogan Highlands and moun-tainous regions of the Kettles and Selkirds (to the north); the vast plateau, marked by lava flows and geological remnants of the last Ice Age; and, to the south, the hauntingly beautiful wheat fields of the Palouse and the rugged northern tip of the Blue Mountains.

In Eastern Washington you will find extremes of weather as well: very cold, even harsh, winters contrasted with still, hot summers. While it's great to visit during these extreme sea-sons, especially for the skiing or the sunning, families might consider spring or fall vacations in this lovely region. Go to enjoy the spring blossoms, or the fall harvest, or just to expe-rience nature as its pendulum swings between extremes.

### GRAND COULEE DAM

Located north of Soap Lake, Coulee City is the former junction of railroad and stagecoach lines that ran along the Columbia River. (According to 19th-century author Guy Waring, the town took full advantage of this junction by pur-posely mismatching travel schedules so that visitors were forced to spend the night here.) Today, however, visitors pass through by choice, intent upon enjoying the weather and see-ing the sights.

#### GETTING THERE

Take I-90 to Soap Lake, then head north 15 miles on Highway 17.

**ROADSIDE ATTRACTIONS.** If you find you need a break along the way, check out "Snoqualmie Pass" and "Cle Elum/Ellensburg: What to See & Do."

## PLACES TO STAY

### COULEE LODGE RESORT

*3017 Park Lake Road NE, 99115*
*509/632-5565*
*Rates: Inexpensive*
*FYI: Kitchens; store; boats, Jet skis; laundry*

This comfortable, low-key resort is located on Blue Lake, in Washington's "Little Grand Canyon." The cabins here are air conditioned, with fully equipped kitchens.

Blue Lake is quiet and uncrowded, and there's a great swimming area with raft, as well as boats for rent. The combination of hot, dry summers and a cool, clear lake makes swimming and boating attractive here.

There's a little store at the resort, and families can bring supplies and cook in their cabins. When you hanker for a night out, there are several family-friendly restaurants in Soap Lake (15 miles).

### ❝❝ PARENT COMMENTS

*"We've been there two years in a row, and plan to return next year. The kids love it and so do we!"*

*"This spot is just what we wanted—comfortable, but not fancy, at a reasonable price."*

### COLUMBIA RIVER INN

*10 Lincoln Ave., Coulee Dam 99116*
*509/633-2100*
*FYI: Kitchens (some rooms); outdoor pool (seasonal); laundry*

For proximity to the Grand Coulee Dam, you can't beat this inn—it's right across the street. Of course, that can be good and bad—there's easy access to the dam, but the summer months bring tourists, traffic, and dust to the area. Still, there is a nice outdoor pool for rinsing off.

The inn's 34 rooms are basic motel faire, but many have balconies with views of the dam.

### ❝❝ PARENT COMMENTS

*"We visited during the off-season, and it was great. The kids learned a lot about the dam, and the whole family sat in the hot tub at night and admired the desert skies."*

## WHAT TO SEE & DO

**GRAND COULEE DAM.** Grand it says, and grand it is! One of the most massive concrete structures in the world, Grand Coulee Dam harnesses the mighty Columbia River for power and irrigation. A visitor center below the dam offers exhibits and movies about the river, the dam, and area geology. Tours of the dam leave daily, every hour on the hour (for group tours, phone 509/633-9265).

Usually the water flows through pipes to turbines inside the dam. If the kids would enjoy watching the water spill over the dam into the river, time your visit for 1:30 to 2 p.m. During the summer, visitors may take a self-guided tour, and enjoy beautiful nightly laser light shows.

*509/633-9265. Visitor Center open 9 a.m.-5 p.m. (Oct.-May), 8:30 a.m.-11 p.m. (June-July), 8:30 a.m.-10:30 p.m. (Aug.), 8:30 a.m.-9:30 p.m. (Sept.). Free.*

**DRY FALLS.** Dramatic changes occurred in this region during the last ice age, and this is one of the best places to view them. The geological centerpiece of the area is Dry Falls, the skeleton of one of the greatest waterfalls in geologic history. (It's 3.5 miles wide and drops 400 feet.) The interpretive center on Highway 17 does a good job of demonstrating the power of nature and what it has wrought. The building overlooks the precipice and affords a panoramic view of the area.

*Four miles southwest of Coulee City on Hwy. 17.*

## RESOURCES

**COULEE CITY CHAMBER OF COMMERCE**
P.O. Box 896
Coulee City, WA 99115
509/632-5043

**COULEE DAM CHAMBER OF COMMERCE**
306 Midway St., Coulee Dam, WA 99133
800/268-5332

## SPOKANE

Spokane is the second largest city in Washington State, but you'd never know it. Full of charming parks and pleasant neighborhoods, it still feels in many ways like a small town. A focal point is Riverfront Park, developed for Expo '74, which covers more than 100 acres along the Spokane River. It might be a major focus of your visit, but you'll find many other interesting attractions to explore with the kids.

## GETTING THERE

**BY CAR.** Spokane is 290 miles east of Seattle, across the Cascades on I-90. Count on about six hours to make the trip, including at least one good rest stop.

From Portland, there are a number of possible routes to Spokane. To mix beauty with efficiency, head east on I-84 (along the gorge) to Highway 97, just past Biggs. Travel north on 97, then east on I-82 until it crosses the Columbia River and intersects Highway 395, which will take you northeast to I-90 and on to Spokane.

**BY TRAIN.** An Amtrak (800/872-7245) train runs from Seattle to Spokane daily, but the schedule isn't particularly convenient for families. The train departs Seattle at 4:50 p.m. and arrives in Spokane at 12:30 a.m.; the return trip leaves Spokane at 2:05 a.m. and arrives in Seattle at 9:50 a.m. Please call for specific cost information (kids ages two to 15 are half-price when traveling with an adult).

**REFUELING.** Approximately 130 miles east of Seattle, as you approach the Columbia River, is the small town of **VANTAGE**—a good place to refuel and refresh. If the weather is suitable, a picnic lunch would be ideal, either at the river's edge or uphill in Ginkgo Petrified Forest State Park (see "Roadside Attractions").

If you want to push on a little farther before you stop and feed the group, there are numerous restaurants and picnic areas in the town of **MOSES LAKE**, about 40 miles beyond Vantage. Watch out if you eat outdoors, though—our parent reviewer watched a seagull snatch a toddler's burger right off his plate!

**ROADSIDE ATTRACTIONS.** Take the Vantage exit from I-90 and follow signs to **GINKGO PETRIFIED FOREST STATE PARK** for spectacular views of the Columbia River. The Interpretive Center (509/856-2700) has Indian artifacts, fossils, and petrified wood. If leg stretching is in order, take one of the short trails through the sagebrush to see the petrified logs close up. There are picnic tables, restrooms, and, just down the road, a gift shop with rocks, crystals, and other treasures.

If the weather is hot, consider a stop at the public beach in Vantage (right side of the road, just before the bridge) for a refreshing dip in the river. There are dressing rooms and picnic tables, as well as a grassy park custom-made for tossing a Frisbee.

Another good stop is **MOSES LAKE STATE PARK** (off the freeway at Exit 175). You'll find a playground, picnic tables, restrooms, concessions, and a swimming beach. However, your young aviator might be most interested in the 747s flying overhead—Japan Airlines trains pilots at nearby Grant County Airport.

At Exit 174 is another interesting attraction: the **SAND DUNES ORV AREA** (known locally as "Four Wheel Drive Park"). With 280 acres, the park provides room for hikers, picnickers, fishermen, and four-wheelers to coexist peacefully (though not quietly).

For more refueling and roadside attractions, see "Cle Elum/Ellensburg."

### PLACES TO STAY

**BEST WESTERN PHEASANT HILL**
*12507 E. Mission Ave., 99216*
*509/926-7432, 888/297-1555*
*Rates: Inexpensive to moderate*
*FYI: Complimentary continental breakfast; refrigerators/ microwaves (some rooms); indoor pool; exercise facility*

About 10 miles east of downtown, this is a convenient location for families who want to enjoy Spokane environs or take day trips outside the city. It's a new hotel, with four family suites: two rooms with king bed, sleeper sofa, two TVs, and a private Jacuzzi. There are standard rooms as well, with two queen beds or one king. The pool and Jacuzzi are open 24 hours a day.

**❝ PARENT COMMENTS**
*"When we needed diapers in a hurry, we discovered Valley Mall (three miles east on I-90). There's a food court, department store, multiplex theater, and several restaurants."*

**CAVANAUGH'S RIVER INN**
*N. 700 Division, 99202*
*509/326-5577, 800/325-4000 (reservations)*
*Rates: Inexpensive to moderate*
*FYI: Restaurant; two outdoor swimming pools (one is covered in winter); game room; playground, tennis court, putting green; pets OK*

There are four Cavanaugh hotels in Spokane. Two of them, the River Inn and the Inn at the Park, are ideally located near Riverfront Park. For families we recommend the River Inn, because the rates are generally lower and the facilities are better for children. The layout and atmosphere are friendly to families (the Inn at the Park has a more corporate feel). River Inn guests enjoy full access to the fabulous outdoor pools at Inn at the Park, just two blocks away via the river walk.

The design of the River Inn complements the nearby river, offering easy access and lovely views. Be aware, however, that the riverbanks are steep and playground and pool areas are unfenced. Kids must be supervised.

**❝ PARENT COMMENTS**

*"The Inn at the Park is located a little closer to Riverside Park, but for us that's not enough to justify the higher price. We stay at the River Inn and take the kids to swim at the Inn at the Park. They love the wonderful pool slides built into the landscaping."*

*"The restaurant, Ripples, is kid-friendly. Our kids loved the food, and we appreciated the great service, reasonable prices, and pleasant river views."*

**COURTYARD BY MARRIOTT**
*N. 401 Riverpoint Blvd., 99202*
*509/456-7600*
*Rates: Inexpensive to moderate*
*FYI: Café; mini-refrigerators (some units); indoor pool; exercise facility*

Located on the south side of the river, across from Cavanaugh's River Inn, the Courtyard offers the same advantages—excellent river views and proximity to Riverfront Park. The suites are a good choice for families; each has a bedroom and a separate living area.

**❝ PARENT COMMENTS**

*"This is one of the newest hotels in the area and one of the best values. Winter rates are excellent,, but when we visit in the summer we opt for a place with an outdoor pool."*

**DOUBLETREE HOTEL**
*322 N. Spokane Falls Ct., 99201*
*509/455-9600, 800/222-TREE; www.doubletreehotels.com*
*Rates: Moderate*

*FYI: Restaurant, café; indoor pool; exercise facility*

Originally a Sheraton, then a Red Lion, the downtown Doubletree is newly renovated. Rooms are comfortable, with little extras like irons and coffeemakers, and some also have nice views. The location is handy—adjacent to Riverfront Park, with easy walking access to downtown shopping.

### HAMPTON INN

*2010 S. Assembly Road, 99204*
*509/747-1100, 800/426-7866; www.hampton-inn.com*
*Rates: Inexpensive to moderate*
*FYI: Complimentary continental breakfast; indoor pool; pets OK (deposit)*

Just five minutes from downtown and the airport, the Hampton Inn is moderately priced and family-friendly. One of its best features is the indoor pool, open 24 hours.

The "deluxe" continental breakfast really is just that—it's served buffet-style and includes cold and hot cereals, muffins and toast, yogurt, fruits, and juices. A deli at the inn serves lunch and dinner at reasonable prices in a relaxed atmosphere. Menu choices include many kid favorites, such as chicken potpie, pizza, sandwiches, and soup.

### 66 PARENT COMMENTS

*"We got back to the inn about 8 p.m. and appreciated being able to get a quick, reasonably priced meal at the deli."*

*"It was great to have the pool open 24 hours. If our kids awoke at the break of dawn, we'd go swimming. It was also relaxing to swim at the end of a long day."*

### QUALITY INN VALLEY SUITES

*E. 8923 Mission Ave., 99212*
*Rates: Inexpensive to moderate*
*F.Y.I.: Complimentary breakfast; refrigerators/microwaves; indoor pool; exercise facility; pets OK*

This is a bright, clean, full-service hotel, located off I-90 about 10 minutes east of Spokane. Though it's not in a notably scenic location, the rooms are pleasant and the indoor pool is a big hit with the kids. Large families, and those who don't want to be limited to sitting on the beds, should consider getting a suite. If your kids are unable to hustle in the morning, be aware that the checkout time here is 11 a.m.

Quality Inn is close to Dishman Hills, a good hiking area,

and the Centennial Trail, which is great for both hiking and biking (see "What to See & Do").

**❝ PARENT COMMENTS**

*"Quality Inn is an ideal place to stay if you are passing through Spokane on your way to Yellowstone or Schweitzer, or if you don't want to stay right in the city."*

## PLACES TO EAT

### AZTECA

*W. 200 Spokane Falls Blvd.*
*509/456-0350*
*Hours: Lunch, dinner daily*

Western Washington residents will recognize this restaurant chain and can expect the same tasty Mexican fare, good service, and good value. In keeping with its family-oriented reputation, Azteca has an exceptional "Little Amigos" menu. When you've had your fill, take a stroll in adjacent Riverfront Park.

### CLINKERDAGGERS

*W. 621 Mallon*
*509/328-5965*
*Hours: Dinner daily, lunch Mon.-Sat.; Sunday brunch*

If you're treating the family to a special dinner out, this is the place to do it. The food and service are consistent; the views of the Spokane River are spectacular. Kids will enjoy the Old English atmosphere and the extensive children's menu (including a small-portion prime rib). Parents will appreciate the warm reception given their kids, along with the good food. Reservations are recommended, especially if you want a table near a window with a view of the river.

Clinkerdaggers is located in the Flour Mill, which houses a variety of shops and merits some after-dinner window shopping.

### CUCINA! CUCINA! INC.

*707 W. Main, Ste. A-1*
*509/838-3388*
*Hours: Lunch, dinner daily*

Another regional family favorite, Cucina! Cucina! Offers all manner of Italian food, and has an affordable kids menu. It's a very kid-friendly place—if the server doesn't offer your child some pizza dough to play with, just ask. The hardest part might be getting the kids to leave the pizza dough behind when you go… although leaving it out overnight can be an interesting science experiment!

### CYRUS O'LEARY'S
*W. 516 Main*
*509/624-9000*
*Hours: Lunch, dinner daily*

Located downtown across from Riverfront Park, Cyrus O'Leary's has a fun atmosphere and an extensive menu. Homemade pies are their claim to fame, but they also serve good sandwiches, salads, soups, and pasta, as well as inexpensive children's entrées. Two recommendations: bring your own crayons and paper, and ask for seating near a window.

### ELK CAFÉ & SODA FOUNTAIN
*1931 W. Pacific Ave.*
*509/456-0454*
*Hours: Breakfast, lunch, dinner Mon.-Sat.; breakfast, lunch Sun.*

The Elk Café is home to Spokane's oldest soda fountain and was previously a drug store (dating back to 1902). Look for some of the original drug store products in the window. In addition to the usual fountain fare, the café serves chiles rellenos, burgers, salads and a hummus platter. In the evening, it's a neighborhood hang-out, and you might even catch some live performers.

### HOT ROD CAFÉ
*1610 Schneidmiller Ave., Post Falls, Idaho*
*208/777-1712*
*Hours: Lunch, dinner daily*

Car lovers will enjoy the hot rod theme of this café, about a 40-minute drive east of Spokane. During the summer, our parent reviewers found the parking lot overrun with hot rods from around the country (devoted hot rodders on their way to an international convention in Spokane). The kids' menu here offers the usual choices, including burgers, chicken strips, grilled cheese sandwich, and fish 'n chips. Grown-ups select from an extensive menu that includes pasta, barbecue, steak, chicken, and seafood. There are also plenty of great desserts to choose! And like so many theme restaurants, the café has their own logo wear—interesting to look at while you await your meal.

## THE MILK BOTTLE RESTAURANT
*802 W. Garland*
*509/325-1772*
*Hours: 11 a.m.-5 p.m. Mon.-Sat.*

Yes, it's true—this restaurant really is built in the shape of a milk bottle. The food is great too, with lots of ice cream (18 flavors of homemade ice cream, sherbet, and yogurt), and soda-fountain fare. For coffee lovers, there's an ice cream latté float and an espresso shake. Entrées include burgers, hot and cold sandwiches, gyros, and a great Greek salad.

## PATSY CLARK'S MANSION
*2208 W. 2nd Ave.*
*509/838-8300*
*Hours: Breakfast, lunch daily; brunch Sun.*

Housed in a mansion built in 1898, this is probably the most expensive restaurant in Spokane, and definitely one of the best. It's a great dress-up, "best behavior" kind of place, offering an excellent Sunday brunch, as well as lunch and dinner. History buffs take note: President George Bush ate here in 1989.

## ROCK CITY ITALIANO GRILL
*505 W. Riverside*
*509/455-4400*
*Hours: Lunch, dinner daily .*

## ROCK CITY GRILL VALLEY
*11003 E. Sprague Ave.*
*509/921-7600*
*Hours: Lunch, dinner Tues.-Sun.*

Locals love these "Italiano" restaurants for their tasty food, hefty portions, and lively atmospheres. This is a good spot to consider an appetizer—perhaps escargot or two decidedly non-Italian Thai satays. Entrées include super-thin-crust gourmet pizza, pasta, panini sandwiches, and calzones, as well as house specialties such as Jack Daniel's Whiskey Steak. There's a kids menu too, with macaroni 'n cheese, pizzas, and burgers.

## THE OLD SPAGHETTI FACTORY
*152 S. Monroe*
*509/624-8916*
*Hours: Dinner daily*

Part of the national chain, this restaurant has been a well-established family favorite for more than 25 years in Spokane.

It's a fun environment and a fun place to do a family birthday celebration, too. Food is inexpensive, portions are generous, and the spumoni ice cream is the perfect end to the meal.

### WHAT TO SEE & DO

#### STROLL & BROWSE

**DOWNTOWN SPOKANE** is good for walking and window-shopping. Pick up a Spokane tour map at the Visitors' Bureau (Sprague Ave. & Monroe St.) or in one of the downtown stores.

**SHOPPING.** If shopping is part of your plan, you'll find a number of options in the area. Even in inclement weather, you can stay dry while you shop; the downtown skywalk area encompasses 15 blocks of second-story shopping, all connected by skywalks (which easily accommodate a stroller). You'll find many little shops, restaurants, and places to sit and rest weary legs.

Not far from downtown, on the north side of the river and connected by footbridge to Riverfront Park, is the **FLOUR MILL**. This century-old building once harnessed energy from the Spokane River to grind wheat. These days it's filled with unique shops and restaurants, as well as historical displays of its milling days. Unless you have older, well-behaved ("hands-in-pockets") kids, stick to window shopping until you come to **WONDERS OF THE WORLD** (509/328-6890), a cornucopia of toys, jewelry, beads and minerals. For "look-don't-touch" collectibles, stop into **CAROLS & CAROUSELS** (509/326-6099). If it's time for a family photo, you can make it fun at **OLD JOE CLARK'S OLD-TIME PORTRAIT PARLOR** (509/327-7915).

Other suggestions include **AUNTIE'S BOOKSTORE** (402 W. Main; 509/838-0206), a cozy place for browsing. A frequent winner of the "Best Family Bookstore" title in a local parenting magazine readers' poll, Auntie's has a fine selection of children's books. Right next door is **UNCLE'S GAMES, PUZZLES & ETC.** (404 W. Main; 509/456-4607). **WHIZ KIDS** (5628 N. Division St.; 509/483-9153) is a notable educational store for kids, parents, and teachers. It offers a good selection of toys, books, puzzles, and science and nature items.

#### PARKS

**MANITO PARK** features a large, modern playground that will entertain young children for hours. If you happen to visit during snow season, the hills offer the best sledding and tubing in town. There's also a duck pond at the park, which often freezes over in winter, providing a good, though not groomed, skating surface for adventurous skaters. (In the summer, bring bread-crumbs for the ducks.) Concessions and a café open seasonally.

For the flower lovers in the family, Manito Park has a conservatory and beautifully groomed gardens in season, including a rose garden, lilac garden, and Japanese garden.

*Located on the south hill, at Grand Blvd. & 18th St. Open daily. Free.*

**RIVERFRONT PARK**, on the former site of Expo '74, is Spokane's centerpiece. Located along the Spokane River on Native American fishing grounds, the park features year-round attractions and activities, including an intricately carved 1909 Looff Carousel, a suspension bridge over the river, a gondola ride above Spokane Falls, and, during summer months, carnival rides and outdoor concerts. The clock tower, four-story IMAX theater, opera house, convention center, and Ice Palace (an outdoor skating rink) are also located in this 50-acre park. A no-cost attraction, which is visible from Spokane Falls Boulevard, is a big red wagon that has a long slide for a handle. For those who enjoy simpler park pleasures, there are plenty of paved pathways to explore on foot, bike, or roller blades.

Accessible from the park is the wide, paved **CENTENNIAL TRAIL**, which follows the Spokane River for 39 miles between Riverside State Park (see "Parks") and Coeur d'Alene, Idaho (see "Excursions"). It's ideal for running, walking, biking, skating, or pushing a stroller.

Skate and bike rentals are available seasonally. **QUINN'S WHEEL RENTALS** (509/456-6545; near Howard Street Bridge at Riverside Park) rents all sorts of fun wheeled toys, including roller blades, bikes of all sizes, tandem bikes, and surreys — pedal-propelled cars that will seat five to eight persons.

If the gang gets hungry, concessions are available at the park. Restaurants are not far away (downtown to the south on Spokane Falls Boulevard and in Flour Mill shopping area, north on Mallong Road.)

*Off I-90, along the Spokane River. 509/625-6600, 800/336-PARK. Attractions open Sun.-Thurs., 11 a.m.-8 p.m.; Fri.-Sat., 11 a.m.-10 p.m. (Memorial Day-Labor Day); Fri.-Sat., 11 a.m.-9 p.m.; Sun., 11 a.m.-4 p.m. Cost: tickets range from $1.50/carousel ride to $3-$6/ice skating or IMAX theater admission. Day pass $11/person, or $10/person for family of four or* more (pass buys a gondola ride, a ride on the Looff Carousel, admission to an IMAX film, and carnival rides or ice skating).

## MUSEUMS

**CHENEY COWLES MUSEUM.** This small museum does an excellent job of providing a historical perspective on this region. Exhibits include a lively presentation of regional history, local artists, and Native American artifacts. Kids will find the lifelike displays in the adjoining **CAMPBELL HOUSE** (an old mansion from Spokane's mining days) particularly interesting.

If the weather's agreeable, walk two blocks up Hemlock St. to **COEUR D'ALENE PARK** (at 2nd Ave.). There's a nice playground and gazebo and, in summer, free outdoor concerts.

2316 W. First Ave. (Exit 280A from I-90, north on Walnut, west on 2nd Ave. Follow signs). 509/456-3931. Open Tues.-Sat., 10 a.m.-5 p.m.; Weds., 10 a.m.-9 p.m.; Sun., 1-5 p.m. Cost: $10/family, $4/adult, $2.50/child 6-16, free/under 6.

**CHILDREN'S MUSEUM OF SPOKANE.** At this new museum, kids can learn about the water cycle in the "Under the Falls" exhibit, build things in the "Fort Spokane Construction Zone," visit an art gallery, and see what life is like in a Greek village. There's a special play area for toddlers and infants, too.

N. 110 Post. 509/624-0435; www.vpds.wsu.edu. Open Tues.-Sun., 10 a.m.-5 p.m. Cost: $4.50/person, free/under 1.

## ANIMALS, ANIMALS

**CAT TALES ENDANGERED SPECIES CONSERVATION PARK AND ZOOLOGICAL TRAINING CENTER** is a family-oriented center that features 33 big cats, including lions, tigers, leopards, pumas, bobcats, black jaguars, servals, and two rare New Guinea singing dogs. Take a tour or enjoy the wildlife on your own. The gift shop is worth a browse.

N. 17020 Newport Hwy., Mead (15 miles north on Hwy. 2). 509/238-4126. Hours: Weds.-Sun.,10 a.m.-4 p.m. (Oct.-April), Tues.-Sun., 10 a.m.-6 p.m. (May-Sept.). Cost: $5/adult, $4/student & senior, $3/child under 12.

**TURNBULL NATIONAL WILDLIFE REFUGE.** Just a half-hour drive from Spokane, this 17,000-acre refuge is replete with lakes, ponds, marshes, and all the wildlife characteristic of these landscapes (especially waterfowl). Visitors can bike, walk, or drive through the refuge on various trails.

*26010 S. Smith Rd. (drive 4 miles south of Cheney on Cheney-Plaza Road, then 2 miles east on Smith Road). 509/235-4723. Open daily, 5:30 a.m.-7 p.m.(until 10 p.m., spring & summer). Cost: $3/vehicle (March-Oct.); free/vehicle (rest of year).*

## EXCURSIONS

**COEUR D'ALENE, IDAHO** is only 33 miles east of Spokane on I-90. Flanked by two outstanding skiing mountains and on the shores of the most beautiful lakes in the country, Coeur d'Alene is fast becoming a vacation Mecca in the Northwest. It is well worth a day trip. Some families stay in Spokane and drive to Silver Mountain, outside Coeur d'Alene, to ski.

**DISHMAN HILL NATURAL AREA.** This 400-acre preserve is home to nearly 40 plant species and 100 species of birds. The area is filled with hikes of varying degrees of difficulty. **NORTHWEST MAP SERVICE** (525 Sprague Ave.; 509/455-6981) sells a good map of these trails.

*Take I-90 east from Spokane to the Sprague Ave. exit, then drive east 1.5 miles to Sargent Road. Turn right and continue for one-half mile.*

**FORT SPOKANE.** This late-19th-century fort was built to maintain peace between settlers and Native American tribes, but it never saw any real action during 20 years of use. Today, Fort Spokane houses visual and audio displays that provide a history of the area. Tours of the grounds are also offered.

It's a bit of a drive from Spokane, but it's certainly a scenic one. The small town of Davenport has a nice city park that surrounds a natural spring—a good spot for a picnic before or after visiting the fort. Kids can play on the playground equipment and maybe even take a dip in the city pool. This is an excellent excursion for budget-minded families who enjoy getting out and exploring small towns and regional history.

*Located 58 miles northwest of Spokane (east on I-90 2 miles to Hwy. 2, then about 35 miles to Davenport. Proceed north on Hwy. 25 about 15 miles). 509/725-2715. Visitors Center open Memorial Day-Labor Day, 9:30 a.m.-5:30 p.m. Free.*

**GREEN BLUFF.** This small farming community, 10 miles north of Spokane, is especially picturesque at autumn harvest time. The fields and orchards of Green Bluff are filled with u-pick vegetables and fruits. On an October visit, pick an

Eastern Washington pumpkin to take home or pluck some apples off the tree. Several of the farms have gift shops where you can buy a jar of apple butter or honey to take along, or some apple cider to sit and sip as you enjoy the scenery.

*Take Hwy. 2 to Day-Mount Spokane Road, and head east.*

**RIVERSIDE STATE PARK.** You'll find places to hike, picnic, fish, and camp in this 7,300-acre park located along the Spokane River, northwest of the city. One trail takes you through a 17-million-year-old fossil forest, set in Deep Creek Canyon. Two easy family hikes begin near the Bowl and Pitcher rock formation, located close to the suspension bridge that crosses the river. Bear right past the picnic shelter to hike the downstream section of the trip (five miles roundtrip) or left at the picnic shelter to hike the shorter upstream section (two miles roundtrip).

The park office is open Wednesday through Friday for trail information. Horseback riding is also available in the park, at **TRAILTON STABLES** (509/456-8249).

There is no food available here, so bring your own picnic or plan to barbecue.

*N. 4427 Aubrey L. White Pkwy. (go north on Division to Francis, then west to Assembly St., where Francis becomes Nine Mile Road. Travel .75 mile northwest to Rifle Road and turn left onto Aubrey L. White Pkwy.) 509/456-3964.*

**SILVERWOOD THEME PARK.** Northeast of Spokane in Athol, Idaho, you'll find a turn-of-the-century theme park complete with rides, air shows, and other live entertainment. Northern Idaho is rich in mining history, and Silverwood recreates the atmosphere of an old mining town—with several modern twists, of course. Come early and plan to stay all day. The admission rates may seem steep, but those with patience for the inevitable lines will certainly get their money's worth.

A new wooden roller coaster, "Tremors," will take the bravest of riders on a harrowing trip that includes going underground five times! Younger children will enjoy "Tinywood," which features a train roller coaster and other kiddie rides, a mine to explore, tree climbs and tunnels, water play, and miniature games. Look for vintage biplanes performing stunts overhead, jugglers tossing all sorts of things on Main Street, and snacks everywhere.

*Located 1 hour northeast in Athol, Idaho. 208/683-3400; www.silverwood4fun.com. Open Sun.-Thurs., 11 a.m.-9 p.m.; Fri.-Sat., 11 a.m.-10 p.m. (June-Labor Day); Sat.-Sun. 11* *a.m.-8 p.m. (mid-May-June & Labor Day-Oct.). Take I-90 east about 30 miles to Hwy 95, then north 15 miles. Cost: $21.99/adult & child 8 and older, $13.99/child 3-7, free/ under 3.*

## CALENDAR

**JANUARY**
Northwest Bach Festival.

**MARCH**
St. Patrick's Day Parade.

**MAY**
Lilac Festival & Bloomsday Run.
Spokane Music & Arts Festival.
Armed Forces Torchlight Parade.

**JULY**
Cheney Rodeo, Cheney.

**SEPTEMBER**
Spokane Interstate Fair.

**OCTOBER**
Family A-Fair.
Green Bluff Apple Festival.

## RESOURCES

**KIDSLINE** provides a taped message about activities for children.
509/458-8800, ext. 3020

**REI (RECREATIONAL EQUIPMENT, INC.) STORE** has clothing, equipment, rentals, and information for a wide variety of outdoor activities.
N. 1125 Monroe, Spokane 99201
509/328-9900

**SPOKANE REGIONAL CONVENTION AND VISITORS BUREAU**
201 W. Main, Spokane 99201
509/747-3230; 800/248-3230

**SPOKANE TRANSIT AUTHORITY**
509/328-7433

## BOOKS AND PUBLICATIONS

*Inland NW Family Magazine* is available at most children's shops, grocery stores and libraries.

*100 Hikes in the Inland Northwest*, by Rich Lander, Ida Rowe Iophin and the Spokane Mountaineers, Seattle Mountaineers, 1987.

## INLAND EMPIRE

This slow-paced and beautiful region offers natural attractions your family won't find anywhere else in the state. Just the drive across these subtle wheat lands is an experience—full of nuances of color and texture. And Pullman has become a worthy destination—it's a cosmopolitan hick town, if such a combination is possible (at any rate, you'll find the Starbucks just a few blocks from the cow barn). Walla Walla is a relaxed and manageable town, and offers families a look at Washington history that will make more impression than any textbook.

## PULLMAN

The largest town in Washington's "Inland Empire," Pullman has only about 24,000 permanent residents—an interesting mix of farmers and faculty—but the town grows exponentially each September with the beginning of the school year at Washington State University. The campus, town, and surrounding area are easily accessible to families, and who knows? Maybe a visit will inspire a youngster to return here for college.

### GETTING THERE

From Seattle, it's a fairly straight shot across the state to the Pullman area, via Interstate 90 and Highway 26. Take I-90 east to Vantage, on the Columbia River (about 140 miles). Exit I-90 and head east on Highway 26, through the small towns of Othello and Washtucna (say that 20 times, fast). Fifty-one miles east of Washtucna, exit to Highway 195 for the last 15 miles into the college town of Pullman.

**ROADSIDE ATTRACTIONS.** Along Highway 26, you'll travel through a hauntingly beautiful terrain of rolling hills and wheat fields known as The Palouse. The scenery will become boring for the youngest ones, but your more sophisticated backseat travelers will appreciate the nuance of light and shadow in winter, or the dancing color and movement of green and gold wheat in spring and summer.

Near Othello, consider a stop at the **COLUMBIA NATIONAL WILDLIFE REFUGE** (735 E. Main St., Othello; 509/488-2668). These basalt cliffs and sagebrush-covered fields provide nesting grounds for a variety of fowl, including red-tailed hawks, American kestrels, owls and great blue herons. Increasing numbers of sandhill cranes are also visiting the refuge. The squeamish will want to take note of the five species of snake found on the refuge, including the western rattlesnake.

### PLACES TO STAY

#### PARADISE CREEK QUALITY INN
*1050 SE Bishop Blvd.*
*509/332-0500, 800/669-3212*
*Rates: Inexpensive to moderate*
*FYI: Refrigerators/microwaves; outdoor pool (seasonal); laundry; pets OK (fee)*

This 66-room motel, located along Pullman's modest "hotel row," is within walking distance of Washington State University and businesses (including the Starbucks). It's quiet and comfortable, and the grounds are enhanced by the pretty little creek running alongside (hence the name). If you visit off-season and the pool is closed, the kids might enjoy a soak in the hot tub.

**66 PARENT COMMENTS**
*"The kids enjoyed this place, especially the fresh-baked cookies and milk served nightly in the lobby. Mom and dad enjoyed quiet relaxation in the spa."*

### PLACES TO EAT

#### HILLTOP STEAKHOUSE
*928 Olsen, adjacent to Best Western Heritage Inn*
*509/334-2555*
*Hours: Lunch Mon.-Fri., dinner daily, Sun. brunch*

You're in cow country: what better reason to break down and have that steak you've been thinking about? Our parent reviewers didn't get a chance to stop here, but the Pullman scuttlebutt is that this is the place to find the juiciest steaks around. If red meat isn't your thing, the eclectic dinner menu offers fresh seafood, chicken, and pasta dishes as well.

Kids can choose from a number of children's menu standards, including hamburgers and fish and chips; if your kids are small eaters, these entræes are big enough to share.

**SWILLY'S**
*200 NE Kamiaken St.*
*509/334-3395*
*Hours: Lunch, dinner Mon.-Sat.*

This intriguing spot, located downtown on the edge of the Palouse River, was once a photographer's studio. It still has many of its original features, such as the exposed brick walls, which give it a rich, bistro-like ambiance. The fare here leans toward the Italian, including fresh pastas and creative calzones, and the younger set can choose smaller portions of similar foods from the children's menu. Attention mom and dad: cuisine options here are nicely complimented by a good selection of imported beer and Washington State wines.

On a nice night, the family can dine on the outer porch overlooking the creek.

## WHAT TO SEE & DO

**LYONS FERRY STATE PARK.** The park was named for the boatman who operated a current-propelled ferry across the Snake River during the last century. The ferry was used by settlers and soldiers alike to access the Palouse region. There are two sights of special interest here.

Located at the confluence of the Snake and Palouse rivers, the **PALOUSE FALLS** drop 198 feet over a basalt cliff into a deep basin. Hiking a short trail provides a scenic perspective from the top of the falls, which are most dramatic in spring and summer.

Just below the falls is the **MARMES ROCK SHELTER**, where 10,000-year-old human remains were unearthed in 1968. The site, accessible from the park via a 2.5-mile trail, has been designated as a heritage site by the Washington State Parks and Recreation Commission.

Lyons Ferry State Park offers overnight camping April through September; the remainder of the year is day-use only.

*Twenty-three miles southeast of Washtucna on Hwy. 261;*
*509/399-2001.*

**WASHINGTON STATE UNIVERSITY.** Founded in 1890, WSU has a pretty campus and a number of interesting museums, including anthropology, art, and veterinary medicine. Campus tours are offered Monday-Friday at 1 p.m. 509/335-5586

It's often possible to catch a "class act"—dance, theater, music or fine arts—sponsored by the University.

No visit to WSU would be complete without a stop at the college creamery, **FERDINAND'S** (509/335-2141; Room 101Food Quality Bldg., on S. Fairway Rd.). This is the home of Cougar Gold (an extra-sharp cheddar cheese), the thickest milkshake in the land, and other creamy delights, all made from the products of the University's own dairy herd. The creamery is open weekdays only.

## RESOURCES

**PULLMAN CHAMBER OF COMMERCE**
N. 415 Grand Ave., Pullman  99163
509/334-3565; 800/365-6948

# WALLA WALLA

Walla Walla is essentially a farming and ranching town, and it's located about as far from Seattle as you can go without leaving the state, but these characteristics are not necessarily negatives! There truly are intriguing family attractions here.

There's a strong sense of history in Walla Walla, which makes it a great place to reinforce the kids' school lessons. Lewis and Clark came through the area in 1805, and passed on information that spurred the tremendous growth of fur trading in the region. One of the earliest settlements in the Northwest Territory was established near Walla Walla in 1836—a mission built just west of the present town.

Today this peaceful town of 26,000 is home to Whitman College, a first-class private institution. The surrounding area is rich in natural resources. Named for the Walla Walla Indian phrase meaning "many waters," the region is watered by numerous rivers and creeks, supporting rich and productive farm and ranch lands.

## PLACES TO STAY

**BEST WESTERN WALLA WALLA SUITES INN**
*7 E. Oak St., 99362*
*509/525-4700*
*Rates: Moderate*
*FYI: Complimentary breakfast buffet; refrigerators/microwaves;*

*indoor pool; exercise facility; pets OK*

This new, three-story Best Western offers families a variety of suites in various configurations. All are spacious and equipped with the basic amenities. The indoor pool keeps kids out of mischief when the great outdoors is too hot or too cold.

**❝ PARENT COMMENTS**

> "We liked the proximity to downtown; we were able to walk to dinner (right next door) and to lunch the next day."

## PLACES TO EAT

### JACOBI'S
*416 N. 2nd St.*
*509/525-2677*
*Hours: Lunch, dinner daily*

What Jacobi's lacks in fine cuisine it makes up for in ambiance. Occupying the old Northern Pacific Railroad depot, it offers the opportunity to dine in a railroad car. The depot itself, which also has tables, is decorated with railroad photographs and memorabilia.

The fare here is fine, if not inspired, and the menu is 20 pages long! The children's menu offers all the most popular kid choices, including a large and luscious cheeseburger.

If the dining car is hot or stuffy in summer, Jacobi's also offers seasonal dining on the patio.

### MERCHANTS LIMITED DELI
*21 E. Main St.*
*509/525-0900*
*Hours: Lunch, dinner daily*

Whether or not your kids find anything to eat here, they'll have plenty to look at. This New York-style deli is piled high with goodies: deli cases are loaded with meats, cheeses, and delicious, fresh salads, as well as a few homemade desserts and cookies. There's also a bakery case offering croissants and bagels. The deli workers will cheerfully serve a Dagwood-sized sandwich on fresh bread, a steaming bowl of homemade soup, or any number of baked delicacies such as quiche or mini-pizza. Don't be shy—belly up and make your choices; you won't be disappointed.

You can eat indoors, or choose one of a handful of tables on the front sidewalk. This is also an excellent place to improvise a picnic lunch.

## WHAT TO SEE & DO

**FORT WALLA WALLA STATE PARK.** The museum complex at Fort Walla Walla State Park gives school-age kids a unique opportunity to step back into the middle and late 1800s. It is built on two levels: on the lower level is the Pioneer Settlement, a grouping of 16 structures (some are replicas, some are actual structures dating to 1859). The upper level has five large exhibit buildings, which house both permanent and changing exhibits. Artifacts displayed here help tell the story of the Oregon Trail pioneers, and those who settled the Pacific Northwest. Be sure to check out the Agricultural Building, with its team of 33 life-sized mules, fully harnessed and driven by a single man.

*755 Myra Road (south end of town off Hwy. 125). 509/525-7703. Open April-Oct., Tue.-Sun., 10 a.m.-5 p.m. Cost: $3/adult, $1/child 6-12.*

**WHITMAN MISSION NATIONAL HISTORIC SITE.** Operated by the National Park Service, the Whitman Mission site interprets historical events pertaining to the lives of Marcus and Narcissa Whitman, their mission among the Cayuse, and the role of the mission as a way station along the Oregon Trail.

Heading westward in 1836, the Whitman wagon (not much more than a cart) was the first vehicle to cross the continent overland. The Whitman mission was established to bring Christianity to the Cayuse, and to persuade them to forsake their nomadic lifestyle in favor of farming. The Cayuse, however, proved indifferent to both farming and Christianity.

Gradually the mission expanded, and became a significant stop for immigrants travelling west on the Oregon Trail. However, growing cultural tensions between the missionaries and the Cayuse heightened when a measles epidemic, introduced to the area by the missionaries, spread rapidly among the Cayuse, eventually killing one-half of the tribe. A band of Cayuse, convinced that the Whitmans were poisoning their tribe, attacked the mission in 1847, killing the Whitmans and 11 others.

At the Visitor Center, the 10-minute slide show and exhibits prepare families to view the site. Although there are no buildings standing—the mission was burned in the mid 1800's—the site is surprisingly affecting. There are lines drawn to show the foundations of the large adobe house, mill, sawmill and blacksmith, and recorders along the trail tell the tale of the mission. (Parents may want to spare younger children the vivid story of the massacre itself, told at the last stop.)

Visitors can walk the short trail to the top of the hill where the Memorial Shaft to the Whitmans is located, and the descending trail to the Great Grave, which contains the bodies of those killed in the massacre. (Parent may wish to provide additional information to "balance" the historical recording here. Our parent reviewer felt it better represented the point of view of the missionaries than that of the Native Americans.) During weekend afternoons in the summer, park rangers and volunteers are on-site to demonstrate pioneer and Native American skills and crafts.

*Located off Hwy.12, 7 miles west of Walla Walla. 509/522-6360 or 529-2761; www.nps.gov/whmi/home.htm. Open daily, 8 a.m. to 6 p.m. (summer); 8 a.m.-4:30 p.m. (remainder of year). Cost: $2/adult, free/under 17, $4/family.*

## CALENDAR

**MAY**
Walla Walla Balloon Stampede.
**JULY**
Walla Walla Sweet Onion Blues Fest.

## RESOURCES

**WALLA WALLA VALLEY CHAMBER OF COMMERCE**
P.O. Box 644, 29 E. Sumach St., Walla Walla  99362
509/525-0850; 877/WWVISIT; www.wwchamber.com

## BRITISH COLUMBIA

British Columbia is larger than the states of Washington, Oregon, and California combined, yet it numbers fewer residents than Washington State: about four million. This Canadian province borders Alberta and the Yukon and Northwest Territories as well as four U.S. states (Washington, Idaho, Montana, and Alaska). Its splendid diversity of land and people makes British Columbia a top tourist destination for visitors from around the world. Here, families can discover unique First Nations cultures, engage in just about every form of outdoor recreation, and sample big-city amenities in a single visit.

**HISTORY.** Home for thousands of years to the Haida, Kwakiutl, Salish, Tsimshian, and Tlingit peoples, among many other First Nations, the area was first explored by Europeans during the eighteenth century, both from sea and from land. By the end of that century, early Spanish dominance had given way to British control. British colonies experienced widespread growth during the 1850s, when gold was discovered in the Cariboo region, opening up what is now the province's interior to settlement. British Columbia became a Canadian province in 1871. Its economy was built largely on timber products, and its importance increased with the completion of the transcontinental railway in 1885 and the opening of the Panama Canal allowing its products to reach markets worldwide. Today, B.C. continues to depend on natural resources as the foundation of its economy, but tourism has become its second largest industry.

**GEOGRAPHY.** Remarkably varied, B.C.'s geography ranges from arid desert to lush, temperate rainforest; from pristine fjords to towering peaks. The province is divided vertically into three mountain ranges that run northwest-southeast: the coast range, the Kootenays (a collection of small, parallel ranges in east-central B.C.), and the Rockies, straddling the border with Alberta. Several major waterways traverse the province including the Fraser, Peace, Stikine, and Skeena rivers. The headwaters of the mighty Columbia are located in B.C. Huge islands dot the waters off the province's west coast. The biggest, Vancouver Island, is North America's largest island. To its north lie the lovely Queen Charlottes, homeland of the Haida people.

B.C. has two principal population centers. Vancouver, sandwiched between the Fraser River delta to the south and Burrard Inlet to the north, is the province's largest city. Victoria, the province's capital, perches on the southwest corner of Vancouver Island, just an hour's ferry ride from Washington's San Juan Island.

The climate along the entire length of the coast is mild and much like that of coastal Washington and Oregon. In the interior, weather can be harsh with snowy winters and scorching summers. Consequently, pretty much every outdoor sport and activity is offered somewhere in the province. Skiing, mountain biking, hiking, camping, cycling, sailing, windsurfing, kayaking and canoeing opportunities are abundant, world class, and family-friendly.

**SPECIAL FEATURES.** The uninitiated U.S. traveler is wise to review the information below before heading into British Columbia. Thanks to Hollywood, American culture is a known quantity up north. However, Canadian culture remains largely a mystery to Americans, who sometimes forget that Canada is a separate country with its own history and culture. This fact affords U.S. families a golden opportunity to combine the excitement of foreign travel with the convenience of a familiar language, just a few hours' drive away.

■ Canadians celebrate a number of holidays not observed in the United States. On these days, public transportation might run on different schedules and businesses might be closed. Visitors can expect to find some popular destinations booked up during these holidays, especially on three-day weekends during summer months. In addition to New Year's, Veteran's Day, Labor Day, and Christmas, Canada observes:

**GOOD FRIDAY:** The Friday before Easter Sunday.

**VICTORIA DAY:** The Monday after the third weekend in May, marking the anniversary of Queen Victoria's birth.

**CANADA DAY:** July 1, commemorating the date in 1867 on which Canada became a country.

**CIVIC HOLIDAY:** The first Monday in August, a drably named holiday that gives residents of most provinces a three-day weekend.

**THANKSGIVING:** The second Monday in October, coinciding with Columbus Day in the U.S.

**BOXING DAY:** Celebrated December 26, a holdover from a British holiday that once included gift-giving between employers and employees.

■ Canadian measurements follow the metric system. Distances and speeds are given in kilometers (km)-1 km equals about .6 mile. Length and height, as in mountain peaks, are measured in meters (1 meter equals about .9 yard). Acreage is given as hectares (1 acre is .about .4 hectare). Rain and snowfall are measured in centimeters (about 2.5 centimeters per inch). Food is measured in grams and kilograms. (A kilogram is approximately 2.2 pounds. An ounce is roughly 28 grams.) Liquids are measured in liters (a quart equals .95 liter).

■ Canadians, as a whole, are more taxed than Americans. Along with sales tax, a Goods & Services Tax (known as the GST) is levied (Oregon visitors, brace yourselves). The combination of sales tax and GST (Goods & Services Tax) in Canada amounts to 14% or more, easily enough to impact travelers' budgets. Luckily, there is relief for non-Canadians: you can recoup all of the GST you've paid for certain items, if you are prepared to keep your receipts and do the paperwork involved. (Begin by picking up the rebate form as you cross the border into Canada.) Recoverable expenses include hotels, gifts, and clothing.

For more information on the GST and how to recover it, call 800/66VISIT (within Canada) or 613/991/3346. Or write to Revenue Canada, Customs and Excise, Visitors' Rebate Program, Ottawa, Canada K1A 1J5.

## PROVINCE-WIDE RESOURCES

### BC PARKS
800 Johnson St.
Victoria, B.C., Canada  V8V 1X4
250/387-4550

### GREAT SPOTS! RECREATION PROPERTIES LTD.
P.O. Box 62001, Arbutus Postal Outlet
Vancouver, B.C., Canada  V6J 1Z1
604/736-0184; www.greatspots.com

### SUPER NATURAL BC INFORMATION/RESERVATION SERVICE
P.O. Box 9830
Stn. Prov Gov.
Victoria, B.C., Canada  V8W 9W5
800/633-6000

# SOUTHERN BRITISH COLUMBIA

The lower mainland of British Columbia runs north from the U.S. border through the Fraser River delta to the city of Vancouver and continues north of Burrard Inlet, through West and North Vancouver, on up to Whistler. East of Vancouver, a chain of suburbs and small communities extends to the mountains and Harrison Hot Springs. The terrain is varied—from the flat river-delta farmlands to the sheer peaks that tower over North Vancouver. Population density may be greater here than in other parts of the province, but the variety of year-round, family-friendly activities available across the region more than compensates.

## GETTING THERE

Vancouver is 150 miles north of Seattle, a straight shot on Interstate 5 (via the Blaine-Douglas border crossing). Driving time is approximately three hours, but will be affected by traffic at the border station. It is not unusual to have a 30- to 90-minute wait, especially on weekends and holidays.

From the United States, **Amtrak** provides train service between Seattle and Vancouver. The train makes one round trip daily, departing Seattle's King Street Station at 7:45 a.m. and arriving at Vancouver's Pacific Central Station at 11:40 a.m. Returning, it departs Vancouver at 6 p.m. and arrives in Seattle at 9:55 p.m. The train is a Talgo—a very comfortable, Spanish-made train with a snack bar and full-service dining car. The latter offers excellent meals that will remind older travelers of the golden days of rail travel.

The train arrives at the Pacific Central Station, in downtown Vancouver. The easiest way to get downtown is to take a cab, for a more exciting (and cheaper) ride, take the SkyTrain. Its Main Street Station is just 100 yards west of the train station. (See "SkyTrain" below.)

**ROADSIDE ATTRACTIONS.** If you're driving into Vancouver from the south or east, consider dropping in at the **Newton Wave Pool.** It has a graduated floor so non-swimmers can enjoy a splash, and two large water slides for older kids. Periodically, three-foot waves are generated and the whole family will enjoy riding them. Refreshments are available and suits, towels, and equipment may be rented.

*13730 72nd Ave., Surrey (Heading north from the border, take*

*Hwy. 99, then Exit 99A. Go north on King George Hwy. and turn right at 72nd Ave.). 604/501/5540.*

**REFUELING.** There are plenty of places to refuel along the way, but for the greatest selection, stop in Bellingham, the last major city before you reach the border. (See "Bellingham: Places to Eat.")

# VANCOUVER

A unique blend of cosmopolitan sophistication and friendly relaxed style in a spectacular setting amid beaches, fjords, and mountains places Vancouver among the world's loveliest cities—right up there with Hong Kong and Rio de Janeiro, but a lot closer to home. The city is compact, defined by Burrard Inlet to the north, Georgia Strait to the west, and the Fraser River delta to the south. Unlike Seattle and Portland, Vancouver is not bisected by a freeway, and there's no bypass around it either. But as a trade-off for occasional congestion, residents and visitors can count on snow skiing within a half-hour drive and great beachcombing just around the corner.

As Canada's gateway to the Pacific Rim, Vancouver has a rich ethnic mixture. An already sizable Asian-Canadian community received a boost from Hong Kong in the '80s and '90s. Thriving South Asian communities, along with substantial Greek, Italian, Japanese, and Indian populations, contribute to Vancouver's vibrant cultural mosaic and eclectic charm.

For families, Vancouver has some especially appealing facets: family-oriented and affordable hotels in the heart of downtown, an equal mix of indoor and outdoor activities for all ages, and some of the best children's attractions in the Pacific Northwest.

## GETTING AROUND

Vancouver has an exceptionally good public transportation system that will get you around town while providing a fun ride.

The **SkyTrain** is an automated, light-rail train that travels on an elevated track, except in the downtown core when it goes underground. The four downtown stations are Stadium, Granville, Burrard, and Waterfront. From these stations the train goes to Main Street Station, which is right next to the train station and Science World.

Trains run about every five minutes. The fare from Main Street to any of the downtown stations is $2.25 per adult and $1.50 per child ages two to 15.

The **SeaBus** is a passenger-only ferry that shuttles back and forth across Burrard Inlet, between downtown Vancouver and North Vancouver. The enjoyable ride affords a great view of the city's major harbor. It leaves from Waterfront Station, the SkyTrain terminus, every 15 minutes. Crossings take 12 minutes. The fare is $2.25 for adults, $1.50 for kids. Return in 90 minutes, and you'll need to pay only one fare.

**City buses** aren't as exciting, but they will get you where you need to go, most of the time. Basic fare is $1.50; each added zone is another $.75. A book of 10 tickets costs $13.75. By picking up a copy of the pamphlet *Discover Vancouver in Transit*, you'll find out how to get to Vancouver's major sights by bus, SkyTrain or SeaBus. It is available at the Tourist Information Centre at 200 Burrard Street and in some hotels. Or you can call B.C. Transit Information at 604/521-0400.

Fares are the same on the buses, SeaBus, and SkyTrain, and you can transfer among the systems.

**False Creek Ferries** operates boats that shuttle between major family attractions on the waterfront, year-round. One route takes passengers to and from the Aquatic Centre across False Creek (see "Swimming") and from there, over to Vanier Park; in the opposite direction, ferries go to Stamps Landing and to Science World (see "Museums"). Service is very frequent in summer, less so in winter. Fares for adults run $1.75 to $5 one way, depending on destination; fares for kids run between $1 and $3.

The **Aquabus** operates daily, 7 a.m. to 8 p.m. from Granville Island to the foot of Hornby Street; 8:30 a.m. to 6:15 p.m. from Granville Island to Yaletown. Ferries leave every half-hour to Stamp's Landing from False Creek and on weekends to Science World. Adult fares are $.75; for travelers with a bike, they run $2.25.

## RESOURCES

### B.C. TRANSIT
604/521-0400
Information about the Bus, Skytrain, and SeaBus

### GREATER VANCOUVER REGIONAL DISTRICT
604/432-6350
Information about Regional Parks

### WEBSITE

At www.findfamilyfun.com/ you'll find lists and descriptions of a variety of family attractions in Vancouver and the lower mainland.

### PLACES TO STAY

If you're new to Canada, read about GST in the Introduction. By mentally adding 15 percent to the rates you're quoted for hotel rooms when making reservations, you'll be spared unpleasant surprises.

Each year in the United States during the off-season (usually November-April), Tourism Vancouver (see "Resources") advertises a wide variety of hotel packages; some are offered in conjunction with Amtrak bookings and include tickets to various attractions. Many of the hotels listed below participate, and savings can be substantial, especially for high-end accommodation. Check your local newspaper in the fall, or contact Tourism Vancouver or your hotel of choice.

### COAST PLAZA

*1733 Comox St., V6G 1P6*
*604/688-7711, 800/663-1144; www.coasthotels.com*
*Rates: Expensive*
*FYI: Two restaurants; kitchens (some units); microwaves (on request); indoor pool; Nintendo; pets OK*

This West End hotel, originally an apartment building, offers rooms and suites that are spacious and comfortable for families, even large ones. Each of the 300 rooms and suites has a balcony and a view of the city, mountains, or bay. Most rooms have been updated recently. You can't beat this location—it's in a residential neighborhood with Stanley Park nearby. Most downtown destinations are only minutes away by car, and easily accessible on foot. The Denman Place Mall, connected to the hotel, has a grocery store, shops, restaurants, ATM machines, and a movie theater. An attractive, if somewhat hidden, feature is the outdoor garden area with fountains, park benches, and tables.

In addition to the pool and sauna, guests enjoy privileges at the squash and racquetball courts next door (Club Cardio). The hotel can provide box lunches for picnics, jogging maps, and playing cards. Rooms have dataports for modems; an office with computer and printer is available for rent.

*"Even in the rain, we enjoy a stay at the Coast Plaza because the accommodations are self-contained and central to the downtown area."*

*"The rooms are so large, it's possible to bring along a teen-aged babysitter."*

*"I chose this location because it's within walking distance of English Bay Beach, and we came to see the Benson & Hedges Symphony of Fire international fireworks competition. I had asked for a room with a view when making my reservation but was told that it would be very expensive due to the show, so I was pleasantly surprised to find that we had an almost unob-structed view of the fireworks show from our balcony."*

## FOUR SEASONS HOTEL

*791 West Georgia St., V6C 2T4*
*604/689-9333, 800/332-3442*
*Rates: Expensive*
*FYI: Three restaurants; pool; exercise equipment; laundry; valet parking (fee); pets OK*

The Four Seasons is well-known for dedication to good service. To parents traveling with children, the staff offers many extras that contribute to a very satisfying hotel experience.

As in other Four Seasons hotels, children receive a toy; a fluffy, little bathrobe just like their parents' to use during their stay; and a cookies-and-milk snack. If you are traveling with an infant, expect whatever special needs you may have to be graciously provided—including strollers, playpens, and baby toys.

The lovely pool is designed so that it lies both indoors and outside. Exercise machines in the pool area let you enjoy the fresh air while working out, and there is a large deck for sunbathing.

The Four Seasons is centrally located in the heart of downtown, and the staff is very helpful about suggesting attractions and activities of interest to families.

*"Two years after our visit, my eight-year-old daughter still talks about the robe and fresh cookies delivered to our room unannounced soon after we arrived."*

*"It has become a family tradition. Every year during the holiday season dad takes his two daughters for a fabulous two-night stay at the Four Seasons. The hotel is beautifully decorated for the holidays. We use our Entertainment coupon for a 50 percent discount on the room price. My only regret is that on my last*

*visit I used valet parking at the hotel. The parking bill was painfully high. Next time I'll look for a better parking deal."*

*"The large swimming pool is half inside and half outside. Our kids loved it."*

### THE GREENBRIER HOTEL
*1393 Robson St., V6E 1C6*
*604/683-4558*
*Rates: Inexpensive*
*FYI: Kitchens; free parking*

This is a good choice if you don't care about being fancy, want the option of cooking your own meals, and appreciate a central location. The newly renovated rooms are large and feature bedroom, living room with hide-a-bed, and kitchenette. There is free underground parking (a real plus in downtown Vancouver).

The heart of downtown is a half-mile walk away; Stanley Park is five minutes away by bus or car. Robson Street is an attraction in itself, with ethnic restaurants, bakeries, corner groceries, and intriguing shops within easy walking distance.

### PACIFIC PALISADES
*1277 Robson St., V6E 1C4*
*604/688-0461*
*Rates: Expensive*
*FYI: Restaurant; refrigerators/microwaves; indoor pool; exercise room; secured underground parking*

A Shangri-la International hotel, Pacific Palisades offers a luxurious stay at a great location. Formerly an apartment building, the hotel has some of the most spacious rooms in the city. All rooms have a view of the water or the mountains.

The indoor recreation area is a real plus for families. The large pool, whirlpool, sauna, and exercise room are located in a separate building. The staff is friendly and thoroughly accommodating.

**❝ PARENT COMMENTS**

*"The concierge was friendly and very helpful. She researched activities for kids and sent a packet of information to our room."*

*"We spent a three-day weekend just playing in the pool and strolling on Robson Street. We found a number of great restaurants within easy walking distance."*

## ROSEDALE ON ROBSON SUITE HOTEL
*838 Hamilton St. V6B 6A2*
*604/689-8033, 800/661-8870; www.rosedaleonrobson.com*
*Rates: Moderate*
*FYI: Restaurant; kitchens; indoor pool; Nintendo; exercise room; outdoor garden terrace; fax, Internet access, voicemail, dataports in rooms*

This suite hotel, new in 1996, is conveniently located about four blocks east of where the main Robson shopping area begins. Rooms are pleasant, and the informal restaurant is good. The Vancouver Library Square (new city library with a variety of shops and sitting area) is across the street; the Yaletown neighborhood, a newly renovated area of shops, restaurants, and designers' studios, begins a block south. The concierge will help plan family outings.

### 66 PARENT COMMENTS
*"The bedroom of our one-bedroom suite was a small sleeping area with a queen bed, separated by a sliding door to the living room which had a sleeper sofa. The suite was convenient and functional, if not particularly large."*

*"Rosie's on Robson is the hotel's New York deli-style restaurant, a casual place with an attached bar area. There's also a deli for take-out, and room service is available. We bought take-out goodies here mostly, including latkes with applesauce, which were quite good, even after the elevator ride up to our room."*

## SHAUGHNESSY VILLAGE
*1125 W. 12th Ave., V6H 3Z3*
*604/736-5511; www.shaughnessyvillage.com*
*Rates: Inexpensive to moderate*
*FYI: Restaurant; refrigerators/microwaves; outdoor pool (seasonal); health club; shuffleboard, crazy-putt golf, billiards; laundry; no in-room telephones*

It bills itself as "Canada's largest bed & breakfast guest house," and it just may be. It's certainly the only high-rise B&B. While the location is residential, it's close to Granville Street shopping and buses to downtown. Room design cleverly re-creates cruise-ship stateroom accommodation, with creative use of storage space. The two-room suites are small, but with the range of child-pleasing amenities to explore, few will want to spend much time in their rooms, anyway. The bathroom amenities are oddly placed, but they're there. Rooms facing north are quiet, with balconies that offer spectacular mountain views; rooms facing 12th Avenue can be noisy.

The staff is friendly and helpful. The Café Helena serves meals all day at low prices and with the usual kid-friendly standbys, from pizza to burgers and pastas. Guests include long-term residents, some undergoing treatment at nearby Vancouver General Hospital or Children's Hospital.

**❝ PARENT COMMENTS**

"*Décor is 'Victorian nautical'—lots of lovely use of wood, model ships, porthole windows, mirrors, velvet furniture, and old-fashioned rugs. Sort of like a land-based Titanic!*"

"*When we checked in, we were a bit surprised when the front-desk clerk suggested we take the key and inspect our room. Apparently, not everyone expects such small rooms— but we thought they were cute and comfortable.*"

### SUNSET INN TRAVEL APARTMENTS
*1111 Burnaby St., V6E 1P4*
*604/688-2474; www.sunsetinn.com*
*Rates: Inexpensive to moderate*
*FYI: Kitchens; exercise room; laundry; free parking*

Families who need room to spread out will appreciate the spacious suites here. A typical suite has, in addition to a bedroom, a full separate kitchen, dining room, and living room with two sofa beds. The location is downtown, with equal access to the seawall walk at Stanley Park (a long hike for small legs) and to the north and east for the SeaBus and Gastown. At the Aquatic Centre, just a few blocks away, you can go swimming or hop on a ferry to Granville Island or Vanier Park.

**❝ PARENT COMMENTS**

"*Handy to downtown. Surprisingly quiet given the location.*"

### SYLVIA HOTEL
*1154 Gilford St., V6G 2P6*
*604/681-9321*
*Rates: Inexpensive*
*FYI: Coffee shop; kitchens (some units); covered parking; pets OK*

For many years, visitors to Vancouver who prefer to save their vacation money for good food and entertainment have taken advantage of the low rates at the Sylvia. The brick, ivy-covered building was originally one of the nicest apartment buildings in town. Now a bit shabby, but still full of eccentric charm, it offers reasonable rooms, a friendly staff, and a sterling location across the street from English Bay and 2.5 blocks from Stanley Park. There is a mystique about the Sylvia; guests come from a long way to stay here, and they return over and over; booking ahead is essential. Rooms vary in size from small to quite large. Some have views.

**❝❝ PARENT COMMENTS**

*"It's a nice walk along English Bay to the playground in Stanley Park. And nearby Denman Street has a nice choice of restaurants and coffee shops."*

*"The newer rooms are less shabby but lack the 'charm' of the older rooms."*

*"We stay here when we are going on to ski at Whistler. An economic choice before we spend big bucks skiing."*

*"Travelers with toddlers take note: windows are low to the ground in some rooms."*

**UNIVERSITY OF BRITISH COLUMBIA CONFERENCE CENTRE**
*Reservations Office, 5961 Student Union Blvd. V6T 2C9*
*604/822-1010; www.conferences.ubc.ca*
*Rates: Inexpensive*
*FYI: Kitchens (some units); refrigerators/microwaves (some units); no TV, baths, or telephones in some units*

For big families and anyone on a tight budget, or for those who simply miss their university dorm days, UBC offers good accommodation at the right price. Where else can you book a six-bedroom suite in summer for $129 a night on one of the West Coast's loveliest campuses? Like other colleges, UBC rents accommodation year round. Unlike hotels and resorts, selection and options are greater in summer, when most students aren't in residence.

At the bottom end, Place Vanier Residence, $50 buys you a basic dorm room with two single beds and male and female bathrooms on alternate floors; it's available May 10-August 26 only. The Walter Gage Residence Court suites, available year round, are one-bedroom units with kitchen, TV, bath, and phone. Rates in winter are low; parking is free in summer. At the high end are the Tower Suites, six bedrooms (five with a single bed each; one with a double bed), kitchen, bath, TV, and phone. Add $10 for each additional guest after the first two.

On campus you can swim (see "Swimming") or check out the anthropology museum (see "Museums"). Families who've just spent a summer night in the dorms, may care to check out the Sunshine Sandwich Shop, at 2756 W. Broadway, a diner that comes recommended for good, inexpensive breakfasts.

**❝ PARENT COMMENTS**
*"Rooms in the Place Vanier Residences have been very quiet when we've stayed. But note that the rooms in the 17-story towers can be noisy at busy times, such as during the Vancouver Folk Music Festival in July."*

## PLACES TO EAT

### APOLLONIA
*1830 Fir St.*
*604/736-9559*
*Hours: Lunch, dinner Mon.-Fri.; dinner only Sat.; closed Sun.*

The Apollonia falls squarely within the Vancouver tradition of Greek/Italian establishments, ideal for pleasing the fussy child (pizza) at the same time as the more discerning parent gourmet (Greek cuisine). At this reasonably priced, friendly family-run café, pizza offerings are limited but appealing; lasagna and gyro sandwiches are also available. To challenge the more adventurous diner are kalamari, dolmades (stuffed vine leaves), and saganaki (fried cheese). Its location close to Granville Island makes it a good destination to head for after a visit there, helping to fill the void left by the closing of Isadora's.

### BUD'S
*1007 Denman*
*604/736-9559*
*Hours: Lunch, dinner daily*

For traditional, English-style fish and chips, you simply can't beat Bud's. The atmosphere is traditional, too: a rather dark, crowded room full of booths and tables. But if you don't mind the occasional spot of grease, it's a relaxed place to take kids. Located just three blocks from English Bay, there's the option of picking up a meal to go and walking down to the waterfront.

### FU WAH RESTAURANT
*555 Gore Ave., 2nd Floor*
*604/688-8722*
*Hours: Dim sum/breakfast, lunch, dinner daily*

This Chinatown restaurant is a great place to go for an authentic dim sum brunch. It's especially bustling with families on Sunday mornings (like the rest of Chinatown). While some may balk at the prospect of recently slaughtered chickens, pigs, and beef on display, not to mention preserved examples of squid, shellfish, and mushrooms, others will be fascinated.

### OLYMPIA PIZZA & PASTA
*3205 W. Broadway*
*604/732-5334*
*Hours: Lunch, dinner Mon.-Sat.*

Another of Vancouver's pizza/pasta bistros, the Olympia has a kids' menu and serves regular entrées in kid-size portions. The location, on Broadway between Alma and MacDonald, is handy for those who've been exploring Kits and the West Side beaches. Service is good and friendly, and patrons include many small children.

### THE PINK PEARL
*1132 E. Hastings St.*
*604/253-4316*
*Hours: Dim sum 9 a.m.-3 p.m. daily; dinner 5-10 p.m. daily (until 11 p.m. Fri.-Sat.)*

Vancouver is famous for its Asian restaurants, and this is one of the best. The Cantonese chefs have built their reputation on fresh seafood dishes. There are live tanks, and servers bring live seafood orders to the table for approval.

Though there's no kids' menu, The Pink Pearl offers plenty of Cantonese favorites. The more adventurous will find some unusual treats, as well. Dare to experiment!

The restaurant is essentially one large room, so it can be quite noisy. Families with talkative little ones will feel right at home. Take your own crayons and paper, or visit the seafood tanks for live entertainment.

### THE RED ONION
*2028 W. 41st Ave.*
*604/263-0833*
*Hours: Breakfast, lunch, dinner daily*

If it's hamburgers, hotdogs, and fries the family craves, look no further than the Red Onion. The French fries are served with a deliciously simple, lightly spiced sauce. If you're interested in lighter fare, they have it here, too, including quiche, homemade soups, and veggie sandwiches. At breakfast, lovely pastries are prepared on the premises.

With its relaxed atmosphere, the Red Onion is a comfortable place to take the kids. Bring along some books, though, as the food preparation can take time. In fact, the menu provides a disclaimer: "We blushingly apologize," it reads, "if your meal seems slow to cook. . ." It's worth the wait.

### SOPHIE'S COSMIC CAFÉ
*2095 W. 4th Ave.*
*604/732-6810*
*Hours: Breakfast, lunch, dinner daily; brunch Sat.-Sun.*

At Sophie's, a fantastically funky spot in the Kitsilano neighborhood, it's tough to decide which is better—the food or the décor. It's a visual cornucopia of kitsch, its walls dripping with paraphernalia. From the rack of antlers that supports a dozen whimsical hats to the BeeGees lunchbox (and don't forget the billiards table with the red lobster crawling out of the corner pocket), this spot will entertain children of all ages. Check out the booth railings made of original Coke bottles. There's also a toy box available, for anyone who tires of looking at the walls.

As if the incredible décor weren't enough, the food at Sophie's is fantastic. There is no kids' menu, but then none is needed—the nine-page menu dares any child to walk out hungry. And don't plan on "cleaning your plate," as the helpings are enormous. Choose from falafel, soups, salads, or deli sandwiches. Try the juicy hamburger with a thick, cappuccino milkshake. Or opt for one of Sophie's lively breakfasts, served all day. For those with iron wills, there's even a "lighter side" section in the menu.

*Our parent reviewers tell us, "There's almost always a line at Sophie's, and another wait for your food to be served. Hang in there—you'll be glad you did."*

### SUN WONG KEE
*4136 Main St.*
*604/879-7231*
*Hours: Dinner daily*

It would be a shame to visit Vancouver without going to at least one restaurant in one of the West Coast's largest Chinatowns. This one specializes in Cantonese seafood dishes and is popular with families. Prices are quite reasonable; entrées range from $7.80 to $16.90, and portions are large. Service is fast, friendly and extra care is taken on the details. The restaurant is all nonsmoking.

### WON MORE
*1184 Denman St.*
*604/688-8856*

*1944 W.4th Ave.*
*604/737-2889*
*Hours: Dinner daily.*
Sometimes, even families need a break from "family fare." This popular Szechuan restaurant fills the bill; mu shu pancakes with all kinds of savory fillings are a specialty. The attractive restaurant is handy to Stanley Park, child-friendly, and service is quick and efficient. The premises are all nonsmoking. There's a second location in Kitsilano.

## WHAT TO SEE & DO

It is well-nigh impossible to be bored in Vancouver. You will find a variety of indoor and outdoor activities, both strenuous and casual.

### STROLL & BROWSE

**COMMERCIAL DRIVE.** Once the center of Vancouver's Italian community, Commercial Drive still has plenty of great coffee bars, Italian restaurants, bakeries, and delis. More recently, the cultural mix has broadened; there's a growing Latin American community, with cafés like the **Havana** (1212 Commercial Dr.; 604/253-9119) offering excellent Cuban food. Crafts, books, music, magazines (check out the Magpie Magazine Gallery): there's an abundance of interesting shops to investigate. When little legs get tired, drop into one of the inviting outdoor cafés and people-watch while recharging your batteries with an Italian soda. In summer, check out **Trout Lake** in John Hendry Park, site of Vancouver's only lakefront beach, with swimming (lifeguards present). No pets, fires, ball-playing, or inflatable devices are allowed at the beach.

*Commercial Dr. runs north-south and is easily accessed from 12th, Broadway, or any of the major east-west arteries. John Hendry Park is at 19th & Victoria Dr. (a block east of Commercial Dr.). For a listing of shops, cafés, and more on Commercial, check out http://thedrive.net/.*

**GASTOWN.** A stroll through this venerable neighborhood is sure to lend historical perspective to your Vancouver visit. A village was founded here in 1876, but burned to the ground 10 years later. As the city grew up around it, Gastown fell into an economic decline and was in danger of being torn down until the community rallied support in 1971. Today, fully renewed, Gastown is a maze of cobblestone courtyards, Victorian architecture, shops, and sidewalk cafés. Kids will enjoy seeing the steam-powered clock which plays tunes on the quarter-hour (at Cambie and Water streets).

*West of downtown on Burrard Inlet, along Powell, Water, Alexander, Carrell & Cordova Streets.*

**GRANVILLE ISLAND.** Tucked away beneath the Granville Bridge, this was once an industrial site. The old warehouses have been remodeled to house artists' studios, craft galleries, shops, theaters, restaurants, and a huge European-style open market. This waterfront development offers lots of options for browsing. Grab a snack at the market and stroll along the dock, watching the boat traffic, feeding the pigeons, or enjoying live entertainment. Poke around the shops and art galleries. When the young ones have had enough shopping, they'll love a stop at the water park. Or stop in at the Kids Only Market, a whole warehouse full of kids' clothes and toy shops.

Bring extra patience, and use the time spent driving around hunting for a parking place to get your bearings; the layout is complex. Consider combining a trip here with a visit to Vanier Park or Science World via one of the False Creek Ferries that leave frequently from the dock near the market.

*Enter Granville Island off W. 2nd or W. 4th from the Granville Bridge or the Burrard Bridge.*

**KITSILANO.** "Kits," as it's known to Vancouverites, includes the small boutiques, cafés, and bookstores that line W. 4th from Burrard Street to just east of Macdonald. After a rather dull residential patch, shops continue west to Alma. Parallel, but five blocks north, is Cornwall Avenue on whose north side lie Vanier Park, Hadden Park, Kitsilano Park, and terrific views. Parallel to W. 4th, five blocks in the opposite direction, is Broadway, with some of the more familiar names in child-friendly retail and fast-food establishments.

*Park on a side street near Burrard & W. 4th or Cornwall, and head west.*

**ROBSON STREET.** If you have window-shopping and people-watching in mind, be sure to stroll Robson Street. You'll find a fascinating collection of upscale clothing stores, novelty shops, and restaurants with an Asian flavor. For a mid-jaunt treat, stop by **Yogurty's** (1194 Robson) for made-to-order frozen yogurt, or get the kids a fancy caramel apple at **Rocky**

**Mountain Chocolates** (1017 Robson). Parents who crave a bit of the bean will find two **Starbucks Coffee** shops nearby (1099 and 1100 Robson).

*Walk west on Robson from Burrard St.*

### KID CULTURE

The **Vancouver Symphony Orchestra** offers a Kids' Concert Series (604/876-3434; www.culturenet.ca/vso). For a complete calendar of cultural events, check Tourism Vancouver's Web site, listed under "Resources."

### SPECTATOR SPORTS

Fans of NHL hockey can check out the **Vancouver Canucks.** For tickets, call 604/280-4400.

As many families discovered during the last major-league baseball strike, attending a AAA minor-league baseball game can be every bit as much fun as watching a big league game, and a lot less expensive. The **Vancouver Canadians** play at Nat Bailey Stadium. Order tickets at 604/872-5232, www.minorleaguebaseball.com/teams/vancouver.

The **Vancouver Grizzlies,** a recent addition to the NBA, play home games at General Motors Place. Call 604/899-4667, or check their Web site, www.nba.com/grizzlies, for ticket information.

### PARKS

**QUEEN ELIZABETH PARK.** The beautiful grounds at Queen Elizabeth Park, the city's first civic arboretum, are simply a joy to walk. Paths wind among acres of native and exotic plant life, sunken gardens, and waterfalls. Worth a visit is the fabulous triodetic **Bloedel Floral Conservatory,** a lush, tropical greenhouse offering collections of 500 species of plants, from jungle to desert environments. Kids will love the pools of colorful koi fish and flocks of tropical birds.

*Enter park at 33rd & Cambie St. Conservatory open Mon.-Fri., 9 a.m.-8 p.m.; Sat.-Sun., 10 a.m.-9 p.m. (April-Sept.); daily, 10 a.m.-5:30 p.m. (Oct., Feb., March); daily, 10 a.m.-5 p.m. (Nov.-Jan.). Cost: $3.30/adult, $2/senior 65 & over, $1.65/youth 6-18, free/under 6, $6.60/family.*

**STANLEY PARK.** Surely one of the most beautiful urban parks in the world, 400-hectare Stanley Park offers outdoor recreation and indoor entertainment. The whole family will enjoy hiking or biking the 9-km seawall promenade around the periphery of the park. You'll find glorious scenery and, for the kids, a fire engine playground. If the weather's warm, pack your swimsuits and stop by the Variety Kids Water Park, which features slides, water cannons, and a full-body blow dryer. If the little ones need incentive on the walk, suggest they watch for the controversial sculpture, *Girl in Wetsuit,* a take-off on Copenhagen's mermaid (hint: this one's wearing scuba gear). Away from the seawall you can check out a game of cricket or lawn bowling. If your family includes any budding young botanists, you may be able to lure them into the famous Rose Garden and Rhododendron Garden.

On the 2.4-km walk around **Lost Lagoon,** family members will likely spot Canada geese, trumpeter swans, raccoons, skunks, and box turtles. (These animals are friendlier than they should be, so be sure your kids don't sneak them any food).

*To get there, follow Georgia St. west through downtown to the park entrance.*

**VanDusen Botanical Gardens.** OK, so gardens are not on every kid's "top ten" list. But these gardens are special, featuring plants from all over the world that blend perfectly with some spectacular indigenous plants. Any time of year, you'll find blooms and shrubs galore, set amid dramatic rockeries and waterways. The Elizabethan hedge maze and floating bridge are attractions, and there's even a special garden for kids. Let them run off their excess energy, then stop in at Sprinklers Restaurant to revitalize.

*37th & Oak St. 604/878-9274. Open daily 10 a.m.-dusk. Cost: $2.75/adult, $1.50/senior & youth 7-18, free/under 7, $5.50/family.*

### ANIMALS, ANIMALS

**Vancouver Aquarium.** What kid doesn't delight in viewing aquatic animals? At Stanley Park you'll find a wide range of fish and mammals in an exceptional setting. Best known for its killer whale show, the Aquarium is also home to two stunning Beluga whales. You'll watch harbor seals and sea otters cavort and discover aquatic wildlife from all over the world, including octopus, sharks, and reptiles. If you've promised the kids a souvenir of Vancouver, the Aquarium gift shop has an especially nice selection.

*Located in Stanley Park. 604/659-3474. Open daily 10 a.m.- 5:30 p.m. Cost: $11.95/adult, $10.55/senior & youth 13-18, $7.95/child 4-12; free/under 4; $39.95/family.*

Also within the park you'll find the **Children's Farmyard** and the wonderful **Miniature Railway.** While the old Stanley Park Zoo is history, the Children's Farmyard contains the expected assortment of farm animals.

*The Railway and Farmyard are open Easter to Oct. and weekends only thereafter, daily, 11 a.m.-4 p.m. Cost: $2.50/adult, $1.75/teen, $1.25/child under 12; $5/family (parents & 2 children). Double rates if you plan to attend both attractions; $8.50/family.*

For the **Greater Vancouver Zoological Centre,** see "South and East of Vancouver."

### THE GREAT OUTDOORS

**HIKING.** For city "hiking," you won't find anything grander than the seawall promenade at Stanley Park. Also check out the beachcombing possibilities on the beaches that march west from Vanier Park toward and around the headland on which the University of British Columbia sits. From Vanier Park, head west on Cornwall, which eventually becomes Point Grey Road. Soon you'll arrive at Jericho Beach, home of the annual Vancouver Folk Music Festival (see "Calendar."); there are trails around and through the marsh here. Hikers can follow the trail of beaches west, including Locarno Beach and Spanish Banks. Steep trails allow visitors to access these beaches from the cliffs above as well. Wreck Beach, around the point on the south side, is a longstanding nude beach, visited by many intrepid singles and families.

### SWIMMING

**SWIMMING INDOORS.** Two excellent indoor swimming pools—**Vancouver Aquatic Centre** and the **University of British Columbia Aquatic Centre**—feature Olympic-size pools and, ever popular with families, whirlpools and toddler pools. Call first for admission fees.

*Vancouver Aquatic Centre, 1050 Beach Ave. 604/665-3424. Open Mon.-Thurs., 6:30 a.m.-9:55 p.m.; Fri., 6:30 a.m.-8:55 p.m.; Sat., 8 a.m.-8:55 p.m.; Sun., 10 a.m.-8:55 p.m.*

*U.B.C. Aquatic Centre, 6121 University Blvd., U.B.C Campus. 604/822-4521. Open daily, 6:30 a.m.-10 p.m. (some days, open until later).*

**SWIMMING OUTSIDE.** For outdoor swimming or beach-bumming, the options are many. In addition to those listed under

"Hiking," Stanley Park has its Second and Third Beaches, which are handy for a quick midday dunk. Along English Bay (west of downtown) you'll find English Bay Beach and Sunset Beach, excellent for swimming, walking, or sunning. Kitsilano Beach, a local favorite, boasts Vancouver's largest outdoor saltwater pool, concession stands, and plenty of parking. It is located just off Cornwall Avenue at the southern end of Burrard Bridge. Also, check out Trout Lake, Vancouver's only lake with swimming (see "Commercial Drive" under "Stroll & Browse" above).

### MUSEUMS

**CANADIAN CRAFT MUSEUM.** This downtown museum can be counted on to inspire your young artists with frequently changing, quirky, and interesting exhibits constructed from all kinds of unlikely materials. One exhibit awhile back featured embroidered bread.

*639 Hornby St. 604/687-8266. Open Mon., Wed., Fri., 10 a.m.-5 p.m.; Sat., 10 a.m.-9 p.m.; Sun., noon-9 p.m.; closed Tues. Cost: $6/adult; $4/senior & student; free/under 13.*

**HADDEN PARK** and **VANIER PARK.** Whether they're fascinated by the sea or the stars (or both), kids will find plenty of interest in the museums at these two connected parks. The **Vancouver Maritime Museum and St. Roch National Historic Site** in Hadden Park offer traveling nautical exhibits and historic sailing vessels. A tour of the Arctic patrol ship RCMP St. Roch will take young imaginations back to an era when sailing ships faced, and not always overcame, the perils of ice, fog, and blizzards.

*1905 Ogden Ave. 604/257-8300 (museum). Open Tues.-Sat., 10 a.m.-5 p.m.; Sun., noon-5 p.m. (winter); daily, 10 a.m.-     5 p.m. (summer). Cost: $6/adult; $3/senior & youth, $14/family.*

Next door at Vanier Park are the **Vancouver Museum** and the **Pacific Space Center,** home of the **H.R. MacMillan Planetarium,** which offers a wide range of astronomy programs for families. Some of the shows are pretty seriously scientific and better for older children or those with a strong leaning toward astronomy. But there are plenty of light, whimsical offerings as well. The Vancouver Museum has a resource room and Toy Timeline, part of the Timeline Wall in the Orientation Gallery. Check their Web site for seasonal children's activities.

*1100 Chestnut St. 604/738-7827 (planetarium); 604/736-*

*4431 (Vancouver Museum); www.vanmuseum.bc.ca. Open Tues.-Sun., 10 a.m.-5 p.m. Cost: $5.50/adult, $3.75/child.*

**SCIENCE WORLD.** This hands-on, high-tech museum is sure to please the science buffs in your family. Science World offers exhibits that make sense of the everyday world. Kids can create a cyclone, blow square bubbles, or discover the science behind today's popular music. There's a search gallery where the youngest visitors will enjoy crawling though a beaver lodge or walking inside a hollow tree. Also located here is one of the world's largest IMAX theatres, with a 28-speaker sound system.

A note of caution: in 1998, parent reviewers had their car burglarized while they were inside. While reporting the incident, they were informed that this is a relatively common occurrence here. This might be a great occasion to check out the SkyTrain.

*1455 Quebec St. 604/268-6363. Open Mon.-Fri., 10 a.m.-6 p.m.; Sat.-Sun., 10 a.m.-5 p.m. Cost: $11.25/adult, $7.50/child, senior & student; free/under 4 (IMAX is extra).*

**UNIVERSITY OF B.C. MUSEUM OF ANTHROPOLOGY.** Older kids and those with a penchant for native lore will appreciate this marvelous collection of Northwest Coast First Nations art, including huge totem poles, feast dishes, war canoes, and carved works in silver, gold, stone, and wood. A signature installation is Bill Reid's amazing sculpture of Raven opening a giant clamshell to release the world's first humans into the world, and it's all housed in an award-winning building, located on the Point Grey cliffs.

*6393 NW Marine Dr. (on the U.B.C. campus). 604/822-3825. Open Tues., 11 a.m.-9 p.m. (5-9 p.m. free); Wed.-Sun., 11 a.m.-5 p.m. Cost: $6/adult, $3.50/child, student & senior.*

**VANCOUVER ART GALLERY.** A short stroll from the Canadian Craft Museum, this excellent art museum welcomes children. Paintings of Canadian artist and Victoria native Emily Carr, form part of the permanent collection. Her frequent subjects were the coastal B.C. landscape and First Nations communities, past and present. Her paintings of the Queen Charlotte Islands are the next best thing to a visit to the Islands.

*750 Hornby St. 604/662-4719; www.vanartgallery.bc.ca. Open Tues.-Sun., 10:30 a.m.-5:30 p.m.; Thurs. to 9:30 p.m.; closed Mon.; statutory holidays, noon-5 p.m. Cost: $8/adult, $6/senior, $4/student, free/under 12, $25/family of 5. Admission by donation on Thursdays.*

### EXCURSIONS

**PLAYLAND AMUSEMENT PARK.** Families will find just the "thrills and chills" they seek at this quintessential amusement park. Recently upgraded, the park offers a choice of 35 rides, including Canada's largest wooden roller coaster. When you've had your fill of thrills, there's more: take in one of the musical revues, visit the petting zoo, play miniature golf, or check out the arcades. Daily admission covers unlimited entertainment.

*At the PNE Grounds, E. Hastings at Cassiar St. 604/255-5161. Open seasonally, during the PNE. Cost: $17.95/person.*

## CALENDAR

#### MAY-JUNE
Vancouver International Children's Festival: Theater, music, dance, and puppetry, 604/687-7697.

#### JUNE
Alcan Dragon Boat Festival, 604/688-2382.

#### JULY
Vancouver Folk Music Festival: Since the early '70s, this annual folkfest has welcomed young and old alike to three days of music from around the world. A children's stage area hosts concerts for children; storytelling, crafts, face painting, and play areas are provided. The adjacent sandy beach is handy for paddling. It's all at Jericho Beach Park, 604/602-9798.

#### JULY-AUGUST
Benson & Hedges Symphony of Fire: International firework competition, 604/738-4304.

#### AUGUST
Abbotsford International Airshow, 604/852-8511.

#### SEPTEMBER
Pacific National Exhibition, 604/253-2311.

## RESOURCES

#### SUPERNATURAL BRITISH COLUMBIA
800/663-6000
Information and reservations

#### TOURISM VANCOUVER
200 Burrard St., Vancouver B6C 3L6
604/683-2000; www.tourism-vancouver.org

#### VANCOUVER PARKS BOARD
604/257-8400

**BOOKS AND PUBLICATIONS**

The *Vancouver Book* is a free visitors' guide provided by Tourism Vancouver (604/683-2000). It lists lodgings, attractions, tours, etc. If you order by phone, allow at least two weeks for delivery.

*Vancouver Parent Newsmagazine* is a monthly publication available free in bookstores, libraries, restaurants.

*WestCoast Families* is a free Vancouver monthly parenting magazine distributed through retailers and libraries.

## SOUTH AND EAST OF VANCOUVER

Those heading for Vancouver sometimes treat the sprawling 'burbs in their path as merely a source of traffic to fight through. In fact, these communities themselves offer plenty of fun, child-oriented things to do. Given the urban density of Vancouver, many of the amenities usually found in a city, such as the zoo, are stashed in Langley or Burnaby instead, where there's more room. And these communities have interesting histories and traditions of their own that repay investigation. Hotels are often less expensive here than in downtown Vancouver.

### GETTING THERE

From the south, visitors to British Columbia crossing from Blaine, Washington, can get their bearings by thinking in terms of west and east of Highway 99 (see "Vancouver"). Major east-west arteries, easily accessed from 99, are Highway 1 (the Trans-Canada), Highway 7, and Highway 10. Frequent exits lead to the lower mainland communities described in this section. For visitors approaching the region from the east, Highways 1 and 10 feed in from south of the Fraser River; Highway 7 from the north.

Coming north from the international border, travelers encounter White Rock to the west and Delta north of that (site of the Tsawwassen ferry dock). North of Delta is Richmond, home of the Vancouver International Airport, and then Vancouver itself, north across the Fraser River. East of Highway 99 are Surrey and Langley, then, further east, Aldergrove, Abbotsford, and eventually Chilliwack. These communities all lie south of the Fraser River. Across the Fraser River, north of Surrey and Langley, are New Westminster and Burnaby.

## PLACES TO STAY

### BEST WESTERN KINGS INN AND CONFERENCE CENTRE
*5411 Kingsway, Burnaby V5H 2G1*
*604/438-1383*
*Rates: Inexpensive (off-season) to moderate (peak)*
*FYI: Kitchens (some units); refrigerators; fenced outdoor pool (May-Sept.)*

Forty miles north of the border and 10 minutes from downtown Vancouver via SkyTrain, this pleasant hotel offers the usual rooms, attractively decorated. But it's the location that makes this a child-friendly choice.

### DELTA PACIFIC RESORT AND CONFERENCE CENTRE
*10251 St. Edwards Dr.; Richmond V6X 2M9*
*604/278-9611, 800/268-1133; www.deltapacific.bc.ca*
*Rates: Expensive*
*FYI: Three restaurants; free continental breakfast and afternoon hors d'oeuvres for Signature Club guests; indoor pool with water slide, toddler slide; two outdoor pools; Nintendo (fee); recreation and fitness center: massage, two squash courts, volleyball court, four indoor tennis courts, tennis lessons, bike rentals; jogging trails; outdoor playground, croquet; children's center and summer kids' programs; baby-sitting; dataport in room; business centre; fee parking*

Even families with small kids need a bit of luxury sometimes. At the risk of turning off its traditional business patrons by installing blatant child-attractants like the 225-foot enclosed water slide, Delta Pacific Resort and Conference Centre aims to appeal to families. Guests who opt for the higher-priced Signature Club get a few additional amenities (their own pool), but all rooms are spacious, with luxury items like bathrobes and blow dryers. There is a negative: mini-bar offerings include overpriced snack items set out in plain view. You may want to ask the hotel to remove these temptations before you arrive.

The Creative Children's Centre, open 9 a.m.-9 p.m. daily, is close to the indoor pool and contains an assortment of toys, games, crafts, art materials, and TV/VCR with videos and games. All the hotel's child guests can get a Kid's Fun Pack here with a scavenger hunt, stickers, crayons, and coloring sheets. To deposit your child here costs $5 per child for two hours. The staff running the recreation center supervises the kids (you may want to observe a bit before entrusting very small children to them).

The hotel is close to the airport and handy to the Richmond Nature Park and other nearby attractions.

**❝ PARENT COMMENTS**

*"The waterslide is an enclosed tube, but actually extends outside, so at night it gets dark in the slide—green lights on the bottom provide the only light. The kids thought this made it scarier and more fun. They went down it for at least two hours, stopping only occasionally to swim in the .92 metre (three-foot deep) pool. To get to the takeoff point, there are 41 steps to climb up an open spiral staircase, then a red/green signal light alerts the next slider whether to wait or go."*

## PLACES TO EAT

### JOE'S PLACE RESTAURANT & SPORTS BAR

*5411 Kingsway, Burnaby*

*(604) 483-1383*

*Hours: Breakfast, lunch, dinner daily*

This family restaurant in the Best Western Kings Inn has a kids' menu and is all nonsmoking. Prices are reasonable, and the cuisine is standard family fare.

### THE WHITE SPOT

*5550 Kingsway, Burnaby*

*604/434-6668*

*Hours: Breakfast, lunch, dinner daily*

This family chain can be found throughout British Columbia. To Americans it may resemble Denny's, but with slightly faster service and a more sophisticated menu. Prices are low to moderate, and it can get crowded. There are quite a few locations in the lower mainland, including downtown Vancouver and North Van. Children 10 and under get crayons with their own coloring menu. Vegetarian entrées are offered. The restaurant is completely nonsmoking.

## WHAT TO SEE & DO

### STROLL & BROWSE

**METROTOWN.** British Columbia's largest shopping complex is in Burnaby and accessible by a 15-minute SkyTrain ride from downtown Vancouver. It consists of three major shopping centers connected by walkways and skywalks, with more than 450 shops and services, including two grocery stores, a food court, a large Toys R Us, a 12-theater multiplex, and a Holiday Inn. There's also a playcare/daycare, called Jelly Bean Park.

The Playdium, a 40,000-square-foot arcade, is an amazing sensory experience with kinetically enhanced games, including motorcycles, snowboarding, horse riding, rafting, Indy 500 races, and a combat game with a six-foot screen. Flashing lights and loud music add to the ambiance. It may be a challenge for parents to summon up the high energy needed to cope with this environment, but kids of all ages should have no trouble.

*4700 Kingsway, Burnaby (head southeast from Vancouver on Kingsway). 604/433-7529. Open daily, 10 a.m.- midnight.*

**RICHMOND CENTRE,** another megamall, features more than 200 stores and has a movie theatre.

*West off Westminster Hwy. onto No. 3 Road.*

**RIVERPORT ENTERTAINMENT CENTRE** includes the Zone Bowling Centre, a 40-lane bowling alley featuring the popular "Cosmic Bowling" on Wednesday and Sunday evenings. In the same building are three restaurants, including a White Spot. The Riverport complex also includes the Richmond Ice Centre, Watermania (a new city aquatics center with Olympic-size swimming pool, indoor water slide, and kids' wave pool), and the 12-plex SilverCity Movie Theaters.

*No. 6 Road & Steveston Hwy., East Richmond.*

### PARKS

**BURNABY LAKE REGIONAL PARK.** The focus of this 800-hectare park is on nature education, and kids can visit the nature house and climb the viewing tower in pursuit of higher learning. From the nature house, loop trails take off to the east and west; some are accessible to strollers. Various lengths are offered.

This area is a wildlife sanctuary, so bring the binoculars. Kids will enjoy searching the marshes for wildlife, including osprey, grebe, muskrat, and turtles.

At the western end of the park is the **Burnaby Lake Sports Complex,** with swimming pools, water slide, sauna, whirlpool, and weight room. Next door is the Burnaby Lake Area office with ice skating and a snack bar. Check out the archery fields, tennis courts, and more.

*Off Winston & Piper Ave., within 1 km of Burnaby Heritage Village. Burnaby Lake Area office, 604/291-1261.*

*C.G. Brown Pool, 604/299-9374. Open Mon.-Wed., 6 a.m.-10 p.m.; Thurs.-Fri., 6 a.m.-9 p.m.; Sat., 1-8:30 p.m.; Sun., 10 a.m.-5 p.m.*

**BURNABY MOUNTAIN PARK.** There are sweeping panoramas of greater Vancouver, Burrard Inlet, and the North Shore mountains from this 525-hectare park. In the park are a small playground, walking trails (not well cared for), the Centennial Pros Garden, benches at scenic views, and the Centennial Pavilion.

Besides the view, the most outstanding attraction is the Playground for the Gods. This is a series of Ainu (Japanese First Nations) totem poles carved by Ainu artist Nuburi Toko and his son, Shusei Toko, commemorating 25 years of good will between sister cities Kushiro, Japan, and the District of Burnaby. The Ainu totem poles stand in harmony with two Coast Salish totems.

The Horizons Restaurant on Burnaby Mountain, located in the park, serves grilled seafood and steak in a formal atmosphere. A concession stand operates during summer months. Picnic tables are also available.

*The park is located next to Simon Fraser University. Visitors can access the park from Curtis or Gaglardi Way. Open dawn-dusk. Horizons Restaurant, 604/299-1155. Open Mon.-Sat., 11:30 a.m.-2 p.m.; daily, 5-9 p.m.*

**CENTRAL PARK,** a 90-hectare parcel of land amid fast-paced Burnaby, has walking trails, a bike trail, and two small playgrounds. From one, you can watch model boats cruise a small pond. The other playground is near a large pond, toward the center of the park. Here, you can watch fishers practice fly-casting techniques. Stroll through lanes lined with deciduous trees and ferns; picnic tables are provided.

*Off Kingsway between Patterson & Boundary; or take the SkyTrain to Patterson Station. Main entrance off Boundary at Imperial Street. Open dawn-dusk. Free.*

**RICHMOND NATURE PARK.** This large park has a boardwalk, trails that wind through the forest, a pond and bog, and a Nature House that has visitor information, hands-on activities and games, live animals, and a gift shop.

*11851 Westminster Hwy., Richmond. 604-273-7015. Open dawn-dusk; Nature House open Mon.-Thurs., 8:30 a.m.-5 p.m.; Fri.-Sun., 9 a.m.-5 p.m. Free.*

## ANIMALS, ANIMALS

**GREATER VANCOUVER ZOOLOGICAL CENTRE.** This is a fun spot for viewing animals. Families will marvel at the giraffe, elephants, lions, tigers, and rhinos that roam the 120 acres of farmland. Young children will get a kick out of the petting zoo, and everyone will enjoy the train ride that skirts the perimeter. Check out the Happy Hippo bus tours; North American wilderness exhibit. During the winter holiday season, nightly laser light shows are offered, with Hay Rides and special train rides through the exhibits.

*5048 264th St., Aldergrove. 604/856-6825. Open daily, 9 a.m.-dusk. Cost: $10.50/adult, $7.50/senior & child 3-15; free/under 3.*

### SWIMMING

**W.C. BLAIR RECREATION CENTRE.** Beat the winter blahs at this big aquatic center that offers pools, whirlpool, sauna, fitness center, refreshments, childcare, and activities for kids of all ages and—of course—water slides. Water is purified by ozone, which supposedly neutralizes the nasty side effects of chlorine (red eyes and itchy skin).

*22200 Fraser Hwy., Langley. 604/530-WAVE. Open daily, 6:30 a.m.-10:30 p.m. Cost: $4/adult, $2.50/youth 13-18, $2.25/child 4-12 & senior, free/under 4, $2.25/family. Admission fee includes lockers, fitness center, pools, and sauna.*

**BONSOR RECREATION CENTER.** This rec center offers a full spectrum of activities with a swimming pool, leisure pool, whirlpool, sauna, racquetball courts, weight room, and café. There's an aquatic lift for wheelchair users. Children seven and younger, or less than 48 inches tall, must be accompanied by an adult (16 years or older) in the pool. Racquetball is for ages 13 and up, and the weight room is for ages 14 and up.

*6550 Bonsor Ave., Burnaby (one block off Kingsway at Nelson & Bonsor, half-block walking distance from Metrotown's back entrance). 604/439-1860. Open daily, 9 a.m.-9 p.m. Cost: complex fee structure; call for details.*

For more watery entertainment, see "Burnaby Lake Regional Park," "Riverport Entertainment Centre," and "Newton Wave Pool."

### EXCURSIONS

**BUDDHIST TEMPLE.** North America's second-largest Buddhist temple welcomes visitors of all ages. The temple has a bonsai garden, Buddhist museum, tea ceremonies, and impressive Chinese artworks and architecture. That may not sound too kid friendly, but in fact the exotic, sumptuous art works, from flying dragons atop the roof to gilded statues of Bodhisattvas, seem to fascinate children.

*9160 Steveston Hwy., Richmond (between No. 3 & No. 4 Roads on Steveston Hwy.). 604/274-2822. Open daily, 10 a.m.- 5 p.m. Free (donations accepted).*

**BURNABY HERITAGE VILLAGE.** This nine-acre re-creation of a village circa 1890 to 1925 is laid out in a park-like setting. Authentically costumed townspeople invite visitors into shops and homes. The approximately 40 exhibits include many demonstrations of old crafts like blacksmithing, along with a variety of hands-on activities and displays. Kids will enjoy the vintage carousel and ice cream parlor.

*6501 Deer Lake, Burnaby. 604/293-6500. Open 11 a.m.- 4:30 p.m.( May 2-Sept. 20); 11 a.m.-9 p.m (Dec. 20-Jan. 3); until 9 p.m.Thurs. evenings in Dec.; 11 a.m.-4:30 p.m. (Nov. 28-Dec. 19-Heritage Christmas). (Days and hours change a little—year to year.) Cost: $6.35/adult, $4.40/student 13-18, $3.80/child 6-12, family rate of $3.80/per person. Carousel ride $1 extra.*

**STEVESTON VILLAGE.** You'll find this historic fishing village near No. 1 Road and the Steveston Highway. There are shops, restaurants, fishermen selling fresh fish, views of the fishing fleet (Canada's largest commercial fishery), and the **Steveston Museum,** offering a historical look at the region's fishing community. Also nearby is the **Gulf of Georgia Cannery.** Built in 1894, it now houses a fishing museum, has canning-line exhibits and machine demonstrations, tours, kids' activities, a theater, gift shop, and store.

*From any major north-south arterial in Richmond, go south until you reach the Steveston Hwy. then go west and follow the signs. Open May-Oct.*

*Steveston Museum, 3811 Moncton Road. 604/271-6868. Open Mon.-Sat., 9:30 a.m.-5 p.m. Free.*

*Gulf of Georgia Cannery National Historic Site, 12138 4th Ave. 604/664-9009.*

## RESOURCES

### GREATER VANCOUVER REGIONAL DISTRICT
604/432-6350
For information about any of the regional parks

### BOOKS AND PUBLICATIONS

*109 Walks in B.C.'s Lower Mainland*, by David Macaree, is recommended reading for those who want to get really serious about hiking British Columbia.

## THE NORTH SHORE

The North Shore, the area that begins north of Burrard Inlet, appears to rise straight up from sea level to towering peaks; seen from Vancouver, houses seem precariously perched on tall cliffs. Side by side with lovely residential neighborhoods and bustling shopping districts are mountains to explore, scary suspension footbridges to cross, and spectacular wilderness of a kind that most residents of big cities have to drive a lot farther to access. Visitors who plan to ski at Grouse Mountain or hop a ferry from Horseshoe Bay can get a head start on adventure by staying on the North Shore.

### GETTING THERE

Getting there can be half the fun on the city's **SeaBus** (604/261-5100). SeaBus is actually two ferries that shuttle passengers between North Vancouver (at the foot of Lonsdale Avenue) and the Skytrain station at the foot of Granville Street, in downtown Vancouver. Boats leave every 15 minutes, and fares are the same as on city buses. It's a fun, inexpensive, and scenic ride. (See "Vancouver: Getting There" at the beginning of this chapter.)

*The SeaBus terminal is at the foot of Burrard St., near Gastown.*

If you choose to drive from Vancouver, be prepared for slow bridge traffic. (Visitors from Portland and Seattle will feel right at home.) Two bridges cross Burrard Inlet. The scenic Lion's Gate Bridge goes from Stanley Park (to access the bridge, go west on Georgia into the Park) to Marine Drive in West Vancouver. The Second Narrows Bridge, often considerably less congested, is part of Highway 1, the Trans-Canada, that runs north-south, just west of the Vancouver-Burnaby boundary. Once on the North Shore, follow Highway 1 west to Horseshoe Bay for ferries to Vancouver Island, Bowen Island, and the Sunshine Coast.

### PLACES TO STAY

#### BEST WESTERN CAPILANO INN & SUITES
*1634 Capilano Road, North Vancouver V7P 3B4*
*604/987-8185; 800/528-1234*

*Rates: Moderate to expensive*
*FYI: Restaurant (breakfast, lunch only); kitchens (some units); free movie channel; outdoor pool*
    The most child-friendly feature of this comfortable hotel may well be its restaurant, de Dutch Pannekoek House (see "Places to Eat"). Rooms are spacious, if generic, and the location can't be beat for easy access to downtown Vancouver, Grouse Mountain, and Horseshoe Bay.

### GROUSE INN
*1633 Capilano Road, North Vancouver V7P 3B3*
*604/988-7101, 800/779-7888;*
*www.grouseinn.bc.ca, admin@grouse-inn.com*
*Rates: Moderate*
*FYI: Coffee shop; kitchens (some units); refrigerators; outdoor pool; laundry; playground*
    Across the street from the Capilano Inn is this definitely funkier but fun and comfortable hotel. Like the Capilano, the Grouse Inn is only a couple of minutes' drive from the Lion's Gate Bridge, but it's set back far enough from Marine Drive that highway noise is minimal. Its recently rejuvenated two stories are a jumble of angled wings with accommodation ranging from the basic two-bed room up to two-bedroom suites with full kitchens. The heated outdoor pool has a slide, and there's a good-sized playground with swings.

### 66 PARENT COMMENTS
    *"As far as we were concerned the pièce de résistance was the pool, which stays open until 11 p.m. We arrived late but there was still time for the kids to change into swimwear and race down to the pool, which also has a waterslide (curvy, with jets of water running down it)."*

### LONSDALE QUAY HOTEL
*123 Carrie Cates Ct., North Vancouver V7M 3K7*
*800/836-6111; LQH@Fleethouse.com*
*Rates: Moderate*
*FYI: Restaurant; whirlpool, exercise room*
    As close to the waters of Burrard Inlet as you'll get onshore, the spacious rooms here are set along the quay over the water, three stories above the public market and boutiques of Lonsdale Quay, and next door to the SeaBus terminal. The views are lovely and, considering the activity below, rooms are quiet and restful. Windows open right out onto the water, so

parental supervision is a must. Downstairs is all the bustle of the market and shops and, outside, the interesting North Vancouver waterfront, undergoing a major facelift.

**❝ PARENT COMMENTS**

*"The staff was very considerate and helped us haul our luggage down to the SeaBus terminal."*

*"There are lots of bakeries in the market for a light breakfast, but if the weather is good, it's worth it to have breakfast in the restaurant. The view of Vancouver across the water is incredible."*

## PLACES TO EAT

### DE DUTCH PANNEKOEK HOUSE
*1634 Capilano Road, in the Best Western Capilano Inn & Suites*
*604/985-0328*
*Hours: Breakfast, lunch daily*

This venerable chain of B.C. restaurants signals its Dutch theme with the windmill on the sign and the décor inside. Often located close to or in family-friendly hotels, they specialize in breakfast. The signature menu offering is the "pannekoek," a thin, crepe-like pancake that patrons can order with a variety of fillings, sweet and savory. The menu is corny, but the food is just fine and low-priced. Order in full or half-pannekoeks. Your young gourmets can order from the kid menu to sample the small pannekoeken ("Dutch babies") with names like "Fruit Loop Baby" and "Chocolate Baby." For the conservative picky eater, there's French toast, "DeBakon," and peanut butter & jelly "samiches."

Lonsdale Quay's public market, in North Van, and the **Park Royal Mall,** in West Van, are both good places to catch a quick bite or a more leisurely meal with plenty of food-court options to choose among.

## WHAT TO SEE & DO

### STROLL & BROWSE
**DEEP COVE.** This charming hamlet on Indian Arm, the fjord that runs north from Burrard Inlet, is adjacent to **Mount Seymour Provincial Park.** Explore the shops and art galleries, stop for a bite at one of the bistros, and let the kids run amok in nearby waterfront **Cates Park** while you take in the awesome view.

*Head east from North Vancouver on either the Mount Seymour Pkwy. or the Dollarton Hwy.*

**HORSESHOE BAY.** If you're heading over to Vancouver Island or up the Sunshine Coast on a sunny midsummer weekend, there's a good chance you'll spend time waiting in line at the ferry dock here. Don't despair; just lock up your car carefully (take valuables with you) and head down to the beach. There's a waterfront park with a playground, souvenir shops, ice cream parlors, fish-and-chips joints, upscale restaurants, and a visitor center to investigate, along with plenty of touristy shops. The ferry will likely arrive before you've exhausted the possibilities.

*Go west to the end of Hwy. 1.*

**LONSDALE QUAY,** next to the SeaBus terminal, houses North Van's public market, a host of upscale retailers, and a hotel, and makes a good place to investigate if the weather pushes you indoors. On the second floor, there's an enclosed toddler play area with slide; on the ground floor, a combination public market and food court rivals Granville Island even to the waterfront setting. If the weather permits, and even if it doesn't, check out Waterfront Park next door or stroll along the Esplanade and make your way uphill to the North Vancouver Museum. (See "Museums.")

*Located next to the SeaBus terminal in North Vancouver.*

**PARK ROYAL.** Homesick for mall culture? No problem; just step into **Park Royal,** the huge mall that straddles both sides of Marine Drive, and feel at home. This was Canada's first mall, built in 1950 but fully updated and expanded. Every major Canadian retailer seems to have a presence here. Among more than 200 retailers are Eatons, supermarkets, pharmacies, bookstores, specialty shops, movie theater, and bowling lanes.

*In West Vancouver, at Taylor Way & Marine Dr.*

**PARKS**

(For the bigger provincial parks in the area, see "The Great Outdoors" below.)

**AMBLESIDE PARK.** Combine a visit to the sandy beach at this waterfront park with a visit to nearby Park Royal Mall. An attractive feature is the West Van Seawalk that runs along the water to Dundarave Pier. There's Pitch & Putt golf here (bring

your own gear), a playground, spray park, and more. The Royal
Hudson Steam Train passes by in summer (see "Excursions").
There are concerts here during the summer, too.

*In West Vancouver at 13th St. & Marine Dr.*

**CAPILANO SUSPENSION BRIDGE AND PARK.** The big draw
here is the 137-meter span bridge that sways 70 meters above
the rushing Capilano River; most kids are invigorated by the
crossing, but some adults may feel queasy. Also fun for kids are
the rain forest trail, forested nature park, trout ponds, totem
poles, and trading post.

*3735 Capilano Road. 604/985-7474. Open 8:30 a.m.-dusk
(summer); 9 a.m.-5 p.m. (winter). Cost: $9/adult, $3/child.*

**LIGHTHOUSE PARK,** for those who can't make it to Meares
Island or the Hoh Rain Forest in Washington State, offers the
best chance to see a bit of the spectacular old-growth coastal
rain-forest that once carpeted the region. About 12 km of
trails wind among the forest giants; the main path leads to
**Point Atkinson Lighthouse,** the first manned lighthouse in
Canada, built in 1874. The park remains wild by design.
There are washrooms, picnic tables, and parking, but no con-
cession stands or playgrounds. Down by the water, you can
watch the huge freighters and cruise ships in Burrard Inlet.
During the summer, the West Van Parks and Recreations
Department (see "Resources") offers nature programs.

*Beacon Lane, at the southwest tip of West Van. (Turn south onto
Beacon Lane from Marine Dr.; the lane leads into Lighthouse Park.)*

**LYNN CANYON PARK AND ECOLOGY CENTRE** and **LYNN
HEADWATERS REGIONAL PARK.** Below the Lynn Headwaters,
Lynn Canyon Park features its own suspension bridge. It's
shorter, but it's higher and, unlike the Capilano Suspension
Bridge, it's free. The Ecology Centre, also free, offers nature
exhibits, films, and other programs. There are a concession
stand and picnic tables here. Hiking trails wind through the
Douglas Fir forest, and the canyon is awesome.

A few miles further up (as you move away from Burrard
Inlet on the North Shore, all directions are up) is the Lynn
Headwaters Regional Park, at the upper edge of North Shore
human habitation. There are many rugged hiking trails along
with some gentle ones, suitable for small children.

*3663 Park Road, North Vancouver. 604/981-3103;*

*www.district.north-van.bc.ca/admin/depart/parks. Open daily, 10 a.m.-5 p.m. (April-Oct.); Mon.-Fri., 10 a.m.-5 p.m.; Sat.-Sun., noon-4 p.m. (Oct.-March).*

**WHYTECLIFF PARK.** This park gets overlooked by those heading to or from the ferries at Horseshoe Bay—a pity, because it's lovely. Trails wind through 4.5 hectares of gorgeous forest, but even more interesting is the rocky beach from which you can often glimpse seals, eagles, and assorted wildlife. There's an observation platform with good views of Howe Sound, a playground, concession area, tennis courts, covered picnic area, and washrooms. A few years back, the **Whytecliff Marine Park** was created, an adjacent underwater sanctuary that attracts plenty of scuba divers. The park can be very crowded on summer weekends.

*7000 Marine Dr., West Vancouver.*

## MUSEUMS

**NORTH VANCOUVER MUSEUM & ARCHIVES.** In this old house in a residential neighborhood, visitors can get a sense of how much this community has grown and altered in 130 years. Special attention is given to the changing waterfront. Along with photos, artifacts, and traveling exhibits, there's a child-size tugboat for hands-on kid exploration.

*333 Chesterfield Ave., North Vancouver. 604/987-5618. Open Wed.-Sun., noon-5 p.m. (open Thurs. until 9 p.m.)*

## ANIMALS/ANIMALS

**MAPLEWOOD FARM.** More than a petting zoo, the two-hectare Maplewood Farm aims to teach kids how a real farm works, from daily milking demonstrations to livestock feedings. There's a full complement of farm animals and open paddocks (Goat Hill and Rabbitat) where hands-on investigation is allowed. A perennially popular destination for North Shore families, Maplewood Farm is open year round and sponsors seasonal events, including the generically named Pumpkin Event, around Halloween, and Country Christmas in December. Pony rides are available, but must be booked in advance.

*405 Seymour River Pl., North Vancouver. 604/929-5610. Open Tues.-Sun., 10 a.m.-4 p.m. Cost: $2.14/adult, $1.61/senior & child, $6.96/family.*

## THE GREAT OUTDOORS

On the North Shore, thanks to the high-elevation terrain,

you can hike in summer and ski, snowboard, and snowshoe in winter at most of the provincial parks and mountain destinations. Each of the destinations below offers summer and winter opportunities. Note that the cheapest and least crowded time of year to visit is off-season: fall and spring.

**CYPRESS PROVINCIAL PARK** and **CYPRESS BOWL.** There's great hiking in summer and the full complement of snow activities in winter here. Cross-country ski lessons are offered for children five to 13, and equipment can be rented.

*Take Hwy. 1, the Trans-Canada, west from the Lion's Gate Bridge to the Cypress Bowl Road turnoff. 604/926-5612; www.cypressbowl.com.*

**GROUSE MOUNTAIN.** Take the Super Skyride to the top, where you can stroll, eat, and enjoy panoramic views. The Peak Chair ride carries visitors to the summit (11 a.m.-7 p.m.) year round, weather permitting. The indoor Theatre in the Sky offers a short multimedia presentation about Vancouver. In the winter there's great skiing and snowboarding, sleigh rides, mountain-top ice skating, snowshoeing, and special kids' programs. Seasonal events include concerts and logger shows. Helicopter tours are offered. Gift shops sell souvenirs.

*6400 Nancy Greene Way. 604/984-0661. Open daily, 9 a.m.-10 p.m. Cost: $16.95/adult, $10.95/youth 13-18, $5.95/child 7-12, $43.95/family of 4.*

**MOUNT SEYMOUR PROVINCIAL PARK.** In summer, the Baden Powell Trail in North Vancouver makes a lovely hike for families who want to escape the city. Access the trail at Mount Seymour Provincial Park (take the Second Narrows Bridge from downtown and follow signs to the park). Three kilometers into the park, you'll see trail signs. There are plenty of other trails, some leading to mountain peaks with panoramic views. There are picnic areas, too.

In winter, every variety of snow activity is offered here, as well as equipment rentals and lessons. New features for snowboarders at all levels have been added recently. There are many children's programs, and equipment can be rented. Food service is available.

*East on Mount Seymour Pkwy. 604/986-2261; 604/718-7771 (snow phone); www.mountseymour.com.*

## EXCURSIONS

**ROYAL HUDSON STEAM TRAIN TO SQUAMISH.** This historic train, operated by B.C. Rail, runs from North Vancouver to Squamish, a two-hour trip through gorgeous mountain scenery. At Squamish, tour the **Railway Heritage Park** where kids can climb onto restored train cars and ride a miniature railway. Grab a bite to eat in town, then return via Howe Sound on the ship MV *Brittania*, or go by boat and return by train.

*Train departs May-Sept., 10 a.m.; leaves Squamish 2 p.m. for return trip. Boat leaves downtown Vancouver (north end of Denman St.) 9:30 a.m.; departs Squamish 1:30 p.m. 800/663-8238 (outside BC); 800/339-8752 (in BC); www.bcrail.com. Cost: train round trip, $46.50/adult, $12.75/youth 12-18 and senior over 60, $12.75/child 5-11, free/under 5; train/boat combo, $77.57/adult, $65.54/youth 12-18 & senior over 60, $21.40/child 5-11, free/under 5.*

*Railway Heritage Park, 39645 Government Road. 800/722-1233; www.wcra.org. Open May-Oct., 10 a.m.-5 p.m. Cost: $4.50/adult, $3.50/senior & student, $12/family.*

## CALENDAR

**JUNE**
Folkfest, 604/984-4484.

**JULY**
Canada Day celebrations, Waterfront Park, 604/987-PLAY.

**AUGUST**
Concerts in the Cove, Deep Cove, 604/987-PLAY.

**OCTOBER**
Pumpkin Event, Maplewood Farm, 604/929-5610.

**DECEMBER**
Festival of Lights, Grouse Mountain, 604/984-0661.
Country Christmas, Maplewood Farm, 604/929-5610.

## RESOURCES

**VISITOR INFO CENTRE**
604/987-4488

**WEST VANCOUVER PARKS AND RECREATION DEPARTMENT**
604/925-7200

## WHISTLER

Located 121 kilometers north of Vancouver in the Coastal Mountain Range of British Columbia, Whistler/Blackcomb is a world-class resort that lies between the two greatest vertical-rise mountains in North America. In all seasons, parents vacationing with their children will find much to like about Whistler/Blackcomb.

In summer, the outstanding interconnecting trail system that runs through the valley is popular for in-line skating, hiking, mountain biking, and skateboarding. Horseback riding and golfing, plus swimming and boating in the five surrounding lakes, will also keep the family busy.

In winter, most people come for the skiing and, increasingly, snowboarding. With more express lifts (12) than just about any world resort, Whistler and Blackcomb combined offer almost 2,800 hectares of skiable terrain.

Families in search of a bargain are beginning to find their way here in spring and autumn—after the snow and before the hot weather. Prices are lowest and crowds thinnest at this time.

In the winter, bitter cold is rare on these mountains, which is an advantage—especially for young skiers. However, the same conditions that make harsh temperatures unlikely occasionally bring rain and fog to the lower slopes. The summer climate is warm and dry.

The resort consists of several communities. The two largest and most developed are Blackcomb and Whistler. The village of Whistler sits at the base of the two mountains. Accommodations are right in the Village, within easy walking distance of the stores, restaurants, and lifts. Cars are parked in an underground parking garage so there is no traffic. If you can afford it, staying in Whistler Village is ideal for families.

The Blackcomb base also is developed with a village and extensive condominiums and houses in the "Benchland" area. It is ritzier than the Whistler Village with the five-star, swank Chateau Whistler Hotel at its center.

Other communities in the area include North Village and Whistler Creekside. North Village (a five-minute walk from Whistler Village) has recently become more developed. With a parking lot in the middle of the village and the largest grocery store in the area, it is not as charming as Whistler or Blackcomb, but accommodations here are more affordable. Whistler Creekside is an area that is older and also less expensive than the Village. It is right off Highway 99 as you enter the area. Located on the backside of Whistler, it has a lift with access to the ski area.

Whistler is a fine place to vacation with kids, but the cost may appear prohibitive. While the strong U.S. dollar helps improve the rates for American visitors, Canadians won't be as lucky. Keep in mind also that rates vary greatly depending on the time of year. Unfortunately, the most expensive winter rates coincide with the school holidays. If you are willing to take the kids out of school, you can save substantially. Package deals on lifts, lodging, and breakfast are another way to reduce your costs—check your local papers or ask your travel agent. With free bus service to the Village from throughout the area, it is also possible to get a good deal by staying in accommodations outside the Village. Finally, many of the condominiums at Whistler/Blackcomb are eager to have families stay at their facilities at rock-bottom rates in exchange for considering a time-share purchase. Central Reservations (see below) can help you find the best rate.

Note: Many lodgings require a three-night minimum stay. You will need to make reservations early, particularly during the "high season." However, be aware that the cancellation policy at most hotels and condos in Whistler/Blackcomb is strict. If you cancel within 30 days of your scheduled arrival you will often be charged the cost of one night of lodging.

One of the most convenient features of the Whistler Resort is the Whistler **Central Reservations,** located at the front of the Whistler Convention Center. It provides complete information about activities, events, restaurants, accommodations, and transportation, and will make arrangements and reservations for you. If you want some help planning your trip, give them a call (800/WHISTLER or 604/932-4222).

## GETTING THERE

Whistler is north of Vancouver. From Seattle, the 121-km drive takes about five to six hours. One of our parent reviewers described the route their family takes:

"We departed from Issaquah and headed north on Highway 405 to Interstate 5. At Blaine we exited and took the truck crossing over the border. We headed east on Highway 1 to Horseshoe Bay, then north on Route 99 to Whistler. It took us six hours to reach Whistler, including stops for meals and several roadside attractions, and 5 1/2 hours to get home."

The drive up Highway 99 from Vancouver to Whistler is on

a winding two-lane road aptly named Sea to Sky. (If you have passengers prone to carsickness, take precautions.) The vistas are spectacular along Howe Sound, with breathtaking views of green fjords and mountain peaks. The once-treacherous road has been straightened in recent years, but it is still a demanding drive on a curvy mountain highway.

A more relaxing alternative is to drive to Vancouver and catch the train from Vancouver to Whistler or take the train from Seattle to Vancouver, spend the night in Vancouver, then catch the train to the ski resort. The beautiful 2 1/2-hour train ride from North Vancouver runs along the coastline through Porteau Cove and Britannia to Squamish before turning inland between snowy mountain peaks en route to Whistler. There is a large parking lot at the Vancouver train station where cars can be parked while you are at Whistler. The train departs daily with one morning departure from North Vancouver and one evening departure from Whistler.

*B.C. Rail, 604/631-3500. Cost: Vancouver-Whistler $31/adult, $19/youth 2-12, $6/under 2.*

**ROADSIDE ATTRACTIONS. Porteau Cove Provincial Park,** just before Britannia beach, is a good place to picnic and enjoy gorgeous views. See "The North Shore" for more ideas.)

If you are driving to Whistler during the summer, consider stopping at the B.C. Museum of Mining in Britannia Beach for an underground tour of a copper mine. Our parent reviewers gave favorable reports on the tour, which includes a train ride into the mountain, live demonstrations of mining equipment, and a tour of Britannia Village. The tour is not recommended for infants.

*Forty-five minutes before Whistler at Britannia Beach. 604/688-8735. Open mid-May–mid-Oct, Wed.-Sun., May, June & Sept, daily, July & Aug. Cost:$9.50/adult, $7.50/child & senior, free/under 5, $34/family.*

At **Murrin Provincial Park,** just past Britannia Beach, there's swimming in the lake, fishing, and nice spots to picnic. Farther on at Shannon Falls, just before Squamish, there is a short trail to a waterfall and a viewpoint with picnic tables, along with old logging and mining artifacts that kids like to climb on. At Squamish there is a McDonalds, with an indoor play area.

## PLACES TO STAY

### CRYSTAL LODGE

*P.O. Box 280, Whistler VON 1B0*
*604/932-2221, 800/667-3363; www.crystal-lodge.bc.ca*
*Rates: Moderate to expensive*
*FYI: Two restaurants; kitchens (some units); fireplaces (some units); outdoor pool; laundry*

Crystal Lodge is a very clean, attractive five-story hotel with an ideal location in Whistler Village. Guests may choose from standard, deluxe, studio, and studio loft-type accommodations. Rooms are spacious and comfortable. The hotel overlooks the Village Square, so noise might be a problem in some rooms. The accommodations with balconies overlooking the swimming pool and the mountain valley are quieter and offer better views.

There are two restaurants in the lodge. Irori is a Japanese restaurant not well suited to young children. **Wainwright's** is highly recommended as a family restaurant (see review in "Places to Eat" below). The large, outdoor (year round) pool and hot tub are located on the side of the lodge.

As with all accommodations in Whistler, rates at the Crystal Lodge vary considerably depending on the time of year and length of stay. Ask about five- or seven-day packages that include lifts, lodging, and breakfast.

**66 PARENT COMMENTS**
*"This is an attractive, friendly place that is in a great location right in the heart of the Village."*

### DELTA WHISTLER RESORT

*4050 Whistler Way, Whistler VON 1B0*
*604/932-1982, 800/877-1133; www.deltahotels.com*
*Rates: Expensive*
*FYI: Two restaurants; kitchens (some units); fireplaces (some units); outdoor pool; tennis (indoor); golf; exercise room, massage; children's games; laundry; pets OK*

The Delta Whistler (formerly the Delta Mountain Inn) is one of the largest (300 rooms) and oldest hotels in the Village. The location is outstanding—about 50 meters from the ski lifts.

At the Delta, the units best suited for families have a loft with a queen bed and a full bath and sauna; downstairs are a sunken living room, two single beds, a queen sofa bed, kitchen, fireplace, and another full bath with a Jacuzzi. The pool is outdoors with a large hot tub both indoors and out.

Dome-covered tennis courts are available year round.

There are two restaurants. The Whistler Garden serves Chinese food, and **Evergreen** is a fun, hip eatery with a toy box and a children's menu. Kids under age six eat for free.

**❝❝ PARENT COMMENTS**

*"The Delta is very comfortable and convenient. It was handy to be so close to the ski lifts and to have two good restaurants right in the hotel. After skiing all day, we enjoyed having everything—food, swimming, tennis—right at our hotel. The Evergreen is a good restaurant for both kids and parents."*

**LAKE PLACID LODGE**
*P.O. Box 1018, Whistler Creekside V0N 1B0*
*800/565-1444;*
*www.whistler-resort.com/accommodations/hotels/lake.html*
*Rates: Moderate to expensive*
*FYI: Kitchens, dishwashers; outdoor pool (heated; open 1-10 p.m., winter; 10 a.m.-10 p.m., summer); gas fireplaces; laundry; ask about pets*

These large condos, with one-, two- and three-bedroom units available, can comfortably accommodate six to eight people. All units are nonsmoking. There's secure underground parking and a barbecue area, along with indoor racks for skis and bicycles. Suites are spacious; living rooms have sofa beds and cushioned window seats that can double as a bed for small people.

**❝❝ PARENT COMMENTS**

*"We stayed on the second floor facing the street (poolside view would have been nicer). It was a bit noisy at night with buses, cars, and motorbikes—and we were there during the off-season. But the room itself was roomy, comfortable, and had everything we needed for an even longer stay."*

*"The biggest hit with our family was the large, super-heated outdoor pool and the hot tub. The pool is kept very warm, and it was fun to swim under the stars and watch the steam rise from the pool."*

**SHOESTRING LODGE**
*7124 Nancy Greene Dr., Whistler V0C 1B0*
*604/932-3338; www.whistler.net*
*Rates: Inexpensive*
*FYI: Common kitchen; shuttle service; no cribs available; pets OK ($100 security deposit)*

The Shoestring is a good option for families on a tight budget. It is similar to a youth hostel, although rooms are private (all have TVs) with private baths. It is very clean, but sparsely furnished. During the ski season it offers some of the cheapest accommodations in Whistler. (A four-bunk room is $20 per person in the summer, $27 per person at the high season.) Families are welcome at the Shoestring. There is a fully equipped kitchen for the use of guests. It is a good place to get to know other parents and kids.

Free shuttle service to the ski area is provided in the morning and afternoon. In the evening there is shuttle service to Whistler Village.

**❝ PARENT COMMENTS**

*"Thanks to the Shoestring we could afford to ski Whistler. The staff was very friendly—meeting other families from all over the world was part of the fun."*

*"Noise could be a problem. The Shoestring has a popular nightclub and is located right off the highway. Ask for a quiet room."*

**TIMBERLINE LODGE**
*4122 Village Green, Whistler VON 1BO*
*604/932-5211, 800/777-0185*
*Rates: Moderate to expensive*
*FYI: Complimentary breakfast; refrigerators; outdoor pool; pets OK*

The Timberline is a casual, comfortable lodge with a good location at the backside of the Village. There is less noise and activity in this part of the Village, and you have an easy walk to the lifts. An enormous stone fireplace in the lobby is a cozy place to congregate after a day on the slopes. Be careful to request a room that is not near the popular nightclub located in the Lodge.

The furnishings in the rooms are "elegant rustic"—lots of attractive woodwork with beds made of rough-hewn frames. The loft-style accommodations are convenient for families—adults can relax in the sitting room while the children sleep upstairs.

**❝ PARENT COMMENTS**

*"The loft-style room worked well when we stayed at Timberline with our kids—ages four and eight. For families with younger children the stairway to the loft might be a safety concern."*

*"The complimentary breakfast helped reduce costs and it was very convenient with our two young children. When we*

*visited, discount coupons for the Lodge were available with Budget Car Rental. Watch out for the cancellation policy—full payment is due (by credit card) within 30 days and there is no refund with cancellation except due to illness."*

Condominium rentals, such as Lake Placid Lodge, described earlier, are an excellent option for families visiting Whistler. For information about location and rates, call 800/944-7853.

## PLACES TO EAT

### CARAMBA

*12-4314 Main St.*
*604/938-1879*
*Hours: Dinner daily; lunch served Sat.-Sun.*

The menu at this dine-in or take-out restaurant is mostly Italian with a few other influences creeping in. Prices are quite reasonable, and families are welcome at this very popular spot. Pizza for grownups is offered, along with a very popular three-cheese macaroni dish and other pasta entrées. There's no kids' menu, but spaghetti and cheese pizza should help.

### LA FIESTA

*4599 Chateau Blvd., at the Canadian Pacific Chateau Whistler Resort*
*604/938-2040*
*Hours: Dinner daily*

The sizzling hot fajitas prepared right at your table get the most attention at this colorful Spanish Mediterranean restaurant in the Chateau Whistler Resort in Blackcomb, but they are only one of the many outstanding entrées. Others include fresh snapper and a sensational paella brimming with prawns, mussels, chicken, chorizo, and more. If you have worked up a good appetite on the slopes, start out with a few of the inspired tapas and save room for a touch of mango sorbet. Prices are reasonable, and there is a good children's menu.

### SPLITZ GRILL

*105-4369 Main St.*
*604/938-9300*
*Hours: Lunch, dinner daily*

You can eat in or take out at this friendly, affordable burger emporium. There's a kids' menu and, for vegetarians, a lentil burger is offered. Save room for ice cream desserts.

**ZEUSKI'S TAVERNA**
*425-4314 Main St.*
*604/932-6009*
*Hours: Lunch, dinner daily*

Vegetarians and meat-lovers alike are well served at this bustling family restaurant. It's surprisingly affordable for Whistler, with most entrées under $15. Young diners are warmly welcomed with a kids' menu, crayons, and an activity page. The cuisine is of the hearty Greek-with-pizza variety. Parents of exuberant youngsters will be grateful for the ambient noise that provides auditory cover. You can even eat outside, under the heat lamps.

## WHAT TO SEE & DO

**WHISTLER ACTIVITY AND INFORMATION CENTRE** provides excellent information about activities and events available in the Whistler/Blackcomb area, including ski rentals and lessons. They will make arrangements and reservations for you or direct you to the right place. Stop by at the front of the Whistler Convention Centre, or call 604/932-2394.

### WINTER ACTIVITIES
### SKIING

**CROSS-COUNTRY SKIING.** More than 22 km of track-set, cross-country trails wind through the scenic Lost Lake and Chateau Whistler Gold Club trails. There are also public trails along the valley floor that are good for beginners and free of charge. The trails at Lost Lake are lit for night skiing. Note: Often there is not enough snow at the Whistler base for cross-country skiing.

There are several shops in the area renting equipment for adults, but fewer serve children. Parent reviewers report that **Sports West** rents skis and boots for children. The smallest boot size is a "one," which would fit about a seven or eight year old. Parents planning to cross-country ski with their kids should check snow conditions before leaving home and bring their own equipment for the youngsters.

*Information available at Whistler Activity Centre, 604/932-2394. The area is open daily, 9 a.m.-11 p.m. Cost at Lost Lake is $10/adult, $5/youth 13-18, $4/youth 6-12, free/under 6, $20/family. Reduced prices for night skiing.*

**DOWNHILL SKIING.** More than 2,794 hectares of skiable terrain and 1,585 meters of vertical drop on two magnificent side-by-side mountains have earned Whistler/Blackcomb a reputation as a world-class ski area.

The area has offered excellent skiing ever since it opened in the late 1960s and continues to improve each year. At Blackcomb in 1994, a new eight-person gondola and connecting high-speed quad were added that link Whistler Village to the Glacier Express and transport skiers more than 1,600 meters high. At Whistler, a high-speed quad opens more than 486 hectares and four bowls. Between the two areas are 12 high-speed lifts.

There is access to both ski areas from Whistler Village. The Gondola takes you up into the Whistler ski area. Also from the Village, the Fitzsimmons chair transports skiers from Whistler Village into the Blackcomb ski area. You can purchase ski tickets for both resorts at the Whistler base area, although skiing both areas in one day would be a challenge. Depending on the amount of snow, you can sometimes ski back to Whistler Village from both ski areas.

All our parent reviewers raved about skiing at Whistler. One mother had this to report: "Whistler was a great place for kids to ski. There are plenty of groomed runs and many areas designated 'Family Only' where skiing speed is well-controlled. The middle of the mountain around the Olympic Station area is best for beginners and there are lots of great intermediate runs off the Green chairs."

"We liked getting a delicious breakfast at the top of the Whistler Express Gondola at "Pika's," said another. "It got us going in the morning and we beat the crowds by riding up the gondola early."

"Whistler and Blackcomb are both large mountains. You would want to make sure kids know their way around before letting them ski alone! Also at both areas, it is so spread out that it is difficult to check in with kids at day care or ski school."

*Lift ticket rates: Whistler, $57-59/adult, $48-50/youth, $28-29/child, free/under 7. Blackcomb, $44/adult, $36 youth, $19 child, free/under 6. Dual mountain 3-day tickets: $132/adult, $117/youth, $63/child, free/under 6.*

**DAYCARE** is not available for non-skiing kids at Whistler, but it is offered at the Kids Kamp at Blackcomb from 8:30 a.m. to 4 p.m. (ages 18 months to three years). The facility is modern, clean, and bright, and a maximum of 10 kids per group is allowed. Cost is $50 a day, including lunch. There is also a "Pepsi Kids Night Out" on Wednesday and Saturday nights. Kids ages

## Downhill Skiing Lessons for Young Learners

The Ski Skamp program at Whistler (604/932-3434) is open to ages two to 12. Half-day to 10-day rates are offered. Our parent reviewer reported the following about the one-day instruction program at Ski Skamp: "Drop-off was at 8:30 a.m. and pick-up at 3 p.m. Kids were transported up the Gondola to the Ski Skamp area. It has easy terrain and a big tent area for lunch and rest periods. Ski rentals with the Ski Skamp program are $10 a day and include a helmet. (Helmets on kids skiing at Whistler are very popular). The lessons worked well for our daughter. Other families we spoke to were very happy with the program."

Blackcomb Resort offers its own Kids Kamp Program. There is a large Kids Kamp building at the base. Lessons are right out the door, so there is less transportation for the kids than at Ski Skamp, but often snow conditions are not as good at the lower elevations. The Kids Kamp program is available for ages two to 12. Rates for day lessons are similar to the Ski Skamp program.

six to 16 may be dropped off from 5:30 to 8:45 p.m. The program includes dinner and entertainment, and the cost is $23 per child.

**GONDOLA AND CHAIR LIFT RIDES.** In the winter, even if you don't ski, a ride in Whistler Mountain's fully enclosed gondola or on one of the Blackcomb express quad chairs is thrilling and offers spectacular views of the surrounding mountains and valleys.

You can ride the **Whistler Express Gondola** weekends from early June to mid-October. You can dine at the **Roadhouse Restaurant** at the top, and frequently you'll find outdoor entertainment. Scenic hiking routes and guided tours are offered.

*604/932-3434. Cost: $20 at either Whistler or Blackcomb—discount tickets often available.*

**ICE SKATING.** The indoor skating rink, Meadow Park Arena, is about 10 minutes from Whistler Village. Operated by Whistler Parks and Recreation, the rink has nifty push-bar devices that kids can use while learning to skate.

*604/938-PARK. Open to public skating most days, noon-3*

p.m., and some evenings. Cost: $6/adult, $3/youth 5-12, free/under 5, $12/family. Skate rentals additional, $2.25.

**INDOOR HEALTH CLUB.** If you have the energy after a day of skiing or if you are having a rainy day, consider an afternoon or evening of recreation at the **Mountain Spa & Tennis Club** at the Delta Whistler Resort. The indoor tennis courts, pool, exercise room, and hot tubs that are free to hotel guests are available for a fee to other visitors. This is a very busy place at the end of the ski day.

Delta Whistler Resort. 604/932-1982. Open 6:30 a.m.-10:30 p.m. Cost: $10/person, $25/family.

**SLEIGH RIDES** through the open fields will thrill the kids. Musical entertainment, a campfire, and food are part of the fun. Departures are from the Chateau Whistler and the Delta Whistler.

Whistler Outdoor Experience Co. 604/932-3389.

**SNOWSHOEING.** If you can walk, you can learn to snowshoe in minutes. Both kids and parents will enjoy the chance to trek tranquil forest trails, far from the crowds. Guiding, instruction, and rentals are available through **Outdoor Adventures @ Whistler.**

604/932-0647; www.adventureswhistler.com. Cost: $29-$58 plus $5 for snowshoe rental.

**THE RAINBOW MOVIE THEATRE** shows first-run movies at the **Whistler Convention Centre.**

### SUMMER ACTIVITIES

**BOATING.** Kayaks, sailboards, canoes, and Laser sailboats can be rented at both Lakeside and Wayside parks on Alta Lake.

**SWIMMING.** Beaches are found at Lost Lake Park, Wayside Park, and Alta Lake. Lost Lake is the warmest and smallest lake.

## CALENDAR

### FEBRUARY
Winter Carnival

### MAY
Lillooet Lake Rodeo

### JUNE
Children's Art Festival

**JULY**
International Fest
**AUGUST**
Whistler Classical Music Festival
**OCTOBER**
Oktoberfest
**DECEMBER**
Christmas at Whistler

## RESOURCES

### THE NANNY NETWORK
9225 Pinetree Lane, Whistler V0N 1B9
604/938-2823; thenanny@direct.ca
Childcare referral service

### WHISTLER SNOW AND INFORMATION LINE
604/932-4191

### WHISTLER ACTIVITY AND INFORMATION CENTRE
Whistler Resort Assoc., 4010 Whistler Way, Whistler V0N 1B4
604/932-2394; 800/WHISTLER
The Centre provides helpful information about activities, festivals, events, restaurants, accommodation, and transportation. Located at the Whistler Convention Centre in Whistler Village. Before you make your reservations, ask for the 'Whistler Vacation Planner."

## HARRISON HOT SPRINGS

The Coast Salish found the waters of these steaming sulfurladen springs healing, and subsequent generations of visitors concur. The setting is restorative in itself, on lovely Harrison Lake, surrounded by mountains. The small community of about 1,000 offers camping along with a well-known resort hotel and assorted other accommodation. The public pool fed from the hot springs is open to everyone, year round. There is plenty to engage kids here apart from the joys of splashing in the pools, from hiking and biking to nearby river rafting.

### GETTING THERE

The resort is approximately three hours and 258 km from Seattle and 129 km from Vancouver. From the United States, take I-5 to Bellingham exit 256A, Highway 539 to Lynden, Highway 546 east to the Sumas border crossing, and head east on the Trans-Canada Highway (Hwy. 1). Take Agassiz/Harrison Hot Springs exit (Exit 135, well signed) and follow signs on Highway 9 north to Harrison Hot Springs. From Vancouver, take Highway 1 or Highway 7. The latter offers a beautiful view of the Fraser River flood plains.

**ROADSIDE ATTRACTIONS.** Fort Langley National Historic Site. This site, reached via Highway 1, re-creates the original 1850s Hudson Bay Company trading post here, the first European settlement in British Columbia. Along with the village of Fort Langley and its shops, restaurants, and galleries, is the **Centennial Museum** and **National Exhibition Centre** with changing exhibits. Children's activities are offered.

*23433 Mavis St. 604/513-4777. Open daily, 10 a.m.-5 p.m. (March-Oct.); open for booked tours (Nov.-Feb,). Call for rates.*

*Centennial Museum: Mavis & King St. Open Mon.-Sat., 10 a.m.-4:45 p.m., Sun. 1-4:45 p.m. (summer); closed Monday (Sept.-May). Special events throughout the year; for details, call Tourist Information for Fort Langley, 604/888-1477.*

**CHILLIWACK.** A little way beyond Fort Langley is Chilliwack, known for its water-based activities from water parks and river rafting to windsurfing. For information on water parks and other options, contact **Tourism Chilliwack,** 800/567-9535.

## PLACES TO STAY

**HARRISON HOT SPRINGS HOTEL**
*100 Esplanade V0M 1K0*
*604/521-8888 (toll free from Vancouver), 800/663-2266;*
*www.tourbc.com/travel/harrison/index.html*
*Rates: Moderate to expensive*
*FYI: Two restaurants, espresso café; indoor and outdoor mineral pools, outdoor swimming pool; bike rentals, tennis courts; fitness center (ages 14 & over); game room (video games), toddler rides, Ping Pong, shuffleboard, indoor and outdoor games (croquet, horseshoes, board games, cards); playground; pets OK in cottages*

At this resort hotel on the shores of Harrison Lake, there's plenty of water-based recreation available seasonally, including swimming (very cold water!), fishing, water bicycle, jet-ski and boat rentals, and cruises. Year-round hotel features include the indoor and outdoor hot springs mineral pools (hot), a free morning nature walk (weather permitting), and complimentary afternoon tea and cookies.

An interesting mix of old and new, the hotel's original building dates back to 1926. (An earlier hotel welcomed visitors in the 1880s.) Today there are outdoor mineral pools, landscaping, and a children's water park, added recently. The staff is pleasant, and this is a popular and comfortable place for families. There's an extra $5 charge for renting terrycloth robes (which aren't especially absorbent); bringing your own is probably a better option.

Rooms range from the standard, with two queen beds, to suites. Larger rooms are available, including some in the newer East Wing, but prices are significantly higher (around $300-$400 for a one-bedroom suite). In the main building, connecting rooms are available, too. Some families opt for the detached cottages, which include a separate sleeping area, but no cooking facilities or bathtub (shower only). These are popular and often booked in advance for the weekends.

In the hotel lobby, next to the fireplace, visitors can sample the hot springs mineral water. Don't expect your kids to go for the taste, which is accompanied by the rotten-egg smell of the sulfur.

The hotel offers organized programs for kids on Canadian long weekends, school spring breaks, summer, and in Easter and Christmas seasons. Prices vary depending on age of child.

**❝ PARENT COMMENTS**

*"All cottages have at least one bedroom and a sitting room with a pull-out bed. This allowed us to stay up after our child went to bed. Indoors there's a hot tub and a warm swimming pool, and you can play Ping Pong and shuffleboard in the game room when it rains."*

*"The main highlight of staying here is the hot-spring-fed mineral pools. While there is a public mineral pool in the town, the convenience of being a room away from these pools can't be beat. (And day use of the hotel's pools only is not really available.) My kids and I preferred the outdoor pools to the indoor ones. The indoor pool area includes both a large hot tub and a very warm swimming pool, and the room is somewhat dark at night and humid. The outdoor mineral pool is freeform in shape, edged by interesting rockery and waterfall effects, and lit at night by color-changing neon-like lights around the edge of the pool. There is also a larger standard-style swimming pool that is not as warm as the other pools."*

*"We've stayed in the west wing, with a lakeside view, which was beautiful—a very serene and spectacular view of the huge lake and the mountains looming above it. This also had good access to the pool area. On our most recent visit, I requested the west tower, facing the poolside. This 3rd floor room included a balcony, but wasn't really practical for overseeing kids in the outdoor pool, since the only really visible pool from there is the "adults-only" one, which is separated by a covered walkway from the all-ages pool area. The balcony did provide a welcome separate sitting area for the two 6th grade girls in our group."*

### THE QUALITY HOTEL
*190 Lillooet Ave. V0M 1K0*
*888/265-1155; www.harrisonhotsprings.com*
*Rates: Moderate*
*FYI: Fireplaces; hot tubs, sauna, steam bath; exercise room; laundry; dataports; pets OK (fee)*

A newer hotel, the Quality has some fireplace suites that provide more space for families. There is a hot tub here, and some of the rooms have lake views (it's one block up from the beach). There's no pool, although the public pool is nearby (in this town, everything is within walking distance).

## PLACES TO EAT

### HARRISON PIZZA & DELI
*On Lillooet Ave., next to the Quality Hotel*
*604/796-2023*
*Hours: Lunch, dinner daily*

This deli is walking distance from the Harrison Hot Springs Hotel and a great place for a low-key family meal. Service is friendly and fast. While there's no children's menu, offerings are good and exceedingly child-friendly, from the inexpensive cheese pizza to chicken and pasta. The old-fashioned chocolate milkshakes are sure to please. Eat in or have your food delivered to your hotel room.

### LAKESIDE TERRACE RESTAURANT
*In the Harrison Hot Springs Hotel*
*Hours: Breakfast, lunch, dinner daily*

This informal hotel restaurant is convenient for guests and there is a kids' menu, but otherwise it doesn't come highly recommended. Prices are high for the quality of the food. You may want to opt instead to walk into town and find a café.

**MISS MARGARET'S ESPRESSO CAFÉ**
*In the Harrison Hot Springs Hotel*
*Hours: 6:30 a.m.-8:30 p.m. daily*

Stop in for a quick bite—a hit of espresso, juice, and other beverages. There's no kids' menu here, but convenient, tasty, kid-friendly snacks abound, including Italian ice cream, bagels and cream cheese, and chocolate-chip muffins. Many are in the $1-$6 price range.

## WHAT TO SEE & DO

### STROLL & BROWSE

The small town of Harrison Hot Springs has the customary souvenir and gift shops, a new-age shop, small grocery store, bakery, candy store, bookstore, and several cafés. The lakeside city park is fun for kids, with a wide, sandy beach, and water-falls and fountains.

**INTERNATIONAL SAND SCULPTURE COMPETITION.** This annual fun event is held every year next to the Harrison Lake lagoon in early September. The impressive sculptures are on exhibit through mid-October (or until weather destroys them). They're kept in a fenced-in area. Visitors can view them from outside the fence, or for an up-close look, pay to enter the exhibit.

*For information: www.harrisand.org. Cost: $5/adult, $2/child.*

### THE GREAT OUTDOORS

There are hiking and biking trails, horseback riding, golf, ten-nis, water activities at the lake, river rafting in nearby Chilliwack.

### EXCURSIONS

**DINOTOWN** is a dinosaur theme amusement park with rides, stage shows, water play area, daily parades, and a toddler area.
*604/794-3733; www.dinotown.com. Open May-Sept. (daily mid-June-Labor Day; then Sat.-Sun. only). $9.50/adult & child, $8.50/senior, free/under 2. Fee covers unlimited use of the park.*

**HELL'S GATE AIRTRAM** is an hour away from Harrison Hot Springs, east of Hope on the Trans-Canada Highway (Hwy. 1). A 25-passenger cable car descends 502 feet above the Hell's Gate in the Fraser Canyon. At the lower terminal are gift shops, interpretive exhibits, a seafood restaurant, and a fudge shop.

604/867-9277; *www.hellsgate.bc.ca. Open April-Oct. Cost: $9.50/adult, $6/youth 6-14, free/under 6, $25/family.*

About 20 minutes from Harrison Hot Springs, just off Highway 1 near the Highway 9 exit to Harrison Hot Springs and near Bridal Falls, are several tourist attractions:

**HISTORIC YALE** is a nearby town of historic interest with a museum and a church built in 1863. Among many attractions are a Fraser River float trip to the town of Hope, 22 km away, gold-panning lessons, a tour of the church, and other tours of various lengths.

*A 15-minute drive north of Hope on Hwy. 1. 604/863-2324. (June-Sept.); Wed.-Sun. (spring and fall). Cost: varies depending on tour chosen.*

**KILBY STORE & FARM,** about 20 minutes east of Harrison Hot Springs, offers a glimpse into the past. Located off Highway 7 in Harrison Mills (follow signs), the site depicts life in the 1920s. The general store operated there from 1922 to1977, and authentic products from the early years are on display. There's also a post office, hotel, and kitchen area with old-time appliances. Outdoors is a playground with a wooden seesaw, swing, and treehouse. Kids will especially enjoy feeding the farm animals from a 50-cent bag of "animal food" and playing on the playground. A gift shop sells present-day products with a historical flavor, including wooden toys, as well as sodas and huge ice cream cones.

*604/796-9576. Open daily, 10 a.m.-5 p.m.; until 8 p.m. in July and Aug. Cost: $5/adult, $2/youth 6-14, $12/family (2 adults & children).*

**MINTER GARDENS** is home to an impressive display of greenery. If your kids like exploring Butchart Gardens, they'll enjoy walking through these variations on the theme, smelling the flowers, walking over bridges, viewing topiary sculptures, and exploring the evergreen maze. The quirky features, such as Victorian topiary ladies and a giant floral peacock, can usually be counted on to entertain even the least garden-oriented kid long enough for parents to check out the offerings.

*888/646-8377. Open daily, 9 a.m.-5 p.m. (April-Oct); closes later in summer. Cost: (peak season) $9.50/adult, $8.50/senior, $6/child 6-18, free/under 6, $26/family. Slight price reduction off-season. Season passes available.*

**TRANSCANADA WATERSLIDES** has mini-slides, several large water slides, a river rapids ride, heated pools, a playground, arcade, and mini-golf.

*604/794-7455. Open daily, 10 a.m.-8 p.m. (mid-June-Labor Day); Sat.-Sun., 10 a.m.-8 p.m. (Victoria Day-mid-June).*

## CALENDAR

**JULY**
Harrison Festival of the Arts
**SEPTEMBER**
International Sand Sculpture Festival

## RESOURCES

**HARRISON HOT SPRINGS VISITOR INFO CENTRE (& CHAMBER OF COMMERCE)**
Hwy. 9, 499 Hot Springs Road, Box 255
Harrison Hot Springs V0M 1K0
604/796-3425; harrison@uniserve.com
On the main road as you drive into Harrison Hot Springs. Open May 4-Oct. 16, 9 a.m.-5 p.m. Maps, travel guides, and brochures are available.

# THE SUNSHINE COAST

Only a short ferry ride from Vancouver, the Sunshine Coast is another world altogether, separated from the lower mainland by Howe Sound and cut off from the east by the towering peaks of the Coast Mountains. Wide, meandering fjords further separate one small community from the next. Driving north from the southern tip of the Sunshine Coast up to Lund, the end of the road, won't take you more than a few hours, but to get even a small glimpse of what this lovely, unique region has to offer will take several days. If your family enjoys hiking, boating, or beachcombing, surrounded by some of the most spectacular scenery on the West Coast, consider making a pilgrimage here.

The name says it all—this is rain shadow country, and the weather can be sunny and warm here when the lower mainland is drenched in drizzle. Further, the warm offshore ocean currents combine with long flat stretches of sandy beach to create some of the warmest saltwater beaches north of California. Locals have occasionally been known to go for a dip in January.

Communities range from small, like Gibson's Landing, to

medium-size, like Sechelt. The Sunshine Coast has just one large town: Powell River, with about 15,000 residents. Resort communities, popular with boaters, are spread out along the coast. Several beautiful marine parks here can be reached only by boat or floatplane. One of the most spectacular is Princess Louisa Provincial Marine Park with Chatterbox Falls, a lovely waterfall at the far end of Princess Louisa Inlet, a small fjord off Jervis Inlet.

## GETTING THERE

It may be on the mainland, but for motorists the Sunshine Coast can be reached only by ferry. B.C. ferries make the short 40-minute run between Horseshoe Bay and Langdale frequently (there are about 10 round trips per day in summer). Other ferries serve Bowen Island, an inhabited island in the mouth of Howe Sound. While smaller than the behemoths that cruise between Vancouver Island and the mainland, the Langdale Ferry is well equipped with a toddler play area, gift shop, restaurant, and plenty of nooks and crannies for small children to explore. Don't despair if you arrive at Horseshoe Bay to encounter what seem like miles of cars lined up for the ferry; chances are they are waiting to go to Nanaimo and your line will be considerably shorter. (Just make sure you're in the right one.) From the ferry dock in Langdale to Earl's Cove is 84 km. Allow at least two hours, even if you plan to make no stops.

To reach Powell River requires another ferry ride, across Jervis Inlet from Earl's Cove to Saltery Bay. The 50-minute crossing is one of the most beautiful ferry rides in British Columbia with about 8 to10 round-trip sailings daily in summer. This ferry is smaller still than the Langdale Ferry but, at least, in summer, offers the same amenities. Ferry service on both the Langdale and Saltery Bay runs stops in late evening, about 10 p.m., and resumes about 6:30 a.m. From Saltery Bay to downtown Powell River is a 30-minute drive.

The artery that knits Sunshine Coast communities together is Highway 101, the world's longest highway. This is the same 101 that runs up the Oregon and Washington coasts. In fact, it extends all the way from southern Chile, in South America, up to Lund, British Columbia, the northern terminus.

B.C. Ferries offers a ticket package known as the Sunshine Circle Tour Pak. Purchasers receive a package of ferry tickets for the runs between Horseshoe Bay and Langdale; between Earl's Cove and Saltery Bay; between Powell River and Courtney-Comox on Vancouver Island; and one sailing between

Vancouver Island and the lower Mainland, from Victoria or Duke's Point over to Tsawwassen, or from Departure Bay to Horseshoe Bay. You can travel in any direction, as long as you go in a circle. Cost savings are substantial, but you'll need at least five days and preferably a week or more to get the most from this package. It's valid for three months after purchase; unused portions are nonrefundable. (For information on the Sunshine Circle Tour Pak, call 888/BC-FERRY from anywhere in British.Columbia, 7 a.m.-10 p.m. daily, or 250/386-3431.)

## LOWER SUNSHINE COAST

There are a variety of family-friendly resorts from funky to upscale along the inlets and beaches of the Sunshine Coast, tucked into hidden spots with enticing names like Halfmoon Bay, Secret Cove, Pender Harbour, and Earl's Cove. From B&Bs to fishing resorts and motels, accommodation is available. The nicest places and campgrounds fill up quickly in the summer, and it's best to reserve in advance. Costs vary considerably. The biggest selection is around Sechelt and Pender Harbour. If you think you'd like to spend a week here—and there is plenty of family fun available to fill one up—consider renting a house or cottage (see "Resources").

The road from Langdale to Earl's Cove is lovely and hugs the water for much of the way. Each small community you encounter has character and a place to stop for snacks or a family picnic. There are a few small museums as well. If you're on the way to Powell River, allow extra time to enjoy the drive, and don't force yourself to hurry just to catch the ferry at Earl's Cove.

**REFUELING.** **Gibson's Landing** is the first town you reach, five km after leaving the Langdale ferry dock, and it's charming—full of quaint older cottages and buildings that hug the cliff side overlooking Howe Sound; views are spectacular. This picturesque village was the setting for one of Canada's longest running TV shows, *The Beachcombers,* which was filmed here. The impact of its cancellation in 1990 after 19 years on the air left an economic crater, and Gibson's is still climbing out of it. For a sense of what you missed (Canadians will know), stop for lunch at **Molly's Reach Restaurant** where the series was filmed (at the corner of Molly's Lane and the public wharf; 604/886-9710; breakfast, lunch, dinner in summer; check for winter hours). Reruns are shown on the restaurant's TV, and photos and artifacts of the show abound.

The food is hearty, plentiful, and decidedly kid-friendly. When they stopped for lunch, our parent reviewers were told the children's menu was available only for dinner, but the staff prepared items off it for the kids, anyway. In summer, dine inside or out. The view is great, but bees may drive you indoors.

For dessert, stroll downtown (there's one street) and stop at Truffle's Café and Confectionery for an ice cream cone or butter tart.

If there's time, you may want to investigate the **Sunshine Coast Maritime Museum** (Molly's Lane; 604/886-4114). It's free, literally down the lane from Molly's Reach, and features an assortment of maritime memorabilia, from model ships to historical exhibits. It's open from 10 a.m. to 4 p.m. daily in summer; 11 a.m.-3 p.m. in winter, when it's closed on Mondays.

## PLACES TO STAY

There are many motels and B&Bs up and down the Sunshine Coast. **Sechelt** makes a good base from which to explore the area if you're coming from Vancouver. There are plenty of recreational opportunities at hand, and until you reach Powell River, you won't find a better selection of amenities.

### ROYAL REACH MOTEL AND MARINA
*5758 Wharf Road, c/o Box 2648, Sechelt V0N 3A0*
*604/885-7844*
*Rates: Inexpensive to moderate*
*FYI: Kitchens (some units); refrigerators; boat charters and rentals*

You'll find the Royal Reach on Porpoise Bay facing away from the coast. (The town of Sechelt is the wasp waist of the Sechelt Peninsula that extends up to Jervis Inlet; the Sechelt Inlet is the eastern boundary of the peninsula; Porpoise Bay is at the bottom of the inlet.) This somewhat basic but comfortable hotel is just outside town.

To refuel in downtown Sechelt, you can pick up some takeout in town or check out one of the town's attractive family-friendly bistros. Then head to Snickett Park, right off Highway 101, for a spot of people-watching on the beach.

## PLACES TO EAT

### KAFE AMIGO
*5685 Cowrie St.*

604/740-0080

*Hours: breakfast, lunch, dinner Mon.-Sat.; breakfast, lunch Sun.*

One of Sechelt's family-friendly cafés, this attractive spot serves up vegetarian and vegan meals with a Mexican flavor.

## WHAT TO SEE & DO

Sechelt has a good bookstore, **Talewind Books** (5494 Trail Ave.; 604/885-2527). And like Gibson's and Robert's Creek, this town, too, has lovely waterfront parks, cafés, and galleries to wander through. Sechelt has a counterculture feel, and if you harbor nostalgia for the '60s and '70s, you'll feel right at home.

North along Highway 101 toward Pender Harbour, communities become more spread out; a drive through the tiny villages, hidden coves, and sudden breathtaking panoramas, with occasional stops to let carsick youngsters get a breath of fresh air (we're in winding-road territory here), will give you a sense of the varied terrain, from peaceful lakes to rocky bays and forested peaks. Detour off 101 to take a look at the small enclaves of Irvine's Landing, Garden Bay, and Madeira Park. Each has services for visitors, from cottages and boats for rent to groceries and cafés.

### PARKS

**PORPOISE BAY PROVINCIAL PARK** has a small beach, and camping and picnicking facilities.

*About 4 miles north of Sechelt on East Porpoise Bay Road.*

**ROBERT'S CREEK PROVINCIAL PARK.** Visitors can camp out, hike, and swim in this 40-hectare park. At the separate picnic grounds, there's a sandy beach and boat launch.

*Entrance off Hwy. 101 in Robert's Creek.*

### ACTIVE FUN

**BOATING.** The following outlets offer boats, from big fishing charters to kayaks for rent: **Lowe's Resort** (604/883-2456) on Lagoon Road in Madeira Park and **Pedals & Paddles** (604/885-6440).

**SWIMMING.** In addition to the many lake and oceanfront beaches in the area, the Sunshine Coast has several indoor pools open to the public. Try **Gibson's Public Pool** (604/886-9415) and **Pender Harbour Aquatic & Fitness Centre** (604/883-2612) for indoor swimming. Call for details.

## CALENDAR

### JULY
Sandcastle Competition

### AUGUST
Festival of Written Arts, Sechelt

### SEPTEMBER
Pender Harbour Jazz Festival

## RESOURCES

### LANGDALE FERRY TERMINAL
604/886-2242

### WEB SITES
For information about the region, try www.bctravel.com/sunshine/ or www.sunshine.net/.

For information on the Sunshine Coast, vacation rentals, activities, and more, see www.bigpacific.com.

### SUNSHINE COAST TOURISM ASSOCIATION
P.O. Box 2573, Sechelt V0N 3A0
604/885-1959

### SUNSHINE COAST TRAVEL INFO CENTRES
Box 1190, Gibson's V0N 1V0
604/886-2325
Box 360, Sechelt V0N 3A0
604/885-0662
Pender Harbour: Box 265, Madeira Park V0N 2H0
604/883-2561

## POWELL RIVER

The north side of Jervis Inlet has a wilder feel than the southern part of the Sunshine Coast. Peaks are higher, stretches of road lonelier. Most of the route from Saltery Bay into Powell River is inland, but as you reach the outskirts of town the vista opens up and you glimpse the full beauty of this waterfront community, with its views of Texada Island and, in the distance, Vancouver Island.

Powell River offers plenty of family entertainment, including some wonderful child-size hikes to nearby summits and wildlife-rich nature trails. Big enough to have urban amenities, the town is actually two towns: there's the original historic logging company town, now a National Historic Site and undergoing restoration, and a modern urban center.

Powell River makes a good home base from which to explore the region's recreational opportunities. In recent years, this community has struggled to stay afloat in the midst of mill closures and recession abroad. Renewed effort has gone into enhancing tourist facilities, yet the region remains one of the best travel bargains in British Columbia. Although the region has become increasingly popular with scuba divers, even in August you can find accommodation. If you're looking for a relaxed, affordable family vacation with just about every outdoor amenity at your fingertips, this could be your best bet.

### GETTING THERE

From the ferry terminal at Saltery Bay to downtown Powell River is a 30-minute drive on Highway 101. Remember that ferry service ceases in late evening. There are washrooms and a small waiting area at Saltery Bay, but no services. The B.C. Ferries phone number at the Saltery Bay Terminal is 604/487-9333.

### PLACES TO STAY

#### BEACH GARDENS RESORT & MARINA
*7074 Westminster Ave., V8A 1C5*
*800/663-7070; bgardens@prcn.org.*
*Rates: Inexpensive to moderate*
*FYI: Restaurant, pub; kitchens (some units); indoor pool (closes 8:45 p.m.); fitness center; extensive grounds; marina, boat charters, dive shop; dataports in some rooms; pets OK*

In 1998, the Beach Gardens, Powell River's only full-service resort, was put up for sale by its owner. Faced with the loss of about 100 jobs and reluctant to accept yet another Powell River business closure, the resort's employees banded together and, with the help of local supporters, obtained financing to buy the resort and operate it themselves. Determined to make the venture succeed, the staff have put their hearts into making guests of all sizes happy, and they do a great job.

The resort has the relaxed, comfortable feel of an earlier era. Set way back from the road, the rooms, suites, and cabins are placed in several two-story, self-contained buildings with decks that overlook beautiful Malaspina Strait to the west. Rooms and suites are spacious and comfortable, but not luxurious.

The pool is on the ground floor of the two-story fitness center with a very vibrant mural on one wall. The pool has no shallow end, so supervision of small children is essential. Water is warm. The grounds have many paths to explore. Dining at the spacious restaurant may be indoors or outdoors. There's a children's menu.

**❝❝ PARENT COMMENTS**

*"We didn't go boating, but we did wander down to the resort's marina and enjoyed watching all the small fishes and seastars in what seemed like very clean water. We discovered a family of mink that had taken up residence by the marina."*

*"Our kids were rowdy after being cooped up in the car most of the day and dashed all around the grounds. No one seemed to mind though, and there was plenty of room."*

**THE COAST CENTRE HOTEL**
*4660 Joyce Ave., V8A 3B6*
*800/663-1144*
*Rates: Moderate*
*FYI: Restaurant, pub; whirlpool; exercise facilities; pets OK*

It's right downtown and lacks the character and charm of the Beach Gardens, but it's comfortable, well equipped, and convenient.

## PLACES TO EAT

**CAFÉ @ THECENTRE.COM, INTERNET CAFÉ**
*4510 Willingdon Ave.*
*604/485-2295*
*Hours: Breakfast, lunch daily; closed Sunday in winter; longer hours in summer*

The teenagers or adolescents in your party will probably enjoy this popular local hangout that features an excellent cappuccino bar. They have wraps and a wide range of vegetarian offerings for lunch.

**DELI TRUCE DUTCH CAFÉ**
*4480 Willingdon Ave.*
*604/485-9224*
*Hours: Breakfast, lunch daily; dinners in summer (call for details)*

This charming, spotless, family-run café, across the street from the ferry to Texada and Vancouver Islands, is full of character. There are Delft tiles on display, and the windows sport lace curtains; the walls are hung with the owner's landscapes in oil, and your breakfast toast will come with a generous serving of his homemade blackberry jam (also for sale in the restaurant). Kids will enjoy a cup of rich Dutch hot chocolate with breakfast. The Dutch cakes are also winners. Sandwiches, salads, and soups are offered for lunch; you can have them packed up for a picnic on Willingdon Beach. When the parent reviewers breakfasted here, the owner brought out a selection of children's books to entertain the kids while they waited to be served.

**JITTERBUG CAFÉ**
*4643 Marine Ave.*
*604/485-7797*
*Hours: Lunch, dinner daily in summer; closed winter (call for details)*

The jitterbug is right downtown, in a pretty white cottage covered with flowers. The location is sensational; dine indoors or outside on the deck overlooking Malaspina Strait. There is a good children's menu, and adults may want to order off it, too, rather than from the overpriced and somewhat disappointing menu aimed at the older set. The elaborate seafood dishes sound good, but don't live up to their hype. Still, service is friendly, and the desserts are just fine. A few vegetarian entrées are offered.

## WHAT TO SEE & DO

Let's face it, there really isn't much to do indoors in Powell River. Shopping is limited, although there are some attractive galleries and local stores can supply pretty much all needs. But the real draw here is the great outdoors. The city, squeezed between mountains and Malaspina Strait, is long and narrow. From the south, Highway 101 becomes the town's main street, Marine Avenue, and shopping district. There is an inhabited stretch before you reach the old town site at the northern end, now a National Historic Site that is slowly being restored. It's full of interesting old buildings and worth a drive through at least, although it probably won't interest many kids enough to go on a walking tour.

If you aren't staying at the Beach Gardens, you can swim at the **Recreation Centre** pool, (5001 Joyce Ave.; 604/485-2891).

### THE GREAT OUTDOORS

**CRANBERRY LAKE WILDLIFE SANCTUARY,** in the Cranberry district of Powell River, is home to all kinds of birds from eagles to ducks.

*Access from Cranberry St. or Manson Ave.; check with the Visitor's Bureau for details.*

**INLAND LAKE.** The 13-km trail around Inland Lake, also known as Loon Lake, is totally wheelchair-accessible and has won awards for its many user-friendly features. Parents with strollers take note; these are the smoothest dirt trails through wild, forested country you're likely to find anywhere. Small cabins and picnic tables with no benches on one side (designed to give wheelchair users tableside access) are other features. On the trail, watch out for young cyclists wobbling along on training wheels.

It's not just the trail that draws families here, though, but the beautiful lake, warm enough for swimming, and the abundant wildlife. Frogs may be endangered, but no one seems to have told the small amphibians who thrive here along with snakes, deer, and bald eagles.

The complete circuit is probably too long for most children, but check out the first few kilometers. Along the trail are occasional wood sculptures; in one spot there's a cheery woodsman, and in another, a small totem pole, about six feet high, with an eagle atop a killer whale atop a fish.

*From Cranberry St., go left onto Haslam St., follow the signs for Inland Lake along the unpaved logging road. There is parking at the park.*

**MOUNT VALENTINE.** Even very small mountain climbers can proudly conquer this 182-meter peak. The hardest part is finding the trail, which begins at the end of Crown Avenue. Park as close to the end of the road as possible. No signs indicate the start of the trail; the only indicator is a gate that bars the road to vehicular traffic. Walk around the barrier and you'll find the trail. It climbs up through salal, Oregon grape, and huckleberry bushes (you may want to stop and sample a few). Eventually you'll reach steep stairs, cut out of the rock, with a metal railing to hang on to. Several flights straight up you'll be rewarded with an incredible view, even by Sunshine Coast standards. Well OK, first look down at the pulp mill below, belching steam and who knows what else. *Then* look at the view; you'll see Texada and Vancouver Islands in glistening sunshine if you're lucky. There are picnic tables here and a few trails that lead to other viewpoints. Allow at least an hour for the round trip.

*Go east on Cranberry Street to Crown. Turn right and drive to the end of the road.*

**SALTERY BAY PROVINCIAL PARK.** Close to the ferry terminal on the north side of Jervis Inlet, this park has camping and picnic facilities. At Mermaid Cove you can snorkle, wade, and do some onshore whale watching. An easy two-km trail leads to Little Saltery Falls. Divers can check out the bronze statue of a mermaid, about 25 meters underwater.

*Off Hwy. 101 just north of the Saltery Bay ferry dock.*

**WILLINGDON BEACH PARK** has a sandy beach, playgrounds, washrooms, picnic facilities, campsites, and laundry. It's very popular and handy to downtown. Note that it can be a noisy choice for family camping; it's great for day use, though.

*On Marine Ave. in Powell River.*

### EXCURSIONS

**LUND.** How can you come to within 30 km of the terminus of the world's longest highway and not go all the way to the end? On the half-hour drive along Highway 101 north from Powell River, you'll pass Sliammon Village, a small First Nations community, marked by totem poles along the roadside, but otherwise there's not much to see along the way. At tiny Lund, you'll find a historic, recently restored hotel (604/483-3187) with a restaurant, post office, and small general store. It has a craft gallery that sells unusual and interesting woodcarvings by local First Nations artists.

The marina is usually full of pleasure boats to investigate, and if you follow the old boardwalk around the small bay, you'll arrive at a small waterside restaurant. Behind the boardwalk is another café, and there is an attractive restaurant in the hotel. But at lunchtime, the line forms at **Nancy's Bakery** (on the pier; 604/483-4180), a compact building above the marina. Favored by boaters, divers, and locals, the bakery has tables and chairs for dining outside. It features fabulous, yet wholesome, baked goodies from whole-grain breads and sandwiches to kid-friendly cheese breads, empañadas, and pizza, and a dazzlingly creative selection of butter tarts. The blackberry cinnamon rolls are justly renowned. Juice, sodas, and lattés are available, too.

From Lund, you can charter a boat, take a cruise to Desolation Sound, or hop a water taxi to **Savary Island,** known, to locals anyway, as "the Hawaii of the North." The island is known for its sandy beaches and exceptionally warm waters. There is no hotel, but a few B&Bs and cottages can be rented. Floatplanes also service the island.

**POWELL LAKE.** This lake is big enough to feature an island that itself has lakes. The setting is spectacular. It's connected to Malaspina Strait by a narrow channel that separates the historic town site from the rest of the town of Powell River. This channel is *the* Powell River, billed as the shortest river in the world. Houseboats and cabins can be rented on Powell Lake. Check with **Floating Cabins** (604/483-4501) or **Sunquest Houseboat Rentals** (604/485-4043).

## CALENDAR

### JUNE-JULY
Kathaumixw International Choral Festival
### AUGUST
Blackberry Festival
### SEPTEMBER
Sunshine Folkfest

## RESOURCES

### B.C. FERRIES, WESTVIEW TERMINAL
### (TO TEXADA AND VANCOUVER ISLANDS)
604/485-2943

### LUND WATER TAXI (TO SAVARY ISLAND)
604/483-9749; 604/483-8078

### PACIFIC COASTAL AIRLINE (SERVING POWELL RIVER)
800/663-2872

### POWELL RIVER VISITORS BUREAU
4690 Marine Ave., Powell River V8A 2L1
604/485-4701

### WEATHER INFO
604/485-6500

### POWELL RIVER WEB SITE
www.prwebs.com.

# VICTORIA AND VICINITY AND SALT SPRING ISLAND

The southern tip of Vancouver Island and the Gulf Islands that sit off its southeastern flank are blessed with a dry climate. Sheltered in the coastal mountain rain shadow, Victoria, the region's largest city, and the islands often experience sunshine and even drought while the rest of the region is waterlogged. Yet there's sufficient rainfall to nourish the beautiful gardens for which the region is known. The mountains, water, and weather have drawn increasing numbers of residents and visitors in recent years, with the usual result: rapid population growth.

Still heavily marketed as a quaint bit of Olde England, Victoria is actually a bustling, modern city of 326,000 residents that has undergone major expansion and development in the 1980s and '90s. Outlying areas have also grown, so traffic on Vancouver Island's major north-south artery, Highway 1, often crawls. Visitors should keep in mind that distances here are deceptive. Allow half an hour more than you think you'll need to reach any island destination by car, and you should do fine.

Salt Spring and other Gulf Islands, while increasingly popular, are still peaceful and unaffected by gridlock. Much like Washington's San Juan Islands in climate and culture, their Canadian counterparts have, in addition, a distinct charm and ambiance that rewards exploring. This section introduces the reader to only one of these gems. B.C. Ferries serve many others, and if you get hooked, you may want to contact some of the listed resources for additional intriguing destinations.

## VICTORIA

This lovely provincial capital is heavily promoted as the home of cricket in the park, double-decker buses, and exquisite flower gardens—an image that attracts many thousands of tourists annually. But don't limit your sightseeing to the most hyped attractions, designed to further the self-created illusion that Victoria is actually a suburb of London, England. A little investigation will uncover breathtakingly beautiful parks and beaches, magnificent cultures of the West Coast's first peoples, and more. And when you see the magnificent Parliament buildings magically lit at night or step into one of the surprisingly realistic dioramas at the Royal British Columbia Museum, you'll discover Victoria's distinctive, family-friendly culture on its own terms.

Seattle residents have a special reason for choosing Victoria for a family getaway: It's easily accessible by boat. Visitors can travel directly from downtown Seattle to Victoria's downtown Inner Harbour and spend a fun and eventful holiday without any need of a car. It is an ideal place to take a child for special time alone with a parent.

Keep in mind that Victoria, like many tourist-oriented communities, is much more crowded and expensive in the summer than at any other time of year. On a midwinter visit you can often get deep discounts at the more expensive hotels (be sure to make clear you are shopping for the best rate) and enjoy a quieter, less-crowded city.

Smokers take note: In 1999, Victoria passed draconian legislation aimed at you. Smoking is now completely outlawed in all public places, including restaurants and even bars.

### GETTING THERE

Unlike many vacation destinations, getting there is half the fun when you are traveling to Victoria. There are several ways to go.

**BY FERRY.** Within Canada, **B.C. Ferries** makes many runs daily, year round, between Tsawwassen, 30 km southwest of Vancouver, and Swartz Bay, about 32 km north of Victoria, on the Saanich Peninsula. Travelers who plan to see more of Vancouver Island than the greater Victoria area can travel from Tsawwassen to Duke's Point, a half-hour drive south of Nanaimo. For those traveling from Vancouver and points north, B.C. Ferries travel daily between Horseshoe Bay, in West Vancouver, and Departure Bay, in Nanaimo, a 90-minute drive north of Victoria (see "Vancouver Island and the Discovery Islands").

Amenities at ferry terminals are limited. At Swartz Bay, there's a cafeteria and a small playground. All terminals have washrooms.

*250/386-3431; 888/BC-FERRY. Frequent sailings daily, year round. Schedules vary with time of year; call for details. Fares vary depending on season (range from low to peak season is given). Cost: $28-32/vehicle (driver not included), $7.50-$9/adult, $3.75-$4.50/child 5-11, free/under 5. Group rates and other dis-*

*counts available; call for details.*

From the United States, **Victoria Clipper** jet-propelled, passenger-only catamarans make the round trip between Seattle and Victoria three or four times daily, depending on the season. Get there early to claim seats by the windows or a seat with a table. Once the boat gets out on the open water, boredom can set in; bring along games and books to help pass the time on the 2 1/2-hour trip.

Warning: If you're traveling during winter or inclement weather, waves can be quite choppy. Anyone prone to seasickness would do well to bring along a motion sickness remedy.

The *Clipper* offers limited food service at your seat. A typical breakfast is yogurt, a bagel and cream cheese, and juice ($4.25 U.S.); supper might offer a choice between a salmon dinner or a croissant sandwich ($6.25 U.S.). Better yet, bring your own picnic.

---

## *Before You Go: Crossing the U.S.-Canada Border*

The United States and Canada have always been fast friends, travelers tend to be quite relaxed about crossing the border. Many times, the border crossing is a simple affair, but at times, though, there may be additional documentation required.

If possible, carry proof of citizenship with picture ID. If someone in your car is not a U.S. citizen, bring additional documents ( such as a "green card."). If you have questions, contact the nearest Canadian consulate before you travel.

When a parent travels alone with children, it s best to bring a letter from the other parent, giving permission to take the kids across the border. Children under 18 traveling to Canada without an adult should bring a letter from a parent or guardian authorizing the travel.

When you travel with the family pet, you'll need to present a certificate from a licensed veterinarian, showing that your pet is vaccinated against rabies (the vaccination must be repeated every three years).

Handguns are not allowed in Canada. Specific rules govern other firearms and weapons. All weapons, including personal protection devices such as pepper spray, must be declared when you cross the border.

*2701 Alaskan Way, Pier 1, Seattle. 206/448-5000; 250/382-8100; 800/888-2535. Cost: round trip, $89/adult, half-price/child 1-11. During the off-season, rates are reduced.*

**Washington State Ferries** run car ferries between Anacortes (85 miles/137 km north of Seattle) and Sidney, near Victoria, on a beautiful, three-hour journey through the San Juans. Arrive at least one hour in advance of your departure time. Reservations are allowed from mid-June through mid-September. You may make a reservation beginning May 1. (See "San Juan Islands" in "Washington" for more information on these ferries.)

Be warned: Ferries fill up quickly in the summer; reservations are highly recommended.

*206/464-6400; 250/381-1551; www.wsdot.wa.gov.ferries. Daily departures from Anacortes, 8 a.m. and 2 p.m. (summer); daily departures, 8 a.m. (winter). Cost: one-way, $24 U.S./car and driver, $8.90 U.S./adult passenger, half-price/child 5-11, free/ under 5.*

**Black Ball Ferry** offers car and passenger ferry service between Port Angeles, Washington, and Victoria on the M.V. *Coho.* The trip takes about 1 1/2 hours. Reservations are not taken.

There's plenty of parking in Port Angeles, should you decide to leave your car in the U.S. If you're traveling in the high season, leaving your car behind makes it more likely your family can be accommodated on the sailing of your choice. In Victoria, the *Coho* docks in the Inner Harbour, within easy walking distance of many hotels and city attractions.

Amenities on board are limited—there's a fairly basic cafeteria, but no duty-free shop. So while you're waiting in Port Angeles, you may want to check out the mall next to the terminal, which has a duty-free shop, several galleries, and restaurants, including a Dairy Queen. The Visitor Information Center for Port Angeles is also next door to the terminal, offering tourist information about both cities.

*In Port Angeles: 101 E. Railroad Ave., 98362. 206/622-2222; in Victoria: 430 Belleville St., V8V 1W9. 250/386-2207. Sailings from Port Angeles, 8:20 a.m. & 2 p.m.; one sailing only on some dates in Jan.-Feb. Sailings from Victoria, 10:30 a.m. & 4 p.m.; one sailing only, at 3 p.m., on some dates in Jan.-Feb. Call for details. Cost: one way, $27.25 U.S./car and driver, $6.75 U.S./adult passenger, $3.40 U.S./child 5-11, free/under 5.*

**BY AIR.** Floatplanes offer a breathtakingly scenic and quick (about one hour) flight between Seattle and Victoria. Kenmore Air offers flights from both Lake Union, in Seattle, and from Kenmore, at the north end of Lake Washington, to Victoria's Inner Harbour, year round.

*800/826-1890; www.kenmoreair.com. Cost: round-trip, $155 U.S./person; weekend discounts available.*

## PLACES TO STAY

A number of Victoria hotels offer transportation and hotel packages at special rates. Ask your travel agent about what's available. Weekend newspaper travel sections also advertise frequent special package rates that combine transportation, accommodation, and Victoria attractions.

### THE BOWERY GUEST HOUSE
*310 Huntington Pl., V8V 2N5*
*250/383-8079*
*Rates: Moderate; no credit cards (personal checks, travelers' checks, and U.S. or Canadian cash are OK)*
*FYI: Complimentary breakfast; kitchens; VCRs; free passes to the Royal B.C. Museum; smoke-free throughout*

The gracious hostess at this attractive and comfortable B&B goes out of her way to make parents and children feel welcome. The upstairs suite has a kitchen, living room, master bedroom (with sofa and chairs), guest bedroom, and loft (with two single beds). The white wicker furniture is charming—but not fragile. Paddington Bear is lent to children during their stay, and pet lovers will enjoy the resident cat and dog. The delicious breakfast includes homemade muffins, bagels and cream cheese, cereal, fresh fruit, juice, and coffee and teas.

The Bowery has an excellent location for families: It is within easy walking distance of downtown, and Beacon Hill Park is nearby with duck ponds, a petting zoo (in summer), and a good playground.

### 66 PARENT COMMENTS

*"The three year old slept in the loft, Grandma got the extra bedroom, the baby was in the porta-crib in the living room, and Mom and Dad got privacy on a family vacation!"*

*"Our daughter was thrilled to find Paddington Bear, complete with sou'wester and boots, waiting in our room for her (on loan). In his paws, he held a brochure about the Beacon Hill Park petting zoo."*

*"What a delight-a B&B that likes kids! The hostess was just right—helpful and gracious but not hovering. Our stay at the Bowery with two kids was relaxing and economical. We will definitely go back."*

*"Owner Beverly Dresen should have substituted for Julie Andrews as Mary Poppins."*

### Clarion Hotel Grand Pacific

*450 Quebec St., V8V 1W5*
*250/386-0450, 800/458-6262*
*Rates: Moderate to expensive*
*FYI: Two restaurants; indoor pool; fitness club*

This rather upscale hotel sits one block away from the Inner Harbour, but when a major remodel in 1999 is completed, the hotel will have expanded out toward the water, encompassing what's now a Quality Inn. Rooms are comfortable, though not huge, with private balconies. The biggest kid-draw is the large swimming pool, open daily, usually 7 a.m.-10 p.m. A glorified lap pool, it's 25 meters long, a little more than one meter deep, and divided into three lanes so that serious swimmers can be separated from the frivolous, splashing set. The large hot tub won't attract kids, but there is a shallow pool for the small fry to frolic in (about a half-meter deep).

The location is convenient to the main Victoria attractions, one block from Parliament and two blocks from the provincial museum. Just around the corner is a touching memorial to the McKenzie-Papineau Brigade, Canadian volunteers who helped to defend the Spanish Republic in the Spanish Civil War of the 1930s. Also around the corner—and unavoidable—are the horse-and-buggy stands, manned by touts who offer horse-drawn buggy tours of the city. Expect to hear begs and pleas for buggy rides from your kids every time you pass by. You may balk at the price, though; a 15-minute ride costs $30.

**❝ Parent Comments**

*"The staff was very pleasant, and no one seemed to mind when our kids rode up and down the elevator, striking up conversations with other guests."*

*"There are large changing rooms with showers, and lockers are free to guests, so you don't have to return to your room dripping and shivering in the elevator. For an hour or two per day the pool is open only to adults. Verify in advance which are the adult-only swim hours (they vary), so the children won't be disappointed."*

## THE EMPRESS HOTEL

*721 Government St., V8W 1W5*
*250/384-8111, 800/441-1414; www.cphotels.ca*
*Rates: Expensive*
*FYI: Three restaurants, seasonal cafés; indoor pool; health club;*
*baby-sitting; small pets OK (fee); historical tours daily*

At first glance, the Empress Hotel appears to be all romance and afternoon tea. It sits regally at the head of the Inner Harbour, where it has welcomed visitors since 1908. From outside, its grandeur and elegance can be intimidating, so it's not surprising that parents with tots in tow sometimes gaze upon it enviously, imagining fine comfort and service within, then turn away, fearing a bull-in-a-china shop experience. In fact, parents should take a second look, because the old queen of Victoria hotels, sporting a 1989, 45-million-dollar facelift, is quite well suited for families.

First: location, location, location. The hotel sits at the center of Victoria's best attractions, with the Royal B.C. Museum on one side and the main shopping district on the other. Second, the pool facilities are excellent. Exhausted adventurers, returning to the hotel for a refreshing swim, will find, in addition to a large swimming pool with hot tub, a much smaller, shallow pool, ideally suited for young nonswimmers. The pools are open from 6 a.m. to midnight, perfect for a late dip before slipping into pajamas.

Negatives here include high prices and small rooms, but if you avoid the high season, rates will be much lower, and the size of the room won't be all that important unless you plan to do more than just sleep here.

The Empress is famous for its afternoon High Tea, served daily in the posh old lobby. However, given the high price, most parents will choose to admire it from afar. On the other hand, Kiplings, a buffet and à la carte restaurant, rather hidden in the hotel's basement, is one of the best places in town to feed a family (see "Places to Eat" below).

### 66 PARENT COMMENTS

*"When we made reservations for a visit to Victoria at Christmas with our five kids, we didn't even consider the Empress, because we thought the prices would be too high. But when we didn't like our first hotel, we called the Empress and got a decent rate (the excellent exchange rate on our American dollars at the time helped)."*

*"The rooms were small, but since we spent very little time in them, it didn't matter to us. The location was perfect: We could even watch the Santa parade from our room! Best of all, there was a real kids' pool that was the best I had ever seen for preswimmers."*

*"The children's clothing store on the second floor, just above the main entrance, has some of the cutest, most original clothing for young kids available. It also has a small assortment of toys."*

### LAUREL POINT INN

680 Montreal St., V8V 1Z8
250/386-8721, 800/663-7667; www.laurelpoint.com
*Rates: Moderate*
*FYI: Two restaurants; refrigerators/microwaves; indoor pool; pets OK (small dogs, first floor only)*

You will likely notice this brick zigzag building as you enter the Inner Harbour by boat. Built in 1979, it lacks the "Olde English" charm of many of Victoria's accommodations. What it does offer are modern, spacious furnishings, great views of the busy harbor, good restaurants that serve three meals a day, and a lovely swimming pool overlooking a reflecting pond. A path between the hotel and the water leads to the Parliament buildings, the Royal B.C. Museum, and downtown—a pleasant, five-minute walk.

**❝❝ PARENT COMMENTS**

*"We got a good discount on our room rate when we visited in February. The staff was exceptionally helpful and warm. We all enjoyed watching the harbor boat and seaplane traffic out our window."*

### OAK BAY BEACH HOTEL

1175 Beach Dr., V8S 2N2
250/598-4556, 800/668-7758; www.oakbaybeachhotel.bc.ca
*Rates: Moderate to expensive*
*FYI: Two restaurants; fishing rentals; baby-sitting*

Sitting majestically by the sea in the elegant Oak Bay district outside Victoria, the Oak Bay Beach Hotel offers guests a retreat into British civility and charm. It is not a place to bring rowdy youngsters, but is suitable if you are planning a special getaway with older children who would be impressed by landscaped gardens and high tea.

Only 10 minutes from Victoria, the Oak Bay is less than a mile from a beautiful public beach, and if you bring bikes you can explore the neighborhood, with its mansions and lovely gardens.

❝he dining room is formal and expensive—not recommended for young kids. Afternoon tea is served daily in the grand lobby, and on the veranda overlooking the sea and gardens if the weather is warm. One kilometer from the hotel is the Oak Bay Marina Restaurant, with moderate prices and excellent food.

### ❝ PARENT COMMENTS

*"We expected to spend more time in Victoria, but our kids just wanted to hang out at the beach near the hotel."*

*"The hotel is truly grand and fine for civilized kids."*

*"I stayed at the Oak Bay on a getaway with my daughter. It was interesting to get out of Victoria. We loved riding bikes through the gorgeous neighborhood where the hotel is located."*

### ROYAL SCOT MOTOR INN

*425 Quebec St., V8V1W7*
*250/388-5463; www.royalscot.com*
*Rates: Expensive*
*FYI: Restaurant; kitchens; indoor pool; game room; laundry; baby-sitting (by pre-arrangement)*

To get you in the right mood for a stay in Victoria, all the employees at the Royal Scot wear beautiful kilts. The inn itself is comfortable, if not fancy, and the landscaped grounds are quiet. Most of the 150 units include kitchens and living rooms. The luxury suites have one or two bedrooms, a living room with sofa bed, and a fully equipped kitchen and dining room.

The indoor pool, shower area, and hot tub are not large, but they are clean and well maintained. Coin-operated washers and dryers take care of wet bathing suits and other laundry. Older kids will like the game room.

In addition to the good value, the Royal Scot is well situated for a stay in Victoria. Its location, just south of the Inner Harbour, at the hub of the city, puts everything this wonderful city has to offer within easy walking distance.

### ❝ PARENT COMMENTS

*"Service was wonderful, right down to our beds being turned down while we were at dinner, with mints on our pillows and our daughter's stuffed animals all tucked in."*

*"We have visited Victoria several times with our three kids—mainly to visit the fabulous B.C. Museum. The Royal Scot works very well for us."*

*"We found it to be an excellent value. Having a kitchen was*

*great for breakfast, and one night when we couldn't stand to take the group out to dinner again, we had Chinese food delivered."*

*"After a busy morning of sightseeing we were all rejuvenated by a long visit to the Crystal Gardens. The parents brought a newspaper to sit and read, and the kids delighted in trying to figure out if the beautiful birds amid the greenery were real or not (they're real)."*

### SHAMROCK MOTEL

*675 Superior St., V8V 1V1*
*250/385-8768*
*Rates: Inexpensive to moderate*
*FYI: Kitchens; small pets OK*

The Shamrock is a 15-unit, three-story motel located right across the street from Beacon Hill Park. The clean units have living rooms with a sofa bed, well-equipped kitchens, bedrooms, and a balcony. The proprietors are very friendly and helpful.

**❝ PARENT COMMENTS**

*"We visited with our two-and-a-half year old and three month old. The location was wonderful. We liked sitting out on the balcony and looking across to the lovely park. We would highly recommend the Shamrock for families."*

### STRATHCONA HOTEL

*919 Douglas St., V8W 2C2*
*800/663-7476*
*Rates: Inexpensive*
*FYI: Restaurant*

It's cheap, reasonably comfortable, and centrally located. The presence of casinos and a nightclub may not thrill every family, but quiet rooms are available. For those who want to conserve their resources for the often-expensive pleasures of Victoria sightseeing, the Strathcona can't be beat.

**❝ PARENT COMMENTS**

*"There's not much in the way of atmosphere, but we were grateful for the low cost. We stayed here one weekend when we had no car and a baby in a baby pack. The location was perfect—a very short walk to just about everything we wanted to see."*

### SWANS HOTEL

*506 Pandora Ave., V8W 1K8*
*250/361-3310, 800/668-7926; www.islandnet.com\~swans*

*Rates: Moderate to expensive*
*FYI: Kitchens*

These 29 attractively furnished suites near the Johnson Street Bridge are well suited to families. Each split-level unit has a fully equipped kitchen and separate dining/living room. An upscale pub, a popular café, and a brewery (with daily tours) share this recently renovated property. Swans is within easy walking distance of the heart of downtown.

**❝ PARENT COMMENTS**

*"We were traveling with three young kids, and the separate bedrooms and spacious living room/dining room were wonderful. The kitchens were also convenient—we saved money and headaches by eating breakfast and lunch in our suite."*

*"Ouch! The crib provided by the hotel cost $15 a night. Since we were already paying dearly, that hurt. But the Swans is a very attractive, small hotel in a convenient location."*

**TRAVELLER'S INN**
*Downtown: 1850 Douglas, V8T 4K6*
*710 Queens St.*
*760 Queens St.*
*888/SLEEPS-4*
*Rates: Inexpensive to moderate (advertised rates can be as low as $29.95/room, off-season)*
*FYI: Complimentary continental breakfast; some locations have kitchens, pool, sauna*

This budget chain offers some of the lowest prices in Victoria, a town where prices, especially in summer, can be very high. Accommodations are basic, but adequate. Their rooms go fast in summer, so book ahead.

**❝ PARENT COMMENTS**

Re: 760 Queens St. location: *"We had to drive quite a few blocks to find a store or restaurant. The lobby, where breakfast is served, was small—your choices are to stand up to eat or carry your food across the parking lot and up the elevator to your room."*

## PLACES TO EAT

**BLETHERING PLACE**
*2250 Oak Bay*
*250/598-1413*

*Hours: Breakfast, lunch, dinner, tea daily*

If you want to treat the kids to an authentic English tea while visiting Victoria, the Blethering Place is a good choice. You'll enjoy excellent scones, jams, Devonshire cream, and tea for $7.95—a good price in this town. And the atmosphere is appropriately civil and leisurely. Local musicians perform most evenings.

The hearty English meals (sandwiches, meat pies), served three times a day, are also very good, if a bit heavy. Well-prepared English food suits many children—plain and simple without fancy sauces.

### CAFÉ MEXICO
*1425 Store St.*
*250/386-1425*
*Hours: Lunch, dinner daily*

Perched on one side of Market Square, this spacious café is decorated in bright colors and serves the usual Mexican family favorites—tacos, enchiladas, salads, and the like—at moderate prices. Most kids will enjoy the cheese pizza (one is big enough to feed two small children). When it comes to dessert, Café Mexico comes into its own. The deep-fried ice cream is a treat, but top honors go to the bunuelos—crispy round, cinnamon-sprinkled wafers sandwiching fresh strawberries and whipped cream.

### CECCONIA'S PIZZERIA AND TRATTORIA
*3201 Shelburne (across from Hillside Mall)*
*250/592-0454*
*Hours: Lunch Mon-Sat.; dinner daily*

Cecconia's is a noisy but relaxed place that is ideal for families. The outstanding wood-oven pizzas and marvelous fresh pasta make this place deservedly popular with the locals.

### EATON PAVILION
*1150 Douglas St.*

This large, indoor shopping mall has a "food circus" assortment of restaurants on its top floor. You'll find pizza, teriyaki, sandwiches, and other fare popular with kids.

### JOHN'S PLACE
*723 Pandora St.*
*250/389-0711*

*Hours: Breakfast, lunch, dinner daily*

John's Place is a top choice among locals when they're in search of a hearty breakfast. The roast potatoes and extensive selection of eggs Benedict dishes are justly famous. The joint is jumping, especially on weekends, and there's not a lot of room in which to wait. But turnaround is quick; and the combination of high-quality dishes, ample portions, and low prices is irresistible. Lunch and dinner offer more of the same: casual, child-friendly, yet high-quality dishes in a bustling, cheery environment.

### KIPLING'S

*721 Government St. (in the Empress Hotel, lower level)*
*250/389-2727; 800/644-6611, or call hotel, 250/384-8111*
*Hours: Breakfast, lunch, dinner daily*

Don't let its upscale location fool you: Kipling's offers excellent family value, especially the hearty buffets that offer a range of dishes from appetizers to seafood, meat and pasta entrées, salads, and desserts.

### PRINCESS MARY SEAFOOD RESTAURANT

*385 Harbour Road*
*250/386-3456*
*Hours: Lunch, dinner daily*

This charming family restaurant, just west of the Johnson Street Bridge, is within walking distance of downtown, but few tourists seem to venture this far. They don't know what they're missing. Crafted from the top stern deck of one of the original, legendary CP Princess steamers, today the Princess Mary sits firmly on dry land, but inside you'd never know it. Gazing through the porthole windows, the kids will swear they're afloat. Hearty, good food of the family-friendly variety is served here, with an emphasis on seafood. Elegant kid cocktails can be ordered from the kids' menu along with the usual offerings.

### RE-BAR

*50 Bastion Square*
*250/361-9223*
*Hours: Breakfast, lunch, dinner daily*

This popular café sits below street level, a few doors away from the Maritime Museum (see "Museums"). No matter when you come, you're likely to find it packed. The food is healthy, delicious, and cosmopolitan, and desserts are justly renowned. If you number adventurous eaters in your family, this is a good option; but if your offspring are inclined to peer narrowly at the dishes set in front of them to verify that no mushrooms or green peppers lurk within, you'll probably do better to dine elsewhere.

### SMITTY'S FAMILY RESTAURANT

*850 Douglas St.*
*250/383-5612*
*Hours: Breakfast, lunch, dinner daily*

This Canadian chain started out as a pancake house, and it still serves up an impressive selection of flapjacks, along with the usual family-restaurant, laminated-menu offerings. Smitty's caters to families, and just about every child-pleaser turns up on the menu someplace. It can be crowded on Sunday mornings. Prices are reasonable.

### WHARFSIDE EATERY AND DECKS

*1208 Wharf St.*
*250/360-1808*
*Hours: Breakfast, lunch, dinner daily; Sunday brunch*

Its harborside location and proximity to major Victoria sightseeing attractions make the Wharfside a good dining option. A warren of rooms on two levels, it's decorated in a rustic, vaguely Italian-villa style with lots of mosaics, pillars, and cast-iron ornamentation. When weather allows, you can dine on one of several multilevel decks.

On your first peek inside, you might get the impression that the Wharfside caters only to adults. But looks are deceiving; kids are welcomed with the traditional menu and crayons, and the noise level (often considerable) is likely to mask sounds emitted by even the most exuberant small fry. Not surprisingly, seafood's the specialty.

## WHAT TO SEE & DO

### STROLL & BROWSE

One of this compact city's greatest charms is that you can see much of it on foot. If you arrive by boat or plane from Seattle, or via the ferry from Port Angeles, you will dock in the Inner Harbour, right in the hub of downtown. Three of Victoria's most famous landmarks—the Empress Hotel, the Parliament buildings, and the Royal British Columbia Museum—as well as the downtown shopping district are within easy walking distance. Many other interesting attractions lie within a few blocks. Pick up a self-guided walking tour map at the **Visitor's Bureau** (812 Wharf St.; 250/953-2033; 800/663-3883), across the street from the Empress Hotel.

Note: Many popular attractions extend their hours during the summer season. Call for up-to-date information on schedules and rates.

**Government Street,** just north of the Empress, is packed with shops that will delight kids who like to look at trinkets, glass figurines, Indian dolls and beadwork, and other assorted wonders. This is the place to spend the souvenir money; plan on at least an hour of browsing. Grown-up shoppers might enjoy checking out the English tweeds, fine china, famous Cowichan sweaters, Scottish tartans, candies, and teas.

As you stroll uptown, you'll encounter **Munro's Books** (1108 Government Street; 250/382-2464), Victoria's premier bookseller, housed in an imposing building, a former bank; its children's section is excellent. Next door is **Murchie's Tea & Coffee** (1110 Government St.; 250/383-3112)—the Starbucks of tea. Along with an impressive selection of brews, the branch here offers fabulous baked goods and salads and, if it's not too crowded, is an excellent place to grab a quick bite. Stroll down Douglas Street, parallel to Government St., for more of the same. In the evening, check out the jugglers, bagpipers, and magicians who perform ceaselessly around the Inner Harbour. Activity drops off but doesn't entirely cease in the winter.

North along the Inner Harbour on Wharf Street, parallel to Government Street, you'll find yourself at **Bastion Square,** home of the Maritime Museum (see "Museums"). If you head east on Johnson Street, you'll arrive at **Market Square,** a complex of shops including toy stores, bookstores, and bistros, housed in a three-story, 19th-century building that surrounds a courtyard. Slightly north of Johnson is Fisgard Street, gateway to Victoria's attractive **Chinatown,** once the largest north of San Francisco. In the 19th century, over 10,000 Chinese Canadians made this their home, working in the coal mines, building the railroad, and taking part in the Gold Rush. Enter Chinatown through the picturesque Gate of Harmonious Interest, flanked by stone lions. After exploring Fan Tan Alley, one block west of Government Street, retrace your steps south. From Johnson Street head east to Government Street, down to Yates, and then stroll back to Wharf Street. If the kids are game, repeat this maneuver going east on Fort Street: The area is packed with antique stores, galleries, shops, pubs, and restaurants.

For something different, check out **Star Fish Glass Works** (630 Yates St.; 250/388-7827). This lovely studio/gallery displays the work of leading-edge West Coast glass artists and features an observation gallery above the studio. Here, visitors can look down on the intently focused artists toiling over medieval-looking ovens into which they insert long rods tipped with glowing, molten glass. The staff say that parents often have a difficult time hauling their offspring away from the mesmerizing sight. The gallery is open daily from Victoria Day to September 15th, 10 a.m. to 6 p.m. In winter, hours are variable, and the gallery is closed on Tuesdays. Glassblowing begins at noon, Wednesday through Sunday.

Free 45-minute tours of the massive **Parliament buildings,** across the street from the Empress Hotel, are offered all day: daily during the summer, weekdays only the rest of the year. The Legislative Assembly, with all its pomp and circumstance, can be observed when it's in session (call for details), offering a view of the magnificently costumed sergeant-at-arms bearing a gold mace and the Speaker sitting on a gilded throne. Tours are conducted in six languages during the summer, three languages during the rest of the year. Don't miss viewing the Parliament buildings at night, outlined by more than 3,000 tiny lights.

*501 Belleville Ave. (on the Inner Harbour). 250/387-3046. Open Mon.-Fri., 8:30 a.m.-5 p.m.; weekends and holidays, 9 a.m.-5 p.m. Free.*

The **CRYSTAL GARDEN** is located in an elegant turn-of-the-century building that originally housed a grand indoor swimming pool. It has been converted into a tropical garden, complete with live flamingos, macaws, and the smallest monkeys in the world. One parent reviewer put the Crystal Garden in the category of an expensive tourist trap not worth visiting, with "tiny cages that are cruel for the animals." But another disagreed, saying it was "a great place to visit when it is raining in Victoria—a restful retreat from the outside hustle-and-bustle" that she enjoyed and that entertained her kids—ages five and seven—for a good two hours.

*713 Douglas St. (behind the Empress Hotel). 250/381-1213.*

Open daily, 10 a.m.-4:30 p.m. Cost: $7/adult, $4/child 5-16, free/under 5.

**MINIATURE WORLD,** located inside the Empress Hotel, will enchant a child interested in dollhouses and miniatures—anyone else will likely be bored and annoyed that they've walked into a tourist trap. One parent reviewer said her nine-year-old daughter voted the Miniature Museum her "second-favorite part of the trip" (the Royal B.C. Museum was first).

Exhibits include a Fantasy Land, with scenes from *Gulliver's Travels*, Santa's Workshop, and more; miniature soldiers in mock battle (providing quick history lessons); a miniature railway; and dozens of exquisite dollhouses with proper period furnishings.

649 Humbolt St. (inside the Empress Hotel). 250/385-9731. Open daily, 8:30 a.m.-9 p.m. (summer); 9 a.m.-5 p.m. (rest of year). Cost: $8/adult, $7/youth 13-17, $6/child 5-11, free/under 5.

## TOURS

**GRAY LINE DOUBLE-DECKER BUS TOUR.** Among the gazillion tours offered in Victoria, the most appealing for young kids are aboard the old double-decker London Transport buses; you can't miss them. OK, they're hokey, but they can be fun, too, and—for the under-10 set—they're a guaranteed hit. If you've never done it before, consider hopping aboard for a trip around Victoria. At the least it will help you get your bearings. The tours depart continuously from the front of the Empress Hotel. Many tours are offered, but some are long, expensive, and not especially child-friendly. Your best bet is to take a 60- or 90-minute trip that ends before the kids get cranky.

Of course, everyone wants to sit on the upper deck; drivers stop halfway to let upper and lower passengers trade places so that everyone gets a chance to ride high. If the bus isn't crowded, though, chances are the kids can stay atop for the entire trip.

Buses turn around at a small waterfront park where kids can dash around and release pent-up energy. The drivers are all tour guide/comedians, with patter that's bound to appeal to smaller audience members. The tours aren't cheap, but check out the happy faces of disembarking passengers.

700 Douglas St. 250/388-5248; 800/663-8390. Open daily, year round. Cost: For a short tour, expect to pay $12-$16.60/ per adult, $6-$8.25/child.

## MUSEUMS

**ART GALLERY OF GREATER VICTORIA.** Housed partly in a historic 19th-century mansion, this lovely art gallery is known for its collection of Japanese art and works by Victoria native Emily Carr. It's a bit of a hike from the harbor (about 10 blocks east on Fort Street).

*1040 Moss St. 250/384-1531; 250/384-4101; www.com/aggv/. Open Mon.-Sat., 10 a.m.-5 p.m. (Thurs. until 9 p.m.); Sun., 1-5 p.m. Cost: $5/adult, $3/senior & student, free/ under 12; admission by donation on Mon.*

**EMILY CARR'S HOUSE.** If you can visit only one of Victoria's historic mansions, make it this one. A 10-minute walk southeast of the Royal B.C. Museum is the home in which artist Emily Carr was born. The 1864 house has been restored to give visitors a glimpse of what life was like for the Carr family in the 1870s. Inspire the young painter in your family with a trip to the birthplace of Canada's most renowned woman artist. A small gift shop on the premises features items by local potters and artists.

*207 Government St. 250/383-5843. Open daily, mid-May-mid-Oct., 9 a.m.-5 p.m. Cost: $4/adult, $3/student, $2/child.*

**MARITIME MUSEUM OF BRITISH COLUMBIA.** This attractive museum, in a historic 1899 building in Bastion Square, once housed the provincial law courts. Well worth a visit, it tends to be less crowded than some of the more touristy attractions and offers an interesting glimpse of the province's watery past. There are three stories of exhibits, but kids may enjoy the trip to the top floor, in Canada's oldest functioning open-cage elevator, most of all. Start your visit in the courtroom on the third floor, which shows nautical films (a hair-raising film of a sailing ship rounding Cape Horn was showing when parent reviewers visited). The second floor contains a host of model ships and wartime memorabilia. Traveling exhibits share the first floor with exhibits on the rich history of regional nautical exploration. Kids will have fun investigating exhibits on the colorful history of piracy, viewing the signature flags of legendary pirates, and climbing up the rigging of a ship to the crow's nest.

*28 Bastion Square. 250/385-4222. Open daily, 9:30 a.m.-5:30 p.m. (July-Aug.); daily, 9:30 a.m.-4:30 p.m. (Sept.-June). Cost: $5/adult, $4/senior, $3/student, $2/child; 15% discount, family discount.*

**ROYAL BRITISH COLUMBIA MUSEUM.** This world-class museum, across the street from the Inner Harbour, will captivate even children who don't like museums. It displays the province's rich natural history and native heritage and is considered by many to be among the finest museums in Canada.

Of special interest to children are the highly realistic, life-size dioramas—complete with authentic sounds and smells. Visitors can observe a lifelike woolly mammoth on the windswept icy plains of the last ice age; walk through a rain forest and along a seashore; sit in a Kwakiutl longhouse; stroll down a Victorian cobblestone street, complete with wood smoke and the smell of baking gingerbread; and stand in Captain George Vancouver's quarters in *H.M.S. Discovery*. Kids will enjoy peering into the store windows of a reconstructed frontier town, visiting a realistic train station into which a train pulls every few minutes, and watching a silent movie in a theater that offers a variety of old favorites.

Children and adults who are subject to claustrophobia may want to avoid the Open Oceans exhibit, whose centerpiece is a simulated—but for many, all too realistic—trip to the deep, dark ocean floor. Some parent reviewers reported that they had to bolt through the emergency exits with a panicked child; however, other families say that this exhibit is a top choice for their kids whenever they pay the museum a visit.

A National Geographic IMAX theater, added recently, rounds out the attractions; admission is extra. As a result of the museum's recent facelift, the gift shop has been greatly expanded. The collection of books for children on science and nature, and about the rich cultures of the region's first peoples, is among the best you will ever find.

*675 Belleville St. (on the Inner Harbour). 250/387-3014. Open daily, 9 a.m.-5 p.m. $8/adult, $5.85/senior, $2.14/child 6-18, free/under 6; $16.05/annual family pass.*

**ROYAL LONDON WAX MUSEUM.** The Royal London Wax Museum is another of the attractions near the Inner Harbour that will put a dent in your wallet, but most kids find it fascinating, if a bit spooky. If mom or dad is in a professorial mood, the highly realistic depictions of historic figures offer a good opportunity for a quick history lesson. Children under seven will likely be bored and, possibly, frightened. Still, one of our parent reviewers who reported going to the wax museum in a spontaneous act of desperation on a rainy afternoon said her eight-year-old son remembers it as the highlight of his trip to Victoria.

Warning: One section of the museum, the Chamber of Horrors, is not a "Disney-style" exhibit meant to give a little frightening fun. It features graphic depictions of barbaric torture methods you might not want your child to see. It is clearly marked and can be easily avoided.

*470 Belleville St. (on the Inner Harbour). 250/388-4461. Open daily, 9:30 a.m.-5 p.m. (winter); longer hours in summer. Cost: $7.50/adult, $6.50/student & senior, $3/child 6-12, $21/family.*

### PARKS

**BEACON HILL PARK.** This lush and elegant 68-hectare park has a gorgeous view of the Strait of Juan de Fuca, plus playgrounds, several little lakes, a petting farm (in the summer), a ceremonial longhouse, a totem pole collection, and numerous places for a picnic. Ponds and flower gardens are scattered about the manicured lawns. If you come on a Sunday afternoon in the summer, you will probably be able to watch a cricket match.

*A short walk from downtown along Douglas St., or take the No. 5 bus.*

**THUNDERBIRD PARK,** an outdoor continuation of the Royal British Columbia Museum, features awesome totem poles, including works in progress. In summer, you might spot carvers at work here. There's also an attractive herb garden. Helmcken House, one of the oldest houses in Victoria, is on the grounds and can be toured during limited hours daily.

*Next to the Royal B.C. Museum, at Douglas and Belleville. Helmcken House, 250/361-0021. $4/adult, $3/senior, student, $2/child 6-12, $10/family.*

**CRAIGDAROCH CASTLE** and **ANNE HATHAWAY'S THATCHED COTTAGE** are popular attractions well worth seeing, but best left for a trip with children over 12. Entrance fees are steep, and few young children care to see historical homes, no matter how exquisite they may be.

**PACIFIC UNDERSEA GARDENS** and the **CLASSIC CAR**

**MUSEUM,** tourist attractions located beside the harbor, are overpriced and not recommended.

### ANIMALS, ANIMALS

**SEALAND OF THE PACIFIC,** a seven-km drive from downtown, is a "mediocre" aquarium in the opinion of several of our parent reviewers. If you'll also be visiting Vancouver or Seattle, you may want to save your money for the superior aquariums in those cities.

**VICTORIA BUG ZOO** is an expensive attraction, but if your family harbors a bug enthusiast, at least one of you will enjoy spending an hour or so here. Wander through the two rooms lined with glass cases featuring an assortment of walkingstick insects, centipedes, some interesting spiders and, the pièce de résistance, an ant—well, let's not call it a farm, but rather a Martian colony. Through clear plastic tubes running along the walls, your young entomologists can observe the ants, nature's little workaholics, going about their daily tasks. Kids can happily spend 10 minutes just trying to spot the queen.

The genial staff is knowledgeable, answering questions and routinely hauling out insects for visitors to handle. Unfortunately, some of the inmates are for sale. Before entering, you may want to think of a few reasons why purchasing a pet tarantula is not an option.

There's a well-stocked gift shop with exactly what you'd expect, from insect lollipops to plastic flies and spiders.

*1107 Wharf St. 250/384-BUGS; bugs@bugzoo.bc.ca. Open Mon.-Sat., 9:30 a.m.-6 p.m.; Sun., 11 a.m.-6 p.m. Cost: $6/adult, $5/senior & student, $4/child 3-16, free/under 3. Annual passes and group rates are available.*

### EXCURSIONS

**BUTCHART GARDENS.** Once a fairly dull experience (from a child's perspective at least), 20-hectare Butchart Gardens today is likelier to please the small fry. On Saturday evenings throughout July and August, fireworks displays are featured along with live music. And all through December, the garden is aglow with thousands of lights. Refreshments are served at a coffeehouse, soda fountain, coffee bar, and two full-service restaurants; the seasonal Blue Poppy Restaurant caters to families. An enormous gift shop carries all kinds of child-pleasing offerings. So no matter how resistant your youngsters are to flowers, the promise of something to eat or buy around the corner can probably motivate them to keep moving.

The real draw—the gorgeous gardens—can be counted on to delight not only adults but many older kids too. Strollers are available, and there are even loan cameras for folks who've left theirs behind. In summer, the gardens are so congested with tours that lines can be long and tempers short. Spring break, off-hour (first thing in the morning or late afternoon), and winter visits are recommended.

*Located on W. Saanich Road at Brentwood Bay, 21 km north of Victoria and 20 km south of the Swartz Bay ferry terminal. 250/652-4422; butchartgardens.bc.ca/butchart. Open daily, 9 a.m.; closing hours depend on daylight and activities offered—anywhere from 4:30 p.m. in winter to 10:30 p.m. in summer. Cost: $6/adult, $3/child 13-17, $1/child 5-12, free/under 5 (mid-Sept.-May, except Dec.) and $15.50/adult, $7.75/child 13-17, $2/child 5-12, free/under 5 (June-mid-Sept.). Dec. admission is higher.*

**VICTORIA BUTTERFLY GARDENS.** Combine a visit to this popular attraction with a visit to Butchart Gardens, which is almost next door. Many butterflies are on display in the attractive indoor garden, but the price of admission may strike some as pretty steep for 12,000 square feet of butterfly habitat. The gardens do help to conserve and breed tropical butterflies, many of which are released back into the big world. A gift shop and food are available on site.

*W. Saanich Road & Keating Cross Road. 250/652-3822. Open daily, 9:30 a.m.-4:30 p.m. Cost: $7.50/adult, $6.50/senior & student, $4.50/child 3-12, free/under 3.*

**FORT RODD HILL AND FISGARD LIGHTHOUSE NATIONAL HISTORIC SITES.** Before your eyes glaze over at the words "gun emplacements and old forts," you should be aware that this two-for-the-price-of-one park is fascinating and well worth a visit. Not to mention that it's hard to imagine a better site anywhere for a game of hide-and-seek. This was an artillery fort for the first half of the 20th century, designed to repel attacks from both sea and land. Visitors needn't be weapons enthusiasts to enjoy viewing the military exhibits that remain. Warrens of rooms are tunneled into the cliff side: Around every corner is another door to open and displays of war time memorabilia, barracks, mess halls, guns (not usable) to investigate. It's all perfectly safe, but it would be easy to lose track of small children here. Holding hands is a good idea.

The lighthouse aficionados in your family will enjoy the beautiful, restored 1860 Fisgard Lighthouse, the oldest on Canada's west coast, still operational and with two floors of exhibits. It's approached on a picturesque causeway from the fort area.

Nature trails, a broad grassy expanse, and picnic facilities round out the attractions.

*14 km west of Victoria, on Hwy. 1A. 250/478-5849. Open daily, 10 a.m.-5:30 p.m. Cost: $3/adult, $2.25/senior, $1.50/child 6-16, $7.50/family.*

**GOLDSTREAM PROVINCIAL PARK.** This lovely, 327-hectare park is full of trails that lead to waterfalls, marshlands, and an abandoned gold mine. Spawning salmon in the Goldstream River and the eagles that dine on them are the major attractions in late autumn. Day-use and camping areas allow short-term or overnight visits. Freeman King Visitor Centre has displays and exhibits, and offers nature programs in the summer and fall. Climb eagle-viewing platforms to observe bald eagles feasting on post-spawning salmon.

*About 19 km northwest of Victoria; entrance is off Hwy. 1. For campground reservations, call 800/689-9025.*

## SOOKE

This small community about 43 km west of Victoria makes an enjoyable side trip. Although primarily renowned as the home of Sooke Harbour House, a lovely, upscale, but definitely not child-oriented small resort, Sooke is well worth a family visit. The village is home to a few shops and galleries and the **Sooke Regional Museum** (2070 Phillips Road; 250/642-6351). The museum, open daily year-round, 9 a.m.- 5 p.m., is worth a visit. It also houses Sooke's Visitor Info Centre. Admission is by donation.

The excellent **East Sooke Regional Park** (250/478-3344, 250/474-PARK) offers 1,422 hectares laced with trails— some along the coast—attractive scenery, and great views. It's not uncommon to spot whales here; there are tide pools to explore and a Coast Salish petroglyph to visit. Washrooms and sheltered picnic areas are available, but there are no food concessions.

*Follow the Old Island Hwy. to Sooke Road; take Sooke Road (#14) toward Sooke to Gillespie Road; turn left and continue down Gillespie Road. Turn right on East Sooke Road to reach park entrances at Anderson Cove and Pike Road, or turn left to reach the park entrance at Aylard Farm; about an hour's drive from downtown Victoria.*

## SIDNEY

On your way to the islands—either the San Juans, in the U.S., via the Washington State ferry, or the Gulf Islands, via B.C. Ferries (see "Getting There: Victoria")—you will pass through the small town of Sidney. As often as not, families rush past on a mad dash to catch the ferry. But should you find yourselves here with a bit of time on your hands, Sidney has several attractions of its own to investigate and a handful of pleasant family restaurants.

Visits to Sidney's two museums can help to break a journey agreeably. The **British Columbia Aviation Museum** features World War II planes, bush planes, and exhibits of related memorabilia.

*1910 Norseman Road. 250/655-3300. Open daily, 10 a.m.- 4 p.m., April 15-Oct. 15; 11 a.m.-3 p.m., rest of year. Cost: $4/adult, $3/senior, student, free/under 13, accompanied by adult.*

**The Sidney Museum** specializes in whales, with exhibits that examine cetacean evolution and biology. Additional installations tell the stories of local First Nations, and European and Chinese settlers.

*9801 Seaport Pl. 250/656-2140. Open daily, 10 a.m.-5 p.m. (May-Labour Day); 10 a.m.-4 p.m., (March-April, Sept.- Dec.); rest of the year, hours vary. Admission by donation.*

### PLACES TO EAT

**PIER ONE RESTAURANT**
*2500 Beacon Ave.*
*250/656-1224*
*Hours: Lunch, dinner daily*
This welcoming family restaurant specializes in Greek dishes—authentic, tasty, and moderately priced. Perhaps more to

the point, they provide the younger set with a menu featuring the usual range of options from burgers to fish and chips and, of course, grilled cheese.

## CALENDAR

**JANUARY**
Polar Bear Swim, Elk Lake.

**MAY**
Victoria Day celebrations and parade, Victoria.
Swiftsure International Yacht Race: Sailboat races across Juan de Fuca Strait, sponsored by Royal Victoria Yacht Club.

**JUNE**
Buccaneer Days: Community festival with parade, midway, and kids' games, Esquimalt.

**JUNE/JULY**
Folkfest, Inner Harbour.
Jazzfest International, downtown Victoria.

**JULY**
A Bite of Victoria, 250/368-6368.
Royal Victoria Flower and Garden Festival, Royal Roads University.

**JULY/AUGUST**
Sooke Fine Arts: Largest juried art show on Vancouver Island, Sooke.
Victoria Shakespeare Festival, 250/360-0234.

**AUGUST**
First Peoples Festival: Showcase for First Nations art, history, culture, and more at the Royal B.C. Museum and nearby sites, 250/384-3211.
Symphony Splash: Victoria Symphony gives a concert on a barge in the Inner Harbour, 250/385-6515.

**OCTOBER**
Salmon Run, Goldstream Provincial Park, 250/391-2300 (See "Excursions").

**DECEMBER**
Eagle Extravaganza: Hundreds of bald eagles come to feast on spawning salmon, Goldstream Provincial Park.

## RESOURCES

**ISLAND PARENT MAGAZINE**
941 Kings Road, Victoria V8T 1W7
250/388-6905; iparentmag@coastnet.com

**TOURISM VICTORIA**
812 Wharf St. (on the Inner Harbour), Victoria V8W 1T3
250/953-2033; www.tourismvictoria.com

**BC PARKS INFORMATION**
www.env.gov.bc.ca/bcparks

**BOOKS**
*Growing Pains*, by Emily Carr. Clarke Irwin, 1966.
*The Book of Small*, by Emily Carr. Clarke Irwin, 1972.
Both books are filled with Carr's recollections of her child-
hood, growing up with her four sisters in Victoria.

## SALT SPRING ISLAND

Salt Spring is the largest and most populated of the beautiful Gulf Islands on Canada's southwest coast. Although it is
also one of the most developed of the islands, it has retained a
rural, relaxed feeling and is renowned for its incredible scenery
and pastoral setting. Its inland lakes, rocky coast, quaint little
towns, and temperate climate make Salt Spring an idyllic
place for a family vacation.

### GETTING THERE

**BY AIR.** Daily service is offered by two airlines that fly
between the Gulf Islands, Vancouver Harbour, and Vancouver.
**Pacific Spirit Air** (250/537-9359; 800/665-2FLY), based on
Gabriola Island, and **Harbour Air** (800/665-0212; www.har-
bour-air.com/), in Vancouver, both offer floatplane service.

**BY FERRY.** B.C. Ferries (250/386-3431; 888/BC-FERRY)
operates daily runs between Vancouver Island, the B.C. mainland, and Salt Spring Island's three terminals. Service is offered
between Swartz Bay (32 km north of Victoria) and Fulford
Harbour; between Crofton (near Duncan, on Vancouver Island)
and Vesuvius Bay; and between Tsawwassen (about 20 km south
of Vancouver) and Long Harbour. The Tsawwassen-Long
Harbour route includes stops at other Gulf Islands. Reservations
are recommended on the Tsawwassen route, and must be prepaid.
There are multiple sailings daily, year round, on all routes.
Fare structures are complex and vary considerably between
high and low season. On average, a round trip between

Vancouver Island and Salt Spring Island, with a normal-size car, two adults and two children, will run under $40 at peak season. A round trip between the mainland and Salt Spring Island for the same configuration will cost about $120. Children under five years travel for free.

Note: B.C. Ferries has been known to cease operation during occasional labor disputes. Further, the Strait of Georgia is notorious for occasional severe storms, so sailings are sometimes delayed or canceled. While it doesn't happen often, it can put a dent in your holiday if it does. Be sure to verify in advance that ferries are actually running.

**Washington State Ferries** currently offers year-round daily service between Anacortes and Swartz Bay, north of Victoria, though there has been talk of ending this service. Currently, there are two sailings each way in summer and one in winter. Schedules vary. See "Victoria: Getting There" and "San Juan Islands" in "Washington" for details.

One of our parent reviewers described a journey to Salt Spring Island this way:

"From Seattle, we took Interstate 5 north and exited to Anacortes (Exit 230). We took Highway 20 west and followed signs to the ferry terminal. The ferry goes to Sidney, B.C., from which we drove to Swartz Bay (about four miles) to take the ferry to Salt Spring Island. The route to the BC Ferries/Gulf Islands ferry terminal is well marked.

"We left at 5:15 a.m. from our Queen Anne home to catch the 8 a.m. ferry from Anacortes (it is about a 90-minute drive to the ferry dock, but the boat fills up during the summer months). We arrived in Sidney, B.C., about 11 a.m. After going through customs at Sidney, we got to the Swartz Bay terminal at 11:35 a.m. and made the 11:45 a.m. ferry. We arrived at our destination about 1 p.m.—tired but happy!"

## PLACES TO STAY

### BEACHCOMBER MOTEL
*770 Vesuvius Bay Road, Vesuvius V8K 1L6*
*250/537-5415*
*Rates: Inexpensive*
*FYI: Beach access*

This could almost be the beach motel you remember from your childhood—the one with the indoor/outdoor carpeting and the plastic furniture you could sit on in a wet bathing suit without anyone yelling at you. Well, the Beachcomber is all that, but it's a bit more. The proprietors have made a real effort to improve on the décor of the motel you remember; this one has floral curtains and bedspreads, and clean, wallpapered walls. The bedroom and living room are all one room, and the bathroom is a one-at-a-time affair.

The rooms vary in size and set up, but all have kitchenettes and small eating spaces. There's a shared patio on the second floor, great for reading the paper or playing a rousing game of cards. The beach is across the (fairly quiet) street, with easy access for the younger members of your clan. The best news is, you can afford to stay here and still pay your way off the island at the end of the week.

**❝ PARENT COMMENTS**

*"We came in late and had to wake the proprietor. He couldn't have been more gracious."*

*"OK, so our shower didn't drain well, and we ended up with a small swimming pool on the floor. Somehow, it seemed like part of the ambiance."*

### CUSHION LAKE RESORT
*171 Natalie Lane, V8K 2C6*
*250/537-9629*
*Rates: Inexpensive to moderate (daily or weekly)*
*FYI: Kitchen; fireplace; swimming, fishing, boating; no TVs or telephones*

The one- and two-bedroom cabins offer kitchens, fireplaces, and private decks and sleep six to eight people. They're far more appealing than the A-frame accommodations, which tend to be dark. There are no telephones or televisions, but the proprietor does rent VCRs for playing videos.

Families can find plenty to do here, and most of it centers around Cushion Lake (where, by the way, powerboats are not allowed). The lake boasts a sandy beach, canoes, and floating docks, and the water is plenty warm for swimming. If all that activity gives you sore muscles, soak in the outdoor hot tub while listening to the lapping lake and gazing at the stars.

**❝ PARENT COMMENTS**

*"This tends to be a romantic getaway in the off-season, but all summer long it belongs to families. The cabins are comfortably close together, and it's easy for kids to make new friends."*

*"We could enjoy coffee or cocktails on the deck, and still keep an eye on the youngsters by the lake."*

## GREEN ACRES RESORT
*241 Lang Road, VOS 1EO*
*250/537-2585*
*Rates: Inexpensive to moderate*
*FYI: Full kitchens; woodstoves; playground*

Green Acres is a family-oriented resort located on about three hectares of south-facing waterfront on the lovely shores of St. Mary Lake. One- and two-bedroom units are available, each with a modern kitchen. Furnishings are comfortable and very clean, but not too fancy. Each cottage has a private deck facing the lake. Most cottages also have new woodstoves that keep them cozy and warm, even in the off-season.

Parents will appreciate the new outdoor play area, the safe and sandy beach, and the dock with canoes and rowboats. In the summer, the lake is warm enough for swimming. During July and August, Green Acres is always booked solid with families.

### 66 PARENT COMMENTS

*"Despite some rain, the weekends we've spent at Green Acres have been memorable. The kids are warmly welcomed."*

*"Though it takes a while to get to Salt Spring, it's a lovely place and well worth the trip. Make reservations with B.C. Ferries, so you don't have to worry about getting on."*

*"Make reservations early if you're going in July or August; it gets booked up fast."*

## MAPLE RIDGE COTTAGES
*301 Tripp Road, V8K 1K6*
*250/537-5977*
*Rates: Moderate*
*FYI: Kitchenettes; swimming, fishing, boating*

This may be the smallest resort on Salt Spring Island, with four cozy little cottages on a ridge above St. Mary Lake. It's located way off the main drag on a dead-end road, so this is the spot to head for if you like privacy and quiet contemplation. That said, don't feel you have to leave the little ones at home; kids are welcome, and there are plenty of woods nearby in which they can run and shout.

The cottages are set on a small ridge, and each has a view of the lake (30 meters away). Built of cedar and decorated with local artwork, the cottages each offer a sundeck, queen bed, and sleeper sofa (the two-bedroom cottage has a double bed as well), and kitchenette.

On the lake are two docks; often, you will have one all to yourselves. You can opt for the great swimming and fishing or take a spin in a canoe, rowboat, sailboard, or sailboat.

**❝❝ Parent Comments**

*"The lake has a gradual walk-in, so little ones can wade and splash."*

*"Our little guy had his first fishing expedition on the lake. He and dad came back with a good-sized bass."*

**Salt Spring Lodge B&B**
*641 Fulford-Ganges Road, P.O. Box 208, Ganges V8K 2V9*
*250/537-9522; www.saltspring.com/saltspringlodge/*
*Rates: Moderate*
*FYI: Full kitchen; no telephone*

Turning into the drive at Salt Spring Lodge B&B, visitors are struck first by the gorgeous setting. Surrounded by bucolic fields where flocks of sheep graze, this spot looks out over Ganges Harbour and the other Gulf Islands, and across to Mount Baker to the south, and Mount Garibaldi and the Coast Mountains to the north. This is a thoroughly peaceful, take-a-deep-breath-and-relax kind of place.

Decked out with Shaker furniture and Persian rugs laid over gleaming hardwood floors, each of the three suites has an attractive, modern kitchen and a private entrance. The two-story suite has a queen-size futon in the living area and two bedrooms upstairs, each with high ceilings and its own bath. The smaller suite, with five skylights, is airy and light. It has one bedroom with futon, full bath, and kitchenette. The third unit is a cute studio space, but it's too tight for a family. Ganges is minutes away by car or bike.

**❝❝ Parent Comments**

*"The two-story suite has a steep staircase seemingly designed to attract adventurous toddlers. Better to choose the one-bedroom if you have really little ones."*

*"Dad took the kids to explore Ganges Village. I sat and read, and looked, and read, and looked some more."*

**Places To Eat**

**Alfresco Café and Restaurant**
*3106-115 Fulford-Ganges Road*

250/537-5979
*Hours: Lunch, dinner daily*

This is a lovely spot, located near the harbor and convenient to prime shopping and browsing areas. The spacious café is downstairs, the more intimate restaurant is above, and the food at both is fantastic. Lunch features robust soups and homemade bread, plus inventive sandwiches and salads. Dinner is served in an atmosphere that might best be described as "informally elegant." Still, the entire family will feel welcome here. A wide range of entrées is served, focusing on delightful pasta and seafood dishes. For kids, the menu includes burgers (beef or chicken), pasta, grilled cheese, and nachos. On Saturday nights, you can enjoy live piano music; the piano player has quite a repertoire, and at some point in the evening takes requests.

### THE BOARDWALK CAFÉ
*104 Fulford-Ganges Road*
*250/537-5747*
*Hours: Breakfast, lunch daily*

This is where the locals go for breakfast; they call the spot "Maxine's," after the proprietress. Located at the edge of the shopping area, overlooking the harbor, this small café has only three or four tables, and they're usually occupied. Don't be discouraged; the food here is more than worth the wait.

Maxine serves every manner of hearty breakfast, from fluffy omelets stuffed with tasty fillings to thick slabs of French toast. As long as you can fit your crew around one of the small tables, everyone is likely to find something appealing to eat. Special orders and substitutions are cheerfully accommodated.

### BOUZOUKI GREEK CAFÉ
*2105-115 Fulford-Ganges Road*
*250/537-4181*
*Hours: Lunch, dinner daily*

The proprietors came to Salt Spring Island from the Greek Islands, and their food is authentic and tasty. Even the décor is reminiscent of a Greek café. If you arrive hungry, have them rush you an order of their delicious hummous and pita bread. Follow up with a bowl of spicy soup, or choose from among a number of Greek favorites, such as souvlaki, moussaka, and spanakopita. Other Greek specialties include roast leg of lamb and chicken in filo pastry. For dessert, try the homemade baklava. Although there's no child's menu, the servers are happy to deliver any entrée in child-size portions. In nice weather, eat outside on the waterfront patio, and take in the action while you nosh.

## WHAT TO SEE & DO

### STROLL & BROWSE

**GANGES VILLAGE.** Most Salt Spring Island residents live in or near Ganges, a pretty town that reflects both the lively artist community and the agricultural roots of the island. Ganges seems to have been designed with strolling and browsing in mind—it's small, quaint, and charming, and the people are friendly and welcoming. In the center of town is tiny, grassy Centennial Park, with a playground and a view of the harbor. Across the street is the fire station; stop and admire the antique engine on display in the window.

Morning coffee and a newspaper await you at the **Moka House** (110 Lower Ganges Road; 250/537-1216) or across the side street at **Salt Spring Roasting Company** (109 McPhillips Ave.; 250/537-0825; 800/332-8858). Cross Lower Ganges Road and stop at the **Chamber of Commerce** (121 Lower Ganges Road; 250/537-5252); the volunteers here are proud of their home and anxious to help you find your way around.

Visit the shops and galleries along Lower Ganges Road, or walk toward the harbor to Grace Point Square. Here you'll find **Muskoka North** (1102 Grace Point Square; 250/537-8999), with its handsome collection of seasonal "island wear" and proprietors who are happy to chat and tell you more about the island. If the kids are along, you won't escape a stop at **Harlan's Chocolates** (100 Lower Ganges Road; 250/537-4434); give in gracefully and let each choose a hand-dipped truffle or some other homemade treat.

Here's something rare: a spot where dads will love to browse! **Mouat's Hardware** (106 Fulford-Ganges Road; 250/537-5551) carries every gadget and gizmo a tinkerer's heart might desire.

**MARKET IN THE PARK.** On Saturdays between April and October, Centennial Park fills up with artists, bakers, and farmers—the market where, say locals, "we have made it, baked it, grown it." Here is where you can see the best aspects of island living: the tight-knit community with all its talents and friendliness. Vendors here sell everything, including handmade knits, fresh island-berry preserves, and graceful, brightly glazed pottery.

*250/537-4448. Intersection of Fulford-Ganges Road & Lower Ganges Road, Ganges. Open April-Oct., Sat., 8 a.m.-4 p.m.*

## EXCURSIONS

**ART STUDIO TOURS.** The island's spectacular scenery and peaceful environment seem to nurture artistic pursuits, and a number of talented artists operate studios here. Thirty-one area artists have banded together to offer studio tours, wherein each opens his or her studio to visitors. Arts and crafts include pottery, clothing, soaps and scents, wind chimes, homemade foods, and much more. As you drive about the island, you will see the "cow signs," indicating studio locations. All studios have individual schedules; pick up a self-guided tour brochure (available at visitor-information outlets and area businesses) or phone 250/537-5538 for more information.

**MOUNT MAXWELL PROVINCIAL PARK.** Open year round, this park offers spectacular views of the southern Gulf Islands and Vancouver Island from atop Baynes Peak. The park is accessible only by a gravel road, which is steep in places. The reward at the end of this trip is an amazing view. There are steep drop-offs here; keep young children firmly in hand and dogs on leashes. The day-use area is equipped with benches and picnic tables.

*On the west central part of the island, off Mount Maxwell Road.*

## THE GREAT OUTDOORS

Families will find recreational opportunities of every description on Salt Spring Island. An excellent guide, *Salt Spring Out of Doors,* is available at the Chamber of Commerce (121 Lower Ganges Road; 250/537-5252) for a nominal fee. The guide tells visitors where to go for everything from boat launching and diving to berry picking and sun worshipping (and an amazing number of things in between).

**HIKING.** There are countless places to hike on the island, many with awesome views of the southern Gulf Islands, Vancouver Island, and points beyond. Be sure to take along binoculars and a camera. Many of the hikes ascend island peaks and are too steep for young hikers; be sure you know the terrain before embarking on an island hike.

At **Mouat Provincial Park** (off Seaview Ave., adjacent to Ganges Village), you'll find a network of relatively flat trails that follow babbling Ganges Creek through old-growth forest. **Ruckle Provincial Park** (on Beaver Point Road, east of Fulford Harbour) also has a number of trails designed for the whole family. This is a particularly beautiful place to visit in spring, when pastures of wildflowers are in bloom. There's a viewpoint here from which kids will enjoy watching for orcas. A map near the camping area shows the various routes.

**HORSEBACK RIDING.** Another great way to enjoy the island scenery is from the back of a horse. **Salt Spring Guided Rides** (9156 Mount Maxwell Road; 250/537-5761) operates on farmlands and in the forests of Mount Maxwell, where riders have access to 325 hectares of land. Caroline Hickman has been offering guided tours for more than 15 years, for groups of two to eight people.

## CALENDAR

### JUNE-AUGUST
ArtCraft: Show and sale of artworks by more than 200 Gulf Island artists, in Ganges.

### JULY
Salt Spring Festival of the Arts

## RESOURCES

### SALTSPRING ISLAND TRAVEL INFO CENTRE
121 Lower Ganges Road, P.O. Box 111, Ganges V0S 1E0
250/537-5252

### B.C. FERRIES
250/537-9921; 888/223-3779

# VANCOUVER ISLAND AND THE DISCOVERY ISLANDS

The term "well-kept secret" is overused for tourist destinations, but it's the best way to describe most of Vancouver Island. The farther north you go, the less traffic and competition for waterfront hotel accommodation you find, and prices come down significantly. The catch is that it takes awhile to get here (a full day from Seattle and half a day from Vancouver). But the trip itself—ferry rides through lovely islands and drives through attractive island scenery—compensates. Plus there are enough interesting attractions on the way to these destinations to entertain even the most restless little ones.

West of Nanaimo and Parksville, past Port Alberni, lies Pacific

Rim National Park, with its network of trails through rain forest and marshland, and miles of white-sand beaches. South of the park is Ucluelet, a thriving fishing and resort town; to the north is Tofino, the starting point for exploring Vancouver Island's wild west coast, with its huge stands of old-growth forest, hot springs, and gray whales. Every spring, these cetacean behemoths migrate up the coast to Alaska. In summer, orcas and humpback whales can be viewed, along with the grays and other wildlife. Accommodation options of all kinds are plentiful.

Off the east coast of Vancouver Island, minutes away by ferry, interesting islands feature some of the best tide pools and water-based family fun in the region. Orcas cruise the waters of Johnstone Strait in great numbers. Farther north are Malcolm and Cormorant Islands, each with a unique cultural heritage and place in Canadian history. If you go all the way to Port Hardy, you can catch a B.C. Ferry up to Prince Rupert and northern British Columbia.

## GETTING THERE

First-time visitors to Vancouver Island need to make a strategic decision: to visit or bypass Victoria on the way. From Victoria, it's a short, if traffic-laden, drive up Highway 1.

But unless you have your heart set on a stay in the provincial capital, you might want to avoid the Victoria–Nanaimo traffic and simply hop a **B.C. Ferries** ferryboat (800/BC-FERRY; www.bcferries.bc.ca/) directly to Nanaimo, which will save you a two-hour drive. Ferry service is offered between Tsawwassen (a half-hour drive north of the U.S.-Canada border via Interstate 5 and, in Canada, Highway 99) and Duke's Point Ferry Terminal, south of Nanaimo. B.C. Ferries also operates between Horseshoe Bay, in West Vancouver, and Departure Bay, in downtown Nanaimo. On all sailings, reservations are taken (604/444-2890, outside B.C.; 888/724-5223, in B.C.). If you're traveling during the high season, during holidays, or just on the weekend, reservations can save you a long, tedious wait with cranky kids at the terminal.

Both routes offer frequent daily sailings: four daily round trips in winter, with additional sailings in summer. The crossing takes about an hour and a half between Horseshoe and Departure bays; between Tsawwassen and Duke's Point, it's two hours. Fares on both routes are the same. During peak season (July to mid-Sept.), two adults and two kids in a car can expect to pay about $120 for a round trip; the figure is slightly lower during the shoulder season (spring and fall), and lower still during the low season (Nov.

to mid-Dec., Jan.-March). Children under five ride free. Recreational and sports-utility vehicles are charged extra on a per-foot basis. B.C. Ferries offers a variety of discounts and promotions, along with special fares. (Also see "Victoria and Salt Spring Island" and "Sunshine Coast" for more ferry information).

Once on Vancouver Island, orient yourself via its north-south axis. The island's main artery runs north from Victoria to Port Hardy and through just about every major community on Vancouver Island's populous east side. From Victoria to Nanaimo, this artery is designated as Highway 1, the final (or first, depending on your orientation) leg of the Trans-Canada Highway; from Nanaimo to Port Hardy, it's Highway 19, the Island Highway. The road is only two lanes most of the way and gets very congested during summer months. Bypasses have been built around the bigger communities, and more are under construction. If you're in a hurry, these bypasses are your best option; but for good scenery and interesting towns, stay on the old road.

**THE E&N TRAIN.** This VIA Rail train connects Victoria and Courtenay, stopping at Cowichan, Duncan, Chemainus, Ladysmith, Nanaimo, Parksville, and Qualicum Beach, as well as a host of smaller communities. One way, the trip takes about four hours. One train runs each way daily (schedule changes on Sundays). There's no baggage checking. Trains stop on request to pick up and let off passengers.

*VIA Rail, 250/383-4324; 800/561-8630 (in B.C.); 800/561-9181 (in U.S.). Cost: Victoria to Courtenay, $35/adult, $32/senior, $21/student.*

## CENTRAL VANCOUVER ISLAND

**ROADSIDE ATTRACTIONS.** If you're driving up the island from Victoria, you'll see many advertisements for attractions seeking to lure you off your chosen path. Some are of family interest; others, while interesting to adults, may not engage kids much or at all.

**THE COWICHAN NATIVE VILLAGE** is located in Duncan, a one-hour drive north of Victoria, and offers multimedia shows, feasts, arts and crafts, and a site tour highlighting Coast Salish First Nations culture. While the shows can be fascinating and a good bet for older kids, they average about $2^1/_2$ hours in length, and the menu may not appeal to young children (octopus, clam fritters, wild venison loaf). Prices are steep, too.

*200 Cowichan Way. 250/746-8119;*

*www.cowichannativevillage.com. Cost: $27.50/adult, $17.50/child 5-12, free/under 5. Call for hours.*

**B.C. FOREST MUSEUM.** Just north of Duncan, off Highway 1, this museum traces the history of logging in British Columbia. Families can watch displays of traditional skills and crafts, explore a demonstration forest, and—the pièce de résistance—take a ride on a steam train.

*R.R. 4, 2892 Drinkwater Road. 250/715-1113; www.bcforestmuseum.com. Museum open daily, year round. Steam train runs May-Sept., only. Cost: $8/adult, $7/senior & student 13-18, $4.50/child 5-12.*

## NANAIMO

Vancouver Island's second-largest city has always had a gorgeous setting—and plenty of visitors, thanks to the Departure Bay ferry terminal serving Vancouver and the Gulf Islands. In recent years, Nanaimo's come into its own with a major facelift of its historic waterfront. Check out the **Bastion,** an octagonal tower dating back to 1853, and the adjacent **Nanaimo Museum** (100 Cameron Road; 250/753-1821; open Wed.-Mon., July-Aug.). Stroll along the four-km Harbourside Walkway. If you have time, **Petroglyph Provincial Park,** two km south of town on Hwy. 19, is worth a visit. It features awesome First Nations rock carvings dating back thousands of years.

### PLACES TO STAY

**DAYS INN HARBOURVIEW**
*809 Island Hwy. S., Nanaimo V9R 5K1*
*250/754-8171, 800/329-7466*
*Rates: Inexpensive*
*FYI: Restaurant, kitchens; indoor pool (7 a.m.-10 p.m.); laundry; pets OK*

Situated south of Departure Bay and downtown Nanaimo, this aging motel could use updating, but it has everything families need at a reasonable price. The family-oriented restaurant offers a kids' menu.

**❝ PARENT COMMENTS**
*"The staff in the lobby were helpful and knowledgeable about the area."*

### PLACES TO EAT

#### LIGHTHOUSE BISTRO
*50 Anchor Way*
*250/754-3212*
*Hours: Lunch, dinner daily*

It's right on the Sea Wall, so diners have a nice view of the waterfront and the walkway lined with shops. You can dine on seafood while your kids order off the children's menu, and all of you enjoy people- and dog-watching. Prices are reasonable.

### CALENDAR

#### JULY
International Bathtub Race: Famous race from Nanaimo Harbor to Departure Bay Beach.

#### AUGUST
Vancouver Island Exhibition: Agricultural fair.

### RESOURCES

#### TOURISM NANAIMO, VISITOR INFO CENTRE
Beban House, 2290 Bowen Road, Nanaimo V9T 3K7
250/756-0106; 800/663-7337; www.tourism.nanaimo.bc.ca

## PARKSVILLE

This resort town about 35 km north of Nanaimo has a lot to offer visitors. First and foremost are its beaches—some of the smoothest sands and warmest waters in the province. Rathtrevor Beach is especially popular, and families return year after year to enjoy its amenities. It is currently overrun with bunny rabbits, but that only makes it more appealing to young visitors. The atmosphere is relaxed just about everywhere in town, with plenty of affordable waterfront resorts, not too close to Highway 19 or each other, in spacious, tree-covered, and self-contained grounds.

### PLACES TO STAY

#### HOLIDAY INN EXPRESS
*424 W. Island Hwy, Parksville V9P 1K8*
*250/248-2232; holidayin-pv@bctravel.com*
*Rates: Moderate*
*FYI: Complimentary continental breakfast; indoor pool; pets OK*

This chain, while not as low-priced as its reputation might suggest, offers predictably comfortable family accommodations.

**❝ PARENT COMMENTS**

*"Pleasant, typical Holiday Inn rooms; near several restaurants and a miniature golf course."*

### RATHTREVOR RESORT

*1035 E. Island Hwy., Parksville V9P 2E3*
*800/661-5494; rathtrevor@bctravel.com*
*Rates: Moderate*
*FYI: Kitchens (all units); fireplaces (all units); two outdoor pools, water slide; playground; video-game room; children's program; beach access; no phones (pay phones on premises); no smoking*

For families who have been on the road a while, Rathtrevor Resort is Shangri-la. The self-contained condo units have just about every amenity parents dream of at this stage of the vacation: well-stocked kitchens (two- and three-bedroom units come with dishwashers), patios, fireplaces, washers/dryers, and plenty of room for all. The office rents VCRs, movies, barbecues, playpens, highchairs, and cots. Options range from one- to three-bedroom units; the latter are two stories.

In warm weather, hang out on Rathtrevor Beach, a short hike down a zigzag cliff-side ramp at the resort's eastern end. A faucet area at the top of the ramp is available for washing sand off after a beach visit. When it rains, kids can amuse themselves with video games in a large game room. The well-treed resort grounds are crisscrossed with bike and stroller paths. Many families stay a week or more, and three-bedroom units go quickly. Kids rule, and the atmosphere is as family-friendly as it gets. In summer, children's programs are offered.

**❝ PARENT COMMENTS**

*"The people in the office were very friendly and offered us AAA rates, which we'd forgotten to inquire about."*

*"Our kids hit it off with a childless couple we met at the pool who lent them their rubber dinghy. The kids then spent the next hour happily giving everyone dinghy rides up and down the pool. The pool area is closed to kids, but not to adults, after 10 p.m."*

### TIGH-NA-MARA RESORT

*1095 E. Island Hwy., V9P 2E5*
*250/248-2072; 800/663-7373; www.island.net/~tnm*
*Rates: Moderate to expensive; minimum stay required, July & Aug., winter weekends & holidays*
*FYI: Restaurant; kitchens (no ovens in lodge rooms); fireplaces; indoor pools, exercise facilities; tennis; playground; children's sum-*

*mer programs; pets OK (off-season and in cottages only); watercraft*

You can rent a spiffy beachfront condo here or stay in the cozier, less-expensive lodge. Even the smallest rooms are big enough for a smallish family (bachelor units with queen and sofa bed). Some of the condos have Jacuzzi bathtubs beside the bed. The two-bedroom cottages can sleep two in each bedroom and provide a sofa bed in the living room as well. We haven't sent a parent reviewer here yet, but the restaurant is exceptionally child-friendly and the presence of many small guests suggests this is a good bet for families.

## PLACES TO EAT

### CAPTAIN JIM'S SEAFOOD GALLEY
*332 W. Island Hwy.*
*250/248-4545*
*Hours: Dinner daily*

Even when measured by the yardstick of child-friendly Parksville, this stands out as a good choice. The specialty is basic seafood dishes, and the décor, featuring nets full of sea stars and fish, should amuse the kids as they wait to be served. Service is good, and portions are large. Next door is an enormous miniature golf course. Even if you don't play, watching those who do can be quite as engaging.

### TIGH-NA-MARA RESORT
*1095 E. Island Hwy.*
*250/248-2333*
*Hours: Breakfast, lunch, dinner daily; Sunday brunch*

The one drawback of Rathtrevor Resort is its lack of a restaurant. However, at the Tigh-Na-Mara Resort next door, there's a great one. Don't let the 'fine dining' atmosphere fool you. It's exceedingly child-friendly, with a kids' menu that includes children's cocktails (not the cheapest items) and a wider than usual selection of the expected pasta and chicken dishes.

## WHAT TO SEE & DO

**RATHTREVOR BEACH PROVINCIAL PARK,** south of Parksville on Rathtrevor Beach, is a large park with an abundance of campsites, picnicking options, nature trails, a playground, free hot showers, and plenty of beach. Pets are OK on leash. It is very popular as a family destination in summer, so if you're hoping to camp, make reservations early.

*Three km south of Parksville on Hwy. 19. 250-/954-4600*

## THE WEST COAST

The 1990s have seen a huge increase in tourism to Vancouver Island's beautiful west coast. From whale watching in spring and summer to the rapidly growing armchair sport of storm watching in winter, the region offers something for all ages to enjoy. For outdoor enthusiasts, the hiking, boating, and kayaking opportunities are just about unlimited.

To reach Tofino, Ucluelet, and Pacific Rim National Park on the Long Beach peninsula, motorists must cross the island on Highway 4, a 3 1/2-hour, very scenic drive with high peaks, lakes, and rushing rivers.

NOTE: For children prone to car sickness, the beautiful but twisty and hilly two-hour drive between Port Alberni and Tofino, as well as much of the 42-kilometer drive between Tofino and Ucluelet, can be uncomfortable. You may want to administer motion sickness remedies before you leave Port Alberni.

**ROADSIDE ATTRACTIONS.** About eight km west of Parksville in Coombs is **Butterfly World,** a popular and well-publicized attraction, featuring the expected hordes of small winged critters fluttering among tropical flowers. There's also a Japanese water garden, with waterfall and koi, and some turtles (on Hwy. 4A; 250/248-7026; open Oct.-Apr., daily, 10 a.m.-4 p.m.; $6/adult, $5/senior & student with ID, $4.50/child 3-12, free/under 3).

Another roadside attraction is **McMillan Provincial Park,** formerly known as Cathedral Grove. This stand of impressive old-growth evergreens straddles Highway 4, serving in part as public relations for the logging industry. Cars park on both sides of the highway; there's lots of fast-moving traffic and crossing can be hazardous. The huge crowds here give it the feel of a theme park. A devastating storm in January 1997 toppled many of the forest giants. Rather than stop here, you may do better to check out the rain-forest nature trails in **Pacific Rim National Park,** which are more interesting and less touristy (see "Tofino: Excursions").

**REFUELING.** About a quarter of the way along Highway 4 is Port Alberni, at the eastern end of Alberni Inlet, an arm of the Pacific that nearly divides Vancouver Island in two. A sizable fishing fleet is stationed here. Just west of town is Sproat Lake, a popular vacation spot with several rustic resorts.

Port Alberni is the logical choice for a lunch break. Deeply impacted by logging and fishing industry downturns, Port

Alberni is struggling to reinvent itself. One sign of its emergence as a tourist destination is the revitalized **Alberni Harbour Quay** complex, on the waterfront at the end of Argyle Street. There's a water-splash park and a playground with a pirate ship for kids to explore, plenty of inexpensive cafés where you can pick up fish and chips or sausage rolls for lunch, craft galleries to wander through, and a clock tower to climb for a good view.

The **Alberni Valley Museum** showcases First Nations and local history (4255 Wallace St.; 250/723-2181; open Tues.-Sat., 10 a.m.-5 p.m.; until 8 p.m. Thurs.; admission by donation). A historic steam train takes passengers around the waterfront on weekends in summer months (check with the museum for details).

### CALENDAR

#### MARCH

Pacific Rim Whale Festival: This festival embraces all of the Long Beach Peninsula, and a variety of events celebrate the return of the gray whales migrating north up the coast.

#### JULY

Pacific Rim Summer Music Festival, 250/-726-7572.

### RESOURCES

#### ALBERNI VALLEY VISITOR INFO CENTRE

2533 Redford St., RR2, Site 215, Comp 10
Port Alberni, V9Y 7L6
250/724-6535

## TOFINO

This lovely town, 131 km west of Port Alberni, has become a world-class resort town thanks to its proximity to the gray whales' migration route. Visitors flock from around the world to see them. A recent building boom has provided new resorts, B&Bs, restaurants, and housing for those who live here. But because Tofino isn't particularly easy to get to, its future as a small town seems assured.

Tofino is surrounded by beaches and is fairly spread out; many hotels are several kilometers outside town, while most restaurants, shops, and tour operators are downtown. The population of around 2,000 can triple during summer months.

Some of the newer resorts, usually the most expensive, cater to honeymooners and adults without kids, as do some tour outfitters. But plenty welcome children, and the community as a whole has some especially child-friendly features, from extensive paved bike trails to good-sized parks and playgrounds and sandy, protected beaches.

Whether you have a telescope or just high-powered binoculars, don't forget to bring them with you for some awesome stargazing. Tofino is so remote from any major urban center that, if the weather is good, you will see stars you may not have glimpsed since childhood. See "Resources" for suggestions on good family stargazing books.

At any time of year, it can get foggy in Tofino, and the sound of foghorns is common at night; often loud, they can be scary for kids. Explaining them to children in advance can help prevent midnight anxiety attacks.

## GETTING THERE

Take Highway 4 west from Highway 19 to Pacific Rim Highway and turn right. Tofino is about 25 km north.

## PLACES TO STAY

### BEST WESTERN TIN WIS RESORT LODGE
*1119 Pacific Rim Hwy., P.O. Box 389, V0R 2Z0*
*250/725-4445, 800/661-9995; www.tinwis.com*
*Rates: Moderate to expensive*
*FYI: Restaurant; beach access*

This comfortable hotel makes a good home base for exploring the area. Some rooms have ocean views. The dining room will prepare tasty box lunches for guests on request to carry on hikes or whale-watching tours, which don't usually provide food. Note: major construction is underway, due to be completed in the spring of 1999.

### 66 PARENT COMMENTS
*"The beach here is great and very close. This was of paramount importance to us because we have three kids under age four (triplets!)"*

### CRAB DOCK GUEST HOUSE
*310 Olsen Road, P.O. Box 121, V0R 2Z0*
*250/725-2911; www.crabdock.com*
*Rates: Inexpensive to moderate*

*FYI: Full complimentary breakfast; guest lounge, patio and deck; pets OK*

This B&B is spacious and offers a nice view. The owners are friendly and knowledgeable. There are three rooms, each with ensuite bath.

Along with the B&B, owners Ray and Camilla Thoroughgood rent a variety of cottages and houses, large and small, by the week. These can be a better bargain than the somewhat pricey local hotels, especially for large families. Call for details.

**❝ PARENT COMMENTS**

*"The big house we rented from Ray & Camilla was a 10-minute walk from MacKenzie Beach on a secluded lot. There was no lawn, but it had a fish pond and shrubs with ripe wild huckleberries that we picked and added to pancakes. We were far enough from neighbors that we didn't worry about the kids making noise. There was a barbecue and crab pot which we didn't use."*

**HIMWITSA LODGE**

*300 Main St., P.O. Box 176, V0R 2Z0*
*250/725-3319*
*Rates: Moderate to expensive*
*FYI: Restaurant, kitchens; VCRs; hot tubs; smoke-free throughout*

With the best location in Tofino, this small First Nations-run hotel is beautiful, with large rooms and balconies overlooking Clayoquot Sound. Downstairs is a gallery selling the work of local First Nations artists and craftspeople. This would not be a top choice for families with very small children, but a good option for those with older kids. This is the only hotel listed for downtown Tofino.

**OCEAN VILLAGE BEACH RESORT**

*555 Hellesen Dr., P.O. Box 490, V0R 2Z0*
*250/725-3755*
*Rates: Inexpensive to moderate*
*FYI: Kitchens, barbecues; indoor pool (9 a.m.-10 p.m.); laundry; nine-hole golf course; boat-launching facilities and beach access; no TVs, telephones, or radios*

From the outside, these rows of wooden cottages with arched roofs resemble vintage World War II housing, but don't let that worry you. The cottages (some are self-contained and some are duplexes) are well equipped with queen, sofa bed, and/or single beds, and a full kitchen in each unit. The cottages are lined up facing MacKenzie Beach, one of the best in an area of great beaches. And the indoor pool, open year round, guarantees that, whatever the weather, your young amphibians can be waterborne. The large number of families here virtually ensures that your kids will have playmates.

## PLACES TO EAT

Tofino attracts health-conscious, but impecunious young whale watchers from around the globe, some of whom have stayed to open restaurants and other businesses. So lucky Tofino diners can choose from a wide selection of bakeries, delis, and cafés serving delicious, affordable, healthy, often vegetarian meals. When it comes to full-service restaurants, prices go up and, in summer, waits for seating can be very long. Reservations are a good idea. If you're renting accommodation with a kitchen, head for the **Co-op** (1st & Campbell; 250/725-3226) for groceries. B.C. has many of these thriving cooperative stores, selling food and produce and some dry goods. They are especially common on Vancouver Island and are often the only supermarkets available. Products sold under the Co-op label also tend to be cheaper.

### BREAKERS DELI
*131 First St.*
*250/725-2558*
*Hours: 10 a.m.-6 p.m daily*
This small deli specializes in excellent, inexpensive fresh sandwiches, subs, wraps, and bagels for take-out. But kids will probably gravitate to the hot-dog menu (five varieties are offered including cheese dog, pizza dog, and veggie dog). For dessert they may go for one of the 32 flavors of ice cream, including Tiger (a blend of orange and licorice) and Worms n' Dirt (chocolate with fruit gummies). The butter tarts are especially terrific here. Wash it all down with a freshly squeezed glass of juice or a fruit smoothie.

### COFFEE POD
*461 Campbell St.*
*250/725-4246*
*Hours: 7 a.m.-5 p.m. daily*
This busy bakery is always crowded; it's not uncommon to stand in line for 15 minutes. They make good sandwiches and sell a variety of pastries by the slice (parent reviewers were not permitted to purchase a whole pie, however). Soup-and-sand-

wich lunch specials are a good value. There's plenty of outdoor seating on spacious decks, but bees can be a problem.

### COMMON LOAF BAKERY
*180 First St.*
*250/725-3915*
*Hours: 8 a.m.-6 p.m. daily (open for dinner in summer)*

Another trendy joint, the Common Loaf is in a distinctive two-story building with seating indoors and on a deck. Their vegetarian sausage rolls are very good, passing muster even with dedicated meat-eaters. Scones are tasty, too. At night, adventurous young diners might be willing to try some of the reasonably priced vegetarian or Asian-accented dishes. Eat here or take out.

### SAND DOLLAR
*120 First St. (in Maquinna Lodge)*
*250/725-3261*
*Hours: Breakfast, lunch, dinner daily; closed Jan.*

When it comes to full-service restaurants in Tofino, prices go up substantially. But the Sand Dollar, in the somewhat down-at-heels Maquinna Lodge, is one of the least expensive. The kids' menu offers meals with fish or chicken and chips in the $5-6 range. Pizza and pasta dishes predominate; the French onion soup and Caesar salad are hearty enough to serve as a full meal. A notch higher in price are the seafood dishes. While not fancy, the Sand Dollar does offer a world-class view of the harbor.

### SCHOONER
*331 Campbell St.*
*250/725-3444*
*Hours: Breakfast, lunch, dinner daily (closed Jan.-Feb.)*

There comes a time when take-out deli meals just don't cut it. When you need a fine-dining fix, head for the Schooner (along with the crowds—reservations are a must). Part of the Schooner Motel, it's easy to see how the restaurant got its name. It consists of two rooms divided by a ship's bow containing the kitchen. It's as if a ship sailed right into the building and got stuck there—quite the conversation piece for children. There's a kids' menu with elegant kid dishes (cheese pizza; noodles with butter and parmesan cheese or tomato sauce). Adult entrées are sophisticated and delicious, of the Pacific Rim-cuisine variety. Seafood is the logical specialty, and options range from shellfish in a Thai red curry sauce to salmon with blackberry sauce. Fresh ingredients and intelligent preparation: you can't go wrong with any of it. And prices somehow manage to be lower than the Victoria equivalent would be. The restaurant is smoke-free throughout.

### SURFSIDE PIZZA
*250/725-2882 (delivery only)*
*Hours: 4 p.m.-midnight daily*
Not a restaurant, Surfside is a delivery-only operation. In addition to a wide variety of pizzas, they provide box lunches and a host of salads, soups, sandwiches, kosher hot dogs, and more. A good selection of vegetarian dishes is available. There's a $2.50 charge on minimum orders.

### TOFINO BAKERY
*445 Campbell St.*
*250/725-3434*
Less appealing from the outside than the more trendy Coffee Pod, the Tofino Bakery may be a better choice for feeding hungry kids. The pizza bread and sausage rolls are excellent. This is a good place to head for breads and desserts if you're renting a house in the area. Pies cost about $4.25 each and a loaf of fresh bread is under $2. It's take-out only, but you can walk to the park and eat on the grass.

## WHAT TO SEE & DO

### STROLL & BROWSE

Take some time to walk around Tofino and get your bearings. Pacific Rim Highway turns into Campbell Street as it comes into town. Parallel to Campbell is Main Street. These short streets and the side streets nearby are lined with interesting shops and galleries, well worth checking out.

A variety of galleries showcase the work of renowned native Canadian artists. The most impressive gallery, **Eagle Aerie** (350 Campbell St.; 250/725-3235; open daily 9 a.m.-5 p.m. in winter; extended hours in summer), is dedicated to the works of internationally known Tsimshian artist Roy Vickers. Inside, it's laid out like a traditional big house (similar to a longhouse). Around the edges are hung Vickers' amazing landscapes, prints, and paintings in rich sunset colors or rain-soaked grays and greens. There are pictures of moons with faces, ghostly totem poles, and native images that shimmer in the background of natural scenes. These and the unusual gallery layout are likely to interest even kids who are normally indifferent to art. A gift store sells reproductions, cards, and other First Nations craft items. Several other galleries in town, most notably the **House of Himwitsa** (300 Main St.; 250/725-3319), sell work of local artists, too.

If Tofino has one serious failing, it's the lack of a dedicated bookstore. But **Wildside Books** (320 Main St.; 250/725-4222), sharing cramped quarters with an espresso bar and the Tofino Sea Kayaking Store on Main Street, tries to fill the gap, and it's amazing how much they fit in. **People's Drug Mart** (360 Campbell St.; 250/725-3101) also carries a selection of books and toys.

**BEAR WATCHING.** Tofino is not just a great place to see whales. Check out the Tofino city dump for its population of industrious bears, out for a spot of recycling. If you do go bear watching, remember to stay in your car with the windows rolled up.

**CITY PARKS.** When the kids tire of the beach (I know, I know—this is theoretical) or you'd like a more structured play environment, head for one of the parks in town. The Village Green, on Campbell Street between 2nd & 3rd, has a large, well-equipped playground, lots of grass for running across, and tennis courts. Another park (1st & Arnet) has a playground as well. Local children have little fear of strangers and are likely to approach you for a push on the swings or ask your kids to play with them.

Should the inevitable bathroom emergency arise, there are public washrooms at the District Office (Campbell & 3rd St.).

**BEACHES.** Tofino is surrounded by water on three sides. To the east are the quieter waters of Tofino Inlet. To the west is the continuation of sculpted white-sand beaches that stretch north up the entire Long Beach peninsula. Look for sand dollars, all kinds of shells, and increasingly rare glass Japanese floats.

A few blocks from downtown is **Tonquin Park** (take Arnet to Tonquin Park Road) with a lovely, though not large, sandy beach. It's reached by a rugged cliff-side trail, including a stretch of 75 steps, but it's all easily negotiated by supervised youngsters. This is a great place to watch the sun set. There are small, safe caves to explore and some nice tide pools. It's not unusual to find European and Australian budget back-packers camping here. The park is named for a 19th-century American ship that sank nearby and has never been found.

A couple of kilometers south of town are two other great family beaches: **Chesterman Beach** and **MacKenzie Beach.**

These long sandy crescents are separated from each other by a headland. Chesterman is bigger, but MacKenzie is more sheltered and a little closer to town.

*Access to Chesterman is from Lynn Road, off Pacific Rim Hwy. To reach MacKenzie Beach, take the Ocean Village Beach Resort turnoff from Pacific Rim Hwy. and park along the roadside. The beach is at the end of the road.*

## MUSEUMS

**FRIENDS OF CLAYOQUOT SOUND.** If your family harbors budding naturalists or environmentalists, you won't want to miss a visit here. This nonprofit, environmentalist organization works to conserve the last Canadian stands of temperate old-growth rain forest on Meares Island and other nearby locales. At their headquarters, visitors can learn about the group's activities and area history. Tee shirts and other items are sold here.

*Box 489, V0R 2Z0. 250/725-4218. Call for hours.*

**RAINFOREST INTERPRETIVE CENTRE.** This small, free museum with hands-on exhibits for kids is a must-see. The foyer as you enter is hung with a series of wildly original appliquéd wall panels that illustrate rain-forest ecology in creative detail. Young visitors are challenged to comb through a well-furnished dollhouse to find rain-forest products; they'll enjoy checking out the miniature postcards, board games, and musical instruments. Art and other activities are offered, and there are programs for kids in the summer.

*318 Main St. 250/725-2560. Call for hours.*

**WHALE CENTRE AND MUSEUM.** A complete gray whale skeleton nearly fills up this tiny museum housed in the ground floor of a house. Exhibits include delicate First Nations basketry and local history; Seattle visitors may be interested in *Seattle Times* articles from 1907 and 1910 on the perils of navigation through this region. Archival photos offer revealing glimpses of Tofino's evolution from quiet fishing village to bustling tourist town.

*411 Campbell St. 250/725-2132. Call for hours.*

## EXCURSIONS

**WHALE WATCHING TOURS.** Over the past decade, whale watching in British Columbia has become a major tourist attraction and big business. Currently, more than 10 tour operators bring visitors to the whales. A family of four can expect to spend $250 for a six-hour cruise, but exactly what that buys will vary from tour to tour.

While most operators welcome children, few feature onboard restrooms or offer food. Many boats afford little protection against the elements, and some are simply big rubber rafts that don't allow for movement by passengers. It can be hard on two year olds—not to mention their parents—to sit for hours without wriggling. Some operators don't allow young children on inflatables.

Tours from two to seven hours' duration are available from many providers. Longer tours offer more hope of seeing whales, but may not be a good choice for very small or restless kids.

When picking a destination, think about what you'd like to see if the whales don't cooperate. Hot Springs Cove, (see travel essay), makes a great family destination, with beautiful scenery, a fun hike, and hot springs to relax in.

There are many whale-watching tour companies from which to choose (see sidebar). Two of the best are listed here. **Jamie's Whaling Station** (606 Campbell St., Box 129 "B," V0R 2Z0. 800/667-9913; www.jamies.com) is an established operator, and the only Tofino company featuring a boat with restroom facilities. Their larger boat has a snackbar and is wheelchair accessible (they also have a glass-bottomed boat). There's a well-stocked gift shop in their store on Campbell Street.

**Sea Trek** (441B Campbell St., Box 627, V0R 2Z0; 800/811-

## *Choosing a Whale-Watching Package*

It's convenient to arrange a trip in advance through your hotel, but the Canadian Coast Guard Division of Boating Safety suggests you take on this responsibility yourself. There are a large number of tours; by booking a day in advance you'll likely have your pick.

To ensure a safe and comfortable outing, ask the following questions:

**DOES YOUR BOAT WEIGH 5 TONS OR MORE AND/OR DOES IT CARRY 12 OR MORE PASSENGERS?**
*If the answer is yes, the service is federally regulated by*

*Transport Canada. Small vessels at present are not subject to any government regulation; thus, most inflatable boats (zodiacs) are unregulated. While many operators are excellent, some may not be. The safest bet is to choose those that must meet regulatory standards.*

### WHAT TRAINING DOES YOUR CREW HAVE?

*Even if they know water safety, it helps to have tour leaders who know whales, too.*

### HOW LONG HAVE YOU BEEN IN BUSINESS?

*New operators may be as good as experienced ones, but the latter have a track record.*

### DO YOU STICK TO PROTECTED INSIDE WATERS OR VENTURE OUT IN OPEN SEAS?

### DO YOU ENCOUNTER OCEAN SWELLS AND ROUGH WATER?

### DO YOU CARRY LIFEJACKETS FOR EVERYONE, INCLUDING KIDS?

*Even big vessels aren't required to carry personal life vests, just the uncomfortable emergency variety. You may want to consider buying or borrowing life vests for your children.*

### FINALLY, CHECK OUT THE BOAT. DOES IT LOOK SEAWORTHY? DOES IT OFFER PROTECTION FROM SUN AND RAIN?

### WHAT TO BRING:

Layers of clothing (bring extras to change into), including raingear, hats, and gloves; even in August you may need them. Sunscreen, motion sickness medication. (To be effective, most medications must be taken at least half an hour before the trip begins. In Canada, Gravol is the most common over-the-counter remedy.)

Sunglasses

Snacks and drinks.

Aqua sox

Binoculars

Camera

## A Whale-Watching Trip to Hot Springs Cove

Half an hour after leaving the dock in Tofino, we spotted our first orcas. John, the skipper of our small powerboat, the *Pisces*, identified them as Panchika's gang, a local family. We marveled as they rose and dove together—whale synchronized swimming. Soon more vessels arrived—orange inflatables and power boats like ours or larger. As our four children, ages six through 11, dashed from one side of the boat to the other so as not to miss a single fluke or dorsal fin, we parents breathed a collective sigh of relief. Whatever happened for the rest of the trip, we had Seen Whales.

We had decided on Sea Trek, a medium-sized tour operator, choosing from their menu of tours a trip that would take us on the 6 1/2-hour return journey to Hot Springs Cove. If we failed to see whales, we reasoned, the charms of bathing in the remote hot springs would compensate. Happily, we didn't have to put this theory to the test.

John brought along his six-year-old son, Colin, whose skillful boat-handling impressed our less water-savvy kids. Leaving Panchika et al., our next stop was a series of rocky islets to the north. Coming in alarmingly close to the rocks, John pointed out a fascinating sight. Scattered over the rocks lay dozens of seals, their light grayish-beige coats blending into the rocks. They resembled well-fed tourists on a Caribbean beach, annoyed at being disturbed during their pleasant nap in the sunshine. One would rise up—as if propping itself with an elbow—stare briefly at us, then snort and turn over.

By now we were well out into the notoriously rough waters off Vancouver Island's west coast. Land appeared very far off. The weather was good and the ocean swells moderate; still, several children got queasy stomachs. Luckily, no one became genuinely ill, and John soon returned us to sheltered waters.

On our way, we encountered a solitary humpback whale quietly feeding, thanks to a nearby vessel whose skipper had alerted John to the humpback's presence. Tour operators cooperate to share information about whale sightings via radio. Often, the result is that a breaching whale is soon surrounded by hordes of boats, tracking its every move, albeit from a safe distance. Thus far, researchers have not determined if these whale paparazzi actually bother the whales or affect their behavior; research is ongoing.

The humpback's long gray form appeared about 100 feet ahead, then dove, daintily waving its flukes at us. John maneuvered us a little closer and we waited. Nothing. Suddenly, fewer than 30 feet off the starboard side, a huge back emerged, close enough to reveal individual barnacles along its length. The majestic creature rose and dove a few times, then disappeared.

Our next stop was the gray-whale feeding grounds, where we encountered three or four, who put on a show for us when they could tear their attention away from lunch. It occurred to us how well the seals, humpbacks, and grays blend into the marine environment, with their hues of gray and brown. On the other hand, orcas make a bold fashion statement—bicolor studies in glistening white and glossy black. Nothing else in the surrounding waters or land is that color. But when you're that high on the food chain, camouflage may be superfluous.

We were running a little late as we turned into Hot Springs Cove, but Sea Trek is casual about time. If passengers are agreeable, Sea Trek extends the trip to maximize wildlife sightings. This spot, an inlet north of Tofino, has long been visited by local residents, fishers, and yachtsmen. Now a provincial park, it features a small resort and has plenty of moorage for pleasure boats. John told us to be back at the boat within three hours. This did not leave a lot of time for loitering, so after paying a visit to the spotless outhouse, we made our way to the two-km boardwalk trail to the Cove.

The lovely boardwalk, with twists and turns and short flights of stairs, is easily negotiated by small children, but not wheelchairs or strollers. At intervals, we inspected the names of ships and pictures carved into the boardwalk.

At the springs were more outhouses, a small changing room, and about 20 tourists from other tours. The hot springs rise out of the ground at a scalding 49 degrees Celsius, a short distance above a connected series of small pools that first cascade down a shower-height waterfall of about 42 degrees. Each succeeding pool is cooler until the final pool—at ocean's edge—reaches a comfortable bath temperature.

We wolfed down our sandwiches, apples, and juice before joining the throng in the water, grateful we'd brought aqua sox for negotiating the rocks. It took a little while to find comfortable perches, given the profusion of jutting rocks at odd angles, but once we did, we experienced pure bliss. Surrounded by tall evergreens and ocean vistas, this is one of Vancouver Island's most enchanting spots, well worth the effort to reach.

Each pool can comfortably accommodate four or five bathers at a time, wedged into crevices in the rocks. The pools are not deep; standing up, our six year old was never in more than waist-high water. But care is needed to avoid cuts and bruises. Deciding the second-to-lowest pool was perfect in size and temperature, the moms relaxed in it, while dads and kids ventured to the lowest level where—to the kids' delight, anyway—they were splashed by icy waves.

Too soon, it was time to pack up and return to the *Pisces*. If we had any complaint this enchanting day it was that time at the hot springs was too short. We noticed a freshly caught large and ugly fish lay on *Pisces's* deck. It didn't look particularly edible, but we learned it had a purpose. Following a shorter, protected route back to Tofino, we encountered a group of nervous sea otters, closely tailed by some very interested orcas. John was masterful at maneuvering the boat around them, guessing where they'd surface next. When we were about 20 feet away, the orcas approached us head on, before turning abruptly and waving their flukes cheekily at us. We left reluctantly, watching as they faded from view, arcing and splashing gracefully in the distance.

Our last adventure was odd and thought-provoking. We passed a forested bank where a lone bald eagle sat near the top of a dead tree. John threw the ugly fish up in the air and the eagle flew down to catch it, just missing. Sulkily, it returned to its perch. John came around and repeated the maneuver. This time the eagle returned, swooping low, and picked up the fish in its talons, without missing a beat. Moving visibly slower (the fish was heavy), the bird returned to its perch—a tame bald eagle.

As we rounded beautiful Meares Island, the lights of Tofino greeted us, twinkling in the twilight. Unusually contemplative, our children shouldered their backpacks, saying fond goodbyes to Colin, with whom they'd bonded closely on the trip back, and we stepped back onto dry land. ■

9155) runs several small boats—one with a glass bottom—on tours of two to 6 1/2 hours in length. Their record for successfully bringing tourists and whales together is impressive. Prices vary, but children under six are free.

**PACIFIC RIM NATIONAL PARK.** This huge national park embraces the West Coast Trail and Broken Islands further south on Vancouver Island's west coast. But the most accessible portion of the park is the Long Beach Unit, on the coast between Ucluelet and Tofino. The park offers the best beaches on the peninsula, a variety of nature trails and guided walks, nature programs, and the Wickaninnish Centre. Campsites here are extremely popular. Booking well ahead of a trip is essential (800/689-9025).

Your first stop should be the **Park Information Center** (follow signs on Pacific Rim Highway, 250/726-4212; open summer, 9:30 a.m.-5 p.m.), where park staff provide information about evening programs, films, guided walks, camping, and more. Here you can pick up brochures, maps, bird- and whale-watching information, and program schedules.

Parking in summer is quite expensive. You pay at trailhead and beach parking lots, with coins, bills, or—sometimes—credit cards (Visa and Mastercard only). Machines issue tickets to place on your dashboard. The cost is $3 per hour, $8 per day, $42 per week. These fees help finance the park's upkeep.

Each beach has its special facets and if you're lucky enough to be in the area several days, you can check out quite a few of them. **Combers Beach** (about 22 km south of Tofino; follow sign from Pacific Rim Highway) lives up to its enticing name; washrooms and changing rooms are available here, along with plenty of parking. When running into the surf and trying to run back ahead of the waves ceases to enthrall, the kids can enjoy a real swim in an inexplicably warm inlet, a watery oasis in the sand, about one-meter deep.

The nature trails were designed with all kinds of users in mind and can safely be negotiated by small kids. The **Rain Forest Trail,** two one-km loops straddling both sides of the Pacific Rim Highway, takes you through magnificent old-growth forest (16 km south of Tofino; follow signs on Pacific Rim Highway.). There are many stairs, so don't bring a stroller.

The **Shorepine Bog Trail** is reached from the Wickaninnish Centre. This wheelchair- and stroller-accessible boardwalk takes you through an unusual stunted forest (take

Wickaninnish turnoff from Pacific Rim Highway, about 16 km south of Tofino; follow signs to parking and trail).

Just beyond the Bog Trail is the **Wickaninnish Centre and Restaurant,** at Wickaninnish Beach, one of the park's most spectacular. Save a trip here for a rainy day and allow an hour or two to explore the exhibits: First Nations culture, local geographic history, films, and a simulated submarine. The beach, protected by a series of jutting headlands, is full of tiny colorful shells that crunch underfoot, red rock scallops, mussels, purple olives, limpets, and more.

From March to October, the **Wickaninnish Restaurant** (250/725-7706) at Long Beach is open for lunch and dinner. Its location, built out over Wickaninnish Beach with windows on three sides (windows sometimes have to be replaced after winter storms take them out), and the huge fireplace, are spectacular. This is the place to splurge; there's fine dining for the grownups and a moderately priced kids' menu with the usual items. Seafood dishes with wild mushrooms are among the excellent adult choices. While waiting, munch on focaccia bread served with olive oil and balsamic vinegar. All seats are good here, but try to snag a window for whale or wave watching. After dinner, wander to the balcony outside and marvel at the surf swirling below you. NOTE: Don't confuse this restaurant with the Pointe at the Wickaninnish Inn, a Tofino resort. While beautiful and elegant, the Inn is not particularly child-oriented, nor is its restaurant menu.

### CALENDAR

**MARCH**
Whale Festival, 250/725-3414.

**JULY**
Pacfic Rim Summer Festival.

**SEPTEMBER**
Tofino Seafest.

### RESOURCES

**PACIFIC RIM NATIONAL PARK**
800/689-9025 (Canada & the U.S.); 604/689-9025 (overseas); pacrim_info@pch.gc.ca
Information or campground reservations.

**SHUTTLE BUS TO PACIFIC RIM NATIONAL PARK AND UCLUELET**
250/726-7779

**TOFINO VISITOR INFO CENTRE**
346 Campbell St., Box 249, Tofino V0R 2Z0
250/725-3414; www.islandnet/~tofino
Open seasonally

**BOOKS AND PUBLICATIONS**
**ABOUT WHALES:**
*I Wonder If I'll See a Whale*, by Frances Ward Weller. Philomel, 1991
*In the Company of Whales: From the Diary of a Whale Watcher*, by Alexandra Morton. Orca Book Publishers, 1993
*Orca Song*, by Michael C. Armour. Smithsonian Oceanic Collection, 1994
*Orcas Around Me: My Alaskan Summer*, by Debra Page. Whitman, 1997
*A Pod of Killer Whales*, by Vicki Leon. Silver Burdett Press, 1995
*The Secret Oceans*, by Betty Ballantine. Bantam Books, 1994

**ABOUT STARGAZING:**
*Exploring the Night Sky*, by Terence Dickinson. Camden House, 1987. This beginner's guide to astronomy, a Children's Science Book Award winner, makes a great introduction to the stars.
*Planets and Galaxies*, by Dan Mackie. Hayes Publishing, 1986
The Practical Astronomer, by Colin A. Ronan. Bloomsbury, 1981 (for older children)
*Sky and Earth*. Time Life Books, 1988

## UCLUELET

"Ucluelet" is the word for "safe harbour" in the Nuu-Chah-Nulth language, and that's just what was needed for mariners struggling up the rugged island coast. While Tofino's primary orientation is recreation, Ucluelet, Long Beach peninsula's southern anchor, is a working town with a bustling fishing industry and less of a holiday focus. This slightly larger town has fewer resorts, hotels, and B&Bs than Tofino, but family-oriented options definitely exist. In general, accommodation, meals, and galleries are somewhat lower-priced than in Tofino. Even if you're staying elsewhere, Ucluelet is well worth a visit.

### GETTING THERE

From Highway 4, take Pacific Rim Highway south. In

Ucluelet it turns into Peninsula Road.

## PLACES TO STAY

### CANADIAN PRINCESS RESORT
*1943 Peninsula Road, P.O. Box 939, V0R 3A0*
*250/726-7771; www.obmg.com/*
*Rates: Inexpensive to moderate*
*FYI: Restaurant, lounges; fireplaces; whale-watching and fishing packages*

Tofino may have more options, but only in Ucluelet will you get the experience this hotel provides: the opportunity to sleep onboard a historic 235-foot survey vessel. Permanently moored in Ucluelet, the *Canadian Princess*, formerly the *William J. Stewart*, served from 1932 to 1975 as a hydrographic survey ship. During World War II, she was given top-secret assignments by the Canadian Navy. In 1944, however, like so many ships before and after her, she struck notorious Ripple Rock in Seymour Narrows (see "Campbell River"); unlike many, she survived and lived to continue charting B.C. waters until 1975. She's been moored in Ucluelet since 1979.

Two very different styles of accommodation are offered: Guests can choose the compact and charming staterooms with room for two to four people; staterooms have sinks, but toilets, baths, and showers are down the hall. Or, for more luxury (but less charm), an onshore addition has many units, somewhat more expensive, with all the expected resort amenities. Some feature fireplaces and lofts, and have balconies and views. The resort's dining room and lounges are onboard ship. Staterooms start at $60, onshore rooms at $105 per night.

During the gray-whale migration, packages are available in which groups of school children can be accommodated, fed, and ferried to the whales. (Call 800/663-7090 for details.)

## PLACES TO EAT

### GRAY WHALE ICE CREAM & DELICATESSEN
*1950 Peninsula*
*250/726-2113*
*Hours: 7 a.m.-6 p.m. daily (winter); 5: a.m.-8 p.m. daily (summer)*

For a quick lunch, your best bet is this pleasant deli across the street from the Canadian Princess. Prices are as low as they get here: $1.65 will buy your child a hefty pb&j sandwich. Pizza subs, a range of soups and sandwiches, and other deli foods are offered.

## WHAT TO SEE & DO

Ucluelet isn't as pedestrian-friendly as Tofino, but it does have its share of galleries and shops. Check out the **Du Quah Gallery** (1971 Peninsula, next to the Canadian Princess Resort; 250/726-7223), designed to resemble a traditional longhouse, for a wide variety of interesting and quite competitively priced First Nations art work, including jewelry, wood carvings, and books.

**AMPHITRITE POINT LIGHTHOUSE** overlooks the site of so many shipwrecks that the waters here are known as the "Graveyard of the Pacific." From the parking lot, walk down the trail past the lighthouse to the overlook. Whale-watching vessels converging on distant dorsal fins and flukes are a common sight here. It tends to be cold and windy, but the view is well worth a few shivers.

*Follow Peninsula Road south; turn right onto Coast Guard Road. Parking is at the end of the road.*

## CALENDAR

**MARCH**
Whale Festival, 250/726-4641.
**JULY**
Pacfic Rim Summer Festival.
Ukee Days.

## RESOURCES

**SHUTTLE BUS TO PACIFIC RIM NATIONAL PARK AND TOFINO**
250/726-7779
**UCLUELET VISITOR INFO CENTRE**
Junction Hwy. 4, Box 428, Ucluelet V0R 3A0
250/726-4641; www.ucluelet.com/ucoc

# CENTRAL AND NORTHERN VANCOUVER ISLAND

The rule is simple: the farther north you go, the wilder it gets, population and traffic thin out, and you realize that you're definitely in "the true north, strong and free." Distances between attractions are greater, but nowhere is there an unrelieved stretch of more than a few hours. Increasingly, family activities are of the outdoor adventure kind, punctuated by some indoor attractions like the world-class museums that showcase the cultures of the region's first inhabitants, including the Kwagiulth and 'Namgis First Nations.

## GETTING THERE

Seventy km north of Parksville are the twin cities of Courtenay and Comox, usually referred to as hyphenated: Courtenay-Comox. From here, you can access two major ski areas to the west: the Forbidden Plateau and Mount Washington. To the east, B.C. Ferries run to Powell River, on the mainland's Sunshine Coast, or halfway there, to Texada Island. In summer and ski season, expect horrendous and frustrating traffic wherever you go in the Courtenay-Comox area. Fixes, including city bypasses, are underway.

Heading north, traffic eases rapidly on Highway 19 until you reach Campbell River, 50 km north of Courtenay-Comox. With a population of 30,000, Campbell River is the biggest city north of Nanaimo on Vancouver Island. Here, you can take a ferry to the magically named Discovery Islands: Quadra and Cortès. If you're headed farther north, this is your last chance to stock up on supplies at a Superstore or Canadian Tire. Be sure to tank up with gas here; there will be few gas stations until Port McNeill.

About 40 km west of Campbell River on Highway 28 is Strathcona Provincial Park, with mountains to climb and lakes to explore by canoe and kayak. Accommodation and camping are available in the park. Another 49 km west is the logging-company town of Gold River, with access to Nootka Sound.

North to Port McNeill, it's a 200 km, 2 1/2-hour drive from Campbell River. Just before you reach Port McNeill is the turnoff for Telegraph Cove, site of a historic community that's now a resort. A major new development is underway here as well. Orca lovers take note: nearby Johnstone Strait is home to some of the largest orca populations in the Pacific Northwest.

From Port McNeill, about 10 km past the turnoff on the Island Highway, ferries run to Sointula, on Malcolm Island, and Alert Bay, on Cormorant Island. Both islands are fascinating and well worth a trip.

Another 50 km north brings you to Port Hardy, a town of about 5,000 and the northern terminus of Highway 19. From here, intrepid travelers can hop a ferry to Prince Rupert, with stops at interesting historic communities along the Inside

Passage. The passage takes about 24 hours, and ferries are equipped with comfortable staterooms and the usual B.C. Ferries amenities, including kid play areas. From Prince Rupert, ferries go west to the Queen Charlotte Islands (see "Northern British Columbia").

## COURTENAY-COMOX

These busy towns seem caught in perpetual traffic gridlock, but once you get off the road, the small-town ambiance comes right back. This is a good place to break a journey to the northern end of the island and check out Vancouver Island's very own dinosaur pedigree (see "What to See & Do"). Comox is about six km east of Courtenay in theory, but in practice it's hard to tell where one leaves off and the other begins.

### PLACES TO STAY

#### KINGFISHER OCEANSIDE RESORT & SPA

*4330 S. Island Hwy., V9N 8H9*
*800/663-7929; www.kingfisher-resort-spa.com*
*Rates: Moderate to expensive*
*FYI: Restaurant, kitchens; fireplaces; VCRs (in new units); indoor and outdoor pools, steam cave; fitness/spa facilities, including massage*

This Quality Inn has recently refashioned itself as a combination timeshare condominium complex and health spa, but has retained, at least for now, its character as a hotel and its family-friendly amenities. The older portion of the hotel features attractive rooms with water views, several acres of lawn, a good stretch of rocky beach teeming with interesting marine life, a small outdoor swimming pool, and a restaurant. The spacious new units down at the beach have full kitchens, Jacuzzi baths, TVs/VCRs, decks, and patios. The intention is to transform this former hotel into a destination for romantic getaways and spa weekends. Kids are welcome to swim, supervised by an adult.

The restaurant is on the expensive side, but has a good selection of dishes, including vegetarian entrées. The kids' menu offers traditional chicken, fish, grilled cheese, and hamburger options at a reasonable price. Dine inside or out; either way, the spectacular view extends across the strait to Powell River.

**❝ PARENT COMMENTS**

*"We stayed in one of the brand-new, one-bedroom condos*

*with a king bed in the bedroom and sofa bed in the living room. The kids immediately ran down to the rocky waterfront, which was studded with shellfish alive and dead and a few wary seals. Then the kids brought back their smelly collection of dead crabs and laid them out carefully on the patio."*

*"The outdoor pool was freezing and there is no lighting around it, so when the sun sets, you leave."*

## WHAT TO SEE & DO

For the young dinosaur enthusiasts in your party, a stop at the **Courtenay Museum & Paleontology Centre,** in downtown Courtenay, is indicated. In 1988, a father and daughter discovered the fossil of a 13-meter elasmosaur near the Puntledge River, a little way out of town. Other fossils were soon uncovered nearby and sent east for identification and restoration. A major custody battle ensued over this find, pitting western against eastern Canada, but in the end this small museum emerged victorious, and visitors can now examine the complete, elegant skeleton of a Cretaceous Period marine dinosaur just a few kilometers from where it was discovered. In summer, the museum conducts tours, several times a week, to nearby dig sites where dinosaur remains continue to be unearthed.

Also at the museum, ammonite fossils, looking like chambered nautiluses carved out of marble, and other remains testify to Vancouver Island's past as a series of islands in a shallow sea. Antique dolls and toys and some reconstructed old-time workplaces, including a blacksmith shop, druggist, and Chinese dry goods store, round out the collection. But the big draw is the dinosaur.

Next door is the **Paleontology Annex,** dusty rooms full of fossils being cleaned, labeled, and stored by local volunteers who welcome young visitors and are happy to take time to explain their work to kids.

*360 Cliffe Ave.; 250/334-3611; www.courtenaymuseum.bc.ca. Open: 10 a.m.-4:30 p.m. daily (May-Aug.); Tues.-Sat. (Sept.-April). Cost: donation requested, of $2 per adult. Kids are free. Call museum for details of paleontology tours.*

## CALENDAR

**FEBRUARY**
Trumpeter Swan Festival.

**JULY**

Comox Valley Festival (MusicFest), 250/336-2694.

Comox Nautical Days.

**JULY-AUGUST**

The Filberg Festival: Arts, crafts, food, and entertainment, 250/334-9242.

**RESOURCES**

**COMOX VALLEY VISITOR INFO CENTRE**

2040 Cliffe Ave., Courtenay V9N 2L3

250/334-3234; www.tourism-comox-valley.bc-ca

## DISCOVERY ISLANDS

The aptly named Discovery Islands, of which Quadra and Cortès are the largest, attract visitors who like to enjoy the outdoors in a tranquil atmosphere and at a relaxed pace. The short trip from Campbell River to Quadra Island is deceptive. It may be close to the mainland, but the culture on the island is distinctly different. Visitors familiar with Washington State's San Juan Islands will recognize the ambiance—everything here runs on relaxed island time.

You can dig shellfish (but be sure to do it legally and watch for red tide alerts), investigate beautiful beaches with some of the Northwest's best tide pools, and learn about First Nations history at the wonderful museum at Cape Mudge.

**ROADSIDE ATTRACTIONS.** Whether you're headed to Quadra Island or points north on Highway 19, **Campbell River** makes a good place to stop for a break. (If you started from Nanaimo, you'll have been driving for more than two hours.) While you're here, check out the large and excellent **Museum at Campbell River** for an overview of the rich First Nations and later history of this region.

In addition to mounting traveling exhibits, the museum houses an extraordinary collection of First Nations masks. They are ingeniously displayed and lighted so as to illustrate the tale of the Siwidi Clan. Told on tape by a descendant of the hero, Siwidi, the tale recounts Siwidi's adventures under the lake with a variety of spirits and monsters, all represented by masks. The enthralling story mesmerizes children; you may want to let them sit through the cycle more than once, while you take the opportunity to tour the museum's less dramatic exhibits.

In the museum's theater, several interesting films are shown, including the story of how nearby Ripple Rock was blown up. This navigation hazard in Seymour Narrows, the channel between Quadra and Vancouver islands, destroyed vessels of all sizes for more than 100 years. The film depicts the staggering engineering feat of 1958, in which workers tunneled under the river and up through the rocks to set off the biggest explosion ever produced by human beings, except those created by nuclear weapons. Thanks to that effort, mariners now safely traverse this once-treacherous passage.

The museum has a well-stocked gift shop with interesting First Nations arts and crafts and some books.

*470 Island Hwy. (entrance off 5th Ave.). 250/287-3103; www.island.net/~crm_chin. Open Mon.-Sat., 10 a.m.-5 p.m.; Sun., noon-5 p.m. (May 18-Sept.) Tues.-Sun., noon-5 p.m.(remainder of year). Cost: $2.50/adult, $2/student & senior, free/under 6, $7.50/family.*

### CALENDAR

**JULY**
Campbell River Children's Festival, 250/287-7465.
**AUGUST**
Campbell River Summer Festival, 250/287-2044.

### RESOURCES

**CAMPBELL RIVER VISITOR INFO CENTRE**
P.O. Box 400, 1235 Shoppers Row, V9W 5B6
250/287-4636

## QUADRA ISLAND
### GETTING THERE

B.C. Ferries (250/386-3431) offers daily ferry service year round to Quadra and Cortès islands from Campbell River. To reach Quadra Island, head to the B.C. Ferries terminal, right off Highway 19 in downtown Campbell River. A 10-minute ferry ride brings you to Quathiaski Cove on Quadra Island. Take West Road across the island to Heriot Bay and the ferry to Cortès Island.

### PLACES TO STAY

**HERIOT BAY INN**
*Heriot Bay Road, P.O. Box 100, Heriot Bay V0P 1H0;*

*250/285-3322; www.nwboat.com/heriotbay*
*Rates: Inexpensive to moderate*
*FYI: Restaurant, kitchens; decks and gas grills; laundry; gift shop;*
*marina, moorage; boat, canoe, kayak rentals; fishing charters and*
*packages; pets OK (on leash)*

It's somewhat funky, but if eccentric charm appeals to your family this is a good bet. The location couldn't be lovelier; it overlooks Heriot Bay and the tantalizingly close ferry to Cortès Island. Next to the inn is an RV park, and the whole place has a 1950s feel, the kind of place where you expect Beaver and Wally Cleaver to turn up. There's been an inn here since 1894, but the two previous incarnations burned down. The small rooms in the main building are charming; however, the best bets for families are the spacious, self-contained cottages out back.

The inside section of the inn's restaurant is small, but the covered deck offers more room and a great view. There is no kids' menu, but then the entire menu is like one big kid's menu. Adults, adjust your expectations accordingly, and you'll enjoy your meal. The specialty, Armadillo Eggs—jalapeños stuffed with cream cheese, then breaded and fried—is surprisingly good.

Old-fashioned lawn chairs are strewn about the spacious gardens. The marina will attract kids, but don't let them visit it alone unless they're good swimmers. Part of the dock consists of loosely connected floats with no sides or railings.

**❝ PARENT COMMENTS**

*"We enjoyed watching huge, plutocratic pleasure boats arrive and dock. For dinner, even though it was chilly, we chose to eat outside; inside reeked of cigarette smoke (there seems to be no area off limits to smokers). Service was a little sloppy, but friendly and cheerful."*

*"Our cottage was huge. There were two self-contained bedrooms-one with a queen bed and one with twins—and the living room had two sofa beds. The view was fabulous and we ate breakfast on the veranda which had a picnic table and benches."*

**TSA KWA LUTEN LODGE**
*Lighthouse Road, P.O. Box 460, Quathiaski Cove, V0P 1N0;*
*250/285-2042; 800/665-7745; www.capemudgeresort.com*
*Rates: Inexpensive to expensive*
*FYI: Restaurant, kitchens (some units); fireplaces; lofts; hot tub,*
*sauna; fitness equipment; fishing charters*

A good choice for a holiday with older children, this beautiful, isolated lodge situated above Discovery Passage means

"Gathering Place" in the Kwakiutl language. It's surrounded by tall evergreens, and the atmosphere is peaceful and relaxed. The rooms are spacious and elegantly decorated with First Nations art; some have Jacuzzi baths. Families with younger kids may prefer the cabins, with kitchenettes and private verandas. All rooms overlook the water.

The common areas and restaurant are also filled with native art and offer breathtaking views. The restaurant is fancy, yet, like the accommodation, quite reasonably priced. There's no kids' menu, but kids who like seafood or pasta should survive. Check out the B&B, cabin, and getaway specials. Rates for some of these bring this resort within our inexpensive price range.

### WHAT TO SEE & DO

**KWAGIULTH MUSEUM AND CULTURAL CENTRE.** This fascinating museum at Cape Mudge is a must-see. Much of the building is round, designed as a spiral, resembling an ammonite shell or chambered nautilus. Visitors move through the spiral, at the center of which is a tall totem pole. The museum was created to house its potlatch collection: a set of First Nations artifacts that had been confiscated by the Canadian government in 1922 and weren't returned to Cape Mudge until 1979. These include extraordinary masks, sacred ceremonial objects, and coppers (a complex and sophisticated form of currency—fascinating to see).

The museum tells the history of the potlatch and its important role in the Kwagiulth culture. Potlatches were the centerpiece of many First Nations cultures and governed relationships and transfer of wealth between families and communities. The hallmark of the potlatch was gift-giving, from the host to the guests. Threatened by what was, essentially, a competing form of government, the Canadian government outlawed all First Nations potlatches for many years. While potlatches are again legal, some confiscated articles have yet to be returned. Many that have been can be seen here.

The echo masks, with interchanging mouthpieces, and cannibal masks are especially compelling. To gain a deeper understanding of what you see here, stop at the Campbell River Museum first and watch the tale of Siwidi. It will give you an appreciation of the important role these masks play in storytelling.

Hands-on exhibits encourage children to touch and investigate different items. Kids can take a rubbing from one of several petroglyphs in the museum (paper and charcoal are supplied) and try on child-size button blankets and dancing aprons hung with little bells.

The museum has an excellent gift shop that sells kits for making dreamcatchers, along with other crafts.

*Cape Mudge, Quathiaski Cove. 250/285-3733. Open: June-Sept., Mon.-Sat., 10 a.m.-4:30 p.m.; Sun., noon-4:30 p.m. Cost: $3/adult, $2/senior, $1/child 6-12, free/under 6.*

**BEACHES AND FOSSIL HUNTING.** One of the charms of Quadra Island is the presence of many inviting small roads to follow and interesting beaches to explore. If your passion is fossils or totally awesome tide pools, head to secluded **Open Bay.** Park at the end of Valdez Drive, and walk down to the rocky beach. You'll be clambering over driftwood, then big rocks, but persevere. Soon tide pools will appear, teeming with life, from pink and deep-purple sea stars (if you're lucky you may catch them in the act of stuffing whole rock crabs into their odd gullets) to myriad crabs, oysters, assorted anemones, and fish of varying sizes. To maximize your marine-life sightings, check a tide table first. The lower the tide, the better. If you can tear your family away from the living world, they may spot some ammonite fossils among the rocks.

*Take Village Bay Road to Valdez Dr.; follow Valdez Dr. to the end of the road.*

## CORTÈS ISLAND

Yes, it's *that* Cortès, the "discoverer" of Mexico. The Spanish charted these waters and named the Discovery Islands, but never colonized them. The Klahoose First Nation, a Coast Salish tribe, were this island's first inhabitants. Today, about 1,000 residents of all kinds live here, and quite a few rent cottages to visitors for a week or more at a time. Families looking for a low-key, affordable, away-from-the-city vacation have gotten hooked and find themselves returning year after year.

Cortès is not for everyone, but if you harbor nostalgia for the '60s, aren't put off by the occasional nude beach, and appreciate the informal friendliness this small and protected community has to offer, this could make a great family holiday.

Parent reviewers highly recommend Cortès for child-friendly outdoor activities, but point out that it takes commitment to get here: it's a long-day's journey from Seattle (11 or 12 hours) and eight or more from Vancouver.

### GETTING THERE

Ferry service to Cortès is limited (B.C. Ferries, 250/386-34331), with about six runs daily each way between the two islands. The last ferry from Quadra to Cortès departs at 6:45 p.m., even in summer. Crossings take 45 minutes.

### PLACES TO STAY

We recommend that you rent a cottage here (see "Resources" below), rather than stay at a motel. Prices for rentals generally fall in our low to moderate range. There are also several upscale lodges, but none is particularly child-friendly, and most restrict guests to ages 12 and over. Another option is to make Cortès a day trip from Quadra Island.

### PLACES TO EAT

While supermarkets exist, they don't carry much in the way of fish or fresh produce. Residents catch their own fish, and produce is purchased from local growers and delivered on an honor system. But deliveries (on Friday or Saturday) aren't convenient for renters, who usually rent from Saturday to Saturday. Visitors who don't plan to stop in Quadra, where there's a good supermarket (the Island Market, open Mon.-Sat., 9 a.m.-7 p.m.; Sun., 10 a.m.-7 p.m.), should shop in Campbell River first. The general store on Cortès has homemade pizza.

As for restaurant dining, there are several good choices on Cortès, and all of them welcome kids. The **Hollyhock Holistic Retreat Centre** restaurant (250/935-6578; see "What to See & Do") serves excellent whole-foods and vegetarian buffet-style meals daily. Dinners feature menus from different countries. After dinner, kids can amble down to the beach and watch the deer. **Caffe Suzanne,** in Squirrel Cove, next to the general store (250/935-6866), is open daily.

### WHAT TO SEE & DO

Urban amenities are nonexistent, but when it comes to the great outdoors, many options exist. Virtually every kind of boating is available, along with lessons. Here's how one parent puts it: "This is a vacation for families who like lake or ocean swimming, kayaking, beach life, beach walks, or just 'staying put.' One must generate one's own night life, except for a weekly community dance. We enjoyed stargazing, flashlight tag, and a variety of table games. My children enjoyed learning about life on Cortès and felt comfortable, after a time, with the nude sunbathers. The children had a hard time at first with the lack of activities—no video arcades, waterparks, etc. But after we got over our initial shock, we decided it was one of our best vacations, and we can't wait to go back."

The **Hollyhock Holistic Retreat Centre,** in addition to offering meals, is a full-service resort with more than 48 acres, offering workshops, trainings, and retreats in many disciplines, from holistic healing and meditation to writing and African drumming. Evening programs, concerts, storytelling, and poetry reading are offered. There are programs for children as well as adults. Prices tend to be on the high side.

*On Cortès, follow signs to Smelt Bay and Hollyhock; P.O. Box 127, Manson's Landing V0P 1K0. 800/933-6339; hollyhock@oberon.ark.com; www.hollyhock.bc.ca.*

The **T'ai Li Lodge** offers kayaking and sailing rentals, lessons for all ages, and tours of various lengths, some in conjunction with Hollyhock.

*P.O. Box 16, Cortès Bay V0P 1K0. 250/935-6749; 800/939-6644; www.island.net/~taili/.*

**BEACHES AND SWIMMING.** Two waterfront provincial parks make good sites for watery exploration. **Smelt Bay Provincial Park** (southwest tip of the island along Smelt Bay Road) allows camping. **Manson's Landing Provincial Park** is a good site for picnicking; there's a lagoon where, at low tide, you can collect clams and oysters for dinner. For water warm enough for real swimming, check out **Hague Lake,** with a sandy beach and surrounded by parkland and a network of trails. No pets or soap are allowed in the water here; the lake provides drinking water for local residents.

## RESOURCES

**ALONG WITH PACIFIC COASTAL AIRLINES, THESE AIRLINES SERVE CORTÈS ISLAND:**

Air Rainbow (direct between Vancouver Harbour and Cortès, June-Aug.)
888/287-8366
Kenmore Air (scheduled seaplane service between Seattle and Cortès, May-Sept.)
206/485-4774

### ON THE ROAD AGAIN

The drive from Campbell River north has a very different feel: the Island Highway becomes virtually deserted. Tall trees, rushing rivers, spectacular peaks, shimmering lakes—no people. Sadly, many of the lovely peaks have been denuded of trees by extensive clear-cutting, an ongoing and controversial issue in British Columbia. Beyond Campbell River, expect to find rest areas about 10 to 15 km apart, with clean outhouses and occasional picnic tables.

In recent years, whale researchers and whale watchers from around the world have discovered Johnstone Strait, one of the best sites anywhere in which to study orcas. Stellar sea lions, bald eagles, bears, and more wildlife are also plentiful here. Scientists and tourists come from every continent and numbers are increasing. To accommodate more people, more services are starting to appear.

Along Highway 19, only two communities offer services for motorists between Campbell River, Telegraph Cove, and Port McNeill. **Sayward,** 70 km north of Campbell River, has camping, a motel, gas station, store, and a few other amenities. **Woss,** 128 km north of Campbell River, has a motel, store, gas station, and rustic café.

## TELEGRAPH COVE

Before it was discovered by whale fanciers, Telegraph Cove was known to boaters for many years as a cool place to drop in for ice cream and take a look at a vanishing breed of waterfront community. Sadly—or not, depending on your point of view—it will soon be small no longer; a huge resort is under construction on the other side of the cove. There will be more accommodation, boat moorage, and services (including a golf course), but unquestionably the atmosphere will change. In the meantime, don't miss an opportunity to investigate what still is one of the most delightful tiny waterfront villages in British Columbia.

### GETTING THERE

Heading north on Highway 19, about 10 kilometers before you reach Port McNeill, a sign beckons you east to Telegraph Cove. Following it, (the road turns to gravel about six km after the turnoff) you begin to feel you've made a mistake—isn't this a logging camp? Huge piles of logs and logging trucks are everywhere.

Don't give up; about 11 km after the turnoff you'll suddenly arrive at Telegraph Cove, a tiny historic community on Johnstone Strait.

## PLACES TO STAY

### TELEGRAPH COVE RESORTS

*P.O. Box 1, V0N 3J0*
*800/200-4665; www.telegraphcoveresort.com*
*Rates: Inexpensive to moderate*
*FYI: Restaurant, kitchens; laundry; store (groceries, tackle); kayak & boat rentals; tent & RV camping, moorage; whale watching, fishing, sightseeing charters; no TVs or phones*

This resort was created out of Telegraph Cove's small collection of historic wooden buildings, built on pilings above the cove and connected by a boardwalk. In other words, the whole village is the resort. The company has simply transformed most of the buildings into overnight accommodation. Outside each is a plaque telling the building's name, age, and history. Some buildings were completely gutted to make sophisticated, comfortable units inside. More renovations are underway. Assorted units are available, from studios to three-bedroom units; the largest sleep up to nine people. Despite the changes, the character of these distinctive buildings, brightly colored with window boxes full of flowers, has been maintained.

There's something fairytale-like about this spot, and children have a ball running up and down the boardwalk and peering inside the older buildings. They're enchanted by the little houses built on stilts over the water. Parents will be glad to know that the wide boardwalk is safe, flanked by the houses. At low tide, these stand in the mud, their stilts revealed; at high tide, the stilts are hidden by the water. Don't let smaller kids wander about completely unsupervised; while it's not easy to fall in the water, once you do, it's deep and cold.

Along the boardwalk is a large restaurant, the **Killer Whale Café** (open daily, 8 a.m.-10 p.m.) with plenty of seating inside and out. It can be noisy at times; consider asking for accommodation as far from the restaurant as possible. The restaurant is the only game in town, so it's lucky that the food is excellent, plentiful, and surprisingly moderate in price. Décor is lovely, consisting of banquettes separated by stained glass partitions featuring orcas in various watery poses. Seafood is, of course, the order of the day; adults may want to wash it down with a glass of excellent beer from the adjacent brewpub. There's a children's menu, too, with the reliable items they know and love.

> ❝ **PARENT COMMENTS**
>
> *"We were housed in a recently remodeled studio. It was very nice, but snug. There was no closet space, and once we brought in our bags, there was no floor space left either. The kids loved it though; it's as close as they've ever come to sleeping on a houseboat."*
>
> *"The restaurant and brewpub are kept very brightly lit at night; this kept our room a little too bright for the kids when they were trying to get to sleep."*

## WHAT TO SEE & DO

Stroll along the boardwalk, stop in the small galleries selling art, crafts, and souvenirs, and check out the store, where you'll find ice cream cones and snacks along with a fairly limited selection of groceries. If you'll be whale watching with Stubbs (see "Whale Watching," below) in the morning, you may want to postpone exploring their gift shop until the tour begins. They require you to be at the pier so far in advance of boarding that there isn't much to do except explore their merchandise while you wait (could this be intentional?).

**WHALE WATCHING.** One of the most respected tour operators on Vancouver Island, with an international reputation for responsible whale watching and respect for the marine environment, **Stubbs Island Whale Watching** offers excellent, reliable service and probably the best chance most of us will have to see orcas in the wild.

Operating two boats, each accommodating more than 40 passengers, they run several trips daily, each about four-hours long. The *Lukwa* is large and a better bet for families who need easy access to a washroom. Be sure to let Stubbs know you want the boat with the washroom at the time you make your booking.

Parent reviewers comment, "Out of about 25 passengers, six countries were represented on our trip. Our family enjoyed our experience aboard the smaller vessel, *Gikumi*, from which we sighted more than 40 orcas. Geraldine, Stubbs's friendly tour guide, brought along a book with drawings and photos of local pod members and took time to show it and explain whale facts to adults and kids. Although there was reputedly a toilet on board, it was located under the engine room, so we decided not to put it to the test. But the coffee, tea, and homemade pastries were superb."

NOTE: The morning whale-watching trips depart before the resort's restaurant opens for breakfast. While Stubbs provides some delectable snacks, you may want to purchase breakfast items like cereal and milk, and breakfast in your suite before joining the tour. It's amazing how that salty air builds an appetite!

*At the end of the boardwalk. 800/665-3066; www.stubbs-island.com. Cost: $65/adult; $58.50/senior & child, $58.50/each person in group of 10 or more.*

## NORTHERN GULF ISLANDS

**REFUELING.** About 10 km north of Telegraph Cove on Highway 19, **Port McNeill** shows its logging-company-town roots. Trees are sparse, and it lacks the charm of many other island towns. Telegraph Cove and Malcolm Island offer more enticing accommodation, but Port McNeill does have several good-sized supermarkets and other stores and an excellent family restaurant, situated across the street from the ferry dock.

Before heading to one of the islands, stop for a bite at the **Sportsman's Steak & Pizza House** (1547 Beach Dr., 250/956-4113; open for lunch, dinner Mon.-Sat.; dinner Sun.)

Facing the waterfront, much of this restaurant is bright and airy. Smokers get the best seats (as is often the case in restaurants in small B.C. towns), with nonsmokers herded to the dark interior. But with luck, nonsmokers can find a table in the good-view area that's not wreathed in smoke and watch a spectacular sunset from front-row seats.

Greek and traditional fine-dining options, from lobster to steak, are the specialties here. An extensive and reasonably priced selection of entrées for seniors and children is offered. And of course there's always pizza, every parent's friend. The Greek-Canadian owners are friendly, and both service and food are excellent.

### RESOURCES

**PORT MCNEILL & DISTRICT CHAMBER OF COMMERCE**
250/956-3131; 250/956-4437 (off-season)

## MALCOLM ISLAND/SOINTULA

From Port McNeill, it's a short hop (about 25 minutes, if you don't go to Alert Bay first) across Broughton Strait to Malcolm Island, birthplace of Canada's longest continuously operating cooperative. In 1901, a group of Finnish immigrants inaugurated their dream of a utopian society on Malcolm Island. (Sointula means "harmony" in Finnish.) Although utopia didn't exactly come about, this early influence is woven into the fabric of island life—from the architecture of the distinctive co-op and other buildings to the friendly, outgoing, and close-knit community who live here.

Disneyland it's not, but Malcolm Island is a good place to come for quiet relaxation and outdoor recreation in a very beautiful part of the world that's a lot less remote than it looks on the map. There are some B&Bs, and cottages can be rented for short stays. Whale watching is excellent here, and you're likely to see a full spectrum of other wildlife, too. From Vancouver, allow at least a full day to get here.

### GETTING THERE

From Port McNeill, get to the ferry dock (take Campbell Way down from Highway 19 to the water). Read your ferry schedule carefully. B.C. Ferries ( 250/956-4533) runs smallish boats in a triangular route between Port McNeill, Alert Bay, and Sointula. Depending on which leg you're on, the trip can take from 25 to 75 minutes. The normally straightforward ferry schedule can be hard to figure out here, and you may find yourself going from Sointula to Alert Bay via Port McNeill. Just relax and enjoy the trip. Orcas are a common sight, and the scenery is lovely. The ferries offer the usual amenities.

### PLACES TO STAY

### MALCOLM ISLAND INN

*210 - 1st St., P.O. Box 380, Sointula V0N 3E0*
*800/735-2912*
*Rates: Inexpensive*
*FYI: Restaurant; store; fishing and whale watching tours*

This small hotel sits above a general store about a block from the ferry dock. It's right on the water, and faces west toward Port McNeill, which looks a lot more attractive from Sointula. The view is world class and can hold its own with any offered by more expensive resorts. Rooms are basic, of moderate size, and each has a private balcony. The stairway up is quite steep. The store serves as hotel office, store of last resort (the owner calls it an "Innconvenience Store," 7 a.m.-10:30 p.m. in summer), and video rental outlet.

The logical spot for breakfast is **Finner's** (7 a.m.-9 p.m. daily), the major island restaurant and part of the inn, situated right next door. It has a children's menu with the traditional offerings. On weekends, Chinese food is sometimes offered. Service is good and fast, and plenty of local families eat here, along with hotel guests.

**❝❝ PARENT COMMENTS**

*"As we were watching the sunrise from our balcony, a great blue heron suddenly flew right by. Harbor seals swam past several times, too."*

*"We noticed a sign in the restaurant asking parents to reign in their kids so they wouldn't disturb other customers. It put us off a bit, but as there were plenty of small children there making noise and no one seemed to mind, we decided not to let it worry us."*

### SEA 4 MILES COTTAGES

*145 Kaleva Road, P.O. Box 421, V0N 3E0*
*250/973-6486*
*Rates: Inexpensive*
*FYI: VCRs; barbecues; playground*

Located next to the Kaleva Shores Campground are the aptly named Sea 4 Miles Cottages, where you can rent one of two cottages. Each has two bedrooms, a TV/VCR, and a covered deck with barbecue. There's a playground on the premises.

### CAMPING

**BERE POINT,** on the north side of the island, has several campsites, picnic grounds, and trails. Best of all, it's free.

**KALEVA SHORES CAMPGROUND** is open May through September and offers potable water, flush toilets, and hot showers. There are no RV hookups.

*Two km from the ferry dock. 250/973-2053.*

### WHAT TO SEE & DO

First, pick up a map of the island at the **Sointula Co-op** (on 1st, across from the ferry dock; 250/973-6912; open Tues.-Sat., 9:30 a.m.-5:30 p.m.; Mon., 9 a.m.- noon). While the current building dates back only to 1953, its design is distinctly Finnish; inside, you'll find a complete supermarket on the ground floor, and dry goods and just about anything else you need on the second.

Before getting into your car, check out Sointula on foot. There are a few galleries and shops in town; the most interesting is **Choyces in Sointula** (on 1st next to the ferry dock; 250/973-6433; Tues.-Sat., 10 a.m.-5 p.m.; Sun.-Mon., 10 a.m.-2 p.m.) Here you'll find arts and crafts for sale, (many from local artists), a selection of books about the region, and an espresso bar. Joyce, the owner, is knowledgeable about family-friendly activities in the area.

After you've exhausted the possibilities on foot, drive around the historic harbor and look at the old houses and buildings.

Community beaches, picnic sites, and campgrounds are scattered across Malcolm Island. There are beaches with tide pools, seals, herons, and more. Check out the beaches on the north side of the island (Mitchell Bay Road runs east-west across the island), especially **Bere Point,** where orcas come for a massage on the rubbing beaches. Nearby to the east, **Shiel's Bay** has a sandy beach.

### RESOURCES

**B.C. FERRIES**
250/956-4533
Call with inquiries about ferry schedules.
**MAGIC DRAGON CHARTER TOURS & FISHING**
250/974-8080
Fishing and whale-watching tours.

**WAYWARD WIND CHARTERS (WHALE WATCHING)**
250/973-6307
Whale-watching tours. (NOTE: There is no ATM on Malcolm Island.)

**BOOKS**
*Sointula: Island Utopia,* by Paula Wild. Harbour Books: Madeira Park, B.C., 1995. Recounts the unique history of Malcolm Island and includes many archival photos.

## CORMORANT ISLAND AND ALERT BAY

This island, the traditional home of the 'Namgis (Nimkish) First Nation, is a 45-minute ferry ride from Sointula and Port McNeill. For years, it has been the site of the world's tallest totem pole, recently relegated to world's second tallest. Alert Bay's biggest draw is the U'Mista Cultural Centre. The island has a small selection of accommodation and restaurants to choose from, but for most families, it will work best as a day trip, rather than an overnight destination.

### WHAT TO SEE & DO

Stop first at the Tourist Info Centre on Fir Street, to your right as you disembark from the ferry, for a map of Cormorant

Island and up-to-date information on hours for attractions. In 1997, the Alert Bay Big House burned down, the result of arson; plans are under way to rebuild it.

**U'MISTA CULTURAL CENTRE.** This wonderful museum, dating from 1980, houses many potlatch artifacts in a remarkable setting. Visitors enter the museum from the right, viewing objects placed in the order in which they would appear at a traditional potlatch ceremony of the Kwakwaka'wakw people. The vivid and powerful masks should appeal even to kids who normally don't get too excited about museums. Traveling exhibits and videos on the culture and history of the potlatch are available for viewing. The gift shop sells a variety of interesting items.

*Drive or walk around Front St. to the left of the ferry dock. 250/974-5403. Open year round, Mon.-Fri., 9 a.m.-6 p.m. (summer); 9 a.m.-5 p.m. (winter). Cost: $6/adult, $4/senior & student, $1/ child.*

Another not-to-be-missed sight is the **'Namgis Burial Ground.** Tourists are asked not to enter this graveyard, but you can stand outside for a good view of the assortment of about 12 totem poles, erected to honor the dead, that mark various graves. Some have weathered badly, as totem poles will (and are expected to do) in this climate, but that just seems to add to their rugged majesty.

*Go east from the ferry dock; burial ground is on the left.*

For something a little different, check out **Gator Gardens,** a small ecological park. A boardwalk takes visitors on a 25-minute stroll through this odd, flooded cedar forest that feels vaguely prehistoric—as if any minute a dinosaur might saunter around the corner. It's home to ravens, eagles, and other birds. Pick up a brochure for a self-guided tour at the Info Centre. The Park is a short walk north of the ferry dock.

The **World's Second Tallest Totem Pole,** 173 feet tall, consisting of 11 different figures, is an awesome sight. You'll see tourists get themselves into all kinds of contorted positions trying to fit it all into one photograph. It's a few steep blocks north of the Cultural Centre.

Sooner or later, they'll be clamoring for food. Stop in at the **Old Customs House Restaurant** (250/974-2282; daily, 11 a.m.-11 p.m.) on Fir Street on the second floor. You can eat inside or out (the covered deck has a great view), and while the premises look fairly dismal, the kid-friendly fast food is actually fine, especially the French fries.

## RESOURCES

### ALERT BAY INFOCENTRE
250/974-5213

### TOURISM ALERT BAY ASSOCIATION
800/690-TABA

### SEASMOKE / SEA ORCA EXPEDITIONS, INC.
P.O. Box 483, V0N 1A0
250/974-5225
This whale-watching tour operator departs from both Alert Bay and Alder Bay Campsite, a 15-minute drive south of Port McNeill. They operate several boats, June to October, one of which, the *Tuan*, is a sailboat. On the *Tuan*, New Zealand-style snacks and tea are served to passengers who are invited to listen to whales through hydrophones.

# CENTRAL AND EASTERN BRITISH COLUMBIA

East of Vancouver, British Columbia unfolds in a series of parallel mountain ranges that run roughly northwest-southeast. The Cascade Range separates the west coast from the arid, high-plateau country of the Okanagan and Cariboo. Still farther east run the Monashee, Selkirk, and Purcell ranges. The Rocky Mountains mark the border between British Columbia and Alberta.

Sandwiched between these ranges is beautiful countryside and two of North America's largest river systems: the Fraser and the Columbia. A series of long lakes—many warm and swimmable with sandy beaches—also lie between the mountain ranges. West to east, they include Harrison Lake, Osoyoos Lake, Okanagan Lake, Shuswap Lake, upper and lower Arrow lakes, Kootenay Lake, Lake Coocanusa, and many more. Some straddle the international border with the United States.

Recreational prospects are rich, from skiing in winter to boating, fishing, and hiking in summer. Many communities are centered on tourism. The region has no large cities, but many of the area's small towns are thriving and distinctive communities, well worth exploring.

## GETTING THERE

**BY AIR.** **Air BC** (800/663-3721, in B.C.; 800/776-3000, in the U.S.) and **Canadian Regional Airlines** (800/665-1177, in B.C.; 800/426-7000, in the U.S.) serve Kelowna and Penticton, Castlegar, and Cranbrook. **Horizon Air** (800/547-9308) in the United States offers direct flights between Seattle and Kelowna.

**BY CAR.** From western British Columbia, several major east-west roads cross the province horizontally. If you're starting out from Vancouver or the lower mainland, you can take the Trans-Canada, Highway 1, east to Hope and continue east on Highway 3, one of the province's most scenic routes. Highway 3 crosses lovely Manning Provincial Park and continues east—roughly parallel to the U.S. border—through Princeton, Keremeos, Osoyoos, Grand Forks, Castlegar, Cranbrook, Fernie, and Sparwood. Spurs run north to encircle Kootenay Lake.

To the north, roughly parallel to Highway 3, Highway 6 runs east from Vernon through Nelson. Still further north is Highway 1, also spectacularly scenic, which takes you through Kamloops, Salmon Arm, Revelstoke, and Golden and continues on to Banff National Park in Alberta.

The bottom line is that you can't go wrong; any of these routes is a winner. The fastest option to reach eastern British Columbia is the Trans-Canada, but to access the Okanagan and Kootenays, Highway 3 is a better bet.

From western Washington and Oregon, the easiest access to the central region (the Okanagan Valley: Osoyoos, Kelowna, Penticton, Salmon Arm, and Sicamous) is via I-90 east, then north onto Highway 97. Cross the border at Osoyoos to reach the Okanagan.

If your destination is the Kootenays and points east, your fastest route will be I-90 to Spokane, from which you can reach Castlegar in fewer than three hours. For a more relaxed and scenic route, but one that requires more time, see "Kootenays: Getting There."

**REFUELING.** Families approaching the region via Vancouver may want to follow one parent's tip: "At Hope, we always stop for potato pancakes at **Polly's.** Exit 170 on Highway 1, turn left at the lights, go straight through into

Hope. Turn right just before the Chevron gas station; you'll find the restaurant behind the gas station."

**BY RAIL.** Scheduled public rail service is no longer provided across southern British Columbia. However, the old Canadian Pacific route (some parents may recall it from childhood) that winds through the Rockies and Banff still exists. A private enterprise, **Rocky Mountain Railtours,** operates sightseeing trains along the route; passengers are billeted at hotels nightly along the way. Some meals are provided. Optional features include dinner theatre, tours of Banff, and more. Travelers can choose none, some, or all of these features. You can travel the full distance from Vancouver to Calgary, or opt for part of it.

*Rocky Mountain Railtours, 800/665-7245; www.rkymtnrail.com. Operates May-Oct., several times per week. Cost: varies depending on package chosen. For two-day Railtour Signature Service, including hotel in summer, $670/adult (double occupancy); $660/child 2-11.*

## RESOURCES

**THOMPSON OKANAGAN TOURISM ASSOCATION**
1332 Water St., Kelowna  V1Y 9P4
250/861-7493
**TOURISM ROCKIES**
P.O. Box 10, Kimberley, V1A 2Y6
250/427-4838

## THE OKANAGAN VALLEY

From Osoyoos on the Canada-U.S. border north to the Okanagan Valley is British Columbia's semi-arid desert, situated between the rugged Coast Mountains to the west and the Rockies to the east. Its numerous lakes, plentiful sunshine, lakefront resorts, and beaches make the area an ideal place to vacation with kids.

Called the "Land of Beaches and Peaches," the Okanagan Valley is dry, but irrigation makes it a rich fruit-producing area. In summer, stands loaded with fresh local fruits, cheeses, and wines dot the roads, and there are plenty of U-Pick orchards. Look for cherries in late June, apricots and peaches in July and August, apples and pears in August and September, and plums and grapes in September and October.

In the winter, there is excellent skiing at Silver Star, Last Mountain, Big White, and Apex.

## OSOYOOS

Just north of the U.S. border, this town is reached via Highway 97. It lies on **Osoyoos Lake,** Canada's warmest fresh-water lake, averaging 24 degrees C year round. Osoyoos serves as an excellent introduction to the south Okanagan region, whose hot, sunny climate produces great fruit and a universal fondness for water-related activities, of which there are many.

### PLACES TO STAY

#### TAMRI LIFESTYLE RESORT
*2019 East Lakeshore Dr., RR 1, Site 26, Comp 10, Osoyoos V0H 1V0*
*250/495-2344*
*Rates: Inexpensive*
*FYI: Kitchens; air conditioned; beach access; grassy play area; small pets OK (fee)*

This pleasant and affordable family resort has several options from which to choose. There are 10 small cabins set in an apple orchard, plus plenty of grassy tent sites across from the cabins. The cabins feature two double beds and a sofa bed in the living-dining-kitchen area.

In addition to the adjacent beach, there are many larger public beaches nearby, along with shady picnic sites and abundant watery entertainment from water slides to river rafting. Weekly packages bring the price down further.

**66** PARENT COMMENTS
*"The campsites have regular washrooms and showers. Older kids can set up tents here."*

### PLACES TO EAT

#### BARRY'S NEIGHBOURHOOD RESTAURANT
*8309 78th Ave.*
*250/495-2224*
*Hours: Lunch, dinner daily*

This restaurant has a children's menu and caters to families, but parent reviewers feel it has gone downhill a bit since a recent change of ownership.

### WHAT TO SEE & DO

What brings our parent reviewers back here, year after year, is the lovely heat. One describes the weather as a kind of

"Canadian Mexico—there's always warm weather in this desert climate."

**Osoyoos Museum** features the interior of a pioneer log cabin dating from 1891, along with mining displays, native artifacts, and town archives.

*End of Main St. in Gyro Community Park. 250/495-2582. Open Victoria Day-Sept., daily, 10 a.m.-3:30 p.m. Cost: $2/adult, $.50/child 6-16, $6/family.*

### THE GREAT OUTDOORS

**Horseback riding.** Indian Grove Riding Stables offer rides and daylong pack trips by reservation.

*About two kilometers east of Osoyoos Lake bridge, turn left onto 45th St. 250/498-4478; 250/495-7555. Trail rides: 9 & 11:30 a.m., 4 & 6:30 p.m.*

**Water Slides.** Wild Rapids has three large water slides, five giant hot tubs, and two mini-slides. If water ceases to amuse, try a round of miniature golf.

*East side of Osoyoos Lake, a few blocks north of Tamri Lifestyle Resort on E. Lakeshore Dr. 250/495-2621.*

## CALENDAR

### JULY

Cherry Fiesta Days: Cherry-pit spit (don't knock it; the kids love it!), parade, fireworks.

## RESOURCES

**Osyoos Travel InfoCentre and Osoyoos Chamber of Commerce**
Box 227, Osoyoos V0H 1V0
250-495-7142; 888-676-9667; tourism@osyooschamber.bc.ca

# OKANAGAN LAKE

Lining 113-km long Okanagan Lake are the resort towns of Penticton, Summerland, Kelowna, and Vernon. Some say the legendary monster Ogopogo lives in Okanagan Lake near the city of Summerland, although Kelownans say it is closer to them, and the folks in Vernon also claim ownership. The creature's name is a palindrome because the beast itself supposedly looks the same from either end. See a statue of the serpent at Kelowna.

## GETTING THERE

Most towns in this section line up vertically along Highway 97. From Osoyoos, it's a 50 km drive north to Kaledon, another 10 km north to Penticton, and another 52 km beyond Penticton to Kelowna. Naramata, on the eastern shore of Okanagan Lake, is a 20-minute drive from Penticton on Naramata Road.

## PLACES TO STAY

### LAKE OKANAGAN RESORT
*2751 Westside Road, Kelowna V1Z 3T1*
*250/769-3511, 800/663-3273*
*Rates: Moderate to expensive*
*FYI: Two restaurants, kitchens; three outdoor swimming pools; boating, water-skiing, tennis (seven courts), golf, horseback riding; laundry; kids' camp; one mile of beachfront*

Once you reach Lake Okanagan Resort, you'll want to settle down for a comfortable and memorable vacation. This 121-hectare spread is everything a family resort should be. Now open year round, the grounds are beautiful and accommodations comfortable, though not fancy. You can choose between large condominiums or Swiss-style chalets—all have kitchens, and most have fireplaces. The rooms in the inns are too small for families. The resort is on a steep hillside, so units are sometimes a good climb from activities but a resort shuttle makes the trip easy.

The fancy "dress-up" restaurant is not for kids, but there is a very good family restaurant. An excellent horseback riding program is available. In the game room, crafts and movies are offered on rainy days (which are rare).

**❝❝ PARENT COMMENTS**
> *"The horseback riding program was very safe and well-supervised. The trail ride was the best we have ever seen for kids."*
>
> *"This place was above our budget, but a good value. We had breakfast and lunch in our room and ate at the family restaurant at night, which was very tasty and reasonable."*
>
> *"There is plenty to keep everybody busy. Our kids enjoyed keeping a lookout for Ogopogo, the local 'Loch Ness monster'."*

### PONDEROSA POINT RESORT
*P.O. Box 106, Kaleden V0H 1K0*
*250/497-5354; www.bcsimpactico.bc.ca.thepoint*

*Rates: Moderate; no credit cards*
*FYI: Kitchens; tennis (lit at night); boats; playground; children's events; smoke-free throughout*

Cozy log cabins and A-frames sit under tall pines on the shores of Skaha Lake, a few miles south of Penticton. Cabins have one, two, or three bedrooms and are immaculately kept and comfortable. Campfires, games, and other activities are organized for the kids.

### 66 PARENT COMMENTS

*"We worried about the one-week minimum but we should have stayed two weeks. It took about four days for us to start to relax and settle into this wonderful family resort."*

*"Our kids quickly met other kids. Ponderosa Point is a very safe, clean, and beautiful place."*

### SANDY BEACH LODGE

*4275 Mill Road, Box 8, Naramata V0H 1N0*
*250/496-5765; www.sandybeachresort.com*
*Rates: Moderate*
*FYI: Kitchens (in duplexes); outdoor pool; rental boats; tennis*

If you are searching for the perfect "cabin-on-the-lake" family resort, you have found your spot. The only drawback to this idyllic place on the shores of Okanagan Lake is that so many families come back every year, you will have trouble getting reservations. A wide lawn gently slopes to a sandy beach on a quiet cove. The nine new duplexes all have decks and barbecues (ask for one next to the beach). If the kids get bored with swimming and the beach, they can frolic in the small swimming pool, rent a rowboat, or play some tennis.

### 66 PARENT COMMENTS

*"The Canadian Okanagan is relatively unknown to Seattle families but it is a fabulous place to vacation. Hot weather, great swimming, and fun, resort-town amusements. The sandy beach is ideal if you just want to kick back and relax. When the kids got restless, we ventured into Kelowna to the waterslides."*

**HOUSEBOATING** on 70-mile Okanagan Lake is as popular as it is on Shuswap Lake (we haven't found any parent reviewers for Okanagan Lake, however). No previous boating experience is necessary, and yes, it is easy to go ashore to explore. Most houseboats sleep at least six and are fully outfitted, including microwaves and water slides.

## WHAT TO SEE & DO

### PARKS

**KELOWNA CITY PARK.** With 13 hectares of recreational space, including a long sandy beach, playground, lawn bowling, tennis courts, paddle and sail boat rentals, and a children's water park (complete with giant body heater/dryers), this is the largest park in the city of Kelowna. There is good swimming for kids, with a very gradual slope into deep water.
*Downtown Kelowna.*

### ANIMALS, ANIMALS

**OLD MacDONALD FARM,** 10 miles south of Kelowna, is fun for younger children. Kids can climb on the "Ladybug Train," feed the animals at the Petting Zoo, enjoy small water slides and a fishing pond, and take a pony ride.
*Eight km south of Kelowna off Hwy. 97. 604/768-5167.*

### THE GREAT OUTDOORS

**SKIING** at the numerous ski areas in the Okanagan is an excellent option for families who want to take a ski vacation but don't want to spend the higher prices at the more glamorous resorts such as Whistler. **Silver Star** (604/542-0224), with many runs suited to novices and intermediate skiers and a full-blown ski village with restaurants, ski shops, hotels, and condos, is especially suitable when winter vacationing with kids. Many resorts at Okanagan Lake also have good ski packages.

**MARINER'S REEF WILD 'N WET WATERSLIDE PARK** (250/768-7600) high above Okanagan Lake, is the largest water entertainment park in the valley. It features two thrilling twister slides, two kamikaze slides, the famous river raging ride, two intermediate and three children's slides, plus hot tubs.

## CALENDAR

### APRIL
Kiwania Music Festival, Kiwania.
### JULY
Westside Daze, Kelowna.
### OCTOBER
Okanagan Wine Festival: Region-wide event, 250/765-2900.

**RESOURCES**

**KELOWNA VISITOR INFO CENTRE**
544 Harvey Ave., Kelowna V1Y 6C9
250/861-1515

**PENTICTON VISITOR INFO CENTRE**
888 Westminster Ave. W., Penticton V2A 8R2
800/663-5052; 250/493-4055

## SHUSWAP LAKE

This area, the northern tip of the Okanagan region, offers more lakes, scenery, houseboating vacations, and watery pastimes. Even if it isn't your final destination, Shuswap Lake—at the junction of highways 97 and 1—makes a good place to stop and catch your breath on your way east to the Rockies, west to Vancouver, or to points north or south.

Salmon Arm and Sicamous, two of the region's larger towns, lie on Shuswap Lake. You'll find a variety of resorts and small communities scattered around the margins of this octopus of a lake with its long, fjord-like extensions (hence the name Salmon Arm). Major tourist destinations in their own right, both offer a full spectrum of accommodation options to families. There's far more here than their small populations might suggest (Salmon Arm has about 15,000 residents and Sicamous has 3,000).

### GETTING THERE

From Vancouver and points west and south, take Highway 1 to Hope, continue on the Coquihalla Highway to Kamloops, then take Highway 1, the Trans-Canada, east to Salmon Arm and Sicamous.

From points south and the United States, take Highway 97. North of Vernon, Highway 97 forks left and right. From the left fork, Highway 97 proceeds northwest to Kamloops and beyond. The right fork soon forks again. Left, Highway 97B, will take you to Salmon Arm. Right, 97A, will take you to Sicamous. The towns lie 32 km apart, each at the junction of its respective fork and Highway 1. Each is about 250 km from the U.S. border, roughly a three-hour drive. From Kelowna, it's about 130 km.

## PLACES TO STAY

### CEDARS MOTEL
*1210 Paradise, Box 294, Sicamous V0E 2V0*
*250/836-3175*
*Rates: Inexpensive*
*FYI: Kitchens; barbecues, picnic tables; near beach*

This charming small motel will appeal to log-house lovers. Units are spacious, with separate bedrooms, and comfortable.

**66 PARENT COMMENTS**
> *"There are always families here; our kids made friends and they spent our stay investigating and comparing the merits of each other's units. The community picnic area makes it easy to meet other families."*

### THREE BUOYS HOUSEBOAT VACATIONS
*710 Riverside, Box 709, Sicamous V0E 2V0*
*250/836-2403, 800/663-2333; www.threebuoys.com*
*Rates: Expensive*
*FYI: Kitchens, microwaves (some boats), barbecues; CD players and hot tubs (some boats); small pets OK (fee)*

A houseboat can make a pretty irresistible vacation, especially if your kids are old enough and able to swim. Even if they're not, you can manage on a houseboat if you take careful precautions (see the sidebar). In recent years, houseboats have acquired new amenities, such as hot tubs, and become larger and more luxurious, although they can still be a tight squeeze. But the prospect of being able to move from gorgeous spot to new gorgeous spot daily on a huge, swimmable lake in hot sunny weather is hard to beat. The novelty alone can make for a cool holiday.

Boats come in different sizes. The largest are about 15-meters long, able to sleep up to 12 people, with one bedroom, a loft, a fold-down dinette and two pullout couches. The bathrooms have showers, and boats can be navigated from outside and inside (if, perish the thought, it should rain).

Fees can be steep. Expect to pay at least $1,500 for smaller houseboats, up to nearly $4,000 for a week on the biggest option during the summer. Still, if two families vacation together, costs become more manageable. And if you choose a trip in spring or fall, your cost will be cut nearly in half.

**66 PARENT COMMENTS**
> *"Kids have lots of fun swimming, going off the water slide*

## The Houseboat Experience

"We have always shared a boat with friends and family. We spend maybe two hours on the move-then you can run the boat right up on a beach for the rest of the day and night (you might share it with two or three other boats). You should be beached by 3 p.m. or you may have to cruise around looking for a spot. Plan on spending two to three hours on the dock on the first day—the captain has to take some training (a half-hour video and talk), and you will make a great many trips up and down the dock with your gear—sleeping bags, pillows, beach gear, food, ice, music, etc.

"The boats can be childproofed (ask staff). We had a two year old along on one trip—she always wore a life jacket (as did all kids under 10) when the boat was moving. Anyone can steer the boats out on the water. Docking is a bit tricky (that's why the boats and docks have big rubber fenders). The trip is much more fun when the weather is good. Campfires on the beach every night were enjoyed by young and old. There's no TV, but there's a tape deck for music. Bring games (cards, Scrabble, etc.) and books (for rain), bedding, beach towels, dish cloths, paper towels, flash light, bug repellant, binoculars, air mattress, lawn chairs, first aid kit, and special cookbooks."

*on the back of the boat."*

*"The holding tank (for the toilet) starts to get fragrant after four days."*

*"The office staff is very professional and helpful."*

*"The kids will enjoy visiting the floating store in the middle of the lake."*

### WHAT TO SEE & DO

If you visit in October, catch the salmon run on the Adams River; it can be viewed at **Roderick Haig-Brown Provincial Park,** which has a visitor center. This is one of the largest salmon spawning grounds in Canada.

*Five km north of Hgwy. 1 at Squilax.*

## PARKS

Salmon Arm has several popular city parks. Take a picnic to **Fletcher Park;** older kids may enjoy skateboarding here (off Highway 1, after 4th Ave., traveling east from Kamloops). **McGuire Lake Park,** (east of town on Highway 1) has a large pond and fountain, and a nice picnic area with ducks, geese, and turtles.

## ANIMALS, ANIMALS

**DeMille's Petting Zoo** gets high marks from parents. There are farm animals large and small for petting.
*3710 10th Ave. SW, Salmon Arm. 250/832-7550.*

# CALENDAR

### SALMON ARM

**FEBRUARY**
Jazz Festival.
International Film Festival.

**MAY**
Grebe Festival.

**JUNE**
Air Show.
Shuswap Rodeo.

**JULY**
Canada Day Children's Festival, Fletcher Park.
Acoustic Festival.

**SEPTEMBER**
Fall Fair.
Harvest Festival.

**OCTOBER**
Roots & Bluegrass Festival.

### SICAMOUS

**JUNE**
Carnival of Arts, 250/836-3057.

**JULY**
Canada Day Parade and Fireworks.

**AUGUST**
Moose Mouse Days, 250/836-3313.

# RESOURCES

### PROVINCIAL PARK WEB SITE
www.elp.gov.bc.ca/bcparks/explore/parkpgs/

**SALMON ARM FOREST DISTRICT**
250/832-1700
Information on wilderness camping.

**SICAMOUS & DISTRICT CHAMBER OF COMMERCE**
110 Finlayson, P.O. Box 346, Sicamous V0E 2V0
250/836-3313

## THE KOOTENAYS

To the east of the Okanagan, the landscape becomes more rugged. The Monashee range separates the Okanagan Valley from the Kootenays—a world of mountains, alpine meadows and valleys, more lakes, and quite a few hot springs. Here you leave the fruit-growing regions behind. Roads are winding, and you definitely know you're in the mountains.

The differences aren't merely in terrain. While the Okanagan region lies squarely within the cultural mainstream, the Kootenays, and especially the Slocan Valley towns of Slocan and Winlaw, have a distinctly countercultural feel. Somewhat off the beaten path (physically and philosophically), east of Highway 97 and south of Highway 1, studded with beautiful provincial parks and lovely towns with unusual histories, this region draws visitors back year after year. The regional center, Nelson, has an established community of artists and craftspeople.

The region's cultural history is interesting and unique. This is silver- and gold-rush country, and many communities arose from the late 19th century population surges that attended the prospectors.

The town of Castlegar is a center of the Doukhobor community, a Russian-originating, pacifist sect that still thrives in British Columbia. In New Denver, a museum tells the story of thousands of Japanese-Canadians interned in camps in B.C. and Alberta during World War II.

A parent reviewer describes area attractions this way: "The natural setting is outstanding. There are rivers, forests, mountains, and natural hot springs. You can hike, canoe, fish, ride, ski, bicycle, or enjoy some of the small towns; see a ghost town, historical sights, and wildlife.

"The West Kootenays have had an influx of a variety of settlers, which accounts for the special flavor of the area. There were First Nations, farmers, miners, Doukhobors. The area includes young people who moved back to the land to live communally and Americans avoiding the draft in the

Vietnam War in the 1960s, and then again young people of the 1990s who want to live in intentional communities in harmony with the natural environment.

"We have found traveling with kids extremely pleasant in this area. We enjoy the diversity and friendliness of the people, along with the heritage towns, the exquisite pristine landscape, and abundance of outdoor activities."

## GETTING THERE

From western or northern British Columbia, you can reach the Kootenays via Highways 3 or 6. Another interesting route is to take Highway 1, the Trans-Canada, east to Highway 23, just west of Revelstoke. Highway 23 goes south along the west shore of Upper Arrow Lake. Cross the lake on the Upper Arrow Lake Ferry that runs from Shelter Bay to Galena Bay, a 30-minute trip, then continue down the east side to Nakusp and Highway 6. This is the route to take from northern B.C. From the junction of Highways 23 and 1 to Nakusp is about 100 kilometers.

If you're traveling from the United States via eastern Washington, one parent reviewer offers these suggestions:

"Take I-90 east to Exit 151, just beyond the town of George. Follow Highway 283 northeast to Ephrata (a good place for a lunch stop; there are several restaurants). Here the name of the road changes to 28. Turn onto Highway 17 north at Soap Lake. Take Highway 17 to Coulee City, then follow Highway 2 east for a couple of miles beyond Creston. Here you can stay on 2 to Davenport and then take 25 north, which you follow along Roosevelt Lake to the Canadian border. You can take the Patterson crossing, Highway 22, or the Waneta crossing, 22A (closes in the evening). Follow 22 through Trail to Castlegar (watch out here; people sometimes get lost). Then follow Highway 3A to Nelson, or if you go to the Slocan Valley, 3A to South Slocan and then north on Highway 6. Traveling with a small child, we usually camp one night."

**ROADSIDE ATTRACTIONS.** If you're following the recommended eastern-Washington route, these attractions make good rest or camping stops:

**SOAP LAKE.** Weather permitting, parent reviewers like to stop for a swim here. The lake is on Highway 17, north of the junction with Highway 28. The water is shallow and feels silky, owing to its high mineral content. The composition of the water is said to be similar to the famous mineral baths at

European spas, and Native Americans value the water for its healing properties. There are public washrooms as well as a playground on the beach.

**DRY FALLS AND SUN LAKES.** East from Highway 17 on Highway 2, this spot makes a good place to camp for the night on your way to the Kootenays. One of the sunniest areas in the state, it can help you dry off after a soggy west-coast winter. The site of a huge (we're talking many times larger than Niagara here) prehistoric waterfall, Dry Falls is an impressive sight. Sun Lakes are popular with campers and offer some services, including showers, a service station, and boat rentals.

**HAWK CREEK.** East from Creston, a few miles northeast of Highway 2, you'll find this other likely camping spot, with a waterfall and the added bonus of bats to watch zigzagging around at night. It's fairly basic: amenities are limited to outhouses and a water pump.

As you follow the east side of Roosevelt Lake up Highway 25, you'll pass great beaches and camping spots (Steamboat Rock is especially popular). Don't miss historic **Fort Spokane** or, if you're in the vicinity on the right night, the laser light show at Grand Coulee Dam (see "Grand Coulee Dam/Dry Falls" in "Washington").

Visitors approaching the Kootenays from eastern Washington or from western British Columbia via Highway 3 have other options, including:

**ROSSLAND.** Just across the border into Canada via Highway 25, Rossland is well known as home of the Red Mountain Ski Area (slopes here have a reputation as best for advanced skiers; this is not the place to take up skiing for the first time.) But it is also home to a cool kid attraction: the **Rossland Museum and Le Roi Goldmine.** Visitors can take a 45-minute guided tour of the mine's tunnel. Visitors are given hard hats to wear; note that the air temperature is a very brisk seven degrees C; bring a jacket.

There are indoor and outdoor exhibits as well, along with a visitor info center and casual restaurant.

*At junction of Hwys. 3B & 22 (the continuation of Hwy. 25 into Canada). 250/362-7722. Open mid-May–mid-Sept., daily, 9 a.m.-5 p.m. Mine tours daily, 9:30 a.m.-3:30 p.m., every half hour, (July-Aug.); every hour and a half (May-June, Sept.) Cost: museum and mine tour, $8/adults, $6/senior 60 & over, $5/student 14 & over, $3/child 6-13, free/under 6, $25/family. If you skip the mine tour and visit only the museum, the cost is 50% less.*

## GETTING AROUND

Once you're in the Kootenays, to hit the region's highlights you'll need to drive in a kind of loop. Take Highway 3 to Castlegar and head north on Highway 6; follow 6 north through Winlaw and Slocan and along the east side of Valhalla Provincial Park, then turn onto 31A at New Denver. You can also follow Highway 6 further north to Nakusp and the Arrow lakes, then retrace your steps back to New Denver and 31A.

On Highway 31A, you'll skirt the southern flank of Goat Range Provincial Park, turn south at Kootenay Lake, then follow the lake down to Kaslo (where the highway loses its "A" and becomes plain Highway 31).

Continuing south along the west side of the lake, you'll pass Ainsworth Hot Springs and two more provincial parks: Kokanee Glacier and West Arm. Continue on to Nelson where you'll find the junction with Highway 6.

Many sidetrips can be taken along this route; ferries cross Kootenay Lake, which is more than 100 km long. All these drives are beautiful, even by B.C. standards, and well worth taking. If your kids are subject to motion sickness, you will almost certainly need to have some remedies on hand. But there are plenty of frequent and interesting stops you can make to break the drive and get fresh air.

The short route, in which you turn onto 31A at New Denver, is about 220 km; but remember, roads can be narrow and winding and they're all two lanes. If you opt for the longer route up to Nakusp and Highway 31, you'll be adding an additional 262 km to your trip.

## CASTLEGAR

Castlegar is an interesting town and makes a good overnight stop for families journeying from western Oregon and Washington. The peaceful environment here can ease your transition from the frantic pace of urban life to the laid-back world of the Slocan Valley.

## PLACES TO STAY

**SANDMAN INN**
*1944 Columbia Ave., V1N 2W7*
*250/365-8444, 800/726-3626*

*Rates: Inexpensive to moderate*
*FYI: Restaurant; indoor pool; pets OK*

This hotel is one of a chain found across B.C. and Alberta. It's conveniently located in downtown Castlegar and a good value. The restaurant, as usual with Sandman Inns, is a Denny's, with the traditional kids' menu and activity booklet.

## WHAT TO SEE & DO

**CASTLEGAR STATION MUSEUM.** This is the original Canadian Pacific Railroad station, dating back to just after the turn of the century. It houses the city museum and contains community archives and a gift shop.

*400 13th Ave. 250/365-6440. Open daily, 9 a.m.-5 p.m. Admission by donation.*

**DOUKHOBOR VILLAGE MUSEUM.** This fascinating museum recreates a communal village of the Doukhobors (the name means "spirit wrestlers" in Russian) who immigrated from Russia, first to Saskatchewan, in 1899, and to British Columbia, a decade later. Doukhobors came to escape religious persecution and were helped in part by the Quaker community, with whom they have much in common. They built communal villages and set up small industries, using a barter system. Their charismatic leader, Peter Verigin, was assassinated in 1924. During World War II, many Doukhobor pacifists were jailed. Today there are still about 30,000 Doukhobors in B.C. A radical branch of the sect, known as the "Sons of Freedom" gained notoriety in Canada for their practice of nudity along with some famous acts of arson. Most Doukhobors do not follow that path.

The museum has several buildings, including the communal house, and many original artifacts; it effectively conveys what life was like in an early Doukhobor settlement.

Nearby are a Doukhobor Bridge, Peter Verigin's tomb, and a statue of Leo Tolstoy, a Doukhobor hero. Ask for directions at the museum. Another Doukhobor village museum is located in Grand Forks, southwest, just north of the Washington-B.C. border, along Highway 3.

*Across from the airport near the junction of Hwys. 3 & 3A. Open May-Sept., daily, 9 a.m.-5 p.m.; other times by appointment. Cost: $3/adult, $2/student, $.50/child, free/preschooler, groups of 10 or more get a 10% discount.*

**ZUCKERBERG ISLAND HERITAGE PARK.** This is a fun spot to explore, where you can let cramped and crabby small people, suffering from car confinement, out for a race around the grounds. The island, at the confluence of the Columbia and Kootenay rivers, is reached via a 150-meter suspension bridge. In addition to the lovely grounds, there's an eclectic assortment of things to investigate: the home of Alexander Zuckerberg, who immigrated from Russia to teach Doukhobor children in the 1930s, a Russian Orthodox chapel, a reconstructed Salish First Nations pit house, and a Hiroshima memorial.

*At the corner of 9th St. & 7th Ave. 250/365-5511. Open May-Aug, daily. Admission by donation.*

## CALENDAR

**JUNE**
Sunfest, 250/365-3386.
**AUGUST**
Oldtime Fiddlers Contest.

## RESOURCES

**DOUKHOBOR WEB SITES**
www.dlcwest.com/~r.androsoff/
www.lightweb.com/doukhobo.htm

**CASTLEGAR VISITOR INFO CENTRE**
1995 6th Ave., V1N 4B7
250/365-6313

## SLOCAN VALLEY

From Highway 3A, take Highway 6 north. Now you're in the heart of the West Kootenays. This was the site of a major silver rush in the 1890s, and some mining continues. Several towns have museums highlighting the boom days, and there's a ghost town, Sandon, to explore near New Denver. Small communities are clustered along the Slocan River. This is a place to explore at a leisurely pace, savoring the beautiful landscape and friendly communities that call it home.

**ROADSIDE ATTRACTIONS.** On Highway 6, along the Slocan River at the tiny town of Passmore (a few kilometers north of the junction with 3A and Slocan Park), look for cars parked along the roadside, then park and follow the trail down to the river; you'll discover a very nice beach that's popular with local kids. The beach is at a river bend, and the water is safe for swimming if you watch out for eddies.

## PLACES TO STAY

### LEMON CREEK LODGE & CAMPGROUND
*7680 Kennedy Road, Box 68, Slocan V0G 2C0*
*250/355-2403*
*Rates: Inexpensive*
*FYI: Restaurant, complimentary breakfast (lodge rooms); shared baths; sauna; Japanese garden; picnic area; kayaking, canoeing, river tubing, mountain bike rentals and packages; guided hikes, snowmobiling, and backcountry ski-touring; smoke-free throughout*

The options at this rustic resort include the lodge's 10 rooms with shared baths, a 28-site campground for tents and RVs, and two cabins: one sleeps four and one sleeps eight. The lodge rooms come with breakfast. Campers get indoor washrooms with hot showers and a covered gazebo. In summer, the restaurant serves meals with fresh-from-the-garden ingredients. There's no kids' menu, but the restaurant will be flexible to accommodate small diners.

## PLACES TO EAT

### HUNGRY WOLF CAFÉ
*Winlaw*
*250/226-7355*
*Hours: Breakfast, lunch, dinner daily*

Hearty, low-priced, good food of all varieties is on the menu here. The kids' bill of fare offers the tried and true. Meat eaters will find plenty to enjoy, while vegetarians large and small can dine on lentil burgers, veggie dogs, and Greek dishes. (Readers of the Quadra Island section will recognize the armadillo eggs.) Works of local artists are on display, and there's occasional weekend musical entertainment. This place is popular on summer evenings, so there may be a wait for a table. Get a feel for the community during your wait by perusing bulletin-board notices for straw-bale house-building workshops or kitten giveaways. Parents give the café high marks for child-friendliness. One noted "When our six year old didn't like the table we were sitting at, he was told in a friendly manner he could sit where he wanted and be served there."

## WHAT TO SEE & DO

**VALHALLA PROVINCIAL PARK.** This wild and lovely park, popular with hikers, extends west of Highway 6 between Slocan and New Denver. There's no car camping, but wilderness camping is allowed. The park is renowned for wildlife including lynx, elk, mountain goats, and—yes—grizzlies. Most trails are challenging to say the least (Valhalla specializes in tall peaks), but there's one good hiking option for families with young kids: follow the trailhead at the south end of Slocan Lake, in Slocan, as far as the small fry are willing to go.

**VALLEY VIEW GOLF COURSE.** Carved out of the pasture on sloping land adjacent to the Slocan River just north of Winlaw, this nine-hole course is relatively short in yardage, well maintained, and offers some golfing challenges. You're welcome to bring small kids as long as you supervise closely. Buy refreshments at the clubhouse. Rates are lower for children.

**WINLAW NATURE PARK.** This park encompasses wetlands along the Slocan River. You'll find a grassy area with swings and restrooms. Locals swim in the river (expect to encounter the occasional skinny dipper). Among the local wildlife spotted here are red hawks and bald eagles. In early summer, mosquitoes may be thick; bring repellant.

*Go left just south of the Hungry Wolf, follow the road by the school over the river, turn right and follow the dirt road about 130 meters past the bridge. From the parking lot, follow the footpath to the boardwalk trail that leads to the river. (There's no railing, so be sure to hold small hands.)*

## RESOURCES

**SLOCAN TOURIST/VISITOR INFO BOOTH**
704 Arlington St., Box 50, Slocan V0G 2C0
250/355-2277

# NAKUSP HOT SPRINGS

Let's face it; hot springs are pretty irresistible to young and old alike. Here in hot-springs country, how can you not take the opportunity to sample at least a few?

## GETTING THERE

Nakusp is about 80 km north of the town of Slocan and 47 km north of New Denver on Highway 6.

**ROADSIDE ATTRACTIONS.** The small, charming historic mining town of **New Denver** definitely merits a stop. There are several museums worth exploring even if the weather is nice. If you have time for only one, make it the **Nikkei Internment Memorial Centre,** with exhibits that tell the story of the 21,000 Japanese-Canadians removed from their homes and forced into internment camps during World War II. Eastern British Columbia was a site of these camps, and here you'll see typical camp accommodation, along with exhibits on Japanese-Canadian history.

*306 Josephine St. 250/358-7288. Open June-Sept.; otherwise, by appointment. Cost: $4/adult; $3/senior & student; $2/child; free/under 6.*

Nearby, you can check out the **Silvery-Slocan Museum,** housed in a century-old Bank of Montreal building, undergoing restoration.

*On Hwy. 31A. 250/358-2201. Open daily (July-Aug.); Sat.-Sun. (Oct.-May). Admission: by donation.*

## PLACES TO STAY

**NAKUSP HOT SPRINGS CEDAR CHALETS**
*Hot Springs Road (12 km north of Nakusp)*
*250/265-4505*
*Rates: Inexpensive*
*FYI: Kitchens; electric heat; small pets OK*

There are only seven units, and they're popular, so you'll need to book ahead. The chalets are roomy and right next door to the hot-springs, but not operated by the same management. There are a few restaurants to the south in New Denver and Nakusp.

**CAMPING.** Opportunities to camp out surround you in this neck of the woods. While the hot springs campground places you squarely in the midst of all the watery action, you may have a more peaceful experience at the provincial park, which is a few kilometers south of town.

**McDONALD CREEK PROVINCIAL PARK**
*RR 3, Site 8, Comp 5, Nelson V1L 5P6*

250/825-3500

*Rates: Inexpensive; cash only; free in April, Oct.; fee, May-Sept. (closed Nov.-March)*

*FYI: Dry toilets; beaches, boat launch; pets OK on leash*

This park is 10 km south of the town of Nakusp on the shores of Upper Arrow Lake.

### NAKUSP HOT SPRINGS CAMPGROUND

*Hot Springs Road (12 km north of Nakusp); Box 280, Nakusp V0G 1R0*

250/265-4528

*Rates: Inexpensive (about $14-16/site)*

*FYI: Flush toilets, hot showers; near pool; pets OK on leash; open mid May-mid Oct.*

This campground is part of the hot-springs establishment, but unlike the hot springs, the campground is closed during the winter. There are 38 sites, and it's lively.

### WHAT TO SEE & DO

**NAKUSP HOT SPRINGS.** There are two hot-spring fed outdoor pools; the smaller is slightly warmer than the larger, and temperatures in each are a few degrees higher in winter than in summer. Kids will probably go for the cooler pool and, thanks to the temperature, never want to leave. There are underwater benches to sit on, and water is never too deep for an adult to stand on the bottom. Small children are welcome to use lifejackets or floatation devices. Parent reviewers observe that warm water seems to spur the children on to make genuine strides in learning and improving their swimming technique. Be sure to rehydrate everyone with plenty of fluids after a session in the pools.

If you can haul the small fry onto dry land for a break, take the 500-meter trail behind the springs, over a hanging bridge crossing a rushing river to a waterfall and the source of the hot springs, where everyone can gaze mesmerized at the hot waters bubbling out of the ground. (Don't get too mesmerized; poison ivy grows luxuriantly here; warning signs illustrate what to look for.)

*Hot Springs Road. 250/265-4528. Open daily, 9:30 a.m.-10 p.m. (June-Sept.); 11 a.m.-9:30 p.m. (Oct.-May). Cost: $5.50/adult, $4.50/senior & youth 6-17, free/under 6, $8/adult day pass, $7/senior & youth day pass.*

**NAKUSP VISITOR INFO CENTRE**
92 W. 6th Ave., P.O. Box 387, Nakusp V0G 1R0
250/265-3808; 800/909-9819
Open daily in summer, 8 a.m.-4 p.m.

## AINSWORTH HOT SPRINGS

The best-known hot springs resort of the Kootenays, Ainsworth is a bargain with remarkably affordable accommodation, more stupendous scenery, and, of course, the deliciously warm waters.

### GETTING THERE

It's about 120 km southeast of Nakusp; retrace your route south on Highway 6, then take 31A to Kaslo, and Highway 31 on to Ainsworth.

**ROADSIDE ATTRACTIONS.** Sandon. On Highway 31A toward Kaslo, this ghost town is not to be missed. The whole town is a museum. Much of the old silver-boom town burned down in 1902; some original buildings remain (the town's population was decimated by the Great Depression and many buildings were swept away in a later flood). The **Sandon Museum** (250/358-2247; open summer to fall; free) tells the town's story. Railway buffs may be interested to learn this was once the terminus of the Kaslo & Slocan Railway, a narrow-gauge mining railway running to Kootenay Lake. The old railbed on the north side of Carpenter Creek has been restored as the **K&S Historic Trail.** Parent reviewers recommend a hike along it where you'll encounter more old buildings, an abundance of wildflowers, and a world-class mountain view.

**KASLO** is an attractive town on the west shore of Kootenay Lake, 47 km east of New Denver, at the junction of highways 31A and 31. Here you'll find some historic buildings, and the S.S. *Moyie*, the oldest intact passenger sternwheeler in the world, now a National Historic Site. Tour this sternwheeler/museum, undergoing loving restoration, on your own or with a guide.

*Docked at the lakefront, next to Visitor Info Centre. 250-353-2525. Open spring-fall, mid-May-mid-Sept., daily, 9:30 a.m.-5 p.m. Cost: $5/adult; $4/senior & student; $2/child 6-13; free/under 6.*

On the first weekend in August, Kaslo Bay Park is host to

the annual jazz festival.
*250/353-7538; kaslojaz@netidea.com.*

## PLACES TO STAY

### AINSWORTH HOT SPRINGS RESORT
*Highway 31, P.O. Box 268, Ainsworth Hot Springs V0G 1A0*
*250/229-4212, 800/668-1171; www.hotnaturally.com*
*Rates: Inexpensive to moderate*
*FYI: Restaurant, kitchens; hot mineral pool, cold plunge, Jacuzzi, cave steam bath; laundry; complimentary hot-springs passes; gift shop*

Most of the rooms here have terrific lake and mountain views. Skiers can unwind in the pools after a day on the slopes. Many rooms have sweeping views of Kootenay Lake. The restaurant gets high marks from parent reviewers.

Except for the last two weeks of December, winter rates are remarkably low. One drawback is small room size—no more than four or at most five people can be accommodated in the rooms here. One parent reviewer recommends the Ainsworth Motel, just down the road, as an alternative.

The pools were originally discovered and enjoyed by First Nations. The larger pool is cooled to child-pleasing temperature, but the biggest draw at the hot springs is likely to be the caves, studded with impressive stalactites formed from the dripping, mineral-rich hot (about 44 degrees Celsius) waters. The water level is about adult-knee deep. The caves are only dimly lit, which adds to their charm, but you'll want to supervise small children closely. Remember to drink plenty of fluids after spending time in the hot water. It can be dehydrating.

### 66 PARENT COMMENTS
*"The glacier-fed cold plunge pool is really cold."*

*"Our kids loved the horseshoe-shaped cave. The cave floor is smooth and the cave is softly lit."*

*"Skiing at Whitewater was great—powder snow and reasonable rates. Blewett Ski hill is very cheap and has a big bunny hill."*

*"Make sure you drink plenty of water here as it's very rich in minerals."*

## WHAT TO SEE & DO

**CODY CAVES PROVINCIAL PARK.** About three kilometers north of Ainsworth Hot Springs, follow the signs from

Highway 31 along about 12 km of gravel road up—and we do mean up—to this interesting park. NOTE: think twice about bringing a motor home or vehicle with low ground clearance along this fairly rough road.

At the park, small spelunkers can satisfy their underground urges on a guided tour through the fascinating world of stalactites, stalagmites, soda straws, waterfalls, flowstones, and draperies. (If you plan a trip here, you might want to bring along a resource book on caves to help you make sense of what you see.)

It is essential to be prepared with warm clothing and appropriate footgear—at the very least sturdy running shoes; hiking boots are even better. Other equipment is provided. No matter what the temperature outside, it will be very cold within the caves. Tours last about an hour. Flashlights are a good idea.

*Follow access road off Hwy. 31. 250/353-2853. Open July-Aug., daily, 10 a.m.-5 p.m. Cost: $12/adult, $8/child. Price includes equipment.*

**Kokanee Creek Provincial Park.** This 235-hectare park is one of the child-friendliest in the region. It features a big playground, plenty of wide open spaces for little ones to explore, and an excellent beach. Parent reviewers report that the water is shallow for a long way out and, consequently, gets quite warm: "Depending on the water level, you can walk 200 to 300 yards out to sand islands in the lake; even our six year old was at most navel-deep in the water."

The park has plenty of grassy campsites, free showers, fire pits, and full hookups. There's a marina, too. Pets are permitted on leash. In summer, the park offers guided walks and interpretive programs, including some for children.

Among the hiking options is the **Old-Growth Trail** (follow signs to trailhead), an easy 1.5-km trail through ancient cedars. You'll reach a nice viewpoint and pass the remnants of the old tramway system that once hauled ore from a mine to the tramway terminus.

*A 20-minute drive south of Ainsworth Hot Springs on Hwy. 3A. 250/825-4421; campground reservations: 800-689-9025.*

Be sure to check out the **West Kootenay Visitor Centre** here. There are displays on local flora and fauna, and regional history, as well as slide shows, films, and children's programs.

*In Kokanee Creek Provincial Park. 250/825-4723. Open daily, 9 a.m.-9 p.m. (July-Aug.); open weekends only, 10 a.m.-4 p.m., (June & Sept.). Admission is free.*

**KOKANEE GLACIER PROVINCIAL PARK.** This park includes some of the high peaks that separate the Slocan Valley from Kootenay Lake. Created in large part to conserve grizzly bear habitat, the park can be accessed from Kokanee Creek Provincial Park and several other routes. Families will find plenty of opportunities for rugged backcountry hiking; while it's not recommended for very young kids, families with teens may enjoy a hike here. One moderate hike takes you past alpine meadows to a 100-year-old mining cabin. Wilderness camping is allowed in the park, and there are several cabins available to sleep in, on a first come, first served basis. Be prepared to camp out.

*Access to the park is from Kokanee Creek Provincial Park, Lemon Creek from Hwy. 6, and several points along Hwy. 31A between Ainsworth Hot Springs and Nelson.*

## NELSON

This town, like most others in the vicinity, was born directly out of the silver and gold rushes of the 1880s. Many original buildings remain intact. In the 1970s, the town undertook an ambitious restoration program so that today these buildings can be seen at their best. While kids may not be especially thrilled by the opportunity to take a long heritage walk around old Nelson, everyone will appreciate the relaxed atmosphere here. This is a beautiful town in an extraordinary setting, shown to advantage in the film *Roxanne*, shot here in 1986.

As the largest community in the area, Nelson offers more amenities than you might expect from a town of only 10,000 residents. The Kootenay School of the Arts has attracted artists and craftspeople of all varieties, and makes a significant contribution to the cultural life of the community. The town sits on the West Arm of Kootenay Lake, close to several provincial parks, with nearby skiing, boating, and hiking opportunities.

### GETTING THERE

Nelson is about 68 km southwest of Kaslo along Highway 31. At Balfour, head west on Highway 3A.

### PLACES TO STAY

**DANCING BEAR INN**
*171 Baker St., Nelson V1L 4H1*
*250/352-7573*
*Rates: Inexpensive; group rates available for parties of six or more*

*FYI: Access to guest kitchen; laundry; ski and storage lockers; smoke-free throughout*

And now for something completely different: this hostel, a member of Hosteling International, offers several styles of accommodation, from dormitory rooms with six beds to family rooms with one double and one twin bed. Rates are exceptionally low, and even lower if you're a member of Hosteling International.

This is a good place to meet other travelers, as the inn attracts guests from around the world. Furnishings are cozy and attractive, and families are welcome.

### VILLA MOTEL

*655 Hwy. 3A; P. O. Box 770, Nelson V1L 5R4*
*250/352-5515*
*Rates: Inexpensive to moderate*
*FYI: Restaurant, kitchens (some units); air conditioning; indoor pool; small pets OK*

Just across the Nelson Bridge, on attractive grounds overlooking Kootenay Lake, this air-conditioned motel welcomes families. If possible, nab a unit with a kitchen and save on family meals.

## PLACES TO EAT

### ALL SEASONS CAFÉ

*620 Herridge Lane*
*250/352-0101*
*Hours: Dinner daily; Sunday brunch*

This smoke-free downtown restaurant in a renovated older house is the place to head for your fine-dining splurge. Prices are high-end but not out of sight (expect to spend about $12-24 for entrées). The menu bills it as "left coast inland cuisine" (read lots of fresh, locally grown ingredients), and it includes yummy-sounding vegetarian options like "Root Vegetable Strata with Carrot & Parsley jus." There's no kids' menu per se, but parent reviewers report that the waitstaff are happy to improvise child-friendly meals. Crayons, coloring books, and sometimes toys are provided. In summer, patio dining is available.

### MAIN STREET DINER

*616 Baker St.*
*250/354-4848*
*Hours: Lunch, dinner Mon.-Sat.; closed Sun.*

We're back in the land of family dining here. The menu is wide-ranging, with hearty burgers, fish and chips, vegetarian entrées, and Greek dishes. There's a kids' menu, and prices are very affordable. The atmosphere is lively and appealing. Dine outdoors on the patio in summer.

**RICKABY'S RESTAURANT**
*524 Vernon Street*
*250-354-1919*
*Hours: Lunch, dinner daily*
This eclectic family restaurant serves up pizza, Tex-Mex dishes, burgers, and pasta. The kids' menu is just what you and they expect: pizza, chicken, burgers, pasta, and an activity-page menu. Prices are low, the atmosphere is casual, and it's full of families.

## WHAT TO SEE & DO

### STROLL & BROWSE

At the Chamber of Commerce, you can pick up walking guides for various tours (guided tours are available in summer). Just wandering downtown is recommended, even if you don't go for the structured approach.

**THE NELSON MUSEUM** has historical exhibits to explore, including First Nations and Doukhobor displays.

*402 Anderson St. 250/352-9813. Open daily, 1-6 p.m. (summer); Mon.-Sat., 1-4 p.m. (remainder of year). Cost: $2/adult, $1/senior & child 5-12, free/under 5.*

If your little ones need room to roam, check out **Lakeside Park** on Kootenay Lake, with its sandy beaches, and picnic and play areas. Also here is **Streetcar 23,** all that remains of Nelson's fleet of streetcars, which operated from the turn of the century through the 1940s. Nicely refurbished by the Nelson Electric Tramway Society, Streetcar 23 is operated by organization volunteers, and runs 2.4 km along Nelson's waterfront.

*At Lakeside Park. 250/352-3971. Operates daily, (Victoria Day-Labour Day); Sat.-Sun. (Labour Day-Thanksgiving (2nd weekend in October) & Easter-Victoria Day.) Cost: $2/adult, $1/senior & youth 6-12, free/under 6.*

**GYRO PARK,** on Gyro Park Road, offers trails through the gardens, a wading pool for kids to splash in, and a good view of the city.

### THE GREAT OUTDOORS

**HIKING. Pulpit Rock** makes a pleasant destination affording a good view of the lake and city. The hike can be fairly steep and is probably best attempted by families with kids of school age and older. Carry water.

*About 122 meters past the eastern end of Nelson Bridge, turn left onto Johnston Road. Parking area is 2 km on the left. Follow the paved road about 30 meters, go right (road is rough) to the trail.*

Check out the nearby provincial parks described in the "Slocan Valley," "Nakusp," and "Ainsworth Hot Springs" sections for more ideas.

**SKIING.** Let's face it; most skiing in this region is geared to the expert, or at least experienced, skier. But **Whitewater Ski and Winter Resort,** renowned for its excellent powder snow, caters to families as well as the hotshots. While it's on the small side, it is well equipped with services that include baby-sitting ($3/per hour per child 18 months and older) and a restaurant. A rental shop can outfit the whole family.

Along with two double chairlifts, there's one handle tow. About 20 percent of the terrain is suitable for beginners. There's a ski school here, with drop-in or long-term classes available for kids and adults.

*About 20 km south of Nelson on Hwy. 6. 250/354-4944; www.skiwhitewater.com/. Cost: half-day pass, $26/adult 19 & over, $20/youth 13-18 & senior 65 & over, $15.50/junior 7-12; full-day pass: $35/adult, $27 youth & senior, $21/junior; 3-day pass: $94/adult, $70/youth & senior; $50/junior; all passes free for children under 6.*

*Lessons: Drop-in half day, lesson only, is $17; lesson & lift are $26; lesson & rentals are $23; full day, lesson only is $27; lesson & lift are $36; lesson & rental are $33.*

*Snowboard lessons and rentals are also offered.*

### EXCURSIONS

**KOOTENAY LAKE FERRY.** To cross the lake and access points east, take the ferry from Balfour (35 km north from Nelson on Hwy. 3A) to Kootenay Bay. Ferry service is frequent and year round. Crossings take 35 minutes. On the other side, Creston, Cranbrook, Kimberley, and the Rocky Mountains await your investigation.

### CALENDAR

**JULY**
Streetfest

**SEPTEMBER**
Heritage Days

## RESOURCES

**NELSON VISITOR INFO CENTRE AND**
**CHAMBER OF COMMERCE**
225 Hall St., Nelson V1L 5X4
250/352-3433; chamber@netidea.com

**CABIN AND COTTAGE RENTALS**
Contact Chamber of Commerce for listings.


# NORTHERN BRITISH COLUMBIA

The wide open spaces begin just north of the lower mainland and extend up to the Alaska and Yukon borders, through thousands of miles of sensational scenery sprinkled with communities large and small, rich in historical interest. The region's long reliance on logging and fishing led to serious economic downturns in the 1980s and '90s, but many communities have begun to successfully redefine themselves as tourist destinations. As the trend continues, access by train and boat is getting easier and more convenient, accommodation options are expanding, and attractions and activities are increasing. For families, there has never been a better time to check out this under-appreciated region practically on our doorstep.

## GETTING THERE

There's simply no unscenic way to get to northern British Columbia. But while all routes are spectacular, some do take longer than others.

**BY AIR.** The fastest and most expensive way to get here is by plane. **Air BC** (800/663-3721 in B.C.; 800/776-3000 in the U.S.) serves Prince George, Quesnel, and Prince Rupert. **Canadian Airlines International** (800/665-1117 in B.C.; 800/426-7000 in the U.S.) serves Prince George and Prince Rupert, while its subsidiary, **Canadian Regional Airlines** (800/665-1117 in B.C.; 800/426-7000 in the U.S.), serves Sandspit, in the Queen Charlotte Islands.

**BY TRAIN.** For a relaxed journey to points north, take the train. **B.C. Rail** (800/339-8752 in B.C.; 800/663-8238 outside B.C. and in the U.S.) connects North Vancouver with Prince George three days a week; the 14-hour trip takes passengers through Whistler and Williams Lake. From Prince George, **VIA Rail** (800/561-8630 in B.C.; 800/561-9181 in the U.S.) trains travel east to Jasper, Alberta, an eight-hour trip. West of Prince George, trains reach the coastal city of Prince Rupert in about 10 hours. All trips are scenic and highly recommended for families.

**BY CAR.** On the shortest routes, driving times are comparable to rail travel. For a straight route east–west across northern B.C., you have only one option: Highway 16, the Yellowhead Highway, a kind of second Trans-Canada, that extends across the province all the way to Manitoba. The B.C. leg runs west from Jasper National Park–Mount Robson Provincial Park on the Alberta–B.C. border, going through Tête Jaune (Yellow Head) Cache, McBride, Prince George, Vanderhoof, Burns Lake, Smithers, and Terrace on the way to Prince Rupert and, hopping across Hecate Strait, to Graham Island.

From Vancouver and other points in the south, two major routes connect northern and southern British Columbia: highways 97 and 5. (The latter is a spur of the Yellowhead Highway.) These highways remain open year round. Other roads can be accessed during the summer or snow-free times of the year.

From Vancouver, the most direct route is east–northeast on the Trans-Canada, Highway 1, to Cache Creek, where you turn north onto Highway 97 to Prince George. For a more scenic trip, follow Highway 99 through Whistler, skirting Garibaldi Provincial Park, and through Pemberton and Lillooet, to join Highway 97. Those approaching from the east can head north on Highway 3 to Highway 97; drivers from the easternmost portion of the province have an additional option: take Highway 3 west to Cranbrook, turn onto Highway 95 north, and follow that route up to the Trans-Canada.

**BY FERRY.** From Port Hardy on northeastern Vancouver Island, **B.C. Ferries** (888/BC-FERRY) offers several sailings per week to and from Prince Rupert. These voyages take 15 hours.

There are plenty of car-rental choices at northern destinations, including the Queen Charlotte Islands, if you opt to leave your car at home.

# PRINCE GEORGE

With a population of 77,000, Prince George is the largest city in the B.C. interior by a fair margin. Positioned at the intersection of highways 97 and 16, and served by VIA and B.C. Rail lines, all roads seem to lead to and through Prince Geroge. Like other Canadian cities that lie far above the international border, it has a distinctive and interesting character that's undiluted by proximity to the United States. The weather, it must be admitted, is not ideal: there are only about 85 frost-free days per year, with some extremely cold days in winter (the average high temperature in January is minus 7.5 degrees C). Summers are another story: comfortably warm, but not hot.

The mighty Fraser River—the same river that eventually flows into the Pacific just south of Vancouver—runs right through town, and several lovely parks offer good views of the river and the city. Big enough to have all the city amenities a family requires, yet small enough so that you can drive completely out of the urban landscape in half an hour, Prince George is well worth investigating.

## GETTING THERE

**BY CAR.** If you push it, you can reach Prince George from Vancouver in 10 to 12 hours, or one very long day. But not only would you miss the scenery and roadside attractions, chances are neither you nor the kids would be in a holiday mood when you arrived. Allow at least two days if possible.

The Coquihalla Highway (Highway 5) runs between Hope, east of Vancouver, and Merritt, where a spur of the Yellowhead Highway runs north to Prince George. While the Coquihalla, a toll road, is fast, it doesn't get high marks from parents owing to the lack of services and amenities along the way. Most will be happier on the Trans-Canada. Unless you're headed to eastern British Columbia, Highway 97 is a better route north than Highway 5, which bends far to the east.

**BY TRAIN.** The route is gorgeous, the train is comfortable, and the price of your ticket includes all meals, plus snacks. How can you go wrong?

The *Cariboo Prospector* is a fun ride, but at 14 hours, it's a long one. Luckily there's lots to see; from the moment you depart from North Vancouver (tunnel buffs will enjoy this part) and head up to Squamish, Lillooet, and Whistler, mountains and breathtaking scenery are your constant companions. Eventually, the landscape broadens out and sweeping vistas appear—you're in the Cariboo, high-plateau cattle country studded with windswept lakes and fissured by deep canyons. At **Williams Lake,** if there's time, get out and browse through the train station's interesting craft gallery. But don't get so engrossed that you let the train leave without you, as happened to one parent reviewer.

The kids will be enthralled by some of the high trestle bridges. Just north of Williams Lake one of the world's highest railroad bridges, the Deep Creek trestle, crosses 312 feet above the creek. This is where the train rejoins the Fraser River and follows it through Quesnel to Prince George. The majestic river, with high tablelands rising in steppes above it, is mesmerizing. For the best views, sit on the left side of the train when heading north.

*800/339-8753 (in B.C.); 800/663-8238 (outside B.C. and in the U.S.); 604/984-5500 (Vancouver area); www.bcrail.com. Trains runs year round. Between North Vancouver and Lillooet, trains run daily; from Lillooet to Prince George, trains run Sun., Wed., and Fri.; from Prince George to Lillooet, trains run Mon., Thurs., and Sat. Trains depart North Vancouver and Prince George at 7 a.m. Cost: One way: $194/adult, $175/senior, $117/child 2-12, $39/under 2.*

### PLACES TO STAY

**ESTHER'S INN**
*1151 Commercial Dr., V2M 6W6*
*250/562-4131, 800/663-6844*
*Rates: Inexpensive*
*FYI: Two restaurants; full kitchens (some units); indoor pool; access to health club with three-story water slide ($6.50/guest); pets occasionally permitted (ask first)*

Some inspired individual realized that what Prince George needed was a South Seas-style family resort, complete with banana and palm trees, steamy tropical landscaping, waterfalls, streams, and fountains. *Voilà!* Welcome to Esther's Inn: northern B.C.'s take on Fiji. From the outside, it looks like a warehouse; inside, it's two stories of hotel rooms and suites built around two connected courtyards filled with watery entertainment: a pool, three hot tubs (one is swimming-pool size), and restaurants interspersed amid the greenery. Benches are set along jungle paths. The air is laden with moisture and the sound of happy kids cavorting in the water.

Rooms are comfortable, but nothing special. The real draw

is the courtyard. Off-season, your fellow guests may well include local families taking a break from the cold.

The restaurants are reasonably priced, and the food is fine. There's a children's menu offering the classics; kids six to 10 years old get the salad bar, buffet, and Sunday brunch at a lower price.

While you have to pay to use it, the three-story health club has just about everything fitness aficionados need. The water slide is closed in winter.

**❝❝ PARENT COMMENTS**

> *"It gets a little steamy from all this water, but it's kind of nice after the dry, gray cold outside (we were here in November). It has a funky charm and the cheery staff reflect it. It's a place with attitude. There's a thatched-roof restaurant that spills out onto the courtyard and plays South Seas music. Everyone has a smile here; you can't help it."*

**RAMADA HOTEL**
*444 George St., V2L 1R6*
*250/563-0055, 800/830-8833*
*Rates: Moderate to expensive*
*FYI: Restaurant (kids 12 and under eat free); refrigerators (some units); indoor pool; fitness equipment (daily, 7 a.m.-11 p.m.); modems; small pets OK*

This is Prince George's flagship hotel. Very comfortable and well positioned within walking distance of the VIA Rail station (but about 20 km from the B.C. Rail station), the Ramada welcomes both families and business travelers. Many units have been remodeled, and more renovations are planned in future; rooms and suites are spacious. The restaurant is reasonably priced; dinner specials are a good value. You can access all of downtown Prince George on foot from here.

**❝❝ PARENT COMMENTS**

> *"There isn't a lot of 'atmosphere' here, but it's very comfortable; and after we got off the train (after 14 hours), comfort was our top priority. The hot tub and sauna were especially welcome."*

## PLACES TO EAT

**CAFÉ VOLTAIRE**
*1685 3rd Ave. (in Books & Company)*
*250/563-6637*

*Hours: Lunch, dinner daily*

Tucked into a far corner of Books & Company, this wonderful café could easily escape your notice altogether. That would be a pity, because it's one of the most charming bistros in a town that has a lot of good ones.

From quiches and sandwiches to salads and baked goods, everything here is tasty. A literary allusion is embedded in the name of every dish, from Miss Marple's Lemon Bars to Salman's Saffron Salad. But however fancy the names, plenty contain the simple, straightforward ingredients our small food critics expect. Juices, soft drinks, and teas are available, and, of course, espresso drinks. (Like Seattle, Prince George has fallen in love with the bean, and this café serves some of the best java in the city.) When you're tired of browsing the bookshelves, have a bite to eat, and then browse some more.

### THE PASTRY CHEF
*380 College St.*
*250/564-7034*
*222-100 Tabor Blvd.*
*250/564-7748*
*5220 Domano Blvd., College Heights*
*250/964-4161*
*Hours: 9 a.m.-5 p.m. Mon.-Sat.*

Although it's at the center of Prince George's somewhat depressed downtown, this bustling, European-style bakery couldn't be busier if it were in Toronto or New York. It's always packed with shoppers, and for good reason: The breads and baked goods are absolutely wonderful. The tone is distinctly continental; try a Black Forest ham and German butter-cheese sandwich on flax bread. The cookies and tarts are to die for. The selection of take-out options includes drinks. Prices are surprisingly low. You can't eat here, but you can order a take-out lunch and pick up some delectable snacks.

### WHAT TO SEE & DO
### STROLL & BROWSE

When you're staying at the Ramada, just go out the front door and turn right onto George Street. Otherwise, head downtown to George and 3rd. You'll find all kinds of interesting shops and cafés. If you're running low on small-fry entertainment, check out **Rainbow Dreams** (345 George St.; 250/563-3932), which has an excellent selection of toys and games.

Be sure to visit the **Native Art Gallery** (1600 3rd Ave.; 250/614-7726). Located in the Native Friendship Centre, the gallery can introduce you to the culture of the Carrier peoples, the First Nations of this area. In addition to exhibited artworks and gifts for sale, the gallery carries many books, including some for children, about B.C. First Nations.

While larger cities to the south struggle to support even one independent bookseller, Prince George has two—and both are excellent. **Books & Company** (1685 3rd Ave.; 250/563-6637) is large, well stocked, and right downtown. Visit at lunchtime, and dine in their café (see "Places to Eat: Café Voltaire"). **Mosquito Books** (131-1600 15th Ave., in the Parkwood Place Mall; 250/563-6495), somewhat smaller, is an excellent resource, too.

**Pine Centre Mall,** off Highway 97 on Massey Drive, is billed as the largest mall in the interior of the province. There are more than 100 stores and services here, including plenty of fast food.

### PARKS

**CONNAUGHT HILL PARK.** Sited on a hill rising above downtown, this park features lovely flower gardens and an impressive view of the city and environs. Since the surrounding region is quite flat, the view is a long one. This is a good spot for a picnic.

*From downtown, go south on Queensway, turn right onto Connaught Dr., and go up the hill to Caine Dr.; turn right.*

**FORT GEORGE PARK.** This large city park sits on the banks of the Fraser River, right downtown. Site of the regional museum (see "Museums" below), it contains a First Nations burial ground. There's also a playground, a picnic and barbecue area, and lots of play space. Most kid-friendly of all is the 1912 miniature steam train that runs weekends and holidays in the summer; rides are $1.

*Enter at the east end of 20th Ave.*

### MUSEUMS

**FRASER—FORT GEORGE REGIONAL MUSEUM.** This delightful two-story museum offers hands-on science exploration and historical exhibits. Installations highlight the region's past, with a re-creation of a general store and an authentic movie theater showing silent films. Traveling exhibits vary (in 1998 this was the only museum in western North America to snag a *Titanic* exhibit of artifacts salvaged from the shipwreck immediately after the sinking). But whatever temporary exhibits may be passing through, kids will enjoy the permanent Northwoods Explorations Gallery, especially its small collection of engaging animals, including the corn snakes, Peaches and Cream. Sally the turtle wins hands down for personality; it's not uncommon to encounter her ambling down the ramp from the second floor to investigate the museum on her own. The gift shop sells interesting educational toys.

*20th & Queensway (in Fort George Park). 250/562-1612. Open daily, 10 a.m.-5 p.m. Cost: $4.50/adult, $3.25/senior & student, $2.25/child 3-12, free/under 3, $8/family (two adults & up to four children).*

**PRINCE GEORGE RAILWAY AND FOREST INDUSTRY MUSEUM.** This museum, appropriately sited north of the train yards and close to downtown, is a work in progress; more exhibits are planned. The big draw for kids is the reconstructed 1914 train station and five passenger cars to explore.

*850 River Road. 250/563-7351; www.pgrfm.bc.ca. Open May-mid-Oct., 10 a.m.-5 p.m. Cost: $4.50/adult, $3.75/senior & student, $2/child, $12/family.*

**SPECTATOR SPORTS**

In winter, the Western Hockey League's **Prince George Cougars** play at the Prince George Multiplex.

*2187 Ospika Blvd. 250/561-7777. Call for schedules and prices.*

**SWIMMING**

**AQUATIC CENTRE.** This impressive new civic center offers public swimming.

*1770 Munro St. 250/561-7787. Open daily; hours vary, but usually 6:15 a.m.-9 p.m. Cost: $4.50/adult; $3.50/senior, student, & youth 13-18; $2.75/child 3-12. Family rates: $3.50/first adult, $2.50/all others. Passes available. Kids six & under must be accompanied and supervised by an adult.*

**FOUR SEASONS LEISURE POOL.** Located downtown, this pool welcomes the public.

*700 Dominion St. 250/561-7636. Open daily; hours vary, call for details. Cost: $3.85/adult 19 & over, $2.90/senior & youth 13-18, $2.40/child 3-12, $2.90/special-needs; family rates: $2.90/first adult, $2.10/all others. Monthly passes available. Kids six & under must be accompanied and supervised by an adult.*

**EXCURSIONS**

**QUESNEL** is a charming town of 8,500, about 116 km south of Prince George on Highway 97. From here, many travelers head east on the famous Cariboo Wagon Road to visit the historic towns of **Barkerville** (site of the province's gold rush in 1862) and **Wells.** There's plenty of child-friendly fun to be had here, from exploring the reconstructed gold rush community to panning for gold. But Quesnel is probably best known as the gateway to **Bowron Lake Provincial Park.** The park, also a wildlife sanctuary, encloses a diamond-shaped series of lakes that are a popular destination for canoeing enthusiasts worldwide. The full canoe route is challenging, but shorter, easier routes can be undertaken. You can camp May through September at Bowron Lake Provincial Park and May through October at **Barkerville Provincial Park;** call 250/398-4414 for reservations.

Quesnel itself is also worth a look, with historic buildings and interesting quirky shops, galleries, and cafés. Most are found on Reid Street.

**Put Spice in Your Life** (331 Reid St.; 250/992-5222) offers fresh herbs and spices, teas, and a vast and eclectic selection of cookbooks new and old (the kids can look at the selection of toys and talk to the affable owner while you browse). **Carryall Books** (329 Reid St.; 250/992-6826) is bigger than it looks from outside; it sells children's books and books of interest about the region.

**Terry's Art Gallery** (351 Reid St.) has a great selection of local arts and crafts, including First Nations work. To recharge everyone's batteries, head for popular **Granville's Coffee** (383 Reid St.) for a restorative potion. Delicious baked goods will perk up the small fry.

Should your family get hooked on the Gold Rush era, you may want to continue your investigations at Wells and Barkerville, which offer more historic sightseeing potential. Wells is 51 km east of Quesnel; Barkerville is 85 km east of Quesnel. Both are on Highway 26.

**CALENDAR**

**FEBRUARY**
Mardi Gras of Winter: A midwinter festival, 250/564-3737.

**MARCH**
Dance Festival: An eclectic variety of dance performances from folk to tap and ballet.

Music Festival: Music of all kinds, including voice and instrumental.

**MAY**

Canadian Northern Children's Festival: Free festival includes theater, music, puppets, and face painting, 250/562-4882.

**AUGUST**

Ol' Sawmill Bluegrass Jamboree.

Prince George Exhibition: Regional agricultural fair, 250/563-4096.

Prince George Sandblast: Skiers race down the sandy banks of the Nechako River.

### RESOURCES

**TOURISM PRINCE GEORGE**

1198 Victoria Street, Prince George V2L 2L2
250/562-3700; 800/668-7646; www.pgonline.com

**QUESNEL VISITOR INFO CENTRE**

703 Carson Ave. (in Le Bourdais Park), Quesnel V2J 2B6
250/992-8716

### BOOKS

*The Boy Who Snared the Sun: A Carrier (Dakelh) Legend,* by Catherine Bird. Yinka Dene Language Institute, 1994.
*Cheryl's Potlatch,* by Sheila Thompson. Yinka Dene Language Institute, 1990.


## PRINCE RUPERT

This gem of a city, with a population of about 17,000, sits more than 800 kilometers north of Vancouver, but you'd never guess it from the city's mild maritime climate. Facing northwest on Kaien Island, at the eastern end of Dixon Entrance and the mouth of the Skeena River, Prince Rupert is the last major Canadian port before Alaskan waters.

Like other B.C. coastal communities, this one presses right up against the mountains, its streets rising in steep tiers above the waterfront. When approached by sea, it's especially striking. Even if you don't plan to fly, consider taking a round-trip ride on the airport shuttle ($18/adult, $10/senior and child under 12 for same-day return; 250/624-3355) to Digby Island, where the airport is located. This scenic bus journey, half an hour each way, includes a ferry ride. The driver acts as tour guide, dispensing interesting facts about the region. If you have a car, you can drive onto the ferry; call for rates.

The Titanic buffs in your family may be interested to learn that Prince Rupert was founded by 19th-century Canadian magnate Charles Hayes, general manager of the Grand Trunk Pacific Railway, who perished in the great ship disaster. His dreams for making Prince Rupert a major seaport like Vancouver went down with him.

Today, this city, struggling to free itself from overdependence on a depressed fishery and logging industry, has much to offer families at a remarkably low price. With one of the highest populations of Native Canadians in any B.C. city, it affords a good introduction to the culture of the region's First Nations, from the totem poles that grace streets and parks to the intricate architectural design of the City Hall. Prince Rupert makes a good rest stop en route to or from the Queen Charlotte Islands, points east in the province, or north to Alaska.

## GETTING THERE

**BY AIR.** **Canadian Airlines** (800/665-1177 in B.C.; 800/426-7000 in the U.S.) flies frequently between Vancouver and Prince Rupert.

**Taquan Air** (800/627-8800; 800/770-8800) offers scheduled service and "flightseeing" charters from Prince Rupert to Ketchikan, Alaska, a 45-minute flight.

Be warned: it is common, at pretty much any time of year, for Prince Rupert's airport to be fogged in. At such times, flights may be delayed, sometimes for hours. This can be a serious inconvenience for passengers leaving the city, since the airport is out on isolated Digby Island with little for young ones to do. If you are traveling by air, pay close attention to the weather report, and pack a few extra toys and snacks, just in case.

**BY CAR.** From Prince George, Highway 16, the Yellowhead Highway, takes you across 600 km of breathtaking scenery. Points along the way include Vanderhoof, Fort Fraser, Endako, and the lovely district surrounding Burns Lake, all offering a host of recreational opportunities. Continuing west, the road passes through the Bulkley Valley and the popular resort and forest-industry town of Smithers, lodged in the shadow of impressive Hudson Bay Mountain.

At its northernmost point, the road passes through the Hazeltons and Kitwanga. Here, you can make a detour north onto Highway 37 to visit Stewart, the northernmost B.C. port that's ice-free all year, and Hyder, just across the Alaska border. These adjacent sister cities lie at the northern tip of the Portland Canal. Highway 37 itself continues north to join with the Alaska Highway, another adventure waiting to happen.

Back on Highway 16, from Kitwanga the road bends south and west and winds along the banks of the wide and ever-more-beautiful Skeena River. After you reach the town of Terrace, the final 153-km stretch to Prince Rupert traverses some of the world's loveliest terrain.

**BY RAIL.** The *Skeena*, run by **VIA Rail,** travels east–west between Jasper, Alberta, and Prince Rupert, three times a week, in two stages. In either direction, the trip takes two days; those going the full distance spend a night in Prince George. Travelers on B.C. Rail from Vancouver, or other points south, arrive in Prince George in the evening and depart on the *Skeena* in the morning, either east to Jasper or west to Prince Rupert. Both B.C. Rail and VIA Rail trains run during daylight hours, so passengers can see as much of the view as possible. This also works well for kids. If all goes well, the trains arrive at their destinations before 9:30 p.m.

The view from the train is wonderful, with many tunnels and exciting trestle bridges along the way. When traveling west from Prince George, you'll want to sit on the left side of the train for the best views. Should you end up with less than optimal seating, you can head for the scenic dome car that affords passengers a sweeping view of river, lakes, and mountains.

Unlike B.C. Rail, on the *Skeena* your ticket price does not include meals. In summer, there's a dining car along with the lounge car that sells snacks; in winter, you're stuck with the limited offerings of the lounge car. The lounge has a TV/VCR, and if you supply kids' videos, the staff will run them for you, should the scenery cease to enthrall the small fry.

*VIA Rail, 800/561-8630 (in Canada); 800/561-9181 (in the U.S.); www.viarail.ca. From Prince George to Prince Rupert, the train departs Thurs., Sat., and Mon. at 7:45 a.m.; from Prince Rupert to Prince George, the train departs Wed., Fri., and Sun. at 8 a.m. Cost: One way, with advance purchase of one week or more for Prince George to Prince Rupert:*

*$67.41/adult, $60.99/senior, $53.50/student 12-17, $34.24/child, 2-11. June 1-Oct. 21, the Totem Class is available; at a higher cost, it includes meals.*

**BY SEA.** If you're traveling to or from Alaska, the **Alaska Marine Highway System** operates ships between Prince Rupert and points north: Skagway, Ketchikan, Wrangell, Petersburg, Sitka, Hyder, Stewart, Juneau, and Haines.

*250/627-1744, 800/642-0066; call for details of sailings.*

From the south, Prince Rupert is served by **B.C. Ferries.** The trip from Port Hardy takes passengers through the beautiful Inside Passage.

*250/386-3431; 888/BC-FERRY. Service mid-May-mid Oct. Call for schedule; ferries depart in either direction at 7:30 a.m. and reach their destination at 10:30 p.m. Cabins are available. Cost: One way: $214/car, $356/RV, $104/adult, $52/child; cabins are $43-52, more for overnight use (on round trips).*

## PLACES TO STAY

### THE CREST HOTEL
*222 W. 1st Ave., V8J 3P6*
*250/624-6771, 800/663-8150; www.cresthotel.bc.ca*
*Rates: Inexpensive to moderate*
*FYI: Two restaurants; outdoor hot tub (under 16 must be accompanied by adult); steam room, fitness equipment for adults; pets OK*

It's not often that the most comfortable and luxurious hotel in town is also the most child-friendly, so make the most of this terrific establishment. Try to get one of the rooms overlooking the harbor, with bay windows and cushioned window seats. The rooms are comfortable, and the staff is accommodating to families. Even if you don't use them, check out the exercise facilities downstairs; they're literally carved out of the rock the hotel is built on.

The Crest hosts conferences and is selected by many cruise and rail package tour operators as the place to billet their passengers. You'll need reservations well in advance unless you're traveling off-season.

**66 PARENT COMMENTS**

*"There was a young, probably middle school, hockey team staying in the hotel. Several kids passed the time practicing shots in the hallway, which was long and wide. The staff let them do this, while keeping an eye on them to make sure they*

*didn't disturb other guests."*

*"The coffee shop does a great breakfast."*

*"When our rental car got a flat tire, the front-desk staff helped us cope admirably."*

### EAGLE BLUFF B&B

*201 Cow Bay Road, V8J 1A2*
*250/627-4955, 800/833-1550; www.citytel.net/eaglebed*
*Rates: Inexpensive*
*FYI: Full breakfast; laundry facilities; private baths (some units)*

In the heart of trendy Cow Bay, the owners of this charming old house welcome families. It's right on the waterfront, and the friendly, knowledgeable hosts can help you get your bearings.

### RAINFOREST B&B

*706 Ritchie St., V8J 3N5*
*250/624-9742, 888/923-9993; Rain4est@citytel.net*
*Rates: Inexpensive*
*FYI: Full breakfast; boat charters*

Set in a residential neighborhood, this B&B will make you feel right at home. There's an extra-big room, with ensuite bath, that can accommodate a large family, along with several smaller rooms. The principal family-friendly feature is the large lounge with kitchen, available for use by guests. The owners have a boat, and you can arrange for them to take your family out on whale-watching and fishing excursions. Prices are quite reasonable; $300 will buy you a half-day boat trip with crew and lunch.

## PLACES TO EAT

### BOULET'S SEAFOOD AND CHOWDER HOUSE

*909 3rd Ave. W. (in the Pacific Inn)*
*250/624-9309*
*Hours: Dinner daily*

On the ground floor of this simple hotel is an excellent seafood restaurant. It's modest and fairly quiet (probably not the best choice for wired kids), but popular with families. The mussels here are superb. They're flown out, for some reason, all the way from Prince Edward Island. (Can you say, "Coals to Newcastle"?) Three kinds of chowder are served. While there's no children's menu, all but the fussiest little diners should find something acceptable.

### COWPUCCINO'S
*25 Cow Bay Road*
*250/627-1395*
*Hours: Lunch, snacks daily*

It has to be admitted: Prince Rupert gets rained on a lot. If it happens to you, raise your spirits and dry off with the rest of the throng at this bustling Cow Bay bistro full of families, rowdy but cheery children, and diehard latte-lovers. The pastries and desserts are wholesome yet fabulous. The scones, muffins, cakes, and Nanaimo bars are good, and the five-fruit crisp, heated up and topped with whipped cream, should help chase away rainy-day blues.

### CREST WATERFRONT RESTAURANT
*222 1st Ave. (in the Crest Hotel)*
*250/624-6771*
*Hours: Dinner daily*

It's fine dining, no question. But the restaurant, like the hotel, has undergone a serious reconstruction since the long-ago days when the menu specialized in frozen snow crab and steak. Today, a sophisticated, fairly high-priced menu offers good Pacific Rim cuisine. Watch the sun set over the water while you dine. There is a children's menu, but this is probably not a terrific choice for very young kids. The hotel's coffee shop is a better bet for the smallest set if you want to dine in the hotel.

### GALAXY GARDENS
*844 3rd Ave. W.*
*250/624-3122*
*Hours: Breakfast, lunch, dinner daily; dim sum on Sunday, 11:30 a.m.-2 p.m.*

This pleasant, moderately priced Chinese family restaurant has a huge menu, but offerings are uneven. Your best bet is to ask for recommendations or closely monitor what the regulars are eating. Dim sum is a good option. Try the fried bread, little crispy chunks that will appeal to kids; dunk them in a bowl of congee (rice gruel—think Cream of Rice). An assortment of aquariums provides youngsters with something to watch while they wait.

### GREEN APPLE
*301 McBride*
*250/627-1666, 250/624-3366*
*Hours: Lunch, dinner, Mon.-Sat.*

You can choose halibut or cod for your fish and chips at this modest little place, around the corner from the Museum of Northern British Columbia. Either way, it's fresh and delicious, and portions are huge. The chips are homemade. There are also burgers and onion rings, chips with gravy, and—for the shellfish enthusiast—scallops, prawns, and oysters. Service is fast and friendly. There are a few tables, but if the weather cooperates, you might do better to order take-out and have a picnic at the Pacific Mariners Waterfront Park.

### TIM HORTON'S
*636 2nd Ave. W.*
*250/624-2999*
*Hours: 24 hours daily*

When do families need a restaurant that's open 24 hours? When they have to take a ferry to the Queen Charlotte Islands or a plane to Vancouver that's been delayed by fog, that's when! Canadians are familiar with this nationwide doughnut-shop chain, but this one stands out, and not only when there's no alternative. For a quick lunch, try their sausage rolls. If you're here in the wee hours, you'll find the coffee excellent, while the freshly made "cruellers" (their spelling) and walnut butter tarts can help boost your energy level.

### ZORBA'S TAVERNA
*715 2nd St.*
*250/624-6999*
*Hours: Dinner daily*

Another Canadian Greek-Italian hybrid, Zorba's is billed as a tavern, but looks and feels like a family restaurant. Choose from among the 44 varieties of pizza, or try the Greek food. Child-pleasing spaghetti dishes are a good choice as well.

## WHAT TO SEE & DO

### STROLL & BROWSE

**COW BAY.** In recent years, Prince Rupert has redeveloped Cow Bay, once a dismal industrial waterfront, into a charming shopping district with renovated historic buildings, wonderful restaurants and cafés, shops, and galleries. If you're staying at Eagle Bluff B&B, you're in the midst of it; from downtown, it's a short walk down 3rd Avenue to Cow Bay Road.

Amid the brightly painted buildings, kids will notice the cow motif: From street lamps and garbage cans to telephone kiosks, telephone poles, and fire hydrants, everything is cow-patterned in black and white.

Check out Eagle Wind Native Arts, the Cow Bay Gift Gallery, and the Loft, all on Cow Bay Road. The Loft is home to an interesting pottery studio and sushi bar—the studio may engage the small fry's interest long enough for you to sample a piece or two of sushi.

If you're traveling with older kids, you may want to try a meal at the tiny, charming waterfront **Cow Bay Café** (205 Cow Bay Road; 250/627-1212). The menu is small and elegant; the food is excellent.

**DOWNTOWN.** You can gauge the gloomy state of much of Prince Rupert's economy by the empty storefronts on 2nd and 3rd Avenues. But there is also plenty to see and celebrate. Many attractive, well-maintained historic buildings give the city character. Take a look at the **City Hall** on 3rd Avenue, an impressive two-story, cream-colored building accented with handsome First Nations ornamentation. The city is dotted with totem poles and other reminders that this is home to a substantial population of first peoples.

The town's bookstore, **Star of the West** (518 3rd Ave. W.; 250/624-9053), is first rate and offers a wide selection of books for all tastes. There's an art gallery in the back, too.

### PARKS

**PACIFIC MARINERS MEMORIAL PARK.** This waterfront park, next door to the Museum of Northern British Columbia, contains a small playground, picnic tables, and a thought-provoking memorial. A modest wall of bricks lists the names of Prince Rupert's fishers and sailors who have given their lives to the sea, in war and peacetime. Kids may be intrigued by a prominent feature of the park: the *Kazu Maru*. This boat was lost at sea in Japan and later washed ashore in the Queen Charlotte Islands. Its owner, a retired Japanese civil servant, had been a resident of Prince Rupert's sister city, Owase. His widow came to dedicate this memorial park.

### MUSEUMS

**FIREHALL MUSEUM.** Next to the fire station on 1st Avenue, a stone's throw from the Crest Hotel, this tiny but irresistible museum contains an original 1925 REO Speedwagon (before the rock band, there was the fire engine) and other interesting and curious artifacts of Prince Rupert's noble firefighting past.

*250/627-4475. Open by request; just ring the doorbell next door at the fire station and someone will come and open it up for you to check out. Free.*

**KWINITSA RAILWAY MUSEUM.** Down by the VIA Rail terminal on the waterfront, you can tour an original Pacific Grand Trunk Railway station that was moved to this location. Inside, exhibits highlight its history. Outside, there's a sculpture of mother-and-calf killer whales.

*On the waterfront, next to the VIA Rail Station. 250/624-3207. Open daily, 9 a.m.-noon and 1-5 p.m. (summer). Admission by donation.*

**MUSEUM OF NORTHERN BRITISH COLUMBIA.** This superb museum is worth a good long look. It's housed in the beautiful waterfront complex that's also home to the Tsimshian Tribal Council, next to the Pacific Mariners Memorial Park. Traveling exhibits augment an excellent permanent collection that includes unique pieces such as a huge, wooden mortuary bear sculpture, antique soul catchers, a very fine Chilkat blanket, Haida argillite (the soft black stone that only Haida carvers are permitted to work), and some incredible beadwork. Installations showcase the history of the Tsimshian people and later settlers. The room facing the harbor contains three rugged totem poles; approaching them down the length of the museum is an awesome experience. The superb gift shop features an especially good selection of First Nations jewelry, and prices are reasonable. A block away you'll find a carving shed where First Nations carvers create their works; check it out in summer.

*1st & McBride. 250/624-3207; 800/667-1994. Open Mon.-Sat., 9 a.m.-8 p.m.; Sun., 9 a.m.-5 p.m. (summer); Mon.-Sat., 10 a.m.-5 p.m. (winter).Cost: $5/adult, $2/student, $1/child 6-11, free/ under 6; group rates available.*

### SWIMMING

**EARL MAH AQUATIC CENTRE.** Water, water everywhere, yet nowhere to swim! Prince Rupert has a mild climate, but it doesn't afford much in the way of warm, sandy oceanfront. So if your kids need a splash or two, head for this aquatic complex where they can be assured of quality time in the wet stuff. There's also a whirlpool, sauna, and workout area.

*1000 McBride St. 250/627-SWIM. Public swimming daily; call for details. Cost: $3.90/adult, $2.10/youth 13-18, $1.65/senior & child 1-12, $3.90/family.*

### THE GREAT OUTDOORS

Looking for a family hike appropriate for all ages? Kaien Island is home to some great options.

**OLIVER LAKE.** Follow a boardwalk trail through an odd, dwarf forest—bonsai in its natural habitat—to a beaver dam and lodge. In summer, guided hikes are offered.

*Take McBride toward Terrace; follow signs to Oliver Lake, about 4 km out of town. 250/628-3298.*

**BUTZE RAPIDS.** A little farther along the highway out of town is Butze Rapids, where four hikes can be accessed from the parking lot. The 18-km trail to Mount Hayes and the 9.6-km hike to Mount Oldfield are classified as somewhat challenging and best not attempted unless your kids are older and experienced hikers, although you can certainly follow the trails part of the way. Tall Trees is a nice but strenuous 3-km loop hike, with some steep terrain. Pick up a trail guide to help you identify the flora. Like the other two, this hike works best for older kids and adults.

The fourth hike, to Butze Rapids, is perfect for all ages. The 4-km loop trail runs east to Grassy Bay. Twice a day, reversing tides churn the waters into a boiling caldron. If you're here at the right time (check the tide tables at the Tourist Info office), you can view this impressive sight. The trail is well maintained by the city and features signs identifying the plants and how they are used by First Nations people. Hikers soon descend into old growth and moss-covered rain forest. This lush terrain turns into wetlands, open bog meadows with stunted shore pines, back to dense forest, and finally beach. Some locals use these trails as jogging paths; the ground is nice and springy. Here and there are picnic tables, but no washrooms.

*Take McBride out of town toward Terrace; follow signs to Butze Rapids and park in the parking lot on the south side of the highway.*

### EXCURSIONS

**NORTH PACIFIC CANNERY VILLAGE MUSEUM.** Don't be fooled by the rather dull name. This museum offers a unique and fascinating look at what was, for many years, an important way of life along the entire Pacific Northwest coast. Now a National Historic Site, the North Pacific Cannery dates back to 1889. Reconstructed buildings (including the old canning lines) and live performances bring this colorful history to life. It's a multi-cultural experience: First Nations, Chinese, Japanese, and European workers and their families all contributed to building the industry. The museum includes a café and gift shop.

*In Port Edward. Take the Port Edward turnoff on Hwy. 16; drive 6 km on Skeena Dr. 250/628-3538. Open May-Sept., daily, 9 a.m.-6 p.m. Cost: $6/adult, $3/youth, free/under 7; group rates available on request.*

After you've explored the museum, you may want to head out on the Yellowhead Highway (Highway 16), which follows the **Skeena River** toward Terrace. The drive is gorgeous. Prince Rupert may seem of a piece with the coastal culture to the south, but once you turn east, you realize you're in the higher latitudes. The Skeena River has a glacial, arctic feel to it—huge boulders are scattered here and there along the riverbed, and hills rise up on either side. Be sure to stop and enjoy the view at one of the frequent vistas with parking lots. Some are equipped with picnic tables and outhouses.

## CALENDAR

### MARCH
Children's Festival, 250/624-9118.

### JUNE
Seafest & First Nations Culture Days, 250/624-9118, 250/627-8888.

### JULY
Canada Day celebrations, Pacific Mariners Memorial Park, 250/624-9118.

### DECEMBER
Winterfest, 250/624-9118.

## RESOURCES

### CITY OF PRINCE RUPERT
### DEPT. OF ECONOMIC DEVELOPMENT AND TOURISM
1st & McBride St., Box 669, Prince Rupert V8J 3S1
250/624-5637; 800/667-1994

# QUEEN CHARLOTTE ISLANDS / HAIDA GWAII

They're called Canada's Galapagos for good reason. This archipelago, homeland of the Haida people for 10,000 years, is separated from coastal British Columbia by Hecate Strait, a shallow and sometimes treacherous body of water about 140 km wide. The isolated position of the islands—there are 150 of them totaling about one million hectares—has allowed many species to develop independently, just as with the Galapagos Islands of Ecuador, thousands of kilometers to the south.

It takes some time and effort to get here. But if you can manage it, you're in for a terrific family holiday in a beautiful environment, interspersed with fascinating communities, and basking in a gentle climate. Amazing wildlife abounds at every turn, and a host of interesting excursions can bring you into contact with the region's unique fauna. The beaches offer the province's best beachcombing. From agates to rare Japanese glass fishing floats and shells of all kinds, you can find it here, somewhere.

The principal islands, Graham to the north and Moresby to the south, are separated by a narrow channel. Graham Island has the largest population. Old Masset, the largest Haida community, sits at the northeast end of Masset Sound, a long arm of water that stretches halfway down the center of the island and ends in wide Masset Inlet. On Graham's south coast are the Haida community of Skidegate and, about 13 km west, Queen Charlotte (QC). The population of Massett is 1,470; QC has about 1,000 residents; and Skidegate has 500 residents.

On Moresby Island, the largest community is Sandspit, with about 800 inhabitants. (The islands as a whole have about 6,000 permanent residents.) In the 1980s, **Gwaii Haanas National Park Reserve** was carved out of a huge portion of Moresby and several adjacent islands. This move was designed to ensure that this unique ecosystem will continue to thrive for future generations to experience. About two-thirds of the way down the reserve is **Ninstints,** a United Nations World Heritage Site. Here you'll find the remains of the abandoned Haida community Ninstints, with the world's largest collection of totem poles standing on their original site. The park contains the remains of other villages as well.

Captain Cook's arrival in the late 18th century and the settlement of Europeans in the 19th century exposed the Haida to smallpox, measles, and tuberculosis, decimating their population. But in recent years, as tribal rights were restored to women who married outside the tribe, allowing them to return and build lives in the Haida communities, the First Nations population has begun to increase again. Today, Haida villages are experiencing unprecedented growth, and new construction is underway throughout the islands.

Haida culture has produced great artists; if you've marveled at the works of Bill Reid or generations of the Davidson family, here you can see for yourself the world that produced them. Jewelry and figures carved from argillite, the soft black stone that only Haida carvers are allowed to work, can be seen and purchased in galleries and museums here.

Then there's the wildlife: bears, deer (not native), all kinds of birds—including some exceedingly rare varieties—and, of course, myriad marine animals, from whales to shellfish.

You can explore the islands in many ways: by kayak, in a seaplane, in a sailboat, by road, and on foot. Each is worth doing, and not all are expensive. If you time your visit outside the peak summer months, prices drop dramatically. Even in winter, temperatures are mild, and there are interesting things to see and do.

Residents of North America's Northwest feel like authorities on mercurial climates. But for weather that *really* changes, the Queen Charlottes have just about anywhere else beat hands down. While extremes of weather are very rare here, it's not at all unusual to go from rain to fog to sun, and back again, in what seems like just a few minutes. Rainbows are common.

### GETTING THERE

**BY SEA.** The most enjoyable route to the Charlottes from Prince Rupert is via **B.C. Ferries** (car ferry). The six- to seven-hour trip to Skidegate is scenic, but some sailings are at night (11 p.m.-6 a.m.). If you take one of these, be sure to reserve a cabin. Sitting up all night with small children is not a happy experience; luckily, the cabins are quite affordable. Accommodations range from small cabins with a toilet and sink to fairly spacious staterooms with toilet, sink, and shower. All have two berths, and because they aren't interconnecting, using them requires some planning if you're traveling with very small kids. You can generally board an hour in advance of sailing, which makes it possible to get a little more sleep. You can also book a cabin for a day trip, which is a good idea if your children are still in nap-taking mode. Should a cabin not be available, all is not lost. While seating in the public areas doesn't allow sleepers to lie down, it's possible to stretch out on the carpeted floor, and many do.

Ferries have two restaurants, a lounge, gift shop, and plenty of room for exploration. A standard play area for young children is also provided.

*888/BC-FERRY. Usually six sailings each way weekly in summer. Cost:One way, $90/car (more for RV), $24/adult, $16/senior, $12/child. Cabin: $32-$50, depending on amenities.*

**BY PLANE.** **Canadian Regional Airlines** (800/665-1177 in B.C.; 800/426-7000 in the U.S.) flies between Prince Rupert and Skidegate. **Harbour Air** (250/626-3225) serves Masset and Sandspit by floatplane.

## GETTING AROUND

**ON GRAHAM ISLAND.** Most of the interesting spots accessible by car are on this island. It takes at least 90 minutes to drive north to Masset from QC on Highway 16, a trip well worth taking, even if you've left your car at home and have to shell out the steep fee to rent a vehicle. With a car you can explore Tlell, a small arts-oriented community 45 minutes north of QC; Port Clements, on Masset Inlet; and go to Skidegate and visit the museum.

Driving to Masset, watch for the wooden carvings of an eagle and a bear along the roadside on your right, a few km past Skidegate.

**BUDGET CAR AND TRUCK RENTALS**
*8-3113 3rd Ave., Queen Charlotte*
*250/637-5688; 800/577-3228*
*Outlets also located in Masset and Sandspit*

**RUSTIC CAR AND TRUCK RENTALS**
*605 Hwy. 33 (at Charlotte Island Tire), Queen Charlotte*
*250/559-4641; after hours call 250/559-4504 or 250/559-8865*
*Note: Hwy. 33 is a continuation of 3rd Ave., to the west.*

**BETWEEN ISLANDS.** It can be fun to take the ferry south to Moresby and tour Sandspit and environs. The small M.V. *Kwuna* connects Skidegate on Graham Island with Alliford Bay on Moresby. Sailings are frequent, about 12 round trips daily, and take 20 minutes each way. Alliford Bay is a 20-minute drive from Sandspit.

*250/559-4485. Cost: $16/car and driver, $4.50/adult.*

**HITCHHIKING.** As in other small communities in northern B.C., hitchhiking is a common, safe, and accepted mode of travel here.

## PLACES TO STAY

### GRACIE'S PLACE

*3113 3rd Ave., Queen Charlotte*
*250/559-4262, 888/244-4262*
*Rates: Inexpensive*
*FYI: Kitchens (some units); pets OK*

For years, Grace Flanagan has been housing travelers in the rooms and suites in or attached to her attractive home. She also runs the local Budget car-rental office and is a good source of information, driving directions, and opinions of all kinds. Some of the rooms are snug; all are charming. Some have antique furnishings, but these are mostly of the sturdy and childproof variety.

### PREMIER CREEK LODGINGS

*3103 3rd Ave., Queen Charlotte*
*250/559-8415, 888/322-3388*
*Rates: Inexpensive*
*FYI: Kitchens (some units); refrigerators*

This historic hotel, nicely restored, has the best view in QC (though plenty of other places have good ones). Premier Creek comes bubbling down at one end of the grounds. Many of the rooms share a wide veranda that runs along the front of the building, where you can sit and watch the world (well, some of it) go by. Most rooms are spacious, with two queen beds, sofa bed, and plenty of room to spread out. A few rooms don't have ensuite bathrooms. The owner, a fabulous cook, is inclined to leave goodies, such as tea breads, for her guests. Don't say no. She'll prepare breakfast on request, too ($5). This is the best option in town for families.

### THE SANCTUARY B&B

*Hwy. 16, Masset*
*250/626-5042; sandj@island.net*
*Rate: Inexpensive*
*FYI: Full kitchens; barbecue; fishing charters*

Perfectly sited across the road from the Delkatla Wildlife Refuge, this double-wide mobile home, a few minutes' drive from Masset, makes a comfortable base from which to explore  the island. It has two bedrooms, a deck with a view, and lots of room. The owner operates M.V. *Olde Tyme* Fishing Charters, at the same phone number.

## PLACES TO EAT

### CAFÉ GALLERY
*2062 Collison Ave., Masset*
*250/626-3672*

Hours: Breakfast, lunch, dinner, Mon.-Sat.

It's an elegant little place, though not a first choice when you're traveling with small kids. But if you have older children, this lovely bistro is worth checking out.

### HOWLER'S PUB AND BISTRO
*2600 3rd Ave., Queen Charlotte*
*250/559-8600*
*Hours: Lunch, dinner daily*

This popular spot is a magnet for local and visiting young people. Downstairs is the pub; upstairs is the bistro, a happily rowdy place with very good, creative cuisine and a kids' menu featuring the usual fare. If the jukebox isn't to your taste, dine outside overlooking the harbor. The appetizers are enticing, and everything is very reasonably priced—a plus in a town where meals can put a dent in your wallet.

### HUMMINGBIRD CAFÉ
*At the Sea Raven Motel, Queen Charlotte*
*250/559-8583*
*Hours: Breakfast, lunch, dinner daily*

This cheery café offers good meals in pleasant surroundings and prepares a great breakfast that can wake you up after a night sailing from Prince Rupert. This is where regulars at Margaret's Café (reviewed below) come on Mondays, when Margaret's is closed.

### MARGARET'S CAFÉ
*3223 Wharf St., Queen Charlotte*
*250/559-4204*
*Hours: Breakfast, lunch, Tues.-Sat.*

Margaret's has been here for many years. If you want to meet locals and get a feeling for the community that calls Queen Charlotte home, head here. The menu is exceedingly child-friendly (hearty breakfasts and a variety of burgers and sandwiches for lunch); coffee is served on the honor system.

### OCEANA
*3119 3rd Ave., Queen Charlotte*
*250/559-8683; oceana@qcislands.net*

*Hours: Dinner daily*

Who would expect to find one of the best Chinese restaurants in B.C. in this far-flung corner of the province? Daily specials are offered, as well as a host of vegetarian entrées. If your kids will eat Chinese, this is a top choice. Prices are not low, but portions are huge. Be sure to have them pack up what you can't finish. It's even better the next day.

## WHAT TO SEE & DO
### STROLL & BROWSE

#### QUEEN CHARLOTTE

Explore Queen Charlotte on foot. There's more here than you'd think at first glance. Don't forget to check out the marina, too.

Along 3rd Avenue, you'll find the **Rainbows Gallery** (3201 3rd Ave.; 250/559-8420; www.cacmall.com), a warren of small rooms, each chock-full of Haida art, argillite carvings, silver jewelry, clothing, all kinds of gifts, and an exceptionally complete selection of books on the region. **Joy's Island Jewellers** (3301-3rd Ave.; 250/559-8890) carries a smaller selection of the same items. Wander down Wharf Street, and investigate the assortment of small shops and cafés. If you need a shot of java or a few calories, check out **Hanging by a Fibre** (off Wharf St.; 250/559-4463). This gift shop features a tiny café serving excellent espresso and delicious soups and baked goods. You may have to keep small hands off the crafts (some are brightly colored animals), but kids are welcome here.

There are no movie theaters in the Queen Charlottes. You can, however, rent a VCR ($8/night) and videos ($5 each) from **Video Gallery** (on Wharf St., south of 3rd Ave.; 250/559-0007), which also sells snacks.

#### MASSET

Tourist accommodations in Masset are limited, which means you'll probably be staying elsewhere and exploring this end of the island by car. Be sure to drive the four kilometers to Old Masset, where you can watch the Haida community expanding before your eyes, with new homes fronted by freshly carved totem poles. A major dock that will accommodate cruise ships and car ferries is under construction here.

**HAIDA ARTS AND JEWELLERY.** You can't miss this long-house-style gallery. Out front are two totem poles carved by Reg Davidson. Inside, a rich and remarkable assortment of Haida arts and crafts are for sale, including wooden masks, prints, clothing, books, and art cards.

*On Eagle Ave, Old Masset. 250/626-5560. Open Mon.-Sat., 11 a.m.-5 p.m.; Sun., noon-5 p.m. (summer). Shorter hours in winter.*

## MUSEUMS

**HAIDA GWAII MUSEUM AT QAY'LLNAGAAY.** This museum houses works by legendary Haida carver Robert Davidson, a vast array of argillite carvings, and exhibits dealing with island history. The museum hosts traveling exhibits as well. Books and Haida art are for sale.

*Skidegate. 250/559-4643; muse@qcislands.net. Open Mon.-Fri., 9 a.m.-5 p.m.; Sat.-Sun., 1-5 p.m. (May-Sept.); Closed Tues. and Sun.; call for hours (Oct.-April). Cost: $2.50/person.*

## SWIMMING

**MASSET REC CENTRE.** Visitors are welcome to use the pool, sauna, gym, weights, and fitness equipment. A snack bar and bowling alley are also on site.

*In Masset; call for directions. 888/627-7388; 250/626-5507.*

## THE GREAT OUTDOORS

**BIRD-WATCHING.** Delkatla Wildlife Sanctuary plays host to some of the rarest birds in North America, who make the Queen Charlottes a stop on their yearly itineraries. Rare sand-hill cranes, trumpeter swans, and cattle egrets have been sighted. More common are bald eagles, ravens, peregrine falcons, and the rest of the 140 species observed here. Climb the towers provided for better viewing.

*A few km outside of Masset, on Hwy. 16.*

**KAYAKING.** Opportunities for kayaking abound throughout the islands. Options range from two-week-long expeditions through the archipelago to shorter adventures closer to civilization. Some outfitters cater to families and some don't; age restrictions may apply. Investigate options carefully and check with the Visitor Info Centre if you're not sure how to make a good selection.

**WHALE WATCHING.** Each spring, after saying goodbye to

Clayoquot Sound off Vancouver Island, gray whales continue their northward journey to Alaska, dropping in on the Queen Charlottes between April and June. Sightings are most frequent off Skidegate, on southeast Graham Island, and Rose Spit, the island's northernmost point. Even if you don't invest in a charter that takes you to the whales, pack your binoculars to one of these viewpoints; chances are good you'll spot some flukes and dorsal fins.

## EXCURSIONS
### GRAHAM ISLAND

**NAIKOON PROVINCIAL PARK.** This park occupies most of the northeast quadrant of Graham Island, between Masset Sound and the island's east coast, and has some of the best beaches, campsites, and hikes in the Charlottes. Some hikes are strenuous for small fry, but many are doable, and all are rewarding.

Park headquarters (open seasonally) are close to the south end of the park, off Highway 16. Nearby, you can hike to the wreck of the *Pesuta*, a log-carrying barge shipwrecked in 1928. This 10-km hike is somewhat strenuous for little legs; allow at least four hours and take a picnic along. Request directions before you tackle this one (check with park headquarters or the Visitor Info Centre).

If you visit in summer and are up for a spot of camping, try to get in at **Agate Beach.** (It's popular with locals too; most head here very early in the day to snag a likely site.) Trees are few, but campsites are hidden from each other behind tall shrubbery, and you're mere feet from a wonderful beach chock-full of agates, glistening in a rainbow of hues. Drift off to sleep to the sound of the waves smoothing the stones, like a million pebbles gently raining down. This campground is open year-round and has outhouses, shelters, stoves, water, and a covered picnic area. There's a small fee May through September; it's free in winter.

Just a little farther north, across the Hiellen River, is **Tow Hill,** a mini-mountain that rises up offering a marvelous view of the beaches nearby. It makes a good, if slightly strenuous, hike. Allow at least an hour and a half.

Don't miss **North Beach,** an endless ribbon of white sand with all kinds of beach-combing goodies awaiting your attention. Locals drive their vehicles out onto the firm sand here. At the far north end is **Rose Spit,** a long sandy point that gives the park its Haida name (*Naikoon* in Haida means "long nose"). This is a good spot to scan the horizon for whales.

On the old Indian reserve are interesting beaches etched with tide pools. You can camp here, but first you'll need to obtain a permit from the Old Masset Band Office (250/626-3337; open Mon.-Fri., 8:30 a.m.-noon).

*Entrance to the park headquarters is off Hwy. 16 shortly after Tlell. For sites in the North Beach area, take Hwy. 16 past the Masset turnoff and continue north; follow signs.*

### MORESBY ISLAND

**SKEDANS.** Farther north and closer to Sandspit than other ancient Haida villages, Skedans is worth a visit. You'll need to make arrangements with one of the tour operators that bring visitors here. As with other Haida sites, there's a Haida watchman here who serves as a guide and tells you about the site's history and the culture of the Haida people.

### GWAII HAANAS NATIONAL PARK RESERVE AND HAIDA HERITAGE SITE.
Created in the 1980s to preserve the unique heritage of the Charlottes—human, animal, and plant—this reserve contains ancient trees (some over 1,000 years old) and 1,600 km of shoreline, with plenty of beaches to explore. The famous villages of Tanu and Ninstints can be found here. (If you plan a visit, take a look at Emily Carr's paintings of Haida sites before you go.)

It's believed that the Queen Charlottes may have escaped glaciation during the last ice age, and many unique plants flourish here, along with assorted varieties of bears, otters, and other animals not found elsewhere. Visitors can expect to see a truly amazing array of wildlife on even a short visit.

**HOT SPRINGS ISLAND.** Long known to the Haida, fishers, and boaters, and now a frequent destination of tour operators, is a lovely spot that features several hot springs. Visitors follow a path across the island from one hot-springs pool to the next, each different.

## CALENDAR

**MAY**
Masset Harbour Days
**JUNE**
Skidegate Days
**JULY**
Juggernaut Jam Music Festival

### OPERATORS, OUTFITTERS, TOURS

Many tour operators have set up shop here, and more are coming. Investigate your options thoroughly, ask for references, and check with the Visitor Info Centre. Consider your priorities: Would you rather see wildlife or visit old Haida village sites? Many operators will gladly customize a trip to client specifications. Interview operators by phone or e-mail and do some comparative price checking, too.

### ECOSUMMERS EXPEDITIONS

*604/214-7484; 800/465-8884;www.ecosummer.com*

This highly rated organization has a long track record leading kayak and sailing expeditions through the Queen Charlottes and other sites worldwide. Most trips are not suited for small children, although ideal for families with teens. There are several options for families with young children.

### GWAII ECO TOURS

*Box 249, Queen Charlotte, V0T 1S0*
*250/559-8333; www.gwaiiecotours.com*

Tour operator Louie Waters takes small groups of two to five people on customized trips lasting four to six hours. His well-organized web site makes a good introduction to the Queen Charlottes.

### SMC

*888/559-8383; smc_123@hotmail.com*

This licensed commercial operator offers boat tours for up to 10 people, lasting three to five days. There's some camping; meals are supplied and prepared by tour leaders. Activities include guided intertidal walks, and visits to Hot Springs Island and Haida village sites.

### SOUTH MORESBY AIR CHARTERS

*Box 969, Queen Charlotte V0T 1S0*
*250/559-4222; 888/551-4222*

If you don't have time to get here by boat, consider visiting Gwaii Haanas by air. Tours to Ninstints, Skedans, and Hot Springs Island cost about $500 to $1,000 per trip (three to four people included).

**AUGUST**
Tlell Fall Fair

## RESOURCES

Be sure to head to the local Visitor Info Centre soon after you arrive in the Charlottes. This is where you will attend the mandatory orientation session required if you're seeking a permit to travel to Gwaii Haanas. (If you're traveling with a licensed operator, attendance is not required, but might still be worth doing. Call 24 hours in advance to make an appointment for an orientation.) The centers show videos about the islands and the park reserve; sell maps, charts, and books; staff are on hand to answer questions.

### QUEEN CHARLOTTE VISITOR INFO CENTRE
On Wharf Street, Queen Charlotte
250/559-8818; 800/663-6000 (orientation reservations)
Open daily, 10 a.m.-7 p.m.(mid-May-mid-Sept.); shorter hours early May and late Sept. Gwaii Haanas orientations: daily, 8 a.m.-8 p.m.

### SANDSPIT VISITOR INFO CENTRE
At the airport terminal, Sandspit
250/559-8818; 800/663-6000 (orientation reservations)
Open daily, 9 a.m.-5 p.m.(mid-May-mid-Sept.); shorter hours early May and late Sept. Gwaii Haanas orientations: daily, 11 a.m.

### BOOKS
*Queen Charlotte Islands Trail Hikes and Beach Walks,* by Fern Henderson. Excel Printing, 1996.